Z
4
M 1.5

Copy

THE BOOK

The Story of Printing and Bookmaking

Also by Douglas C. McMurtrie

THE BOOK

THE STORY OF
PRINTING & BOOKMAKING
BY DOUGLAS C. McMURTRIE

OXFORD UNIVERSITY PRESS

London   NEW YORK   *Toronto*

Author's Preface

TEN years ago Pascal Covici, then publishing books in Chicago, proposed to me the writing of a book aiming to cover the history and development, and the art and technique, of bookmaking. Acting on this suggestion, I wrote *The Golden Book*, the first edition of which he published in 1927. That the subject was one of wide interest was demonstrated by the fact that this book, with many defects known to no one better than to its author, ran through four editions in eight years, selling approximately twenty thousand copies, some of which have found their way into all parts of the world.

A continuing demand made it desirable to issue a fifth revised edition. But when I undertook this revision, I found that the state of knowledge regarding the history of printing and bookmaking had changed considerably during the past ten years. I found also that in many places I had repeated the accepted stories regarding certain events, which a wider reading of the scientific literature has shown to be false. Certain features of bookmaking had been inadequately dealt with, and mention of some important points had been omitted entirely.

These circumstances made me unwilling to do anything other than start all over again, with the same subject assignment, and write a new book. The present volume is the result of that effort. It follows a somewhat similar outline; it includes some of the same illustrations, and a few of the chapters which I felt unable to improve. But in most respects the present volume presents a fresh survey of printing history and practice. Many subjects which received only cursory mention in the previous work are here dealt with

v

in considerable detail, as, for example, the beginnings of writing, book illustration, printers' marks, special problems of early book-making, and modern typography and illustration. In the chapter on bookbinding history, a large proportion of the statements have been radically revised as well as expanded.

As the present volume has some degree of kinship to *The Golden Book,* I desire to renew my expressions of gratitude to those who aided me in preparing the text and illustrations of that volume. Many of the illustrations were reproduced from rare books in the Newberry Library, for which courtesy I am indebted to Mr. George B. Utley, the distinguished librarian of that institution. Appreciated assistance was also given me by Dr. Pierce Butler and Dr. Edwin E. Willoughby, both of whom were then on the staff of the Newberry Library. Various readers wrote me comments on or corrections of certain statements, which I have been able to use to advantage in the present book. Among these helpful correspondents were Messrs. Charles H. Douglas, Louis N. Feipel, J. U. Nicolson, Lee Grove, Solomon R. Shapiro, and R. H. Stetson.

In the writing of the present volume, my obligations to the authors of published studies of various aspects of bookmaking are numerous indeed, but I have endeavored to acknowledge them all in the bibliographies and notes at the end of this book. The authorities of the Henry E. Huntington Library, of San Marino, California, have been kind enough to supply me with photographs of some of its treasures and have granted permission to reproduce them. Like courtesies have been extended me by the John Rylands Library, of Manchester, England, which numbers among its collections some of the rarest known specimens of early printing. Mr. W. A. Marsden, Keeper of Printed Books of the British Museum, has graciously accorded me permission to reproduce numerous subjects, the originals of which are in that library. The Gutenberg

Gesellschaft of Mainz has placed essential material at my disposal and consented to its reproduction in this book. The Museum of Modern Art has been kind enough to lend the blocks of book illustrations by a number of the eminent modern painters and sculptors. Mr. Arthur Hind, of the British Museum, has accorded me permission to reproduce certain illustrations from his notable recent treatise on fifteenth century woodcuts, and Mr. E. P. Goldschmidt has consented to my reproducing several illustrations from his scholarly monograph on Gothic and Renaissance bookbindings. For all of these courtesies I am grateful.

The Library of Congress, the University of Chicago Library, the New York Public Library, and the library and print department of the Art Institute of Chicago, have extended me appreciated privileges, without the benefit of which I should have been unable to do much of the research on which the present book is based. The J. Pierpont Morgan Library extended me the courtesy of checking against its rare original editions my quotations from several of William Caxton's prefaces. Miss Margaret Bingham Stillwell of the Ann Mary Brown Memorial Library kindly supplied information regarding incunabula in American ownership. The Kommission für den Gesamtkatalog was kind enough to give me an up-to-date estimate of the known number of issues of the fifteenth century press. And many other libraries and librarians answered by letter numerous inquiries addressed to them.

Mr. Will Ransom, leading authority on the private presses, has kindly read the manuscript of my chapter on this subject and made many valuable suggestions. Mr. William M. Ivins, Jr., of the Metropolitan Museum of Art, made, in correspondence, numerous helpful comments on early wood engraving. Mr. Ben Abramson made some appreciated suggestions after reading the chapter on modern book illustration.

Finally, I wish gratefully to acknowledge the indispensable assistance of my colleague, Albert H. Allen, in preparing the text of this book. He has assumed almost complete responsibility for the chapters on the beginnings of writing and the history of the alphabet and has made a useful contribution on the intellectual status of Europe at the beginning of the fifteenth century to the chapter discussing the stage-setting for typography. He has also suggested desirable revisions of statement at many points through the book and accepted the task of preparing the index of the volume. To Harold Strauss, Wallace Brockway, and Miss Frances Broene of the Covici-Friede staff I am indebted for special interest and helpfulness in seeing this book through the press, and for their patience in dealing with an author who has been under necessity of doing his writing on evenings, Sundays, and holidays.

I am deeply appreciative of the interest in this book taken by the distinguished American artist, Gustav Jensen, and evidenced by his design of the jacket, binding, and the title page decoration of this volume.

To Robert Josephy, who has made such a consequential personal contribution to the art of the book in America, I desire to express my appreciation for his interest in and able oversight of the typography of this volume. I recall with pleasure my first collaboration with him, almost fifteen years ago, in the printing of books.

To Pascal Covici I am indebted not only for the original suggestion responsible for the writing of this book, but also for constant encouragement—along with not infrequent prodding—during the preparation of the manuscript. I only hope that *The Book* measures up to his expectations.

That I have drawn heavily on the knowledge and experience of others in the writing of this book will be apparent from the bibliographies of works consulted, which will be found at the end of the

present volume. It could not be otherwise, with an attempt to present an authoritative statement covering a subject so wide in scope as the history, art, and technique of printing and bookmaking. For source material, except in the chapters dealing with American printing history, I have had to depend largely on others, but for the arrangement and presentation of the material I must myself accept responsibility, as well as for attempted evaluation of work and expression of opinion regarding styles and trends.

A sincere effort has been made to have the statements throughout the book as accurate as possible, but I am not visionary enough to expect that some faults will not have slipped through. I am hoping, therefore, to receive from readers suggestions for improvements of the text, of which I can avail myself if the market demand for this book is such as to require subsequent editions.

Douglas C. McMurtrie

July 20, 1937

In sending to the press this third revised edition of *The Book,* I feel bound to express my grateful appreciation of the favorable reception which this work has experienced since it first appeared in 1927 under the title of *The Golden Book,* of which four editions appeared before it was almost wholly rewritten in its present form. The widespread sale of these editions throughout the world gives me the satisfaction of knowing that the publication of this history of printing and bookmaking has filled an actual need for such a work.

In the course of the years that this book has been in circulation, I have been favored with correspondence from a large number of interested readers in all parts of the world; some of the writers have taken issue with me on points of fact; others have called attention to minor errors in the spelling of names or to a few typographical

slips. All such comments have been gratefully received and have been taken into consideration in the revision of the text for the present edition. And I have also endeavored to bring the bibliographies at the end of the volume up to date by the inclusion of some recent titles deemed to be of importance.

It gives me real satisfaction to have this volume now issued under the publishing auspices of the Oxford University Press, an organization which has been making history in printing and bookmaking for over four hundred years. My respect and admiration for this institution was heightened a number of years ago by the opportunity of spending a week in its historic but efficiently equipped printing plant at Oxford, England—an experience which could not fail to inspire any printer with sincere respect for the traditional background of his profession.

DOUGLAS C. MCMURTRIE

November 2, 1942

Contents

Illustrations

Introduction

THE most cursory reflection will make it clear beyond doubt that books are a primary necessity of life in any civilized community. Yet, while there is widespread appreciation of literature, that is, of the art of writing books, there is comparatively little popular appreciation of the art of bookmaking. Nevertheless, the design of books is as much an art as architecture, or painting, or sculpture—and perhaps of more import to the population at large, in that it exerts an esthetic influence upon more people more frequently than any other art. And the setting of type and the printing of books is as truly a craft susceptible of high standards as the craft of the weaver or potter or goldsmith.

That much present-day bookmaking is sadly deficient in design and quality of execution is, of course, owing to the lack of popular appreciation of what excellences of craftsmanship go into the making of a really fine book. For when a demand exists for good work in any field, that demand is inevitably supplied. It is perhaps because of this lack of appreciation and interest that there are but few "books about books" addressed to the general reader and making clear to him the essentials of good bookmaking.

But while the average of bookmaking has been and is poor, there is evidence of light amidst the shadows. There is even now a dawning renaissance in the book arts, an awakening that needs and deserves the encouragement of all booklovers. With patronage, the art of book design will flourish; the craft of the printer will be brought once again to a station of dignity, to a pride in fine work.

So while deploring some prevailing standards of bookmaking, our view may be optimistic rather than the reverse. Conditions are

on the mend rather than the decline. And those who are making good books find that they sell, which indicates an appreciation not only potential but actual—though perhaps yet limited in extent. This evidence of an improvement in public taste, so far as bookmaking is concerned, is sufficient to indicate still greater potentialities of appreciation. The existence of this incipient renaissance is the reason for the present volume, and perhaps its justification.

Among the influences contributing to improvement, two can be singled out for comment. The first is an enlightened interest on the part of publishers of good taste in bringing out well designed and soundly made books. In the United States the palm for pioneering in this direction must be awarded to Alfred A. Knopf, who, from the very start of his publishing career, has made an earnest effort to produce books creditable in both design and execution. His example has exerted a good influence on the design of "trade books" produced by his fellow publishers, many of whom have evinced a sincere interest in typography, presswork, and binding.

The second important factor in this contemporary renaissance of bookmaking has been the annual "Fifty Books" exhibition, conceived by the late Burton Emmett and sponsored by the American Institute of Graphic Arts. When this show first began in 1923, the larger publishers were sparsely represented in the fifty volumes deemed worthy of exhibition by the jury of selection, and they evidenced little concern in the failure of their books to win a showing. However, as the show gained annually in prestige and public interest, many of the great book houses became interested for the first time in sound typography and workmanlike printing, and made deliberate efforts to produce books which would merit selection. The later exhibits, after being shown in New York, have been sent for showing in a number of other cities from coast to coast.

There is no question that the "Fifty Books" show has had a

highly beneficial influence on standards of American bookmaking, particularly in the design and manufacture of trade books published for sale in unlimited quantities at moderate prices.

In judging the books to be selected, all elements of bookmaking are taken into consideration, and a serious deficiency in any feature is likely to disqualify the book. Design, composition, presswork, paper, and binding are all weighed in the jury's balance. The number of titles entered has constantly increased. In reference to progress in the quality of books exhibited, Frederic G. Melcher, editor of the influential journal of the book trade, the *Publishers' Weekly,* has recently written:

The indifference to style which tended several years before to make all trade books look alike, all equally drab and uninviting in appearance, seemed to be replaced by a growing desire for character and "spark" and individuality. Many observed at that time that well designed books were issuing from an increasing number of plants and that new designers and more of them were doing good work. In addition to the many new and pleasing treatments of title pages, chapter headings and of the other problems in pure typography, much fresh thought had been given to bindings, and this was particularly welcome in trade editions.

Three other countries have followed the American example by organizing similar annual exhibits of currently produced books: Great Britain, Germany, and Sweden.

Recently a Book Clinic, a group of designers and production men and women working for trade publishers, was organized in New York under the auspices of the American Institute of Graphic Arts. It holds interesting meetings to discuss highly practical questions regarding the planning and manufacture of books. A similar group has recently been formed in Chicago.

This discussion of books and their makers is written from the viewpoint of the designer and printer. Personally, I confess to a

real enthusiasm for good books—primarily for their content. But I take a further pleasure in a fine work of literature interpreted in physical form by an artist, just as I most enjoy a great symphony played by a great orchestra under a conductor of real inspiration. To convey a beautiful passage to our minds through a medium which esthetically affronts us cannot fail to handicap its full appreciation. To clothe it in simple, appropriate, yet withal beautiful typography, is to treat it only as it merits. Such presentation cannot help giving us, subtly and perhaps unconsciously, added pleasure in the reading of the text.

The ambition of the true artist in the bookmaking field is to present fine works of literature in a fine format. With reprints of the classics he occasionally has this opportunity, but almost never with the best modern literature. Most books of this character are planned to sell in large quantities and are ground through the usual mill of manufacture in form or manner not one whit better than the most mediocre novel preceding them on the publisher's list. In my esthetic anguish over the modern books I most enjoy, it almost seems that the good books are, if possible, a little worse than the average in design and production. A glance through the shelves of any collection of modern first editions will demonstrate how shabbily present-day authors have been treated by the printers who introduced the children of their brains to a critical world.

The average publisher, reading the preceding paragraph, will immediately retort that there are economic limitations imposed by costs of production and the sale prices of current books. This moves me to make a statement that cannot be too clearly emphasized: *Good book design has almost no bearing on expense of manufacture.* Taste and judgment are the only additional ingredients required. The artist in bookmaking, if he has his feet on the ground and is not merely a dilettante, can take a barbarity in the form of a book

and make out of it a good volume—at no increase in cost. The manner of doing this will later be discussed in detail. Let us, how-ever, remember this precept: Sound bookmaking is not necessarily expensive bookmaking.

There is an element of public service in improving the design of printed matter of wide circulation, for the improvement exerts its influence on the taste of numberless readers. The typographer who has opportunity to plan a popular novel, the cover of a tele-phone book, the headlines and layout of a metropolitan newspaper, may make the same contribution to raising standards of public taste as the architect who designs inexpensive workingmen's houses of real beauty and charm. The campaign against banality is one in which we can all enlist with a will.

There is still another caution. By fine bookmaking we do not mean elaborate book design. Some of the finest books are made with simple types plus only the elements of taste and judgment in their setting, spacing, and positioning on the page. While a little appropriate decoration, used with discretion, often adds greatly to the charm of a volume, it is in no way essential to achieving the finest results in book design, as has been demonstrated by many master printers of ages past and present.

As in all other arts, the best in present practice is based on tradi-tion evolved during centuries past, with admixture in limited degree of principles of modern genesis, the whole colored by the personal interpretation of the designer. The best printing of any period has not been revolutionary, but evolutionary, the individual printer of genius adding some new note to the work of his predecessors. The sane book designer, therefore, studies carefully the history of his art and familiarizes himself with the printed masterpieces produced since the invention of movable types. These will be of value not only in the development of his own taste, but in affording him sound

models from which to work. If his work is to be more than routine, however, he must introduce some new note that will make it his own, that will make it creation rather than reproduction.

There is still another reason for acquaintance with the historical aspects of typography, since certain periods and countries have developed specific and individual characteristics of type design and book planning. When the typographer has before him for design the manuscript of a book dealing with the American Continental Congress, he will not want to set it in a type of wholly Italian inspiration which dates from the sixteenth century. He will choose rather a typeface in keeping with the character of our own Colonial typography and in all likelihood will set the title page in the same spirit. Yet when we deal with a volume made up of translations of French eighteenth century essays, it would be desirable, in absence of reasons to the contrary, to give the volume some of the highly characteristic feeling of French printing and decoration of that century.

Any appreciation of modern book design is therefore based, to a considerable degree at least, on an acquaintance with and understanding of the historical development of the book. For that reason many of the chapters in the first three parts of this volume are historical, beginning with the origins of writing and of our alphabet and then tracing in brief outline the making of books from the earliest times, with some reference to the work of outstanding individual printers, and attempting some appraisal of their contributions to the art of book design. Later chapters are devoted to a discussion of the various features of bookmaking which enter into the planning and production of various kinds of books. In the concluding chapter, which is brief, is attempted some orientation of our present status and the formulation of a program for still further improvement of bookmaking, looking toward an ideal within the limits of practical accomplishment.

THE BOOK

The Story of Printing and Bookmaking

I

Primitive Human Records

IN the inconceivably remote past, man was able to communicate with his fellows only by means of grunts or cries, supplemented no doubt with gestures or a sort of sign language. The sign language persisted even after man became capable of articulate speech; even today, primitive peoples eke out their inadequate speech with meaningful gestures. But speech and gestures were not enough for the imperative needs of the growing human spirit. And so we find men having recourse, in the dim prehistoric past, to drawings or pictures in order to express themselves. This was a development of immeasurable importance in the evolution of man—it was his first effort *to make thought or feeling visible in a lasting form*.

The paleolithic cave dwellers of Europe have left behind them, on the walls of their caves, drawings and even paintings of amazing representative accuracy, showing the bison, the reindeer, the wild horse, and other animals now extinct in that region, even including the hairy mammoth. These records were commemorative, no doubt, of some notable experiences in the lives of those prehistoric peoples. But the thing of outstanding importance to our present purpose is that the men of that far-off time not only made accurate representations of animals and human beings, but also used what might be called shorthand equivalents of them—linear outlines which even today are perfectly intelligible as meaning "mammoth," or "goat." In other words, quite unconsciously and without knowing what a mighty power they were unleashing in the world, they had made a beginning of *writing*.

But many thousands of years passed before man, though everywhere using such picturizations of things, really awoke to a realization of what he had created with these pictographs. No doubt, there were innumerable beginnings throughout the world of quite independent systems of using pictographs as records. In fact, there are still peoples in the world today who have a Stone Age culture, or who have barely evolved out of that stage, and in quite recent times such systems of pictographic records have been in use among the Indians of America, the Eskimos of the arctic regions, the Hottentots and Bushmen of South Africa, and many other primitive races. But most of these systems perished without trace, or else never developed beyond their crude beginnings.

But at certain points in the world these pictographic records developed into systems of what can truly be called writing in almost the modern sense of the word. Innumerable objects of the neolithic period and the Bronze Age of Europe have been found, weapons and other utensils of bone, stone, and metal, inscribed with pictographic symbols. Some of these can be quite clearly identified with the things they represent. Other unexplained signs, if not mere attempts at ornament, are symbols so far removed in form from their pictographic originals that they cannot now be recognized, although they undoubtedly had definite meanings for the men who made them. In all parts of the Mediterranean world, from the Spanish peninsula to the Valley of the Nile, there have been found objects marked with such signs, which Flinders Petrie called the "Mediterranean signary." Some of them seem to have been totems or, perhaps, makers' or owners' marks. Sir Arthur Evans found primitive substrata of linear pictographs in Crete, where later there developed a true script. With the appearance of a script in the world, it might be said that the history of the book begins.

Primitive pictographs served as aids to memory or to convey

suggestions rather than precise indications of what they represented. How did such pictographs develop into what we call writing? A full and exact answer to that question cannot be given, because the circumstances of that momentous step in human progress are hidden in the dimmest reaches of prehistoric times. But the general nature of the process is perfectly clear from the earliest specimens of true writing which have been found and studied. It is evident from the form and interpretation of the characters used in these very earliest written records that ancient races of men, accustomed for many generations to the use of pictographs, grasped in time the advantage of definitely associating certain pictographic symbols with certain objects or ideas. The pictographs thus gradually evolved into ideograms, or symbols representing generalized ideas derived from objects. In developing a system of ideograms for the representation of thought in written form, the human intellect uncovered a capacity for method that is little short of miraculous.

It seems perfectly clear from all the available evidence that in every part of the world in which writing developed, its earliest form was ideographic. It must have taken a long time to work out ideograms for the expression of abstract ideas, but even that was done by imaginative uses or combinations of symbols for concrete things. Thus, by figures of speech, so to speak, the symbol for "ear" also meant "hearing," the symbol for "sun" also meant "day," and so on.

Ideographic writing has had an unbroken history from the time of the very earliest written records down to the present day. The outstanding representative of this system of writing today is the Chinese. But ideographic writing was found, even in the very earliest times, to have certain serious limitations. As human activities became more complex and the range of ideas more extended, ever increasing ingenuity was required to devise new ideograms for putting new ideas into writing. Furthermore, it became more and

more difficult, even for a man who devoted his whole time to their study, to learn and remember the always increasing number of ideograms. The Chinese have labored with this problem for centuries. A fairly diligent Chinese student is an adult before he has acquired a facility in reading and writing equivalent to that of a fairly diligent child of twelve in a country with an alphabetic system of writing. Especially in this highly technical modern age, the Chinese find themselves handicapped with a cumbersome system of writing. Only in recent years has the Chinese government authorized and undertaken to introduce a system of simplified phonetic writing.

But other peoples, even as far back as four thousand years or more before the Christian era, had already begun to work their way out of the difficulties imposed by a purely ideographic writing. For the very earliest written records which have been found show the beginnings of the change from ideographic writing, in which the symbols stand for ideas, to phonetic writing, in which the symbols stand for sounds.

To complete this change, which Mason called "the most signal intellectual achievement ever attained by man," required several thousand years. This seems an excessively long time, even if allowance is made for the slowness with which new ideas took root and grew in the early centuries of human history. But an explanation of the extremely slow emergence of a purely phonetic system of writing may be found in the fact that writing from the very beginning seems to have been the prerogative of the priestly and ruling classes, which doubtless had their reasons for not allowing this mysterious process to become too well known to the masses and therefore kept it as abstruse and esoteric as possible. Thus, even at the sacrifice of developing the full utility of writing, the conservative forces kept it more or less fixed in the form which would best serve the purposes of the ancient representatives of "special privilege."

Another obstacle in the way of substituting phonetic for ideographic writing was found, in the case of the Egyptians, for instance, in the large number of homophones—words of identical sound but of different meanings—in their language. Even after they had achieved a satisfactory method of writing phonetically, the Egyptians still clung to a number of symbols used as ideograms to identify the meanings of words. It was as if we found it necessary to use a little picture of an insect together with the written or printed word to distinguish "bee" from "be," or as if we had to use a special symbol with the word "fast" to indicate whether we meant "securely attached" or "to abstain from food."

It is quite easy to see how the transition was made from ideographic to phonetic writing. Inevitably, most of the ideographic symbols in the ancient systems of writing became associated closely with the sounds of the spoken words which named the things for which the symbols stood. What was more natural than to use such a symbol to represent the sound of a word, if such a use of it became desirable? We may suppose that this change in use began with some ancient scribe faced with the problem of writing some foreign name, or even the name of one of his own countrymen, for which he had no ideogram. He could best do this by using ideograms which called to mind the sounds occurring in the strange name. Thus, if we had to write the name "Manhattan" and had only a set of ideographic symbols to do it with, we could use the symbols for "man," "hat," and "ten" and get a quite satisfactory representation of the name. And if the symbol for "man" could be used in this way for the sound *man,* it could also be used for the same sound in such words as *"man*date," "hu*man,"* and so on.

Something like this was the beginning of phonetic writing which, as has been said, is found in rudimentary form in the very earliest written records. But the process gradually went farther.

A written symbol which could be used to represent the sound of an entire word could also come, in the course of time, to be used for the initial syllable or sound of that word. Thus, our hypothetical symbol for "man" could be used not only for the sound *man,* but also, with the continued development of phonetic writing, for the sound *ma,* and eventually for *m.*

The Egyptians successfully reached the point of being able to write either ideographically or phonetically, or both ways together. Reproduced herewith are two cartouches from Egyptian monuments,

  in which the name "Cleopatra" is written phonetically. The characters are read from top to bottom. It will be noted that the little figures in the two cartouches face in opposite directions. The one on the left stood in an inscription of which the text was to be read from right to left, while the text of the other inscription was read from left to right. It can readily be seen that the nature of the Egyptian characters made it possible for their inscriptions to be carved so as to be read with equal facility in either direction.

The Egyptian words used to "spell" the name Cleopatra in these cartouches are the following:

Kne	angle
Labo	lion
Ake	reed
O——	noose (name unknown)
Pu	mat (shutter)
Ahom	eagle
Tot	hand
Ro	mouth
Ahom	eagle

The "reed" character seems to have been used for A or E or I. Egyptologists do not always agree on these names.

In the cartouches are also found some Egyptian determinatives or explanatory symbols. The little semicircle at the bottom indicates that the name is to be read phonetically. The little oval, or egg, tells the reader that the name is that of a female person. And in the right-hand cartouche the little seated figure means that the person named has been deified.

In their development of such a phonetic system of writing, the Egyptians became confused with too many symbols. They used about twenty for *A*, about thirty for *H*, and so on, having in all between three hundred and four hundred symbols which were capable of being used phonetically, together with about ninety determinatives to aid identification. Some of these symbols were restricted by custom to use only in certain connections. Though there came to be many different symbols which might be used for *A*, for *M*, and for *N*, only one form of symbol for each was ever used in writing the name of the god Amen. And certain symbols were preferred as phonetic signs in writing the names of royal personages. But otherwise the choice of symbols seems to have been more or less unfettered, one or another being preferred for reasons of symmetry or appearance in the inscription. In the times of Greek and later Roman domination, Egyptian writers of monumental inscriptions liked to display their versatility by varying their "spelling." In one inscription there have been found ten variations in the phonetic writing of the name of one town.

In another part of the ancient world, another mighty race was working out its solution of the problem of phonetic writing. In Mesopotamia, the Babylonians and their successors, the Assyrians, in very early times developed a system of phonetic symbols. But these symbols, instead of tending to become alphabetic, like their

Egyptian contemporaries, became syllabic. Thus there was a separate written sign for each of the syllables *ba, be, bi, bo, bu, ab, eb, ib, ob, ub,* and so on. Similar systems of syllabic writing are still in use for many of the native languages of India, Burma, Siam, and elsewhere. The Assyrians developed more than five hundred phonetic symbols, together with a considerable number of determinatives.

Other widely separated systems of writing developed at least to some extent along phonetic lines. Many of the Chinese ideographs contain phonetic elements. Sylvanus G. Morley suggests that even the yet undeciphered symbols of the ancient Aztec and Maya monuments of Mexico and Central America had reached the point of beginning to have phonetic values.

The story of how our present alphabet came into being has been reserved for another chapter. But as the implements and materials used for writing have had an enormous influence upon the development of that art, some mention of them is appropriate here.

The natural surfaces of the rock walls of caves or cliffs offered the most obvious opportunities for mankind's first attempts at pictographs. At a much later time it was possible to smooth and plane the face of a cliff for monumental inscriptions such as the gigantic record left by Darius the Great on the cliff of Behistun, in Persia. Or huge boulders and great slabs of rock (megaliths) were artificially set in place and inscribed. If the stone was dressed before being set up, such monuments as the Egyptian obelisks resulted.

Small stones were also used. Possibly the very oldest specimens of true writing that have yet been discovered have been found on two well-prepared pieces of black stone, about four inches square, one (the Hoffman tablet) in the possession of the General Theological Seminary in New York City and the other in the museum of the University of Pennsylvania in Philadelphia. Both came from Mesopotamia and show a very primitive pictographic form of the pre-

cuneiform characters of that region. Their age can only be guessed—possibly 6000 B.C. is approximately right. Almost as old, and also inscribed with pre-cuneiform characters, are two pieces of thin greenish stone, known as the "monuments Blau," which are now in the British Museum. These have been dated between 5500 and 5000 B.C. If nothing of equally remote antiquity has been found in

THE SEND INSCRIPTION, ABOUT 4000 B.C.

Egypt, it is possibly because the Egyptians first developed their system of writing on perishable materials. The earliest Egyptian inscription on stone, the Send inscription of about 4000 B.C., now preserved in the Ashmolean Museum of Oxford University, is carved in characters so completely conventionalized that they must have had a long ancestry, even though no trace of it has yet been found.

These ancient inscriptions on rock and stone are important in the history of writing because they show us how men of remote antiquity made intelligible symbols which can still be interpreted. But stone-cutting is hardly writing in our sense of the word. However, men who could cut inscriptions on stone could also write on perishable materials and undoubtedly did so, using hides, or wood, or bark—just as in quite recent times our American Indians drew their pictographs on buffalo skins or on birch bark. At the dawn of history, writing was unquestionably done on a variety of accessible materials, but nothing of it has survived except such as was done on stone, on metal or pottery, or on the baked clay tablets of the Tigris-Euphrates region. The most ancient form of archaic Chinese writing has been found on bone rings, possibly used as amulets, which some scholars date as far back as 1500 B.C., or even earlier.

The earliest true writing material that has survived—used for the purposes for which we use paper and ink—is probably the curious baked clay brick-like tablets of Mesopotamia. No doubt those ancient Akkadians, Babylonians, and Assyrians had other writing materials. Certainly during centuries of their history the papyrus of Egypt was accessible to them. But in the valleys of the Tigris and Euphrates there was no stone or other durable material available for their permanent records, so tablets of clay were used.

Characters which in their earliest beginnings had been linear and pictographic were jabbed rather than drawn upon these tablets while still soft, with a stylus which made wedge-shaped marks. Hence this writing has received the name "cuneiform," from the Latin word *cuneus,* "wedge." When the writing was finished, the tablet was baked until it was as hard as a brick. Literally tons of these tablets, of all sizes and shapes, have been removed from the ruins of the ancient cities of Babylonia and Assyria. Their contents range from state documents, codes of laws, treaties, and the like,

through religious treatises and works of science, history, and literature, to court actions, partnership agreements, contracts, and even
promissory notes.

A relief carving of the eighth century B.C., at the time of the
Assyrian Empire, shows the process of writing on a clay tablet,
described by Breasted as follows: "At the left is an official reading
from a tablet, while before him stands a scribe with a thick clay

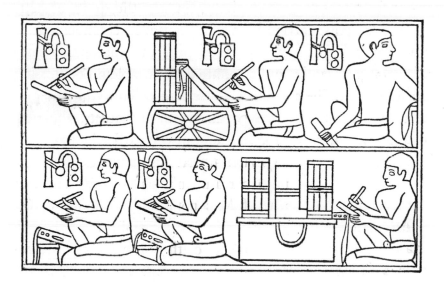

EGYPTIAN SCRIBES AT WORK.

tablet supported in his left hand. He has paused for a moment in his
writing and raises his right hand with the stylus poised between the
thumb and the palm of the hand, the fingers being stretched straight
out. . . . When the scribe actually applied the stylus to the clay, he
bent all of his fingers and held the stylus in the closed fist."

The characteristic writing material and implement of the ancient
Egyptians was the papyrus sheet or roll and the reed pen-brush.
Older than any surviving scraps of the material itself are monumen-
tal representations of it. A relief from the tomb of Ti, at Sakkara,

Egypt, dating from the twenty-seventh century B.C., shows a pair of scribes at work, squatting before two small desks on which are stacked their rolled-up records, like bundles of college diplomas. The reproduction on the preceding page shows also four clerks or assistants, in similar posture, holding in their left hands the papyrus rolls on which they are writing.

Much of the Egyptian scribes' work was done in the open, and many ancient monuments depict them as writing in a standing position. The scribe carried his writing outfit in a convenient form. Its essential elements were two reed pens in a protective carrying case, a little jar of water, and a palette with two round depressions in which to mix his red and black inks. The palette and water bottle were often tied to the pen case with a cord, so that the whole equipment could be slung over the shoulder or carried in the hand. A pictorial representation of this outfit naturally came to be the ideographic symbol for "writing," "to write," and "scribe." This symbol will be seen above the scribes depicted in the illustration on page 11.

When writing, the scribe made his ink as he needed it, using one of the compartments of his palette. For black ink he mixed lampblack with an aqueous solution of a vegetable gum which held in suspension the nonsoluble black. For carmine ink a red oxide of iron was used. The use of both red and black ink accounts for the numerous representations of scribes with two pens behind their ears.

The red ink was used for the introductory words of paragraphs. This conventional use of red was adopted by the Greeks and later by the Romans and survived in the rubrics (from the Latin *ruber,* "red") of European manuscripts and early printed books. The word "rubric" is used to the present day in almost the same meaning, although our rubrics are no longer necessarily printed in red.

The writing implement of the Egyptian scribe was a cross between a pen and a brush. Perhaps by chewing the end of a reed

the scribe frayed the fibers, giving him a soft tuft with which to work. His writing was a sort of brush painting on papyrus. Only with the coming of parchment did the split pen come into use.

Though for some of his work the Egyptian scribe adhered closely to the forms of the characters which were used for monumental inscriptions, a cursive form of writing also developed—the hieratic or "priestly" writing in which the pictured ideograms of the monuments were reduced to the barely recognizable essentials. This was necessary, of course, if writing was to be done at all rapidly. The oldest papyrus rolls which have been found, taken from mummy cases of about 3500 B.C., were written in hieratic. In fact, hieratic characters have been found even in inscriptions dating from the earliest Egyptian dynasties.

Out of the hieratic there came, in the course of time, a still more simplified cursive, the demotic, or "popular" script, in which the pictographic origin of the characters had disappeared as completely as they have in the modern Chinese ideographs. Both the hieratic and the demotic scripts were made possible by the availability to the Egyptians of a material which readily took their thin inks, which retained the color of the pigments, and which was smooth enough to permit free movement of the raveled fiber pen brush. This material was papyrus, made from the fibrous lining of the marrow of the papyrus plant, a kind of sedge native to the Nile region, once gathered there in almost unlimited quantities, but now almost extinct. The Roman writer Pliny, in his *Natural History,* describes for us the method of fabricating a writing material from this plant. The stalks were cut into lengths of about sixteen inches. The marrow was then slit into thin strips, which were laid flat side by side. A second layer of these strips was then laid over the first and at right angles to it. The two layers were then treated with a gum solution and pressed, pounded, and smoothed until the surface was suitable

for writing. In fresh condition the resulting sheets were of a yellow-ish white color, later turning to various shades of yellow.

The papyrus plant was used by the Egyptians for other purposes than the making of a writing material. Its roots were dried and used for fuel, its fibers were made into ropes, its stalks were used for thatching and for making light rafts. In time of scarcity, its tender shoots supplied food. Thus the papyrus harvest was of great importance to Egyptian life.

For extensive manuscripts a number of papyrus sheets, each approximately twelve by sixteen inches in size, were pasted end to

PAPYRUS HARVEST, FROM AN INSCRIPTION OF ABOUT 1475 B.C.

end and made up in the form of a roll, usually containing twenty such sheets. If more than one roll was needed, the scribe pasted on additional sheets, but this was often done so clumsily that the writing over the seams suffered accordingly.

The height of the papyrus rolls was usually a little more than twelve inches. The rolls were then cut into small rolls about six inches tall, or sometimes into rolls a little over three inches tall. These smaller rolls had the advantage of being easier to handle and less liable to injury. For a letter the normal sheet halved vertically was used, but if necessary a whole sheet was used, or it was cut into four strips.

Writing on papyrus was done in columns arranged something

like the columns of a newspaper. Each column was the equivalent of a page in a modern book. A section of a roll looked something like this:

```
XXXXX    XXXXX    XXXXX    XXXXX    XXXXX    XXXXX    XXXXX
XXXXX    XXXXX    XXXXX    XXXXX    XXXXX    XXXXX    XXXXX
XXXXX    XXXXX    XXXXX    XXXXX    XXXXX    XXXXX    XXXXX
XXXXX    XXXXX    XXXXX    XXXXX    XXXXX    XXXXX    XXXXX
XXXXX    XXXXX    XXXXX    XXXXX    XXXXX    XXXXX    XXXXX
XXXXX    XXXXX    XXXXX    XXXXX    XXXXX    XXXXX    XXXXX
```

Normally the lines were of a length to contain about thirty-eight characters or letters.

The tops and bottoms of the rolls were the parts most exposed to wear and were therefore often reinforced with pasted strips. The side of the sheet on which the layers were horizontal was the smoothest and considered the "right" side. In ancient times the reverse side was not used, but later, in a pinch for space or because of a shortage of material, the back of the sheet was also used for writing. A number of the ancient Greek classics, including Aristotle's famous *Constitution of Athens,* are known to us today only because of copies made about A.D. 300-400 (when papyrus was becoming scarce) on the backs of rolls which had previously been used for such mundane purposes as reports of stewards in charge of property and the like.

Papyrus as a material for the preservation of records was far from satisfactory. There was danger of punching through in the process of writing, and in guarding against this the up strokes and the down strokes of the pen often became almost indistinguishable. Papyrus was also most susceptible to damage from water or dampness; on the other hand, when it had dried out, it became highly fragile— almost as brittle as dead leaves. Nowhere but in a rainless land such as Egypt could ancient papyrus have been preserved for centuries.

Quantities of papyrus rolls have been found in mummy cases, and others have been dug up from the ancient rubbish heaps of a bygone civilization. Covered centuries ago with Egypt's drifting

sands, these emptyings of the waste baskets of two thousand years and more ago, brittle and delicate, carefully treated with restoratives and kept between sheets of glass, have told us in fascinating detail of the everyday life of those ancient people. Of all the ancient papyrus rolls discovered, the most remarkable are those excavated from the little city of Herculaneum, which was destroyed by the lava of Vesuvius in A.D. 79. Treated with all the resources of modern science, many of these little rolls, mere lumps of charcoal, have been so restored as to become legible again.

Not only in Egypt but throughout the ancient Mediterranean world, papyrus was the accepted writing material for ages. The latest known use of it is a papal bull of A.D. 1022, long after parchment had become the common material for writing and just before paper began to come into general use in Europe. It is impossible to overestimate the importance to human culture of this material, which served the needs of mankind probably for fifty centuries.

Parchment, which eventually succeeded papyrus as a writing material, is known to have been used as early as about 500 B.C., but it did not become a successful rival of the popular papyrus until a few centuries later. This material was the prepared skins of animals, principally of the sheep or of the calf. That which was made from calfskin, known as vellum, was the best. Skins had been used, of course, in extremely ancient times, but only in the form of tanned leather. The Egyptians used hides for writing as early as 2000 B.C. But parchment did not begin to come into general use until about two centuries before the Christian era, and then under the pressure of necessity.

The story goes that Eumenes II, king of Pergamum in Asia Minor in the second century B.C., incurred the ill will of the Ptolemies, then rulers of Egypt, who imposed an embargo on the exportation of papyrus to Pergamum. The people of Pergamum then re-

verted to the use of skins. But the preparation of this material was much improved, by more skillful processes of splitting, tanning, and bleaching, into a product of fine quality which soon gained renown. It was especially welcomed because it was much more durable than the fragile papyrus, though it was heavier and also more expensive. When it was exported into the Roman world, it became known, from the place of its origin, as *pergamena,* from which the name in time found its way into English as "parchment."

By the fourth century A.D. parchment had become the dominant writing material in Europe. It yielded slowly to the advantages of paper after that substance was first introduced, and it is still used occasionally for certain engrossed documents, such as diplomas —which are fittingly known as "sheepskins."

The general use of parchment had a far-reaching effect upon the development of writing. For writing upon its smooth surface a broad-pointed pen, made of reed or quill, came into use. It was inevitable that writing done with such an implement on such a surface should assume an appearance quite different from writing done with a reed brush on papyrus.

In all parts of the world men have used for writing material whatever was most available for the purpose. Early Chinese writing, before the advent of paper, was done on silk or other textiles. The Egyptians made not infrequent use of linen, and the ancient Romans kept some of their official records on strips of linen. The Romans also used waxed tablets for personal correspondence and for records of business transactions and the like. These tablets, of wood and sometimes of ivory, had slightly raised borders, the depression being coated with a thin layer of blackened wax. A pointed stylus was used for tracing the letters in the wax, and the other end of the stylus was blunted and widened for making erasures by simply smoothing out the wax. Two or three or more of these tablets were sometimes

hinged together to make the prototypes of the pages of our books. A number of such tablets, their writing still intact, have been recovered from Pompeii, destroyed by Vesuvius in A.D. 79 as was Herculaneum, but with ashes and not with molten lava.

Perhaps the strangest of all writing materials, from our point of view, are the palm-leaf strips used in some parts of India, in Burma, and in Siam. Writing on these strips was—and still is—done with a sharp-pointed implement. Pigment is then rubbed into the finely

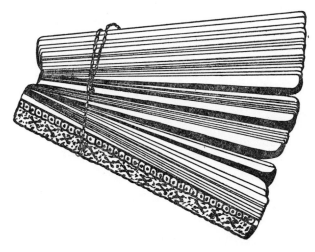

A HINDOO PALM-LEAF "BOOK."

incised lines to make them visible. The strips are then "bound" by stringing them on cords, for all the world like the slats of Venetian blinds.

The peculiarities of each kind of material used for writing have profoundly influenced the character of the writing done on them. Thus we have the linear style as incised on bone, stone, pottery, metal, and the East Indian palm-leaf strips; the peculiar stencil-like linear of the Roman script written in wax, where the closing of a circle or loop in a letter would cut out a bit of the wax; the jerky

staccato of the cuneiform jabbed into soft clay; the gracefully shaded and sweeping brush strokes of the ancient Egyptian calligraphers and of the modern Chinese and Japanese; the easy, fluent, cursive movement of the pen on the smooth surface of parchment or paper. All these modes of writing had their effects on the shapes of the written characters. It is safe to say that whatever beauty the letters of our modern European alphabets may have, we owe largely to the efforts of medieval scribes to write beautifully on their parchments.

II

The Origin of the Alphabet

ALMOST from their very beginnings, systems of writing, as we have seen, tended to become phonetic—that is, capable of representing the sounds of spoken languages. But if writing was to become truly useful to mankind, it was necessary that the complicated systems of phonograms should be simplified so that the art of writing could be acquired and used by the ordinary man. The process of simplification has resulted in the relatively small group of written and printed characters which make up what we today call the alphabet.

We use the letters of our alphabet every day with the utmost ease and unconcern, taking them almost as much for granted as the air we breathe. We do not realize that each of these letters is at our service today only as the result of a long and laboriously slow process of evolution in the age-old art of writing. The centuries during which mankind learned to write alphabetically are now telescoped into a few years of school life, from the primary school youngster awkwardly tracing his first ABC's to the grammar-school child who can (sometimes) make more or less legible letters.

What is our alphabet? It is a set of symbols, seemingly of quite arbitrary form, which we use to represent the elemental sounds of our spoken language. It is perfectly obvious to all who use it—and especially to those who use it for writing the English language—that the alphabet as we know it is at best only a makeshift as a means of representing spoken sounds. But mankind, curiously enough, has a way of getting along nicely with makeshifts. The alphabet, as nearly

as we can judge, has been in process of development for about four thousand years and is still far from a perfect implement. In fact, a perfect, truly phonetic alphabet, except as invented by scholars for the scientific study of human speech, seems to be impossible of realization. For our letters have now become so imbedded in usage that it is almost hopeless to try to dislodge or change them.

But, imperfect though it is, where did this alphabet originate? For an answer to this question, as with our inquiry about the beginnings of writing, we must go back to remote antiquity. And even from the evidence to be found there we can make no more than shrewd conjectures. An enormous amount of study has been devoted to the subject, but scholars still disagree widely on many important details. We have a very good clue, however, in the very word "alphabet," to guide us at the start of our search. For the word "alphabet" is nothing more than the names of the first two letters, *alpha, beta,* in the alphabet of the ancient Greeks. Following up this clue—first noting that many letters in the ancient Greek alphabet had true *names,* such as *alpha, beta, gamma, delta, iota, kappa, lambda,* and so on—we are next impressed by the fact that the letters of the Semitic alphabets (ancient Phoenician, ancient and modern Hebrew, Arabic, and others) also had names, and that the Semitic names (in Hebrew *aleph, beth, gimel, daleth, yod, kaph, lamed,* and so on) have a striking similarity to the Greek names. The conclusion seems inescapable that the ancient Greeks got the names of their letters, at least, from a Semitic source.

But it seems unlikely that the Greeks could have taken the names alone, without the characters to which the names belonged. The names unquestionably had some meaning for the Semites who first used them, but they were meaningless to the Greeks, who could not even pronounce them correctly. To those Greeks of a very ancient day who first learned to use the alphabet, the strange-sounding and

meaningless names must have been identified with the separate letters which some strange-speaking foreigners taught them.

In pursuing the search for the land from which the letters first came to Greece, scholars have made careful studies of ancient inscriptions. In Phoenician inscriptions there have been found abundant evidences of a system of alphabetic characters. Most of these characters have been clearly identified as the prototypes, if not as the actual models, of letters with the same phonetic values as those in very ancient Greek inscriptions. Greek tradition, also, credits the Phoenicians with being the "inventors" of writing. The accumulated evidence is convincing that at some remote time the inhabitants of various parts of the Greek world acquired the alphabet through contacts with the seafaring Phoenicians.

We are speaking now of the Greek alphabet which became in time the ancestor of the Roman alphabet and thus of ours. The progenitors or predecessors of the ancient Greeks, on the coast of Asia Minor, on the islands of the Aegean Sea, and on the Greek mainland, have left evidences of a system of writing possibly derived from the linear script of prehistoric Crete. But when the alphabet as we know it first made its beginnings in ancient Greece, all knowledge of that earlier script seems to have been wiped out completely, except perhaps on one or two of the islands and a few localities in Asia Minor. On the island of Cyprus a local syllabary remained in use until the sixth century B.C. And Lycia and Lydia in Asia Minor also had ancient syllabaries. But these were so exceptional that it truly may be said that from the Phoenicians the Greek world learned all over again the art of writing.

We now confront the critical question: how and when did the Phoenician alphabet come into being? In their search for an answer to this question, scholars have long been groping in a realm of historical obscurity. Monuments of vast age have been found, bearing

inscriptions in Phoenician characters. But these characters are already wholly alphabetic, with apparently no trace of ideographic phonograms in them. Without an ideographic ancestry, how did they originate? Did some brilliantly inspired Phoenician, once upon a time, just "make them up"? Such an explanation makes too great a demand upon credulity. But where are the ancestors of these twenty-two Phoenician letters to be found?

The first serious attempt at an answer to this question was made in 1859, when Emmanuel de Rougé, a French scholar, presented before the French Academy a memoir in which he sought to show that each one of the known Phoenician characters was derived from a corresponding character in the Egyptian hieratic writing. For many years this answer to the question was generally accepted as final and conclusive. But the work of later scholars, based upon more recently discovered inscriptions, in characters more archaic than any to which De Rougé had access, so thoroughly discredited the Frenchman's theory that the question again became an open one.

Sir Arthur Evans in 1895 advanced the suggestion that the Cretan pictographs and the later Cretan linear characters lay behind the Phoenician alphabet. It is not out of the question, of course, that Cretan refugees, fleeing from the catastrophe which overwhelmed their civilization about 1200 B.C., found their way to Palestine with their peculiar script. But the Cretan characters at best are only imperfectly understood, and until more is known of them the suggestion of a connection between them and the Phoenician alphabet must remain only a suggestion.

In general appearance the Phoenician characters can be compared with some of the characters found in the Cretan script or in the scripts of prehistoric Cyprus or Asia Minor. But nowhere are appearances more deceitful than in tracing the descent of the letters in a primitive alphabet. Religious and governmental conservatism

fixed the forms of the Egyptian hieroglyphic characters and to a large extent those of the Mesopotamian cuneiform writing. Thus the characters on the very latest Egyptian monuments are practically identical with the same characters as found on the very earliest. But when alphabetic writing made its start, conservative forces had no control over it. Writing became purely utilitarian, the tool of traders and men of business who refused to be bothered with the complications of the older systems. Those who used the primitive alphabets did so with perfect liberty—not to say license—to do with them as they saw fit. The forms of the letters were fluid, so to speak, and changed from place to place and from time to time all through the ages as they spread from Phoenicia through Greece to ancient Rome and from Rome throughout Europe, until the invention of printing fixed them in their present almost unalterable forms.

Thus we find the ancestor of the letter A, for example, lying on either side, standing on its apex, or canted at all possible angles, and with its crossbar across its feet, tangent to its point, or crossing anywhere between. In some archaic Greek inscriptions the characters for M and for S can barely be differentiated. If these mutations and variations are found in inscriptions that can be read, in which the values of the letters are accurately known, how uncertain must it be on the basis of appearance alone, to identify characters in unknown scripts with the known letters of primitive alphabets!

Other possible sources of the Phoenician alphabet have been sought in the characters developed by the ancient Hittites of Asia Minor and in the linear script of the Akkadians, Sumerians, and earliest Babylonians in Mesopotamia. A Hittite origin cannot be intelligently discussed as yet, since next to nothing is known of the meanings of the Hittite characters. A Babylonian origin seems much more plausible. The Phoenicians, according to tradition, had migrated from the region of the Persian Gulf in the third pre-Christian

millennium, just as Abraham had led the ancient Hebrews out of Chaldea to Canaan at about the same time. The linear Babylonian script had not been entirely displaced by the cuneiform writing at the traditional time of the Phoenician migration, and it is interesting to speculate that the emigrants may have taken a knowledge of writing with them. At a much later time, about 1400 B.C., it is known from Egyptian records that Babylonian was the language of diplomacy and officialdom in international communications. Babylonian and its script must have been known in Palestine and among the Phoenicians, at least in official circles. But no conclusion can be drawn from this fact as to the language and script (if any) used by the Phoenician populace for internal communication. French was for many years the diplomatic and "polite" language of Europe, but its use in this way did not perceptibly affect the vernaculars of the different European nations.

Of all the ancient cultures which hemmed in that little strip of seacoast inhabited by the Phoenician people and from which they may have derived their alphabet, none remains to be considered— unless we should find that in some bygone time there was an ancient culture south of the Phoenicians and between them and Egypt. When we turn in this direction, we are getting "warm," as children say. For in quite recent years there has been found evidence of just such a culture, though a quite primitive one, between Phoenicia and Egypt and, what is more, inscriptions which offer a most intriguing clue to the origin of the Phoenician alphabet.

On the Sinai Peninsula, the wedge-shaped land mass which juts into the Red Sea southeast of the Isthmus of Suez, Sir Flinders Petrie, the famous English Egyptologist, discovered in 1904 and 1905 some stone objects inscribed with characters which seemed to be alphabetic. In all, about fifteen such inscriptions have been found, containing in all about 225 characters, of which about thirty are highly

problematical because of the wearing away of the soft sandstone in which they were cut. About twenty-five distinctly different forms have been sorted out. Unfortunately, the inscriptions are all quite short, and very few identical groups of characters (that is, identical words) recur. But there is one group of four characters which recurs several times, and these have been quite conclusively identified by

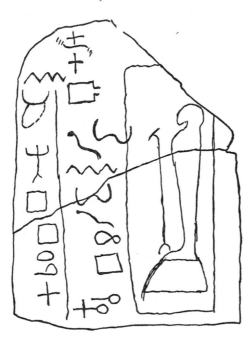

Alan H. Gardiner, another English scholar, as Bʿʟᴛ, spelling the name of the primitive Semitic goddess Baʿalat, who was identified with the Egyptian goddess Hathor.

This was enough to make it reasonably clear that the characters were truly alphabetic and also that the language of the inscriptions was Semitic. Many scholars have busied themselves with the problems of deciphering and interpreting the inscriptions, with varying results. In 1931, Martin Sprengling, an accomplished Arabist, published

SINAITIC INSCRIPTION, ABOUT 1800 B.C.

what seem to be highly satisfactory interpretations of the inscriptions. As Sprengling reads them, they are mostly votive in character and are inscribed on objects that a primitive Semitic people, working in the mines of the Sinai region, used as offerings to the tribal goddess.

The accompanying illustration shows in outline drawing (after Sprengling) the inscription on one of these Sinaitic stones. Sprengling translates the characters thus: "The gift of Benshemish, sculptor

of Upwawet, beloved of Ba'alat." Upwawet was the name of the Egyptian deity whose statue, possibly the one carved by Benshemish, is sketched at the right of the inscription. The name of the goddess is spelled with the four characters, interpreted as b'lt, below the crack in the left-hand column, reading downward.

For the probable date of the origin of these inscriptions Sprengling refers us to James H. Breasted's *History of Egypt*: "While operations in the mines of Sinai had been resumed as early as the reign of Sesostris I, . . . it remained for Amenemhet III to develop the equipment of the stations on the peninsula, so that they might become more permanent than the mere camp of an expedition while working the mines for a few months. . . . Amenemhet III made the station at Sarbut el-Khadem a well equipped colony for the exploitation of the mineral wealth of the mountains." Details of this account by Breasted, supplemented by extracts from his *Ancient Records,* include the mention of a stele set up by an Egyptian official, barracks for the workmen, fortifications against the marauding tribes of the desert, a temple of the local Hathor, mine shafts each under the charge of a native foreman after whom it was named—all of which fits in with the tentative translations of the inscriptions as made by Sprengling.

Amenemhet III reigned in Egypt from 1849 to 1801 b.c. It seems almost certain, therefore, that the Sinai inscriptions date from the last half of the nineteenth pre-Christian century, when the Sinai mines were being worked by crews of local Semitic natives under the direction of Egyptian officials. Not long after this date the Egyptian Empire suffered reverses which caused the mines to be abandoned.

How did an alphabet come into being under such circumstances? Before attempting an answer to this question, we must recall that the Egyptian system of writing at that time was already well on its way toward becoming alphabetic. It had reached the point of iden

tifying some of its ideographic characters with the initial sounds of the spoken words which corresponded to those characters. But it never reached the point of assigning *one* character to the function of representing *one* sound; for each sound it preferred to have a wide range of characters from which to choose. What happened in Sinai, we may imagine, was the reduction of this complicated formula to its simplest terms—only one character for each sound.

The method by which this came about might be compared with what the electricians call "induction." As an electric current passing through a coil of wire somehow causes an independent current to flow through another wire which moves in the field of this coil, so the influence of the Egyptians in Sinai set in motion an impulse to write among those ancient Semites. One may suppose that some Egyptian scribe connected with the management of the Sinai mines lightened the tedium of his exile in that desolate place by "teaching" an intelligent native foreman the rudiments of writing. This foreman, or perhaps several foremen, could use these rudiments in keeping simple records, thus no doubt saving some labor for Egyptian clerks. The few characters which the natives learned were written for them, no doubt, with the Egyptian pen brush on papyrus. They may have been in the cursive, hieratic form, or they may have been in the more easily identified form of the hieroglyphic pictographs. But when the Semites came to using them on stone, as they saw their Egyptian masters doing, some modification and simplification of the forms were doubtless necessary. Still, some of the characters as they stand can be quite easily identified with Egyptian characters, although, it is important to note, they were not used with the same phonetic values as in Egyptian, but with phonetic values derived from the *Semitic* words for the objects which the Egyptian symbols represented.

The system of writing which thus developed was a bare skeleton

of some two dozen consonantal characters. How condescendingly
the Egyptians may have smiled at the pathetic efforts of those natives
to write with an equipment so pitifully meager! But those efforts
were the beginnings of the alphabet—one of the mightiest implements of power now at man's command. Those primitive natives of
Sinai were intelligent enough to grasp the principle of alphabetic
writing that their Egyptian superiors were much too learned to perceive. They discovered the advantage of having a few characters
which could be used in innumerable combinations over a system of
innumerable characters to serve the same purpose.

From Sinai this primitive alphabet seems to have been carried
on currents of migration and trade southeastward into what is now
Arabia and northward into Palestine. The two branches became
markedly differentiated, but the northern branch may well have
been the progenitor of the earliest Phoenician alphabet.

Even if this latest theory as to the origin of the Phoenician
alphabet is not completely established in all details, it is at least the
most credible theory thus far advanced. No doubt the Phoenicians
may have modified their alphabet under influences from other
sources, but the Sinaitic origin of its beginnings seems to be quite
satisfactorily established.

The earliest known inscription in which the Phoenician alphabet
appears dates from an era about six hundred years after the probable
date of the Sinaitic inscriptions. Six centuries allow plenty of time
for experimentation with alphabetic writing and afford plenty of
opportunity for other systems of writing—Cretan, Hittite, Babylonian, Egyptian—to contribute whatever they had to offer for its
improvement. The Phoenicians were a practical people. In business
and trade they had contacts everywhere. It is not at all unlikely that
they borrowed letter forms from other peoples; but if they did so,
they modified the borrowed forms and adapted them to their own

uses. But it is important to keep in mind that what persisted throughout those six centuries was the tradition of the *function* of the letters rather than of their *form*. Through all possible changes or even substitutions of forms, the function of that little group of symbols for the sounds of human speech remained essentially unchanged. The principle of writing alphabetically survived among a few Semitic peoples occupying a relatively unimportant geographical area, while mighty nations such as Assyria and Egypt continued their cumbersome methods of writing with hundreds and hundreds of symbols.

And it does not seem likely that alphabetic writing, after its principle had once been discovered, fell entirely into disuse and had to be discovered anew. Durable objects bearing clearly alphabetic inscriptions may be lacking—but the users of the alphabet, the ancestors of the Phoenicians, were not builders. They were not prepossessed, as the ancient Egyptians so evidently were, with the idea of projecting themselves into the future by means of imperishable monuments inscribed with records of their deeds. They were concerned with practical day-to-day affairs, and their notes and records of these were made on perishable materials. Even though the Babylonian language and script came to be used in official and diplomatic correspondence, we may quite reasonably suppose that in their own private affairs the Phoenicians used their own alphabet, just as they used their own language.

The earliest known Phoenician inscription shows the alphabet in a mature and well-developed state, which gives the impression that it had been in use for a considerable time. This inscription was found in 1923, by a French archaeological expedition, on the sarcophagus of a Phoenician king of Byblos named Ahiram. Scholars have determined that the tomb and the sarcophagus date from the middle of the thirteenth century B.C., in the time of Rameses II,

king of Egypt. Byblos (the Gebal of the Old Testament) was then under strong Egyptian influence.

In the inscription, of which a portion of the first line is here reproduced, the son of the deceased king dedicated the tomb with a curse on any person who should dare to violate it. It is read from

PORTION OF THE AHIRAM INSCRIPTION OF ABOUT 1250 B.C.

right to left. The alphabet, as in the case of the Sinaitic inscriptions, is still almost purely consonantal, with no letters for true vowel sounds. Weathering of the stone has obliterated a few letters in the name of the king's son, but following the break the letters shown in the reproduction, reading leftward, are TB'AL BN ACHRM MLK GBL, or, *. . . tbaal ben Ahiram melek Gebal—*". . . tbaal son of Ahiram king

PHOENICIAN INSCRIPTION ON A BRONZE BOWL, ABOUT 950 B.C.

of Gebal." With an effort of the imagination the reader may be able to recognize ancestors of A, H, L, and T; perhaps of R and M. It should be noted that the occasional short vertical strokes are not letters but indications of divisions between words or word groups.

A fragment of a bronze bowl found at the site of a Phoenician colony or outpost on the island of Cyprus carries an inscription

which has been interpreted as referring to that Phoenician King Hiram who was the friend of King Solomon. If that interpretation is correct, the fragment dates from about the middle of the tenth pre-Christian century, and the inscription on it is the next earliest known use of the Phoenician alphabet. An outline drawing of this interesting relic appears on page 31. The inscription reads leftward, so that the letters must be reversed before any possible resemblance to our letters can be recognized. The primitive forms of K, M, and N are fairly easy to distinguish. But the letter that at first sight looks like K is really A, lying on its side and with its crossbar at or near the angle. And the letter that resembles W is an archaic letter with a value similar to that of S.

This Cypriote bowl has also been ascribed to the time of another Hiram, king of Sidon, in which case its date is about two hundred years later, or in the eighth century B.C., and the next earliest known inscription in the Semitic alphabet would then be the famous Moabite stone now in the Louvre at Paris. This monument was found in 1868 by a missionary in the vicinity of the Dead Sea. As soon as the local Arabs saw that it was of some interest or value to the Christian intruders, they tried to destroy it by heating it in a fire and then pouring water over it, thus splitting it into scores of pieces. Fortunately, "squeezes" had already been made of the inscription, so that it was possible to restore the stone in part to its original condition.

The inscription on the Moabite stone is the record made by Mesha, king of Moab, of the rebellion of his people against Jehoram, king of Israel, some time between 896 and 884 B.C. As was the case with conflicting *communiqués* from the opposing forces in the late war, the story of the rebellion as told by Mesha differs considerably from the account of it in the second Book of Kings in the Old Testament. Of more immediate interest to us, however, is the fact

that the letters of the inscription show recognizable resemblances to those of our own alphabet. Below are shown the letters of the Moabite stone (but reversed, to face rightward, in the direction in which we read), with our modern equivalents under them.

There is still much controversy as to the date when the Phoenician alphabet found its way into Greece. Rhys Carpenter had no sooner made it clear, by an excellent line of observation and reasoning in an article published in 1933, that the Greeks could not have received the alphabet much earlier than 700 B.C., than Mrs. Agnes Newhall Stillwell showed, by an inscription on a vase fragment found at Corinth, that "by the period 775-750 B.C. writing must have already become a permanent feature of Greek civilization."

A B C D E F Z H Th I K L M N S O P Ts Q R Sh T

THE ALPHABET OF THE MOABITE STONE.
(*Reversed, so as to read from left to right.*)

Carpenter then pointed out that the evidence of this vase fragment was inconclusive by itself. If we were to "split the difference" and say that alphabetic writing was probably introduced into the Greek world between 800 and 700 B.C., we should be reasonably safe—at any rate until some inscriptions come to light which are much more archaic than any yet found.

It would seem that the Phoenicians, in their active commercial exploitation of the Mediterranean region, were in contact with the Greek-speaking peoples, particularly in Asia Minor and the islands of the eastern Mediterranean, for an indefinitely long time, and that it was possibly in Rhodes or in Cyprus that their alphabet was first adapted so that it might be used efficiently for writing the Greek language. The Phoenicians had colonies, or trading posts, in

Melos, Rhodes, and other Aegean islands as early as the thirteenth century B.C, and somewhat later at Thasos, Samothrace, Corinth, and other points. Writing first took root in some of the islands.

PRIMITIVE GREEK WRITING FROM THE ISLAND OF THERA.

Herodotus, the first Greek historian, tells of the coming of Cadmus, the legendary hero, with a company of followers whom he brought from Phoenicia, and of how Cadmus first stopped at Thera, an island in the Aegean Sea, and later settled in Boeotia, on the mainland, where he introduced the art of writing to Greece.

Cadmus in Greek legend has been explained as the personification of the forces of a foreign culture which profoundly affected ancient Greek life. It may be significant that what seems to be the most archaic form of the Greek

AN ANCIENT GREEK INSCRIPTION FROM ATTICA.

alphabet has been found in inscriptions from the island of Thera. The letters of these inscriptions are described as being almost pure Phoenician and in the earliest cases are written leftward, as the Phoenicians wrote. The Thera inscriptions have been ascribed to about the ninth or eighth century B.C. The earliest surviving Phoenician inscriptions, as has been noted, date from about the same period.

CORINTHIAN VASE INSCRIPTION, THOUGHT TO DATE ABOUT 750 B.C.

But even with the alphabet safely on Greek soil at about 800 B.C., we find difficulty in recognizing our familiar letters in the characters at first used by the Greeks. Here are shown drawings of

some very early inscriptions from Thera, from Attica, and from Corinth, and especially a few lines from the famous inscription in which were published, about 650 B.C., some of the laws of the ancient Cretan city of Gortyna. From a casual inspection of these specimens it would seem that the Greeks, in their first struggles with alphabetic writing, were somewhat like our primary-school children. They apparently felt quite at liberty to write as they pleased, with the characters sideways, hindside before, or upside down, and in a delightful variety of forms. To them, it would seem, a letter was a letter, no matter in what position it was written or carved. The

VA23113WSO1O△32O9Э⊗VƎ 13ꓘMO
CSⱮⱳOꮁƎⱮCPO△SꓘAⱮⱲEA△EⱮΛS△
9Ǝ⊗VŞ·· OTOTAⱮꓘAꓘS△ATAꓘSƎΛAꓘƎ
O△EꓘAⱮTATEPAⱮⱮTO△OᒥⓄCEⱮT
ꙄAⱮAΛAꓥOTAⱮꓘAꓘS△S△Aꓘ2ƎΛA·TOƎ

LINES FROM THE GORTYNA INSCRIPTION, ABOUT 650 B.C.

Gortyna inscription, however, is a striking illustration of how Greek genius, even at a very early date, was able to bring order into confusion and create proportion and beauty.

But Gortyna was a shining exception for its time. Elsewhere for another century or so the Greek use of the alphabet was quite notably "free style." The creative spirit of the Greeks was at work in making the alphabet over to suit their own purposes. They introduced two important innovations: they fixed for all the western world the convention of writing from left to right, and they adapted some of the Phoenician letters to the representation of vowel sounds.

Whether writing is done from left to right or from right to left is more or less a matter of convention, fixed by age-old usage. The Phoenicians wrote leftward. The first experiment of the Greeks was in writing alternate lines in opposite directions. In the Gortyna

inscription, for example, the first line shown in the illustration reads leftward, the second rightward, and so on alternately. This forward-and-backward method of writing the Greeks called *boustrophedon,* meaning literally "ox-turn-like," the term having reference to the movement of the animal pulling a plow up one furrow and down the next. In boustrophedon writing the letters in alternate lines are reversed as in so-called mirror writing, so as to make them face in the direction of the reading.

The earliest Greeks wrote leftward, boustrophedon, and rightward, but finally settled upon the rightward direction. We write and read from left to right, and our letters face the way they do, because the Greeks of about twenty-five centuries ago decided to have it so. On the other hand, the Semitic alphabets, such as Hebrew and Arabic, are still written in the direction preferred by their Phoenician ancestor—from right to left.

The Phoenician alphabet as first introduced into Greece was almost purely consonantal. The vowel sounds, unless we except certain voiceless breathings, were mostly taken for granted. It was somewhat as if our writing were restricted to such groups of consonants as *bldg, mfgr,* and the like, which we know how to expand to their fullness of sounds when they are read. This method of writing only the consonants was more or less suitable to the characteristic word structure of the Semitic languages. Classical Hebrew is still written and printed this way. To simplify matters for students or learners, the proper vowel sounds are indicated in Hebrew by means of a system of diacritical marks, or points, written or printed under or over the consonants.

But the ancient Greeks found this lack of vowel signs an inconvenience in writing their language, in which a variety of vowel sounds played an important part in inflections. At a very early date, therefore, they adapted some of the Phoenician characters for ob-

scure or voiceless breathings to represent some of the Greek vowels. The earliest inscriptions from Thera show five true vowel signs in use. Later on, the Greeks introduced some additional characters to represent other vowel sounds, and also cleverly combined vowel signs in pairs to form diphthongs such as *ai, ei, oi, ou,* and so on.

The Greeks likewise created, or derived from non-Phoenician sources, a few characters to represent certain consonantal sounds peculiar to their language, such as *ks, ps, ph,* and *ch.* But the addition of the vowel signs was the outstanding contribution of Greek genius to the alphabet as we know it.

In different parts of ancient Greece the alphabet developed along somewhat different lines. For the Greeks, although of one race and speaking different dialects of the same language, were far from being a unit politically or culturally. They were divided into a number of groups, each of small geographical extent, but with marked individualities—so marked, in fact, that the different groups found it hard to get along with one another. It is not surprising, therefore, that no uniform use of the alphabet was established among them until a relatively late date. Almost every Greek state had its own alphabet, at least ten of which can be distinguished by the shapes or functions of the letters.

But disregarding many local variations, we can distinguish two main lines of evolution in the alphabet as the Greeks used it. These resulted in what may be called the eastern alphabet and the western alphabet. The eastern, the earlier of the two, came to be the alphabet of the Ionian branch of the Greek race, at first on the islands of the Aegean Sea and in the many Greek cities on the coast of Asia Minor, later reaching the Greek mainland. It became the alphabet of ancient Athens after the Peloponnesian War, displacing an earlier Attic form. With hardly any change since about 400 B.C. it has been revived as the alphabet of modern Greece, and some of its

letters, with only minor changes, have found their way into the alphabets of Bulgaria, Serbia, Russia, and other Slavic nations.

The eastern Greek alphabet, even in its modern form, has a number of characters which cannot be recognized without some study as having anything in common with our letters for the same sounds, although they actually have a common ancestry. But its outstanding characteristic, from the point of view of the history of the alphabet, is its use of two letters, identical in form and origin with letters of our alphabet, but having entirely different functions. These are H and X. The form of H was derived from the Semitic letter *cheth,* a heavily aspirated breathing. In the earliest Greek inscriptions H was used for an aspirate, but in early times the Ionian division of the race settled upon the use of H as a vowel, with a value something like that of *a* in "cane" or of *e* in "they." The X was an added character, not in the Phoenician alphabet, which the eastern Greeks used for a sound like that of *ch* in the Scotch word "loch."

The western Greek alphabet is of importance to us because it passed into Italy and there became the ancestor of the alphabet that we use. Most of its characters were the same as those of the eastern alphabet, although some of the letters had quite decidedly changed their shape and posture. But the outstanding difference was in the functions of H and X. In the west the letter H was used in its original value of a strong aspirate, and X was used for the sound of *ks*—just as we use those letters today. For the long vowel that the eastern alphabet represented with H, the western used the diphthong *ei* and for the sound of *ch* it used the letter which the eastern Greeks used for *ps*.

Among the Ionians the characters for F and Q were dropped quite early, as the sounds they represented disappeared in speech. In the west they were retained long enough to be transported to Italy, although they were later dropped by the western Greeks also.

We have traced our alphabet back to its beginnings in the desert of Sinai (if that was indeed its place of origin) and have seen it planted and taking firm root in ancient Greece. Before we go on to its later history in western Europe, we may digress long enough to notice quite briefly some of its distant relatives of the same ancestry. For the Phoenician alphabet spread not only westward through the islands to Greece. It also grew prolifically eastward.

Before the Babylonian Captivity the Jewish people used the Phoenician alphabet in its pure form, as is attested by Hebrew inscriptions and coins. Towards the end of the seventh century B.C. an offshoot of the Phoenician alphabet began to come to the fore in the Aramaean alphabet of ancient Syria. As the commercial supremacy of Phoenicia fell before the onslaughts of the Babylonians, ending with the destruction of Tyre by Nebuchadrezzar, the Aramaean alphabet spread in influence. It was used by the Jews during their captivity by the waters of Babylon, and also by the civilian population of Assyria and Babylonia, becoming a powerful competitor of the ancient cuneiform.

After the Captivity the Jews brought the Aramaean alphabet with them to Jerusalem, where it developed into the old Hebrew script of the second and first centuries B.C. From this, but many centuries later, there came the "square" Hebrew which is commonly in use today. The Yiddish alphabet is a modification of the Hebrew.

In another direction the Aramaean alphabet spread through Syria where, through a long series of changes, it became the Syriac of the early Christian centuries and eventually appeared, quite unrecognizable, in the swinging curves of the modern Arabic. A curious side issue of the ancient Aramaean, while it was still quite close to the Phoenician, was the Samaritan, which seems to have adhered to the Phoenician tradition while the Aramaean was being trans formed in Babylonia.

III

The Alphabet in Western Europe

ALL authorities agree that the alphabet adopted by the ancient peoples inhabiting the Italian peninsula was of Greek origin. But as to how it got to Italy, when it was introduced, and from what source it came, there are almost as many differing opinions as there are students of the subject. Nor is there convincing agreement as to which of the peoples then dwelling in Italy was the first to receive and use it. Was it the Pelasgians, that almost mythical aboriginal race in Italy as well as in Greece? These people were prehistoric even to the ancients, who wondered at the walls of massive masonry which an unknown race had left behind them. Very few specimens of writing have been found among Pelasgian remains in Italy, and some scholars have speculated on the possibility that the alphabet was transmitted from Greece to Italy in the movements of trade and migration within this race.

But what little the Pelasgians (whoever they were) knew about the alphabet they most probably acquired from the Etruscans, who eventually expelled or absorbed the aborigines. The Etruscans, a race whose origin is still one of the most baffling problems of history, are said by some ancient writers to have migrated to Italy from Lydia in Asia Minor. Whatever their origins, they settled on the west coast of Italy, probably about the twelfth or eleventh century B.C. The Tyrrhenian Sea, between Italy and Sardinia, still bears the ancient Greek name (*Tyrrhenoi*) of that mysterious race, as Tuscany (Italian *Toscana*) still reminds us of the Latin name (*Etrusci*) for the same people.

The Etruscans used the alphabet at a very early date. Innumerable objects found in their tombs and burial places bear inscriptions in letters almost identical in form with those of archaic Greek alphabets. But, except for the names of divinities and some proper names, the inscriptions cannot be read, as the Etruscan language remains unknown.

It has long been quite generally assumed that the Etruscans received the alphabet from Greek colonists who settled at Cumae, not far from the later settlement at Naples, some time about the middle of the eighth century B.C. These colonists came from Chalcis and brought with them their alphabet, one of the variants of the western group of Greek alphabets. During the period of active colonization, in which the Greeks succeeded the Phoenicians in the exploitation of the Mediterranean region, the Chalcidians assumed the leadership in the Greek penetration of Italy, and consequently the western form of the Greek letters predominates in the early Italic alphabets. It did not seem unreasonable to suppose that the Etruscans, who must have come very soon into contact with the newcomers at Cumae, acquired the alphabet from the Chalcidian Greeks.

But a little object found in one of the Etruscan tombs has made it doubtful that Cumae was the sole, or even the principal, source of the Etruscan alphabet. That object is an ivory writing tablet, about 3½ by 2 inches in size, with a raised border. The sunken part of the tablet once contained a thin coating of wax in which the written letters were traced with a sharp-pointed stylus. Interesting enough merely as an ancient writing tablet, this little piece of ivory immediately became one of the rare archaeological discoveries of incalculable importance when it was found that it had a complete alphabet of twenty-five letters carefully incised in the ivory of its raised upper border. Once, no doubt, the "copybook" of some Etruscan youngster, it has survived to give instruction to learned men. For

the alphabet it carries, while of an archaic Greek form, is not Chalcidian, nor even of the characteristically western form of the Greek.

The tomb in which this tablet was found, at Marsiliana, in the valley of the Albegna River, has been determined to be of the second half of the eighth or the beginning of the seventh century B.C. Other objects found with it are described as not at all Greek in type, but showing the influences of an oriental art. The tablet itself was undoubtedly imported, ivory not being a product native to Italy, but the alphabet was probably engraved on it after it had been brought to Etruria. The fact that any Etruscan would be interested in acquiring an imported writing tablet seems to indicate

ETRUSCAN ALPHABET OF THE MARSILIANA TABLET, ABOUT 700 B.C.
(*Read leftwards.*)

that writing was already well established in that region at a time when the Greek colony at Cumae either did not yet exist, or before it could have exercised much if any cultural influence in Etruria.

The Marsiliana alphabet was written from right to left. An outstanding peculiarity of it, and of other Etruscan alphabets of later date, was its retention of a letter which all the Greek alphabets had long since dropped. In the reproduction shown herewith it is the eighteenth letter counting from the right, closely resembling our M. It is the Phoenician *tsade,* representing the sound of *ts.* The fifteenth letter represents *ks,* while the Etruscan X represents *ch.* The Chalcidians at Cumae had no *tsade* and used an entirely different letter for *ch.*

The evidence seems to exclude a Cumaean origin for the earliest alphabet used in Italy. The fact remains that the letters are Greek,

but they are Greek of a kind which has not yet been satisfactorily identified elsewhere.

The archaic form of the Etruscan alphabet remained in use until about the beginning of the fifth century B.C. Thereafter it was modified somewhat, doubtless to make it conform more closely to the pronunciation of the Etruscan language. But it was in its earliest form that it was transmitted to the Etruscans' neighbors on the south—the *Latini*. Very early Latin tradition fixed the year 753 B.C. as the date of the founding of their principal city, Roma, on the Tiber. But it seems more likely that this was the traditional date of the Latin declaration of independence from Etruscan domination. Typical of the legends of Rome's infancy is the story of Horatius at the bridge, barring the way of the Etruscans led by Lars Porsena of Clusium, whose purpose was to destroy the upstart on the Tiber which had expelled its hated Etruscan kings.

Although Roman culture from the very beginning was deeply rooted in Etruscan institutions, relations between the two races, while often peaceful, were never wholly cordial. Their rivalry for the control of Italy continued for nearly five hundred years from the legendary date of the founding of Rome, until in 281 B.C. the power of the Etruscans was finally destroyed and their country absorbed in the growing Roman domain.

But in spite of stubborn incompatibilities, the early Romans learned their letters from their Etruscan neighbors, just as they took their religion, their early laws, their architecture, and other fundamentals of civilization from the same source. Just how and when the intellectual contagion of writing first spread among the Latins we do not know. The earliest surviving specimen of writing in Latin has been dated at about 600 B.C., when Etruria was still the dominant power in central Italy. This writing is incised on a gold fibula, or brooch, discovered at Praeneste (modern Palestrina), not far

from Rome. Written in the archaic manner from right to left, it reads MANIOS MED VHEVHAKED NUMASIOI, which means "Manius made me for Numasius." The four words of this inscription present not only the oldest known form of the Roman alphabet, but also some peculiarities of the archaic Latin language. Those who remember their Latin may compare *vhevhaked* with its later equivalent *fecit*. In the alphabet of this inscription, F still represented the softer sound of V. The spelling with VH was doubtless an expedient to represent the *f* sound. Other Roman inscriptions of very remote date show other equally interesting peculiarities both of the alphabet and of the language.

THE PRAENESTINE FIBULA OF ABOUT 600 B.C.

It was two hundred years or so from the date of the Praenestine fibula before the Romans had reduced their alphabet to very nearly the form in which we now know it in our capital letters. Changes caused it gradually to differ from the Greek alphabets of corresponding periods, not only in the shapes of the letters, but in the letters which were used. The Romans for some reason discarded the letter K except in the spelling of two or three words; thus *kalendae,* "the calends," in Roman dates, continued to be written with K. But elsewhere in place of K they used the letter C, the rounded form of the gallows-shaped *gamma* of the Greek alphabet which had the value of G. For a time the Romans made no distinction between the sounds of G and C, using the same letter for both.

On the other hand, the Romans kept the ancient letter F (called by the Greeks *digamma,* or double gamma) which the Greek alphabets had dropped in very early times. It represented a *v* sound which early disappeared from Greek pronunciation, but the Romans, after experimenting by strengthening it with H, finally conferred upon F by itself the value which it has today.

The letter Z, seventh in the ancient Greek alphabet, stood for a sound which did not occur in the pronunciation of Latin. It was therefore dropped entirely, but in its place was substituted a new letter, G, which the Romans made by putting a little "beard" on the letter C. The earliest known appearance of G as distinct from C was in the epitaph, carved in stone, of that famous old Roman, Cornelius Lucius Scipio Barbatus, about 250 B.C., but the new letter was doubtless in use for some time before that date.

As in the western Greek alphabets generally, and in the Etruscan, H was used by the Romans for an aspirate. In the eastern Greek world, as we have seen, H represented a vowel sound, as it still does in modern Greek. The next letter in the Greek alphabet, *theta,* representing the sound of *th,* was useless in writing Latin, so it was discarded almost at the very beginning. Centuries later, when Greek names and words began to find their way into Latin speech, the Romans did not restore the Greek letter *theta,* but used the combination TH for its sound, as we still do today.

The Greek letter *xi,* for the sound of *ks,* which came after N in the Greek and Etruscan alphabets, was dropped by the Romans. For *ks* they used the non-Phoenician letter X. Its place well towards the end of all the archaic alphabets still bears witness to the fact that it was not one of the letters which the Greeks originally received from the Phoenicians but an addition of Greek creation. When the Romans later found it necessary to write the sound that the eastern Greeks represented by X, they used the combination CH, which has

become fixed in the usage of many languages using the Roman alphabet today.

Another letter, Q, fell entirely out of use among the Greeks and was later dropped by the Etruscans also. But it proved indispensable to the Romans, although, curiously enough, they very soon thought it necessary to add another letter to it to aid its pronunciation. Thus Q has become a letter which, in the European languages at least, never stands alone. There is no reason why Q should not be understood as having a definite value by itself so that we might write *qeen, qick, qote,* instead of *queen, quick, quote,* and so on. But the ancient Romans established the usage of always writing QV, and we have never broken from that tradition.

The letter V was used by the Romans both as a vowel and as a semivowel. As a vowel it represented the sound usually expressed in English by doubling the letter O, as in *tool.* As a semivowel it was used as we use W. In later Roman times V tended to become rounded at the bottom until it took the shape of U, and then V was sometimes used for the semivowel and U for the vowel. But not until quite late in the history of the Roman alphabet was V ever used for the sound originally represented by F, which V now has in the English word *save.*

The letter V was derived from the Greek letter *upsilon* (Υ), one of the non-Phoenician letters added to represent a Greek vowel sound which seems to have been something like the *u* in French or the *ü* in German. In later times, when Greek culture was penetrating the Roman world, another letter was needed to represent in Latin the peculiar sound of *upsilon* in Greek words and names. So the Greek Υ was again taken into the Roman alphabet, in the form Y. The Romans used Y only as a vowel, never as a semivowel as in the English word *you.*

Under the same Greek influences the Romans restored the letter

Z, which centuries earlier they had discarded as useless. The position of Y and Z at the end of our alphabet is evidence of their very late adoption by the Romans.

Thus the Roman alphabet was finally completed with twenty-three letters. We miss our J, U, and W. The Romans used I both as a vowel and as a semivowel. As a semivowel it had the value of the English Y in *you*. The Romans never knew the sound of the English J in *joy*. The addition of the curved tail to I to distinguish its function as a semivowel was a relatively late innovation. To the ancient Romans, also, V and U were simply different forms of the same letter; only in very late Roman times was U specifically detailed to the function of representing the vowel. As to W, its form and its English name "double-U" show that it was "made up" from VV to take over the old function of V as that letter came to be used more exclusively for the fricative sound of V in the English words *very* or *ever*.

"RUSTIC" CAPITALS, FROM A PAPYRUS OF THE FIRST CENTURY, A.D.

The alphabet as the ancient Romans used it in monumental inscriptions and for such formal purposes as the writing of books had only *one* form for each letter until well after the beginning of the Christian era. These were the forms which we now recognize in our capital letters. True, there were some variations in the way those letters were made. For books and other kinds of formal writing there eventually developed a modification known as the "rustic" capitals. But they were still capitals, easily identified with those we still use. Our "small" letters came into being in the course of time, through a long series of transitional changes, as the result of the scribes' perfectly natural impulse to write more smoothly and rapidly than could be done with the conventional forms of the monumental letters. This impulse received great encouragement from

the increasing use of the smooth-surfaced parchments and vellums in place of papyrus, and it was constantly abetted by the cursive handwriting of the time, in which the letters were adapted for everyday personal and business purposes.

The early Roman man of affairs, of course, did not carefully form his letters one by one in copybook style when he wrote his personal letters or his notes of business transactions. Instead, he (or his clerk) took all manner of short cuts in shaping the letters so as to write them rapidly. The practice of writing on the waxed tablets described in an earlier chapter also had much to do with the way the letters were shaped. The result was a cursive style of writing

ROMAN HANDWRITING OF THE FIRST CENTURY A.D.

that had even less resemblance to the original shapes of the letters than our ordinary handwriting has to the printed letters in our books today.

We do not know anything about the appearance of Roman handwriting in its earlier phases. Written on perishable materials, it has all completely disappeared. But from the Egyptian waste heaps of the years after Egypt became a Roman province and from the buried cities of Pompeii and Herculaneum, destroyed in A.D. 79 by the ashes and lava of Vesuvius, there has been recovered an abundance of documents written in the cursive hand of the Romans of the first Christian century. Even the casual scribblings on the walls of the houses of Pompeii have been instructive in this connection. To test the ingenuity of the reader in identifying the letters, we

here show one of these *graffiti,* or wall scribblings. It quotes two lines from the works of Ovid, a popular Roman poet, in the handwriting of a rather well-educated person. The lines are

SURDA SIT ORANTI TUA IANUA LAXA FERENTI

AUDIAT EXCLUSI VERBA RECEPTUS [A]MA[NS]

Two marked characteristics of this Roman cursive handwriting were influential in the later development of the forms of our letters. One was the tendency to make curves of straight lines, and the other was the conspicuous ascenders and descenders—the strokes which extended above and below the line of writing. In the making of books, even though written more and more upon vellum instead of

IESTATVRQVEDEOSITERVMSEADEROELIACOGI
BISIAMITALOSHOSTLSTAECAUTERAFOEDERA

RUSTIC CAPITALS, FROM AN EARLY MANUSCRIPT OF VIRGIL
("*testaturque deos iterum se ad proelia cogi
bis iam Italos hostis haec altera foedera*".)

papyrus, literary usage was notably conservative, and the traditional capitals continued to be used in the manuscripts of books until the fifth or sixth century. But there were also innovators among the scribes, and little by little changes in the forms of the letters crept in. Some straight lines gave way to curves, and distinguishing strokes in some of the letters were extended above or below the line of writing.

The traditional capitals, which scholars of a later age have named "majuscules," took two forms, the so-called "square" capitals, which kept rather close to the forms of the letters seen in monumental inscriptions, and the somewhat more informal "rustic" capitals, in which the letters are thinner and more elongated. But by the fourth

century the modifying influence of the contemporary cursive scripts, together with other influences, had become so marked in the writing of book manuscripts that an entirely new style of letter could be clearly recognized. This is now known as the "uncial," from the Latin word *uncia*, "inch," because of the exaggerated size in which those letters were sometimes written.

The uncial style clearly shows the beginnings of our small letters. In the letter A, the right-hand slanting stroke was curved to the left at the top, while the left-hand slanting stroke together with the crossbar degenerated into a narrow loop which tended in time to become rounder until the result was "a." The upper loop of B became

ITEMAPOSTOLUS
ADROMANOS

ROMAN UNCIALS, FROM A SEVENTH CENTURY
VELLUM MANUSCRIPT.

smaller than the lower, and also narrower as the vertical line was gradually extended upward, until the upper loop merged with the vertical line and the form became "b." In the cursive writing of D, the earliest Roman scripts that we know already show the tendency to make the vertical line curve outward to the left, while the original curve is straightened out and extended upward, at first with a pronounced leftward slant, but later becoming vertical, as in "d." E was rounded into something like ϵ, from which "e" resulted. The "beard" of G grew downward and finally curled up under what had been the body of the capital letter, so that progressively the form "g" developed. H was more easily written by suppressing the upper half of the right-hand vertical stroke; then, with a rounding of the crossbar, "h" resulted. L grew taller while the horizontal stroke at the

bottom grew shorter so that it became more and more like "l." The straight lines of M and N were easily modified into curves resembling those of "m" and "n," although N kept its original form much longer than M. The vertical stroke of P grew downward to make "p," and the "tail" of Q was carried to the right and made into a straight descender, as in "q." As far as the uncial style is concerned, R, S, and T changed relatively little. V had almost disappeared in the form of U.

The uncial was the prevailing style until the eighth or ninth century, particularly in the writing of religious or ecclesiastical manuscripts. The older capitals were reserved for the making of fine copies of the pagan authors. The extraordinary popularity of the works of the poet Virgil had much to do with the persistence of the capitals in use until a quite late date. No copy of the Bible and almost no Christian works have been found written in capitals, and on the other hand relatively few of the pagan authors have been preserved in uncial manuscripts.

But even where the uncial style had become prevalent, the old majuscules were not entirely discarded, but were relegated to special use in such parts of the manuscript book as the headings (Latin *capita*), whence their present name "capitals." They also came to be used now and then as the initial letters of chapters and sometimes of paragraphs.

The four or five centuries during which the uncial style developed saw political and social unrest throughout Europe. In the early centuries of the Christian era the imperial power of Rome was slowly but steadily disintegrating while the power of the church was growing. The incursions of Germanic tribes from the north in the fifth century brought the centers of the old Roman civilization face to face with readjustments which seriously disrupted the established order. Italy and Rome became separated from the provinces,

and as the old imperial controls weakened, new nationalities began to assert themselves. Old traditions died, and the new national customs and usages, combined with the influence of the church, produced changes in institutions, just as the national vernaculars broke down the prevailing Latin language into the various Romance, or Romanic, languages which survive today, or in some parts supplanted Latin altogether. In those troubled times the industry of book publishing, which had once flourished in Rome and other centers, came to an end. Learning, including the writing and transcribing of such books as remained in use, took refuge with the church, in monasteries, cloisters, and other religious establishments, which thus became the sanctuaries of the few remaining scholars.

But Latin, however debased, was still the language of law and government, and of the church, and Roman Italy was still the center and source of such culture as survived, as well as of all ecclesiastical authority. This high source sanctioned the uncial book-hand. Although it varied somewhat with different scribes at different places and times, it maintained a fairly uniform appearance throughout the duration and extent of its vogue. An uncial manuscript of the seventh century is strikingly similar, in the forms of its letters, to one of the third.

Long before the uncial style finally went out of use, its successor was developing, just as the uncials themselves developed before the majuscule capitals entirely lost their vogue. First came the so-called half-uncials, an intermediate step on the way to the "minuscules," or small letters, now familiar to us. The earliest examples of half-uncials appear in the form of notes written by scholars on the margins of majuscule or uncial manuscripts. The forms of the letters in these marginal notes show a sort of informal compromise between the bookish uncials and the cursive script of the time and place. These forms vary considerably in different places and with

different scribes, but they have in common a distinctly cursive character in certain letters.

The half-uncials also showed the beginning of a tendency to run certain combinations of letters together into ligatures. In time, these ligatures multiplied enormously, and in many of them the original forms of their letters almost entirely disappeared. One of these ligatures which has survived to the present day is the character &, in which only a trained imagination can still see the letters *et*. A few other ligatures have survived in such forms as *æ, œ, ffi,* and the like.

It was the half-uncial style which was carried into Ireland by Saint Patrick and other missionaries in the fifth century. In that far-off land, sequestered and secure from the turmoils of the Con-

ꞏꞏꞏ *adilledantur rerpondir*

HALF-UNCIALS, FROM A MANUSCRIPT OF THE SEVENTH CENTURY.

tinent, utterly free from the restraints of convention, and with no other national script of their own to conflict with it, the Irish monks cherished the only style of writing that they knew and lavished upon it a peculiar genius. The result was a startlingly distinctive script, which was also one of the most beautiful book-hands ever developed. This Irish half-uncial shows so many well-developed transitions to the minuscule forms of the letters that Ireland may claim with much justice to be the real birthplace of the minuscule book-hand, even though minuscule letters were appearing in cursive scripts a full century earlier in other places.

The pinnacle of Irish calligraphy was reached in the immortal Book of Kells, containing the Gospels in Latin, produced in Saint Columba's monastery in the seventh century. It has justly been called the most beautiful manuscript book in the world. Certainly in

the unbelievably delicate tracery of its lavish ornamentation it is without an equal. For some reason it was never completed, much of its ornamentation being left unfinished. A sudden raid of the savage Danes may have caused work on it to stop. At any rate, the devoted solicitude of its custodians saved it from destruction when the Danes were ravaging both Ireland and Anglo-Saxon England, and also from the disasters of the later English conquest of Ireland, and it is now preserved in the library of Trinity College, Dublin. Any lover of beautiful books who has not already made its acquaintance will do well to repair to the nearest library which has a reproduction of it, and there enjoy at leisure its endless fascination.

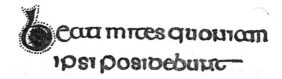

IRISH HALF-UNCIALS, FROM THE BOOK OF KELLS.

From Ireland in time went monks and missionaries to England and to the Continent. Wherever they went they took their distinctive script with them. In England, the Saxons and then the Danes had almost obliterated all traces of the Roman civilization which had once flourished there. The art of writing was revived very largely under Irish influences. About A.D. 700, in the north of England, Eadfrith, bishop of Lindisfarne, produced under Irish tutorship the famous Lindisfarne Gospels, the finest example of Anglo-Saxon manuscript writing of the period. But in time the Anglo-Saxons modified the rounded Irish letters into angular forms distinctively their own, which, however, still showed many evidences of their parentage.

By the eighth century the uncial style was definitely on the wane everywhere. It required too much skill and care for an age in which scribes were no longer trained in the ancient traditions of their craft but were drawn from the ranks of the public writers, notaries, scriveners, conveyancers, and others, who used the cursive handwriting. Also, the uncial style required space in which to display itself, and vellum was becoming scarce and expensive while papyrus in most places could no longer be procured. It was an age of palimpsests—old parchments with their writing carefully erased and then rewritten. The much more facile and condensed minuscule style was well on its way to prevalence in the eighth and ninth centuries.

But with the victory of the minuscule there came a steady degeneration of the art of writing into a confusion of local and per-

MINUSCULE WRITING OF THE BENEVENTAN SCHOOL, FROM A MANU-
SCRIPT OF THE ELEVENTH CENTURY.

sonal peculiarities. There were mixtures of uncials, half-uncials, cursives, and imitations of various kinds, cluttered with an ever increasing multitude of ligatures and abbreviations derived from cursive writing, and adulterated even with a number of shorthand signs for certain words—arbitrary symbols which had nothing to do with the letters of the alphabet. Each center of book production developed its own style of penmanship, and these styles became so widely different that a scholar from one locality had considerable difficulty in reading even a familiar text written by a scribe in another center.

At the close of the eighth century Charlemagne assumed a power in Europe that made some pretense to the universality of the old

Roman dominion. He gave powerful aid to the cause of scholarship and even before he became emperor had established a school of writing at Tours. Here was developed the so-called Caroline minuscule. This style of writing was not a new creation, but was based on a careful selection from other styles. It consciously sought to emulate the legibility and beauty of the old manuscripts which were being copied under Charlemagne's imperial encouragement. The Tours school did away with hosts of unsightly ligatures and also made general the practice of leaving a space between words, an aid to ease in reading which had only recently become optional with European scribes.

From Tours the new style spread with extraordinary rapidity throughout Europe, its standards set in a large number of manuscripts turned out at Tours by scribes who assembled there from all parts of the European world. In some countries, as in England, the established national scripts continued to be used for books written in the vernacular, but the new minuscule style was everywhere adopted for manuscripts written in Latin.

The Tours school effected far-reaching and valuable reforms, but after the days of its influence had passed, local and national peculiarities in penmanship once more reasserted themselves, so that down to the time of the invention of printing the development of writing followed several different lines. An increasing tendency towards angularity in the formation of the letters resulted in the Gothic style of the twelfth century. In the course of this development writing became once more an art in which scribes received professional training. Fine, large volumes were produced, with carefully exact lettering, and ornamented with handsomely illuminated initials and borders.

In the Gothic period some fairly distinct national alphabets appeared. In England, the Netherlands, and most of **France, the**

letters tended to be tall and narrow, with moderately heavy pen strokes. Southern France, Italy, and Spain still inclined towards rounded letters. The Italian Gothic never entirely lost the good features of its Carolingian predecessors. Germany developed a distinct style, with heavy strokes, increasing angularity, and much elaboration of the letters, especially of the capitals. The Gothic styles also brought back many of the old abbreviations and fusions of letters, with a tendency towards compression and crowding.

In all the Gothic book-hands the changes in the forms of the capital letters were particularly striking. The old majuscule capitals were abandoned in favor of those made on the uncial pattern. Especially in Germany, these capitals were elaborated in a most remarkable way, with scrolled serifs, hairlines, hooks, and other excrescences of ornamentation, until their kinship with the severely simple ancient Roman capitals was quite unrecognizable. These highly artificial capitals, and the Gothic style of letters generally, have survived in the printed types that we call Old English.

The Gothic style, in its turn, began to degenerate into confusion and artiness, and was not at its best when the invention of printing put a stop to its evolution. Fortunately for those of us who prefer the simplicity of our roman types to what is sometimes called "black letter," a revulsion against the Gothic artificialities set in at the beginning of the Renaissance, especially in Italy. Stimulated by fresh contacts with the classic literature of ancient Rome, scholars expressed abhorrence of later barbarisms by applying the term Gothic in contempt to the crudities of their own times, so far from the classical beauties that the invading Goths had once destroyed. For manuscript copies of the Latin classics they felt that a purer, simpler letter form was more suitable than the elaborate scripts then in use. They therefore went back to the admirable Caroline minuscule of five or six hundred years before—influenced, no doubt, by the clear

and legible penmanship of the old manuscripts that they were copying, and also by the fact that the Caroline script was supposed to be
somehow more purely Roman than the scripts later developed in the
provinces. The result was the so-called humanistic book-hand of the
early fifteenth century, a form of writing which has a remarkable
resemblance to our roman letters of today. A later chapter will
disclose how the early printers seized upon this style of writing and
fixed it lastingly in their metal types.

The metamorphoses of the alphabet from the austere capitals
of ancient Rome to the forms of the letters we now read have resulted in giving us really two alphabets—our small letters and our
capitals. The latter are letter forms which are now detailed to special
functions. They appear in headings, as the initial letters of proper
names and of the first words in sentences, and so on. A book printed
entirely in capitals would be quite difficult for us to read, so accustomed have we become to their successors, the so-called minuscules
or small letters.

In preserving a really archaic form of letters for such limited
functions, the alphabets that developed in Europe are peculiar. No
other alphabets have a similar specialized kind of letters. Attempts
have occasionally been made in printing to dispense with our capitals, but there is no indication at present that this proposed reform
will ever become universally accepted for our books and newspapers.
So for some time to come, it seems, we shall continue to employ
those forms of our letters in which can still be traced some resemblance to their Phoenician prototypes of more than thirty centuries ago.

In a history of the book we are really not concerned with cursive
handwriting except in so far as we have briefly noted that the cursive
hands have intruded, from time to time, upon the penmanship with
which books were written. But since the advent of printing, the

book forms of our letters have become quite definitely set and fixed, and there is very little likelihood of any such marked changes in the future as were made during the centuries of their evolution under the hands of scribes. So far as the letters are concerned, a book printed by Nicolas Jenson or by Aldus Manutius at the beginning of the sixteenth century is as easily legible to our eyes as a book printed yesterday. In four hundred years, changes in the forms of printed letters of the roman alphabet have been only in minor details of proportion, shading, serifs, and the like. The characteristic shapes by which we recognize our letters have been very little altered. But in the same space of time, handwriting has been changed enormously; only an expert in the scripts of different periods and places can read, say, a letter written in the days of Queen Elizabeth. Although we can merely mention the fact here, our alphabet as we use it in handwriting and the alphabet as we see it printed have developed along distinct lines of evolution, with their two routes through the centuries only occasionally uniting with, or crossing, each other.

Although they are in no sense a part of the alphabet which has come down to us from most ancient times, our Arabic numerals are now an indispensable part of the system of symbols with which we write and print. The Moors in Spain are said to have introduced these numerals into Europe in the eighth century. If so, they did not come into anything like general use for five hundred years. Before their advent, even the simplest calculations required the aid of the abacus, and arithmetical notation was limited by the cumbersome Roman numerals or various abbreviations of them.

Even after Arabic numerals came into use in the fourteenth and fifteenth centuries, the forms of most of them were so different from the forms with which we are familiar that we would scarcely recognize them even as being numerals. Like our letters, they passed

through a succession of changes in form, strangely modified at different places and at different periods by the hands of copyists or in cursive handwriting. The illustration here shows, for example, how the figure 2 came to be written "upside down" if compared with its original form.

SOME STEPS IN THE EVOLUTION OF THE ARABIC FIGURES 2 AND 4.

Europe took a long time to settle finally upon what the forms of the numerals should be. Furthermore, it also took the Europeans a long, long time to learn their use—particularly that of the zero and of the designation of tens, hundreds, thousands, and so on, by the relative location of the figures. It seemed impossible for the people to learn, for example, how 3 was to be understood as "three" in the units place and as "thirty" in a combination such as 35. So we find them writing "302" for 32—what was more logical, if 30 was "thirty" and 2 was "two"? They even used the new numerals in combination with the Roman numerals which were more familiar to them, producing such strange hybrids as "X3" for 13, "C25" for 125, "M.CCC.35" for 1335, "M.CCCC.8.II" for 1482, and the like.

Even at the time of the invention of printing the forms of the numerals had not become completely standardized, although they were then very close to their present shapes. But we still have "old-style" figures. And convention still sanctions the use of the Roman numerals for dates on title pages and in monumental inscriptions.

IV

Paper and Its Origins

INDISPENSABLE to the successful development of printing was the availability of a material less costly and more easily worked than parchment or vellum. It is true that some of the earliest typographic books were printed on vellum, but the substance which really gave printing its initial impetus was paper.

Paper as a substitute for vellum had been slowly making its way into favor in Europe for about three centuries before the first metal types were cast, but it was not a product of European origin. On the contrary, it found its way to Europe, through a long, slow series of intermediate steps, from the land which was the most distant of all lands in the then known world. For paper was first made and used in China.

The year A.D. 105 seems to be established with approximate accuracy as the date of the invention of paper. It was in that year that the new process was first reported to Emperor Ho Ti by Ts'ai Lun, to whom Chinese tradition gives credit for the invention. It is by no means certain, however, whether he was actually the inventor or merely the official through whom an important discovery was made known. A record of the event, which was written in the fifth century by Fan Yeh in his official history of the Han Dynasty, runs as follows:

"In ancient times writing was generally on bamboo or on pieces of silk, which were then called *chih*. But silk being expensive and bamboo heavy, these two materials were not convenient. Then Ts'ai Lun thought of using tree bark, hemp, rags and fish nets.

In the first year of the Yüan-hsing period [A.D. 105] he made a report to the emperor on the process of papermaking and received high praise for his ability. From this time paper has been in use everywhere and is called the 'paper of Marquis Ts'ai.' "

For the emperor ennobled Ts'ai, and after the death of the marquis, although he poisoned himself when he was found to be implicated in a palace intrigue, a temple was erected to his memory. And even to this day, among the old-fashioned Chinese paper dealers, the apocryphal portrait of Ts'ai Lun is sometimes found with incense sticks burning before it.

This tradition of the invention of paper received amazingly clear confirmation from discoveries made in China by Sir Aurel Stein in 1907. In the sealed dustbin of a watchtower on an outlying segment of the Great Wall, near Tun-huang in Chinese Turkestan, this explorer made a rich find of a mass of documents written on wood and one or two on silk, and with them nine letters written on paper in the Sogdian script. None of these letters is dated, but as the Chinese documents found with them all belong to a period of not later than A.D. 137, it seems safe to say that the paper of the letters was made within fifty years from the date of Ts'ai Lun's official announcement. One of these letters, written on one of the oldest pieces of paper now in existence, is reproduced in the plate facing page 64, from the original in the British Museum.

Microscopic examination has shown this ancient specimen to be a pure rag paper. Other specimens of paper of only slightly later date have been discovered by other explorers at various points in central Asia, usually with documents written on wood or on silk, showing that the use of the earlier writing materials had not been entirely supplanted. By the fifth century, however, the use of paper had become universal in China.

A mere recital of the dates of the earliest known occurrence

of paper at different points tells much of the history of this now universal material for writing and printing and of its gradual movement westward. After its origin in central China in A.D. 105, it was in use at Tun-huang in Chinese Turkestan by A.D. 150; also in Chinese Turkestan but farther west, at Lou-lan, in A.D. 200 and at Turfan in 399; at Gilghit in Kashmir in the sixth century; at Samarkand in 751; at Bagdad in 793; in Egypt in the year 900 or perhaps earlier; at Fez in Morocco about 1100; at Jativa (or Xativa), Spain, in 1150; at Fabriano, Italy, about 1270; at Nuremberg, Germany, in 1390; in England not until 1494; and finally it was manufactured for the first time on the American continent at Philadelphia in 1690.

How graphic a story even this brief schedule tells! Chart it on a map, and it is still more impressive. Set it beside the outstanding dates in the history of Europe and try to visualize all that befell European civilization while the manufacture and use of paper was so slowly spreading. Long before paper became the helpmate of printing in Europe, it had played its part in the vast movements of races in Asia and in the minglings and interchanges of Oriental cultures for centuries.

Powerful forces helped the spread of paper and also prevented its earlier arrival in the western world. Three mighty religions played their part in its history before it ever reached Europe. The zeal of Buddhist missionaries, with their peculiar enthusiasm for the endless repetition and multiplication of their sacred texts, seized on paper as a means of spreading their faith throughout China and Japan. The Nestorian Christians, penetrating central Asia in the fifth and sixth centuries, must have known of it and used it, although none of their documents written on paper have survived. On the other hand, the Mohammedans, represented by the all-conquering Arabs, closed to Europe the ancient trade routes, and thus

diverted the spread of paper into the Moslem world exclusively.

Military conquest also played an important part in the diffusion of papermaking. During the early part of the eighth century the Arabs, aflame with zeal to conquer the world for Islam, overran what is now Russian Turkestan and in the course of a battle there made prisoners of some Chinese papermakers. The prisoners taught their craft to their captors, and the making of paper was thus introduced into the Mohammedan world at Samarkand in A.D. 751—the first step on its momentous travels from its Chinese birthplace into Europe.

Samarkand, where fine crops of hemp and flax were grown, was a favorable location for the making of paper. An Arabian writer of the eleventh century tells us: "Among the specialties of Samarkand that should be mentioned is paper. It has replaced the rolls of Egyptian papyrus and the parchment which was formerly used for writing, because it is more beautiful, more agreeable, and more convenient. . . . The manufacture grew and not only filled the local demand, but also became for the people of Samarkand an important article of commerce. Thus it came to minister to the needs and well-being of mankind in all the countries of the earth." But though Samarkand continued to be a papermaking center for centuries, the craft had soon spread to other cities. Harun-al-Rashid, the well known caliph of the Arabian Nights, brought Chinese papermakers to Bagdad in A.D. 793, and soon thereafter the craft reached Damascus, which became for several centuries the world's principal source of supply.

Paper was still a mere upstart in the world when it first appeared in Egypt and there confronted the ages-old papyrus, whose use was already on the decline. By A.D. 850 paper was displacing it. The older material was becoming outmoded; an Egyptian letter written towards the end of the ninth century closes with the apologetic

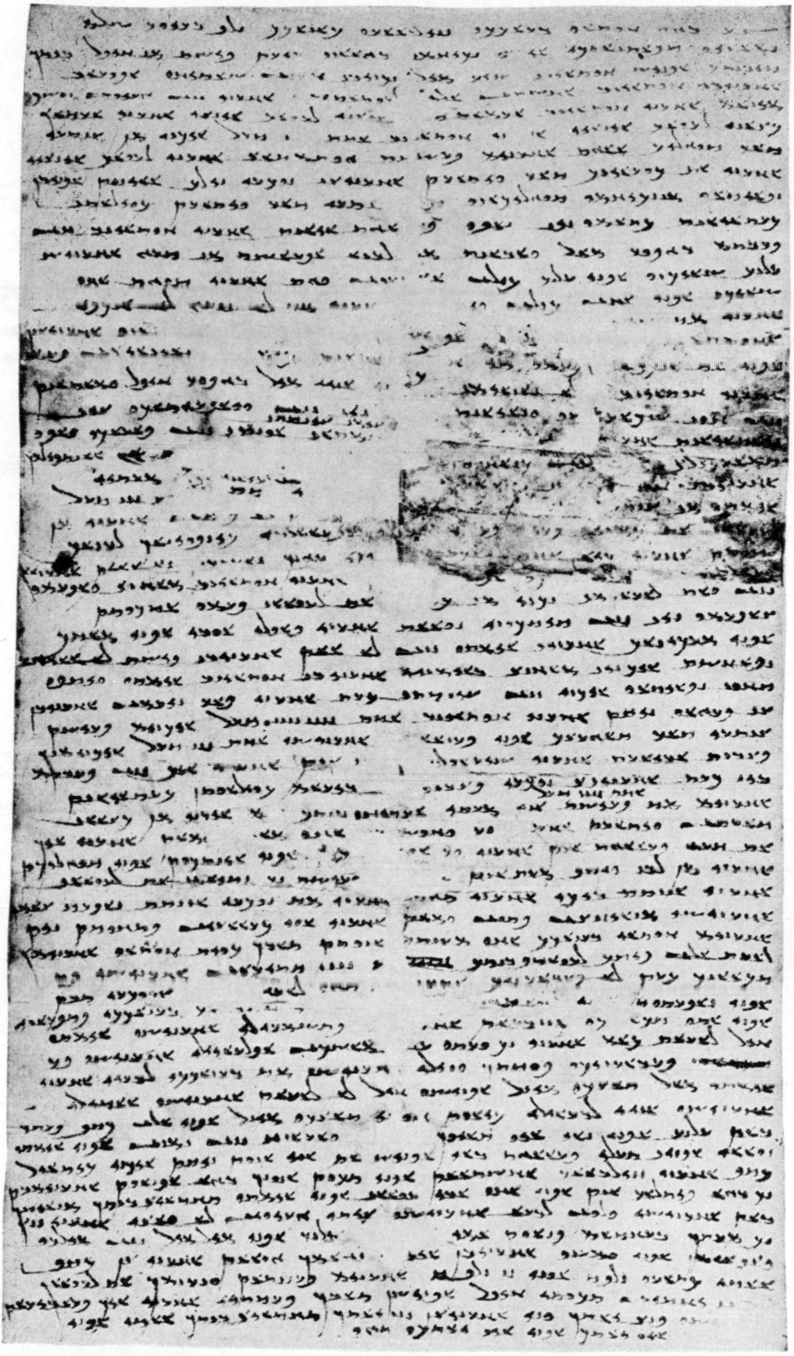

SPECIMEN OF CHINESE PAPER, A.D. 137

PAGE FROM A FRENCH MANUSCRIPT BOOK OF
HOURS, ABOUT 1450.

words "Pardon the papyrus." Paper was then the vogue for stylish correspondence, and by the year 950 papyrus was entirely supplanted—but not until it had passed on to its successor the name by which it is still known.

The rainless climate of Egypt, like that of the deserts of Turkestan, is favorable to the preservation of paper. Thousands upon thousands of paper documents, ranging from the ninth to the fourteenth century, have been found in Egypt and have contributed richly to our knowledge of the Moslem civilization of those centuries, as well as to the history of paper and papermaking. Egypt was peculiarly favorable to the manufacture of paper. For thousands of years it had grown flax and woven linen, and it had abundance of the raw material for making paper. Even the ancient tombs were rifled by the roving Bedouins for the strips of linen in which mummies had been wrapped, and this stuff went into the making of a coarse stock used for wrapping paper.

Still confined in its range to the Moslem world, papermaking slowly moved from Egypt across northern Africa and finally reached Morocco by the beginning of the twelfth century. By that time this substitute for parchment was not entirely unknown in Europe, though it was not yet made there, and not much of it seems to have been imported for use. Some European trade in paper had begun, however, with supplies arriving from Damascus through Constantinople and from Africa through Sicily. The oldest extant European paper document is a deed of Count Roger, of Sicily, written in Latin and Arabic and dated 1109.

Papermaking came into Europe under Mohammedan auspices when the Moorish rulers of the old kingdom of Valencia, in Spain, provided for the erection of paper mills in the town of Jativa about 1150. Even after the conquest of the region by the kingdom of Aragon nearly a century later, the paper industry, though still con-

ducted by infidels, received royal protection, as the export of paper from Jativa had grown to impressive proportions.

The earliest paper mill in Christendom was probably that erected about 1270 at Fabriano—an Italian city which is still one of the

THE STROMER PAPER MILL, NUREMBERG, ABOUT 1390.

world's most important centers for the production of fine handmade papers. Through improved technique the Italian papermakers at Fabriano, and a little later at Bologna, Padua, Genoa, and other centers, so far surpassed the product of the Spanish mills that in the fourteenth century Italy had supplanted Spain and even Damascus as the source of Europe's supply.

For some time France and Germany were satisfied to import such paper as was required for their needs. But by 1348 we find that paper was being made in the Saint Julien region near Troyes, in France; and at about 1390 the famous Stromer mill was in operation at Nuremberg, Germany, but manned by Italian craftsmen. Flanders is said to have had a paper mill at Huy about 1405, but no paper was made in England until the end of the fifteenth century.

Paper, we have now seen, was a Chinese monopoly for some six hundred years and then passed into the almost exclusive control of the Moslems for another five hundred years. After its introduction into Europe its advance in favor there was painfully slow. There were several impediments to the general acceptance of paper in Europe. In the first place, parchment was still a highly satisfactory material and was, indeed, much better than the earliest paper made in Europe. In the second place, education in Europe was backward, and there were relatively few who could read. In the making and use of books, the differences between European civilization and that of the Arabs of the eleventh century, for example, was startling. The library of the caliph at Cairo contained some 150,000 books at a time when even a flourishing European monastery was notable if it had copies of 150 titles. For a long time there was no European demand for paper such as an active book publishing industry would have created.

Furthermore, paper at first lay under the displeasure of the church because of its exclusively Moslem or Jewish origin. And it also suffered at first from laws which forbade its use for public documents and important written instruments. A decree of Emperor Frederick II in 1221 declared that instruments written on paper had no validity in law. Hence paper long had the status of a very poor relation of the lordly parchment and had to be satisfied with lowly employment for unimportant writings.

But with the entrance of printing upon the European stage, paper came into its rich inheritance of usefulness. It can truly be said that if paper, more than anything else, made printing successful, printing reciprocated by making the use of paper universal.

What were the methods of manufacturing the paper used in the first European printed books? It is worthy of note that the methods of the early papermakers differed only in slight details from those in use today in the mills that turn out the handmade papers found in our finest books. Like the crafts of the weaver and the potter, papermaking has changed but little since its early days. Its essence is still to mix disintegrated vegetable fibers with water and then to spread the mixture evenly over a screen or mold through which the water drains off, leaving a film of matted fibers which, when dried, is paper. The only changes of method have been in the preparation of the fibers and the construction of the molds.

In the operations of the old-time papermakers, linen rags were first macerated in water, and the resulting pulp was put into a tub or vat. The mixture was kept warm whenever possible, and a workman constantly stirred it with a pole until it reached a satisfactory consistency, ready for the next step.

The mold was a wire screen bordered with a strengthening frame. Another removable frame placed over it, and known as the deckle, determined the size of the sheet of paper to be made. The mold was plunged into the liquid perpendicularly and then turned to a horizontal position. It is possible that the Oriental papermakers may have poured the water-mixed fibers or pulp onto the molds, but at least since the twelfth century, when the art came into Spain, the method has been to dip the mold into the tub of pulp and bring to the surface on the screen the desired quantity of fiber.

The vatman, on lifting his mold from the liquid, then shook the pulp that lay on the screen, first in one direction and then in

THE OPERATION OF AN EARLY EUROPEAN PAPER MILL.

another, at right angles. This process crossed and matted the fibers and made paper as strong in one direction as in the other. Incidentally, papers with most of the qualities of handmade products are being manufactured today by machine. These are called mold-made papers.

When the fibers were adequately matted, the wooden deckle which limited the size of the sheet was removed, leaving the paper with a feathery and slightly uneven edge which has come to be known as the "deckle edge" or even as the "deckle." The mold was then passed to a second workman known as the coucher, while the vatman started to dip another sheet, using a second mold but the same deckle. After the proper quantity of water had drained from the sheet, the coucher turned the mold face down on a piece of wool cloth or felting. As the mold was lifted again, the wet sheet of incipient paper adhered to the fabric. Another felt was laid on top of it, ready to receive the next sheet from the vatman.

These operations were repeated until there was a pile of sheets of paper separated by sheets of felt. The pile was then put into a screw press, and pressure was applied to expel as much water as possible. After the pressing, the felts were removed and returned to the coucher for further use, while the pile of paper, with nothing now between the sheets, was pressed again. The sheets were then separated, placed in different order, and pressed again. The oftener this pressing was repeated, the smoother the finish of the paper became. This finishing was a refinement, however, and many of the earliest papers show no evidence of any further treatment after the removal of the sheets from the felts.

The paper was next dried by hanging it in "spurs" of four or five sheets together, over cowhair or horsehair cords. If the sheets had been hung up separately, they would have wrinkled badly, but in groups of four or five sheets they dried fairly flat.

A final process, more necessary for writing papers than for book papers, was the sizing of the sheets by dipping them into a glutinous liquid or "size" and then pressing and drying them. Size made the paper impervious to ink. The Chinese, Arabian, and Spanish papers were sized with starch or some kind of vegetable glue. The thirteenth-century paper mills at Fabriano, in Italy, achieved their outstanding success in part through the introduction of animal glue in sizing, an innovation which vastly improved the quality of their product and made them the foremost producers of paper in Europe.

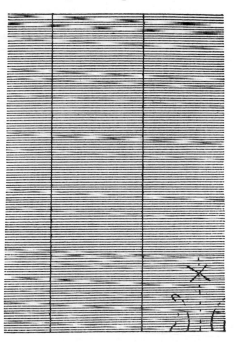

The molds of the early European papermakers, just like those still in use today for hand-made papers, were constructed of fine wires laid close together and held in place by somewhat heavier wires crossing them at right angles at intervals of about an inch. The pattern of these wires appears in the texture of

THE LAID MARKS AND PART OF THE WATERMARK OF THE PAPER OF THE FRAGMENT OF THE WORLD JUDGMENT.

the paper and forms what are known as the "laid marks"—the closely spaced "wire lines" crossed at wider intervals by the heavier "chain lines."

Another innovation introduced by the Fabriano papermakers about the year 1270 was the watermark. This was produced by a design of some kind made of fine wire and superimposed upon the screen of the mold. Like the laid marks, this design showed in the

texture of the paper. The position of the watermark, or a portion of it, on a page, together with the direction in which the chain lines run, is often useful to scholars in their investigations of early printed books as determining the manner in which the printed sheet was folded for binding, or as indicating the part of the sheet to which some rare printed fragment of a page once belonged.

The designs used for watermarks are of the utmost variety. Some of them are house marks and identify quite clearly the mill from which the paper came. Others, however, were used generally by a number of mills simply to indicate the quality of the paper or its size. The study and identification of watermarks has become an important branch of the science of bibliography, particularly in connection with the investigation of the very earliest printed books.

All the earliest papers were laid papers made by hand in the manner just described. It was not until the middle of the eighteenth century that "wove" paper first appeared. Its introduction is credited to John Baskerville, the fastidious printer of Birmingham, England. It was made over a wire screen of extremely fine texture which showed no pattern of laid lines in the finished sheet. The French called it *papier vélin,* or "vellum paper," and the members of the celebrated Didot family of French printers did much to bring its manufacture to perfection.

Though centuries have passed, handmade paper, both laid and wove, is still manufactured by practically the same methods as at the beginning of European papermaking. The greatest changes in the manufacture of paper have been introduced by machinery. The process in use today for the mass production of paper was invented in 1798 by Louis Robert, who was in the employ of the Didots in their Essonnes mills in France. It was later introduced into England by Henry Fourdrinier, after whom modern papermaking machines have been named.

In the making of paper by machine, the screen of the single hand mold is replaced with an endless belt of wire mesh, over which the pulp, prepared in mechanical beaters, is caused to flow. As the screen, which is constantly shaken from side to side, moves forward, the water in the pulp drips through it, leaving the film of fiber on top. A roll of felt then meets the moving screen and with its greater adhesiveness picks up the web of matted fibers and carries it through steam-heated drying rollers, which serve the double purpose of pressing out and also evaporating the moisture.

Soon the web of paper is well enough formed to hold together; it is then detached from the felt to continue its way through further drying rollers. At the end of the machine—and some Fourdriniers are several hundred feet long—the completed paper is wound on a roll. If it is an uncoated paper, such as that on which this book is printed, it is then finished except for being later "sheeted," or wound off the roll and cut into sheets of suitable size. Newsprint and the paper for large-edition magazines go in rolls directly to rotary presses without being first cut into sheets.

Among uncoated papers the two main varieties are the wove and the laid, distinguished by their texture as in the case of the hand-made papers. Modern wove papers are classified according to the smoothness of their finish. A rough paper entirely free from shine is known as "antique" or "eggshell." A moderately smooth sheet is called "machine finish." When compressed between the finishing rolls of the Fourdrinier machine to a still smoother surface, suitable for the printing of half-tones, the product is known as "English finish" paper. Wove papers as well as laid may also be "super-calendered" by a process of burnishing between rollers turning at different speeds. "Plate-finish" papers, either laid or wove, are produced by pressing between polished plates to make them smooth.

The papers ordinarily used for printing fine illustrations, for

color printing and the like, before being sheeted go through another process called coating, in which a mixture of casein or of glucose, clay, and some other ingredients is applied to the surface, making it extremely smooth and suitable for receiving the impression of fine-screen half-tone plates. This product is known in the United States as "coated" paper; in Great Britain as "art" paper. The first coated papers were all objectionably glossy, but in recent years an improvement has been introduced in the form of a clay-coated paper without gloss. This is known as "dull coated" and is the paper generally used by the best printers for work in which half-tone illustrations of fine quality must be used.

The technique of paper manufacture today makes it possible for the printer to select from a great variety of qualities and textures the paper most suitable for his purposes, from the cheapest kind of a handbill to the most beautifully printed book. But the modern papermaker faces an insistent and vexing problem in the quality of the raw materials entering into the manufacture of his product, particularly in the case of paper intended for the printing of books. The cost of linen rags makes it impossible to use them for paper produced in any more than limited quantities. So it has come about in comparatively recent years that most modern papers are composed principally of wood pulp, much of it in a very crude state. The newspapers of today are printed on paper which will disintegrate in the course of twenty years or so. Already the problem of preserving the most important of our newspapers for the use of future historians is a most serious one. By contrast, newspapers of our Revolutionary period, printed on all-rag stock, are in almost as good condition as the day they were first published. Some modern newspapers, such as the *New York Times* and the *Chicago Tribune,* for example, now print a special edition of each issue on an all-rag paper for permanent preservation in a few important libraries.

If properly treated, however, so as to reduce it to almost pure cellulose, wood pulp makes a fairly durable paper, and for economic reasons we must content ourselves with it for ordinary uses. Perhaps it is a boon to posterity that a vast quantity of the printing now being done in books, magazines, newspapers, and so on, will soon crumble to dust. But for books and records entitled to survive at least as well as the books of the fifteenth century have survived, no substitute has yet been found for paper manufactured from good old-fashioned linen rags.

V

Handwritten Books

BOOKS in the form with which we are familiar, made up of leaves bound together at the side, were a relatively late development in Europe and did not appear there for many centuries later than the papyrus or parchment rolls of the ancients. Although occurring now and then at much earlier dates, this form of book did not begin to come into general use until about the fourth Christian century, when the jurists of the later Roman Empire found that it was more convenient than the roll for their lawbooks. In the *codex,* as a book of this form was called, the parchment sheets, instead of being pasted end to end and then rolled up, were folded to make two leaves each, and collections, or gatherings, of these folded sheets were fastened together along their folds.

The Christian church, as well as the jurists, had much to do with making the codex popular. The old *volumen,* or roll, was associated with the literary works of a pagan culture which the early church fathers sought to supplant. Thus the writings of Christian authors were thought to be more appropriately presented in the codex form. But strangely enough, it is the old pagan *volumen* which survives in our word "volume," while we use the words "codex" and "code" only in specialized meanings.

The codex, of course, as well as the roll, was written by hand. Both classes of ancient books are therefore known as manuscripts, from the Latin designation *libri* (or *codices*) *manu scripti,* "books (or codices) written by hand." It was books such as these, laboriously written by scribes, that have preserved to us all that we have

of the history and literature of ancient times. Manuscripts, therefore, in addition to inscriptions on stone, metal, or wood, are an extremely important factor in the cultural heritage of mankind. Some of our most precious intellectual treasures have been saved only by the tenuous thread of a single copy, discovered by an appreciative enthusiast and made part of our spiritual endowment, first through duplication with the pen of the scribe and later through the medium of printing.

During the so-called "dark ages" following the barbarian invasions of the Roman Empire, men who preferred the quiet life of scholarship took refuge under the protection of the church, and the making of books, so far as that art survived at all, became more and more exclusively a monastic function. Monasteries and other churchly places of retreat from the turmoil of worldly life assumed the neglected task of making copies of books, both for the enrichment of their own libraries and, to a lesser extent, for the use of the fraternity of readers and scholars elsewhere. The methods and facilities of the monastic scribes differed, of course, with time and place, but generally speaking were centered in the monastery's *scriptorium,* — or "writery."

The *scriptorium* of a typical Benedictine monastery has been well described for us by Falconer Madan, in the delightful volume entitled *Books in Manuscript.* The workshop of the scribes was a large room usually over the chapter house, but when no special room was assigned for this work, separate studies were sometimes made for the writers in the cloisters, each scribe having thus a window to himself, but with his den always open to the cloister walk. It was only in special cases that a scribe was assigned a private room in which to work.

To guard against irreparable loss by fire, artificial light was forbidden to the scribes, so all work had of necessity to be done during

the daylight hours. Access to the scriptorium was denied to any except high officials of the abbey, so as to protect the scribes from interruption. The scriptorium was in charge of an officer known as the *armarius,* whose duty it was to provide parchment, pens, ink, knives, awls, and rulers. Absolute silence was the rule during the hours of work. If a scribe wished to consult a book, he made certain signs to his fellow workers. For example, in asking for a pagan work, he made the general sign, followed by scratching the ear after the manner of a dog!

In addition to regular scribes who were members of the monastic community, there were some secular scribes who were brought to the monasteries for special duties, such as rubrication or illumination. But many of the monasteries and other church institutions developed highly competent rubricators and illuminators among their own members.

The monastic scribe worked about six hours daily. He received his parchment in sections, each sheet separate but folded and arranged in the order in which it should appear in the book as finally bound. After the decision as to the style and size of the writing to be used, the limits of the written page were ruled in with "blind" marginal lines, the parchment being held in place with awls. In addition to the lines limiting the margins, guide lines for the individual lines of writing were ruled upon the parchment with a blunt instrument which made a little furrow in the material. Inasmuch as parchment has two distinct sides, a quaternion, or signature, was arranged so that each two facing pages had the same character—that is, both were hair side or both were flesh side.

After the scribe had finished his quaternion, or group of four sheets in eight leaves, his work was proofread in comparison with the original by a second person, and the sheets were then sent to the rubricator, who inserted titles, headlines, chapter or other initials,

notes, and the like. If the book was to be illustrated, the sheets next went to the illuminator. After he had completed his work on the volume, it was ready to be bound.

Accuracy in the transcription of classical texts was, of course, of primary importance, for the tendency to error in successive recopyings by different hands at different times was very great. Scribes were usually forbidden to make changes in the text before them even when the original which they were copying was obviously in error. But the monastic scribes were only human and not infrequently worked unwillingly at a task which was distasteful to them, so it is by no means surprising that their minds sometimes wandered and that slips occurred. The ingenuity of expert textual criticism in repairing these mental lapses of the scribes and in unraveling the meaning of passages that a careless copyist had left obscure is in some instances remarkable.

Illumination added much charm to manuscript books. The earliest texts were, as a rule, the plainest, but as wealth increased and the demand for beautiful books in manuscript form become greater, the first move was to make the first letters of new sentences larger and sometimes to color them. Then the extremities of these initial letters were flourished, and soon these flourishes were elaborated until they ran into the page margins. Next the margins of opening or of important pages were decorated with an independently designed border. Finally, miniatures were introduced into books, and when the miniaturist was a real artist, the results were superb indeed.

The principal colors used in the embellishment of manuscript books were red, blue, and gold. Less frequently, purple, yellow, green, or plain black and white were used. Sometimes whole manuscripts were lettered throughout in gold or in silver; in these cases the parchment itself was often dyed purple, producing a sumptuously rich effect. Until the twelfth century, gold was applied in

powder form, but after that usually in gold leaf and burnished, resulting in a glittering effect of much splendor.

The first really great development of manuscript books took place, strange to say, in Ireland, in the sixth, seventh, and eighth centuries. Within a century of the coming of Saint Patrick to the Emerald Isle—then lying remote from all the active cultural influences of the time—there was a vivid flowering of the intellectual as well as of the religious spirit. The influence of this almost self-created culture went far beyond the insular limits of Ireland and Britain, and Irish missionaries invaded the Continent, while, reciprocally, continental students made pilgrimages to Ireland to study the classical languages under Irish teachers. During this time there were produced, in the Irish monasteries, manuscripts of splendid calligraphy and illumination, in workmanship which has never been surpassed in originality of design and skill in execution. The most celebrated example of the work of the Irish school of calligraphy and illumination is the famous Book of Kells, hailed by more than one writer as "the most beautiful book in the world."

The history of the manuscripts through which we know what little is known of the ancient world is one of the most interesting chapters in the record of human endeavor. The very oldest manuscripts that now survive, with the exception of some discoveries of Egyptian papyri, were written centuries after the works which they contain were first penned. How great is our indebtedness to the generations of nameless scribes who copied and recopied, again and again, through those centuries, so that we might have the immortal epics of Homer, the plays of the great Greek tragedians, the dialogues of Plato, the scientific works of such great ancient thinkers as Aristotle and Euclid, the poetry of Virgil and Horace—to mention only a portion of the priceless total! To the busy hands of innumerable scribes, too, we owe the preservation in written form of

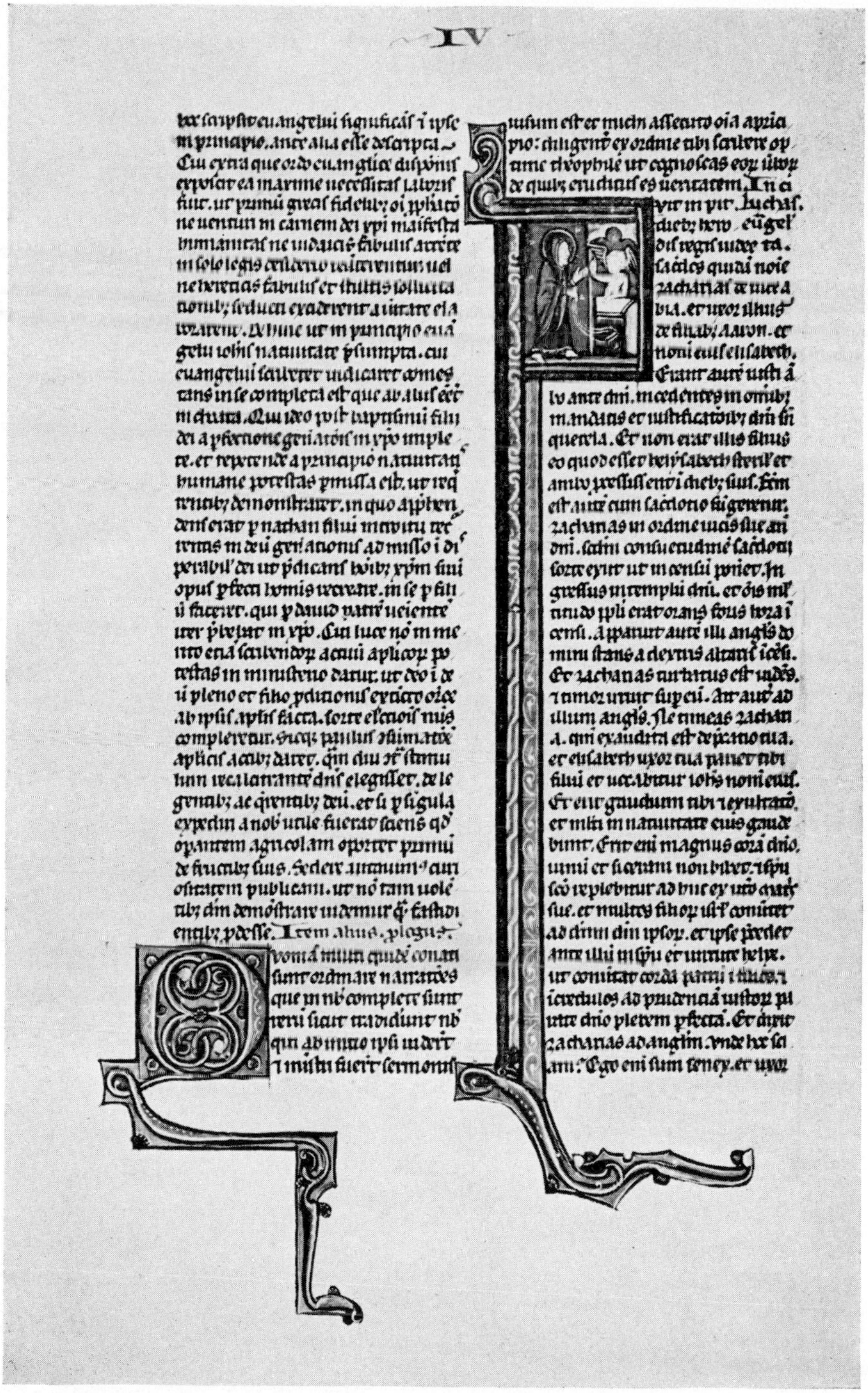

PAGE FROM A FRENCH MANUSCRIPT BIBLE ABOUT 1300.

PAGE FROM AN ENGLISH MANUSCRIPT OF
THE GOLDEN LEGEND, ABOUT 1300.

the books composing our Bible, for centuries known in manuscript form only to the chosen few, until printing made it the most widely distributed book in all history.

There is romance and adventure in the stories of how many a precious manuscript was preserved from destruction in the ravages of war or in the perils of fire or flood, or of how some were lost for ages, only to be discovered again in some obscure hiding place. None of these stories is more romantic than the tale of the discovery of the manuscript of the Bible in Greek, written not later than A.D. 400—the oldest, and in many respects the most interesting, text of the New Testament that has been preserved to us. Falconer Madan tells us about it thus:

Constantine Tischendorf, the well-known editor of the Greek Testament, started on his first *mission littéraire* in April, 1844, and in the next month found himself at the Convent of St. Catherine, at the foot of Mount Sinai. There, in the middle of the hall, as he crossed it, he saw a basket full of old parchment leaves on their way to the burning, and was told that two baskets had already gone! Looking at the parchment leaves more closely, he perceived that they were parts of the Old Testament in Greek written in an extremely old handwriting. He was allowed to take away forty-three leaves; but the interest of the monks was aroused, and they both stopped the burning and also refused to part with any more of the precious fragments,

Tischendorf departed, deposited the forty-three leaves in the Leipzig Library, and edited them under the title of the Codex Friderico-Augustanus, in compliment to the King of Saxony. But he wisely kept the secret of their provenance, and no one followed in his track until he himself went on a second quest to the monastery in 1853. In that year he could find no traces whatever of the remains of the MS. except a few fragments of Genesis, and returned unsuccessful and disheartened.

At last, he once more took a journey to the monastery, under the patronage of the Russian Emperor, who was popular throughout the East as the protector of the Oriental churches. Nothing could he find, however; and he had ordered his Bedouins to get ready for departure, when, hap-

pening to have taken a walk with the steward of the house and to be invited to his room, in the course of conversation the steward said: "I, too, have read a Septuagint," and produced out of a wrapper of red cloth "a bulky kind of volume," which turned out to be the whole of the New Testament, with the Greek text of the Epistle of Barnabas, much of which was hitherto unknown, and the greater part of the Old Testament, all parts of the very MS. which had so long been sought!

In a careless tone Tischendorf asked if he might have it in his room for further inspection, and that night (February 4-5, 1859) it "seemed impiety to sleep." By the next morning the Epistle of Barnabas was copied out, and a course of action was settled. Might he carry the volume to Cairo to transcribe? Yes, if the prior's leave were obtained; but unluckily the prior had already started to Cairo on his way to Constantinople. By the activity of Tischendorf he was caught up at Cairo, gave the requisite permission, and a Bedouin was sent to the convent and returned with the book in nine days.

On the 24th of February, Tischendorf began to transcribe it; and when it was done, conceived the happy idea of asking for the volume as a gift to the Emperor of Russia. Probably this was the only possible plea which would have gained the main object in view, and even as it was, there was great delay; but at last, on the 28th of September, the gift was formally made, and the MS. soon after deposited at St. Petersburg. . . .

In this manner were preserved some sheets of old parchment which, but for Tischendorf's timely arrival, would have gone into the fire as waste! But the adventures of this manuscript were not yet over when it arrived at St. Petersburg. Since Madan wrote his account of it, the government of Soviet Russia offered it for sale, and the British government, with the assistance of private individuals, acquired it for an enormous sum equivalent to approximately half a million dollars. It is now among the priceless treasures in the library of the British Museum, in London.

For every sheet of parchment or papyrus which has been preserved to the present day, it is safe to say that thousands of such

sheets have been destroyed forever. The ravages of time, the excesses of military conquest, the bigotry of religious zealots, the fury of fire and flood, and the carelessness of the ignorant and unthinking have all taken their toll, and what is left is but a fragment of the records once written in ages past. Yet even in recent times, surprising recoveries of such records have been made. Just as an example, mention may be made of the finds at Herculaneum. When the lava of Vesuvius poured over that little Roman city in A.D. 79, it charred and apparently destroyed many rolls of papyrus in private libraries in the devastated area. But, strange to say, what seemed to be destruction turned out to be preservation. For it has been found that these charred and blackened rolls, by very careful treatment, could be restored to a condition which would permit unrolling them. Many of these rolls, recovered in excavations at the beginning of the nineteenth century, have since been deciphered, and some consequential additions were thus made to our store of Greek and Latin literature. Very fortunately, copies of these manuscripts were made at the time, for the originals have since suffered disintegration, and it is the facsimiles of them which are now of the greatest value.

Books in manuscript are still treasured in many a library as monuments of bygone ages. But the slow-moving pen of the scribe has long since ceased to write. The texts of ancient manuscripts, on which our cultural foundations are established, are now reproduced as needed in another way, and since the middle of the fifteenth century all the world's wit and wisdom has taken form "without help of reed, stylus, or pen, but by the wondrous agreement, proportion, and harmony of punches and types."

VI

Printing in the Far East

I N the history of the making of books, the beginning of printing
in the Far East must be considered entirely independently of
the origins and progress of printing in Europe, for in the Orient
books were printed nearly six centuries earlier. Just as paper was first
made there, so also the first printed books were produced in China.

Those earliest books were block books—that is, books printed
from wooden blocks on which text and illustrations had been
engraved. But movable types were also made in China long before
Gutenberg's epochal invention. They would undoubtedly have been
invented even earlier had they been suitable for the printed reproduction of the Chinese written language. But because of the vast
number of separate characters required for writing the Chinese language, movable types offered no great advantage. Even after they
had been invented they eventually fell into disuse, because it was
easier to engrave on wood a page of the ideographic symbols than it
was to compose a page with types for the separate characters.

In Europe, with its alphabetically written languages, the invention of printing, to all intents and purposes, consisted in the invention of a satisfactory process for making any desired quantity of
movable types. In China, however, the invention of printing as a
practical method of making books consisted in the invention of
block printing.

The essential feature of printing in the most widely accepted
sense of the term is a form of some kind bearing in relief the characters to be printed—a form which can be inked and from which suc-

cessive impressions can be drawn. In this broadest sense, printing by means of seals or stamps impressed on paper with ink was done in China as early as the fifth or sixth century of the Christian era. It is significant that the Chinese word for printing of any kind is *vin*, which also means "seal." From the use of seals as a means of the identification or authentication of documents, the transition seems to have been to the use of similar stamps for the printing of charms. The very oldest extant specimens of printing from blocks of wood are in the form of paper charms produced in Japan about A.D. 770.

At that time, Japan was under strong Chinese influence—an influence traceable to a great extent to the Chinese origin of Japanese Buddhism. Shotoku, empress of Japan from A.D. 748 to 769, in her zeal for Buddhism, ordered a "million" Buddhist charms to be printed and placed in miniature pagodas for distribution among the people. This work was completed about the year 770. The facts are clearly attested by Japanese historical records, but even better evidence are the charms themselves, a number of which are still extant. Several of them can be seen today in the British Museum. These charms are not only the earliest known specimens of printing but are also the oldest extant specimens of paper made in Japan.

There can be no question that similar printing from wooden blocks was done in China long before the appearance of the process in Japan, though no specimens of it appear to have survived. With the beginning of the T'ang Dynasty in A.D. 618, China entered upon one of the most glorious periods in her history, in which art and literature flourished and a succession of enlightened rulers permitted the most impartial freedom to all religious teachings. Buddhism then took deep root, and one of the ways by which the devout Buddhist then acquired merit was by the ceaseless repetition, orally or in writing, of passages from the Buddhist scriptures. A method of endless reduplication of such merit-bringing passages

by means of impressions on paper from wooden blocks was too precious an opportunity for Buddhist zeal to have overlooked. Among the priceless finds of ancient documents in Turkestan are thousands upon thousands of little images of Buddha impressed on paper with stamps. One roll in the British Museum contains nearly five hundred such impressions from the same stamp. It seems almost certain that the Buddhists made the transition from the little hand stamp to impressions from larger wooden blocks in the seventh or eighth century, and some day, perhaps, specimens of such impressions may yet be found.

The period of religious toleration came to an end in A.D. 845, and for a long time thereafter Buddhism was relentlessly persecuted in China. When we read that at the beginning of this persecution 4600 Buddhist temples were destroyed, we can understand why we have no definite record of any Buddhist printing before that time: the evidence of it was all wiped out. But there is indirect evidence of block printing in an imperial edict of the year 835 ordering that the private printing of calendars be stopped, and in the record that an effort was made to reprint a printed Buddhist work which was burned about 845.

The earliest *certain* date of printing in China is A.D. 868, a century after the little printed Japanese charms of the Empress Shotoku. But the evidence in this case is not a mere slip of printed paper, but a complete printed book and, what is more, a book *with a woodcut frontispiece*. The circumstances of its discovery read like a fairy tale.

The scene of the discovery is once more that far western finger of civilized Chinese territory which projects into the desert of Turkestan and once more in the vicinity of Tun-huang. Near that city are the Caves of the Thousand Buddhas cut into the face of a cliff. From an early stone inscription there we learn that this colony of religious cave dwellers dates from A.D. 366. In 1900 a mendicant

Taoist priest raised the money for the work of restoring one of the caves to its former magnificence and was engaged in "improving" one of the early frescoes on its wall when he found that the wall behind the fresco was not of stone but of brick. Investigating a little farther, he found that the brick closed the mouth of a chamber which was piled high with manuscript rolls. Seven years later, Sir Aurel Stein, the British archaeologist celebrated for his researches in the field of Chinese history, came to Tun-huang and learned about the secret chamber. In his *Serindia* he tells of his nerve-racking negotiations for a part of its treasures.

The earliest identified date among the documents found in the walled-up chamber is A.D. 406 and the latest is 997. It is thought that this hiding place was made and sealed up in 1035 to prevent its precious contents from falling into hostile hands and that for some reason the very existence of the vault was forgotten. In it were found 1130 bundles, each containing a dozen or more rolls. Of these, Stein was able to procure about 3000 rolls for the British Museum. All the rolls were found to be in almost perfect condition, which was possible only because of the dry climate of the desert. In another part of China the same documents would probably have disintegrated from dampness.

The documents found were of the utmost variety of contents. They were written in Chinese, Tibetan, Sanskrit, Iranian, Sogdian, Uigur (ancient Turkish), and even included some selections from the Old Testament written in Hebrew. But among them was one of the most precious monuments of mankind's cultural history— a copy of the oldest printed book now extant. This is a Chinese version of the so-called Diamond Sutra, one of the most highly favored of the Buddhist scriptures, and it is now among the proudest possessions of the British Museum. It was literally startling to the scholars who first examined it to find at the end of the text the

explicit printed statement that it was "printed on May 11, 868, by Wang Chieh, for free general distribution, in order in deep reverence to perpetuate the memory of his parents." Here we have the oldest known book imprint and the name of the first printer of books of whom the world has record.

This book is the work of no tyro and gives evidence of a considerable antecedent period of evolutionary development of the art of reproduction by means of printing. In other words, in this copy of the Diamond Sutra we find the arts of book printing and of illustration in an advanced rather than in a primitive stage. This is most graphically shown by the woodcut frontispiece which is reproduced in the plate facing page 96. It is the earliest dated woodcut, antedating by many centuries the earliest European woodcuts, to be discussed in Chapter VII. The plate presents Sakyamuni seated on his lotus throne, attended by a host of divine beings and monks and discoursing with Subhuti, his aged disciple.

Printed throughout from wooden blocks, this copy of the Diamond Sutra is in a roll sixteen feet long and about one foot wide, made up of seven sheets of paper pasted end to end—six sheets of text, each about thirty inches long, and a shorter sheet on which the woodcut appears.

In the whole immense collection taken from the walled-up chamber there were only three other printed books, but there were a large number of single-sheet prints, which served as charms or votive offerings. On these were printed both illustrations and text, so that in many respects they have a kinship with the early European *Heiligen,* or block prints of sacred subjects. Of the three other printed books, one is the oldest extant representative of a new form of book. This is a small Buddhist sutra, or collection of aphorisms, dated A.D. 949 and is also in the British Museum. It was printed on one side of a long strip of paper but with its text divided into pages.

The strip was then folded in the manner of accordion pleating, and the unprinted backs of the pages were then pasted together, the final result resembling to a surprising degree the form of the modern book. Printed books made in this manner are still common in China and Japan.

The Chinese province of Szechuen (then known as Shu) was evidently the center of the early printing activities in China. A government official named Liu Pin made mention of books which he had seen there in the year 883. After some account of their contents, he wrote: "Most of these books were printed with blocks on paper, but they were so smeared and blotted that they were not readily legible." In 907 the province asserted its independence as the empire of Shu, and the making of books received renewed impetus from the interest of a farsighted statesman, Wu Chao-i, about whom this story is told: "When Wu Chao-i was poor, he wished one day to borrow some books from a friend. The friend showed by his look that he did not wish to lend them. Wu was grieved and said, 'Some day, when I come into a position of power, I shall have books cut in blocks, so that all scholars may have the opportunity of reading them.' When later he served the king of Shu as prime minister, he fulfilled his promise. This was the beginning of printing."

This story about Wu Chao-i must be understood as meaning that this statesman was responsible for the beginning of *official* printing under governmental direction. Chinese authorities differ as to the date of Wu's efforts to foster printing, but the undertaking had far-reaching consequences. For the central empire, though torn with civil dissensions, had strength enough in 929 to conquer the independent state of Shu and to hold it for five years, and during this short time absorbed the idea of printing as a government function. Fêng Tao, a wise and capable statesman, whose ability kept him in office, in spite of civil strife, under four dynasties and seven emperors,

was the prime minister of the conquering power, and he was quick to recognize the importance of printing under government auspices such as he found in Shu. In the year 932 he and his associates presented the memorial which initiated the printing of the Confucian classics, one of the greatest enterprises in Chinese cultural history.

The memorial declared: "During the Han dynasty, Confucian scholars were honored and the classics were cut in stone. . . . Our dynasty has too many other things to do and cannot undertake such a task as to have stone inscriptions erected. We have seen, however, men from Wu and Shu who sold books that were printed from blocks of wood. There were many different texts, but there were among them no orthodox classics. If the classics could be revised and thus cut in wood and published, it would be a very great boon to the study of literature. We therefore make a memorial to the throne to this effect."

The emperor issued his decree which ordered the proposed revision of the classics. The editorial task was entrusted to the Kuo-tzu-chien, or National Academy, composed of the leading scholars of the empire. The most expert calligraphers were chosen to write the accepted text, which would then be transferred to the wooden blocks and cut by careful workmen. Through twenty-one years, during which the empire continued to be torn by civil strife, the work went on until the monumental project finally reached a successful conclusion, in the year 953, in the completion of the full text, commentaries included, in one hundred and thirty volumes.

In spite of the fact that the memorial of Fêng Tao himself mentions the printing that was already being done in Shu, and in spite of a number of records of earlier printing in the works of Chinese chroniclers, Fêng Tao has been given a place of honor in Chinese tradition as the inventor of printing—the Gutenberg of China. As a matter of fact, Fêng Tao was not at all interested in printing except

as a means to an end. His object was the establishment of an accurate and officially authenticated text of the ancient Chinese classics. The traditional method of preserving the text of these classics had always been to have them cut in stone, from which rubbings on paper were taken for the use of scholars. Wooden blocks were admittedly a makeshift to which Fêng resorted because of the poverty of the empire.

No specimen of the printing instituted by Fêng Tao has survived. The specimens of printing of the same period found at Tunhuang are Buddhist, not Confucian. But the printing of books from wooden blocks became the accepted thing in China. Some of the blocks themselves have survived, the oldest now in existence, dating from A.D. 1108, being preserved in the Field Museum, in Chicago. A copy of a block-printed book dated 1167, the *T'ang Liu sien shêng wên tsi,* the earliest printed book preserved in America, is now in the fine Chinese collection of the Newberry Library, in Chicago. A page from it is reproduced herewith. This work, in twelve volumes, contains the collected poems and essays of Liu Tsung-yüan, one of the most celebrated writers of the T'ang dynasty, who lived A.D. 773-819.

An important influence in the spread of the art of block printing was the manufacture and use of playing cards. These are clearly of Chinese origin. Cards were first known as "sheet dice." When made on bone or ivory, they evolved in simple forms into dominoes and in more complicated forms into *mah-jongg.* When made on paper, they became playing cards.

The use of playing cards in China is traced with certainty as far back as A.D. 969, but they are probably still more ancient. When first known in Europe, in the closing decades of the fourteenth century, they were recognized as an eastern invention. In China they were early produced by the method of block printing, and in Europe,

臨淄王隆基起兵討韋氏并其黨皆伏誅隆基

PAGE FROM A BLOCK PRINTED BOOK OF A.D. 1167.

soon after their introduction, the same process of manufacture was called into use.

Again, the evidence regarding the transmission of this form of the printing art is not conclusive. The adoption of playing cards by the Europeans has been attributed to contact with the Saracens during the Crusades; but there is no mention of them in medieval Arabic literature, and the Koran forbade games of chance. To quote Professor Carter: "While it is not safe to say with certainty that playing cards in coming from China brought block printing with them, the evidence is at least sufficient to suggest that among the possible ways by which block printing may have entered the European world, the use of playing cards holds an important place."

The art of block printing spread into Korea and Japan, and also westward in Asia. But it met in the Mohammedan world, which lay between Asia and Europe, a seemingly impenetrable barrier. Islam, in marked contrast to Buddhism, was uncompromisingly opposed to the reduplication of its sacred writings through the medium of print. The reason for this opposition is not clear, but in all probability it was simply religious conservatism. The Koran had been given to the Moslems in written form, and writing, therefore, was the only means by which it might ever be transmitted. To this day the Koran has never been printed from type in any Mohammedan country; it is always reproduced by lithography.

But the Asiatic peoples used printing at an early date for many purposes—not only for books, but for playing cards, paper money, and many other miscellaneous purposes, including, of course, the printing of charms. In Europe at the same period the monasteries were busily at work copying manuscripts by the most laborious method possible, and for centuries there was no penetration of the art as practiced in the East among the peoples of the West. The conquests of the Mongols under Genghis Khan, however, broke

through the barrier. From the middle of the thirteenth century to the midpoint of the fourteenth, Asia and Europe were in contact. The contact was often violent, to be sure, but there was cultural and commercial interchange at many points. The Mongols penetrated into Russia, Hungary, Poland, and even into Germany. At Tabriz, in Persia, there grew up a colony of international character which served as the crossways between the East and the West.

With the fall of the Mongol Empire in 1368 the tradeways were closed again. If the Chinese art of block printing actually reached Europe, it must have done so before that date. There is no categorical evidence attesting the direct transmission of the art, but the late Professor Carter, in his very thorough study of the origins of printing in China, concluded on the basis of much circumstantial evidence that such transmission took place.

Until comparatively recent years we knew of no early block printing at any point between the Asiatic and European worlds. In 1880, however, in excavations in Egypt near El-Faiyûm, there were discovered a great quantity of ancient documents which are now preserved in the Archduke Rainer collection of the National Library in Vienna. The documents range from the fourteenth century B.C. to the fourteenth century A.D., or through twenty-seven centuries— a range that testifies to the spectacular importance historically of this find. Among the thousands of bits of paper in the collection there were about fifty examples of block printing. These are all in Arabic, and their subject-matter is religious—passages from the Koran, prayers, charms, and so forth. There are text and decoration, but in accordance with Moslem precept there is no illustration representing living things. The style of writing varies widely, and from the differences in writing they have been dated approximately between A.D. 900 and 1350—but with a suspicion that specimens assigned to the earlier date may have been later imitations of an archaic script.

There is no definite evidence, either in the Archduke Rainer documents or in contemporary records, as to the origin of block printing in Egypt, but the prevailing opinion is that it came from China by way of Persia. Nor is there evidence of any connection between the Egyptian prints and European block printing. All that can be said is that the later Egyptian specimens synchronize quite closely with the probable beginnings of the art in Europe.

Not only block printing but also movable types originated in China. The Chinese invention of separate types antedated the experiments of Gutenberg by more than four hundred years. The inventor was Pi Shêng, and his types were made of baked clay and not of metal. As the event is one of major importance in cultural history, I am quoting the original record in full, as translated from the essays of Shên Kua, a Chinese writer who was contemporary with the invention and possibly a personal friend of the inventor. Shên Kua wrote as follows:

Under the T'ang dynasty, block printing, though carried on, was not fully developed. In the time of Fêng Ying-wang [Fêng Tao], first the Five Classics and then in general all the ancient canonical works were printed.

During the period Ch'ing-li [A.D. 1041-1049] Pi Shêng, a man in cotton cloth [i.e., a man of the common people], made also movable type. His method was as follows: He took sticky clay and cut in it characters as thin as the edge of a cash. Each character formed as it were a single type. He baked them in the fire to make them hard. He had previously prepared an iron plate and he had covered this plate with a mixture of pine resin, wax, and paper ashes. When he wished to print, he took an iron frame and set it on the iron plate. In this he placed the type, set close together. When the frame was full, the whole made one solid block of type. He then placed it near the fire to warm it. When the paste [at the back] was slightly melted, he took a perfectly smooth board and rubbed it over the surface, so that the block of type became as even as a whetstone.

If one were to print only two or three copies, this method would be neither convenient nor quick. But for printing hundreds or thousands of

copies, it was marvelously [literally "divinely"] quick. As a rule he kept two forms going. While the impression was being made from the one form, the type were being put in place on the other. When the printing of the one form was finished, the other was all ready. In this way the two forms alternated, and the printing was done with great rapidity.

For each character there were several type, and for certain common characters there were twenty or more type each, in order to be prepared for the repetition of characters on the same page. When the characters were not in use, he had them arranged with paper labels, one label for each rhyme, and thus kept them in wooden cases. If any rare character appeared that had not been prepared in advance, it was cut as needed and baked with [a fire of] straw. In a moment it was finished.

The reason why he did not use wood is because the tissue of wood is sometimes coarse and sometimes fine, and wood also absorbs moisture, so that the form when set up would be uneven. Also the wood would have stuck in the paste and could not readily have been pulled out. So it was better to use burnt earthenware. When the printing was finished, the form was again brought near the fire to allow the paste to melt, and then brushed with the hand, so that the type fell of themselves and were not in the least soiled with clay.

When Pi Shêng died, his font of type passed into the possession of my [a later text reads "his"] followers, and up to this time it has been kept as a precious possession.

Other Chinese historians confirm the record of Pi Shêng's invention. Types are also reported to have been made of tin, but these, as well as the earthenware types, did not work well with the watercolor ink. So wooden types were made, in spite of the objections which Pi Shêng had raised against them. There is a record of the making of wooden types in 1314 by Wang Chêng, who first cut the characters on a block of wood and then sawed them apart. Wang is said to have arranged his types in a case in the form of a revolving table and to have provided something over sixty thousand types for the printing of a book on agriculture, and other works. But the text in which Wang's types are described is of uncertain authenticity, so

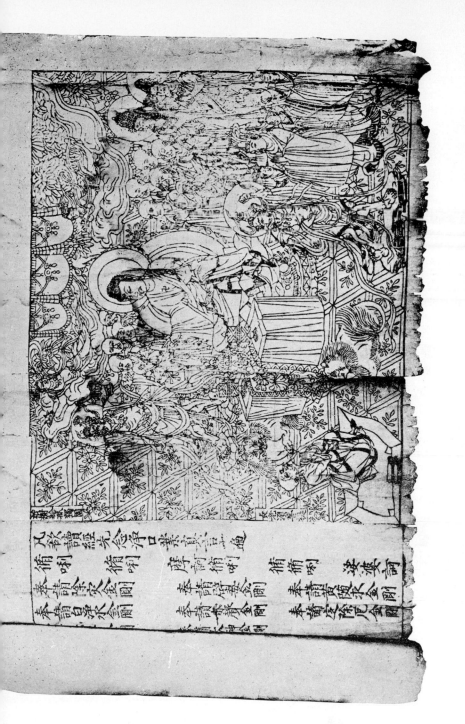

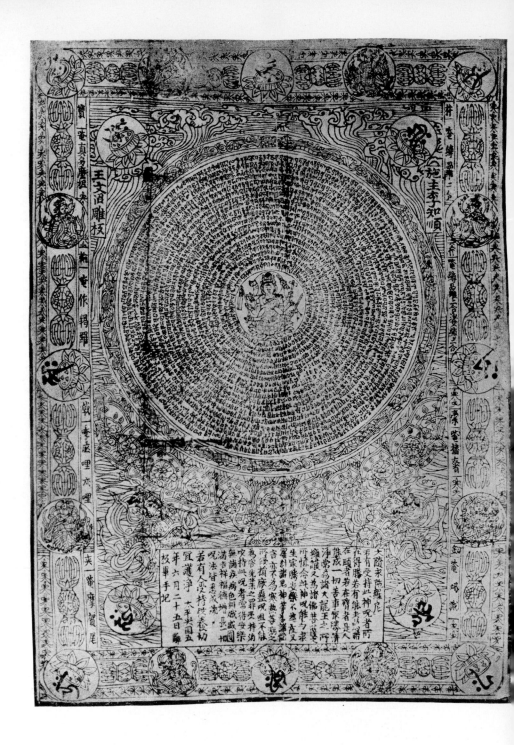

BLOCK PRINT OF A CHINESE CHARM, A.D. 940.

the story of how he made his types and of his ingenious revolving type case requires confirmation.

There is no question, however, about the fact that wooden types were actually made in China, for some of the types themselves have been discovered. They were found in the caves at Tun-huang by Paul Pelliot, a French archaeologist, and are still to be seen in Paris and in New York. They date from the beginning of the fourteenth century and, though made in China, are in the Uigur script of Central Asia. This script was *alphabetic,* derived ultimately from the ancient Aramaic, but the types found are *word* types and not *letter* types. So narrowly did the genius of the Far East miss the pith of Gutenberg's invention!

Our scene now shifts to Korea, a kingdom which had nominally acknowledged the sovereignty of the Mongol Empire, with its kings of the Koryu line occupying the throne under "appointment" from the Mongol khan. But with the Mongol overthrow, Korean government became rather chaotic, and things went from bad to worse until the country was redeemed by the Korean hero, General Yi. Yi founded a new dynasty of rulers, who gave Korea a vigorous and enlightened administration and encouraged literature and the arts. In the Korean annals for 1392—still antedating Gutenberg by half a century—we find record of the establishment of a department of books, among the responsibilities of which were "the casting of type and the printing of books."

There are records that printing with movable types had been known in Korea as far back as the first half of the thirteenth century, and the activities at the close of the fourteenth century should perhaps be regarded as a revival of a method of printing which had fallen into disuse. In this revival, however, the types to be used were made of metal. The "department of books," after some delay, actually began work in 1403, in which year, at the private expense

of T'ai Tsung, General Yi's son and successor to the throne, "several hundred thousand type had been cast" of bronze.

Here in Korea, printing with movable metal type became more than an experiment. Between 1403 and 1544 there were eleven royal decrees concerning the casting of new fonts of type. A type of small size was produced in 1420, but it was found to be difficult to read, so a larger face was cast in 1434. In two months' time over two hundred thousand type of the new face were produced.

There is no doubt that large quantities of books were printed in this splendid period of Korea's history. A chronicler in 1422 ecstatically wrote: "There will be no book left unprinted, and no man who does not learn. Literature and religion will make daily progress, and the cause of morality must gain enormously. The T'ang and Han rulers, who considered the first duty of the sovereign to be finance and war, are not to be mentioned in the same day with the sovereign to whom this work is due." A large number of fifteenth-century Korean incunabula are still to be found in the libraries of Korean and Japanese monasteries.

In this same period, too, the Koreans came perilously close to the creation of types for single letters. Large numbers of Sanskrit and Tibetan books were imported by the Korean Buddhist monks, and the study of foreign languages flourished. Korean scholars thus learned to read alphabetic scripts, and finally, in the first half of the fifteenth century, a Korean phonetic alphabet was evolved, based largely on Sanskrit. Types were actually cast for this alphabet, and one book printed from that type has been recorded. It was printed in 1434—but the Koreans, like the Uigurs more than a century earlier, just stopped short of going over wholly to alphabetic printing. For they combined their new phonetic alphabet with the old Chinese ideographs in such a way that each piece of type carried a Chinese character together with its corresponding Korean phonetic symbols.

A method of printing which was so complicated was inevitably doomed to failure.

The Koreans also developed a primitive type mold or method of casting types. Their types were cast in sand, with wooden types used as dies in forming the sand matrix, as is recorded by Song Hyon, writing at the end of the fifteenth century. Some eighteenth-century Korean types preserved in the American Museum of Natural History, in New York, give unmistakable evidence in the texture of their metal surfaces that they were sand-cast. In my opinion, when set up for printing they were imbedded in a plastic base which was ribbed with half-round or round rods which fitted into a semi-circular groove in the feet of the types, serving as guides to alignment.

Printing with movable types ceased in Korea about 1544 but was resumed again for a time in 1770. The first book printed in Japan with movable types was dated 1596, but this method of printing came to an abrupt end in 1629. In China the use of movable types continued through the eighteenth century. There are several reasons why this method of printing failed to become permanently established in those countries, even after several centuries of use. In the first place, the Chinese system of writing, with its thousands and thousands of separate characters, is unsuitable for reproduction with separate types. Too many types are necessary, and too much time and labor are needed for the work of composition, to say nothing of distribution. Although Korea and Japan developed phonetic rather than ideographic systems of writing, tradition and usage had so firmly established the Chinese ideographs among them that they never succeeded in shaking them off entirely and developing systems of alphabetic printing. All things considered, printing from characters cut a page at a time on wooden blocks was much more practical and much less expensive for private and commercial use. The printing from movable types never flourished at all in those Far Eastern

lands except under governmental auspices involving heavy subsidies from imperial or royal treasuries.

Another reason for the Chinese preference for block printing was—and still is—the Chinese estimation of calligraphy as one of the fine arts. A book to be cherished by a Chinese scholar had to offer him not only a correct and authentic text, but also the brush strokes of a master in the formation of the characters. The beauty produced by the masters of the brush could be more satisfactorily reproduced for admirers by means of carefully cut wood blocks than with separate wooden types, which had to be used monotonously again and again—to say nothing of metal types cast in sand.

The final effort to print with movable types in China was a glorious one, involving the casting of 250,000 copper type for printing a Chinese encyclopedia which was completed, in 6000 volumes, in 1726. Soon thereafter a serious deficiency of small coinage made it necessary to melt down this enormous font of type and turn it into cash. Some printing with wooden types was done after that, but with the supreme effort of 1726 printing with movable types, either of wood or of metal, practically died out in China, to be resumed only in quite recent times under European auspices.

Much as was achieved in the Orient in printing from wood blocks and from type, there is not the slightest evidence that the Chinese inventions had any influence whatever on the invention of movable types in Europe. It was in Europe, with its alphabetically written languages, rather than in the Far East, that the invention of typographic printing opened a new era in the intellectual history of all mankind.

VII

Early European Woodcuts

PRINTING of woodcuts in Europe goes back quite certainly into the fourteenth century. The earliest work known to us from extant prints is represented by pictures of religious character. Scenes from the life of Jesus or of the Virgin Mary, and pictures of saints, accounted for the great majority. Some of the latter were combined with prayers for protection against the plague. New Year's greetings are found in woodcut form. The inevitability of death was pictured in many forms, and a series of nine famous heroes was represented in a number of series of prints.

The original intention was that the prints should be colored by hand, and they were designed with that purpose in view. In the natural course of events, however, the coloring of many was never completed. As the quantity produced increased, more and more were left in the black-and-white form in which they were printed.

But another product of the block printer's art may well have antedated the earliest prints of religious subjects. I refer to playing cards. Dice may originally have been an invention of the Egyptians, which was then transmitted eastward to China. Certainly dominoes, which represented a modification of dice, were of Chinese origin, as were also playing cards, which were early referred to as "sheet dice" or "flying dice." Cards were in use in China by the tenth century and perhaps earlier. Thin dice, elaborated considerably, became known to us a few years ago as the tiles of *mah-jongg*.

When St. Louis returned to France from the Crusades, he found the people addicted to the vice of card playing. We have record of

the use of playing cards in Germany in 1377. Gambling, which has always seemed an inevitable concomitant to card playing, became so serious that cards and their use were forbidden: at Nuremberg, for example, in 1380, at Ulm in 1397, and at Augsburg in 1400. The vice of card playing was widespread in France also, and we find a decree issued at Paris in 1397 forbidding working people to play, on working days, certain games, among which cards and dice were specified. The Synod of Langres in 1404 interdicted card playing by the clergy.

There is a story, more or less authenticated, that St. Bernardino preached at Rome a sermon inveighing so eloquently against the sin of gambling that the people brought from their homes playing cards and other gaming equipment and burned them in the public square. A local card maker, believing his business ruined by this change of heart on the part of his customers, complained to the saint that his only means of livelihood was gone and that he and his family would starve. St. Bernardino handed him an image of Jesus, saying, "If you know how to paint, paint this image."

Of course, the earliest cards were drawn and colored individually, perhaps with the aid of stencils. But the widespread popularity of playing cards among the working classes offered a potent incentive to the development of some more expeditious and economical method of manufacture. Such a method was, of course, offered by printing from woodcuts and coloring the printed cards. We have record of the manufacture at Ulm of large quantities of playing cards which were exported to other cities of Europe. In 1430 an artist stated in a declaration to the tax office at Florence that he was the owner of many wood blocks for the printing of playing cards and images of saints. We know that playing cards were being printed at Venice in 1441, for in that year the importation of such cards was forbidden as a means of protecting local block printers.

FRENCH PLAYING CARDS OF ABOUT 1470, SIGNED J. DE DALE.

The oldest printed cards preserved cannot be much older than 1455, but in view of the perishable character of playing cards, this constitutes no disproof that they were printed at much earlier dates. Let any reader of this book see how old a pack of cards he or she can find around the house.

Fragments of printed playing cards were found at Rome in the binding of a manuscript register of 1465, indicating that the blocks must have been cut at a still earlier date. In comparatively recent years, there has been found a pack of woodcut playing cards, signed by Jean de Dale, or de Dalles, an engraver known to have been working at Lyons between 1450 and 1480. Bouchot, who reported on their discovery, dated them about 1470. Six of these interesting playing cards, now in the Bibliothèque Nationale at Paris, are reproduced on the preceding page.

While our definite knowledge regarding block-printed playing cards is far from satisfactory, there is yet reason to believe that these perennially popular pasteboards may have contributed in an important way towards introducing block printing into Europe.

As block printing made playing cards available to the poor as an inexpensive means of amusement, it also made possible to them the ownership of sacred image prints. In the German-speaking regions, these prints were generally known as *Heiligen*. They met a need aroused by the growing wave of austere, puritanical, and deeply religious feeling which was pervading the lower and middle classes, particularly in Germany. It would appear that the printing of *Heiligen* was carried on, strange to relate, along with the manufacture of playing cards, the same craftsman producing the instrumentalities of God and the devil! Both were made by the same process, both were sold to the same classes of people, and both were coupled together in the Florentine artists' declaration of 1430 and the Venetian edict of 1441.

JESUS IN THE GARDEN OF OLIVES, A BLOCK PRINT
OF ABOUT 1400.

The practice of going on pilgrimages increased greatly towards the end of the fourteenth century, when Pope Boniface IX added to the number of authorized places to which such pilgrimages might be made. Many woodcut prints of sacred subjects were sold to the pilgrims, who took them home to insert into books of devotion or put up on the wall, thus establishing, in effect, private shrines.

As representative of the earliest extant woodcuts Arthur Hind, in a recent masterly treatise, lists four prints which both provenance and appearance justify dating about 1410. These are the *Rest on the Flight into Egypt,* the *St. Jerome,* the *St. Dorothy,* and the *Martyrdom of St. Sebastian.* Hind believes these were stamped by pressing the block, inked with an oily ink, face down on the paper.

There are other prints for the dating of which there is no evidence other than their style and technique. Judging from these, however, competent authorities agree in ascribing a not inconsiderable number of woodcuts to the first quarter of the fifteenth century. The *Christ before Herod,* two prints of which, extracted from the binding of an incunabulum, are preserved in the British Museum, is believed to be of French origin, about 1400. Another print assigned by Schreiber to the same approximate date is *Jesus in the Garden of Olives,* believed to be of German origin and preserved today in the collection of the Bibliothèque Nationale at Paris. The dark background, shown in my reproduction on page 105, has been painted in on the print.

Almost as early is a print of two subjects on the same block, the *Annunciation and Nativity,* reproduced on page 107 in the size of the original, which is in the Graphische Sammlung at Munich. It is to be specially noted that this block is in the double-subject style of the *Apocalypse* block books, to be later discussed.

Prints of woodcuts of a slightly later period appear to have been made by the method of rubbing, whereby the inked block is laid

BLOCK PRINT OF THE ANNUNCIATION AND THE NATIVITY.

face up on the work table, the dampened paper laid on top of it, and the impression taken by rubbing the sheet against the block with a *frotton*—a small cushion of cloth stuffed with wool—or some other similar implement. In this classification are two dated prints: the Brussels *Madonna* of 1418 (a date which has been questioned), and the *St. Christopher* of 1423 (a date generally accepted as authentic). Both were printed in a thin ink which today shows a brownish cast.

This brownish, or sometimes grayish, cast is noted in many of the early prints and in practically all the block books printed by the rubbing process. The brown cast indicates the use of an iron-gall ink, the making of which was described about 1100 by Theophilus in his *Diversarum artium schedula*. From this time onward, this kind of ink was in common use. The ink may have printed black at the time the prints were made. Permanence of the black color in such prints may have resulted from addition of oak galls or of carbon, or from the use of more oil, which would help to prevent oxidation.

We may pause here to describe in some detail the *St. Christopher* which, because of its specific dating in the first quarter of the fifteenth century as well as for its artistic merit, is the best known of all the early single woodcuts. This print, as Dr. Guppy tells us, owes its preservation to the fact that it was pasted inside the oak board, covered with undressed deer skin, of the binding of a Latin manuscript, *Laus Virginis,* written in the Carthusian House at Buxheim in 1417, according to a note in the manuscript itself. This convent, one of the oldest in Germany, was within fifty miles of Augsburg, where there is record in 1418 of the activities of a *Kartenmacher,* or playing-card maker.

The print pictures St. Christopher bearing the youthful Jesus across a stream. Dr. Guppy writes: "The whole treatment of the subject seems to breathe of the East, as though it had been suggested from some Chinese model. The saint carries a palm-tree as his staff,

Criſtofori faciem die quacunqʒ tueris ·:· Millefimo ccccᵒ
Illa nempe die morte mala non moriaris ·:· | rrᵒ tᵃno ·:·⚔

while the treatment of the water is distinctively Chinese, and the perspective of the scene, or the absence of it, points to the same influence. To the left of the picture the artist has introduced, with a noble disregard of perspective, a bit of nature. In the foreground a figure is seen driving an ass loaded with a sack towards an overshot water mill, while up a steep path the miller is seen carrying a sack from the back door of the mill towards a cottage. To the right is a hermit, known by the bell over the entrance to his cell, holding a lantern to direct St. Christopher, as he crosses the stream." To the left of the date, 1423, is a Latin couplet which may be translated:

> *Each day that thou the likeness of St. Christopher shalt see*
> *That day no frightful form of death shall make an end of thee.*

To understand the story behind this picture it will be helpful to quote the legend of St. Christopher as it is told by Voragine in the *Legenda aurea,* or *Golden Legend:*

Reprobatus was a heathen giant who was determined to serve the strongest king he could find. He goes to the mighty Pharaoh and serves him, but whenever the devil is mentioned the king crosses himself. Reprobatus perceives that he fears the devil, consequently he goes off in search of the devil to serve him. Satan takes him into his service, but one day Reprobatus sees the devil start aside at a cross. Thus he sees there is one stronger than Satan, so he leaves his service and goes in search of Christ. He finds a hermit who orders him to pray. That I cannot do says Reprobatus. Then you must carry travellers over the deep river. So Reprobatus who had been a reprobate became Christophorus and undertook his good work. One night a voice calls to him. He goes out to find a little child, and puts him on his shoulder to carry him over. But the child nearly weighed him down. When he placed the child on the other bank he said: "You seemed to weigh as heavy as the world." "Well said, Christopher," answers the child, "I created the world, I redeemed the world, I bear the sins of the world," and he vanished. Thus Christopher saw that he had borne Christ over the river. It is thus that St. Christopher is represented in Western art.

JESUS IN THE GARDEN OF OLIVES. A WHITE-LINE
METAL CUT OF ABOUT 1470.

It should be here pointed out that not all the prints of the early fifteenth century were woodcuts. In addition to intaglio copperplate engravings, which will be dealt with in a later chapter, metal blocks, cut to print in relief, were frequently used. These were engraved in much the same manner as was employed in cutting wood blocks, but the material cut away was exactly opposite to that cut out in making black line woodcuts, in that the outlines of figures were cut into the block of metal, usually copper, showing, when printed, in white against a background of black. To cut down the area of black, the backgrounds were stippled or worked in various patterns, with punches or gravers. Prints from such metal plates are known as dotted prints, or prints in the *manière criblée,* or dotted manner, or, in German, *Schrotschnitt.* Nail holes in the corners of many of them indicate that they were probably mounted on wooden blocks for printing. While most of the metal cuts reproduced white-line designs, a few black-line designs cut on metal are found in use during the latter half of the fifteenth century.

The engravers of such metal blocks were goldsmiths, or allied to that craft, rather than painters and carpenters, who co-operated in the production of woodcuts. It seems probable that these goldsmith-engravers, being of necessity men of considerable artistic ability, were often responsible for the design as well as the production of the block. They worked with the knife, the burin, and various punches and stamps used to produce the dots and ornaments such as stars, rings, fleurs-de-lis, and lozenges pierced by a round hole. Dots of different sizes, used to break up black areas, are sometimes skilfully grouped to produce the effect of modeling of figures or objects. A network of white lines was sometimes graved over a dotted area to produce a still lighter tone.

A particularly fine example of white-line metal cut in the dotted style, preserved in the John Rylands Library, is reproduced on page

ILLUSTRATION FROM A MANUSCRIPT APOCALYPSE.

ILLUSTRATION FROM A BLOCK BOOK APOCALYPSE.

111. This print, showing Jesus on the Mount of Olives, with his apostles behind him, is believed by competent authorities to date not later than 1470.

Since this book does not undertake to outline the history of the woodcut, the points already established regarding the dating of the earliest extant single prints, many years in advance of the first efforts looking towards the invention of printing with movable types, will suffice for our present purposes. It is clear that the art of cutting blocks of wood or metal for relief printing was well known in many centers during the first half of the fifteenth century.

VIII

The Block Books

FROM a picture with a simple Latin couplet like the St. Christopher to a series of pictures with a more or less connected text was a simple step. When this step was taken and the prints were bound together, the block book had evolved. There have been preserved to us a considerable number of books of this character. The late W. L. Schreiber, author of the standard manual on fifteenth-century woodcuts, listed the titles of thirty-three different books, but as the blocks for some of these were re-engraved for the printing of a number of successive editions, we therefore have to deal with over a hundred different series of blocks.

The purpose of the early block books was to popularize the stories or teachings of the Bible in pictorial form, which even those who could not read, or could read but little, might comprehend. Most of them were first made up in hand-drawn and handwritten form and duplicated in the same manner. When the xylographers began to cut the pages of these books on wood blocks, they faced no problems of design or authorship. All they had to do was to obtain a hand-drawn copy as a model, trace it, and cut the picture and lettering on the wood. Some of the extant manuscript forerunners of the block books are dated as early as 1350.

The extent to which the block books followed the manuscript originals in composition and text can be judged by comparison of two volumes of the *Apocalypse* in the John Rylands Library, corresponding pages in which are here reproduced. A page from a manuscript version of about 1350 is shown by the plate facing page 112,

while the corresponding page of the block book may be seen in the plate facing page 113.

To our eyes, the illustrations may seem strange and perhaps irreverent, though such an intention was far from the designer's mind. As Dr. Guppy points out, they "took the Bible stories and clothed them in a mediaeval setting, so that they might the better be understood by the illiterate. For example, we find Gideon arrayed in plate-armour, with mediaeval helmet and visor, and a Turkish scimitar in his hand. Or, we have David and Solomon represented in rakish wide-brimmed hats with high conical crowns. The translation of Elijah takes place in a four-wheeled vehicle resembling a farmer's waggon, or an early type of motor-car. The Israelites are represented in slouch hats, puffed doublets, tight-legged breeches, and pointed shoes."

Schreiber's opinion, which was accepted by most other writers, was that none of these could be ascribed to a date much earlier than 1460. In view of the fact that some of these books exist in hand-drawn and handwritten versions produced as early as 1350, that they were popular in appeal, and that the art of producing woodcuts was known in 1400 and widely practiced in 1425, this late dating by Schreiber, in the absence of very specific evidence, has appeared unconvincing. Because of the wide differences in technique and style between editions of the same book, a fairly wide spread in date of production would seem possible and probable. Informed opinion has tended in this direction.

Paul Kristeller, who has studied intensively and edited many of the important block books in facsimile reproductions, considers Schreiber's dating of the early editions far too late and has stated in detail in several publications his reasons for this belief. More recently Arthur Hind, with the resources and facilities of the British Museum behind him, has analyzed the more important block books most

searchingly and has arrived at individual estimates of date at striking variance with Schreiber's generalization.

There is, for example, one exceedingly primitive block book, the *Exercitium super Pater Noster,* in which the illustrations are printed from woodcuts and the text added in manuscript. The edition is hence designated as chiroxylographic. The costume is that of the Burgundian court of the second quarter of the century, and this feature, in conjunction with the technique of design and cutting, led Hind to date the book about 1430 and hardly later than 1440. There was a second edition with the illustrations printed from a new set of blocks and with woodcut text in Flemish and Latin. A similar volume, which I have but recently seen, is described in the notes.

The block books of the *Apocalypse* constitute a highly important series. Both Hind and Kristeller agree in dating the first two series of blocks within the second quarter of the fifteenth century. Six different editions, printed from five distinct sets of blocks, have been identified, the second being printed from the blocks of the first, with page signatures added. Each page is divided horizontally into two compartments, in each of which is a different subject telling pictorially the story of the Revelation of St. John the Divine.

The next block book of real importance is the *Ars moriendi,* in its first edition second only in artistic quality to the *Apocalypse.* Twelve different editions, with certain variants between individual copies of the editions, have been identified and described by Schreiber. The pictures vary, but the text continues relatively uniform. The text appears in Latin, French, and German. Some editions were printed on one side of the paper, others on both sides. Some were printed in brownish ink, some in black ink.

The original authorship of pictures and text is unknown. The *Ars moriendi* sets forth the art of dying becomingly. Again to quote Dr. Guppy: "The object of the book is to describe the temptations

that beset the dying. The first picture represents the dying man as tempted by devils concerning his faith. The succeeding picture shows the good angels who enable him to remain steadfast. In like manner the dying man is tempted by devils to despair, to impatience and to avarice, but through the help of the angels he triumphs over all his adversaries. In the last of the series of pictures the spirit of the dying man is being exhaled from his mouth, and is received by the angels, to the utter disgust of the baffled devils who display frightful contortions as they beat a retreat."

This is the most medieval of all the block books, yet its appeal is universal, for in it, despite theological language, is heard the lyric cry of the human soul as it comes face to face with the unknown.

The first edition of the *Ars moriendi,* which may be dated about 1450, is a superior example of engraving, thought by many authorities to be the work of the "Master E. S." who is known to have executed a notable series of engravings—the Grotesque Alphabet of 1464. Over the pros and cons of this ascription much printer's ink has been consumed.

The *Biblia pauperum* was another block book of wide popularity. Ten block-printed editions have been identified, and there is one chiroxylographic copy. No title is attached to these issues, but a manuscript version of the fourteenth century opens with the words *Incipit Biblia pauperum,* and from this the series has derived its name. The central panel in each picture shows a scene in the life of Jesus, while on both sides are parallels from the Old Testament, teaching the same moral lesson. It presented a series of sermons in pictures, with texts to refresh the memory, and proved highly valuable to the less learned among the clergy. Its original authorship is variously ascribed to a monk named Wernher, celebrated as painter and poet, who was living in 1180, and to St. Ansgarius, archbishop of Hamburg in the ninth century.

PAGE FROM A BLOCK BOOK ARS MORIENDI.

Temptacio dyaboli de vana gloria

Quarto dyabolus temptat hominem infirmũ p̃
simp̃us complacenciam que est sup̃bia spiritualis
p̃ quã deuotis et religiolis atqz pfectis magis est ifes-
tus Cum eũ hominẽ ad deuiandũ a fide aũt ĩ despacio-
nem aũt ad impaciencia non potest ĩdũcere time aggre-
ditur eum p̃ sũi ṕmo complacencia talẽ ĩ eũ iaculans
cogitaciones. O qz firmus es ĩ fide qz fortis ĩ spe et qz con-
stanter pacies ĩ tũa infirmitate oquam multa bona opatus
es maxime gloriari debes quia non es licut cetri qui ifi-
nita mala petrariũt et tamen solo genitu ad celestia reg-
na peruenerũt igitur regnũ celorũ tibi iure negari
non potest quia legittime certasti. Accipe ergo coronã
tibi paratam et sedem excellenciorem pre ceteris optinebis
Per ista et similia dyabolus istantissiue laborat hominem ĩdũcere ad spirituialem superbiam siue ad sui iṕius
complacenciam.

Pro quo notandũm qz ista superbia multũ est vitanda
Primo quia per eam homo efficitur similis dyabolo nam
per solam sup̃biam de angelo factus est dyabolus.
Secundo quia per ipsam homo videtur committere blas-
phemiam per hoc qz bonũ qd a deo habet a se presũmit
habere. Tercio quia tanta posset esse sua complacencia
qz per hanc dampnaretur. Unde gregorius Reminiscẽ
do quis boni qd gessit dum se apud se erigit apud auc-
torem humilitatis cadit. Et augustinus. Homo sise
iustificauerit et de iusticia sua presũmpserit cadit.

One page, for example, advocates the necessity of curbing appetite. In the central panel Jesus is pictured resisting the temptation of the devil in the wilderness. On one side we see Adam and Eve and the forbidden fruit, and on the other Esau receiving from Jacob the mess of pottage.

There are many other block books which cannot be here described in detail, since our interest is limited largely to the earliest editions. Among the more important may be mentioned the *Historia seu providentia Virginis Mariae ex Cantico Canticorum,* the *Ars memorandi,* the *Life of Saint Servatius,* the *Symbolum apostolicum,* and the *Decalogus.* Some of the later block books dealt with secular subjects.

The Netherlands, which comprised roughly the present Holland and Belgium, constituted the region which was most active in the production of early block books, with Germany following slightly behind. France did practically nothing in this field, and Italy was responsible for but one important early block book.

The production of block books continued many years after the invention of printing, competing with typographically produced books in certain fields. For small works reprinted many times without change, the wood blocks had many of the merits of present-day stereotypes or electrotypes. We thus find some comparatively late editions of schoolbooks such as the Latin grammar of Donatus xylographically produced. Although it was eventually destroyed by typography, the block book did not, however, abandon the field without a struggle.

With the trend of authoritative opinion towards a conclusion that the earlier of the extant block books were produced in the second quarter of the fifteenth century, let us turn to documentary records clearly or apparently relating to block books. Let us here bear in mind that single copies only of the earliest extant block books have

been preserved, and that many block books produced during the same period have certainly succumbed to the ravages of time and the mischances of fate, and are therefore represented by no existing copy. This would be particularly true of schoolbooks, which, then as now, were likely to be "chewed to pieces" in the course of daily usage. It is to be noted that practically all the early block books which have been preserved are of a devotional character and thus used and treasured by adults rather than children.

The diary of Jean le Robert, abbot of Saint-Aubert at Cambrai, in the Netherlands, shows that he sent to Bruges in 1445 for two copies of a doctrinal *gette en molle,* which were purchased from Marquet, an *escripvand,* or scribe-vendor, of Valenciennes. In 1551 the abbot sent to Arras a doctrinal on paper, bought at Valenciennes, which was *jetté en molle* but was full of errors. Since some of the earliest *doctrinales* were simple metal plates on which appeared the letters of the alphabet, what the abbot sent for might have been prints from duplicate casts of such alphabet plates.

At Bologna, Italy, records show the use in 1446 by Zuane de Biaxio, an illuminator, of *forme de stampar donadi e salterj,* terms undoubtedly referring to wood or metal blocks for printing grammars or psalters as "cast in a mold," and would seem to refer to booklets printed from plates cast from some patterns. Whether the latter were wood blocks or not, we have no way of determining.

In 1450 the chronicle of the Weidenbach church at Cologne records the bequest by Wymandus de Roremundis of printed books (*libris impressis*) to the value of twenty florins.

In 1452 the town council of Louvain heard the petition of the wheelwrights, carpenters, turners, and coopers that Jan van den Berghe should be required to become a member of the carpenters' guild. The latter argued that his work of cutting letters and pictures (*letteren ende beelde prynten*), which was not among the regular

crafts practiced in that city, was related to the clergy more closely than to the guild of carpenters. On the showing, however, that other printers of letters and pictures had been previously assigned to membership in the carpenters' guild, Van den Berghe was ordered to follow this precedent. He is known to have continued work at Louvain until 1480. His reference to the clergy would make it seem likely that he was cutting blocks for illustrated books of devotion, of the character of the block books already described.

These records appear to show that, at least as early as 1445, books or pamphlets of an educational or devotional character were available on the market. The presumption that some or all of these were block books of one kind or another seems inescapable, especially when viewed in the light of the established facts regarding typographic printing, which will be discussed in succeeding chapters.

Opinion is divided as to whether these publications were printed from wood blocks or from engraved metal plates, and the question may never be finally resolved. Both techniques were certainly known and practiced earlier than 1445, and the market demand may have been met in one technique or the other, and perhaps in both. With a revision of dating of the earlier of the extant xylographic block books, we are justified in concluding, on the basis of all the evidence, that printed books were in circulation before the earliest claimed dates for the production of either pamphlets or books printed from movable types.

IX

The Stage Setting for Typography

PRINTING as it made its appearance in Europe in the fifteenth century was an altogether independent outgrowth of
its own times and conditions. It cannot even be said with
any certainty that the idea of printing, though not the processes,
found its way to Europe from the Far East. It is not impossible,
of course, that Europeans in their varied contacts with the Orient
learned something of printing and perhaps even saw documents
and books printed on paper. But if they did, the idea—with the
possible exception of its application in block printing—did not take
root and grow on European soil. For an idea is not an invention.
Leonardo da Vinci had the idea of the airplane in the fifteenth
century, and over fifteen hundred years earlier than that, the Greek
scientist Hero, of Alexandria, had the idea and even the principle
of the steam engine.

Two sets of conditions are prerequisite to the development of
any creative idea into a useful invention. One is the existence of
facilities and materials for converting the idea into physical form.
The other is a social need or demand, or at least a mental readiness,
for the invention. Of the two prerequisites, the latter is the more
essential for success, for if society is not ready for it and does not
accept it, an invention is to that extent useless and cannot live.

It will be instructive to consider briefly the Europe into which
printing was born. During the time of its gestation, which we may
say was between 1436 and 1450, Germany, its birthplace, was hardly
even a geographical term. Politically it was a muddle of petty princi-

palities with no head except that of the shadowy historical ghost known as the Holy Roman Empire. Italy was also a mess of political confusion. But the foundations of modern literature had been laid there by Dante, Boccaccio, and Petrarch, who wrote in the language of the people instead of in Latin, the language of scholars and of the church. Venice was then the chief trading power in Europe, though already threatened by the rising power of the Turks. The French were ending the series of conquests, begun under Joan of Arc in 1428, which in 1450 finally ended the centuries of English domination over a large part of the French territory. France was still a feudal association of provinces. Spain contained four Christian kingdoms, warring among themselves and all four warring against the Moorish kingdom of Granada, which was not conquered until 1492. The English realm, deprived of its French domain, was reduced to its island homeland and contained no cultural center such as Venice, Rome, or Paris. Scotland, Wales, and Ireland were still independent countries. Chaucer, known as "the father of English poetry," had died in 1400. He wrote a language which is hardly intelligible to ordinary readers of today.

The dukes of Moscow were just throwing off the yoke of the Mongolian Tartars, and Russia was only beginning to take form. The Christianizing of portions of Europe was still in progress. Parts of Norway and Sweden, and even Denmark, had only recently become Christian. Prussia, though conquered by the Teutons a century and a half before, was still a frontier, inhabited by a barbarous and pagan Slavic people.

To Europe, China and India—Asia generally—were lands of fancy. All that was really known of Africa was its Mediterranean coast and parts of Egypt. Not until 1487 did Bartolomeu Dias discover the Cape of Good Hope, and it was ten years later before Vasco da Gama sailed into the Indian Ocean. All Europe was appre-

hensive before the rising Turkish power. Constantinople fell to the
Turks in 1453, and the long tradition of Greek culture, perpetuated
for centuries at that ancient capital of the Byzantine Empire, was
threatened with extinction. It was the menace of the Turks across
the old trade routes to the Orient that started Columbus on his
momentous voyage westward to find the East. Even at the time of
the death of Johann Gutenberg, the existence of the American continents was still unknown and unsuspected.

It is significant that the first European printed matter which
bears a date appeared in 1454, the year after the fall of Constantinople, and heralded the coming of a power greater than the Turk
to save what the barbarian threatened to destroy. It might seem to
us of today that the time of the invention of printing was a dark and
desperate one. But quite on the contrary, it was a time of intense
intellectual activity. Forces in human affairs which had been slowly
gathering their lost momentum throughout the centuries of what are
called the Dark Ages were culminating in the fifteenth century in
the Renaissance, the great rebirth. Minds were once more becoming
eager and inquisitive. Scholars were active, studying not only the
Christian literature, but also the pagan Latin classics. Other scholars,
fleeing from Byzantium before the advancing Turk, brought with
them the treasures of Greek literature to a Europe which had almost
forgotten Greece. An era of exploration dawned as new opportunities were sought for trade.

Then, too, there was a quickening of interest in orthodox
religion. In the fourteenth century the Christian church was, as
Goldschmidt has pointed out, in a state of unprecedented decadence.
The Great Schism had brought about deterioration of churches,
abbeys, and schools, and a great falling off in the devotion, enthusiasm and discipline of the clergy. The renaissance of piety and energy
within the church which followed upon the Councils of Constance,

Pisa, and Basel had an invigorating influence on the worthwhile activities of priests and monks, and among these the writing and binding of manuscript books came in for an important share of their attention.

Two orders, both founded by Gerard Groot, the Windesheim Congregation and the Brothers of the Common Life, had as their primary aim the production and dissemination of literature, the former producing scholarly works, and the latter prayer books, schoolbooks, and manuals for the common people. These are typical of fifteenth-century activities which made it almost imperative that an improved method of producing books be found.

If there had been a darkness covering Europe before, it was the darkness of a fog rather than of night, and the fog was now lifting. It was under just such circumstances that there existed in an extraordinary degree a social need for printing to help dispel that fog. It would be difficult to name any invention at any time for which the world was more eagerly ready.

Europe was fortunate in the middle of the fifteenth century in having ready for the inventive mind not only an urgent need for the service which printing could render, but also all the material means required for working out the practical problems of creating a new craft. For any invention depends quite as much on the state of knowledge in related arts as on the creative idea in the mind of the inventor. The inventor borrows one known process here, finds a suitable method or material already in use there, adapts a scientific principle from still another source, and combines these and other available materials and processes for his invention. The first railroad cars were stagecoaches adapted to run on metal tracks; the first automobiles were buggies and surreys with mechanical motive power in them; the first airplanes were adaptations of box kites with internal combustion engines to keep them moving.

It is of interest, therefore, to consider what the related industrial arts had ready to offer to the inventor of printing in his quest for the one best way to produce books quickly and economically. Without any one of the following essentials, printing as it developed in Europe would have been impossible: (1) an abundant and easily procurable substance such as paper for taking printed impressions; (2) an ink that could be applied to metal surfaces and transferred to paper under pressure; (3) a press for bringing the inked metal and the paper firmly into contact with each other; and (4) all those materials and processes of the worker in metals which could provide a proper alloy for type metal and which made possible the cutting of dies or matrices, the construction of molds, and a convenient method of casting.

If paper had been unknown, printing could still have been done on vellum, though less satisfactorily; had there been no suitable ink, some other kind of pigment might have served; if the principle of the press had not been available, some other method of bringing type and paper together might have been used. But without the types, the printing of the European alphabetical languages in any serviceable way would have remained an insoluble problem. The very essence of the European invention of printing, therefore, was a method of producing accurately proportioned types in the desired quantities at a reasonable cost.

Paper, as we have already seen, was available in Europe and was used even for the making of manuscript books for some time before the advent of printing. It is significant that a paper mill had begun work at Strasbourg about 1430, or just about the time when, as we shall see, Johann Gutenberg took refuge in that town. The spread of printing gave an immense stimulus to the manufacture of paper, but even at the very outset of printing, paper was so abundant that the material on which to print his books was among the least of the

inventor's problems. Availability of this almost indispensable material vastly favored the early development of the typographic craft.

For printing from wood blocks, the Europeans, like the Chinese before them, used what may be called a "water-color" ink. The pigment, made from lampblack combined with gum or gluten, was dissolved in a little water before use. This was quite satisfactory for block printing, but would not do at all for printing from metal types, as the watery ink would not "stick" to the metal surfaces. We do not know exactly what kind of ink the Chinese and the Koreans used with their metal types, but it must have been some kind of oily substance that could be applied evenly on metal.

In Europe, when printing was invented there, a satisfactory ink was readily available. Before the close of the fourteenth century, painters had begun the use of drying oils and varnishes as vehicles for their pigments. The invention of paints with a varnish base has been traditionally credited, on the testimony of Vasari, to the Flemish painter Jan van Eyck in the year 1410. But while it is certain that the artistic abilities of Jan and Hubert van Eyck brought deserved attention to the merits of their improved materials, it seems probable that they simply improved certain processes which were already known. For the Strasbourg Manuscript, probably older than 1400, contains a recipe for preparing "oil for the colors" by boiling linseed, hempseed, or nut oil with certain dryers. This oil, which the unknown writer called *oleum preciosum,* was, after bleaching in the sun, of a thick consistency and transparent. But not all painters, he added, were familiar with it.

Cennino Cennini, in his treatise on the arts written in 1437, speaks of painting in oils as "much practiced by the Germans," indicating that the process was not at that time regarded as a new invention. Alberti, writing in Italy about 1450, mentions "a new discovery of laying on colors with oil of linseed so they resist forever all injuries

from weather and climate." And Filarete, writing about 1464, spoke of German painting with linseed oil as a medium. As a matter of fact, Theophilus several centuries earlier (about 1100) had given directions for mixing colors with prepared linseed oil, and Heraclius at about the same period described oil colors to the admixture of which driers were added. From the sixth century onward, varnish made from nut oil was used as a protective finish over paintings done in tempera or encaustic. And there are many references in early English and continental documentary records and accounts mentioning oils supplied to medieval artists for use in painting.

The production of a suitable ink, therefore, was a problem of no particular difficulty to the first experimenter with printing from movable types. The oil paints of the artists required only slight adaptation to make them available for printing on paper or vellum.

The ancient Oriental printers did not resort to the mechanical principle of the press in making impressions from their wood blocks and types. They laid their paper on the inked form and took the impression by rubbing or brushing down against the form. The early European printers of block books used the same method. But to the German inventor of typography a press of some kind seemed to be the most practical means of procuring a firm, even impression from a form of separate types. In the earliest document alluding to the invention, the record of the Dritzehen lawsuit of 1439, there are references to a *presse,* and no other method of making the impression seems ever to have been considered.

For industrial applications of the principle of the press Gutenberg did not have far to seek. Screw presses were used for the pressing of olives and wine grapes, for the printing of designs on textiles, and—in crafts closely associated with printing—for expelling the moisture from damp sheets in the process of making paper, and for pressing the covers of manuscript books in the process of binding.

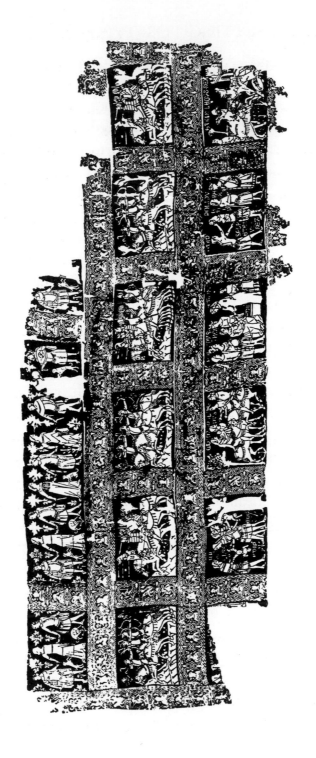

So all that was necessary was to devise a proper base on which the type might rest and an impression member in the form of a platen.

As a matter of fact, the printing of textiles had been a flourishing industry for several centuries before Gutenberg's time. The process was most frequently used in the portrayal of religious subjects for altar cloths and other church decorations, which could be produced by this process much more cheaply than tapestries. Early printed textiles are to be found in a number of museums or other collections of antiquities. One of the earliest and historically most important is the Sion textile, reproduced on the opposite page from the original in the Historisches Museum in Basel, which is dated by competent authorities at about the end of the fourteenth century.

Not only have there been preserved specimens of early printed textiles, but through a stroke of good fortune one of the wood blocks used for printing textiles was discovered in 1898, in the course of demolishing the Cistercian convent at La Ferté-sur-Grosne, in the department of Saône-et-Loire, France. Cut in relief upon this block was a depiction of part of the scene of the crucifixion, with an inscription of several words in uncial letters. The large size of the block, which measures approximately nine by twenty-four inches, points to its use for printing a fabric intended to be viewed at a distance. The costumes and arms of the centurion and two soldiers shown in the picture indicate a date in the last quarter of the fourteenth century.

Textiles were printed by laying the cloth on a flat surface and placing the inked block face downward on it. The block was then stamped or pounded sufficiently to transfer the ink to the fabric. After being re-inked, the block was laid down in the next position, and the process was repeated.

Finally, for the method of producing the separate types, the medieval workers in metals were well prepared with processes which

the inventor of printing could use or adapt to his purposes. In fact, there was nothing altogether new even about the fundamental idea of separate types. The use of them for the imprinting of letters of the alphabet and the *successive,* interchangeable use of them to make words and sentences was already known in Europe. For this procedure had been developed by the bookbinders for stamping letters on their bindings, and these letters were made in much the same form as the gilding tools used by hand finishers today—the only difference being that these letter stamps were cut in intaglio instead of relief. Dr. Franz Falk has made record of lettered inscriptions on dated bindings of 1436, 1442, and 1451.

Letter stamps for bookbinders were also cut in relief, as exemplified in the binding of a fifteenth-century manuscript missal described by Gottfried Zedler. On the cover of this book the word *Missale* and the binder's name *Hene Crans* are impressed with relief stamps, and a manuscript note inside, complaining that several of the signatures were transposed by the binder, makes reference to that craftsman as the *impressor.*

As early as the thirteenth century, metal founders had made use of single letters engraved in relief on metal or on wood to impress in the sand in which the molten metal was poured the letters of an inscription which was intended to appear in relief on the finished casting. Also in the thirteenth century, there is attributed to Étienne Boileau, then provost of Paris, a regulation forbidding the guild of metal founders to produce castings bearing legends similar to those on coins or seals, but making an exception in favor of those which bore only letters impressed one at a time. Letter punches were used also by the founders of bells, pewter vessels, and other metal objects. Punches were also used by early engravers of dies for coins and medals, some being used for parts of the design and others for single letters in the inscription.

Processes for casting small objects in metal were well known, of course, to the medalists and goldsmiths of the time, both of whom had carried the art to a high degree of perfection. It is interesting to note, in this connection, how often a goldsmith figures in the first experiments at printing with movable types. Hans Dünne, for example, plays a part in the Gutenberg lawsuit at Strasbourg in 1439 as one who had furnished the inventor with "what pertains to printing." Waldfoghel at Avignon (see page 180) was a silversmith, Nicolas Jenson was skilled in the making of coins, and there are other instances of a like association. The services of a capable goldsmith must have been indispensable to the success of experiments with the whole process of making small separate metal types. He would have been able not only to engrave the dies or punches for the letters, but would also have been skilled, from his experience in casting gold and silver, in methods of casting the types in sand molds, if indeed that process was used in the production of the most primitive types.

So far as engraving on metal was concerned, the art was well known at the time when the invention of printing was brewing. A spectacularly early testimony regarding it appears in the records of the dukes of Burgundy under the date of 1398. A "block of lead" costing twenty-two livres was then provided for the painter Jehan Malouel "to cut in it several stamps [or prints] necessary for making the pictures of several subjects for the said church"—the Eglise des Chartreux at Dijon. And in another reference the *ciripagus* is described by Paulus Paulirinus, in a manuscript on the industrial arts written between 1459 and 1463, as an artificer who engraves skillfully in brass, iron, or wood both pictures and text with the object of printing them on paper.

We thus see that the inventor of typography had more or less at hand, subject to his observation, all the elements of printing except

two. One element which his genius had to supply was a satisfactory method of producing separate types of such accurate quadrature that they could be assembled easily and when assembled could be held firmly together so that successive impressions could be made from them with reasonable convenience and speed. This was by no means easy. The earliest specimens of printing clearly show several stages of experimentation with various methods of making dies, punching matrices, and casting the type. The other element was a method of combining the types so that a series of them, assembled to reproduce the letters of a text, could be printed together at one impression and after printing could be distributed and at any time re-assembled in another order.

The time was ripe. A re-awakened Europe was demanding books. The need for a method of producing books rapidly and in quantity was acute. The block books already in circulation made it clear that books could be produced in quantity by printing. The separate letter stamps used by the bookbinders perhaps suggested the one best method—the most flexible, practical, and economical method—of composing texts for printing. The arts and crafts of the period had ready for use or adaptation the materials, processes, and mechanical appliances requisite for working out the technique of printing. All that was needed was a mind capable of grasping clearly and steadfastly the result to be accomplished and then of assorting and selecting the essential elements and welding them into a new industrial engine—the practical process of printing.

It does not at all minimize the importance of the invention of printing or the genius of the inventor to point out that the invention was the result of a process of synthesis or combination of known elements. For that power of the human mind which can visualize known and familiar facts in new relations, and their application to new uses—the creative power of synthesis—is one of the highest and

most exceptional of mental faculties. Others had seen the need which Gutenberg saw, and others had experimented with printing and had at their disposal all the elements essential to success. But with every condition favorable towards the middle of the fifteenth century, the invention of printing still awaited the patient labor of a man with a truly creative mind.

X

Johann Gutenberg's Invention

IN the cultural history of mankind there is no event even approaching in importance the invention of printing with movable types. It would require an extensive volume to set forth even in outline the far-reaching effects of this invention in every field of human enterprise and experience, or to describe its results in the liberation of the human spirit from the fetters of ignorance and superstition. The mighty power of the printed word to influence human thought and action, for good or ill, has seldom been more clearly shown than in our own day and age, when we see the governments of great nations enforcing a rigorous control or even suppression of the press as a necessary means of controlling the opinions and activities of their people. Since printing has exerted so immense an influence upon the course of civilization, the question of who invented it becomes one of high historical interest and importance.

We have seen that printing, and even printing with movable types, had been practiced in China and other Oriental lands long before the appearance of printing in Europe. But we have also seen that in those Far Eastern lands the conditions were unsuitable for the acceptance of printing, so that the invention did not take root and flourish there. From the point of view of its effects on history, printing as it was done in China was sterile. The epochal event was the appearance of printing in Europe, about the middle of the fifteenth century.

Yet the first appearance of the printed word in Europe was so unobtrusive that it left no clear historical traces of its beginning.

A CONJECTURAL SIXTEENTH CENTURY
PORTRAIT OF JOHANN GUTENBERG.

Before the end of the fifteenth century, the fame of the new art of printing was reverberating throughout Europe. But in spite of the fact that the first printer had in his hands the very tools of advertisement and publicity, he remained—deliberately, it would seem—in nameless obscurity. So we are left in almost total ignorance of just how and where printing actually was first begun. And when the question is asked, "Who invented printing?" the answer must be that we do no not know with conclusive certainty what man first made types in Europe and printed with them.

As to the identity of the inventor of printing, historical research has amassed a considerably body of evidence, a very small proportion of which is direct evidence, most of it being indirect and circumstantial. This evidence has been sifted and resifted until it can safely be said that no smallest item of it has escaped searching and critical examination by competent scholars. From this evidence there emerges the figure of Johann Gutenberg, of Strasbourg and Mainz, as the most firmly established claimant to the honor of being the inventor of printing.

Johann Gänsefleisch, or Gensfleisch, who according to the then prevailing custom used his mother's family name, Gutenberg, was born at Mainz of a patrician family about 1400. In his early manhood an uprising of the popular faction in the city resulted in the banishment of his family from Mainz. It may have been about 1430 that Gutenberg, in exile, took up residence in Strasbourg, where he seems for a time to have lived in comparatively easy circumstances on an inherited income.

It is from Strasbourg that we get the first faint hint that Gutenberg was beginning his experiments with printing. In 1439 we find him engaged in a lawsuit there. From the documents in the case, so far as copies of these have been preserved, we learn that a few years previously he had entered into a partnership with two associates to

engage in several crafts in which Gutenberg was to instruct the others. On the death of one of the partners, his brother demanded that he be admitted to the partnership, or else that the capital invested by the deceased partner be refunded. About forty witnesses testified in the case, and the testimony of sixteen of them has been preserved. But in all this testimony there are only the most casual references to the enterprises in which the partners were engaged. These references, obscure though they are, can quite convincingly be interpreted, however, as showing that Gutenberg and his associates were actively engaged in working out some kind of a process resembling printing.

What later became of the partnership and its enterprises, we do not know. The case against Gutenberg, however, was dismissed by the court for the reason that the partnership agreement provided for the manner in which a deceased partner's interest should be disposed of, and that the plaintiff had no case until the time came for the dissolution of the partnership according to the agreement.

In 1441 Gutenberg borrowed a sum of money from the funds of the parish of Saint Thomas in Strasbourg and presumably used it in furthering his work. Then for nearly five years there is no record of him. In 1448, however, he was back in Mainz, having finally decided to take advantage of a permission to return which had been granted to him many years before. Strasbourg at that time was threatened by disturbances arising out of the Peasants' War in France, and Gutenberg may have found it an unsuitable place in which to continue his experiments. In 1448, in Mainz, he negotiated another loan through a relative for 150 gulden, a considerable sum of money for those days. Then for another period of nearly five years the records are silent about him.

Finally, in 1455, Gutenberg reappeared in history, and once more as the defendant in a lawsuit. From the records in this case it is clear

that in 1450 he had borrowed the impressive sum of eight hundred gulden from Johann Fust, a goldsmith and capitalist of Mainz, the purpose being "to finish the work." Toward the end of 1452, Fust advanced eight hundred gulden more, this time with an agreement that he was to share as a partner in Gutenberg's enterprise. In the lawsuit of 1455 Fust sued to recover the total amount of money advanced, together with interest, the total amounting then to a little over two thousand gulden. Fust also demanded the forfeiture to him of the tools and equipment which were made with the proceeds of the first loan.

In this case we find quite specifically that the enterprise in question was printing. In Gutenberg's reply to Fust's demands there is mention of expenditures for workmen's wages, for house rent, for parchment, paper, ink, and so on, and also of money to be devoted to "the work of the books." For Fust his later partner and son-in-law, Peter Schoeffer, appeared as a witness, and there appeared for Gutenberg two of his employees, Bertolf von Hanau and Heinrich Keffer, who are probably the men we later find working as printers at Basel and Nuremberg. The whole case gives the impression of being concerned with a loan of a large sum of money advanced to finance a printing project of considerable importance.

There is no record of the outcome of Fust's suit, but later events make it seem likely that Fust became the owner of at least so much of the printing equipment as had been acquired or made with his first eight hundred gulden. At any rate, when printing finally emerged from experimental obscurity, Fust and Schoeffer in partnership were the outstanding printers at Mainz.

Gutenberg, on the other hand, seems to have become bankrupt after the breach with Fust. The account books of the parish of Saint Thomas in Strasbourg show that his regular payment of interest on his loan ceased about 1457 and never was resumed. In 1461 the

parish laid a complaint against Gutenberg before the imperial court sitting at Rottweil, but without effect. If Gutenberg was engaged in printing, or in any other form of business, after Fust foreclosed on him, there is no direct evidence of it, but it is a not unreasonable conjecture that he may have operated a small printing shop, although not very successfully from the financial standpoint.

On January 17, 1465, Archbishop Adolf of Mainz appointed Gutenberg as his servant and courtier for life by reason of the "grateful and willing service which he had rendered to him and to his order [*Stift*] and may and will render in the future." Whether this was for political service in support of Adolf's cause or a reward for his achievements in the typographic field, we have no certain means of knowing.

From a document dated February 26, 1468, we learn that Dr. Konrad Humery, of Mainz, gave a quittance to the archbishop for "certain forms, letters, instruments, tools, and other things belonging to the work of printing which Johann Gutenberg left after his death, and which were and still are mine." From this it appears that Humery at some time or other had procured for Gutenberg some printing equipment with which to work. From it we also can fix with reasonable certainty the date of Gutenberg's death, which must have occurred somewhat earlier than the date of the Humery document. But where Gutenberg died, and the place of his burial, are as deeply hidden from us as the other facts of his life. There was a tradition that his remains were interred in the Church of Saint Francis at Mainz, and that Adam Gelthus, a relative and friend, caused a tablet to be erected to his memory with an inscription, thus translated: "To Johann Gensfleisch, the inventor of the art of printing and deserver of the highest honors from every nation and tongue, Adam Gelthus places this tablet in perpetual commemoration of his name." But the church was torn down in 1742, and later search on its

site for the tomb (and tablet, if there was one) has been fruitless up to the present time.

Just thirty documents, of accepted authenticity, have been discovered to give contemporary evidence of the facts of Gutenberg's life. Only three of these (the Strasbourg lawsuit, the Fust lawsuit, and the Humery quittance) contain anything which refers to printing. Some relate to Gutenberg's borrowing money, others are concerned with annuities payable to Gutenberg, to duties paid by him in Strasbourg on a large store of wine, to a suit brought against him, presumably for breach of promise, by Anna zu der Iserin Thure, a noble lady of Strasbourg, and to the arrest in Strasbourg of the secretary of the city of Mainz whom Gutenberg sought to hold as a hostage for a debt claimed to be due him from that city. If there were nothing else upon which to rest the case, the claim that Gutenberg was the inventor of printing would indeed be questionable. But quite aside from the documents, there are two other sources from which is drawn evidence which gives significant weight to the claim. These sources are the surviving specimens of printing produced in Gutenberg's time, and the practically unanimous testimony of contemporary writers to the effect that he was the inventor.

When we come to consider the earliest products of the German press, we find that they are represented only by fragments, no one of which bears any indication of the name of the printer, the place of printing, or the date of issue. Many of these fragments have survived only because some fifteenth-century binders found them handy for use in making their bindings of other books. These precious scraps of parchment or paper have been subjected to the most painstaking examination, and innumerable scholarly articles or monographs have been written about them. Though there are many differences of opinion about details, they all have been found to have one characteristic in common: we are able to associate all the types

used in them with types which were later used by known printers who were all located at Mainz or in the immediate vicinity.

This does not mean, of course, that these fragments were all printed with the same type. It does mean, however, that they were printed with various fonts of type which show such close resemblances in detail as to indicate that they all originated in, or were developed from, a common pattern or design. The obvious modifications of this design may mean that the differing types of our fragments may have been made by different hands at different times. But the basic features of the design appear so markedly in all the modifications as to demonstrate their derivation from one and the same creative idea.

The sequence in time of these fragments can be determined only by deduction from what is known of the types used in them—the condition of the types with respect to wear, the degree of skill shown in setting them, and the progressive modifications in their forms in the direction of improvement. The sequence of development ends in the type known as that of the 36-line Bible, which was certainly printed, at Mainz or at Bamberg, not later than 1460. The same types are also known to have been in the hands of Albrecht Pfister at Bamberg and used by him in books printed in 1461 and 1462. The types of the fragments, through all their variations, are therefore generically known as the 36-line Bible types.

These 36-line Bible types are classified by German scholars (who are the outstanding specialists in the study of them) as having passed through three successive states of development: (1) the types of the Paris Donatus; (2) the types of the astronomical calendar; and (3) the types of the 36-line Bible. Within each "state" there are a number of minor variations.

It is the consensus of present-day bibliographical judgment that the earliest and most primitive of these fragments which have been

preserved to us is a part of a single leaf of a sibylline poem in German. This precious scrap of paper is generally referred to as the "Fragment of the World Judgment" because of the fact that the particular portion of the poem which it contains deals with the Last Judgment. It was found in Mainz about 1892 and some ten years later became the property of the Gutenberg Museum in that city, where it is most carefully preserved.

From the position of the watermark in this fragment (see the illustration on page 71) it has been possible to compute its probable position in the full sheet, and from the known text of the complete poem it has been estimated that the book from which the fragment was cut was originally made up of 37 leaves, or 74 pages, with 28 type lines to a page. No trace of any other leaves of this book has ever been found. The fragment itself shows signs of having been used in the making of a bookbinding, and it is not impossible that other portions of the same book are still hidden away in some old fifteenth-century binding which has not yet been dissected.

As the "Fragment of the World Judgment" is considered more primitive in its type forms and in the technique of its composition than the other fragments still to be mentioned, it is believed to belong to the very earliest years of experiments with printing. Gottfried Zedler concludes that it was printed between 1444 and 1447, or just at the close of Gutenberg's sojourn in Strasbourg. There is some speculation in this deduction, of course, but there is much more evidence in favor of this conclusion than against it. Competent authorities therefore regard it as the earliest piece of printing with movable types now extant, and as such it is a very precious document indeed. A reproduction of it faces this page.

Closely related to the "World Judgment" fragment in type and technique are certain fragments from pages of copies of Aelius Donatus' widely used Latin grammar, which was a standard text-

leben wil nutze do nien do got orcel wil
gebē Sie gene mir schreckē do hien Die
got nye erkante noch forchte zu Niema
mag sich obergē nicht Vor d̄ gotlichē
angesiecht Cristus wil do urtel spreche·
Vn wil alle boszheit rechen Die nie ge-
dacht den willē in Den wil er gebē ewige
pin Vn wil den gudē gebē By ym freude
vn ewig lebē Sist die werlt vn alle ding
Die in d̄ werlt geschaffē sint Czu gene
vn werdē auch zu nicht Als man wol

er werde do pine erlon · wer in d̄ hymel
rich ist Der hat freude mit ihesu crist Der
von d̄ hymel her nidd ist komen Vnd
mentschlich natuer hat an sich gnōm̄
· Vn an d̄ mentscheit ist erstorbē Vn m̄
dem dode hat erworbē Dz wer do glaubt
hat an en Mynne vn zuusiecht d̄ sal zu
ym · wir sollē gantzē glaubē habē Da
wir vō ihesu crist horē sagē Vnd sollen
alle vnß werck vn sene Czu xpo keer̄ yn
liebe vn yn mynne Vn zu ym habē zu ō

THE "FRAGMENT OF THE WORLD JUDGMENT."

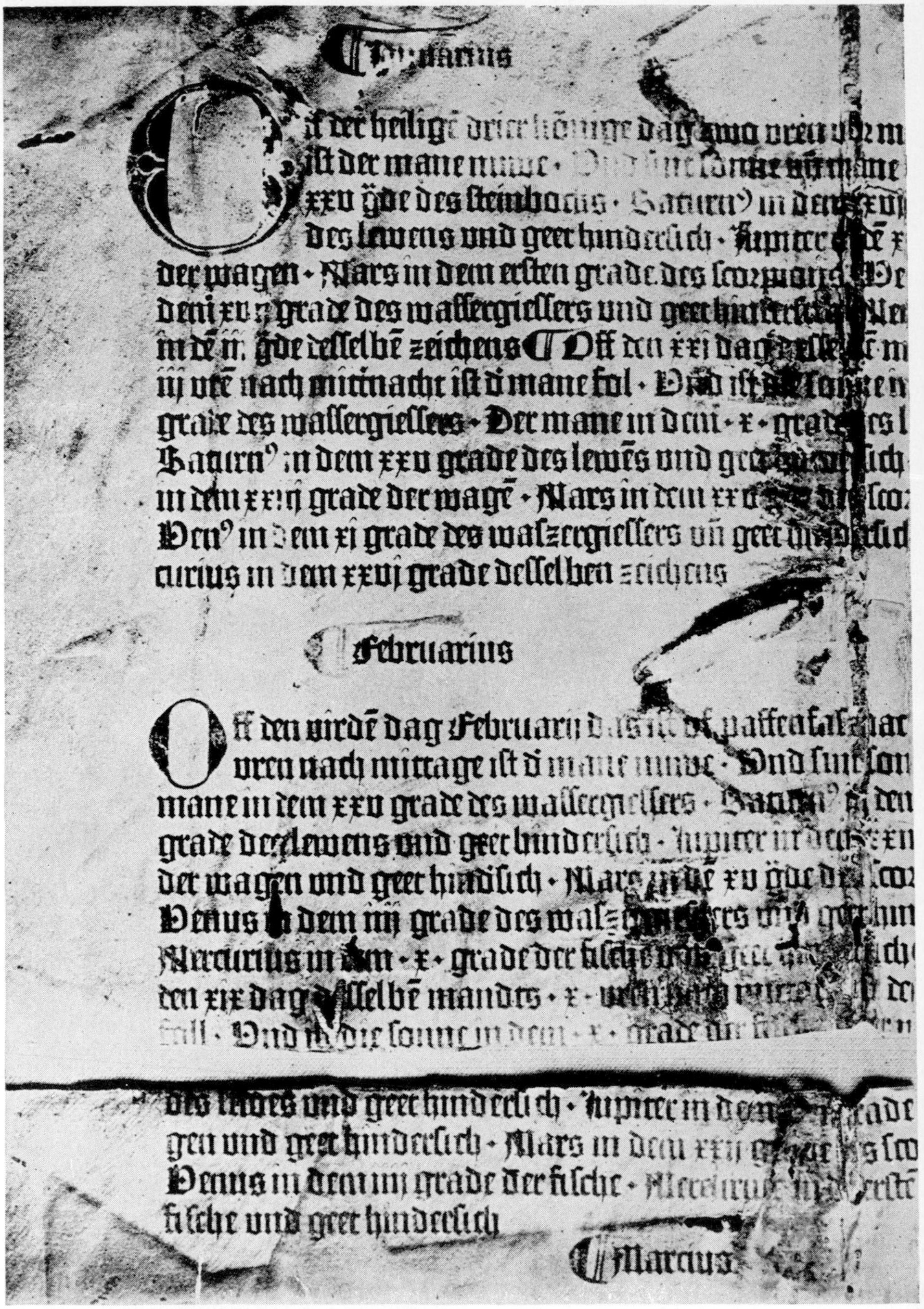

book of its time. Three different issues of this work belong, on excellent authority, to the period before 1458, arranged in order of time according to the peculiarities of their types. The earliest of the three is represented by two full leaves printed on parchment, the second by two very small parchment fragments, and the third by another pair of full parchment leaves. The remains of the first two issues are preserved in the Preussische Staatsbibliothek at Berlin. The two leaves of the third issue, which first were brought to light about 1800, are in the Bibliothèque Nationale at Paris. The types in this group are generally known as the "Paris Donatus" types, from the pages in which they were first studied.

The earliest representative of the second "state" of the 36-line Bible type is a large piece of parchment, nine inches wide by nearly two feet long, in two segments. It was discovered in 1901 in an old bookbinding in Wiesbaden and contains a portion of a single-sheet astronomical calendar or ephemeris. It bears no indication of the year for which it was printed, but astronomical calculations from the data it contains lead many authorities to relate it to the year 1448. If this is so—and the sequence of many other identified pieces of printing, in their relation to issues of known date, makes it quite possible—the calendar was printed at the end of 1447. It seems to have been printed with a freshly cast type, and its typographical execution gives evidence of considerable previous experience with type and printing.

Who was responsible for the production of these specimens of printing in its primitive or formative state? The only man whom we can so much as suspect, on the basis of existing evidence, of being interested in or engaged in the practice of printing in Mainz or in that vicinity at that period was Johann Gutenberg. The majority of scholars unite in ascribing the "World Judgment," the three issues of the Donatus, and the astronomical calendar to Gutenberg's experi-

mental workshop, whether the work on them was actually done by Gutenberg in person or by his associates.

Bear in mind that the "World Judgment," a book of seventy-four pages or thereabouts, was set in type and printed a full ten years before the probable date of the 42-line Bible (the so-called Gutenberg Bible), which has been widely celebrated as the first book printed in Europe. There were also at least sixteen additional issues of the Donatus, as well as a number of other minor pieces of printing which appeared, in all probability, before that Bible. Then again, we must realize that the primitive issues of the press which are known to us, largely through the preservation of fragments, probably represent only a small proportion of all that was printed then, most of which has disappeared without trace.

On the basis of all this evidence it seems likely that printing was being done at Strasbourg and later at Mainz for a period of at least ten years before the appearance of the celebrated Bible. The same evidence shows, too, that this earliest printing was experimental or in a state of development, with improvements constantly being made. This accords perfectly with what we know of the development of other inventions. The first telephone was not a perfect instrument, nor was the first phonograph, nor the first radio. It would be unreasonable to assume that the art of printing sprang at once full-grown and perfect from the mind of its inventor. And it is no detraction from the fame of the inventor to point out that, beginning with a great creative idea, he had to find his way toilsomely to the means of making his idea take effective form. The greatest honor we can attribute to the name of Gutenberg is to say that he produced that 74-page "World Judgment" ten years or more before the appearance of the great Bible on which his fame has been mistakenly made to rest. For in that first production he was blazing the way into virgin territory, encountering problems the difficulty of

which we can only surmise, and evolving from his own mind the fundamental principles of that art which of all arts has made the greatest impress on civilization.

If scholars are correct in determining the date of the calendar which has been ascribed to 1448, it was printed at about the middle of that period of nine years (1444-1453) during which Gutenberg, his activities and even his whereabouts, almost wholly disappear from our scanty knowledge of him. But there have been recorded no fewer than sixteen issues of the Donatus printed with the so-called "calendar" type, showing that the inventor and his associates were decidedly active in carrying forward the invention of printing. These grammars were all printed on vellum and show in some cases a marked improvement over the first three in printing technique.

It has been shrewdly suggested that in those beginning years the inventor devoted himself to the solution of technical problems and left to his associates the first efforts to put printing to practical use. We know that Gutenberg at Strasbourg was imparting instruction in his "secret" art in return for the investment of rather large sums of money by his partners. It is certainly plausible to suppose that those Strasbourg partners, and probably other men later associated with Gutenberg, tried to turn their new craft to profitable use by printing the various editions of the Donatus which we have noticed, as well as other works which may have been in demand. The very imperfections in their work would then have suggested to the inventor new ways of improving the technique of types and their use.

The dates of many of the earliest products of the European press are matters of conjecture. The first *dated* piece of printing preserved to us appeared in 1454, which is thus the earliest date that can be set beyond any speculation or controversy. In that year four different issues of a papal indulgence appeared in printed form. The occasion was historic. Constantinople had fallen to the Turks the year before.

Vniuersis christifidelib; psentes litteras inspecturis Paulinus Chappe Consiliari? ambassiator et pcurator generalis Serenissimi Regis Cypri Thac pte Salute in dno Cui Sactissim? Xpo pr et dns Nicolaus diuia. puidetia. papa v?. afflictioni Re-
gni Cypri misericorditer cpatiens et hostibus crucis xpi hostes. Theucros et Saracenos gratis cocessit omib; xpifidelib; vtriusq;
sexus vere penitentib; et confessis...

Forma plenissime absolucionis et remissionis in vita

Misereatur tui &c. Dns noster ihesus xps p sua sctissima et piissima mia; te absoluat Et auctoe ipi? beatoq; petri et pauli
apłoru; ei? ac auctae apłica michi cmissa et tibi cocessa Ego te absoluo ab omnib; peccatis tuis cotritis cofessis et oblitis...

Forma plenarie remissionis in mortis articulo

Misereatur tui &c Dns noster ihesus xps p sua sctissima et piissima mia; te absoluat Et auctoe ipo beatoq; petri et pauli...

THE 1455 INDULGENCE OF 31 LINES.

At the solicitation of the king of Cyprus, Pope Nicholas V granted indulgences to those of the faithful who should aid with gifts of money the campaign against the Turks. Armed with papal authority, Paulinus Chappe, as representative of the king of Cyprus, went to Mainz to raise money for this cause. Ordinarily, these indulgences would have been written out by hand, but in this case, as there were a considerable number to be distributed, the aid of the new art of printing was enlisted, and forms were printed with blank spaces left for filling in the dates, the names of the donors to whom they were issued, and other details.

All these printed indulgences which have been discovered look remarkably alike, but on close examination we find that three of the issues, although differing in slight details of spelling, are alike in having 31 lines of type, while the fourth issue has 30 lines. It was then recognized that the type in the 31-line indulgences was different from that in the 30-line issue—different, yet so similar that they could indicate only the independent use of similar types by different printing offices.

The 31-line indulgences make use, in addition to the small type in which their text is set, of a large type which has already been classified as the 36-line Bible type—essentially the same typeface that was used for printing the "Fragment of the World Judgment" and therefore, in all probability, belonging to Gutenberg.

The 30-line indulgence of 1454, on the other hand, employed for its display lines a slightly smaller type which very closely resembles that of the 42-line Bible, although not identical with it. There is one clue, however, to the identity of its printer—there was used in it a decorative capital M which we later find in the possession of Peter Schoeffer, at Mainz.

Of the 31-line indulgence, in addition to the three varieties dated 1454, a fourth variety appeared later with the date changed to 1455.

A copy of this fourth variety is reproduced on page 148. There are also two known issues of the 30-line indulgence dated 1455.

It is interesting to note that these indulgences were printed at just about the time of the breach in the partnership between Gutenberg and Johann Fust. It was a most important turning point in the development of printing, and there has been much ingenious speculation as to what the relations between the two partners actually were in those critical years. But from this speculation nothing has yet emerged which can be stated as established fact, although it seems quite clear, from the evidence of the indulgences, that a split had taken place and that there were two rival printing offices in Mainz in 1454.

To the same period belongs a leaflet of twelve pages with the title *Eyn Manung der Cristenheit widder die Durken,* or "A Warning to Christendom against the Turks." It is in the 36-line Bible type, and internal evidence shows that it was printed in December, 1454. It is ascribed to the press of Gutenberg, now operating in competition with Fust. It ends with the earliest printed New Year's greeting in the words "Eyn gut selig nuwe Jar."

The next important date in our chronology is the year 1456, in which, on August 15, Heinrich Cremer, vicar of a church at Mainz, completed the rubrication and binding of a copy of the great Latin Bible already referred to as the 42-line Bible—so called from the fact that there are 42 lines to the column on most of its pages. Cremer made note of the date at the end of the two volumes of a copy of the book (from the Mazarin library) which is now preserved in the Bibliothèque Nationale at Paris. The printing of this Bible was completed, therefore, not later than 1456, and probably earlier.

This is the book commonly named the "Gutenberg Bible" and generally regarded as Europe's first printed book, as has already been noted. The book itself bears no indication of the date or place

Left column

eſt anima ei⁹ cū ea: triſtemqʒ deliniuit
blandicijs: et pergens ad emor patrē
ſuū. accipe inquit michi puellā hanc
ōiugem. Quod cū audiſſet iacob: ab-
ſentibus filijs et in paſtu pecoꝝ occu-
patis ſiluit donec redirēt. Egreſſo au
tem emor patre ſichem· ut loqretur ad
iacob· ecce filij eius veniebāt de agro:
auditoqʒ ꝙ acciderat· irati ſunt valde.
eo ꝙ fedam rem opatus eſſet in iſrl̄: et
violata filia iacob· rem illicitā perpe-
traſſet. Locutus eſt itaqʒ emor ad eos.
Sichem filij mei adheſit anima· filie
veſtre. Date eam illi uxorē: et iunga-
mus viciſſim ꝯnubia. Filias veſtras
tradi.e nobis: et filias n̄ras accipite:
et habitare nobiſcū. Terra in ꝓteſtate
veſtra eſt: exercete· negociamini· ⁊ poſſi-
dere eam. Sed ⁊ ſichem ad patrē et ad
fratres ei⁹ ait. Inueniā graciā coram
uobis: ⁊ quecūqʒ ſtatuitis dabo. Au-
gete dotem· ⁊ munera poſtulate: ⁊ liben-
ter tribuā qd' pecieritis: tantū date mi
chi puellā hanc uxorē. Reſpōderūt filij
iacob· ſichem ⁊ patri eius in dōlo: ſeui-
entes ⁊ ob ſtuprū ſororis. Non poſſu-
mus facere ꝙ peritis: nec dare ſororē
noſtrā homini incircūciſo: qd' illicitū
⁊ nephariū eſt apud nos. Sed in hoc
valebim⁹ federari. Si voluitis eſſe ſiles
n̄oſtri: ⁊ circūcidaẜ i uobis ois maſcu-
lini ſexus: tunc dabim⁹ ⁊ accipiemus
mutuo filias uꝼas ac n̄ras· et habita-
bim⁹ vobiſcū: erimuſqʒ un⁹ ꝑls. Si
autē circūcidi noluicitis: tollem⁹ filiā
noſtrā ⁊ recedem⁹. Placuit oblatō eoꝝ
emor ⁊ ſichem filio ei⁹: nec diſtulit ado
leſcens quin ſtatim qd' ꝑebaꜩ explere.
Amabat eni puellā valde: et erat in-
clitus i omni domo pris ſui. Ingreſſi-
qʒ portam urbis locuti ſunt ad ꝑslm.
Viri iſti pacifici ſūt: ⁊ volūt habitare

Right column

nobiſcū. Negocientur in terra et exerceāt
eam: que ſpacioſa et lata cultoribꝰ in-
diget. Filias eoꝝ accipiem⁹ uxores: et
n̄ras illis dabim⁹. Vnū e quo differt
tantū bonū. Si circūcidam⁹ maſclos
noſtros· ritum gentis imitātes: et ſub-
ſtancia eoꝝ ⁊ pecora ⁊ cuncta ꝗ poſſidēt
noſtra erūt. Tantū i hoc acquieſcām⁹:
et habicātes ſiml̄· unū efficiam⁹ ꝑslm.
Aſſenſiqʒ ſūt omnes· cūctis circūciſis
maribꝫ. Et ecce die tercio ꝗndo ꝗuiſſi-
mus uulnerū dolor eſt· arreptis duo
filij iacob· ſimeon ⁊ leui fr̄es dine gla-
dijs· ingreſſi ſunt urbem confidēter:
interfectiſqʒ omnibꝫ maſculis· emor et
ſichem pari�териͨ necauerūt: tollentes dinā
de domo ſichem· ſororē ſuā. Quibꝰ
egreſſis· irruerūt ſup occiſos ceteri filij
iacob· ⁊ depopulati ſunt urbem i ulci-
onem ſtupri: oues eoꝝ et armenta· et
aſinos· cunctaqʒ uaſtantes que in do-
mibꝫ ⁊ i agris erant: paruulos qʒ eoꝝ
et uxores duxerūt captiuas. Quibus
perpetratis audācter: iacob dixit ad
ſimeon et leui. Turbaſtis me: et odio-
ſum feciſtis me chananeis ⁊ pherezeis
habitatoribꝫ terre hui⁹. Nos pauci ſu-
mus: illi congregati percutiēt me: ⁊ dele-
bor ego ⁊ dom⁹ mea. Rūderūt. Nūqd
ut ſcorto abuti debuere ſorore noſtra?
Interea locut⁹ eſt deus ad
iacob. Surge· ⁊ aſcēde bethel· ⁊ habita
ibi: facqʒ altare dn̄o ꝗ apparuit tibi:
quādo fugiebas eſau frā tuū. Iacob
vero ꝯuocata omni domo ſua ait.
Abicite deos alienos qui i medio uꝼi
ſūt· et mūdamini: ac mutate veſtimē-
ta uꝼa. Surgite ⁊ aſcendam⁹ in bethel·
ut faciam⁹ ibi altare dn̄o· qui exaudi-
uit me i die tribulacōnis mee: et ſoci⁹
fuit itineris mei. Dederūt ergo ei omes
deos alienos quos habebāt: ⁊ inaures

of printing or of the identity of its printer. The warm adherents of Gutenberg, whose name is legion, confidently regard this Bible as the masterpiece of his career. But I think I am stating the truth when I say that the majority of temperate bibliographers, who are not special pleaders, believe that the book was either produced in its entirety or in any event was carried through to completion by Fust and Schoeffer, under whose remarkably competent auspices the magnificent Psalter was brought out just one or two years later. The plan for the book was perhaps Gutenberg's, the technique of its manufacture was unquestionably his, and it is not unlikely that work on it began while Gutenberg and Fust were still in partnership. But we certainly cannot believe that it was printed by Gutenberg personally or that he had much more to do with it than to supervise the preparation of its types and the other initial steps in its production.

Every detail of the 42-line Bible has been studied with meticulous care by Schwenke, Dziatzko, and other German bibliographers, and many facts have been learned about the manner of its production. The body size of the type used at the beginning was such that forty lines made a column. The size was then reduced so that forty-one lines could be set within the same space. It was finally reduced again to a size that permitted forty-two lines to a column throughout most of the book. After printing began, it was evidently decided to increase the edition, for the early pages were reset and sent to press a second time. Six presses were at work on the book simultaneously. Paper was purchased in large quantities rather than in job lots, and the total consumption of paper and vellum was extremely large. Altogether, the book was the product of a printing shop liberally equipped with type and with all other essential apparatus—a shop which represented the outlay of large sums of money such as Johann Fust is known to have advanced.

With the production, or at least the completion, of the 42-line Bible, leadership in the practical use of the new craft of printing definitely passed from Gutenberg and such associates as he may have had to the new firm of Johann Fust and Peter Schoeffer. These two made the year 1457 stand out as one of the most conspicuous landmarks in all the five centuries of typographic history by producing the first edition of their famous Psalter—a book which is a never-failing source of amazement and an object of almost idolatrous admiration to all amateurs of early printing. The Psalter is also distinguished as the first *dated* and *signed* printed book. On the last page appears a colophon in Latin, which is thus translated:

The present copy of the Psalms, adorned with beauty of capital letters, and sufficiently marked out with rubrics, has been thus fashioned by an ingenious invention of printing and stamping without any driving of the pen, and to the worship of God has been diligently brought to completion by Johann Fust, a citizen of Mainz, and Peter Schoeffer of Gernsheim, in the year of the Lord 1457, on the vigil of the Feast of the Assumption.

Here at last printing has emerged from its shelter of anonymity, and we stand on firm ground regarding the identity of the printer and the place of issue. The capitals mentioned in the colophon are floriated initials of lacy design printed in three colors. The register of these colors in all the existing copies is so perfect that typographic experts remain puzzled in their efforts to discover the method by which it was obtained. The large type is printed throughout in red and black, and the entire effect cannot be otherwise described than as magnificent.

There are two editions of the Psalter which are easily distinguished the one from the other. The first has 143 leaves, the second contains some added rituals and comprises 175 leaves. There are also at least three variations in the typography of the first page of the text. The differences have been studied and a number of cases have

been recorded of typographical errors which were found and corrected as the work of printing proceeded, but there is more work to be done before we can come into possession of all the facts about this book. Ten copies have been found to be still in existence, together with a number of separate leaves and other fragments—all, by the way, printed on vellum. The copy in Vienna is known as the virgin copy. It was apparently never used in a church, and its vellum pages are practically as pure and white as the day it was printed. Under the colophon of this copy only appears the printers' mark of Fust and Schoeffer.

Two other early books printed at Mainz demand special mention because of the problems which arise in the effort to identify their printer or printers and because of their presumed connection with the later part of Gutenberg's career. These are the 36-line Bible and the *Catholicon*.

The 36-line Bible is much rarer than the 42-line Bible. Only eight copies even approximately complete are known to exist, whereas thirty-two practically perfect copies of the other edition were recorded by De Ricci in 1911. As we have already noted, the typeface in which it is set is that which was used for the earliest German printing. Because of the early origin of this type, it was natural to assume that this Bible was printed before the 42-line Bible. But although there is some reason to suspect that a few leaves of it may possibly have been printed about 1450, the patient studies which Dziatzko has made of its text reveal that it contains numerous errors which can be accounted for only by assuming that it was set up from the printed 42-line Bible as copy. This circumstance, together with the known dates on which was completed the rubrication of copies of the book, and other evidence, point to its having been printed about 1460, or perhaps a little earlier. The extant copies are all printed on paper, but the existence of some separate leaves

THE FIRST PAGE OF THE FUST AND SCHOEFFER BIBLE
OF 1462, WITH HAND-DRAWN BORDER (MUCH REDUCED).

and fragments printed on vellum indicate that there must have been at least a few copies issued on that material. Only one complete copy of this famous book has been recorded as being still in the possession of a private owner. Should it ever come on the market for sale, we may confidently expect the bidding for it to reach truly dizzy heights.

The types of the 36-line Bible were Gutenberg's, made from the original designs with which he had been experimenting for years. Apparently they did not become part of the partnership property acquired with the money invested by Fust about 1452 and hence remained in Gutenberg's possession after the two separated. It has been surmised that Gutenberg planned and even began the printing of this Bible about 1450 (there are known to be two different printings of the first few leaves of the book) and then set it aside in order to work on other things, including the smaller typeface used in the 42-line Bible. According to this line of conjecture, Gutenberg returned to his original project about the time that Fust and Schoeffer were completing and bringing out the 42-line Bible. Albrecht Pfister, later the first printer at Bamberg, eventually came into possession of the 36-line Bible type and possibly of the copies of the book itself which remained unsold. Hence it has been assumed that he was Gutenberg's financial backer, partner, and technical assistant in the task of producing the 36-line Bible itself. But when Pfister printed his first books at Bamberg about 1461, he showed himself to be an inexperienced printer and surely not a man who had had any important part in the printing of a great Bible. All in all, there are many reasons why we should ascribe this work to Gutenberg and no very weighty reason why we should not. Certainly, on the evidence now available, this second Bible has a much better claim than the 42-line edition to be called the "Gutenberg Bible."

The *Catholicon,* a Latin dictionary written by Joannes Balbus in

the thirteenth century, was printed at Mainz in 1460. It bears its
date, but not the name of its printer. It appeared as a folio volume of
373 leaves, printed in two columns to a page of a small type which
was none too good, and of which three varieties have been differentiated. Some copies were on vellum and some on paper. It ended
with a colophon which in translation reads as follows:

By the help of the Most High, at Whose nod the tongues of infants
become eloquent, and Who ofttimes reveals to the lowly that which He
hides from the wise, this noble book, *Catholicon,* in the year of the Lord's
Incarnation, 1460, in the bounteous city of Mainz of the renowned German nation, which the clemency of God has deigned with so lofty a light
of genius and free gift to prefer and render illustrious above all other
nations of the earth, without help of reed, stylus, or pen, but by the wondrous agreement, proportion, and harmony of punches and types, has
been printed and finished.

Hence to Thee, Holy Father, and to the Son with the Sacred Spirit,
Praise and glory be rendered, the threefold Lord and One;
For the praise of the Church, O Catholic, applaud this book,
Who never ceasest to praise the devout Mary.
Thanks be to God.

Many have professed to see in these lines the authorship of
Gutenberg himself, preserving to the end his policy of anonymity—
perhaps for cogent business reasons. The identity of the printer of
the *Catholicon* has been argued pro and con with much vigor and
occasional asperity, but at present the question must be considered
as still an open one. The printing office in which it was produced
had a short life, and the stock of the book was "remaindered" to
Schoeffer not later than 1469 (at which date it appears in his list of
books), and perhaps earlier.

It is perhaps significant that the types of the *Catholicon* were
used by the Bechtermünze brothers, Heinrich and Nicolaus, in
printing the *Vocabularius ex quo* (an excerpt from the *Catholicon*)

at Eltville in 1467. The Bechtermünzes were distant relatives of Gutenberg; and Eltville, not far from Mainz, was the residence of Archbishop Adolf who admitted Gutenberg to his retinue in 1465. But whether or not Gutenberg had any actual connection with the Eltville printing office we simply do not know.

While Gutenberg, perhaps, was struggling to re-establish himself as a printer at Mainz, the Fust and Schoeffer firm was prospering, turning out excellently printed books with regularity. The so-called Bishops' War in 1462 resulted in the sack of Mainz, which must have had disastrous effects upon business there, including the new-born printing business. But in 1465 Fust and Schoeffer were publishing some editions of the classics. The firm had extensive business connections, with agencies in several European cities. Fust died in 1466 while on a business trip to Paris, and Schoeffer continued alone. But though he was successful in a business way, his publications never rivaled the brilliancy of the earlier fruits of the partnership. In 1469, as we have intimated, Schoeffer issued a single-sheet list of books, constituting the first printed publisher's list. A reproduction of it is presented in the plate facing page 161. The first four lines tell us that "Those desiring to procure the books listed below, which are edited with great care, printed at Mainz with a type like this, and well collated, should come to the address written below." It is also the first printed type specimen, the last line, set in large type, reading *hec est littera psalterii,* "this is the type of the Psalter."

To return now to the evidences supporting the claim that Johann Gutenberg was the inventor of printing, we find strong support for the claim in the testimony of a large number of fifteenth-century contemporaries, in documents or in books. A few of the more significant of these testimonies deserve our attention here.

First in point of date is an interesting extract from the manu-

script records of the French royal mints. Here is found a notation to the effect that on October 4, 1458, the king of France (Charles VII), having heard that Johann Gutenberg, of Mainz, a man adept in the cutting of punches and *"caracteres,"* had brought to light the invention of printing, ordered the directors of his mints to select a competent man to be sent secretly to Mainz to learn the new art. The note goes on to say that Nicolas Jenson was selected for this important mission, and we shall have more to say about this royal order when we come to tell about the work of Jenson at Venice. The manuscript in which this note occurs was written in the sixteenth century, but it gives evidence of having been copied, or condensed, from an actual fifteenth-century record which cannot now be found. Dziatzko, after searching study of this document, found no reason to suspect that it was not a genuine transcript of a fifteenth-century record actually contemporary with Gutenberg's life and work. It is significant also that the sixteenth-century transcript was made long before there was any interest in proving or disproving Gutenberg's claim to the invention of printing and, further, that it is found in a manuscript record dealing, not with books or printing, but solely with numismatics.

Next we must note the colophon on the last page of a volume of the *Institutes* of Justinian printed by Peter Schoeffer at Mainz in 1468. Here, in a Latin poem of twenty-four lines, an unknown writer extols the new art of printing and designates "two Johns, both born in the city of Mainz," as the renowned first printers of books. With these Johns, the writer adds, was later added a Peter. It would seem that this must necessarily be interpreted as referring to Johann Gutenberg, Johann Fust, and Peter Schoeffer. It is important to note that these verses were printed about two years after the death of Fust and presumably shortly after the death of Gutenberg.

Two years after the publication of the Justinian at Mainz, an

152 v°

PAGE FROM THE RECORDS OF THE FRENCH ROYAL
MINTS IN WHICH GUTENBERG IS MENTIONED AS
THE INVENTOR OF PRINTING.

A PAGE FROM THE FUST AND SCHOEFFER PSALTER OF 1457 (MUCH REDUCED).

Voletes tibi oparare infrascriptos libros mag̃
cũ diligẽtia correctos.ac in hm̃oı lra mogunũe
impssos·bñ õũnuatoſ·wm̃ãt ad locũ habitatio=
nis infrascriptũ.

Primo pulcram bibliam in pergameno.
Item scõam scõe trati thome de aquino.
Item quartũ scriptũ eiusdẽ.
Itẽ tractatũ eiusdẽ de eccie sacris a articlis fidei.
Itẽ Augustmũ de doctrina xpiana·cum tabula
notabili p̃dicantibs multũ p̃ficua.
Itẽ tractatũ de róne et õscieãtia.
Itẽ m̃gr̃m iohãnẽ gerson de custodia lm̃gue.
Itẽ õsolatoriũ tim̃ oeate õscie venerabilis fratris
iohãnis nider sacre theologie p̃fessoris eximij.
Itẽ tractatũ eiusdẽ de õtractibs mercatorz.
Itẽ bullã p̃ij ip̃e seõi contra thurcos.
Itẽ historiã de p̃sentacõe beãte marie v̊ginis.
Itẽ canonẽ misse cũ p̃facõibs a ip̃aratorijs suis.

ãntiphonis in magna ac grossa littera.
Itẽ iohannẽ ianuensem in catholicon.
Itẽ sextũdecretaliũ.Et clemẽũnã cum apparatu
iohannis andree.
Itẽ in iure ciuili·Jnstitucõnes.
Itẽ arbores de õsanguinitatea affinitatẽ.
Itẽ libros tullij de officijs·Cũ eiusdẽ paradoxis.
Itẽ historiã griseldis.de maxia õstantia m̃ulierũ
Item historiam Leonardi aretini ex bocatio de a=
more Tancredi filie sigism̃udẽ in Duiscardum.

ħec est littera psalterij

important French witness spoke for Gutenberg. Printing had been established in Paris in 1469 by three Germans who had been brought there by Guillaume Fichet and Jean Heynlin, as will be told in more detail in Chapter XII. We cannot conceive of two intelligent men who were better informed regarding the beginnings of the art of printing, which it is evident they had followed closely, or who had a more disinterested point of view regarding the invention and the identity of the inventor. On New Year's day, 1471, Fichet wrote to Robert Gaguin, a scholar and author of eminence, a letter in praise of printing and its service to humane letters. In the course of this letter the writer said, "It is said that there [in Germany], not far from the city of Mainz, a certain John surnamed Gutenberg first of all men thought out the art of printing." This statement from a well-informed and non-partisan source can hardly be impeached.

The Fichet letter, which was printed and bound in a copy of Gasparino's *Orthographia* dedicated to Gaguin, was discovered in comparatively recent times. I consider it the most weighty document bearing on the invention controversy. Because of its importance, I published a few years ago a transcript of its text and a full translation into English, with an introduction and notes.

In the text of a number of books printed in the fifteenth-century are statements that printing was invented in Germany, but with no mention of the name of the inventor. We shall note just a few references in which the printer is named. There are errors of fact in some of these statements, but it must be remembered that in the fifteenth-century news still traveled mostly by word of mouth and that dates, of all items of fact, always suffer most from oral transmission.

In 1474 Johannes Philippus de Lignamine published at Rome the *Chronica* of Riccobaldus Ferrariensis, in which the first reference to printing is under the year 1459, with the statement that "Jacob, surnamed Gutenberg, a native of Strasbourg, and another

man whose name was Fust, being skilled in printing letters on parchment with metal types, are known each of them to be turning out 300 sheets a day at Mainz, a city of Germany." In 1483 Matthias Palmer, of Pisa, under the year 1457, wrote that Johannes Gutenberg zum Jungen, knight of Mainz, invented the art of printing in 1440. By this full and accurate entry of the inventor's name, the writer gave evidence of clear knowledge as to his identity.

Adam Wernher and Johann Herbst, two professors at Heidelberg, wrote some verses in 1494 in honor of Johannes Gensfleisch (Gutenberg's family name), whom they called "the first printer of books" and "the first inventor of the art of printing." In 1499 Jacob Wimpheling praised Joannes Gensfleisch for his invention of printing. Wimpheling's verses were preceded by an epitaph on Gensfleisch, "inventor of the art of printing," by Adam Gelthus, a relative of Gutenberg—whose remains, it is added, rest in peace in the Franciscan Church at Mainz. Also in 1499, Polydore Vergil wrote that a certain Peter, a German, invented printing at Mainz in 1442, but in later editions of this book "Joh. Gutenberg" is substituted for "Peter." In the same year we have a passage in the *Cologne Chronicle* naming Yunker Johann Gutenberg as the inventor of printing at Mainz—but with a "prefiguration" of the invention in Holland at an earlier date. This prefiguration will be discussed in the following chapter.

In 1501 Jacob Wimpheling came forward again with the statement that the invention was made at Strasbourg by Johann Gutenberg, of Strasbourg, and that it was perfected later at Mainz. Finally we will note a bit of testimony from an important source from which, if from anywhere, we might expect a dispute of Gutenberg's claims. It is in a German translation of Livy printed at Mainz in 1505 by Johann Schoeffer, the son of Peter Schoeffer and the grandson of Johann Fust. In this book is a reference to Johann Gütten-

bergk as the inventor of printing in 1450 and to Johann Fust and Peter Schoeffer as improvers and perpetuators of the art. This statement was repeated in a number of subsequent editions before Johann Schoeffer, in books which he printed later, changed his testimony to speak for his grandfather as the inventor of printing. It is interesting to note that the date 1450 is the year in which Johann Fust presumably made his first advance of money to Gutenberg. The younger Schoeffer doubtless had information from family sources as to that transaction.

One of the strongest arguments in support of Gutenberg is the fact that the firm of Fust and Schoeffer, and later Peter Schoeffer, though they were aggressive self-advertisers in their colophons, never during Gutenberg's lifetime claimed credit for the invention—a distinction which they would unquestionably have claimed had they been entitled to it.

It remains to be said, in concluding the presentation of evidence in favor of Gutenberg as the inventor of printing, that Gutenberg's cause was seriously hurt by some over-enthusiastic advocates who, in the last half of the eighteenth century, unblushingly forged a number of "original" documents in support of his claim. These forgeries have now been exposed, but they have served to cast suspicion on the authenticity of all the Gutenberg documents.

The situation is further complicated by the fact that the original record books of the Strasbourg trial of 1439 have perished and that we have to depend, therefore, upon the text at second hand. It is one of the little ironics of history that these records, foundation stones in the edifice of fame erected to one of Germany's national heroes, were destroyed in the taking of Strasbourg by the Prussians in 1870. The text of the Helmasperger notarial instrument of November 6, 1455, from which we derive what little information we have about the Fust-Gutenberg lawsuit, was long known only from tran-

scripts or extracts, but after a disappearance lasting a century and a half the original again came to light about fifty years ago in the library of the University of Göttingen.

The records of the Strasbourg trial of 1439 have been denounced as wholly forged to serve the cause of Gutenberg. If we have to deal with a forgery in this case, it would be hard to think of a more ineffective one. Had some ingenious fabricator written the extensive records of this trial with the idea of furthering the cause of Gutenberg, he would certainly have made the references to printing somewhat clearer. As they now stand, the allusions to printing could not well have been more cryptic. It is not worth while to review here all the conflicting arguments and interpretations which have been built up on the testimony given at that trial. Even if we leave these trial records out of consideration by our jury, the case is still strong enough to justify a verdict in Gutenberg's favor.

This verdict may thus be stated: on the basis of present knowledge, we must conclude that printing with movable types of metal cast in matrices (which constitutes the invention of printing) was invented, so far as its epoch-making appearance in Europe is concerned, at Mainz or in that vicinity at some time between 1440 and 1450; and, on the basis of the evidence now before us, we must assign credit for that invention to Johann Gutenberg.

XI

The Case of Rival Claimants

THE claim that Johann Gutenberg was the inventor of printing has been left by no means uncontested. At some time or other, almost every European country has named some contender for this distinction. These rival claims have been mostly inspired by national pride, and since they were first advanced, centuries ago, little or nothing has been done to support them with argument or proof. But there is one contestant whose claim cannot be lightly dismissed, as his cause has been championed by serious and scholarly advocates in a controversy which is not yet ended. This is the claim of Lourens Janszoon Coster of Haarlem in the Netherlands, who, it is said, began to print with movable types at Haarlem some time in the vicinity of 1430.

The Dutch claim to the invention of printing was not advanced until some years after the invention is supposed to have taken place. The first rumor of it appeared in the *Cologne Chronicle,* which has already been mentioned in the preceding chapter. This book, printed at Cologne in 1499, contained a passage of which we here give Pollard's translation or paraphrase:

This right worthy art was invented first of all in Germany, at Mainz, on the Rhine. And that is a great honour to the German nation that such ingenious men are found there. This happened in the year of our Lord 1440, and from that time until 1450 the art and all that pertains to it was investigated, and in 1450, which was a Golden Year, men began to print, and the first book that was printed was the Bible in Latin, and this was printed with a letter as large as that now used in missals.

Although this art was invented at Mainz, as far as regards the manner in which it is now commonly used, yet the first prefiguration [*Vurbyldung*] was invented in Holland from the Donatuses which were printed there before that time. And from and out of these the aforesaid art took its beginning, and was invented in a manner much more masterly and subtler than this and the longer it lasted the more full of art it became.

A certain Omnibonus wrote in the preface to a Quintilian, and also in other books, that a Walloon from France, called Nicolas Jenson, was the first inventor of this masterly art—a notorious lie, for there are men still alive who bear witness that books were printed at Venice before the aforesaid Nicolas Jenson came there and began to cut and make ready his letter. But the first inventor of printing was a burgher at Mainz, and was born at Strassburg, and called Yunker Johann Gutenberg.

From Mainz the art came first of all to Cologne, after that to Strassburg, and after that to Venice. The beginning and progress of the art were told me by word of mouth by the Worshipful Master Ulrich Zell, of Hanau, printer at Cologne, in this present year 1499, through whom the art came to Cologne.

Ulrich Zell, a cleric of the diocese of Mainz, learned the new art of printing at Mainz and probably as early as 1460. He introduced printing at Cologne in 1462. The statement in the *Cologne Chronicle* which was based on his "word of mouth" testimony states very clearly that printing was invented by Johann Gutenberg at Mainz, but qualifies this by suggesting that there had been a still earlier prefiguration of printing in Holland. This word "prefiguration," *Vurbyldung,* has been the theme of hundreds of pages of learned research and argument. But before attempting an account of what this prefiguration may have been, let us first examine some of the other witnesses who have spoken for a Dutch origin of printing.

Next in point of time, although two generations later than the cryptic allusions in the *Cologne Chronicle,* is Jan van Zuren, of Haarlem, who wrote in Latin, at some time between 1549 and 1561, a "Dialogue on the first and as yet commonly unreported but still

more veritable invention of the art of printing." According to the
word of Petrus Scriverius, a Haarlem writer of the seventeenth century, this dialogue existed in a manuscript of which all had been lost
except the first few leaves containing the introduction. From this
introduction, as transmitted by Scriverius, we translate:

That rightly honored city [Mainz] developed the art [of printing]
conceived by us, into common property and drew it into the light. She
gave to the generally crude and ill-shaped invention a neater form, as the
circumstances of that day required.... Meanwhile,... remember that in
this our city Haarlem the foundation of this art was laid—crude indeed, but
nevertheless the first. Here the printing art was born,... For many years
it was located here in a private house which, although dilapidated, is still
preserved and unharmed,... Here in fact the art was nurtured,... was
indeed too economically nourished and restricted, until, disdaining the
restricting poverty of a private house, it attached itself to a foreigner and,
leaving the limited circumstances of the paternal home behind it, multiplied its equipment and at last appeared publicly in Mainz.

In this account, the story of the Dutch invention of printing
becomes somewhat circumstantial in that Haarlem is named as the
birthplace, where the invention was made in a private house which
seems to have been known to the writer, and from which it departed
with an unnamed stranger, to reappear in a neater form in Mainz.

Next appears Dirck Volkertzoon Coornhert, writing in Latin
a dedication to the governing powers of Haarlem in an edition of
Cicero's *De officiis* which was printed at Haarlem in 1561; again
we translate:

It has sometimes been said to me in good faith... that the useful art of
printing was discovered here in Haarlem, though true enough in a very
crude manner,... This art, which later was taken by an unfaithful servant
to Mainz, was there so much improved... that that town has been given
the credit for the invention. Our citizens have little faith in this statement,
even though it is believed by many and considered as being based on indis-

putable knowledge of the matter;...Since I firmly believe in the above, on the basis of trustworthy evidence of distinguished gray heads, who not only gave me the descent of the discoverer, but also his name and surname, and have pointed out to me the very house of the very first printer, I cannot refrain from bringing this before you.

This writer, although distinguished elderly men had told him the name and surname of the Haarlem inventor and had even pointed out to him the house in which he had lived and worked, did not disclose these important facts—perhaps believing it not worth while, because, as he complained, the fame of Mainz "has become so deeply rooted in everybody's opinion that no proof, no matter how convincing, how clear, and how indisputable it may be, can root out this antiquated delusion from the minds of mankind."

A few years after Coornhert, an Italian, Ludovico Guicciardini, published at Antwerp in 1567 his *Descrizzione di tutti i paesi bassi,* or "Description of all the Low Countries." In this he wrote:

This land, according to the public voice of the citizens and other Hollanders, as well as that of several authors and some memorials, is the land where the art of printing by means of letters and characters, according to the manner of today, was first discovered. Since, however, the originator died before the art was developed and brought to public attention, it is said his servant removed to Mainz, where he received a warm welcome because he was a printer. There...complete mastery and highest development [of printing] was attained. This gave rise to the rumor that Mainz was the town where this art originated. What truth there is in this, I cannot and will not judge; I content myself with having mentioned the matter, in order not to appear to this land and this locality as being prejudiced.

Guicciardini's book was later translated and published in Dutch, French, English, and German, and had much to do with spreading broadcast the claim of the Netherlands to the invention of printing.

Thus far, the story of an invention of printing in Holland offers

nothing but the vaguest kind of rumor. It remained for Adraen de Jonghe, a Dutch physician and historian also known as Hadrianus Junius, to give this story a definite form and substance. Before his death in 1575, this writer had completed his *Batavia,* a history of Holland in Latin, which was finally printed at the Plantin office in Antwerp in 1588. The book had been written, however, about 1568, and the latter year is generally accepted as its date. Since a passage in the *Batavia* is the principal foundation of the Dutch claim to the invention of printing, we give a full summary of it here.

Junius advanced a positive claim for the city of Haarlem to the credit of the invention of printing. The information on which his account of the invention is based was obtained, he tells us, from aged residents of Haarlem of unimpeachable reputation. According to this account, a certain Lourens Janszoon Coster (*Coster* meaning "church warden" or "sexton") had lived in Haarlem 128 years earlier (that is, in 1440), and members of his family were still living there at the time that Junius wrote. One day, while walking in the forest, Coster cut some letters from the bark of trees and found, by impressing them on paper, that they made a print of the letters. Having a keen mind, he was led by this first essay to attempt greater things. With the help of his son-in-law, he then invented a superior kind of black ink, as he had found that the use of ordinary ink smeared the impressions of the letters. This son-in-law, Thomas Pieterszoon, had four children who all later held positions of honor in Haarlem. Thus, Junius explains, the invention did not originate in a lowly or mean family.

Coster next began to make pictures and to explain them with printed words. Junius had actually seen one of the inventor's first works along this line. It was in Dutch, with the title *Spieghel onzer Behoudenisse* ("Mirror of our salvation"). The leaves were printed on one side only, with the blank reverse sides pasted together so

that they might not appear unpleasing. The essence of the story continues thus:

Then he substituted lead forms for the beechwood ones; still later he made them of tin that they might be more resistant and durable. From the remnants of these tin forms were cast wine pots which are still shown as antiques in the Lourens Janszoon house on the market place. This house was later occupied by his great-grandson, Gerrit Thomaszoon, a prominent and excellent citizen who died only a few years ago at a ripe old age.

The new invention thrived because of the readiness with which the people bought the novel product. Apprentices were taken on—the beginning of misfortune; for among them was a certain Johann. Be it, as is suspicioned, the one with the surname Faustus, who was to his master a faithless servant and a messenger of misfortune, or another man of this name, that is all the same to me, since I do not wish to make restless the shades of the dead, who during their lifetime were tortured enough by conscience.

This Johann, after he had learned the art of casting types and combining them—in fact, the whole trade—took the first favorable opportunity, on Christmas Eve, when everyone was at the church, to steal the whole type supply, with the tools and all the equipment of his master. He went first to Amsterdam, then to Cologne, and finally to Mainz, which was out of striking distance, and there opened a printing establishment and reaped the fruits of his theft.

It is known that within the year, in 1442 A.D., there appeared with the same letters [*iis ipsis typis*] which Lourens had used in Haarlem his first work, the *Doctrinale* of Alexander Gallus, a grammar at that time in general use, accompanied with the tracts of Petrus Hispanus.

This is about the story as I heard it from aged and trustworthy men to whom it had been handed down from their forefathers. Nicolaus Gaal, the teacher of my youth, a man of an iron memory, worthy of honor because of his long, white hair, used to tell me that as a boy he had often listened to a certain Cornelis, a bookbinder, then a man eighty years old, who had been an apprentice in that same printing establishment. This Cornelis used to tell how the art had been discovered, as he had heard it from his employer, how the art had developed, and also the story of the

theft, which enraged him so that he wept and cursed the thief, and even cursed the nights when he had slept in the same bed with him.

This story as told by Junius is not a fabrication. It undoubtedly represents a tradition which was current in Haarlem—the same tradition upon which were based the earlier accounts by Van Zuren, Coornhert, and Guicciardini. The strongest point in the story, as Pollard has indicated, is the mention of Cornelis, the bookbinder. There is documentary evidence that a binder of that name was employed between 1474 and 1514 to bind the account books of the cathedral at Haarlem. This Cornelis continued in the binding business, in conjunction with which he was also a bookseller, until his death in 1522. The first known printer at Haarlem was Jacob Bellaert, whose first recorded work was dated 1483. Cornelis had a shop on "der Cruysstraet," and we know that in 1492 he there sold a book printed by Bellaert. We also know that in that same street there was a house known as "Den Bellaert." Kruitwagen, in a recent attack upon the Junius story, has suggested that Cornelis may have woven into his narrative about Coster some facts recalled from his associations with Bellaert. This, however, is pure speculation.

The identity of Coster has also been established. Contemporary records show that he was a resident of Haarlem from 1436 to 1483 and that he was an innkeeper and also a dealer in wine, candles, oil, and soap; also that he held the appointive position of "coster," or custodian, of the church at Haarlem, a position of some responsibility to which were attached some valuable perquisites. Other members of the family had held the same office, so that the title in time became the family name.

No one of the official records connects Coster in any way with printing. But a manuscript pedigree of the Coster family, prepared about 1559 and now preserved at Haarlem, refers to Lourens Coster as "having brought the first print into the world" in 1446.

The foregoing pages contain the essentials of all the affirmative evidence upon which rests the case of Haarlem and of Lourens Coster. In weighing this evidence it is necessary to bear in mind certain facts about it. One is that Hadrianus Junius, to whom alone we owe the identification of Coster with the Haarlem printing, was not at all critical of the facts which he narrated. It is held against him, for instance, that he recorded a legend of Loosduinen, according to which the Countess Margarethe von Henneberg gave birth to 364 children at one time. Mother and children died and were buried in the same grave, and the event was noted on a tombstone. Junius says the story is incredible—but there was the record on the tombstone. He merely recounted the record as it stood. Thus in regard to the invention of printing at Haarlem, he set down with thoroughness and in categorical detail the story as it came to him. His narrative appears to me to present truthfully the Haarlem tradition of his day. In other words, there actually *was* such a tradition, whatever may have been its basis.

It is furthermore to be noted that the first statement of any kind, either in manuscript or in print, in which the name of Coster is connected with the invention of printing is dated over one hundred years after the event—the Coster pedigree of about 1559 and the narrative of Junius written about 1568. Of earlier testimony we have only the cryptic allusion in 1499 to a Dutch prefiguration of the invention perfected at Mainz and the rather vague references of some writers of the early sixteenth century to an invention at Haarlem which, in some discreditable manner, was brought to Mainz. All the testimony for Haarlem, by the way, includes testimony to the effect that Mainz was the place where the invention was first brought to public notice.

Another significant fact is that the early printing done in Mainz or vicinity, of which a considerable quantity of specimens are avail-

able for study, was not any of it done in the types of the primitive Dutch printer, supposedly carried to Mainz by the perfidious "Johann," but in types totally different in character. On the basis of technical evidence it can be confidently asserted that there is not the slightest likelihood that the art of printing as developed at Mainz was derived in any way from the typographical practice of the unidentified primitive Dutch printer or printers. And especially it cannot be shown by any evidence that the primitive Dutch printing antedated the beginnings of typography in Germany.

In a case as important as a claim to the invention of printing, testimony resting on a tradition which circulated for a hundred years before it was published in any definite form would have to be rejected as having insufficient foundation in historical facts. If this were all that had to be considered, the Haarlem claim would be thrown out of court without further ado. However, the case cannot be so easily disposed of. There is still other evidence presented by supporters of the Dutch claims to the invention of printing.

This evidence consists of a considerable body of primitive Dutch printing which is clearly shown to be Dutch, not only by the fact that the text of some of the items is in the Dutch language, but also by the fact that the type used in this printing is designed on the model of manuscript letter forms which are distinctively Dutch in character. Of some of these books and pamphlets there are preserved a few complete copies, but most of them are known to us through fragments only. These, as in the case of the fragments of early German printing, have been found in the bindings of other books. And in this connection it is interesting to note that some Donatus leaves of primitive Dutch printing have been found in the bindings of the Haarlem church account books of 1474, 1489, and 1514—in bindings which are known to have been made by the Haarlem bookbinder Cornelis.

By the study of these specimens of Dutch printing we are able to identify, not one or two, but *eight* distinct types. Not one of these types can be tied up with the work of any known printer, nor is it possible to establish the place of printing or the date of issue of any one of the dozens of publications represented.

Inasmuch as the history of printing in Holland from 1473 on—at which date printers of the German school introduced the art at Alost and Utrecht—has been exhaustively studied and is well known, the existence of this body of unidentified printing presents a puzzle which challenges the wits of any student of the subject who is not blindly committed to one camp or the other. When we add that the technique of this printing is primitive to a degree, the puzzle becomes still more complicated.

When, where, and by whom was that primitive printing done? The answer to these questions is perfectly clear: we have not a shred of definite evidence on which a conclusive answer can be based—except that the printing was probably done in Holland. The identity of the primitive Dutch printer—or printers—is still a mystery. The *Gesamtkatalog der Wiegendrucke,* the latest and most complete catalogue of the incunabula, with praiseworthy conservatism lists these titles as produced by the "Printer of the *Speculum.*"

There is just one thread of connection between the unidentified early Dutch printing and the work of known printers. In 1481, Jan Veldener, an itinerant printer then working at Utrecht, issued an edition of Epistles and Gospels in the Dutch language in which he used two halves of one of the double-compartment woodcuts which had earlier been used in printing an edition of the *Speculum.* In 1483, while at Kuilenburg, the same printer used a number of the *Speculum* woodcuts cut in half so that they would fit a smaller book. This shows that Veldener must have acquired all, or nearly all, of those historic woodcuts. As he is known to have used them first at

Utrecht, the assumption is, in the absence of evidence to the contrary, that he found them there. For this reason, Bradshaw provisionally attributed to Utrecht the various editions of the *Speculum* and also of other works that proceeded from the unknown Dutch press. As Pollard says, "The presumption that Veldener found the blocks of the *Speculum* there constituted a grain of evidence in favour of Utrecht; and if a balance is sufficiently sensitive and both scales are empty, a grain thrown into one will suffice to weigh it down." But this attribution of the primitive Dutch printing to Utrecht has been often repeated without emphasis on the provisional character which Bradshaw assigned to it, and there has been considerable resultant confusion. I share with Mr. Pollard the opinion that it would have been better to disregard the "grain of evidence" and not attempt, in our present lack of knowledge, to assign these books and fragments to any one city.

Mention has just been made of editions of the *Speculum*. The *Speculum humanae salvationis* (the Latin title) or *Spieghel onzer Behoudenisse* (the Dutch form of the title) was the most interesting product of the primitive Dutch press. This "Mirror of Human Salvation," which has already been mentioned in the chapter on early woodcuts and block books, was a series of scenes from Bible history presented in pictures with explanatory text. The pictures were placed two on a block, each picture being enclosed in a border of architectural design. A column of descriptive matter was printed under each picture. There are four known editions of the *Speculum* from the unknown Dutch press. Two of these have the text in Latin and two in Dutch. The pictures in all of them are obviously from the same wood blocks, but there are individual peculiarities in each edition in the letters of the text. The woodcuts appear to have been printed first in a watery ink which has since turned brown, after which the text was printed in a black, oily ink.

In three of these editions of the *Speculum* the text is set in movable types, while in a fourth the text of some of the pages is set in movable types but for the other pages is engraved on a wood block. For three and a half centuries this mixture of type and block printing was interpreted as meaning that this edition was the earliest of all and marked the transition from block books to books printed with movable types. Ottley, however, in 1816, upset this neat hypothesis, which seemed so beautifully to fit the facts, by demonstrating from the comparative wear and tear on the blocks in the various editions that the "mixed" edition came third instead of first. This circumstance seemed to indicate that the printer of the *Speculum* became weary of setting the type all over again each time the book was reprinted and in consequence decided to replace the type composition with engraved blocks which could be used again and again without undue labor—much as modern printers resort to stereotyping under similar conditions. But this supposition, too, has been vigorously contested, with much show of reason. In fact, the problem raised by this combination of type and wood blocks for printing text matter must be regarded as an open question until there has been opportunity for further study of the existing copies and fragments of the different editions of the *Speculum*.

In addition to the four editions of the *Speculum,* the primitive Dutch press produced an extensive series of different editions of the omnipresent Latin grammar of Aelius Donatus, which remind us that the *Cologne Chronicle* mentioned the Donatuses printed in Holland as the "prefiguration" from which the German invention of printing was developed. Some of these Donatus fragments appear to have been printed on one side of the leaf only and with an extremely primitive technique.

Other titles from the unknown Dutch press—or presses—include several editions of the *Doctrinale* of Alexander Gallus de Villa Dei

Lameth oscidgit a inas suus vroribus — Job flagellabat a demone et ab vxore

Genesis iij capto

Job ij° capto

PAGE FROM THE "MIXED" EDITION OF THE SPECU-
LUM, WITH THE LATIN TEXT PRINTED FROM A
WOOD BLOCK.

(another popular schoolbook of the day), the *Disticha* of Dionysius Cato, the *Facetiae morales* of Laurentius Valla, the *De salute corporis* of Gulielmus de Saliceto, and the *Singularia juris in causis criminalibus* of Ludovicus Pontanus. The last-named volume also contains, but in a different type, some abstracts from the works of Aeneas Sylvius, who is designated therein as Pope Pius II.

There are a good many examples of this early Dutch printing now to be seen at Haarlem, but, as Kruitwagen has pointed out, not many of them were found there but have, on the contrary, been acquired by purchase in comparatively recent times.

Efforts to date these primitive Dutch books have produced only negative evidence. A fragment of a Dutch *Doctrinale* has been found in the binding of a manuscript which its writer completed in 1462 and which was probably bound soon thereafter. A copy of Saliceto's *De salute corporis* has a note that the rubrication of it was finished in 1472, and a copy of a Latin edition of the *Speculum* from the unknown Dutch press was rubricated in 1471. The abstracts of the works of Aeneas Sylvius, already mentioned, could not have been printed before 1458, because it was in that year that the writer became Pope Pius II and the fact that he was pope is mentioned in the volume. In other words, direct evidence that any of this printing was done before 1458 is as yet entirely lacking.

The work of the primitive Dutch printer—or printers—was crude indeed. It appeared in pamphlets rather than books, produced for distribution among people of the simplest tastes or for the uncritical use of schoolboys. The different types used show no stages of improvement, as with the earliest German types, but only variations of forms produced by the same process. Clearly, if the early Dutch printing was indeed the prefiguration of the invention perfected at Mainz, it could have contributed little more than the suggestion that it was possible to reproduce books by a mechanical method.

S ymoīs ar moīꝰ máimona breuiaē folemꝰ
T anoīs nīto breuis cū dembē ſydoīs vñ vīs
P ſubeūte breuē facīt o. caropꝰ dabo teſtē
Q ſopū retrahas europā ſiue piropū
V ñ placet ē canophꝰ pſopꝰ qꝫ iūgē debes
P ſup r bremas. ſephorā teſtē tibi ſumas
D iriuatiua palſ ꝓduc pateī erre ſonorus
N oīs obliquos qd ī oꝛ ſīt iūge. ſed arbor
E ñ meoꝛ et rethoꝛ caſtoꝛ ſeu marmoꝛ ꝗ eſt
C orripuē ſuos. ſed lōgis adde paloꝛ
E ñ quedā ꝓpria ſūt obliꝗs breuiādi
N as facīt os oris ꝗ dat oꝛ et vs breuiamꝰ
M ſup o lōga. ſicut teſtar aloſa
T ſubeūte dabis o longā ſicut azotū
Q ue componitur diſcreta mēte notetur
M ſup v vro. ſed compoſitiua notato
A nte b corripis v. ſz demit inde ſaluber
v c ꝓtrahunt qꝫes a l vm ſubit ā vs
C etera corripies. ſed polluē tibi demas
N anduco iūges fiducia conſociato
A nte d lōga die v. ſz pecud retrahat
V re g longa ſit v. tñ hīc tibi cōiuge cēpta
S ugo ꝓducis ſed ſanguiſugā breuiabis
V ſup l breuia gemulus adulor adempta
Q ue declinabit tibi tercia lōga notabis
N oīa ſed ſabulon breuiat hercule iūcto
D ijs ſorilar ſocio ſpecular breuiabit origo
O bliꝗs breuies vñ pſulis et nebulonis
N dabimꝰ ſup m. tibi lōgā. ſicut alumē

PAGE FROM AN EDITION OF THE DOCTRINALE OF
ALEXANDER GALLUS FROM AN UNKNOWN DUTCH
PRESS.

But what was the method by which these early books were produced? Gottfried Zedler, who has made an exhaustive study of the Dutch incunabula, believes that they were printed from movable types made by a primitive and tedious process of casting in sand, with wooden hand-engraved originals used as patterns. Zedler further believes that Coster was the inventor of this process, which, however, was sterile because it was incapable of development into a practicable method of casting types.

It remains now to note that there have been several other pretenders to the honor of being the inventor of printing. According to an obscure chronicle of the seventeenth century, Pamfilo Castaldi, of Feltre, Italy, was the inventor of movable types, and his native town gave the story such credence that in 1868 a monument was erected in his honor. The story has not been taken seriously by historians, but, though denying him the chief honor, recent researches have shown that Castaldi was the first printer in Milan. One wild story places the invention at Kuttenberg, in Bohemia, of which city Johann Gutenberg is asserted to have been a native. Another story ascribes the invention to Jean Brito, who printed at Bruges about 1477 to 1488. And the honor has been claimed by some advocates for Johann Mentelin, the early printer of Strasbourg. None of these tales, however, appears to have any foundation except a local legend.

But there is one rival claim to the invention of printing which has some basis of fact, and the circumstances of it are of considerable interest. In 1890, the Abbé Requin discovered at Avignon, France, five notarial protocols in Latin, dated 1444 and 1446, which show that Procopius Waldfoghel, a silversmith from Prague then residing in Avignon, was interested in a method of "writing artificially" and in painting colors on textiles. One of the documents mentions "two

alphabets of steel, two iron forms, one steel screw, forty-eight forms of tin, and various other forms pertaining to the art of writing." Another document deals with a promise made by Waldfoghel to give instruction in his art of writing. We hear further of promises not to disclose to others the art so taught, of making twenty-seven Hebrew letters cut in iron "according to the science and practice of writing," and of instruments of "wood, tin, and iron."

But the references in the Avignon documents do not point clearly to an invention of printing with movable types, although there is an indication of some process in which metal letters were to be used—perhaps for being successively impressed on paper in the "writing" of a text, somewhat after the manner of the letters of our rubber stamps. No scrap of printing at Avignon produced within fifty years of the Waldfoghel dates has ever come to light, and no writer has ever seriously maintained that the Waldfoghel experiments, even if they had to do with printing, antedated the Strasbourg experiments of Gutenberg. The suggestion has been advanced, however, that Waldfoghel may have picked up the idea of printing from something or other which became public at the Gutenberg trial in Strasbourg in 1438. There are records of several former Strasbourgers in Avignon at about that time, including one Walter Riffe, who was a silversmith.

XII

The Dissemination of Printing

OUTSIDE of Mainz and its immediate environs, the first cities into which the new typographic art was introduced were Bamberg and Strasbourg. Some authorities have suggested that Gutenberg himself may have printed the 36-line Bible at Bamberg about 1460, but this must remain a matter of speculation. However, Albrecht Pfister, beginning at Bamberg in 1461 with types which had been Gutenberg's, is known to have printed there at least ten books, to some of which we shall refer in a later chapter. Most of Pfister's publications were addressed to a popular audience, and few copies have survived their contemporary popularity. Typographically they were so inferior as to weigh against the supposition of some scholars that Pfister had been closely associated with Gutenberg in the production of the 36-line Bible. Whatever this association may have been, it does not seem to have involved close attention on Pfister's part to the technique of printing.

At Strasbourg, Johann Mentelin was printing by 1460, and perhaps earlier, turning out for the most part large and unwieldy volumes which defied everyday use and have thus come down to us in better condition than most incunabula. Mentelin's associate and successor was his son-in-law, Adolf Rusch, whose name, however, does not appear on a single one of the books he printed. Rusch was the first to print with a type of a strongly roman character, and his font was distinguished by a capital R of bizarre design which has led to his being usually designated as the "R-printer." Heinrich Eggestein, who began printing at Strasbourg about 1464, was another who sel-

dom put his name to his typographic productions, and many of the other early books printed in that city are without indication of the names of their printers. Eggestein was one of the first printers to receive a special privilege to follow the new craft, under a grant conferred upon him by Landgrave Friedrich in 1466.

Soon after the beginnings of printing at Strasbourg and Bamberg, internal dissensions in Mainz came to a head in the so-called "Bishops' War" between rival claimants to ecclesiastical authority. In October, 1462, the victorious party of Archbishop Adolf entered and sacked the city. Adolf represented the patrician party, and with his accession it seemed likely that things would go hard with the guilds and crafts. Possibly in the industrial dislocation of this period a number of printers trained in their craft at Mainz found themselves without prospect of employment and left the city to seek their fortunes elsewhere. At any rate, we find that almost all the first printers in Italy, France, and Spain were men either with German names or specifically designated as Germans. And many of them, not always truthfully, claimed to have come from Mainz.

Among those printers who are known to have lived and worked in Mainz was Conrad Sweynheym. This craftsman, with a partner named Arnold Pannartz, left Mainz apparently with the intention of carrying the printing craft to Rome. But instead of proceeding directly to the Eternal City, they stopped and set up a printing office in the ancient Benedictine monastery at Subiaco, some thirty or forty miles away. No one knows why they tarried at the monastery instead of seeking opportunities at Rome. It has been suggested that they were invited to do so by the learned Spanish prelate, Cardinal Juan de Torquemada, known also by his Italian name, Giovanni di Turrecremata, who acted on the earnest plea of a brother cardinal, recently deceased, that the new art of printing be introduced into Italy. At that time, the Subiaco monastery was under the charge of

Torquemada and was logically the place at which he would wish to see a press erected.

However this may have been, the two German printers established their press in the monastery and proceeded to print, in 1465 or possibly a year earlier, an edition of Donatus, of which no copy has survived. They next produced two books, Cicero's *De oratore* and an edition of the works of Lactantius. The latter noted in its colophon that it was completed October 29, 1465, and it was long considered the earliest extant book printed in Italy. But the priority of the Cicero has been made known by a copy of it which contains a handwritten notation by its first owner that the volume had been "carefully corrected and emended" on September 30, 1465.

The Lactantius, in addition to being a handsome volume, is distinguished by being the first book in which Greek type appears. A page of this volume is here reproduced. The type, it will be observed, is a condensed roman of considerable color but retaining many of the characteristics of the rounded gothics. It is a type which Sweynheym probably cut and cast in Italy, in deference to the Italian preference for the humanistic roman letter. This type has served as the model for one of the private types cut by the Ashendene Press and used in its books.

The foregoing is the story of the introduction of printing into Italy as it has been told for the last century. Recently, however, Konrad Haebler, one of the world's leading authorities on fifteenth-century printing, has proposed a correction in the record of early Italian printing, based on his studies of some printed fragments of an Italian translation of the German *Sieben Leiden vom Christi.* Haebler believes that this translation was printed in Italy about 1462 by an itinerant printer who came into Italy, found the field unpromising, and returned to Germany. The only clue to the place of printing is the fact that the translation is in an Italian dialect peculiar to

magis utimur.Recte si ita uixisset ut locutus est. Seruiuit ei fedissimis uo-
luptatibus:suáq; ipe sentétiam uitę prauitate dissoluit. Quod si aía ignis
est ut ostendimus:in celũ debet eniti sicut ignis ne extinguatur. Hoc est ad
imortalitaté quę i cęlo ē. Et sicut ardere ac uiuere nõ põt ignis:nisi aliqua
pingui materia teneať in qua hęat alimentũ:sic aię materia & cibus ē sola
iustitia:qua teneť ad uitã.Post hęc deus hoiem qua exposui rõe generatum
posuit in paradiso:idest in̄orto fecũdissimo et amenissimo.quę in partibus
orientis omni genere ligni arborũq; conseruit.ut ex earũ uariis fructibus
aleretur. Expersq; oim laborũ deo p̃ri summa deuotione seruiret. Tũ dedit
ei certa mãdata quę si obseruasset:imortalis maneret.si trãscendisset:morte
afficereť.Id aũt preceptũ fuit:ut ex arbore una quę fuit in medio paradisi
non gustaret.in qua posuerat intelligétiam boni & mali. Tũ crimiator ille
inuidens opibus dei:oēs fallacias & calliditates suas ad decipiendũ hoiez
intendit.ut ei adimeret immortalitatem. Et p̃mo mulierem dolo illexit.ut
uetitũ cibum sumeret. et per eã ipi quoq; hõi persuasit:ut transcenderet dei
legem.Percepta igiť scia boni et mali:pudere eum nuditatis suę coepit.ab-
scõditq; se a facie dei:qď antea nõ solebat.Tum deus snía i peccatores lata
eiecit hoiem de paradiso.ut uictum sibi labore cõgreret:ipmq; paradisum
igni circũuallauit:ne homo posset accedere.donec summũ iudiciũ faciat in
terra.et iustos uiros cultores suos i eũdem locũ reuocet morte sublata.sicut
sacrę litterę doceť.et Sibilla erithrea cum dicit.Οἱ δὲ θεόν αἰμωντεσ
ἀλίθιμομ αεμμαομ τε ζωὴμ κλήρομομουσὶ τομ αἰῶμοσ χρό-
μομ αυτοι οἰκουμτεσ παραδεισομ ὅμωσ ἐρίθηλεα κὴπομ .
Qui aũt deũ honorãt uerũ:sempiternã utiq; uitã hereditario iure possidét
seculi tpus ipi habitãtes ad paradisum similiter florétissimũ ortũ.Verũ qm
hęc extrema sunt:rota in extrema opis huius pte tractabimus. Nunc ea
quę p̃ma sunt explicemus. Mors itaq; sequuta est hoiem secũdũ dei sníam.
quod etiam Sibilla in carmine suo docet dicens.Αμθρωπομ πεπλα-
σθαι θεου παλάμαισ ομ και πλάμησεμ οφισ διολίῶσ ἐπι
μοίραμ αμελθειμτου θαμάτου γμωσιμδε λαβειμ αγαθομ
τε καλου τε .idest.hoiem fictũ dei mãibus quę et seduxit serpés dolose
ad fatũ ascendere mortis:notionéq; boni et mali hoiem plasmatũ dei ipius
palmis.quę dolis fefellit serpés:ut uim mortis incurreret:et sciam accipet
boni & mali.Sic facta hois uita est tparia:sed tñ longa.quę in mille annos
,ppagareť.qd diuinis lr̃is,pditũ est.et per oēm sciam publicatũ. cũ Varro
nõ ignoraret argumétari nisus ē:cur,putareñt antiq mille ãnos uictitasse.

the region of Bologna. It is not possible here to discuss in detail the evidence on which Professor Haebler's contention is based, but the weight of his opinion on the matter is very great. His argument will at least afford a variant on the commonly accepted account of Italian typographic origins.

To return to the two German printers at the Subiaco monastery, we find that they did not tarry there long, nor did they do much printing there. In addition to the works already mentioned, they printed an edition of Saint Augustine's *De civitate Dei,* which was completed June 12, 1467, and in the same year moved on to Rome. Whether the first printing in that city was done by Sweynheym and Pannartz or by Ulrich Han, another German who set up a press there, cannot be stated with certainty.

Sweynheym and Pannartz at Rome worked not wisely but too well. By 1472 they had produced about forty titles in editions of 275 to 300 copies each. They printed mostly editions of the Latin classics, and their output flooded the market. In 1472 they presented to Pope Sixtus IV an appeal for aid of some kind, in return for their great service in bringing the printing art to Rome. So many other printers had followed them to Rome, they said, that they could not sell what they had printed. Their house was full of printed books, but empty of the necessities of life. This petition is of interest to bibliographers because there was printed with it a list of the books produced by the two Germans. The petition apparently had no immediate result, and the two printers, in spite of their houseful of unsold books, produced seven more in 1473. In 1474 the two parted company. Pannartz continued to print at Rome until his death in 1476. Sweynheym turned his attention to the engraving of copper-plate maps for the use of another printer. He died about 1477. By that time, ten or a dozen other printers, all Germans, were operating presses at Rome.

As Rome was the center of culture and of ecclesiastical authority, so Venice was the leading commercial center of Europe in the fifteenth century. The first printer at Venice was John of Spire, known from contemporary documents as having been a goldsmith at Mainz in 1460 or 1461. His first book at Venice appeared in 1469. He shrewdly procured for himself a five-year exclusive patent or privilege for printing in Venice, which was destined soon to become the queen city, typographically, of Italy, if not of all Europe. But this monopoly was short-lived, for John died the following year, and his brother, Wendelin of Spire, who took over the business, did not fall heir to the special privilege, as the Venetian authorities held that it had lapsed with John's death. The field was thus open to all comers, and the entrants were many. In fact, the developments of typography at Venice were so important under Jenson and Aldus, two of the outstanding early masters of the craft, that their contributions to bookmaking have been reserved as the subject of the following chapter.

After Italy, the next country of modern Europe in which printing began was Switzerland, although Basel, where the press was first set up, was in the domain of Germany in the fifteenth century. It is not known just when printing began in Basel, nor who was actually the first printer there. The first *dated* book produced in that city was printed in 1474 by Bernhard Richel, who was not, however, the first to print in Basel. The generally accepted tradition is that the first printer was Berthold Ruppel, whom some writers have unsuccessfully sought to identify with the Bertolf von Hanau mentioned in the Fust-Gutenberg lawsuit of 1455 as one of Gutenberg's servants. But it is not at all certain that Michael Wenssler has not some claim to priority here. The early printers of Basel as a rule neither put their names to their books nor dated them, and the facts of the introduction of printing there must be sought in contem-

porary town records and other indirect sources, which are not conclusive. It seems likely, however, that the first printing office in Basel
began work about 1467.

The next country into which typography was introduced was
France. The story of its coming there reveals to us the zeal of two
enthusiasts for the service of printing to the cause of learning. These
men, still in their thirties, were Johann Heynlin, a German by
birth, who had been rector and librarian of the Sorbonne at Paris,
and Guillaume Fichet, professor of philosophy and rhetoric and also
former rector and librarian of the same institution. Heynlin had
come to Paris from Germany in 1459, but after a few years had gone
to Basel in 1463 for further study at the university there. There is
no doubt that Heynlin and his scholarly associates at the Sorbonne
were already quite familiar with books produced by the new process
of printing, and it is known that Heynlin in Basel was acquainted
with some of the printers who came there to practice their craft.

After his return to Paris in 1468, Heynlin associated himself with
Fichet, who had important and influential connections, in the enterprise of establishing a press for the service of scholars at the Sorbonne. At their instigation, three German printers were induced to
come to Paris. They were Ulrich Gering—generally regarded as the
ranking member of the group and in consequence looked upon as
the Caxton of France—Michael Friburger, and Martin Crantz.
Friburger had been a student at the University of Basel at the time
Heynlin was there and probably had learned printing in that town.
It is not unlikely that Gering and Crantz also came from Basel.

These three printers worked for a time in the employment of
Heynlin and Fichet, who were the real conductors of the enterprise.
They set up their press within the confines of the Sorbonne and
there, in the space of two years, printed more than a score of books—
all of them, it may be noted, in a very fair roman type and all

re intelligā amari! nullū ego modū offi/
ciif meif/aut amori meo in illū faciā·Sed
ne ab ōnibus te defertū effe iudices! ego
(quem forte in numero amicoꝝ nō habe/
bas)polliceor tibi operā meā· &(qꝗ illi
non fine fcelere neglexerūt)ego paratus
fum defenfionē tuam fufcipere · Tu uero
admonebis/quibus adiumentis opus tibi
fit·& ego necꝫ pecunia!necꝫ confilio tibi
deero · Vale ;

Foelix Epſaꝝ Gafparini finis;

Vt fol lumen!fic doctrinam fundif in orbem
  Mufarum nutrix/regia parifiuf ;
Hinc prope diuinam/tu quā germania nouit
  Artem fcribendi!fufcipe promerita;
Primos ecce librof!quos hæc induſtria finxit
  Francorum in terrif·ædibuf atꝗ tuif;
Michael Vdalricuf/Martinufꝗ magiſtri
  Hof impreſſerunt·ac facient aliof;

addressed to an academic circle of readers. Their first book was a collection of letters in Latin of Gasparino Barzizi, edited by Heynlin, which appeared probably in the latter half of 1470, with a colophon of four Latin distichs offering to Paris this product of the almost divine art invented in Germany and practiced by the printers Michael, Ulrich, and Martin. Their next work was probably the *Orthographia* of Gasparino, also edited by Heynlin, which was completed January 1, 1471. It was this volume which contained, in some of its copies, the famous letter of Fichet to Robert Gaguin in which Gutenberg was hailed as the inventor of printing.

Towards the end of 1472, Fichet, the more influential of the two backers of the press, departed for Italy to accept an appointment from the pope. A few months later Heynlin, too, left Paris to return to Basel. Deprived of professional patronage, the three German printers had to leave the Sorbonne and set up shop in the Rue Saint-Jacques—a street destined to be the haven of printers for centuries to come. In 1476 they issued from the sign of the Soleil d'Or the first Bible printed in France. In January, 1478, Friburger and Crantz dropped out of the partnership and disappeared from printing history. Gering continued to print alone at Paris, with only indifferent success, until his death in 1510.

Competitors appeared in the Paris field soon after the three pioneers left the Sorbonne. In 1474 Pieter de Keysere, from Ghent, and Johann Stoll, a German, were printing in partnership in the Rue Saint-Jacques, and in the following year a third printing office, the first in Paris conducted by Frenchmen, was opened on the same street by a group of printers working at the sign of the Soufflet Vert.

The first printer at Lyons was Wilhelm König, better known by the French form of his name, Guillaume Le Roy, who was brought thither by Barthélemy Buyer, a wealthy merchant of that city, who employed him. Le Roy's first book, *Lotharii compendium breve*,

a volume of miscellaneous religious essays, appeared in September, 1473, printed by the order and at the expense of Buyer.

Lyons was a commercial city, situated on many trade routes. Most of the early books printed there were for a popular rather than a scholarly public. They included many French books of literature, romances of chivalry, fables, and histories; also a number of law-books for the law schools at Lyons. The city soon became an important center of the French book trade. Before the end of the fifteenth century more than 160 printers had worked there. Among these printers, Germans so far predominated that printers as a class came to be known collectively as *les Allemands* (the Germans). At Lyons, also, was established the first typefoundry in which types were cast for sale to other printers.

Printing was established in nearly forty towns and cities in France during the fifteenth century, but in most of them the functioning of the press was ephemeral. In only about four localities was printing established on a solid and permanent basis. Most of the French incunabula were, as we might expect, printed at Paris, but the history of the first printers in the provincial towns offers an intriguing field of research—an opportunity embraced by the late Anatole Claudin, who issued a number of monographs on the genesis of printing in many of these communities. He had planned a general history of printing in France, but this commendable project was unhappily cut short by his death.

We have already discussed in an earlier chapter the question of when and where the first printing was done in Holland. The earliest Dutch books which were signed and dated by their printers were produced by Gerardus Leempt and Nicholaus Ketalaer at Utrecht in 1473. The irrepressible art raised its head in 1477 at Delft (Jacob Jacobszoen and Maurice Yemantszoen) and at Gouda (Gerard Leeu). Printing also began at Deventer in 1477, at Zwolle

in 1479, and at Leiden in 1483, in addition to several less important towns into which the press had meanwhile been introduced. Not until December, 1483, do we find issued at Haarlem a book ascribed to a specific printer, in the person of Jacob Bellaert.

We next come to a region of extraordinary interest, in its typographic history, to people of the English tongue, for here was the cradle of the first book ever printed in our language. This region was the southern portion of the Low Countries comprising approximately the area of present-day Belgium. The first printing here was done in the town of Alost in 1473 by Johann of Paderborn, also known as John of Westphalia, who moved in 1474 to the city of Louvain, famed for the treasures of its university library which was so regrettably destroyed in the World War. Here he found a competitor, Jan Veldener, already at work, but managed to dispose of him by fair means or foul.

But our interest in this region centers at Bruges, where it behooves us, as members of the English-speaking fraternity, reverently to doff our hats. For here was produced, in 1476, the first book printed in the English language—the *Recuyell of the Histories of Troye,* the printers being Colard Mansion and William Caxton. To Caxton and his work a separate chapter will be devoted, so we shall not here discuss in more detail his activities at Bruges. After Caxton left for England, Mansion continued to print in that city until 1484.

Until recent years, early printing in Spain was the *terra incognita* of bibliographers. But thanks to the labors of Dr. Konrad Haebler in the public, monastic, and private libraries of the Iberian peninsula, we now have a fairly wide knowledge of the work of the typographic pioneers in Spain. The earliest product of the Spanish press has long been supposed to be a small volume of poems laudatory of the Blessed Virgin, printed at Valencia, in Castile, by Lam-

bert Palmart, probably in 1474. Palmart, who was brought to Valencia by Jacob Wisslandt, a German bookseller then active in Spain, put neither his name nor the dates on his earlier works. From the colophon in a later book we learn that he, like so many other pioneering printers of the time, was an *Alemanus,* which in this case is thought to mean that he was Flemish. The peculiarities of his types and other evidences indicate that he learned printing in Venice.

But the priority of Palmart, and of Valencia, in the Spanish field has recently been disputed by an unpretentious little piece of print-ing—an indulgence, in the Spanish language, issued by Cardinal Rodrigo Borgia under a papal bull dated March 5, 1473. As the cardinal's mission to Spain ended in October, 1473, it seems clear that the indulgence must have been printed between the two dates mentioned. The printer and the place of issue remain unknown, but as the price of the indulgence is given in the money of Aragon, it is safe to say that it was not produced in Valencia. It may have been printed in Saragossa. A document recently discovered in the archives of that city gives some plausibility to this conjecture. It is a three-year contract, made at Saragossa and dated January 5, 1473, between Heinrich Botel, of Embich, Georg von Holtz, of Halting, and Johann Planck, of Halle, whereby Botel undertook to impart the secrets of the printing art to the others, who were to invest a modest capital in establishing a printing business. But nothing is known of any printing actually done by these three partners, although they remained in association of some kind until 1478. Botel in 1479 set up a printing establishment in Lerida, where he worked for about sixteen years.

Matthaeus, another native of Flanders, is known to have brought the art to Saragossa in 1475, when he printed a single book there and then disappeared from all records. At the end of the same year two German printers, Johann of Salzburg and Paul Hurus, of Con-

stance, produced the first printing at Barcelona. A much disputed Barcelona imprint, *De condendis orationibus,* by Bartolomaeus Mates, bears the printed date MCCCCLXVIII (1468) and the name of Johann Gherling as printer. The date as printed would establish this as the first book printed in Spain, but Dr. Haebler has brought to notice the fact that contemporary records of Gherling at Barcelona make it highly probable that the date on the volume was misprinted and that it should have been 1488.

At Tortosa the total fifteenth century output of the press consisted of one book printed there in 1477 by Nicolaus Spindeler and Peter Brun, two Germans, who used the same types that Matthaeus the Fleming had used at Saragossa two years earlier. In 1478 the transient printers of Tortosa set up their press at Barcelona. Also in 1477, printing began at Seville, a city which was soon to become an important center for the production of books. Another important Spanish center of book production was Salamanca, where, however, printing did not begin until 1481.

The earliest printing in Spain, as in Italy and France, was in roman types. Later the gothic came into use, particularly for liturgical books. Characteristic of the earliest Spanish printing was the extensive use of Hebrew. The Spanish Jews, in spite of the Inquisition, were an important factor in the spread of printing in that country, producing not only works in Hebrew, but also a quantity of Christian writings.

The last important country of Europe to receive the benefits of the press was England, where printing was first done at the end of 1476. Of the coming of the press into the Anglo-Saxon domain we shall defer discussion to a later chapter.

During the fifteenth century, however, printing was introduced into many of the lesser countries of Europe, the art becoming much more widely distributed than is generally realized. In addition to the

countries already mentioned, the first known printing in Bohemia (now a part of Czechoslovakia) was done in 1468, at Pilsen, by the unnamed "printer of the Guido della Colonna"; in Hungary in 1473, at Budapest, by Andreas Hess; in Poland in 1475, at Cracow, by Caspar Hochfeder; in the Balearic Islands in 1480, at Valdemosa, by Nicolaus Calafat; in Austria in 1482, at Vienna, by Stephan Koblinger; in Denmark in 1482, at Odensee, by Johann Snell; in Sweden in 1483, at Stockholm, by the same Johann Snell (in both Denmark and Sweden, the first printing offices were branches of Snell's principal printing plant at Lübeck, in Germany); in Portugal in 1489, at Lisbon, by Rabbi Elieser; in Montenegro in 1494, at Rieka, by the monk Makario; and in Turkey in 1494, at Constantinople, by David and Samuel ibn Nachmias. So far as is now known, no printing was done in Russia in the fifteenth century. But the origins of Russian printing have not yet been subjected to careful study, and in Dr. Haebler's opinion it is not unlikely that Russian printing of the incunabula period may yet be discovered.

Hundreds of printers, some of whom worked without leaving any records of their names, swarmed to the adventure of carrying the new art into all parts of Europe before the end of the century in which printing was first made known to the western world. In a great many cases, these typographic missionaries carried their entire equipment "under their hats," so to speak. In other words, all that many of them took with them to a new location was a knowledge of how to cut punches, strike matrices, make molds, cast the type, and then set it and print from it on presses which were also of their own construction. This explains why, in certain places—Subiaco and Paris, for example—considerable time seems to have elapsed between the first arrival of the printers and the first product of their presses; the printers had to make all their equipment on the spot before they could begin to print. It also explains the great variety of

typefaces found in the works produced by the earliest printers. Many printers, of course, transported from place to place, if not the actual types, at least their punches, matrices, and casting molds, or else came into possession of this equipment in taking over the shop of a predecessor.

XIII

The Master Printers of Venice

VENICE in the fifteenth century had become the outstanding European center of commerce and industry. It was inevitable that such a center should seize upon the opportunities offered by the new craft of printing, and it was just as inevitable that the merchants of Venice should see in printed books not only aids to scholarship or to the service of the church, but also valuable commodities in trade. It is at Venice, therefore, that we first clearly see the printing industry regulated by business methods rather than by the preferences or whims of individual printers or their patrons. Venice at a quite early date became an important printing center, and by the end of the fifteenth century more books had been published there than at all the other principal Italian centers of the press put together.

But much more important to the future of typography than the large-scale production of books at Venice was the work done there by two men of particular eminence in printing history. The ordinary printer of today, however vague may be his knowledge of the history of his craft, is almost sure to know the names of Jenson and Aldus nearly as well as the name of Gutenberg. Gutenberg is generally recognized as the traditional inventor of printing. The name of Jenson, even if recalled in no other connection, is associated with a widely known family of typefaces, while many brands of paper and the like have taken as their trade names the adjective Aldine.

There is a certain historical justice in the survival of these three names, for the men thus honored stand out in a group by themselves

as three great benefactors of modern civilization through their achievements in typography. If the German, Johann Gutenberg, invented the process of printing with movable types, it was a Frenchman, Nicolas Jenson, who first put the designing of typefaces on a high artistic level, while Aldus Manutius, an Italian, first showed the way by which the benefits of printing could best be disseminated among the greatest number of people, by producing books of convenient size and selling them at a reasonable price.

Jenson and Aldus worked at Venice. Nicolas Jenson was certainly the world's first great type designer, perhaps the greatest in all typographic history. Of his life and personality we do not have extensive information, though what we do know is of the highest interest. The date of his birth is not recorded, but from his own statements it is clear that he was born at Sommevoire, in the Department of the Aube, in north central France. He had a brother, Albert, who entered the priesthood. When Nicolas died in 1480, his mother, Zanetta (Jeanette), and his brother were still living, as were his three daughters and his wastrel son, the last then resident at Lyons. For all these relatives Jenson made ample provision in his will, besides numerous bequests to charity. The considerable estate of which he thus disposed is an indication that he was a man of commercial as well as artistic ability.

Tradition informs us that after an apprenticeship at the art of making dies for coinage, Jenson became master of the French royal mint, but whether at Tours or at Paris remains obscure. From this obscurity his name emerges for a time in one of the most interesting documents thus far discovered in the search for evidence of the origin of printing. This document, already mentioned in Chapter X as one of the foundation stones on which rests the fame of Johann Gutenberg as the inventor of printing, is the famous order of Charles VII, king of France, that the directors of his mints select a suitable

man to be sent secretly to Mainz to learn the new art of cutting punches and letters.

This order of the king, dated October 4, 1458, has been discovered in a manuscript chronicle of the French royal mints made about the middle of the sixteenth century, in which the substance, if not the exact wording, of the original order appears to have been carefully followed. In this sixteenth-century manuscript, which is now preserved in the Bibliothèque Nationale at Paris, the tenor of the royal order is followed by a brief statement to the effect that Nicolas Jenson was the man chosen for the king's mission, that he arrived at an understanding of the art of printing, and that he was the first to introduce that art into the kingdom of France.

As to the statement that Jenson was the first to introduce printing into France, we can only surmise that possibly he submitted some specimens of printing as a kind of a voucher for the successful completion of his mission—specimens which the writer of the sixteenth century chronicle may possibly have seen in the archives of the French mints. But that is pure and unsubstantiated surmise. However that may be, at about the time of Jenson's probable return from Mainz, Charles VII died and was succeeded by Louis XI. This change of sovereigns involved a fundamental change of policy and personnel in the government of the kingdom, which may have made France at that time an unsuitable field for the introduction and development of the art of printing.

But Jenson himself seems to have formed so favorable an opinion of the future of the new art that he decided to entrust the course of his life to it, although the reasons which caused him to leave his fatherland are wholly unknown. Nor do we know what he was doing during the years that intervened before the appearance of his first known printed work in Venice in 1470. He must have spent some of that time, we may be sure, in the study and practice of type

design and type casting, for the earliest types with which he printed under his own auspices show the design and workmanship of a master. It does not seem unlikely that he was in Italy for several years, employed by the first German printers there to cut their punches, before he opened his own establishment at Venice in 1470.

Since Jenson's fame is derived chiefly from the beauty of his roman types, we must note once more the historical origin of that form of letter. As mentioned in Chapter III, students of the classics, or "humanities," in the times of the Renaissance revived the admirably legible Caroline minuscule of four or five centuries earlier, believing it to be more truly Roman than the book-hands prevalent in the manuscripts of their own time. Thus developed what has become known as the humanistic script, as distinguished from the prevalent scripts which the Renaissance scholars contemptuously called "gothic," or barbarous. The convention arose, principally in Italy but to a certain extent elsewhere, that manuscripts of the Latin classics, poetry, and belles lettres generally, should be written in this humanistic form of calligraphy, while theological works, law, medicine, and logic should appear in the more conservative dress of the gothic letter.

This convention certainly prevailed in Italy, where, moreover, the influence of the humanists was so great that there developed a tendency to modify the angularity of the gothic letters to something approaching the more graceful humanistic forms. Thus the early printing in Italy at Subiaco (see page 185) was done in what must be called a semi-gothic, a letter which has a distinct resemblance to the roman type in which this book is printed no less than to the true gothic black letter. We are tempted to describe this first Subiaco type as a modified gothic such as one who admired the humanistic letters might produce in working from a German black-letter model.

The next types produced in Italy were definitely of the form

which we now call roman, and they take their name from the city in which they were cast. These, strangely enough, were not so well done as were the types of like character which had already been cut by Adolf Rusch, the "R-printer," at Strasbourg. Similarly, the first Venetian types, those of John of Spire, although infinitely more beautiful in design than their immediate predecessors at Rome, were extremely unsatisfactory in their irregular alignment. It would seem that the simpler the letter form, the more difficult it was for the early craftsmen to reproduce it satisfactorily in type.

It was not until Nicolas Jenson printed with his own letter in 1470 that there was produced a successful combination of a pure letter of great beauty in design, accurately placed on the type body so that it harmonized perfectly with the other characters which preceded and followed it. What is more natural, then, than to suppose that the craftsman who achieved this result had learned by the slow process of trial and error, or, in other words, that he had been employed in the service of one of the earlier printers and had perfected his technique in another man's workshop? It is altogether improbable that Jenson's admirable type of 1470 was the result of a first effort.

Whether or not we can assume that Jenson worked for a time with Sweynheym and Pannartz at Rome is not to be decided hastily. That John of Spire, with his brother Wendelin, had done so before he set up shop for himself in Venice seems quite definitely established, while the supposition that Jenson left the workshop of Ulrich Han at Rome to join John of Spire's new establishment at Venice is quite within the range of probability. In fact, it would not be wholly absurd to imagine that the first roman types used at Rome and at Venice were trial flights of Jenson's genius. At any rate, the fact that Jenson was able to produce a whole series of editions dated 1470 and 1471 implies that he was already in Venice and had done con-

siderable work on his new type before the death of John of Spire late in 1469.

Jenson's earlier editions were largely texts of the Latin classics for which his new letter was perfectly adapted. In 1471 he brought out a Greek type which was almost as excellent in its field as his roman, and he was not so wholly committed to the classics that he could not also design a gothic letter in 1473 or 1474 for the production of legal and theological texts. In addition to being a type designer of distinction, Jenson was also a careful publisher, employing competent scholars as editors and revisers of the texts he published. He gradually diversified his output so that in the ninety-eight works which he is known to have produced nearly every phase of the intellectual activities of his day was represented. But theology in twenty-nine titles and the classics in twenty-five were preponderant. A few medical and legal works were included, as well as several Italian translations, and finally one work of pure literature, Boccaccio's *Fiametta*.

By 1475 Jenson enlarged his organization and formed a company, but this was probably concerned only with the selling of books, and not with their production. As legal custom required at that time, this partnership could exist for only a limited term of years, and the organization was therefore dissolved in 1480. It had been so profitable, however, that a new company was immediately formed on June 1, 1480, for another term of five years, but with a larger number of partners. Included in the company was Johannes de Colonia, or John of Cologne, who had married the widow of the late John of Spire and had been one of the successors to the failing business of Wendelin of Spire. Thus we have here an early instance of a merger of competing concerns engaged in printing and publishing.

By this time, however, Jenson was planning to take a less active part in business affairs, perhaps because his health was already

Meminit quippe illius ī protagora illū pro periādro cōſti⁄
tuens.Dicebat autē nō ex uerbis res:ſed ex rebus uerba eſſe
inqrenda:neqʒ propter uerba res perfici:ſed rerū gratia uer⁄
ba conſumari.Defunctus eſt autē ætatis anno.lxxyii.

Epimenides.

e   Pimenides ut ait Theopompus:aliiqʒ complures
         patrē habuit Phæſtium: alii Doſiadē:alii Ageſar⁄
         chum tradūt Cretenſis genere:gnoſo uico oriū⁄
dus effigiē immutaſſe perhibetur.Miſſus enim aliqñ a pa⁄
tre ut ouem rure deferret:meridiano tēpore diuertit ex iti⁄
nere:atqʒ ī ſpelunca ubi ſe iactarat:quinquaginta & ſeptē
annos perpétuo ſopore acquieuit.Dehinc ſomno excitatuſ
quæſiuit oué:putabat ſe enim parū obdormiſſe : quam cū
nō iueniſſet:in agrū reuertit.Cum uero rerū omniū faciem
immutatā cerneret:agrūqʒ in alterius ius cōceſſiſſe:ſtupore
attonitus:& cunctabūdus rediit in oppidū:ibi cū domum
ſuā uellet ingredi:quiſnā eſſet interrogatus:uixqʒ agnitus
a iuniore fratre iam uetulo omnē ex illo didicit rei ueritatē.
Porro illius fama per græciam uolante deo eſſe cariſſimus
exiſtimatus eſt.Vnde & Athenieſes cum aliquādo peſte la⁄
borarent:reſponſo a Pythia accepto urbem expiari oporte⁄
re:Niciam nicerati filiū miſere epimenidemqʒ ex creta ad⁄
uocarūt:profectus autē olympiade.xxvii. luſtrauit urbem
peſtéqʒ repreſſit hoc modo.Sumpſit oues nigro & candido
uelere:duxitqʒ in ariū pagū:atqʒ inde quo uellet abire per⁄
miſit:his qui illas ſequebātur mandās ubicūqʒ illæ accubu⁄
iſſent:ſingulas mactare propicio deo:atqʒ in hūc modū q⁄
euit lues.Ex eo iā hodie qʒ per athenienſiū pagos aras ſine
noīe iueniri certū eſt:In eius quæ tūc facta eſt expiationis
memoriā.Alii cām dixiſſe peſtis celonīum ſcelus:liberatio⁄
nemqʒ ſignaſſe:atqʒ ideo mortuos duos adoleſcétes cratinū
& lyſiniū:ſicqʒ cladē quieuiſſe Athenienſes ea pnicie liberi

broken. For the new partnership, instead of being titled Nicolas Jenson and Company, as the first one had been, was named John of Cologne, Nicolas Jenson, and Company. Its first book appeared on November 30, 1480, but before that date Jenson had been taken by death. The company imprint, however, continued to be used in 1481 and 1482.

Jenson's will, which was drawn on his deathbed, was dated September 7, 1480. From our point of view, it is one of the most interesting fifteenth-century documents which have been preserved. It is a complicated document replete with details, but the outstanding features of immediate significance to us are three: the great wealth accumulated by the testator, which seems to have been acquired solely through his activities as printer and publisher; the complexity and wide ramifications of his business relations; and the fact that he seemed to value more than anything else his set of type punches. The disposal of these implements he hedged around with numerous provisions, but he evidently desired his closest friend, Peter Uglheimer, of Frankfort, to become their owner. Evidently this transfer took place, for Jenson's types continued in use for many years thereafter.

That Jenson's judgment of the value of his type punches was well founded and that his distinctive type design was indeed his most precious possession is borne out by the high esteem in which those letters have been held by every succeeding generation which has had any concern for the quality of its typography. As early as 1483, Andrea Torresano, later the father-in-law of Aldus Manutius, boasted of printing with "the illustrious equipment and famous types of the late great master in this art, Nicolas Jenson, the Frenchman." And from that day to this the masters of typography have harked back to those types as a standard for beauty and balance in the design of letters for printing.

In marked contrast with Nicolas Jenson, who was primarily a craftsman, stands the second great Venetian in printing history, Aldus Manutius, who was first and foremost a scholar. Aldus turned to printing as a means to an end, his main interest being focused on the buyer and user of his books. Himself a profound scholar, imbued with the spirit of the Renaissance, he never lost faith in his conviction that books should be made so as to be read and he never faltered in his missionary zeal to put what he considered the best books into the hands of the largest possible number of readers. The ingenuity with which he developed methods for achieving these results and the success he won by them have set him apart as the first great publisher who created a demand for an entirely new form of book.

Aldus was born in 1450 in the village of Bassiano, near Velletri. He was a student at the universities in Rome and in Ferrara and became an enthusiast for the recently rediscovered masterpieces of ancient Greek literature, now brought in manuscripts to Italy by Greek refugees from Constantinople. He next received appointment as tutor to the sons of the prince of Carpi. This proved to be an important connection, for the elder of his pupils later supplied him with funds to embark on his career as a printer and publisher.

In 1490, in his fortieth year, Aldus went to Venice prepared to establish a printing office primarily for the printing of the Greek classics. His enterprise was carefully planned and was set in motion by first assembling a group of learned humanists, both Greeks and Italians, as well as a corps of technical assistants necessary for operating an ample printing establishment. Some time was devoted to this preparatory work, as the first product of the Aldine press did not appear until 1494, in the form of two little works, the poems of Musaeus in Greek and Latin, and the anonymous *Galeomyomachia* in Greek. In February, 1495, according to the modern calendar, appeared the *Erotemata,* a Greek grammar, by Constantine Lascaris,

which Aldus himself described as the first fruits of his labors in Greek typography after five years of experimentation. Work on the Lascaris volume was undoubtedly begun before the other two, but the two minor works were undoubtedly published earlier.

Aldus held as his primary purpose the not inconsiderable task of getting into printed form all the important ancient Greek classics which had so far remained unpublished and also to issue revised and corrected texts of those which had been printed only in corrupt and inaccurate versions. Up to July, 1499, eighteen out of thirty titles from his press were Greek texts or Greek grammars and dictionaries. But although he was primarily an enthusiast for the literary treasures of classical antiquity, he was fortunately more than that. He was also gifted with a sense of practical values and he intended that the books he made should not be the expensive playthings of learned amateurs, but marketable merchandise. If these books were to have the wide sale which their publisher desired, their price must not be too high for the buyer of modest means. As a practical executive, Aldus met this problem of price by reducing the cost of production. His purpose could not be served by the publication of ponderous folios; he conceived the idea of printing all the best works in volumes of handy size, rather closely printed in small type. The typical Aldine, of which one or two specimens can be found in almost any large library, is a handy little volume bound in parchment-covered boards. The roaming scholar could easily pack a dozen such volumes in his saddlebags and thus carry his working library with him, and the traveling bookseller of the day had little difficulty in transporting a considerable stock of such books.

Aldus was not himself a printer, but he was evidently capable of grasping the essential points of a technical problem. It must have been under his direction that his artisans cut the small types which are characteristic of so many of his editions, and his must have been

POLIPHILO QVIVI NARRA, CHE GLI PARVE AN‑
CORA DI DORMIRE, ET ALTRONDE IN SOMNO
RITROVARSE IN VNA CONVALLE, LA QVALE NEL
FINE ERA SERATA DE VNA MIRABILE CLAVSVRA
CVM VNA PORTENTOSA PYRAMIDE, DE ADMI‑
RATIONE DIGNA, ET VNO EXCELSO OBELISCO DE
SOPRA. LA QVALE CVM DILIGENTIA ET PIACERE
SVBTILMENTE LA CONSIDEROE.

A SPAVENTEVOLE SILVA, ET CONSTI‑
pato Nemore euaso, & gli primi altri lochi per el dolce
somno che se hauea per le fesse & prosternate mebre dif‑
fuso relicti, me ritrouai di nouo in uno piu delectabile
sito assai piu che el præcedente. Elquale non era de mon
ti horridi, & crepidinose rupe intorniato, ne falcato di
strumosi iugi. Ma compositamente de grate montagniole di non tro‑
po altecia. Siluose di giouani quercioli, di roburi, fraxini & Carpi‑
ni, & di frondosi Esculi, & Ilice, & di teneri Coryli, & di Alni, & di Ti‑
lie, & di Opio, & de infructuosi Oleastri, disposti secondo laspecto de
gli arboriferi Colli. Et giu al piano erano grate siluule di altri siluatici

A PAGE FROM THE HYPNEROTOMACHIA POLIPHILI
PRINTED BY ALDUS, VENICE, 1499.

the deciding voice, doubtless in conference with his learned associates, in the unfortunate choice he made of a type for his Greek texts. It must have been an undertaking of great difficulty and expense to create the enormous fonts of contorted ligatures and contractions with which he sought to reproduce the appearance of contemporary Greek handwriting. By all standards of typographical esthetics, the ligatures of the Aldine Greek are hideous monstrosities which disfigure the printed pages on which they appear. But the scholars of the day were accustomed to reading Greek in that form, and a clear and graceful Greek type such as Nicolas Jenson had created only a few years earlier may have been rejected by the Aldine staff of scholars as an objectionable archaism.

The first really important work that Aldus published was the first volume of the works of Aristotle, which appeared in 1495. This undertaking, completed in five volumes, was not finished until 1498. The typographic masterpiece of the Aldine press was issued in 1499 in the famous *Hypnerotomachia Poliphili,* a bizarre and curious mixture of pedantry and sensualism by a Dominican monk named Francesco Colonna, who wrote in Italian weirdly mixed with Latin, Greek, and even Hebrew. Though no one takes the trouble to read the text of this extraordinary work any more, the volume itself, a folio of 234 leaves, displays a harmony of illustration and text which is truly amazing for its day and age and establishes it among the master works of printing of all ages. Unfortunately, the artist who made the remarkable illustrations which adorn this volume has not been conclusively identified.

In February, 1495, Aldus made use for the first time of a roman typeface of notable legibility and merit which has recently been brought from obscurity to the attention it deserves by Stanley Morison, who considers it the model for the admirable fonts cut by Claude Garamond and other sixteenth-century typefounders. How-

Itaq;,quas pueri miserimus ad te lucubra
tiones nostras; numerare aliquas possumus; quas adolescentes, non possumus:
quo in consilio nobis diutius permanen
dum esse non puto: nam ut interdum nó
loqui moderati hominis est; sic semper
silere cum eo, quem diligas, perignaui:
neq; Hercule; si in officio permansimus
in prima aetate; debemús nunc, tanq̃
inexercitati histriones, in secundo, aut
tertio actu corruisse. praesertim cum
aemulatio tuorum studiorum Angéle
nos non excitare modo languentes possit,
sed etiam incendere; quippe, qui multa,
et praeclara habuimus a te semper, habe
músq; quotidie et consuetudinis nostrae
testimonia, et doctrinae tuae. Quare si
cuti pueri scriptiunculas nostras, quasi la
ctentis ingenii acerbitatem, detulimus
ad te; sic nunc deinceps etiam ad te adole
scentiae nostrae primos foetus deferemus;
non quo me ipse plus ames: nam iam id

P abula parua legens, nidisq́; loquacibus escas,
E t nunc porticibus uacuis, nunc humida circum
S tagna sonat, similis medios Iuturna per hostes
F ertur equis, rapidoq́; uolans hic ostendit ouantem
I amq́; hic germanum, iamq́; hic ostendit ouantem
N ec conferre manum patitur, uolat auia longe.
H aud minus Aeneas tortos legit obuius orbes,
V estigatq́; uirum, et disiecta per agmina magna
V oce uocat, quoties oculos coniecit in hostem,
A lipedumq́; fugam cursu tentauit equorum,
A uersos toties currus Iuturna retorsit.
H eu quid agat, uario nequicquam fluctuat aestu,
D iuersaeq́; uocant animum in contraria curae.
H uic Mesapus, uti laeua duo forte gerebat
L enta leuis cursu praefixa hastilia ferro,
H orum unum certo contorquens dirigit ictu.
S ubstitit Aeneas, et se collegit in arma,
P oplite subsidens, apicem tamen incita summum
H asta tulit, summasq́; excussit uertice cristas.
T um uero assurgunt irae, insidiisq́; subactus,
D iuersos ubi sensit equos, currumq́; referri,
M ulta Iouem, et laesi testatus foederis aras,
I am tandem inuadit medios, et Marte secundo
T erribilis saeuam nullo discrimine caedem
S uscitat, irarumq́; omnes effundit habenas.
Quis mihi nunc tot acerba deus, quis carmine caedes
D iuersas, obitumq́; ducum, quos aequore toto
I nq́; uicem nunc Turnus agit, nunc Troius heros,
E xpediat tanton? placuit concurrere motu
I uppiter, aeterna gentes in pace futuras?

A eneas Rutulum Sucronem (ea prima ruentes...
P ugna loco statuit Teucros) haud multa moratus
E xcipit in latus, et qua fata celerrima, crudo
T ransadigit costas, et crates pectoris ense.
T urnus equo deiectum Amycum, fratremq́; Diorē
C ongressus pedes, hunc uenientem cuspide longa,
H unc mucrone ferit, currusq́; abscissa diuorum
S uspendit capita, et rorantia sanguine portat.
I lle Talon, Tanaimq́; nea, fortemq́; Cethegum
T res uno congressu, et moestum mittit Onyten
N omen Echionium, matrisq́; genus Peridie.
H ic fratres Lyciam missos, et Apollinis agris,
E t iuuenem exosum nequicquam bella Menoeten
A rcada, piscosae cui circum flumina Lernae
A rs fuerat, pauperq́; domus, nec nota potentum
M unera, conductaq́; pater tellure serebat.
A c uelut immissi diuersis partibus ignes
A rentem in syluam, et uirgulta sonantia lauro,
A ut ubi decursu rapido de montibus altis
D ant sonitum spumosi amnes, et in aequora currunt
Q uisq́; suum populatus iter, non segnius ambo
A eneas, Turnusq́; ruunt per praelia, nunc nunc
F luctuat ira intus, rumpuntur nescia uinci
P ectora, nunc totis in uulnera uiribus itur.
M urranum hic atauos, et auorum antiqua sonantem
N omina, per regesq́; actum genus omne Latinos
P raecipitem scopulo, atq́; ingenti turbine saxi
E xcutit, effunditq́; solo, huic lora, et iuga subter
P rouoluere rotae, crebro super ungula pulsu
I ncita, nec domini memorum proculcat equorum,

X iii

ever that may be, it is indeed a fine, vigorous roman typeface. It has now been revived in England under the title of Bembo, so named because the volume in which it was first used by Aldus in 1495 was the *De Aetna* by Pietro Bembo. A page of this book may be seen on page 209, reproduced in actual size. The same type, modified only by being fitted with a set of more appropriate capitals, was later used in the *Hypnerotomachia.*

Up to the time of his death in 1515, Aldus continued to print the Greek classics, although his zeal for things Hellenic brought him more honor than profit. But he also undertook the printing of authoritative texts of the Latin classics, as well as the best works in the Italian contemporary vernacular. In his Latin and Italian texts Aldus introduced a highly important innovation by turning to a form of letter which had previously been ignored by type designers —the cursive script of the Italian humanists.

We have already mentioned the two prevalent forms of writing of the period—the gothic, which was currently used for the books of the professional classes, and the humanistic, or roman, preferred for classical texts and for literary works. These two were formal book-hands used by professional scribes and hence as a matter of course were selected as models for the design of types for printing. But there was still a third form of handwriting, known as the "chancery" script from its development in the Vatican chancery. This was used for the common, everyday purposes of business and correspondence and for the writing of documents of minor importance. It was much closer, however, to the formal roman book-hand than the handwriting of our day is to the letter forms of our printed books.

A type representing this chancery script seemed to Aldus to be appropriate for his inexpensive books in small formats. In 1500, therefore, he had his typefounders make a font of this new type

from punches cut by Francesco Griffo, of Bologna, a goldsmith then resident in Venice, and thus introduced into printing the letter form which has ever since been called *italic*. Its first appearance was in the few words of the title of a woodcut illustration used in the *Epistole* of Saint Catherine of Siena, which Aldus published in September, 1500.

The chancery script was written either vertically or with a forward slant. The earliest Aldine chancery types had a very slight forward slant (see illustration on p. 210) and were used with capital letters of a roman font. Even after the italics developed a more pronounced forward slant under the hands of later designers, roman (upright) capitals continued to be used with them for thirty or forty years before real italic (slanting) capitals were designed.

The first book printed throughout in the new italic was the works of Virgil published by Aldus in April, 1501—a volume of 228 octavo leaves. There followed a long series of compact editions of Latin and Italian texts printed largely in italic—a series which Mr. Winship has aptly called the Everyman's Library of its day. These books, of handy pocket size, were sold at a price approximately equivalent to fifty cents in our present money.

The Aldine italic has been described as "much less elegant than serviceable," and even its utility was questionable, from the point of view of modern type composition, because of the large number of ligatures in its font. Updike has counted no fewer than sixty-five tied letters in the Aldine Virgil of 1501 and the Dante of 1502. While Aldus was the first to see the value of the chancery script as a model for printing types, the design which he used was far surpassed, in beauty of form, by those cut later at Rome by Ludovico degli Arrighi, of Vicenza. It was the Arrighi italic, and not the Aldine, which was followed by the French type designers of the sixteenth century.

Aldus sought protection for his italic letter by procuring an exclusive privilege for its use, which was granted by the Venetian senate in November, 1502, and a month later a similar privilege was accorded him by the pope. These privileges were valid, however, only within limited areas, and the new type was soon pirated. Girolamo Soncino, of Fano, for example, issued a counterfeit of the Aldine Virgil with types from punches which, it is said, were provided by the same Francesco da Bologna who had cut the punches for Aldus. And an unknown printer of Lyons not only counterfeited the Virgil, type and all, but put the Aldus trade mark on the books and sold them as products of the Aldine press.

In March, 1503, Aldus was moved to publish a vigorous protest, of which De Vinne gives the following version:

When I undertook to furnish good books to lovers of letters, I thought I need only see that the books issued by our Academy should be as correct as care could make them. But four times within the past seven years I have had to protect myself against the treachery of our workmen. I have defeated their plots and punished their perfidy. Yet, in the city of Lyons, books are fraudulently printed under my name. These books do not contain the name and place of the real printer, but are made in imitation of mine, so that the unwary reader will believe them printed in Venice. Their paper is inferior and has a bad odor. The types displease the eye and have French peculiarities. The capitals are deformed. The letters are not connected, as mine are, in imitation of writing.

The Academy referred to was an organization of scholars which Aldus founded in 1501 and to which was entrusted the editing of classical texts for publication.

The pirating of his types and books was not the only difficulty which Aldus encountered. As a business venture his handy little volumes were not successful, for there were altogether too many books on the market. There was not a sufficient number of scholars, to say nothing of educated and intelligent laymen, to absorb all the

books that were produced by a constantly increasing number of printers. In Venice alone, we are told, exactly one hundred printing offices had been in operation, for longer or shorter terms, between 1481 and 1501, and they had produced a total of about two million volumes. Horatio Brown counts 268 printers who worked in Venice in the fifteenth century—one hundred more than could be counted in Milan, Rome, Florence, and Naples taken together in the same period. From a condition, before the invention of printing, of having too few books, the rapid exploitation of the new art had brought not only Venice, but all of Europe to the condition of having more books available than could be bought. Aldus was only one of the printers of his time who suffered financially from a glutted market. We have already reported upon the troubles of Sweynheyn and Pannartz at Rome.

In addition to an overstocked book market, the vicissitudes of war afflicted Aldus. In 1503 Venice became involved in one of the many conflicts between the Italian city-states, and in 1506 Aldus was compelled to close his shop and leave the city. He even experienced the indignity of being arrested as a spy and imprisoned for a time in Mantua. In 1507, impoverished but undaunted, Aldus resumed operations again at Venice, but was stopped by a conflagration which ravaged the city. He printed nothing in the years 1510 and 1511. When he began again in 1512 it was with the aid of his father-in-law, Andrea Torresano, the successor to the printing establishment of Nicolas Jenson, himself experienced in the printing business. When Aldus died in February, 1515, he disposed by will of his remaining interest in the business he had founded, which was then but a one-fifth share.

Characteristic of the lasting concern of Aldus Manutius with the interests of his printing business was one of the provisions of his will which may be thus translated from its original Latin:

Furthermore, since a certain cursive type which they call Chancery is still to be perfected, I beg Andrea my father-in-law that he will have this type perfected by Giulio Campagnola, to make capital letters which are written by themselves and which are used in conjunction with the Chancery letters.

The significance of the achievements of this great Venetian publisher is often overlooked today, though as we have said, the name of Aldus is still current in the technical vocabulary of the printer. Similarly the famous Aldine trade-mark is still frequently used for various purposes. The familiar anchor with the dolphin entwined around its shaft often appears in typographic decoration. Perhaps it may be in order to remind those who use this emblem of its significance. The dolphin is a symbol of speed and activity as the anchor is of stability and firmness. The two together are a pictorial representation of the good old motto "Make haste slowly."

Long after the death of Aldus Manutius in 1515, the business which he founded was carried on by his family, at first by Torresano until the sons of the founder came of age. It continued to function in one form or another until it finally ended in the year 1597, a little over a century after its beginning. But the later productions of the Aldine press are of little interest either for content or for printing. It is the early record of the house of Aldus which is written upon a bright particular page in the history of bookmaking.

XIV

The First Printing in English

THAT the first printed book in the English language is one
of the great landmarks in Anglo-Saxon cultural history will
hardly be denied. Strange to say, it was not printed in England, but on the Continent. The manner of its printing was thus:

William Caxton was born about 1422 "in the weald of Kent"
and in 1436 was apprenticed to a prominent London merchant, a
member of the Mercers' Company, who soon thereafter was made
Lord Mayor of London. His master died five years later, and Caxton
went to Burgundy, where the English cloth merchants carried on an
active business. He prospered there, and in 1462 or 1463 we find him
filling the post of "governor" of the Merchant Adventurers at
Bruges—an accredited representative of the English king. William
Obray had been named for this position for the years 1462-1463,
but a record recently discovered shows that he was discharged in
June, 1462, for malfeasance in office. Though we have no record
of the appointment, it is probable that Caxton was designated as his
successor. The functions of this post were approximately similar to
those of a consul at the present time. Caxton was commissioned by
the English government to negotiate, in conjunction with Sir Richard Whitehill, a diplomat of some eminence sent from home, a
renewal of the commercial treaty between England and Burgundy
which was due to expire in 1465. The mission reached an apparently successful conclusion, but Philip the Good, duke of Burgundy,
yielding to insistent internal demands for protection of home indus-
tries, ordered the exclusion of English cloth from his dominions.

The English merchants therefore withdrew from Bruges and moved in a body to Utrecht, which city received them eagerly. Full protection for their persons and goods was formally issued to William Caxton as "Governor of the English Nation" on November 24, 1464. During their stay in Utrecht, according to Crotch, who has made the most recent contribution to our knowledge of Caxton's record on the Continent, the governor was empowered to control the merchants, regulate trade, and settle all disputes of a commercial nature. The town reserved only the right to deal with cases involving life and limb.

In 1465 the House of Commons recommended to the king that he should retaliate for the Burgundian embargo by excluding from his realm all merchandise except food of the "growing, working, or making" of Burgundy. But in 1466 we find under way a negotiation of more peaceful character, plans being matured for the marriage of Margaret of York, sister of Edward IV, and Charles, son of the Duke of Burgundy. Charles was antagonistic to this plan, but when it became apparent that such a marriage alone could bring about a protective alliance against his enemy, France, he was won over to the project.

Meanwhile Philip the Good died, and Charles the Bold succeeded to the throne. In November, 1467, was effected a commercial treaty with England to endure for thirty years. This was ratified early in 1468, and the marriage of Margaret and Charles was solemnized in June or July of that year. No longer, however, was Charles reluctant, for his first glimpse of Edward's sister "had so enchanted him that he was in all haste to return and claim the kisses she was not loath to bestow."

The merchants now returned to Bruges. How long Caxton continued as governor we cannot say with certainty, but he must have relinquished the office some time in the neighborhood of 1470. We

know from his own account that he was in the service of the new duchess of Burgundy in the early part of 1471.

In March, 1469, Caxton, "having no great charge of occupation," had undertaken the translation into English of the *Recueil des histoires de Troies,* "to eschew sloth and idleness and to put myself into virtuous occupation and business." The text he selected was one which was very popular at the time—a compilation from Latin sources by Raoul le Fèvre. When he had completed five or six quires of the manuscript he laid it aside until "on a tyme hit fortuned" that he showed them to the duchess, who commanded him to revise his English and carry the task to completion. So the translation begun at Bruges was continued at Ghent and completed at Cologne in 1471. The magnitude of the task is noted by Caxton in the epilogue to the third and last part of the tale:

And for as moche as in the wrytyng of the same my penne is worn, myn hand wery and not stedfast, myn eyen dimmed with overmoche lokyng on the whit paper, and my corage not so prone and redy to laboure as hit hath ben, and that age crepeth on me dayly and febleth all the bodye; and also because I have promysid to dyverce gentilmen and to my frendes to addresse to hem as hastely as I myght this sayd book. Therefore I have practysed and lerned at my great charge and dispense to ordeyne this said book in prynte after the maner and form as ye may here see, and is not wreton with penne and ynke, as other bokes ben, to thende that every man may have them attones, for all the bookes of this storye named the Recule of the Historyes of Troyes thus enprynted as ye here see, were begonne in oon day and also fynysshid in oon day.

In the quaint English of this passage we find the clear statement that Caxton learned the printing art in order that he might produce copies of the translation in book form and make possible its general circulation. It is thought that Caxton became familiar with the printing process during his stay at Cologne, to which city there is reason to believe he went in a voluntary and protective exile due to the in-

Hus endeth the seconde book of the recule of the historyes of Troyes/ Whiche bookes were late translated in to frensshe out of latyn/ By the labour of the vene
able persone moul se feure preest as a fore is said/ And
by me Indigne and vnworthy translated in to this rude
englissh/ By the comandement of my said redoubtid lady
Duches of Bourgone : And for as moche as I suppose
the said two bokes ben not had to fore this tyme in oure
englissh langage, therfore I had the better will to accom-
plisshe this said werke/ whiche werke was begonne in
Brugis/ and contynued in gaunt And finysshid in Coleyn
In the tyme of the troublous world/ and of the grete deuy-
sions beyng and regnyng as well in the royames of
englond and fraunce as in all other places vnyuersally
thrugh the world that is to wete the yere of our lord a
thousand four honderd lxxi. And as for the thirde book
whiche treteth of the generall and last destruccion of Troye
hit nedeth not to translate hit in to englissh/ ffor as moche as that worshipfull and religyo9 man dan John lidgate
monke of Burye dide translate hit But late/ after whos
werke I fere to take vpon me that am not worthy to bere
his penner and ynke horne after hym. to medle me in that
werke. But yet for as moche as I am bounde to con-
template my sayd ladyes good grace and also that his
werke is in ryme/ And as ferre as I knowe hit is not
had in prose in our tonge/ And also parauentur/ he
translated after some other Auctor than this is/ And
yet for as moche as dyuerce men ben of dyuerce desyres.
Some to rede in Ryme and metre. and some in prose
And also be cause that I haue now good leyser beyng in
Coleyn And haue none other thynge to doo at this tyme

A PAGE OF CAXTON'S RECUYELL OF THE HYSTORYES OF
TROYE, PRINTED AT BRUGES ABOUT 1475.

surrection of his native county of Kent. The Register of Aliens shows him to have been in Cologne on July 17, 1471, permission being that day extended to *Will. Caxton uyss Engelant* to reside in the city until August 16—a permission thrice extended, the final extension valid to December, 1472.

The hypothesis regarding Caxton's instruction in the printing art during his stay at Cologne is reinforced by a statement by Wynkyn de Worde, the successor to his printing business in London, in *De proprietatibus rerum* by Bartholomaeus Anglicus, printed in the year 1496:

> *And also of your charyte call to remembraunce*
> *The soule of William Caxton first prynter of this boke*
> *In Laten tonge at Coleyn hymself to avaunce*
> *That every well disposed man may theron loke.*

An obscure edition of Bartholomaeus Anglicus, printed some time about 1471, in the typography and style of Cologne printing of that period, indicates the probability that in the production of this volume Caxton learned the printing processes.

On his return to Bruges, Caxton presented his translation to Margaret, who "well accepted hit and largely rewarded" him. He now undertook in earnest the establishment of a printing office, enlisting as an associate a talented calligrapher by name Colard Mansion, who had in his early youth been given a position in the library of the Duke of Burgundy. The first production of the press was the *Recuyell of the Hystoryes of Troye* which Caxton had translated, a small folio of 351 leaves, the first of which, containing the prologue, was printed in red. This first book printed in English appeared some time between 1474 and 1476.

The most interesting example of this book is the Chatsworth copy, now in the Henry E. Huntington Library at San Marino, California. In this copy is bound a slip on which it is noted in a

fifteenth-century hand that the volume belonged to Elizabeth, the wife of Edward IV and thus sister-in-law to Duchess Margaret of Burgundy, for whom the translation was completed. But the outstanding feature of the book is that it contains an inserted leaf bearing a probable picture of Caxton presenting his book to Margaret of Burgundy. There is considerable likelihood that this copperplate engraving, which is reproduced in the plate facing page 228, was of a date contemporary with the printing of the book itself, since Colard Mansion used engravings of somewhat similar style to illustrate another volume of approximately the same date. At any rate, the print is one of great interest, showing as it does a man in plain citizen's garb, kneeling to present two bound volumes to a lady of rank surrounded by her women.

The next book to be issued at Bruges was *The Game and Pleye of the Chesse,* which, contrary to general belief, is not a treatise on the rules of the game, but a "morality" with the characters presented in the guise of chessmen. One other book, in French, for which a new type was cut, probably completed Caxton's product as a printer on Burgundian soil. Mansion continued the press, the first book bearing his own name, Boccaccio's *De la ruine des nobles hommes et femmes,* being dated 1476.

Caxton left for England, taking with him the new type recently cut, and by September, 1476, had become the tenant of a shop in the Almonry, near Westminster Abbey, marked by a sign with a red pale or band across it. *The Dictes or Sayengis of the Philosophers* was the first dated book printed in England, the Epilogue being dated 1477 and in one copy November 18. Though this was the first *dated* book, it was not certainly the first issue of the press, Caxton's translation of Jason and a few other publications of slight extent having probably preceded it.

The next publication of importance was an edition of Chaucer's

Canterbury Tales, a very considerable volume of 374 leaves, appearing in 1478. Typography was now firmly established in England.

Most of Caxton's early publications were of a popular character and are, in consequence of the usage they received, very rare. He printed most of Chaucer's other works, Gower's *Confessio amantis,* Malory's *Morte d'Arthur,* the *Chronicles of England* (a page of which is here reproduced), Higden's *Polychronicon,* and the *Golden Legend.* Poems by Lydgate, translations of French romances, the *Fifteen Oes* (fifteen prayers), and many other publications to a total of one hundred (in which are included several indulgences) issued from his press. An excellent census of extant copies has been compiled by De Ricci. In all, Caxton made use of eight different types. Attention has recently been called to the existence of textual variations in the colophons of different copies of several books printed by Caxton, showing that corrections were made while the type forms were being printed.

The first of Caxton's books to contain woodcut illustrations was the *Myrrour of the World* which appeared in 1481. The year previous he had used a woodcut initial letter in printing an indulgence. *The Golden Legend,* the translation of which Caxton completed in 1483, was illustrated with seventy woodcuts.

Caxton could not by any stretch of the imagination be regarded as a fine printer. He was more interested in the textual content of books than in their appearance, and his work was, technically and artistically, below the standards of his continental contemporaries.

The first English printer died in 1491, his business being continued by his foreman, Wynkyn de Worde, who had worked for him since 1480. The latter's output of books was large. In his edition of Higden's *Polychronicon,* dated April 13, 1495, a page of which is reproduced on page 225, music was first printed in England.

Printing was introduced at Oxford in 1478 by Theodoric Rood

¶ How the land of Englond was fyrst named Albyon/And
by what encheson it was so named?

IN the noble land of Sirrie/ther was a noble kyng & myghty &
a man of grete renome/that me callid Dioclisian/that well & wor
thely hym gouerned & ruled thurgh his noble chyualrye/so that
he coquerd all the londes about hym/so that almost al the kynges
of the world to him were entendant/Hit befel thus that this dyoclisian spoused a gentil damisel/that was woder fayr that was
his emes doughter labana/and she loued hym as reson wold/so
that he gate vpon hir xxxiij doughters/of the which the eldest me
callid Albyne/& these damisels whan they come vnto age bicome
so fair that it was woder/wherfor that this dyoclisia anon lete
make a somenyng/& comauded by his lres/that all the kynges
that helden of him shold come at a certayn day.as in his lres we
re conteyned to make a ryal feste/At whiche daye thider they co-
men/& brought with hem amyrals prynces & vnkes,& noble chy
ualrye/The feste was ryally arayed/ & ther they lyued in ioye
& myrthe ynough.that it was wonder to wyt/And it befel thus
that this dyoclisian thought to marye his doughters amonge alle
tho kynges that tho were at that solempnyte/& so they spaken and
dide that albyne his eldest doughter/& al hir sustres rychely were
maried vnto xxxiij kynges/that were lordes of grete honour and
of power at this solempnyte/And whan the solempnite was done,euery kynge toke his wyf & lad hem in to her owne countrey/&
ther made hem quenes/And it befel thus afterward/that this da-
me Albyne bycome so stoute & so sterne/that she told lytel prys
of her lord/& of hym had scorne & despyte/& wold not done hys
wyll/but she wold haue hir owne wyll in dyuerse maters/and
all hir other sustres euerychone bere hem so euyl ayenst hir lordes
that it was wonder to wytte/& for as moch as hem thought that
hir husbondes were nought of so hye parage comen as hir fader /
¶But tho kynges that were hir lordes wold haue chastysed hem
with fayr speche & bekestes,and also by yeftes/& warned hem in
fair maner vpon al loue & frendship that they shold amende her
lither condicions/but al was for nought/for they dyden her owne wyll in all thynge/that hem lyked.& had of power/wherfore
tho xxxiij / kynges vpon a tyme & oftymes beten theyr wyues
for they wende that they wolde haue amended her tatches / & hyr
wicked thewes/but of suche condicions they were/that for fayr
speche & warnynge,they dyden al the wers) and for betynges

a   2

of Cologne. In 1479 or 1480, the anonymous "schoolmaster-printer" began work at St. Albans, issuing eight books up until 1486. He apparently borrowed some type from Caxton, and it was probably with the latter's consent that he reprinted the Caxton version of the *Chronicles of England,* adding to it an appendix entitled *Fructus temporum.* In Wynkyn de Worde's 1497 reprint of this edition we have our only hint of the printer's identity, it being stated that it was "compiled in a booke and also emprynted by one sometyme scole-mayster of saynt Albons, on whose soule God haue mercy."

John Lettou, or John of Lithuania, began to print in London City proper in 1480. In the opinion of Gordon Duff he learned to print at Rome, bringing his punches to England with him, his type being very similar to that used at Rome by a printer whose name—strange to state—was John Bulle, though he hailed from Bremen. Lettou was joined in 1482 by William de Machlinia, the latter being the Latinized form of the name of the Belgian city of Malines After printing five lawbooks in partnership, Lettou disappeared and Machlinia continued the business alone. But by 1490 he, too, had dropped out of sight, and his stock of books appears to have been acquired by Richard Pynson, a Norman, who began printing in 1491 or 1492.

Julian Notary was the last printer to begin work in England during the fifteenth century. He started in 1496 with two partners, an I. B., who was Jean Barbier, and an I. H., who in all probability was Jean Huvin of Rouen. In 1498, Huvin had left the firm and Notary and Barbier were at Westminster. It will have been noted that all these printers, with the exception of Caxton and the printer of St. Albans, were foreigners.

The most important of the fifteenth-century English printers was Caxton, not only because he was the first, but also because of his consequential contributions to English literature. He was the

de of twelue/the thyrde of eyght/the fourth of .ix. as this fygure sheweth.

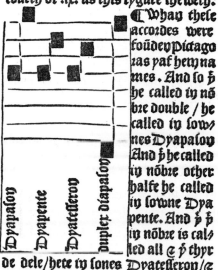

Dyapason   Dyapente   Dyatelleron   Duplex diapason

Whan thele accordes were foūdeŋ piẟago ras pas heŋ na mes. And so þ he called iŋ nō bre double / he called iŋ sow nes Dyapason And þ he called iŋ nōbre other halfe he called iŋ sowne Dya pente. And þ þ iŋ nōbre is cal led all ҩ þ thyr de dele/hete iŋ sones Dyatelleron/ҩ that þ iŋ nombres is called all ҩ the eyghteth dele / hete iŋ tewnes double Dyapason.As iŋ melodye of one ftre ge/yf the ftrynge be ftreyned enlonge vpoŋ the holownelle of a tree / ҩ de parted euen a two by a brydge lette there vnder iŋ eyther parte of þ ftren ge/the lowne lhall be Dyapason/yf the ftreng be ftreyned ҩ touched.And yf the ftreng be departed euen iŋ thre ҩ the brydge lette vnder/lo that it de parte bytwene the twey deles ҩ þ thyr de/thaŋ the lenger dele of the ftreng yf it be touched lhall yeue a lowne cal led Dyatelleron.And yf it be depar ted iŋ nyne/and the brydge lette vn der bytwene the laft parte and the o ther dele / thaŋ the lenger dele of the ftrenge yf it be touched lhall yeue a lowne/that hete Tonus/for nyne cō teyneth eyght/and the eyght parte of eyght as iŋ this fygure that foloweth

C Del Anno Transmi. ronim9 Ab Vrbe.

contra Ruf.Many of piẟagoras dyf cyples kepte her mayftres heeftes iŋ mynde and vled her wytte and myn de iŋ ftudye of bookes / and taught that many luche prouerbes lhall hyt te and departe lorowe from the bo dye/vnconnynge from the wytte/le cherye from the wombe/trealoŋ oute of the Cyte / ftryfe out of the hous: Incontynence and haftynelle oute of all thynges.Also all that frendes ha ue lhall be compyn . A frende is the o ther of tweyne . Me muft take hede of tymes . After god lothnelle lhall be worlhypped that maketh meŋ be next god. C Ylydorus libro octauo ca pitulo lexto.

C Cap.iŋ   .xii.

The name of phylosophres hadde begynnynge of piẟa goras.for olde Grekes cal led hyŋ lelfe lophiftris that is wyfe/ But piẟagoras whaŋ me axed what maŋ he was/he anlwerde and layde that he was a phylolopher /that is a louer of wytte and of wyfedome for to calle hyŋ lelfe a wyfe maŋ/it wol de leme grete booft ҩ pryde.Afterwar other philolophres hadden her names of her auctours.And so they that hel de piẟagoras loore/were called piẟ tagoraci . And they that helden pla toos loore / were called platonici . C Pot.libro pri9.Some phylolophres hadden names of contrees / ҩ lo they þ helden piẟagoras loore were called

translator of more than twenty of the books he printed, and many others he provided with prologues or epilogues of rare good humor and charm. He also did yeoman's service in crystallizing and establishing the forms of English speech, our mother tongue being in a fluid state, to say the least, at the time his labors began.

Before we leave this great figure in English literary history it may be interesting to achieve a more intimate acquaintance with his work. With reference to the chaotic state of the English language he writes in the prologue to his translation of the *Eneydos* [*Aeneid*]:

I confess me not lerned nor knowing the arte of rethoryke, ne of suche gaye termes [the slang of Caxton's day] as now be sayd in these dayes and used. . . . Having noe werke in hande, I sittyng in my studye where as laye many dyvers paunflettis & bookys, happened that to my hande came a lyttyl booke in Frenche, which late was translated out of Latyn by some noble clerke of France . . . whiche booke I sawe over and redde therin. . . . In whiche booke I had grete plesyr, by cause of the fayr and honest termes and wordes in Frenche, which I never sawe tofore lyke, ne none so playsaunt ne so well ordred . . . And whan I had advysed me in this sayd boke, I delybered & concluded to translate it in to Englysshe. And forthwyth toke a penne & ynke and wrote a leef or tweyne, whyche I oversawe agayn to correcte it. And whan I sawe the fayr and straunge termes therin I doubted that it sholde not please some gentylmen whiche late blamed me, sayeng that in my translacyons I had over curyous termes whiche coude not be understande of comyn peple, & desired me to use olde and homely termes in my translacyons. And fayn wolde I satisfye every man, and so to do toke an olde boke and redde therin, and certaynly the Englysshe was so rude and broad that I coude not wele understande it. And also my Lorde Abbot of Westmynster ded do shewe me late certayn evydences wryton in olde Englysshe for to reduce it in to our Englysshe now usid, and certaynly it was wreton in suche wyse that it was more lyke to Dutche than Englysshe. I coude not reduce ne brynge it to be understonden. And certaynly our language now used varyeth ferre from that whyche was used & spoken whan I was borne. For we Englysshe men ben borne under the domynacyon of the moon, whyche is never stedfaste but

ever waverynge, waxynge one season and waneth and decreaseth another season. And that comyn Englysshe that is spoken in one shyre varyeth from another. Insomuch that in my dayes happened that certayne marchauntes were in a ship in Tamyse for to have sayled over the see into Zelande, & for lacke of wynde they taryed at Foreland, & went to lande for to refreshe them. And one of theym named Sheffelde a mercer came in to an howse & axed for mete, & specyally he axed after eggys. And the goode wyf answerde, that she coude speke no Frenche. And the marchaunt was angry, for he also could speke no Frenche, but wolde have hadde egges & she understode hym not. And thenne at laste another sayd that he wolde have eyren, then the good wyf sayd that she understod hym wel. Loo what sholde a man in thyse dayes now wryte, egges or eyren? Certaynly it is harde to playse every man bycause of dyversite & chaunge of langage. For in these dayes every man that is in ony reputacyon in his countre, wyll utter his comunycacyon and matters in suche manners and termes, that fewe men shall understonde theym. And som honest & grete clerkes have ben wyth me and desired me to wryte the most curyous termes that I coude fynde. And thus bytwene playn, rude, and curyous I stand abashed. But in my judgemente the comyn termes that be dayly used ben lyghter to be understonde that the old & auncyent Englysshe.

Finally, let us enjoy the humor of his comment on the relative virtues of Greek women and English women. The queen's brother, Earl Rivers, had translated the *Dictes or Sayengis of the Philosophers,* which, as we have already noted, was the first dated book issued from his press. In comparing it with the original, Caxton found the earl had omitted portions of the text which comprised "certayne and dyverse conclusions touchyng women," and wrote:

Whereof I mervaylle that my sayd Lord hath not wreton them, ne what hath movyd hym so to do ne what cause he hadde at that tyme. But I suppose that some fayr lady hath desired hym to leve it out of his booke, or ellys he was amerous on some noble lady, for whos love he wold not sette yt in hys book, or ellys for the very affeccyon, love & good wylle that he hath unto alle ladyes and gentyl women, he thought that Socrates spared the sothe and wrote of women more than trouthe.

But I appercyve that my sayd Lord knoweth veryly that suche defautes ben not had ne founden in the women born and dwellyng in these partyes ne regyons of the world. Socrates was a Greke. I wote well that of whatsomever condicion women ben in Grece, the women of this contre ben right good, wyse, playsant, humble, discrete, sobre, chaste, obedient to their husbondes [it is supposed that Caxton married not long before he settled down at Westminster] trewe, secrete, stedfast, ever besy and never ydle, attemperat in speking, and vertuous in alle their werkis, or atte leste sholde be so, for whiche causes so evydent my sayd Lord as I suppose thoughte it was not of necessite to sette in his book the saiengs of his auctor Socrates touchyng women. Therefore in accomplisshing his commandement to correcte & amende where as I sholde fynde fawte and other fynde I none . . . for as muche as I am not in certayn whether it was in my Lordis copye or not or ellis peraventure that the wynde had blowe over the leef at the tyme of translacion, I purpose to wryte the same sayings of that Greke Socrates, which wrote of the women of Grece & nothyng of them of this Royame, whom I suppose he never knewe.

Among the typographers of the past, we may well consider William Caxton one of the leaders in weight of contribution to the advancement of culture. First English printer and first English editor, his must certainly be ranked with the great names in English literary history.

CAXTON PRESENTING HIS BOOK TO MARGARET OF BURGUNDY.

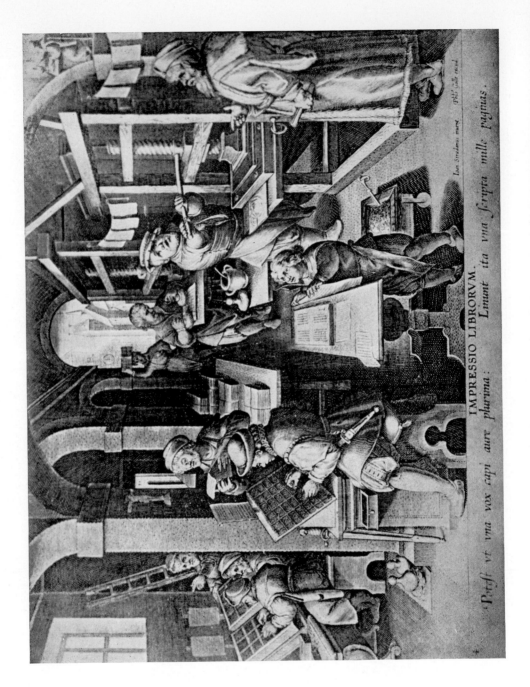

IMPRESSIO LIBRORVM.

Preß vt vna vox capi aur plurima:
Lmunt ita vna scripta mille paginas.

Ioan Stradanus inuent   Phls Galle excud

A PRINTING OFFICE AS REPRESENTED BY STRADANUS, ANTWERP, ABOUT 1600.

XV

The Production of the Incunabula

THE first equipment requirement of the fifteenth-century printer was a font of types, accurately rectangular in body so they could be set together and locked up for printing, and reasonably uniform in height to paper. There has been much discussion of the material and method of manufacture of the first types. There have appeared in the literature numerous statements that they were made of wood, but this would involve individual engraving by hand of the face of each letter in the font, which would have introduced inevitably wide variation in the printing face of different letters, which is not to be observed in the earliest extant specimens of typography produced by the earliest printers either in Germany or in Holland.

On the contrary, there is a uniformity between numerous examples of the same letter occurring in any one page which points to their production from a single model, which would, in turn, necessitate the use of some process of casting.

Another theory of early type manufacture, advanced by Gerardus Meerman in 1765, was that types were made by what he called the sculpto-fusi process, whereby the shanks of the types were cast type-high in metal molds and the letters were then engraved on the faces by hand. In support of this theory, Meerman called attention to the frequent use of the word *sculptus,* in one form or another, in the colophons of the early printers. It is the generally accepted opinion, however, that *sculptus* referred to the cutting of punches rather than to the making of types.

Granted a casting process, there are still several possible alternative methods. First, pattern letters the size and shape of the finished types may have been cut in wood. A number of these at a time may have been molded in fine sand and cast in lead or a lead alloy, the jets broken off, and the resulting casts perhaps touched up by hand to correct imperfections. A modern reconstruction of this method was undertaken by Gustav Mori in co-operation with the Stempel typefoundry at Frankfort, using a casting frame such as was in use during the fifteenth century. In a thought-provoking essay Mori showed in 1921 photographs of the frame, the cast types as they came from the mold, and also a remarkably perfect impression of a piece of composition set in the types so produced.

Knowing the perfection to which the art of casting was carried by the medieval goldsmiths, we can easily conceive the production of primitive leaden types by this method. Furthermore, it seems logical that this would be the first and most obvious method to occur to one familiar with the goldsmith's craft who desired to produce numerous duplicates from a simple model.

A variation of this method was suggested by Dr. Charles Enschedé, the eminent Dutch typefounder. This is known as the *Abklatsch* method, whereby the face of the letter only, forming a thin metal plate, was cast into a matrix. This plate was then placed face down under a casting mold and the shank of the letter cast onto it, the two sections fusing at the point of contact. Enschedé thought this system practicable only for the larger types, but most authorities think it impracticable for any.

Gottfried Zedler, who has exhaustively studied the Costerian printing, advanced the hypothesis that these thin type heads might have been pasted on paper, and thus printed from. He points to the thin strokes tying the contraction marks above the Dutch type letters to the letters themselves as proof of this theory, but inasmuch

as the plates must have had a square base below the counters of the letters, those strokes would play no essential role in tying together two parts of a letter.

Whether or not sand casting was the process first experimented with, it is probable that some crude metal-casting mold was devised at a very early period. As the height of all types in any given font was uniform, all that was needed was two L-shaped pieces of iron shaped in cross section like this ⌐▭⌐ . These would go together ⌐▭⌐ to form a casting cavity of variable width, the matrix being placed face up at the bottom of the well thus formed. When hot metal was poured into this cavity a type would be formed. This could easily be released by separating the two pieces of the mold. To obviate differences in height to paper, all the types could be locked up, face down on a level surface, and their bases or feet trimmed or planed off evenly. Such a primitive process could and would, of course, be soon refined and improved in many respects. But it provided all that was needed for a successful start in printing with movable types.

Any casting process naturally required matrices, and the production of these in turn required punches or patrices. There are many possible ways in which both these essential elements may have been produced, but the weight of opinion favors the following as the probable procedure: Patterns of the individual letters were engraved on wood or on soft metal. From these, brass patrices were cast in fine sand, just as were the bookbinders' stamps in general use many years before the invention of printing. It is also possible, of course, that these patrices may have been engraved directly in brass.

To form matrices, hot lead was either poured over these brass patrices, or the patrices were pushed or driven into lead heated to a point of comparative softness. Strange as it may seem, lead, if it is not too hot, can be cast into leaden matrices without spoiling them,

though deterioration is rather rapid. When a matrix did wear out in use, it was only necessary to make another from the patrix.

In support of the hypothesis as to leaden matrices, it is interesting to observe that one of the earliest fonts of matrices which has come down to us, though for quite large letters, is made of lead.

The next important development was the cutting of a patrix or punch on a billet of soft steel, which could subsequently be

hardened and driven into copper, which proved to be an ideal matrix material. The pioneer typemakers soon learned to "justify" the matrices, cutting them down to the right width, so that when the jaws of the type mold closed on them, the width of the mold was set automatically for casting the particular letter. Once a font of matrices was correctly fitted, therefore, it was easy for the workman doing the casting to obtain a uniform result each time the type supply needed replenishment. The steel punch and copper matrix, which have

CASTING TYPE, AS REPRESENTED BY JOST
AMMAN IN 1568.

often been credited to Peter Schoeffer, made possible the production of small types and the reproduction of more detail.

There was no particular requirement as to the height of the types except that they had to be of a height sufficient to lock up firmly in a page. The types of one fifteenth-century printer varied in height from those of another, though it is evident, from impressions of pulled-out letters as they lay on top of the form, that they were all

somewhat similar in height to the types in use today. Some of these impressions, which date as early as 1470, show a round hole in the side of the type, which does not seem to extend through the body. It is thought that these holes served the same purpose as nicks in modern types in helping the compositor to place them rapidly in his stick right side up. The fact that types such as these pulled out of the form seems to disprove the rather improbable theory sometimes advanced that each line of types was pierced by a wire to hold it securely in the form.

The admixture of tin to improve the flow of lead in casting was known to the early printers, as is evidenced by documentary records, but we hear nothing of antimony as a hardening agent. The fact that the paper was wetted before printing helped, of course, to reduce the wear on the type which would otherwise, with the use of all-rag handmade paper, have proved serious.

It is a noteworthy fact that, during the fifteenth century, the complete process of type production remained a function of the individual printing office. The first tasks of any printer setting up an office were to cut punches, drive matrices, and cast a supply of types. These requirements account for delays between the known arrival of a new printer in a town and the appearance of his first book.

Since type was a universal requirement of all printing offices, it might be expected that, when printers became numerous, there would have grown up a typefounding industry to supply the demand. Or, even if fonts of cast types were not offered on the market, we might reasonably expect to find a lively and flourishing business in the sale of matrices, since any number of sets of matrices could be driven from one set of punches. Such opportunity to purchase "strikes" would have spared many printers the slow and troublesome task of cutting new alphabets.

Yet the types used by almost every fifteenth-century printing

office show that they were independently produced, for the exclusive use of one particular shop. And a painstaking examination by Dr. Konrad Haebler of the documentary evidence available shows that there was no organized trade in cast type or matrices during the fifteenth century, and for some years thereafter. As the industry developed, functions inside the larger offices became specialized, so that different workmen specialized in certain operations. We find references to some workers who devoted their attention particularly to punch-cutting and typefounding, such as Nicolas Wolff, *fondeur de lettres* at Lyons, or Hendrick Lettersnider at Antwerp; but such men were either master printers themselves who had risen above their original specialty, or employees of a particular printing office, rather than suppliers to the trade.

There were, of course, sales of printing-office equipment from one printer to another, and sales of or foreclosures on offices, in the course of which matrices and types passed from one ownership to another. But these were individual transactions. It might be added here that when typefounding did begin to emerge as an industry distinct from printing, it was matrices struck from a master set of punches that were sold, printers continuing for a considerable period to cast and recast their types in their own shops.

We get a good idea of the arrangement of the type cases of the early printers from engravings showing the interior of ancient printing offices. The cases were considerably larger than those in use today, probably because of the greater average size of the typefaces used, and were set on the frames supporting them at a much sharper angle than is the custom today.

As type was first set and made up directly in page form, rather than set up in long columns on galleys to be made up into pages in a later process, it may well have been that the setting was done directly into the frame or chase into which the page was wedged

or locked in some manner not exactly known to us. The compositor's stick must have been developed rather early, however, as a matter of convenience, though I do not recall any fifteenth-century references to such sticks.

A PRINTING OFFICE AS REPRESENTED IN THE DANCE OF DEATH, LYONS, 1500.

The next major requirement was a press, with which the inked type form could be firmly and evenly impressed on the sheets of paper or vellum. It has already been pointed out in Chapter IX that screw presses were already in use during the fifteenth century in a number of other crafts, so the pioneer printer had only to adapt such presses to his particular technical requirements.

We have no knowledge of the construction of the press used by

EPISTOLAE

Gullielmi Budęi, Secretarii Regii, Posteriores.

Vęnundantur Iodoco Badio, cum gratia
& priuilegio in triennium.

THE PRESS OF JODOCUS BADIUS, 1520.

Gutenberg and his immediate successors. It probably did not differ much, however, from the presses used by later printers, of which there are a number of representations in prints of the sixteenth century. The earliest representation of a printing press was printed in an edition of the *Dance of Death* produced in Lyons, France, in 1500. The illustration on page 235 shows the symbolic grisly figure of Death summoning a group of printers from their work. In this drawing, in which the equipment of a printing office was only incidental to the purpose of the illustration, not much is shown us of the details of the press or of its operation.

But in 1507, Jodocus Badius Ascensius, who printed at Paris, began to use as his printer's mark a spirited representation of (presumably) his own printing office, in which the press formed the principal feature. There were several variations of this printer's mark between its first appearance and 1532, but all show the press in action at the moment when the pressman put his strength into pulling the lever which caused the screw to force the platen down upon the bed of the press to produce an impression.

Still later, Jost Amman, a well-known wood engraver, made a woodcut used as an illustration in Hartmann Schopper's *Panoplia omnium artium* printed at Frankfort in 1568. This drawing was made specifically for the purpose of showing the operation of a printing press. It represents the moment when the type form has been run out from under the platen just after taking an impression. One operative with two ink balls is inking the type for the next impression. Another operative is removing the recently printed sheet from the tympan, which is hinged to the type form. The drawing shows, probably in somewhat exaggerated size, the two points or pins on the tympan which pierced the sheet of paper to hold it in proper register. Hinged to the other edge of the tympan, and in open position in the drawing, is the frisket, a frame over which is

stretched a sheet of paper cut out so as to cover the sheet on the tympan except for the area intended to receive the impression of the type. When the form has been freshly inked, a new sheet of paper will be placed on the tympan and held there in position by the two pins. The frisket will be folded down over the tympan and the tympan, shielded by the frisket, will then be folded down over, but not touching, the type form. The form will then be run back under the platen, the long lever will be pulled, and another impression will be made.

The illustrations all show a press frame of sturdy construction supporting a firmly fixed horizontal bed on which the type form rests when in position under the platen. The platen is raised and lowered by a screw mechanism turned by a long lever. Considerable power was exerted in making the impression, as is shown by the fact that the illustrations all show a conspicuously heavy and solid construction of the top of the press to give a rigid resistance to the downward pressure of the screw. The top of the press is also firmly braced against the ceiling—in the Ascensius illustrations by means of jacks and in the Amman illustration by means of strong timbers. The strength required for operating a press of this type is also indicated by the fact that in the illustrations the pressman, who pulls the lever, is represented by a powerfully muscled individual.

In the early days of printing there were no specialized manufacturers of printing presses. A press was no part of the paraphernalia which a roving printer had to take with him in moving from one place to another. Some local artisan at the printer's next stopping place could construct a press according to his specifications.

XVI

Woodcut Book Illuſtration

THE art of the woodcut was well known and widely practiced in Europe many years before the invention of printing, as has already been indicated in Chapter VII. Although the printing of type forms and the printing of woodcuts were technically co-ordinate, and the idea of illustrating books had been well established by the practice of illuminating manuscript volumes, no printer undertook to illustrate a book with woodcuts until about fifteen years after typography had been brought to a practical basis. Even then, only one printer made the apparently revolutionary experiment, and the next one to follow his example did not venture upon the production of pictured books until eleven years later.

The first illustrated books were printed from 1460 onward at Bamberg by Albrecht Pfister, whom we find then in possession of the types previously used, probably by someone else (perhaps Gutenberg) in printing the 36-line Bible. Pfister's publications had one other distinction in addition to their illustrations, in that they presented texts of popular character, unlike the plethora of theological or academic works which issued from other early presses.

Pfister printed nine editions of five books, all of which, with the single exception of the *Belial,* by Jacobus de Theramo, were planned to be adequately illustrated. In or about the year 1460 he printed the first edition of the *Ackermann von Böhmen,* by Johannes von Saaz. Only one copy of this edition, that in the library at Wolfenbüttel, has been preserved to us, and this one lacks the five full-page woodcuts for which spaces had been left. As Pfister printed his blocks

ILLUSTRATION FROM THE ACKERMANN VON BÖH-
MEN PRINTED BY ALBRECHT PFISTER, BAMBERG,
ABOUT 1463.

subsequent to the printing of the type matter, it seems reasonable to assume that we have here to deal with a set of sheets on which the printing of the woodcuts was inadvertently omitted. The illustrations allowed for appeared in the second edition, which was printed about 1463. There is here reproduced the best known of these illustrations, representing Death sitting as a king on his throne. At the left is a widower with his child, at the right the body of his wife lying in an open coffin.

The next text to be published by Pfister was *Der Edelstein,* by Ulrich Boner, a series of fables in German, which appeared in 1461, illustrated with the impressive total of 101 woodcuts. This had the added distinction of being the earliest *dated* book printed in the German language. An undated edition, in which two more illustrations were added, appeared probably in 1464. The other illustrated texts printed by Pfister were the *Vier Historien,* in which one of the cuts was carelessly printed upside down, and the *Biblia pauperum,* that favorite subject of the block-book printers, three editions of which appeared from 1462 to 1464.

All Pfister's woodcuts are in simple outline and were obviously designed to be colored by hand, perhaps in the printing office where the books were produced. Practically all the extant copies of these volumes have been so colored.

With the termination in 1464 of Pfister's activity in the production of illustrated books, we find no further attempt of like character for seven years. The next undertaking in this field encountered a number of difficulties, suggestive of jurisdictional disputes between modern labor unions. Only through the good offices of the abbot of SS. Ulrich and Afra, did Günther Zainer manage to obtain citizenship rights and the license to engage in printing after his arrival in Augsburg in 1468. At first, he was denied the right to use in his books woodcuts of illustration or ornament, but later gained this

privilege upon engagement to use only the services of members of the local guilds in cutting the blocks. When all obstacles had finally been surmounted, Zainer embarked in 1471 on an ambitious program of illustrated book production.

Zainer's first illustrated book was the *Wintertheil* of Voragine's *Leben der Heiligen,* or *Lives of the Saints,* which appeared in 1471.

ILLUSTRATION FROM VORAGINE'S LEBEN DER HEILIGEN (WINTERTHEIL) PRINTED BY GÜNTHER ZAINER AT AUGSBURG, 1471.

As is clearly apparent from the illustrations here reproduced, the woodcuts and the type were printed in separate operations following the practice of Pfister. This was probably due to the fact that the blocks were different in height to paper from the type forms. This deficiency in technique had, however, been remedied before the appearance in 1472 of the *Sommertheil* of the same work, in which

the register of illustrations and text indicates that they were printed in the same impression.

In 1473 Zainer, at the invitation of the abbot of SS. Ulrich and

Er lieb het fat ieronimus
ift geborn von der ftat ftri
damie/vnd was ein criften
vnd hett got lieb/vnd hett einen
reinen müt/da ließ man in fchier

ILLUSTRATION FROM VORAGINE'S LEBEN DER
HEILIGEN (WINTERTHEIL) PRINTED BY GÜNTHER
ZAINER AT AUGSBURG, 1471.

Afra, co-operated with the monks at that convent in printing with his types an illustrated edition of the *Speculum humanae salvationis*. The identity of neither the designer nor cutter of the blocks is known. The cuts were simple and strong in line and harmonized with the type pages which they illustrated.

Zainer printed a number of other well-illustrated books before his death in 1478. One of these was a folio Bible in German, which was one of the three earliest illustrated Bibles printed in Germany, and perhaps the first. The illustrations, however, were represented largely by pictorial initials.

Johann Bämler and Anton Sorg were also known as printers at Augsburg of creditably illustrated books.

Erhard Ratdolt, a German, did distinguished printing at Venice. At the urgent invitation of Bishop Friedrich von Hohenzollern, he returned in the year 1486 to Augsburg where, until 1516, he printed liturgical works chiefly, and mathematical and astronomical works secondarily. Here he used some of the attractive decorative initials he had produced in Italy, and added new ones.

Ratdolt had printed in Venice astronomical works in which the diagrams of heavenly bodies were printed in colors. The first book he printed at Augsburg, the *Obsequiale,* which appeared in 1487, contained the first regular woodcut illustration ever printed in colors, thus marking a milestone in the technical development of the printing art. This woodcut, printed in black and two or three colors, pictured Bishop Friedrich von Hohenzollern, who was responsible for Ratdolt's setting up a press at Augsburg. Other subjects printed in colors are found in later books. The authorship of some of the woodcuts in Ratdolt's books issued from 1491 onward are attributed to Hans Burgkmair the elder.

Ulm was the next German city in which important illustrated books were produced. During the latter part of the fourteenth century and the early years of the fifteenth, this city had been known as the principal center for the production and distribution of playing cards. Here Johann Zainer, of the same family as Günther Zainer who worked at Augsburg, established himself about 1472 as a printer. His first book, which appeared early in 1473, contained

Ionas missus est in mare· ⁊ deglutiꝰ a pisce· Ione⸗
primo ca.   Ionas der ꝓphet ward geworffen in das
mör vnd von dem walfisch verschlicket.

Seda figura·
⸿ Sepultuꝛam ꝑpi etiam filij Iacob ꝑfiguꝛaueꝛůt.
Qui fratrem suum Ioseph in cÿsternam miseꝛunt·
Filij iacob fratrem suum sine causa vsꝗ ad moꝛtem
oderunt· Ita iudei fratrem suum ꝑpm gratis odio ha
babueꝛunt· Filij iacob fratrem suum ꝓ triginta de⸗
narijs vendebant. Iudei ꝑpum ꝓ triginta denarijs
iuda emebant. Filij iacob tunicam fratris sui dilace
raueꝛůt. Iudei carnem ꝑpi virgis flagellis spinis cla
uis verbeꝛaueꝛunt· Tunica ioseph nō sensit aliquam
penam vel doloꝛem. Sed caro ꝑpi in omnibꝰ mēbris
sustinuit passionem. Tunica ioseph vsꝗ ad talos de⸗
scendebat. Et in ꝑpo a vertice vsꝗ ad talos nulla sa⸗
nitas erat. Filij iacob tunicā ioseph sanguine edi asp⸗
gebant. Sed iudei tunicam Cristi ꝓprio sanguine
ꝑfundebant. Filij Iacob patrem suum nimis turba
ueꝛunt· Sic iudei marie tristiciam maximů intuleꝛt
Ioseph fratribus suis ꝗ in eo reliquerant relaxauit·

ILLUSTRATION FROM THE SPECULUM HUMANAE
SALVATIONIS PRINTED BY GÜNTHER ZAINER, AUGS-
BURG, ABOUT 1473.

woodcut embellishment which included one pictorial initial, but his first fully illustrated book, Boccaccio's *De claris mulieribus,* appeared in 1473 in two editions, each containing about eighty woodcuts.

The art of the woodcut reached a high at Ulm with the appearance from Zainer's office in 1476 or the year following of Aesop's *Vita et fabulae.* Other printers at Ulm produced illustrated books of high quality, but few were commercially successful, possibly because the plague ravaged the city again and again. Conrad Dinckmut and Lienhart Holle were among the better known printers who produced pictured books in this city.

Printing had started at Basel far earlier than at Augsburg or Ulm, but the illustration of books in this city came later, the earliest local work reflecting some influence of the woodcut work at the two other cities named. Bernhard Richel printed at Basel in 1476 the ubiquitous *Spiegel Menschlicher Behältnis,* the woodcuts in which show the influence of illustrations in the block-book editions of the *Biblia pauperum* produced in the Netherlands. Johann Amerbach began the issue of woodcut books in 1489, and illustrations of mediocre quality are found in books printed by M. Furter at Basel from 1491 onward.

We find evidence of a new virtuosity in book illustration at Basel in 1492 and 1494, during which period young Albrecht Dürer was in the city. The original block of a woodcut of St. Jerome, which appeared in the *Epistles* printed by Nicolaus Kesler in 1492, bears the signature of Dürer on its back. Other cuts attributed to Dürer appeared in books printed at Basel, notably those richly illustrating Sebastian Brant's *Narrenschiff* printed by Johann Bergmann von Olpe in 1494.

From this point on, we can refer only to a few highlights of woodcut illustration in Germany. Among these must be numbered one of the greatest illustrated books of the fifteenth century, the

THE FRONTISPIECE OF BREYDENBACH'S
PEREGRINATIONES, MAINZ, 1486.

Sanctae peregrinationes of Bernhard von Breydenbach, which was illustrated and printed at Mainz, cradle of typography, in 1486. Breydenbach, who was a member of the nobility, in 1483 and 1484 went on a pilgrimage to the Holy Land as a penance for the misdeeds of his youth. As artist of the expedition he took along the gifted Reuwich, who made drawings of actual scenes and views as he observed them. This feature places the book he illustrated upon his return in a category quite different from most other early books with illustrations, nearly all of which were conceived in the mind of the artist, rather than being drawn from life.

The frontispiece of the *Peregrinationes,* which is reproduced on page 247, is a noble composition, ably rendered. In addition to many other woodcuts, the book includes folding plates authentically picturing cities passed through on the journey. Of these the view of Venice is the best known.

This was not the earliest illustrated book printed at Mainz, for Peter Schoeffer had issued three: the *Herbarius Latinus* in 1484, the *Gart der Gesuntheit* in the following year, and the *Cronecken der Sassen* in 1492. The frontispiece to the *Gart der Gesuntheit* was a woodcut of fine quality picturing a group of thirteen physicians, authorship of which can safely be attributed to Erhard Reuwich.

At Cologne, an important commercial center on the Rhine, there was done relatively little distinguished work in book illustration. The celebrated Cologne Bible printed about 1478 by Heinrich Quentell was, however, a notable exception to the general rule. This large folio, set in double-column arrangement, appeared in two editions in two different German dialects. There are well over a hundred illustrations, the bulk of which relate to the Old Testament. In addition, a number of type pages are surrounded by three-piece borders in varying arrangements, one such page being reproduced on page 251. The drawing of the illustrations, the author-

FRONTISPIECE TO THE GART DER GESUNDHEIT, PRINTED
BY PETER SCHOEFFER, MAINZ, 1485.

ship of which is unknown, is rather angular and heavy-handed, but this edition of the Bible is important for the influence it exerted on other illustrated editions of the Scriptures.

Considerable activity in the illustration of books is observable in the early issues of the Nuremberg press, but the books issued by Anton Koberger overshadow in importance the work of his local competitors. Koberger, who is reputed to have operated twenty-four presses and employed a hundred printers, developed a successful business of international scope. He was fortunate in enlisting the services of two distinguished artists, Michel Wolgemut and Wilhelm Pleydenwurff, whose designs were apparently cut on wood by various hands. Two celebrated volumes were the fruit of this association of talent. The *Schatzbehalter,* explained in its subtitle as being a "treasury of the true riches of salvation," written by Stefan Fridolin, was printed by Koberger in 1491. The volume contained nearly a hundred illustrations, mostly of scriptural subjects.

The second celebrated book pictured by the same illustrators was Hartmann Schedel's *Weltchronik,* generally referred to as the *Nuremberg Chronicle,* which Koberger printed and published in Latin and German editions in 1493. The contract between publisher and illustrators was dated 1491, but there is evidence that the work was at that time already well under way.

The *Chronicle* was a monumental undertaking for all concerned, 645 separate woodcuts being presented in the German edition. As some blocks were used several times, the count of printed illustrations reaches the amazing total of 1809. This repetition makes it apparent that the woodcuts represented imaginary rather than real illustrations. The views of cities are of the most value, but most of these are not authentic—in marked contrast to the faithfulness of the Reuwich illustrations in Breydenbach's *Peregrinationes.* The magnitude of the undertaking in printing and illustrating the

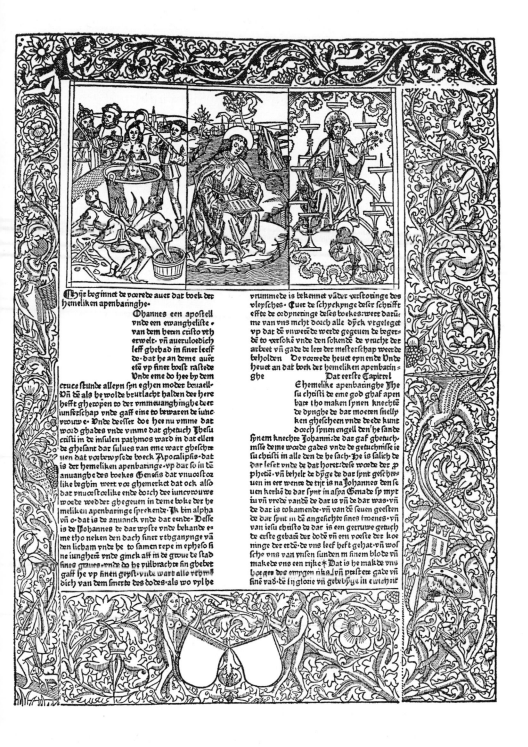

ILLUSTRATED PAGE FROM THE COLOGNE BIBLE
PRINTED BY HEINRICH QUENTELL, 1478.

Chronicle, and the speed with which it was carried through, undoubtedly detracted from the merit of the work.

There was a still brighter chapter in the history of illustrated bookmaking at Nuremberg, for in this city the great master of woodcut, Albrecht Dürer, did much of his best work. Arthur Hind tells us that Dürer "found in woodcut the most perfect medium for the expression of his genius, and is perhaps the greatest figure in the whole history of the art." Dürer was enrolled as an apprentice in Wolgemut's studio during the three years ending December, 1489, a period preceding the latter's work on the illustrations of the two books just referred to. In 1490, Dürer left Nuremberg on his *Wanderjahre,* during which his activities are not clearly known, though it is evident he did some work at Basel in the field of book illustration. Returning to his home city in 1494, he married and took a trip to Italy, perhaps to escape the plague, a local epidemic of which was raging in that year.

Evidence of a matured genius is found in the fifteen large woodcuts of the *Apocalypse,* printed with the text set in Koberger's types, which appeared in German and Latin editions at Nuremberg in 1498. One of these illustrations, *The Riders on the Four Horses,* which is reproduced on page 257, is artistically in a different class from the woodcut book illustrations heretofore discussed. In the design of Dürer's woodcuts we find evidence of both Gothic and Renaissance influences. The technical excellence of his illustrations was contributed to by the master's practice of drawing his design directly on the block, thus eliminating necessity for tracing, and of closely supervising the cutting and printing of his subjects.

Since Italian book illustration, having an individuality all its own, is being dealt with in another chapter, we have now to discuss fifteenth-century woodcut illustration in Holland.

Apart from the blocks in the editions of the *Speculum* discussed

ILLUSTRATION FROM SCHATZBEHALTER PRINTED BY
ANTON KOBERGER, NUREMBERG, 1491.

in Chapter XI, the earliest woodcut used in the Netherlands was a portrait of Johann of Westphalia, cut in reverse, and serving as his printer's mark in the *Justinian* which he printed at Louvain in 1475, and in subsequently issued volumes. Jan Veldener used, also at Louvain in 1475, the printer's mark reproduced in Chapter XX, and another portrait mark was used by Conrad of Paderborn in the same city during the following year.

Jan Veldener used the first series of woodcut illustrations to appear in a book printed in the Netherlands in an edition of Rolewinck's *Fasciculus temporum,* which he completed in the closing days of December, 1475. Veldener moved his press first to Utrecht and later to Kuilenburg. In the first-named city he printed another edition of the *Fasciculus,* in which additional blocks appeared.

While at Utrecht, Veldener printed a book which has been the object of acute attention from typographic historians. The *Epistelen en Evangelien,* which came from the press in 1481, contained thirty-nine biblical illustrations. On the two final leaves appeared halves of a block used in the early Dutch-printed *Speculum* referred to in Chapter XI. Two years later Veldener printed the *Spieghel onzer Behoudenisse,* an edition of the *Speculum* in the Dutch language, in which all the original blocks (cut in half) were used, along with twelve additional subjects cut in like style. Two of the cuts appeared in the *Kruidboeck* in 1484.

Here is the important link between a known printer of the later period and the work of the unidentified early Dutch "printer of the *Speculum*." But there was also a link with the printer of the *Biblia pauperum* block book and Pieter van Os, who printed at Zwolle in 1487 another edition of the *Epistelen en Evangelien,* containing forty-four pieces cut from the blocks of the earlier publication. Some of these blocks reappear in books produced later by this same printer. Finally, the upper half of one subject in the block book *Canticum*

Qᵁ Uneß suggerente diabolo in forma ser/
pentis, pthoparētes mandatuz dei trãſ/
greſſi fuiſſent: maledixit eis deus: et ait
serpenti. Maledictᵒ eris inter omnia animãtia
τ beſtias terre: ſuper pectus tuuin gradieris: et
terram comedes cunctis diebus vite tue. Muli/
eri quoqß dixit. Multiplicabo erūnas tuas: τ cõ
ceptus tuos: in dolore paries filios τ ſb viri po
testate eris: τ ipe dominabitur tibi. Ade vo dixit
Maledicta terra in opere tuo i laboribus come
des ex ea: spinas τ tribulos germinabit tibi: in
sudore vultus tui vesceris pane tuo: donec reuer
taris in terram de qua sumptus es. Et cū feciſſz
eis deus tunicas pelliceas eiecit eos de paradi/
so collocans ante illum cherubin cum flammeo
gladio: vt viam ligni vite custodiat.

Adam primus homo formatus de limo
terre triginta annorū apparens imposi/
to nomine Eua vxori sue. Cuz de fructu
ligni vetiti oblato abvxore sua comediſſet: eie/
cti sunt de paradiso voluptatz: in terram maledi
ctionis vt iuxta imprecationez domini dei. Adã
in sudore vultus sui operaretur terram: et pane
suo vesceretur. Eua quoqß in erūnis viueret fili/
os quoqß pareret in dolore. quam incompabili
splendore decorauit. eã felicitatis sue inuid⁹ ho
stis decepit: cū leuitate feminea fructus arboris
temerario ausu degustauit: τ virū ſiẽ‚ſn sentēti/
am suam traxit. Deinde perizomatibus foliorū
susceptis ex delitiaz orto in agro ebron vna cuz
viro pulsa exul venit. Tandem cuz partus dolo
res sepius expta fuiſſet cuz laboribus in senū τ
tande in mortez sibi a domino predictã deuenit.

ILLUSTRATION FROM THE WELTCHRONIK PRINTED
BY ANTON KOBERGER AT NUREMBERG, 1493.

canticorum is found in a *Rosetum* printed by Van Os in 1494. It is significant to note the relatively late dates of the reappearances of these blocks from the equipment of the early Dutch printer or printers. Because of the perambulatory habits of some of the early printers, it is not safe for us to draw conclusions from these reappearances as to the locale of the earlier printing office or offices. Regarding this we are still left in ignorance.

At Gouda, woodcuts made their first appearance as book illustrations in 1480 in the *Dyalogus creaturarum,* a book of fables printed in the office of Gerard Leeu. This work was so popular that many editions, in both Latin and Dutch, were brought out in the Netherlands during the fifteenth century. A series of cuts of better design, closely related to the technique of the block-books, illustrated the *Gesten van Romen* printed in 1481 by Leeu.

Satisfactory but by no means distinguished book illustrations were executed by Dutch designers and craftsmen for books printed at Antwerp, Delft, Deventer, and other cities. The designer who illustrated for Jacob Bellaert, the first known printer at Haarlem, also gave evidence of a technical kinship with the illustrators of the *Speculum* and the block books, but with this slender clue ends the relationship of the later printing to the works believed by some to have been printed earlier in that city.

None of the Dutch book illustrations approach the quality of the German and Italian contemporaneous work. As they are of interest chiefly to the specialist, we are not warranted in dealing with them here in more detail.

In books printed in France during the fifteenth century, the most important function of the woodcut was to provide borders and initials to decorate books of hours and other liturgical works. Such use, being decorative in purpose, rather than illustrative, will be dealt with in Chapter XVIII. There was, however, a reasonable

DÜRER'S FOUR HORSEMEN, FROM THE APOCALYPSE
PRINTED AT NUREMBERG IN 1498.

amount of true book illustration which was characteristically French. But here again the great majority of the French illustrative work did not measure up in virtuosity of design to the contemporary work of the Italian and German artists.

The French illustrations that persist in my own memory, because of their dramatic quality, are those in numerous editions of the *Dance of Death,* or a similarly cheerful treatise on the art of dying becomingly. The earliest French book illustrations are found in books printed at Lyons, a city located on the important routes of international commerce. The first book with woodcuts, the *Mirouer de la Redemption,* was printed at Lyons in 1478 by Martin Huss, who used the blocks of the edition printed at Basel two years earlier by Bernhard Richel. This popular book ran through many editions.

Among the earliest work of local authorship were the rather primitive woodcuts illustrating *L'Abusé en court,* a satire on court life, produced by an anonymous printer, who also issued other illustrated books.

Guillaume Le Roy, the first printer at Lyons, began work in 1473. Until 1483 his operations were financed by a local merchant, Barthélemy Buyer, whose name appeared in the joint imprint. In 1483, after Buyer's death, Le Roy brought out a French edition of the *Aeneid,* illustrated with woodcuts of amateurish execution.

The outstanding Lyonnese illustrated book is the *Comoediae* of Terence, printed in 1493 by Johann Trechsel, a printer who emigrated to Lyons from Mainz, quite likely bringing with him a German artist whose handiwork is seen in this volume. The frontispiece, showing a theater of the period, with the cubicles of the prostitutes underneath, is reproduced on page 259.

A book of special interest to those interested in printing is the edition of *La grant danse macabre* printed by Matthias Huss, early in 1500, according to the modern calendar. In this book the agents

ILLUSTRATION FROM THE COMOEDIAE OF TERENCE
PRINTED BY JOHANN TRECHSEL, LYONS, 1493.

of death are seen calling people away from various trades and professions. This is, however, the only French fifteenth-century edition picturing the grim reapers summoning printers from their work at case, press, and bookstore. This celebrated illustration is reproduced on page 235.

Well-illustrated books were produced at Toulouse, Abbeville, Rouen, and in other French communities, but limitations of space restrict our further discussion to the work produced at the capital.

Jean Dupré, in collaboration with Desiderius Huym, was responsible for the first illustrated book printed at Paris, a Paris missal which was completed in 1481. A number of missals for other dioceses were issued by the same press. The first book in the French language to be illustrated was of quite different character. Boccaccio's *Les cas et ruynes des nobles hommes et femmes* was also printed by Dupré in 1484. The illustrations are well done.

Pierre le Rouge, member of an extensive family of scribes and illuminators, turned printer and brought out highly creditable illustrated books, his *chef d'œuvre* being *La mer des hystoires,* brought out in two folio volumes in 1488 and 1489. The woodcuts are of excellent quality, but many are repeated again and again.

The first illustrated book to be printed on the Iberian peninsula was an edition of the ubiquitous *Fasciculus temporum* produced by Alfonso del Puerto and Bartolomé Segura at Seville in 1480. The blocks, however, were of slight artistic significance. Pablo and Juan Hurus operated an important printing office at Saragossa, from which issued from 1489 onward a succession of illustrated books, which were also of slight interest because of the fact that they either used the blocks cut for earlier European editions, or unblushingly copied them.

The earliest illustrations which were characteristically Spanish were, according to the competent opinion of Arthur Hind, those in

81

Eydelhart was vol böser list
Dann Er aus vil vrsachen wist
Wurd Er wider dem Tewren mann
Geleich ein anndre schalckheit tan
So mocht Ers newr böser machen
Darumb Er still stund in sachen
Ein klein zeit bis Er kunndt ermessen
Das Tewrdanninck des het vergessen

A PAGE FROM THE
THEWERDANCK, 1517.

the *Doze trabajos de Hercules,* by Enrique de Villena, printed by Antonio de Centenera at Zamora in 1483. Another typically Spanish subject is found in the frontispiece of the *Regimiento de los principes,* by Egidio Colonna, printed at Seville in 1494 by Ungut and Stanislaus Polonus.

The most important illustrated book produced in Portugal within the period of the incunabula was the *Vita Christi* by Ludolphus de Saxonia, printed at Lisbon jointly by Valentin Fernandez and Nicolao de Saxonia.

Woodcut illustration did not appear in any book printed in England until about 1481, when Caxton used some highly amateurish blocks in the *Mirrour of the World,* an English version of the *Speculum historiale* by Vincent de Beauvais. At about the same time, Caxton used some of the blocks cut for the *Mirrour* in his third edition of *Cato parvus et magnus.*

In the second English edition of the *Game of Chesse* by Jacobus de Cessolis, which came from Caxton's press some time about 1483, appeared some illustrations more vigorous in style but only slightly better in design and cutting. The woodcuts illustrating the *Subtyl Hystoryes and Fables of Esope* were obviously inspired by the illustrations in continental editions of this classic. Other important English works of the fifteenth century, such as the *Canterbury Tales,* the *Golden Legend,* the *Fifteen Oes,* books of hours, and many others, were illustrated with woodcuts; but none of these latter were of marked artistic merit and in none do we observe the emergence of a characteristic national style.

Of the illustrated books of the fifteenth century the German are the most numerous and the Italian are the finest. France also made notable contributions, resembling the Italian more than the German work but marked by distinctive national characteristics. The most famous of the illustrated books produced on German soil during this

period—the *Schatzbehalter,* the Nuremberg *Weltchronik,* and the Breydenbach *Peregrinationes*—are all executed in a finished technique which, while it accomplishes much in elaboration, has lost something of the naive charm which one finds in such illustrations as those produced at Augsburg in the seventies.

In Italy the best illustrated book of this century is undoubtedly the *Hypnerotomachia,* although here again its more conscious artistry has nothing of the direct effectiveness shown in earlier and more primitive works such as the Florentine editions of Savonarola's tracts. The blocks of the *Hypnerotomachia,* however, provide an outstanding example of observance of one of the cardinal principles of good book illustration: that the plates should key, in color and weight of line, with the color and weight of the type, so that both together form a harmonious ensemble.

During the sixteenth century Germany still specialized in the wood block. The *Thewerdanck* of 1517, a page of which is reproduced on page 261, is probably the finest book ever achieved by the craftsmen of that nation in the point of the successful welding of decoration and typography in a unified design.

Engraved Book Illustration

NOT all of the early printed books which were illustrated depended on woodcuts. Illustrations engraved in intaglio on copperplates were also used, but to a very limited extent. The results obtained with this method were not, apparently, satisfactory, for we find that most of the printers who tried engraved illustrations did not continue their use. Books first illustrated by engravings are found in later editions with the copperplates replaced by woodcuts, affording clear evidence that the increased ease of printing justified the expense of making over the plates.

The difficulty, of course, was that intaglio engravings did not print by the same process or on the same press as the type forms. This necessitated two entirely independent printings to impress text and picture on a single sheet, whereas the printer depending on woodcuts accomplished the same result with a single pull of the press. And with labor and press equipment doubled, there still remained the difficulty of registering the picture in proper position with respect to the text.

Because of this latter difficulty, the earliest books in which engraved illustrations appear have the plates printed on separate leaves and inserted into the book, or printed on thin paper, trimmed, and pasted into position. This cumbrous procedure quite naturally contributed to the virtual abandonment of intaglio engravings for use as book illustrations.

The fine detail possible to the engraver, however, made his plates especially suitable for maps and charts which had to be

rendered minutely. This led to a wider use of intaglio plates in geographies and other works of like character.

With intaglio engravings, it is the line which is incised into the plate which shows in black on the printed sheet. The whole area of the plate is covered with ink, the top or flat surface is then wiped free of ink, the dampened sheet of paper placed on the plate. Paper and plate are then subjected to heavy pressure between two rollers, through which they are drawn so that the ink is sucked out of the depressions in the plate onto the surface of the paper.

It is clear that woodcuts antedate intaglio engravings, the earliest of which were probably produced by goldsmiths. The first dated intaglio print is of the year 1446: one in a Passion series preserved at Berlin, ascribed to an anonymous engraver referred to as the Master of the Year 1446. Other undated engravings are believed to have been executed at least a decade earlier.

One group of early engravers was apparently working in the region of the Upper Rhine; another contemporary group shows evidence of a Flemish or Burgundian locale.

An unknown engraver, known as the Master E. S. (the initials with which he signed some of his plates), who worked from 1466 onward, exerted a great influence on the technical progress of intaglio engraving. He was probably a native of the region around Strasbourg, originally a goldsmith, who is thought to have served an apprenticeship as an engraver somewhere in the vicinity of Basel under the Master of the Playing Cards. The art was carried still farther by Martin Schongauer, who was more of an artist than a goldsmith. Many of his plates give evidence of real genius, emancipated from Gothic limitations.

In what printed book engraved illustrations first were used is a question not easy to resolve. In one copy only of the *Recuyell of the Hystoryes of Troye* translated by William Caxton and printed

by him in collaboration with Colard Mansion at Bruges between 1474 and 1476, is inlaid on the first leaf an engraving apparently showing Caxton presenting a copy of his book to Margaret of Burgundy. It is probable that this engraving was nearly if not exactly contemporary with the printing of the book, though it was not intended to serve as an illustration for all copies of the edition, but merely for insertion in the one presentation copy. This hypothesis is supported by the appearance in the third of four distinct issues of Boccaccio's *De la ruine des nobles hommes et femmes,* printed by Colard Mansion alone in 1476, of nine engravings unquestionably made to illustrate the text, and subsequently colored by hand. Two copies of a fourth issue have but eight engravings. All are printed separately and pasted in rather than printed directly on the same sheet as the text. Arthur Hind, of the British Museum, believes the Caxton plate was executed by "an engraver of the same school as the Boccaccio illustrator, if not by the same hand." Hofer believes we have to deal with two different artists.

Though dated 1476, there is some question as to the exact time of appearance of the third and fourth issues of the Boccaccio, containing the pasted-in illustrations. It is, however, certain that they appeared before 1483, in which year Mansion, having abandoned the engraving technique, brought out a new edition of the same text illustrated with woodcuts!

Another contestant for the distinction of being the first book illustrated with engravings is Ptolemy's *Cosmographia,* which has recently been proved by contemporary documentary evidence to have been printed at Bologna by Dominicus de Lapis on June 23, 1477—in spite of the fact that its obviously inaccurate colophon gives the date as 1462. In this volume are included twenty-six maps engraved by Taddeo Crivelli of Ferrara.

In 1477 (a date questioned by one authority in spite of the

colophon) was printed at Florence by Niccolo' di Lorenzo the *Monte Sancto di Dio* by Antonio Bettini, which is important in that the third of three plates by an unidentified engraver is printed on the same paper as the text of the book. The printing of the plates is indifferent and, as Hofer tells us, the register of the third plate in all five of the known copies is poor, providing additional evidence of the difficulty experienced by fifteenth-century printers in combining the techniques of letterpress and intaglio. In the second edition the engraved plates were replaced by woodcuts.

A finer edition of Ptolemy was printed at Rome in 1478 by Buckinck, with twenty-seven well-printed maps designed, if not engraved, by Conrad Sweynheym, the pioneer Italian printer whom we have already encountered. As Sweynheym died in 1473 or 1474, the designs at least may have antedated Crivelli's engravings for the 1477 edition.

In spite of difficulties, Niccolo' di Lorenzo continued to attempt the illustration of books by copperplate engravings. He ambitiously projected the first illustrated edition of Dante, planning to print an engraving at the head of each of a hundred cantos, on the same sheet of paper as the text. The outcome was little short of ludicrous. Only nineteen illustrations for the *Inferno,* out of the hundred projected, were ever completed, and only three of these are known to have been printed on the same paper as the text. The remainder of the nineteen are found in some copies only, but printed separately and pasted in. The printers neglected to leave space for the engraving to head the first canto, so it was printed in the bottom margin of the page! Here the knife of the binder has invariably cropped it. This was the printer's last attempt to use intaglio illustrations.

There was almost no use of engravings as book illustrations in Germany, France, or Spain. An isolated exception was a French translation of Breydenbach's *Peregrinationes* printed at Lyons in

1488, illustrated by engraved copies of the noble woodcuts in the original Mainz edition, which had appeared two years earlier. The experience of book printers in the fifteenth century with engraved illustration appears, therefore, to have begun and ended in frustration and disappointment.

XVIII

Early Book Decoration

IT was not long after man had learned to print books set in movable types that he gave thought to their embellishment and beautification. There were two ways in which books could be made more interesting and attractive to their readers: one, by illustration; the other, by ornamentation. It so happened, however, that the ornamentation came first in the evolution of the printed book from the crudest of experimental impressions to the pinnacles of bookmaking art.

The first appearance in printing of elements disparate from the individual types in the case is found in the large initial letters, apparently cut on metal, which were used in printing the papal indulgences at Mainz in 1454 and 1455. In these, one of which may be seen in the reproduction on page 148, the decorative element was modest indeed.

The next appearance of printed book decoration was of outstanding importance, reaching a high peak of artistic and technical excellence. In the Psalter of 1457, printed at Mainz by Fust and Schoeffer, appeared a number of purely decorative initials of much beauty, printed or stamped in one and in two colors. The simpler letters are printed in one color, generally red, while the more elaborate ones are printed or stamped in two colors, usually red and a rather light blue. The noteworthy point is that the register of the two colors is exact.

There has been considerable difference of opinion regarding the material of the blocks and the method used in printing these cele-

brated initials, one of which, on the colophon page, is reproduced on page 290. Hind believes they were originally cut on wood, metal casts from the wood blocks being used for printing or stamping. To the present writer it appears more likely that they were engraved directly by a goldsmith on a reasonably hard metal, such as brass. These same blocks were used in a number of different editions of the Psalter that appeared in succeeding years. In the 1490 edition the blocks show signs of wear, which appears to me to support the hypothesis that they were engraved directly on metal, rather than stamped from casts of the original woodcuts.

Since the ornamental portion of the letters prints over the type matter in some places, it is evident that the initials were added after the printing of the black forms. Since a small "director" letter appears under some of them, and since a copy of the 42-line Bible contains the same design of two-color initial added by the hand of the rubricator, it seems at least likely that the initials were stamped on the pages in the rubricator's studio.

Similar initials appear in two other books printed by Fust and Schoeffer, the *Durandus* of 1459 and the *Canon missae* of about the same date. After this date, except for the later issues of the Psalter, printers at Mainz and elsewhere confined themselves to single-color initials. Perhaps this first great experiment in book decoration proved to cost more in time and effort than it was worth.

The next appearance of book decoration was in Italy about 1470, but while allowed for by the printer, the decorative elements were stamped in later, probably by the rubricator. These initials and borders were actually intended as aids to the illuminator, who was expected to go over them with colors and gold. Such ornamental features are found in certain copies of a Suetonius printed at Rome in 1470 by Sweynheym and Pannartz, a Virgil printed at Venice by Bartholomaeus Cremonensis in 1472, and in many other books

P. Candidi in libros Appiani fophiſtę Alexandrini ad Nico-
laum quintū ſummū pontificem Pręfatio incipit feliciſſime.

Ppiani Alexandrini hiſtoriā ſeu ue-
terū incuria: ſeu temporū iniquitate
deperditā: & ueluti longo poſtlimi-
nio ad nos redeunte optime: ac maxi
me pōtifex Nicolae ǫuinte tuo nutu
tuoǫ imperio e gręca latinam facere
inſtituiſ ut non modo apud noſtros
nota eſſet ſedulitas mei obſequij: ſed
ad poſteros quoǫ uirtutis tuę fama
tranſiret. Quid enim dignius tuis meritis impendi poteſt/ǫ ut
ij: qui in ſequenti ęuo hęc aliquando legent cum ędificiorum
magnitudinem ornatū intuebunt: quę ętate noſtra tuo auſpi-
cio confecta ſunt/ te Nicolaū eum eſſe intelligant: qui nō mi-
norem in recuperandis libris/ ǭ in reſtituendis moenibus huic
urbī adhibueris curam. Et pfecto licet illa pręclara: & magna
ſint: quę manu & arte conſtant: & a plurimis ſūmmo ingenio
diligentiaǫ parantur/ pręſtantiora tamen habenda erunt: quę
ſtudijs adiunctaſ monumentis quoǫ ſeruantur litterarū. Itaǫ
qui Petri Baſilicę contiguam domum admirant a te ſtructam
quadrato lapide: qui Hadriani molem uiciſſim reſtitutā: qui
deorū templū ab Agrippa conditū a te ſuffectū ętate noſtra :
qui plura alia breui ceſſura uetuſtati ni tua caritas admouiſſet
pias manus/ eoſdē quoǫ admirari cōueniet tot illuſtres libros
ad nos tua opera traductos e gręcis: nec tuam ſapientiā nomen
dignitatē cōmemoratione laudis ſuę immunes pręterire: etſi
non huius temporis eſſe putem uirtutes tuas elegantioti ſtilo
debitas in mediū proferre hoc ſolū dixerim te bis rebus geſtis
aſſecutūm ut uerus pręſul digniſſimus princeps habetere. Sed
ut ad Appianū redeam Doleo equidē ſumme pater bis i libris

printed by Jenson, John and Wendelin of Spire, and others. The blocks thus stamped in were in pure outline specifically intended for subsequent coloring.

The next important step in the progress of book decoration was the development of ornaments, designed to print in the same form with the type and be sufficient in themselves, not requiring any attention from the hand of the illuminator. Such work was first seen in the books printed at Venice from 1476 onward by Erhard Ratdolt, a native of Augsburg, Germany, and his two partners; Bernhard, designated as *Maler* or "painter," also of Augsburg, and Peter Löslein. It was undoubtedly Bernhard, the painter, who designed the fine initial letters, borders, and border units which are the glory of the Ratdolt books.

We see some of the border units in the world's first complete title page, reproduced on page 563, and the border and an initial letter in the illustration on page 271. Some were done in delicately drawn outline, but the majority were white designs of floral motif against black backgrounds. These woodcuts established a standard in book decoration which passed unchallenged until the time of William Morris and his disciples.

Decorative effects can also be achieved by the combination of ornaments cut on punches, driven into matrices, and cast as type units. The earliest use of type ornaments, or fleurons, known to me was in Capranica's *Arte di ben morire,* printed by G. and A. Alvise, at Verona, Italy, in 1478, a page from this volume being reproduced on page 273. It was in later centuries, however, that type ornaments were used most extensively and effectively.

At Augsburg and Ulm, in Germany, the printers responsible for the issue of illustrated books were also making use of woodcut initials and border ornaments from 1473 onward. And, starting about 1475, pictorial initials, with scenes in the book shown inside

a lo feruo tuo o ancilla tua laborante in le extre
me anguftie necceffitade la facia tua gloriofa e
difpergi tutti li foi inimici in uirtute del tuo dile
ctiffimo figliolo fignor noftro Iefu Chrifto e in
la uirtute de la fua fanctiffima croce libera da o-
gni anguftia lanima del corpo acio che lui reda
a lo figonre dio eternalmente . 🌸❖🌸🌸❖🌸

A LAVDE DE LO OMNIPOTEN
TE DIO E DE LA SVA MADRE
VERGINE MARIA E TVTA LA
CORTE CELESTIALE FV CON
PITA QVESTA OPERETA MOL
TO SALVTIFERA A LE ANIME:
CHE PASSANO DE QVESTA
VITA:IMPRESSA IN VE
RONA DE ❖ LANNO
.M.CCCC.LXXVIII.
A DI XXVIII
DE APRI
.LE.

🌸❖🌸🌸❖🌸🌸❖🌸

.FINI.

🌸❖🌸 :S: 🌸❖🌸

🌸

the letter, began to appear in books printed in these and other German cities. These latter must be considered as hybrids of decoration and illustration. A similar crossing of the two elements is seen in the borders appearing in the Bible printed about 1478 at Cologne by Heinrich Quentell, one page of which is reproduced on page 251.

The next point of interest from the decorative viewpoint is France in the last two decades of the fifteenth century. In 1481, Jean Dupré printed at Paris the Verdun missal, one of the illustrations enclosed within a four-piece woodcut decorative border. Dupré, according to his own statement, made use of craftsmen from Venice, then a leading center of liturgical printing, in the printing of many missals, breviaries, and other works of like character.

One of the early books in which decorative borders played an important role was in the *Mer des hystoires,* in two volumes, printed at Paris in 1488 and 1489 by Pierre le Rouge, the outstanding member of a family of French printers. In 1488, at Rouen, Jean le Bourgeois printed the first volume of *Le Livre des vertueux faix de plusieurs nobles chevaliers,* using blocks for border units and illustrations undoubtedly supplied by the printer Jean Dupré of Paris, who printed the second volume in the same year.

A characteristic element of decoration in French books was the calligraphic L, for the first letter of the definite article, which graced many a title page. Interwoven with the letter we find figures and faces which are often grotesque. A particularly fine example of one of these initials may be seen on page 567.

The small books of private devotion, the *Horae Beatae Virginis Mariae,* or books of hours, had been produced for several centuries, in the most elaborate form, by scribes and illuminators. When the printers turned their hands to producing *Horae,* the most distinguished work was done first in France at Paris, though soon copied in other countries. Following the manuscript models, each page

Dyalogus Salomonis et marcolfi.

Alomon cū staret sup solium dauid prīs sui plenꝰ sapiētie z diuicijs vidit quendā hoiem Marcolfū noīe a pte orientiꝭ veniētem facie turpissimū difformē·z tn̄ eloqn̄tissimū Vxor eius erat cū eo q̄ nis erat terribilis z rustica Cū eos ābos ꝺspectui suo pic exhiberi iussissz·stabāt ambo an̄ eū se mutuo ꝺspiciētes Statura itaq; Marcolfi fuit cur ta z grossa·caput habuit grāde·frōte latissimā rubicūdā et rugosā· aures pilosas z vsq; ad mediū maxillaꝝ pendētes·ockos grossos z liꝯosos·labium sꝭcominꝰ q̄si caballinū· barbā sordidā z fetosā q̄si hirci·manꝰ trūcas·digitos breues z grossos Pedes rotūdos·nasū spissū z giꝲposū·labia magꝲ z grossa·faciē azininā·capillos veluti sūt spinule hircoꝝ· Calciamta pedū eiꝰ rustica erāt nimis Et cingebat renes eiꝰ ꝺimidiꝰ gladiꝰ tirpatā Et in sumo capite repalatū capiculū ꝺ|tilia factū eiecit

A PAGE SHOWING A PICTORIAL INITIAL AND DECO-
RATIVE BORDER UNITS, FROM A BOOK PRINTED BY
KNOBLOCHTZER AT STRASBOURG, ABOUT 1482.

whether it was made up of text or illustration, or a combination of both, was enclosed within a decorative border, usually made up of four or more separate blocks. Most of the decorative blocks were cut on wood, though metal was often used, it being stated by Dupré in an edition of 1489 that the pictures were *imprimées en cuyure,* or "printed in copper."

Antoine Vérard, a Paris publisher, was most active in the production of books of hours, entrusting their production to various printers, but depending principally on Jean Dupré, whose work we have already noticed in other connections.

Philippe Pigouchet, the printer, working in collaboration with the publisher Simon Vostre produced many fine books of hours, in which there is an even gray tone in the decorative border units achieved by delicate stippling of the black backgrounds. Much of the best work in this field carried over into the early years of the sixteenth century.

The *Horae* printed in Germany, though inspired by the French work, did not measure up to it in virtuosity, giving us the impression of having been executed by heavier hands. The contrast between the German and the French styles is well exemplified by the reproduction on the opposite page from a *Zeitglöcklein* printed at Basel in 1492.

Borders appeared in *Horae* printed in England by Machlinia, Caxton, and Wynkyn de Worde during the last fifteen years of the century, but they were crude in design as compared with the excellent French work of the period.

Really distinguished book decoration is observed in the work of Spanish and Portuguese printers of the fifteenth century. An especially fine one-piece border was used about 1487 at Hijar by Alfonso Fernández de Córdoba, and later, with Hebrew initials of similar design, in Hebrew books printed at Lisbon by Rabbi Elieser.

Borders which are unmistakably Spanish in design were used at Valencia in 1490 in the edition of *Tirant lo blanch* printed by Nicolaus Spindeler. This border, apparently cut on metal, was in

DECORATIVE BORDERS IN A ZEITGLÖCKLEIN, BASEL, 1492.

five parts, the fifth being a decorative band separating the two columns of text. Coats of arms, ably rendered in woodcut, are also encountered frequently in early Spanish printing.

XIX

Some Special Problems

W HEN the earliest printers, trained in Mainz or elsewhere, confidently set out to carry their wonderful new
craft into all parts of Europe, they soon discovered that
they had command of only the rudiments of printing. So long as
they were called upon to print only books in Latin or in the vernacular languages of western Europe, they managed very well with
their fonts of the commonly used gothic or roman types. But the
widening range of the literature presented to them for reproduction
in type soon demanded of them the cutting of types for other and
different alphabets.

Greek was the classic language second in importance to Latin,
and even in the works of the standard Latin authors there were
quotations in Greek. But Greek had an alphabet of its own and
could not be represented satisfactorily with roman letters. The first
printers who really confronted the problem of supplying Greek
types were Sweynheym and Pannartz, who found a Greek font
necessary for their edition of the works of Lactantius, completed in
1465. Work was begun on this book, however, before the Greek
font had been finished; in the earlier pages of it there are only
occasional uses of Greek, a word or two here and there; for the
longer Greek passages, blank spaces were left in the printed text
for the later insertion of the Greek by hand. But later pages show
extensive use of a quite presentable face of Greek type.

A page of the Sweynheym and Pannartz Lactantius is reproduced on page 185. The Greek characters shown there are western

rather than Hellenic, but they have the feel of the roman letters with which they were used. The many accents were added by hand.

In the same year, 1465, Peter Schoeffer at Mainz also made some Greek types for use in the first printed edition of Cicero's *De officiis* and *Paradoxa*. But Schoeffer's Greek characters were crude and bungling, evidently designed in complete ignorance of the Greek language. Only ten or a dozen distinctively Greek letters were provided, the rest of the Greek alphabet being eked out with roman letters which were thought to approximate the Greek forms. Even if Schoeffer's attempt at Greek type should be found actually to antedate the Greek font of Sweynheym and Pannartz, the credit would still rest with the Subiaco printers for the earliest successful use of Greek in printing.

Some fifteenth century printers got around their lack of Greek types by transliterating Greek in roman types. Schoeffer himself did this in 1470, but as he knew no Greek he simply used the roman types that looked to him most like the Greek letters in his copy. The results were truly remarkable!

Nicolas Jenson in 1471 cut a beautifully clear and legible Greek font, which deserved to become a standard for future designers, as did his roman letters. A derivative of this Jenson font was used in the first book of which the text was entirely in Greek—an edition of the pseudo-Homeric *Batrachomyomachia* ("Battle of the Frogs and Mice"), which was printed, presumably, by Thomas Ferrandus at Brescia about 1474. The earliest book wholly in Greek which was dated and signed by its printer was an edition of the *Epitomé*, a grammar by Constantinus Lascaris, printed at Milan by Dionysius Paravisinus in 1476. A page of this volume is reproduced on page 281. The type shows a tendency to imitate the ligatures and contractions of Greek manuscripts of the time—a tendency which Jenson in his Greek type had almost entirely disregarded. The font of the

Epitomé is the first in which Greek capital letters were used, but the capitals are not at all in harmony with the lower-case letters.

Aldus Manutius, at Venice, devoted himself especially to the publication of Greek classics. But most unfortunately for the fame of Greek literature, he took as pattern for his Greek types the cursive handwriting used by fifteenth-century Greeks in Italy for correspondence and business. But it must have been inconceivably difficult to set—the first Greek font which Aldus used is said to have contained, with its innumerable ligatures and contractions, over 1,400 sorts! This preposterous number was soon reduced, but the sorts in the Greek case still remained high in the hundreds. In spite of its cumbersomeness, however, the cursive Greek introduced by Aldus became the typographic norm, with the result that one of the most beautiful of all the world's languages continued to appear in an almost illegible and hideous printed form for some two hundred and fifty years.

France, Germany, and England eventually accepted the Aldine style of printing Greek. In Spain, however, the first book printed there in which Greek was used—the so-called Complutensian Polyglot New Testament printed at Alcalá by Arnaldo Guillen de Brocar in 1514—shows a most beautiful Greek font modeled, apparently, on a manuscript by a tenth-century Greek calligrapher. In quite recent years an attempt to revive this type was made by Robert Proctor, in England, in a font which was used for printing his edition of some of the plays of Aeschylus, published in 1904, just after the death of that brilliant young editor and bibliographer.

Any possible improvement in Greek type was halted when Francis I, king of France, ordered the cutting of his Royal Greek type for editions of the Greek classics to be printed at his command by the Estiennes. This type, first used in 1543, was cut by Claude Garamond from designs by Angelos Vergetios, a distinguished

ΡΗΜΑ ὈΡΙΣΤΙΚὸΝ ἘΝΕΡΓΗΤΙΚὸΝ
ΣΥΖΥΓίΑΣ ΠΡῴΤΗΣ ΤῶΝ ΒΑΡΥΤό –
ΝΩΝ ·   Ἐνεστὼς.

Τύπτω Τύπτεις Τύπτει / Τύπτετον Τύπτετον / Τύπτομεν Τύπτετε Τύπτουσι ·

Παρατατικὸς.

Ἔτυπτον ἔτυπτες ἔτυπτε / ἐτύπτετον ἐτυ.
πτέτην / ἐτύπτομεν ἐτύπτετε ἔτυπτον.

Παρακείμενος

Τέτυφα Τέτυφας Τέτυφε / Τετύφατον Τετύφα
τον / Τετύφαμεν Τετύφατε Τετύφασι.

Καὶ μέσος Διὰ π.

Τέτυπα Τέτυπας Τέτυπε / Τετύπατον Τετύπατον / Τετύπαμεν Τετύπατε Τετύπασι.

Ὑπερσυντέλικος.

Ἐτετύφειν ἐτετύφεις ἐτετύφει / ἐτετύφειτον ἐτε
τυφέτην / ἐτετύφειμεν ἐτετύφειτε ἐτετύφεισαν

Καὶ μέσος Διὰ π.

Ἐτετύπειν ἐτετύπεις ἐτετύπει / ἐτετύπειτον ἐτε
τυπέτην / ἐτετύπειμεν ἐτύπειτε ἐτετύπεισαν.

Ἀόριστος πρῶτος.

Ἔτυψα ἔτυψας ἔτυψε / ἐτύψατον ἐτυψάτην /
ἐτύψαμεν ἐτύψατε ἔτυψαν.   Ἀόριστος β.
Ἔτυπον ἔτυπες ἔτυπε / ἐτυπέτον ἐτυπέτην /
ἐτύπομεν ἐτύπετε ἔτυπον.

Greek scholar. It was a technical triumph in its precision of execution, but it followed the Aldine tradition; a font used by Robert Estienne contained 430 sorts, of which 367 were ligatures and contractions.

The Royal Greek became all the style and delayed the development of Greek printing for another two centuries. The shackles of its oppressive tradition were not loosened until 1756, when Robert and Andrew Foulis, at Glasgow, produced an edition of the epics of Homer with a type designed by Alexander Wilson, in which the Greek language could move with something of its native grace and power. But not until 1826, when the Cambridge University Press adopted the Porson Greek designed by Richard Porson, was the last of the Aldine peculiarities removed from the printing of Greek.

Hebrew, which also called for the cutting of another alphabet, was a living language in the fifteenth century. The earliest use of Hebrew type was probably in the first volume of Jacob ben Asher's *Arba Turim,* printed at Piove di Sacco, near Venice, by Meschullam Cusi about 1474. The fourth and last volume of this work was completed on July 3, 1475. In the meantime Abraham Gorton, at Reggio di Calabria, had completed the printing of Solomon ben Isaac's *Perusch ha tora* (a commentary on the Pentateuch) in February, 1475. But the first volume of the *Arba Turim* had undoubtedly been finished earlier.

Soncino and Venice, in Italy, became important centers of fifteenth-century Hebrew printing, but the production of Hebrew works was also an outstanding feature of the early press of Spain and Portugal, where not a few of the fifteenth-century printers were themselves Jews.

While Hebrew scholars have never been completely satisfied with the typographic rendering of their distinctive alphabet, it at least escaped the fate of Greek and has remained, at the hands of all type

designers who have essayed Hebrew fonts, reasonably simple and therefore legible.

But the providing of type for unfamiliar alphabets was among the least of the early printer's difficulties. His training included the art of preparing punches and striking matrices, so that, if he could procure the necessary materials and a satisfactory specimen of the required alphabet from which to make his type designs, he could provide himself in time with the requisite types. Of course, the best results with Greek or Hebrew types could be attained only by type designers who knew those languages. In this connection it is important to note that many of the early printers were university men and scholars and that types for Hebrew and Greek were first cut successfully by learned Jews and Greeks, or under their direction.

A greater problem was presented by the printing of books on mathematics. Even with all the facilities of today, the type composition of mathematical works is a job for printing plants with special type equipment and with compositors experienced in that sort of work. For the early printers, even with the relatively simple notation of fifteenth-century mathematics, books in this field were severe tests of their ingenuity, and for that reason the number of such books is relatively small.

The *Elements of Geometry* of Euclid, a Greek mathematician who lived at Alexandria about 300 B.C., was in liveliest demand among fifteenth-century scholars, who had for the most part to be satisfied with manuscript copies. The first printed edition of the *Elements* appeared at Venice in May, 1482, from the press of Erhard Ratdolt, the first printer to solve the problem of producing mathematical diagrams typographically. The result of Ratdolt's efforts was not only successful, but brilliant. The book was adequate mathematically and it was a thing of beauty as well, thanks to the characteristic borders and initials which this distinguished typo-

graphic innovator introduced. A page of this important mathematical and typographical monument is reproduced on page 285.

Ratdolt, however, left no clue to his method of making the geometrical diagrams which occur in profusion throughout the book, and to this day there are differences of opinion as to the printing elements with which these diagrams were produced. Gilbert Redgrave, in his standard monograph of Ratdolt, held that the printer used in this work upwards of 420 different woodcuts, not counting about two hundred diagrams which might have been made with metal rules. De Morgan, on the other hand, expresses the belief that "though at first sight they seem to be woodcuts, yet a closer inspection makes it seem probable that they were produced from metal lines."

I incline to the latter view, believing that an ingenious and patient craftsman could achieve the result by bending or fitting metal rules and filling in the spaces with molten lead. The inclusion in the diagrams of words set in type, inside of circles and other figures, would be relatively easy by this method, but exceedingly difficult, if not impossible, if woodcuts had to be mortised to hold the short lines of type.

Although we credit Ratdolt with the first successful solution of the problem of geometric diagrams in a printed book, it must be added, in fairness to a less distinguished craftsman, that similar diagrams had been printed in 1481 or 1482 at Milan by Petrus of Corneno, but in a far less celebrated book, the *Perspectiua communis* by Archbishop Peckham.

Another typographic problem which long baffled the early craftsmen was the printing of music. In the Middle Ages, music had a definite place in the scheme of education. It was included among the seven sciences and also among the seven liberal arts and was closely allied, in medieval theory, with mathematics. The literature

Præclarissimus liber elementorum Euclidis perspi/
cacissimi:in artem Geometrie incipit quāfoeliciflime:

Unctus est cuius ps nō est. ℂLinea est
lōgitudo sine latitudine cui⁹ quidē ex/
tremitates ſṫ duo pūcta. ℂLinea recta
ē ab vno pūcto ad aliū breuiſſima exté/
sio ī extremitates suas vtrūq₃ eoꝛ reci
piens.ℂSupficies ē q̄ lōgitudinē ꝛ lati
tudinē tm̄ h₃:cui⁹termi quidē ſūt linee.
ℂSupficies plana ē ab vna linea ad a/
liā extēsio ī extremitates suas recipiēs
ℂAngulus planus ē duarū linearū al/
ternus �practus:quaꝝ expāsio ē sup sup/
ficiē applicatioq₃ nō directa. ℂQuādo aūt angulum ꝑtinēt due
linee recte rectilineꝰ angulus noiať. ℂ Qn̄ recta linea sup rectā
steterit duoq₃ anguli ꝟrobiq₃ fuerit eqles:eoꝝ vterq₃ rectꝰerit
ℂLineaq₃ linee supſtās eī cui supſtat ꝑpendicularis vocať.ℂAn
gulus vo qui recto maioꝛ ē obtusus dicit.ℂAngul⁹vo minoꝛ re
cto acutꝰappellať. ℂ Terminꝰē qd vniuscuiusq₃ finis ē. ℂ Figura
ē q̄ t̄nino vl termis ꝑtinet. ℂCirculꝰē figura plana vna q̄dem li/
nea q̄ circūferentia noiať:in cui⁹medio pūctꝰē : a quo⁹oēs
linee recte ad circūferētiā exeūtes sibiinuicē ſūt equales. Et hic
quidē pūctꝰcentrū circuli dř.ℂDiameter circuli ē linea recta que
sup eī centꝝ trāsiens extremitatesq₃ suas circūferentie applicans
circulū ī duo media diuidit.ℂSemicirculus ē figura plana dia
metro circuli ꝛ medietate circūferentie ꝑtenta.ℂPortio circu
li ē figura plana recta linea ꝛ parte circūferēne ꝑtenta: semicircu/
lo quidē aut maioꝛ aut minoꝛ. ℂRectilinee figure ſūt q̄ rectis li/
neis cōtinent quarū quedā trilatere q̄ trib⁹rectis lineis: quedā
quadrilatere q̄ q̄tuoꝛ rectis lineis. q̄da mltilatere que pluribus
q₃ quatuoꝛ rectis lineis continent. ℂ Figurarū trilaterarū:alia
est triangulus hn̄s tria latera equalia.Alia triangulus duo hn̄s
eq̄lia latera Alia triangulus triū inequalium laterū. Maꝝ iterū
alia est oꝛtbogoniū:vnū.ĺ rectum angulum habens.Alia ē am
bligonium aliquem,obtusum angulum habens.Alia ē oꝛigoni
um:in qua tres anguli sunt acuti. ℂFigurarū autē quadrilateraꝝ
Alia est q̄dratum quod est equilateru atq₃ rectangulū. Alia est
tetragonꝰlong⁹:q̄ est figura rectangula : sed equilatera non est.
Alia est helmuaym: que est equilatera : sed rectangula non est.

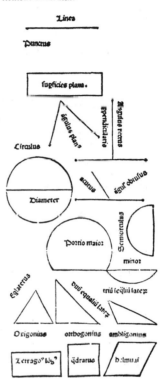

De principijs ꝑ se notis:ꝛ ꝑmo de diffini·
tionibus earandem.

Linea

Punctus

Supficies plana.

Angulus perpēdicularis

angulus planꝰ

Circulus

Diameter

acutus

ꝫgur obtusus

Semicirculus

Portio maioꝛ

minoꝛ

Eq̄laterus

duū equaliū laterū

triū sequliū lateꝝ

Oꝛigonius   orthogonius   ambligonius

Tetragoꝰlōg⁹   q̄dratus   helmuaī

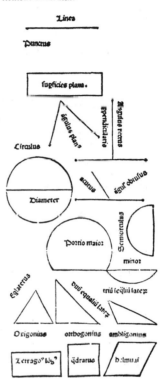

A PAGE FROM RATDOLT'S EUCLID, VENICE, **1482**.

of the fifteenth century included a number of works on musical theory. But music was also a practical part of the life of those times. It held a fixed place in the services of the church, and there was demand for service books containing the musical notation of the plainsong and chants used with the church rituals.

But the printing of musical notation was indeed a problem for the early printers. It involved printing the lines of the staff and of the variously shaped symbols for notes accurately placed upon those lines—a much more difficult matter than the setting of straight text in movable types or even than constructing geometric diagrams with pieces of metal rule. At first, the difficulty was simply avoided by leaving blank spaces on the page, to be filled in by hand with the lines and notes, as in the famous Fust and Schoeffer Psalter of 1457.

An obvious solution of the problem was to have the musical notation cut on a block of wood (or metal) which was inserted in the form and printed with the type, as was done with the *Musices opusculum* of Burtius, printed at Bologna in 1487. A number of musical incunabula show the use of this method. Another attempt at a solution was to print accurately spaced and positioned black squares representing the notes, leaving it to the rubricator, or the purchaser of the book, to draw in the staff lines.

A method which was found still more satisfactory in liturgical books was to print only the staff lines. The purchaser was then free to supply the notes of the particular chants preferred in the ecclesiastical center for which the book was bought. This left opportunity for the expression of a local choice in church music, but poor penmanship and carelessness in writing in the notes often resulted in marring an otherwise handsome service book.

Ingenious craftsmen next turned to printing the notes in black, together with the words of the text, and then supplying the staff lines, often in red, by giving the sheets a second impression. The

A PAGE FROM THE MUSICES OPUSCULUM, THE
EARLIEST BOOK CONTAINING MUSIC PRINTED FROM
BLOCKS, BOLOGNA, 1487.

first printer to use this method was Ulrich Han, or Hahn, who printed a missal for the Roman curia in October, 1476, in which the musical notation was quite successfully achieved by two impressions. In his colophon to this book the printer emphasized the fact that music had never before been printed in that manner.

For the relatively simple chants and plainsong of the church service this method of two impressions served satisfactorily, but for the more complicated notations of polyphonic choral works the printers long preferred woodcuts to the difficult process of setting the music with type elements. The most successful attempt of any early printer to print mensural music in two impressions was made by Ottaviano dei Petrucci da Fossombrone. His *Harmonice musices odhecaton,* printed at Venice in 1501, was so outstandingly successful, in its precision of register and in its graceful, dainty note forms, that this artisan has been generally hailed as the real inventor of the printing of music with movable types.

Such works as hymn books and popular songbooks, in which letterpress text accompanies the music, are still printed today with a special case containing about 460 sorts or type elements for the musical notation. But most sheet music and instrumental music is now printed by a lithographic or offset process. Musical notation, however, has not kept pace with typographic advances in other directions. Its forms are rigidly cast in a very few slightly different patterns which afford almost no flexibility to fit the kind of musical theme presented. To the music printer there is practically no difference, so far as the form of the printed representation is concerned, between a Beethoven sonata and the latest product of Tin-Pan Alley.

Desultory efforts at improvement in this respect have been made, but typographers generally seem to consider the printing of music as foreign to their concerns. Hence they have given little attention to the demands of musicians for a better style of printing music.

XX

Printers' Marks

SOON after the invention of printing, the custom arose among printers of using, under the printed statement of their part in the making of a book, a cut displaying a personal emblem or device, symbolic of the printing craft, or of the printer's name or ancestry. To a limited extent, this custom still prevails, although it is more often the publisher rather than the printer who now puts his device on the title pages of his books.

The use of distinctive marks to identify the ownership of movable property goes back to remote antiquity—even to prehistoric times. In Europe the marks of merchants on their bales and packages of goods were common in the thirteenth century and probably earlier. From a mark or device to identify ownership it was an easy transition to the trade-mark, which was used to identify the source of a product handled as an article of merchandise. It seems clear that it was the idea of a trade-mark that the printers adopted.

It is significant that practically no manuscript books ever bore producers' marks indicative of their origin, though some have been found with devices indicative of ownership, serving the same purpose as our more modern bookplates. In adopting the idea of the trade-mark, therefore, the early printers recognized that the books which they produced were different from the books made by scribes. Printed books were thus early identified as articles of commerce, moving in the channels of trade.

The earliest known printer's mark was the well-known double shield of Fust and Schoeffer. This first appeared in 1457, but strange

to relate, it has been found in only one of the surviving copies of the famous Psalter of that year—the copy in the national library at Vienna. Why the printers did not use it in all the copies they printed is one of bibliography's baffling little riddles. The device was next used in the Fust and Schoeffer Bible of 1462.

COLOPHON, WITH PRINTER'S MARK, OF THE FUST AND SCHOEFFER PSALTER OF 1457.

This earliest of printers' marks—which, incidentally, has been adopted as the emblem of the Printing House Craftsmen of America—consists of two shields hanging from a branch. On the shields are representations of some indeterminate angular objects with the addition of three stars on the right-hand shield. Some authorities have described the objects on the shields as printers' rules, but Hugh William Davies considers this description of them very doubtful, though conceding it as just possible that one or the other of them

resembles some tool used by typefounders. It is more likely, in his opinion, that the odd-looking objects were derived in the first place from early German house marks.

The device of two shields hanging from a branch became popular among the early printers. The Fust and Schoeffer mark was quite boldly counterfeited in a tract printed at Rome about 1470 in the types of Ulrich Han. Other printers, however, while using the theme of the two shields, put different emblems on them, as, for example, Jan Veldener, reputed to be the first printer to use a trademark in the Netherlands, at Louvain in 1475. Still other printers used a single pendent shield.

THE PRINTER'S MARK OF JAN VEL-DENER, LOUVAIN, 1475.

The symbolism of the emblems used by the early printers falls into a number of classifications. Many of them are imitations of armorial bearings, such as the devices using the theme of the shield or shields. Knighthood was still in flower at the time, and many a printer "made up" for himself a pseudo coat of arms, though of doubtful heraldic validity. Here and there, however, a printer was actually entitled to display armorial bearings. Thus Richard Pynson, in England, on receiving a royal appointment as king's printer became *ex officio,* so to speak, an esquire and therefore entitled to bear arms. A reproduction of his armorial device adorned his printing from 1509 to 1526.

Another numerous classification of printers' marks used pictorial representations of the printers' names. Thus the device of Richard Pynson, just mentioned, displayed three birds which are interpreted as being "pinsons," or chaffinches. Gilles Couteau displayed a number of knives in his device. The mark of Michel Le Noir, in 1500,

shows the head of a negro heraldically supported by two negresses; those of Denis Roce, or Rosse, of Paris, and of Germain Rose, of Lyons, use a rose; the two Maillets, also of Lyons, exhibited a mallet in the center of their shield. The family of Sebastien Gryphe, of Lyons, used a griffin in a number of different emblems. J. du Moulin, of Rouen, as we might expect, adopted a mill as his symbol, and so did Androw Myllar, the first printer of Scotland. The mark of

THE PRINTER'S MARK OF GILLES
COUTEAU.

P. Chandelier, of Caen, showed a candlestick, while Adam du Mont made use of the figures of Adam and Eve at the tree of forbidden fruit. Others of these so-called "punning" devices will be mentioned later, and references to them could be multiplied.

Hugely popular among early printers was the orb-and-cross design—the type of emblem made familiar in modern times by the label on the end of the carton containing soda biscuits of a well-known brand. It was the basis of the mark of the partnership of John of Cologne, Nicolas Jenson and Company, at Venice. Roberts showed in one plate, reproduced on the opposite page, thirty marks with this underlying motif, thus illustrating the persistence of the idea and the variety of its expression.

The exact significance of the symbolism in the orb and cross has never been satisfactorily determined. But Davies is perhaps on the right track when he traces the design in its primitive forms to the symbols in pagan times of the Roman divinity Mercury (the Greek Hermes), patron of merchants. But Paul Delalain thought the orb

and cross implied the connection of the printer with some religious order. There may have been such a connection in some instances, but in a great many cases pure imitation was probably the sole explanation of the use of the orb and cross in printers' marks.

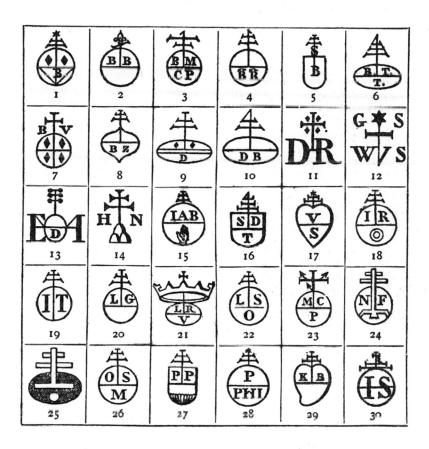

SOME VARIANTS OF THE ORB-AND-CROSS SYMBOL IN PRINTERS' MARKS.

A special class of printers' marks, of unusual historical interest, is made up of those which depict the printing press or printing implements. The best-known example of a press so used was the mark of Josse Bade, better known by his latinized name, Jodocus Badius

Ascensius, first of Lyons and later of Paris. This mark first appeared in 1507. A revised form of it, which is reproduced on page 236, appeared on the title page of a book issued in 1520. In its amended form, the compositor's stick is changed from the right hand to the left hand, the press shows an improved construction and greater strength, and the seated figure is that of a woman instead of a man.

Other sources of symbolism were myriad. Animals were introduced in some devices, also birds, serpents, fish, trees, and flowers, as well as a variety of human figures. Some of the devices tended to become elaborately pictorial. Altogether, some fifteen hundred fifteenth-century printers' marks have been depicted or described. In the space here available, we are able to discuss only a few individual marks of interest.

A device of great interest to Anglo-Saxons is, quite naturally, that used by William Caxton, the first printer in England, here reproduced in full size. The device is rather cryptic, and the authorities on Caxton have been hard put to it in their attempts to explain the significance of its elements. William Blades, the biographer of Caxton, accepted the usual interpretation of the central lettering as "W74C," the figures (note the archaic form of the figure 4) standing for the year 1474. It has been urged by some that this refers to the date of the introduction of printing into England. But this contention is obviously impossible, as the "Chess" book was printed by Caxton at Bruges, on the Continent, in 1476, and the first printing office on English soil was not established until late in that same year. Roberts considered it probable that the date is that of some epochal event in the printer's life, and this appears to be a not unreasonable conjecture. At the lower left and upper right of the design are two other symbols which Madden reads as "S" and "C" and interprets as standing for "Sancta Colonia," the city of Cologne, possibly indicating that the epochal event, whatever it may have

been, occurred when the printer was in that city in 1474. On the
other hand, Davies suggests that the central emblem may not be in-

WILLIAM CAXTON'S PRINTER'S MARK.

tended for numerals at all, but is merely a merchant's mark. He also
thinks the supposed "S" and "C" can be no more than ornaments.
Curiously enough, Caxton's device did not make its first appearance

until 1487, a considerable time after printing had been brought to England. Ten years after Caxton was established in what is now a part of London, he wished to print a Sarum missal—that is, a missal following the usage of the Salisbury diocese. As he did not have suitable types available, he sent the job to Guillaume Maynyal at Paris for printing, with the distinct understanding that the French craftsman print the book at the expense of William Caxton, of London. When the printed sheets, which were undoubtedly shipped flat, were received at Westminster, Caxton printed on the last page, which happened to be blank, his strikingly bold device, which was here used for the first time. It is thought that the English printer had it engraved especially for this purpose, in order to emphasize his own part in the publication of the book. Only one imperfect copy of this Sarum missal is known to exist.

THE SAINT ALBANS PRINTER'S MARK, 1483.

Caxton's mark is here mentioned first because of his primacy in the history of English printing. The first printer's mark to be used in England, however, appeared in two of the books issuing from the anonymous press at Saint Albans. This mark, which is here reproduced, is one of the many variants of the orb-and-cross theme, with a shield bearing the Saint Andrew's cross displayed within the circle. This was printed in red in the *Chronicles of England* in 1483 and also appeared in the *Book of Hawking,* dated 1486. Davies suggests that the mark was probably of foreign origin.

Wynkyn de Worde, a native of Lorraine, who was Caxton's successor, evidently had a distinct flair for printers' marks, for he made

use of no fewer than nine. This rather unusual diversity in trade-marks would seem almost to defeat their very purpose. The earliest of the nine much resembles Caxton's, with whose mark it is some-times confused, differing only in that it is smaller, has a different border, and a flourish inserted above and below the lettering. The second is an elongated varia-tion of the first, with the name Wynkyn de Worde in a narrow white space beneath the device.

ONE OF WYNKYN DE WORDE'S MANY PRINTER'S MARKS.

Richard Pynson, who worked at London during the last of the fifteenth and the first quarter of

MARK OF JOHN SIBERCH, CAM-BRIDGE, ENGLAND, 1521.

the sixteenth centuries, used six marks, five of which, however, were very similar. His title to heraldic bearings and the nature of his device have already been mentioned. Rich-ard Fawkes, another English printer of the early sixteenth century, used a mark which showed distinctly French influence. Richard Grafton, an author and scholar as well as a printer, who worked during the middle years of the sixteenth century, used but one mark. It was one of the "punning" devices, indicating Grafton's own name by a tree grafted on a hogshead, or "tun." The same kind of an allusion was borrowed and used by William Myddleton, in whose mark a tun appears in the middle ground of a shield.

From a purely graphic point of view the best of the early English printers' marks was one of the two used by John Siberch, the first Cambridge printer. It appeared in his first book, Galen's *De temperamentis,* about 1521, and is reproduced on page 297.

THE "WILD MAN" OF REINHARD BECK, STRASBOURG.

Finally, mention may be made here of the mark of that press which has rendered so great a service to English letters, learning, and typography—the Oxford University Press. This device has passed through several forms, but it was derived originally from the mark used by John Scolar, printer to the university in the year 1518.

Only a few of the more interesting marks used by German printers can be noted here. One of the most fascinating of the early German marks depicts "ein wilder Mann" leaning on a shield which bears the initials of Reinhard Beck, a Strasbourg printer of the early sixteenth century. Although "wild," the old fellow shown in the reproduction appears to be rather attractively good-natured. This mark, reproduced on the opposite page, with its trees and animals, also shows the tendency of some printers' marks to become pictorial.

ANTONIO BLADO'S MARK, SHOWING MOTH AND FLAME, ROME, 1548.

A novel motif chosen by Valentin Kobian, who printed at Hagenau in the second quarter of the sixteenth century, was a peacock with one foot on a cock and the other on a crouching lion, perhaps symbolical of beauty triumphant over belligerency and force.

A very handsome mark was used by Matthias Schürer in Strasbourg in the early years of the sixteenth century. If I may be permitted a digression, I would remark that I have a soft spot in my heart for this printer, because he was the first, to my knowledge, to make use of quotation marks, and quotation marks are among the minutiae of typography the history of which I have been studying off and on for a number of years past. Some day, if I am spared from the various hazards to which a typographer is exposed, I shall yet perpetrate a book of several hundred pages entirely devoted to quotation marks, their origin and their development.

Sixtus Riessinger was the first printer at Rome to adopt an em-

blem. A handsome printer's mark used in Palatino's treatise on calligraphy, printed by Antonio Blado at Rome in 1548, is here shown.

The Italian printer whose mark is of the greatest interest to book lovers is, of course, Aldus Manutius, who began his work at Venice in 1494. Not until 1502 did he adopt a mark—the famous Aldine anchor and dolphin. This mark first appeared in a volume of the works of Sedulius and other Christian poets in June, 1502. A few months later it was used in *Le terze rime di Dante* of August, 1502, a duodecimo, the first edition of this classic of Italian literature in conveniently portable form.

With slight variations this mark was used by the Aldus family until 1546. From that date until 1554 the family usually surrounded the anchor with an embellishment made up of cornucopias, cupids, and the like, approximately square in contour. From 1555 to 1574 the decorative frame was oval, and from 1575 to 1581 the anchor was almost submerged in a coat of arms granted to the family by the Emperor Maximilian.

Another famous family of early Italian printers was that which bore the name of Giunta, members of which were printing at Florence and Venice from 1480 to 1598. In all their marks a lily has a place of more or less prominence. The mark of Lucantonio Giunta is perhaps the best known. Lucantonio, who was an engraver of merit as well as a printer, was responsible for many of the engravings with which his books were illustrated, and it is probable that he engraved his own mark.

Berthold Rembolt, successor to Ulrich Gering who was one of the three pioneers who jointly introduced the art of printing into the French capital, is believed to have been the first to use a printer's mark in Paris. He is known to have used four different marks, the later ones showing a variant of the familiar orb and cross. The marks of the French fifteenth-century printers soon came to be quite

elaborate and probably surpassed in beauty those used by printers in other countries during the same period. A typical one is that adopted by Philippe Pigouchet, justly celebrated for the beautiful books of hours that he produced. Another mark of much charm, which may possibly have been drawn by Geofroy Tory, is that of Simon de Colines, who was likewise a major contributor to the renown of French printing.

One form of the olive-tree mark of Robert Estienne had reference to the address of his shop, "At the Sign of the Olive." A number of other members of this famous family of printers made use of variations of the olive-tree mark. A different mark associated with the name of Robert Estienne is that of the serpent on a rod intertwined with the stem of a climbing plant. This mark, however, was that of the "Printers of Greek to the King." Estienne was the first printer holding this office to make use of it, the mark not appearing on any books printed by Conrad Néobar, his predecessor. From Robert Estienne the serpent mark passed in succession to Charles Estienne in 1551, Adrien Turnèbe in 1553, Guillaume Morel in 1554, Morel's widow in 1564, Jean Bienné in 1565, Fédéric Morel I in 1577, and finally to Fédéric Morel II in 1581.

Jumping to the end of the sixteenth century, we find a fascinating mark used then at Paris by Sebastian Nivelle, who, at the time of his death at the age of eighty, was the dean of the typographic craft in that city. His shop, as we might expect, was in the Rue St. Jacques, "At the Sign of the Two Storks." This sign inspired Nivelle's mark, in which the corner medallions depicted scenes of filial piety.

Among the earliest printers' marks to appear in the Low Countries was that used by Jan Veldener, reproduced on page 291. Veldener printed in a number of Dutch cities between the years 1475 and 1484. The design of the two shields dependent from a branch is strongly reminiscent of the earliest of all printers' marks, that used

by Fust and Schoeffer at Mainz. Thierry Martens, one of the first printers of Alost, used a four-pronged anchor as his emblem. Colard Mansion, who was William Caxton's associate at Bruges, used a single shield dependent from a bough. Jacob Bellaert at Haarlem,

A FORM OF CHRISTOPHER PLANTIN'S DEVICE, ANTWERP.

1483-1486, used a handsome device showing a griffin bearing a blank shield displayed between two columns, the tops of which merge into an intricate ribbon pattern supporting the arms of Haarlem. This was the handiwork of Jacob Cornelis, one of the outstanding Dutch wood engravers of the fifteenth century.

Christopher Plantin, the celebrated printer of Antwerp, whose

life was full of vicissitudes, took as his printer's device a compass describing a circle and guided by a hand emerging from a cloud, as shown on the opposite page. The device bore the motto *Labore et Constancia* (By Labor and Constancy); and if ever a motto epitomized a man's life, this one expressed the life of Plantin.

The members of the Elzevir family used five different emblems of importance. Louis, the first of the family, used an eagle with a quiver of arrows together with a motto and the date 1595. The younger Louis continued this emblem with certain changes, and Isaac, the grandson, likewise used it, although he also adopted a new device, referred to as the "sage," or "hermit," who is depicted standing beneath the branches of a tree. The third Elzevir mark consisted of a palm tree bearing the motto *Assurgo pressa,* which was a device previously used by Erpenius, the professor of Oriental languages at the University of Leiden, who conducted a printing office of which the Elzevirs took over the equipment. The fourth mark showed Minerva with her attributes—the breastplate, the olive tree, and the owl. The fifth was the "Elzevir Sphere," the geographer's usual representation of the globe.

The printers' marks doubtless served some useful economic purpose in the early days of printing. But with time this means of identifying the source of production became unnecessary, and printers' marks survived, if at all, mainly as a form of title page decoration.

XXI

The Study of Incunabula

EFORE we finally take leave of the printing of the fifteenth century and proceed with our story, it will be instructive to consider briefly some of the general characteristics of our earliest printed books. What were the outward forms, what was the subject matter, what is the present inventory, of the books that are called incunabula?

First, by way of definition, the term "incunabula" (plural form of the Latin word *incunabulum,* "cradle") is used by bibliographers to refer to printed works of a time so early in the history of printing in any given locality that this printing may be said to be in its infancy. Thus it is not altogether improper to speak of American incunabula, Illinois incunabula, or even of Chicago incunabula. But *specifically,* and unless otherwise explained, the term is used to refer to the products of the European press in the fifteenth century—thus including all printing which can be dated before the year 1501.

The dating of many incunabula is by no means easy. For the most part, they had nothing corresponding to our title page, to which we look for information, not only as to the title of the book and the name of its author, but also as to the date and place of its publication and sometimes as to the name of the printer or publisher. Such incunabula as bear the information as to place of publication, name of printer, and date, carry it in a colophon at the end of the book. But about one-third of the known incunabula have no colophons, and their dates and the names of their printers and places of issue must be inferred from a study of their contents, from care-

ful scrutiny of their types and comparisons with the types of other books, from the watermarks of the paper used in them, and from references to the books or their printers in contemporary documents or other books. And not infrequently, after all such evidence has been gathered and weighed, only conjectures can be offered as to the dates and origins of a large number of these early volumes.

The paper of the early printing period was mainly of two sizes, a large, or "royal," folio, and a small, or "medium," folio, printed in sheets which were folded once to make two leaves, or four pages. For books of smaller size, more pages were printed on each sheet, which was then folded so as to make four leaves, or a "quarto," or even eight leaves, or "octavo." Page numbers were unknown in incunabula; Dr. Haebler was able to cite only one book, produced at the very close of the incunabula period, which had its pages numbered. The printers of Venice, however, introduced the practice of numbering the *leaves* of their books. It had long been the practice to number the leaves of manuscript books, but the first printers were slow to follow this usage. Our table of contents was foreshadowed by a printed "register" which in a great many cases was merely a printed list of the first words of the sheets or gatherings in a book, intended mainly to guide the binder in putting the book together correctly. This list could serve the reader, after a fashion, as a guide to the order of the chapters, or divisions, of the volume. Many other peculiarities of incunabula might be mentioned to show that, even after the problems of type production and use had been solved with considerable success, there was still much experimentation needed to determine the most satisfactory structure of the book after its sheets had been printed with its text.

A common impression is that the books of the "cradle" period of printing were mostly ponderous folios or quartos. Many of them were indeed unwieldy tomes, but the octavo format was also widely

popular, and we have already seen that Aldus Manutius, at Venice, made a specialty of handy editions of even smaller size. It seems to have escaped general attention, however, that among the incunabula are also to be found a few tiny volumes that may fairly be classed among the miniature books which are so dear to the hearts of the collectors of "64mos."

In the nature of things, books of small size will hardly be found among the incunabula of the earliest years of printing—say from 1450 to 1470. Type at first was cast only in relatively large sizes, unsuitable for pages of small dimensions. But by the last decade of the fifteenth century the refinements in the arts of punch-cutting and typecasting made it possible to produce types in sizes so small that miniature books could be printed with them. One of the earliest books printed in a type of really small size was the Latin Bible produced by Johann Froben at Basel in 1491. A page of this Bible is reproduced in its actual size on page 307.

Strictly speaking, however, this Froben Bible was not a miniature book. For the sake of definition, it is suggested that any volume to qualify as a miniature among incunabula must have a page not larger than about 85 millimeters in width by 120 millimeters in height (about 3⅜ by 4¾ inches), provided that the type area is not larger than 56 by 75 millimeters (about 2¼ by 3 inches). Some will be found to come within the indicated page size but with type pages out of proportion. These, however, are dwarfed books, crippled by the binder's knife, rather than true miniatures.

The earliest book of really small size which I have noted is the *Diurnale Moguntinum,* printed presumably by Peter Schoeffer, at Mainz, about 1468. Unfortunately, only two imperfect leaves of this volume, printed on vellum, have survived, being now preserved in the Bibliothèque Nationale in Paris. Gotthelf Fischer, however, had four leaves of this little book in his possession in 1803 (they can-

oblationē tibi. Tradidus sū ꝶ nō egrediebar: oculi mei languerūt ꝓ iopia. Clamaui ad te dñe: tota die expandi ad te manꝰ meas. Nūqd mortuis facies mirabilia: aut medici suscitabunt ꝶ ꝓfitebunt tibi? Nūqd narrabit aliqs i sepulchro miꝓicōiꝰ tuā: ꝶ veritatē tuā in ꝑditiōne? Nūqd cognoscēt i tenebris mirabilia tua: ꝶ iusticia tua i ꝑrā obliuionis? Et ego ad te dñe clamaui: et mane oꝛo mea ꝓueniet te. Ut quid dñe repelles oꝛonē meā: auertis faciē tuā a me? Pauꝑ su ego ꝶ in laboribꝰ a iuuētute mea: exaltatꝰ aūt húiliatꝰ sū ꝶ conturbatꝰ. In me trāsierūt ire tue: ꝶ ꝶroꝛes tui cōturbauerūt me. Circūdederūt me sicut aqꝺ tota die: circūdederūt me simul. Elōgasti a me amicū ꝶ ꝓximū: et notos meos a miseria

Intellectus ethan ezraite. LXXXVIII

m Isericordias dñi: i eternū cātabo. In generatione ꝶ generatiōnē: annūciabo veritatē tuā i ore meo. Qm dixisti in eternū misꝛicōia edificabit i celis: ꝓparabit veritas tua i eis. Disposui testamentū electis meis: iuraui dauid seruo meo vsqꝺ i eternū ꝓparabo semē tuū. Et edificabo i generatiōe ꝶ generatiōe: sedē tuā. Cōfitebūt celi mirabilia tua dñe: eteni veritatē tuā in ecclesia sctōꝝ. Qm quis in nubibꝰ eqꝰbit dño: sitꝰ erit deo in filiꝭ dei? Deꝰ qui glorificaꝶ in cōsilio sctōꝝ: magnus et terribilis sup oēs qꝺ in circuitu eius sunt. Dñe deus virtutū qs siꝭ tibi: potēs es dñe ꝶ veritas tua in circuitu tuo. Tu dñaris ꝑsti mari]: motū aūt fluctuum eius tu mitigas. Tu húiliasti sicut vulnerarū supbū in brachio virtut] tue: disperdisti inimicos tuos. Tui sū celi ꝶ tua est terra: orbē terre ꝶ plenitudinē eius tu fundasti: aquilonem ꝶ mare tu creasti. Thabor ꝶ hermon in noie tuo exultabūt: tuū brachiū cū potētia. firmeꝶ manꝰ tua ꝶ exalteꝶ dextera tua: iusticia et iudiciū ꝓpatio sedes tue. Misericordia ꝶ veritas ꝓcedēt faciē tuā: beatus pplꝭ qꝺ scit iubilationē. Dñe i luie vultus tui ābulabūt: ꝶ i noīe tuo exultabūt tota die: ꝶ i iusticia tua exaltabūt. Qm glꝛia virtutis eoꝝ tu es: ꝶ in bñplacito tuo exaltabiꝶ cornu nfm. Quia dñi est assumptio nꝛa: ꝶ sci isrꝉ regis nꝫi. Tūc locutꝰ es i visiōe scis tuis: et dixisti posui adiutoꝛiū i potēte: ꝶ exaltaui electū ꝺ plebe mea. Inueni dauid

seruū meū: oleo scto meo vnxi eū. Manꝰ eni mea auriliabiꝶ ei: ꝶ brachiū meū cōfirmabit eū: Nihil ꝓficiet iimicꝰ i eo: ꝶ filius iniqtat] nō apponet nocere ei. Et ꝓcidā a facie ipi iimicos eiꝰ ꝶ odiētes eū infuga cōuertā. Et veritas mea et misericordia mea cū ipo: ꝶ i noīe meo exaltabiꝶ cornu eius. Et ponā in mari manū eiꝰ: ꝶ in flumibꝰ dexterā eiꝰ. Ipe iuocabit me pꝶ meꝰ es tu: deꝰ meꝰ et suceptoꝛ salut] mee. Et ego ꝓiogenitū ponā illū: excelsū ꝓ regibꝰ terre. In eternū ꝼuabo illi miꝓicōiā meā: ꝶ testamentū meū fideli ipi. Et ponā in seculū seculi semē eiꝰ: ꝶ thronū ei sicut dies celi. Si aūt dereliqerit filii eiꝰ legē meā: ꝶ in iudiciꝭ meis nō ābulauerit. Si iusticiꝭ meas ꝓphanauerit ꝶ mandata mea nō custodierit. Visitabo in virga iniꝗtates eoꝝ: ꝶ in verberibꝰ pctā eoꝝ. Misericordiā aūt meā non dispgā ab eo: neqꝝ nocebo in veritate mea. Neqꝝ ꝓphanabo testamētū meū ꝶ qꝺ ꝓcedunt de labiꝭ meis nō faciā irrita. Semel iuraui in scō meo si dauid mētiar: semē eiꝰ i eternū manebit. Et thronꝰ eiꝰ sicut sol i cōspectu meo: ꝶ sicut luna ꝑfecta i eternū ꝶ testis i celo fidelis. Tu vero repulisti et despexisti: christū tuū: Auertisti testamentū sui tui: ꝓphanasti i terra sctuariū eiꝰ. Destruxisti oēs sepes eiꝰ: posuisti firmamētū eiꝰ formidinē. Diripuerūt eū oēs trāseūtes viā: factꝰ e opꝓbriū vicinis suis. Exaltasti dexterā deprimētiū eū: letificasti oēs iimicos eiꝰ. Auertisti adiutoꝛiū gladii eiꝰ: ꝶ nō es auriliatꝰ ei i bello. Destruxisti eū ab emūdatiōe: ꝶ sedē eius in terra collisisti. Minorasti dies tpis eius: pfudisti eum pfusiōe. Usqꝝ dñe auert] in finē: exardescet sicut ignis ira tua? Memorare qꝺ mea substātia: nūqd eni vane ꝺstituisti oēs filios hoīm? Quis e hō qꝺ viuet et nō videbit moꝛte: eruet aīam suā ꝺ manu inferi? Ubi sū misericoꝛdie tue ātique dñe: sicut iurasti dauid in veritate tua? Memoꝛ esto dñe opꝓbriū seruoꝝ tuoꝝ: qꝺ ꝓtinui in sinu meo multaꝝ gētiū. Qꝺ exꝓbrauerūt iimici tui dñe: qꝺ exꝓbrauerūt ꝓmutationē christi tui. Bñdictꝰ dñe in eternū: fiat fiat.

LXXXIX

Oꝛo moysi hois dei.

b Dñie refugiū factꝰ es nobis: a generatōe i generatiōe nꝫi. Priusꝗ mōtes fierēt aut formareꝶ terra ꝶ orbis a seculo ꝶ i seculum tu es deus. Ne

not now be located) and he described them in some detail, indicating that the type page measured 65 by 94 millimeters, or about 2½ by 3¾ inches. Though this height considerably exceeds the limit suggested above, an exception must be made in order to include among miniature incunabula this very early specimen of the making

FACING PAGES OF ALPHABETUM DIVINI AMORIS, BASEL, ABOUT 1491, ACTUAL SIZE.

of small books. The *Diurnale* was set in the small rounded types used in the composition of the Bible of 1462 and is hence ascribed to Schoeffer, although the existing fragments give no other clue to its typographic authorship.

More truly a miniature is the *Officium Beatae Mariae Virginis* printed by Moravus at Naples in 1490, a chunky little sextodecimo of 106 vellum leaves. The type page measures only 40 by 62 milli-

meters on a leaf of 70 by 100 millimeters. The proportions of these dimensions indicate that this little volume has not suffered from undue trimming.

Another miniature fifteenth-century book, now one of the treasures of the Newberry Library in Chicago, apparently unrecorded and perhaps unique, is an edition of the *Alphabetum divini amoris,* attributed to Johannes Gerson. It bears no indication of the printer or place of printing, but its type discloses that it was undoubtedly printed by Johann of Amerbach at Basel about 1491. It has a type page of 41 by 58 millimeters on a leaf measuring about 61 by 86 millimeters. Two facing pages of this interesting little book are here reproduced in the actual size of the original.

Also in the Newberry Library is a copy of the *Breviarium monasticum Sancti Benedicti,* edited by Bartholomaeus de Mantua, which was printed at Venice, November 15, 1491, by Andrea Torresano, the father-in-law of Aldus Manutius. The leaf of this volume measures only 60 by 82 millimeters. The final page, with colophon, is here shown.

COLOPHON PAGE OF THE SAINT BENEDICT BREVIARY, VENICE, 1491, IN ACTUAL SIZE.

About 1492, Ulrich Zell, at Cologne, printed two companion volumes of diminutive size—the *Horologium devotionis,* of Bertholdus, in 122 leaves, and a work entitled *Meditationes,* in 128 leaves. In each case the type page contains 22 lines of text, the whole

measuring 50 by 74 millimeters, on a page of 83 by 119 millimeters. The sequence of signatures shows that the two were closely connected in the printing process, and the copies in the Pierpont Morgan Library in New York are bound in one volume. A third book, *De spiritualibus ascensionibus,* by Gerardus Zutphaniensis, is also related typographically with these two.

Also outstanding among miniature incunabula is a beautiful little *Horae* in Greek, printed by Aldus at Venice in 1497. This is a sextodecimo of 112 leaves printed in black and red. The type page is 50 by 74 millimeters and the leaf 80 by 111 millimeters. A page of this fascinating little book is here reproduced in actual size.

PAGE FROM A GREEK HORAE, PRINTED AT VENICE, 1497.

The very smallest fifteenth-century book of which I know is the *Horae ad usum Sarum,* issued April 2, 1500, from the press of Julian Notary, the Frenchman who printed in Westminster and in London. All that remains of this, so far as has ever been discovered, is an unfolded half-sheet on which are printed, in black and red, six-

teen of the tiny pages. The type, set in 11 lines to the page, measures 26 by 33 millimeters, or about 1 by 1⅜ inches. The imposition of the pages on the sheet shows that if the sheet were to be folded, the leaves of the book would measure about 37 by 52 millimeters (1½ by 2⅛ inches). This unique fragment is now preserved in the Public Library of Victoria, in Melbourne, Australia.

Among the many thousand known issues of the press in the fifteenth century there are still many surprisingly interesting and delightful discoveries to be made by some investigator who has a love for diminutive books. The subject seems to me to deserve more attention than it has yet received.

The subject matter of the incunabula depended, of course, on what the printers thought was in sufficient popular demand to insure sales or on what their employers or backers required of them. But for the fifteenth century, as for every succeeding age, the kind of reading matter which the presses turned out reveals the prepossessions of the reading public and is some expression of what most concerned the thought of its time and place. What do the incunabula tell us about the thought currents and interests of Europe in the latter half of the fifteenth century?

Typography was born in a time of change and trouble. The glories of the Middle Ages which culminated in the great thirteenth century were past. Europe was not only crushed by devastating plagues, but was menaced by the Turks, who stormed Constantinople in 1453 and early in the next century were standing before the walls of Vienna. The old order of society, the feudal system, though still strong, was declining under the rising power of commercialism and absolutism, while craftsmen and merchants, politically unimportant in the order which was passing, were growing in wealth and influence. In this newly developing class of Europe's citizenship were included the makers and sellers of books.

Intellectually, Europe was being swept by two forces which were to transform western civilization. The first, which took form in Germany, was a religious movement among the lower and middle classes, personal and pietistic in temper, which to a large extent found expression outside of formal worship. Huss at the beginning and Savonarola at the end of the fifteenth century are representatives of the extreme form of this religious awakening, which later culminated in the Reformation.

The other great movement was Humanism. For more than a century, Byzantine Greek refugees from the advancing Moslem armies sought shelter in Italy, bringing with them manuscripts of the Greek classics, which western Europe had almost forgotten, and opening schools in Italian cities. They were welcomed by scholars like Petrarch, and soon old monastic libraries were being ransacked in an eager search for codices of classic authors. Under the influence of the rediscovered literature of ancient Greece and Rome, human vision was broadened, and in place of the narrow medieval conception of life as a somber preparation for the next world, there arose a new striving for culture and beauty, while faith, the ideal of the Middle Ages, was slowly supplanted by free inquiry, the ideal of the dawning Renaissance.

At a time, then, when the mighty forces which were to transform civilization were gathering strength, typography was born. How it hastened the process of change by making possible the wide dissemination of knowledge is well known. The books which the printing press produced during the first fifty years of its existence, however, were for the most part the classics of the Middle Ages, the theology and liturgy of the church, the law of the sixth century, and the science of the twelfth—in other words, the literature of the old order of things. Yet, along with these medieval classics, appeared tracts of popular devotion and the writings of the philos-

ophers of pagan Greece and Rome—forerunners of a great religious and intellectual upheaval in which the printing press would have an ever enlarging share.

Almost half of the books printed in the fifteenth century were religious in subject matter. This is not surprising when we remember that a large proportion of the literate population were ecclesiastics. Ample funds, too, for the purchase of such books were available to the monasteries through the bequests of benefactors who had died in the recent plagues. Even among the laity, especially in the northern countries, the religious awakening created a demand for devotional works.

The Bible may be justly termed the favorite book of the fifteenth century, for, in spite of its great size, which rendered it difficult to print and expensive to buy, it was issued more frequently than any other single work. The popularity of the Latin Vulgate version of the Bible is evidenced by the fact that at least 133 editions of it are known to have been printed in the fifteenth century and that after 1475 not a year elapsed without the production of at least one edition. Vernacular editions were sought by laymen. In the different dialects of German were issued fifteen editions of the Bible; in Italian, thirteen; in French, eleven; in Bohemian, two; and one each in Spanish and in Dutch.

The writings of the church fathers also were much read. Of these, Saint Augustine was the favorite, with Jerome, Chrysostom, and Gregory as his closest rivals.

Theology, too, was in great demand. In the doctrinal aspect of the subject, Saint Thomas Aquinas, with over three hundred editions of his separate works, was pre-eminent. Disputation on such doubtful points of theology as we find collected in the *Sentences* of Peter Lombard was an intellectual exercise of which medieval scholars were extremely fond, and numerous works of this nature,

by writers like Duns Scotus, and usually in the form of small tracts, made their way into print.

Parish priests sought from the early printing press books which would aid them in the performance of their duties. Manuals such as Gregory's *Pastoral Care* and Nider's *Instructions to Confessors* found a ready market, as did also compilations of the lives of the saints, such as Jacobus de Voragine's *Golden Legend,* which contained stories that a medieval audience delighted to hear. And many fifteenth-century priests were in full accord with the sentiment which Addison's famous character, Sir Roger de Coverley, later expressed, that it was better for a congregation to have read to them a discourse by a famous preacher than that they should hear a mediocre one composed by their own pastor. This probably explains the great demand for the printed sermons of such men as Caraccioli, Meffreth, and that master of eloquence in an age that dearly loved oratory, Savonarola.

The liturgy of the church called forth many of the most sumptuous products of the fifteenth-century press. Besides missals and other service books for public worship, private devotion made a ready market for the books of hours, which today are so eagerly sought because of their exquisite decoration.

Religious tracts designed to stir the reader to greater piety, such as the *Art of Righteous Living and Dying,* circulated widely among the middle classes, while meditation, an important spiritual exercise, called forth many mystical treatises, the most important of which was the *Imitation of Christ,* by Thomas à Kempis.

Closely allied with theology is ecclesiastical or canon law. The *Decretals* of Gratian and of Pope Gregory IX, with their many commentators, were in great demand in the early years of printing.

Outside the Church, Roman law and procedure were still in force in Germany and the greater part of Italy, and even where it

was not the law of the land, Roman law was much studied and admired. For this reason the codes of Justinian, often with annotations, were frequently printed. Local ordinances and the decrees of kings, despite their limited appeal, were fairly numerous in book and pamphlet form. Textbooks on national law, such as (in England) those of Stratham and Lyttleton, also found wide circulation among lawyers.

Encyclopedias were popular in the Middle Ages, for when books were scarce it was but natural that a volume which could pretend to be an epitome of human knowledge would be greatly desired. Pliny's *Natural History,* Isidore's *Etymologies,* Vincent of Beauvais' ponderous *Mirrors,* and especially *The Properties of Things* by Bartholomaeus Anglicus were eagerly bought by students.

Fifteenth-century science was still thoroughly medieval. Works upon physics, for instance, were almost exclusively comments upon Aristotle. Important among these were the disquisitions of Averroes, Albertus Magnus, and Saint Thomas Aquinas.

Medicine, in a time when pestilences were sweeping Europe, was a subject frequently treated in books printed in the fifteenth century. The works of such classic writers as Galen and of Arabian physicians like Avicenna, along with those of fifteenth-century writers on the plague, were repeatedly issued. Herbals, also, which told of many marvelous and infallible cures for all the ills to which man is heir, were read and believed in by many.

The first book to contain a chapter on medicine was the *Opus de universo,* by Rabanus Maurus, which was printed at Strasbourg by Adolf Rusch in 1467. From that date through the year 1480, there were printed more than two hundred books which were wholly or partly of medical interest. In 1497 was printed, also at Strasbourg, the first edition of the illustrated *Buch der Chirurgia,* a manual of surgery by Hieronymus Braunschweig. This was promptly pirated

by Schönsperger, of Augsburg, later in the same year. An interesting illustration from this important work is reproduced opposite.

For two of the most important occupations of the time—war and agriculture—little practical help could be derived from fifteenth-century books. Treatises like *Management of an Army,* by the Roman Vegetius, or Columella's commentary on Virgil's *Georgics* were of great interest to antiquarians, perhaps, but of little value to soldiers or farmers.

Books on mathematics were then, as now, difficult to print, and for that reason their number was small. Euclid's *Elements of Geometry* was the most popular. Although only two editions appeared in the fifteenth century, the numerous editions of the succeeding half-century may still be called mathematical incunabula. The first edition of the *Elements* was printed at Venice by Erhard Ratdolt in May, 1482. The text was that of a twelfth-century Latin translation said to have been made by Adelard of Bath, the "English philosopher," a striking personality of the later Middle Ages. It is not clear, however, whether this translation was made directly from the original Greek or from an intermediate Arabic translation.

In the letter in which Ratdolt dedicated this monumental work to the Doge of Venice, the printer expressed his wonderment that, among the great output of the Venetian press, the mathematical works were so few and of so little importance. He ascribed this to the difficulty of printing the mathematical diagrams without which such books would be relatively unintelligible. This difficulty, the printer said, he had endeavored to overcome.

Astronomy was much more liberally represented than mathematics among fifteenth-century books. Calendars are numerous, beginning with the celebrated astronomical calendar believed to relate to the year 1448. These were usually printed in single-sheet or broadside form. Dr. Haebler reproduced an even hundred of them in

Die fahet an der erste tractat dis büchs mit hülfe deß Almechtige gottes, on den kein güt werck angefangen oder vollent mag werde. Das wiurt dich lere/wyssen vn vnderichte wz eine yede wundartzt E sitte vn wessen not ist/warnug prenostiratio erkenug des krancke/vn d wunde

ILLUSTRATION IN THE BUCH DER CHIRURGIA, STRASBOURG, 1497.

facsimile in one publication. The first known prognostication of the weather, by Franciscus de Gascono, was printed at Venice in 1470, but no copy of it is thought to have survived. Astronomy was also represented by such works as Holywood's *Spheres*.

Closely connected with astronomy was astrology, one of the occult sciences which, though frowned upon by the church, still survived. The *Times of Birth,* by the Spanish Jew Ibn Ezra, was a favorite treatise on this subject, while the dream books and alchemical manuals of Arnold of Villa Nova and numerous treatises on witchcraft, like Institor's *Malleus maleficarum,* were representatives of the fifteenth-century literature which dealt with other forbidden fields of knowledge.

Geography was an important branch of science in that century which began a great era of discovery. The classic writers, Strabo, Pomponius Mela, and Ptolemy, were printed, often with additions of new knowledge made by their editors, while the marvelous tales of travel by such men as Marco Polo, Breydenbach, and that Prince of Liars, Sir John Mandeville, fired the imagination of many a fifteenth-century boy whose name is now written in the annals of continents which were then unknown. The Breydenbach *Peregrinationes* has already been mentioned in connection with its illustrations. The first edition of Ptolemy's geography was printed in 1475.

Turning to literature, we find the Latin classics dominating the fifteenth-century book market. Cicero, with over three hundred editions of his different works, was the favorite, German readers being attracted to his ethical discussions quite as much as were Italians to his literary style. Virgil followed in popularity, with over one hundred and eighty editions. Ovid, Lucan, Horace, and the Roman historians were also frequently published.

The Greek authors, although they were greatly admired, were printed less frequently. The many-sided Aristotle unquestionably

had the greatest appeal of any Greek writer, and over one hundred and sixty editions of his separate works, both in the original and in Latin translations, appeared before the end of the century. Aesop, whose works had a great attraction for the common people, was Aristotle's nearest rival, while the works of Homer, Herodotus, Plato, and Josephus, disseminated by the fifteenth-century press, either in Greek or in Latin, created a great impression upon the succeeding generation.

Vernacular literature was less liberally represented in the products of the early press, yet among them are many distinguished names. Dante, Boccaccio, Petrarch, Villon, and Chaucer were repeatedly published, as were also several of the prose and metrical romances in the national languages of the day.

The dramatic literature available in printed form to the fifteenth-century reader is of especial interest to us because of the great activity in that field in the following century. Besides the classic dramatists like Aristophanes, Euripides, Plautus, Terence, and Seneca, there appeared also the comedies of Hrosvitha, the medieval nun, and some French mystery plays.

The principles and methods of education were much discussed in fifteenth-century books. One of the most popular treatises on this subject was the *Training of Children,* by Aeneas Sylvius, a work of pronounced humanistic tendencies. Grammars such as the *Eight Parts of Speech,* by Aelius Donatus, and disquisitions of a more philological nature like Lorenzo Valla's *Elegancies of the Latin Language* found many buyers in an age which was becoming sophisticated and careful of good form, and in which a command of Latin was indispensable to the serious student.

What we call commercial printing was firmly established in the fifteenth century. In fact, the famous Mainz indulgences of 1454 were just printed forms, pieces of job printing. Advertising, espe-

cially of books, by means of printed handbills, like Peter Schoeffer's list of books for sale in 1469 or Caxton's famous placard of 1477, was not an unusual procedure.

Though the newspaper did not come into being until the seventeenth century, printed epistles or pamphlets dealing with current events served as effectual disseminators of news. An example of special American interest is the famous *Letter of Christopher Columbus Concerning the Newly Discovered Islands,* which was printed at Barcelona in 1493 as a two-leaf folder of folio size, to announce to the Spanish authorities the discovery of the "islands of the Indies." This discovery was news indeed, and the printers of Europe gave evidence of their recognition of its importance by bringing out twelve editions of the *Letter* within a year, at Rome, Paris, Antwerp, Basel, and Florence. Within five years of the discovery by Columbus of a continent misnamed for a later explorer, the report was printed in at least seventeen editions, in four languages, in six different countries.

Incunabula, we see, treat a large variety of subjects. Adopting a rough and rather arbitrary division, we may say that approximately forty-five per cent of them are concerned with religion, ten per cent with law, ten per cent with science, thirty per cent with literature, and the remaining five per cent with miscellaneous subjects.

Before the invention of printing, students must have heard or read of many books of which it was impossible to procure a copy. For this reason the early printers found the old standard authors in great demand and for this reason, until 1485, issued them almost exclusively. But after that date the works of contemporary writers were printed with increasing frequency until, when the end of the century was reached, they formed fifteen per cent of the total number of incunabula. The most popular contemporary author was Aeneas Sylvius, afterwards Pope Pius II, whose novel, *Concerning*

Two Lovers, was the outstanding best seller of fifteenth-century fiction. Chronicles of past and current events, such as those of Schedel and Rolevinck, and the sermons of the fiery preacher, Savonarola, also attracted the attention of their contemporaries. But only one work by a writer who saw his work appear in a fifteenth-century book is likely to prove immortal. That work is the *Imitation of Christ,* by Thomas à Kempis.

The book production of different parts of Europe was by no means uniform. Germany's contribution was largely religious, and no consideration of the struggle of the early sixteenth century can ignore the literature with which the minds of German youth had been saturated. It is very significant that the Bible and the works of Saint Augustine, powerful weapons in the hands of the reformers, were the favorites in the German book trade. Italy, on the other hand, produced the Latin and Greek classics. In fact, printing in the Greek language in the fifteenth century was confined to that country in which the Greek refugees from Constantinople provided a ready supply of compositors and proofreaders. From Italy came those influences which, in the sixteenth century, redeemed Europe from her crudeness and superstition and called forth that matchless blossoming of the human spirit which we call the Renaissance.

We are prone to think of incunabula solely as objects of art or as monuments of the pioneer efforts of the printer's craft, and to forget that they were factors in a great intellectual struggle. We shall better appreciate the significance of the invention of printing if we bear in mind that even in the fifteenth century the power of the press was a mighty power.

For a long time after printed books first began to appear, they were valued for their contents, or else not at all. Scholars gave a full measure of appreciation to the service which printing rendered in making books accessible to all who wanted them, but a "dated"

book was as quickly discarded then as now. The intellectual and religious upheaval of the sixteenth century made a considerable portion of the fifteenth-century books so outmoded as to be useless to readers, and in the case of standard texts, improvements in the art of printing constantly produced new editions which were better printed and more convenient to use than their quaintly printed and cumbersome predecessors. Thus innumerable incunabula, as we now call them, were thrown away and destroyed as "useless old books," or else set aside and neglected in forgotten alcoves or basement storage heaps in libraries.

In 1640 the printers of Germany celebrated the second centenary of the invention of printing. On what evidence they based their choice of that year, rather than 1645 or some other year, is quite another story. The point of interest for us here is that then, for the first time, efforts were made to bring to light, as historical exhibits of interest, old books of the cradle days of printing. Since that time, fifteenth-century books have been collected for their own sake, as curiosities or rarities, as historical sources or landmarks, and as monuments marking the beginnings of typography's course through the succeeding centuries.

This desire to collect incunabula—at first an inexpensive hobby—called forth bibliographies to serve as guides for purchasers. The earliest of any note was Cornelius Beughem's *Incunabula typographiae* (1688), a small work which, though it contains brief accounts of the authors of the books listed, omits the names of their printers and publishers. More pretentious was the *Annales typographici* (1719-1741) of Michael Maittaire, the classical scholar. But not until the appearance of the large work of the same title by Georg Wolfgang Panzer (1793-1803) did the interest in incunabula become definitely typographical. In eleven volumes Panzer gathered the titles of all incunabula known up to that time and arranged them

in chronological order under the names of the towns in which they were printed, adding invaluable information as to the location in which he found each individual book or the sources from which he derived his knowledge of it.

Modern bibliography of incunabula may be said to begin with Ludwig Hain's *Repertorium bibliographicum* (1826-1834). In this monumental work Hain describes, usually in detail, over 16,000 issues of the fifteenth-century press. So successful was Hain that to this day his work is probably the most frequently cited catalogue of incunabula. Two later works, the *Supplement* (1895-1902) of the versatile lawyer, theologian, musician, and antiquarian, Walter A. Copinger, and the *Appendices* (1905-1911) of the German scholar, Dietrich Reichling, rectify, to some extent, the errors and omissions of Hain. The task of Copinger and Reichling was made easier by the labors of Marie Pellechet, who, after compiling catalogues of the early printed books of several French libraries, prepared her *Catalogue général des incunabules des bibliothèques publiques de France* (1897 ff.). Mlle. Pellechet died while the publication of her great work was still in progress, and the French ministry of public instruction has printed but one-third of her manuscript.

The bibliographies mentioned above contain much material of value to the student of printing. With the exception of Panzer's *Annales,* however, they all have the titles arranged alphabetically by authors, a feature which makes them primarily guides for collectors. Progress in the study of early typography was seriously hampered for a long time by the fact that a large proportion of the books printed in the fifteenth century bear no indication of place, printer, or date. A method of determining the press of issue by comparing the types of books of unknown origin with those of books of which the printers are known was developed by Henry Bradshaw and was used with great success by Robert Proctor in his

Early Printed Books in the British Museum with Notes of Those in the Bodleian Library (1898-1906). In this work, which revolutionized the study of early printing, the titles are arranged chronologically by printer, town, and country. Proctor's method of identifying incunabula of unknown origin was systematized by Konrad Haebler in his *Typenrepertorium der Wiegendrucke* (1905-1910). The great possibilities of bibliographical scholarship are in a large measure realized in a work which follows and perfects Proctor's scheme of identification and arrangement—the *Catalogue of Books Printed in the XVth Century now in the British Museum,* begun in 1908 and still in process of publication. This is by all odds the most valuable work to date for students of typographic history.

The foregoing titles, however, represent but a few of the productions of the many able and industrious men who have been attracted to the study of early printed books. Bibliographies of rare books such as Graesse's *Trésor* or Brunet's *Manuel du libraire* often contain notices of incunabula, while almost every large library has published a catalogue of its own fifteenth-century books.

A bibliography of incunabula may attempt, like Campbell's *Annales de la typographie néerlandaise au XVe siècle,* to describe the fifteenth-century books printed in one country, or, like Voulliéme's *Der Buchdruck Kölns,* those printed in a certain town. Again, it may confine itself, as does Blades' *Caxton,* to the output of a single press. Of late years some bibliographers, like Osler in his *Incunabula Medica,* have been dealing with the fifteenth-century books which treat with particular subjects. Information about early printed books, therefore, must be sought in many different places. Robert A. Peddie, for example, in his still unfinished *Conspectus incunabulorum* (1910 ff), a concordance to bibliographies of incunabula, cites descriptions from over two hundred reference works.

To meet the need of an all-inclusive bibliography of fifteenth-

FORMS OF THE CAPITAL M, AS COMPILED BY HAEBLER TO FACILITATE THE IDENTIFICATION OF INCUNABULA.

century books, the Prussian commission of education in 1904 appointed a commission to make "a complete catalogue of all known incunabula." With the assistance of almost all the large libraries of the world and of many private collectors, full descriptions of about 40,000 different issues of books printed before the year 1501 have been gathered and are now being published in the *Gesamtkatalog der Wiegendrucke* (1925 ff.), which it is expected will be complete in twelve large quarto volumes.

As a result of these two hundred and fifty years of bibliographical scholarship, fifteenth-century books, in spite of the great difficulties which they present, have been more minutely and successfully studied than the books printed in any other period. The literary taste of the half-century in which they were published can now be studied in great detail, and an intimate understanding may be had of the practices of the early printers, whose number and activity have been proved to be far greater than any but the boldest could have conjectured.

XXII

Typography's Golden Age

THE sixteenth century was an age of strife and glory. Europe was rapidly casting from her the shackles of the Middle Ages under the leadership of daring scholars who were fired with the Renaissance ideal of free inquiry. It was the age of the Reformation when a philosophical justification was demanded for many beliefs which preceding generations had accepted without question, when the traditions of centuries were fiercely assailed and vigorously defended. It was a time when men had at last discovered the meaning of intellectual freedom and found it delicious but dangerous. It stimulated art, literature, and learning till they reached heights seldom attained in human history. But the stake and the block stood as grim reminders to the sixteenth-century scholar that those who upheld the medieval ideal of authority would suppress free inquiry by force.

Education was quickened by this intellectual and religious upheaval. Among all classes of society, except the very lowest, there arose an intense desire to learn to read. Books, as a result, could no longer be considered the exclusive property of a small class. Instead, the popular demand for such widely circulated works as Luther's translation of the Bible was so great that to meet it mass production was introduced into the printing industry.

Paris, in the sixteenth century, was favorably situated to have a leading part in any movement in typography. It was probably the largest and most important city of Europe. Far enough removed from the religious controversy which was raging in the north to

escape its violence, it was at the same time quickened by the intellectual excitement that the conflict engendered. It was also fortunate in that the successive kings who resided in it were for the most part patrons both of letters and typography. It was the seat, too, of a university which, although in a state of decline, was still in the earlier decades of the sixteenth century the largest and most important institution of learning in Europe. Even if the University of Paris was extremely conservative and unduly fond of medieval traditions, the campaigns of Francis I in Italy had brought to Paris a realization of the highest ideals of Renaissance scholarship. It was this happy combination, then, of material prosperity and intellectual stimulation which served to make the first sixty years of the sixteenth century in Paris the Golden Age of typography.

Prominent in this notable period was a family of scholar-printers, the house of Estienne, perhaps better known by the Latin form of the name, Stephanus. Henri Estienne, the first of the family, in 1502 took over the business of Jean Higman whose widow, Guyonne Viart, he had married in the previous year. Greek and Latin classics were the chief products of his press, and the high scholarly character of his work is evidenced by the fact that he had among his editors Jacques Le Fébvre d'Etaples, the teacher of Calvin, and among his proofreaders Geofroy Tory. Despite the fact that during the eight years in which he printed he produced more than a hundred editions, many fine books, such as Valla's translation of Galen's *De sectis medicorum* (1518), show his skill in combining the best features of French and Italian typography. He died in 1520 and his widow promptly married Simon de Colines. The influence of Guyonne Viart as the wife of three and the mother of two of the city's best printers still remains an unwritten chapter in the history of Parisian typography.

Robert Estienne, the second son of Henri, put to good use the

Nobiliſſimi Principatus fundamenta feliciter Otho iecit, Vberti filius, qui ab Aſiatico Othone proauo nomen acceperat. Natus eſt Inuorio in pago ad Verbanum lacum, magnis quidem natalibus, ſed patrimonio tenui, & tum adeò afflictis totius familiæ fortunis, vt quatuor tantum & planè ignobilium vicorũ ditione, propinqui Proceres maiorum ſuorum nomen tuerẽtur. Hi fuere, Inuorium, Maſſinum, Vergantum, & Olegium: ſed fundos etiam peramplos Mediolani extra portam Iouiam à Sultano Vicecomite emptos conſtat. Frequentibus enim Barbarorum irruptionibus, & ciuili præſertim bello, cuncta apud Inſubres conturbata proſtratáque erant, vt non mirum ſit, tantas opes in publica calamitate corruiſſe. Sunt qui ex genitura, propter admirabiles ſiderũ concurſus, imperiũ ei à Mathematicis prænuntiatum fuiſſe aſſeuerent. Verùm ipſe repudiatis prorſus Aſtrologis, id vnum pro inſigni oſtento iocabundus accepit, quòd Vicecomite Placentino, Mediolani Prætore (qui tum erat ſupremæ poteſtatis magiſtratus) & Othone Cæſare imperante, in lucẽ eſſet editus. Enituit ſatis maturè in adoleſcente ingenium alacre, præaltũ, ardens, & quod mirabile erat, graui prudẽtia temperatuím: acceſſerat corporis atque oris dignitas maximè excellens. ſtatura enim erat excelſa, & nexu neruorum longè firmiſſima: pectore autem lato atque extanti, & radioſis prægrandibuſque oculis. eloquentia verò illuſtri, exquiſitíſque literis, quũ oporteret, ad

instruction of his stepfather. In 1524, at the age of twenty-one he took over the paternal printing office, Colines having set up another shop close by; and soon after he married Perrette, the daughter of Jodocus Badius. His wife was a thorough scholar, and they worked together editing the many Greek and Latin classics which he printed. Latin, in fact, was the language of the Estienne home, spoken even by the servants and the children.

Robert Estienne attained fame by compiling, with the assistance of others, dictionaries of the Latin, Greek, and Hebrew languages, works which were soon adopted by most of the universities of Europe and which unfortunately were pirated by unscrupulous printers. His ability as a scholar was equaled by his success as a typographer. His books, many of them printed with types designed by Claude Garamond and with borders, initials and ornaments engraved by Geofroy Tory, are extremely beautiful. The happy combination of the efforts of these three artists may be seen in the page of Paolo Giovio's *Vitae duodecim vicecomitum Mediolani principum* of 1549 reproduced on page 329. He strove for accuracy even more than for beauty. To attain this, so it is said, he was accustomed to hang up his proof sheets in the streets by his shop, and near the university, and to offer a reward to anyone who could discover an error in them. His typographic ability was recognized by his title, "Printer to the King for Hebrew, Greek, and Latin."

Robert Estienne, then, during the twenty-six years in which he worked in Paris, produced many beautiful and scholarly books and this in spite of the fact that he was hampered by an irritating quarrel. During his lifetime the University of Paris, though the largest in Europe, was steadily declining both in numbers and in learning. The faculty of the Sorbonne was gradually being filled by doctors who attempted to conceal their ignorance by attaining a reputation for orthodoxy. The Greek and Roman classics, for example, some

of the doctors denounced as pagan, while they stoutly maintained that "a knowledge of the Greek and Hebrew languages would operate to the destruction of all religion." Robert Estienne printed a number of editions of the Bible in Latin, in Greek and in Hebrew. Besides introducing the verse division which is still retained in the King James and Douai versions, Estienne employed the critical method to restore the text and made free use of the emendations and notes of the humanist scholars, especially those of Erasmus. This aroused the enmity of the doctors of the Sorbonne, who thundered against him in their pulpits but who, when called upon to point out specific errors in Estienne's editions, were seldom able to prove anything but their own inability to translate Greek. With the aid of the King, Francis I, a patron of typography and Renaissance learning, Robert Estienne was able to defy the faculty of the Sorbonne, but on the death of his supporter, fearing persecution, he fled, in 1550, to Geneva which, ruled over by John Calvin, had become the refuge of many scholars. Here he set up his press and continued to issue books of the same high character until his death in the year 1559.

The two brothers of Robert played less important roles in the history of Parisian printing. His elder brother, François Estienne, was a publisher who sold the books of his stepfather and brothers. François seems to have shared Robert's love of intellectual freedom, for in 1542 he was ordered to surrender certain prohibited books found in his possession. He died in 1553. Charles Estienne, the younger brother of Robert, was born about 1504. After a thorough classical training he studied medicine and became a *docteur-régent* to the faculty of medicine of the University of Paris. Famous for his learning, he attracted many pupils. He compiled also, usually from material gathered from ancient authors, works on medicine, agriculture and pedagogy. As the Estiennes labored under royal dis-

pleasure after Robert's flight to Geneva, Henry II did not confer the title of Royal Printer of Greek upon Charles, but gave it to Adrien Turnèbe, to whom Charles was compelled to turn over the matrices of the royal Greek types. When Turnèbe retired in 1555, Guillaume Morel succeeded him as royal printer and held that office until his death in 1564. Charles Estienne, however, was allowed to take charge of the family printing office in 1551 as guardian for Robert's children and was permitted to assume the rather colorless title of "Printer in Ordinary to the King." He suffered business reverses, however, and in 1561 became bankrupt. He died, so it is said, in 1564, in prison where he was incarcerated either because of his religion or for debt.

The fortunes of the other members of the Estienne family are somewhat outside the scope of this chapter. Henri (usually called Henri II), the son of Robert, was a precocious child. After completing his education at an early age he traveled through Europe gathering manuscripts and conversing with learned men. At the death of his father he took charge of the printing press at Geneva and produced numerous editions of the classics, many of them edited by himself with the help of newly discovered manuscripts. In 1572, after many years of labor, he produced his great *Thesaurus,* a dictionary of the Greek language which is still used by scholars. His satire, *An Apology for Herodotus, or, A Treatise on Ancient and Modern Marvels,* was popular with readers but was little relished by the Consistory of Geneva. The publication in 1578 of his satirical *Dialogues* so aroused the consistory that he decided to leave the country for his own safety. He remained an exile and wanderer until his death in the year 1598.

Besides Henri, Robert Estienne had two other sons. Robert II succeeded to the office of printer to the king after the retirement of his uncle Charles. He died in 1571. François II, the remaining

son, printed both at Paris and Geneva, and his descendants followed the printing trade until late in the seventeenth century.

Simon de Colines may in many respects be considered a member of the Estienne family. An associate of Henri Estienne, the husband of his widow and the instructor of his son, he left his impress upon Estienne typography. He is said to have designed the first good Greek type with accents and also a beautiful italic, both types appearing in his books in 1528. The books which he printed are for the most part small quarto and octavo editions of the Greek and Latin classics, cheap in price but tasteful and workmanlike in execution. In this and in his successful use of roman type in books where more conservative printers still employed black-letter, Colines was a typographic reformer bringing to Paris the best features of the books of the Aldine Press. He was, on the other hand, no servile imitator of the Venetian printers. There is a certain delicacy of execution and a tendency to variety in the books of Colines that is distinctly French in tone. This may be seen by a comparison of the title pages of Colines, sometimes plain, sometimes decorated with exquisite woodcut borders, with the set pattern of the Aldine title page. Frequently his works are illustrated with excellent wood engravings, examples of which may be found in his books of hours or in the *De dissectione partium humanae corporis* by Charles Estienne (1545), the author of which, it would seem, preferred to have his stepfather rather than his brother print his scientific works. Simon de Colines continued the exercise of his craft until his death in 1546.

Another printer who was influential in changing French typography from the ornate black-letter to the magnificent roman of the Golden Age was Michael Vascosan, printer to the king. His books, such as the *Caesar* of 1543, are plainer and more Italianate than those of Colines, but his type is excellent and his maps and illustrations are noteworthy. He died in 1547.

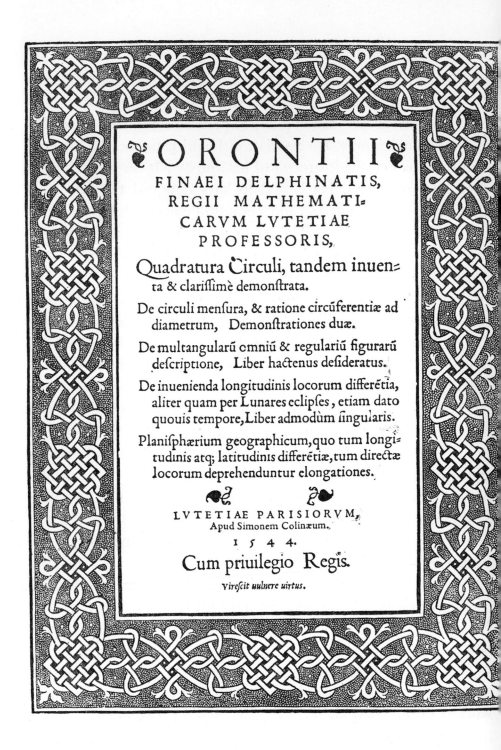

ORONTII
FINAEI DELPHINATIS,
REGII MATHEMATI=
CARVM LVTETIAE
PROFESSORIS,

Quadratura Circuli, tandem inuen=
ta & clariſſimè demonſtrata.

De circuli menſura, & ratione circũferentiæ ad
diametrum, Demonſtrationes duæ.

De multangularũ omniũ & regulariũ figurarũ
deſcriptione, Liber hactenus deſideratus.

De inuenienda longitudinis locorum differẽtia,
aliter quam per Lunares eclipſes, etiam dato
quouis tempore, Liber admodùm ſingularis.

Planiſphærium geographicum, quo tum longi=
tudinis atq; latitudinis differẽtiæ, tum directæ
locorum deprehenduntur elongationes.

LVTETIAE PARISIORVM,
Apud Simonem Colinæum.

1544.

Cum priuilegio Regis.

Vireſcit uulnere uirtus.

A COLINES TITLE PAGE, WITH BORDER
BY ORONCE FINE, PARIS, 1544.

No account of this period in French typography would be complete without a mention of Jodocus Badius Ascensius (1462-1533), the father-in-law of both Robert Estienne and Michael Vascosan. His typography, though excellent, does not compare with that of his sons-in-law, and his reputation rests chiefly upon his scholarship. He edited with comment the editions of the classics which he printed and wrote a life of Thomas à Kempis and a famous satire on the follies of women, *Navicula stultarum mulierum*. Today he is best known by the woodcuts which appear on his title pages showing scenes in an early printing office.

There were numerous other printers during this period who brought out books which were at once scholarly and beautiful. Gilles de Gourmont first printed in 1507 and 1508 respectively books in Greek and Hebrew, with the editorial co-operation of François Tissard. Chretien Wechel, apparently a native of Basel, was an able printer of scholarly works. Conrad Néobar, who began printing in 1538 and died in 1540, gave promise of a brilliant career as a printer of Greek. Maittaire quite properly says that there was scarcely any typographer who practised the art for so short a period and attained so much credit in it. Other printers of distinction were Pierre Vidouvé and Gerardus Morrhius.

The brothers Gryphe, or Gryphius, whose printer's mark of the griffin is well known, printed in two different cities; Franciscus working at Paris, Sebastien at Lyons.

Charlotte Guillard was the first woman printer of importance. Widow successively of two printers, Berthold Rembolt and Claude Chevallon, she operated in Paris an office with the motto of *sub sole aureo*. Studious of accuracy in her books, she printed up to 1556, the year of her death. According to her own account, she worked in the typographic profession for fifty-four years.

Etienne Dolet, the printer-martyr in the cause of a free press,

was several times jailed for expressions in print which were displeasing to constituted authority. In 1544, after liberation from a Paris prison, to which he had been committed on a charge of contravening religion, he promised to be a good Catholic. But we find him, the following year, accused of atheism and condemned, at the early age of thirty-seven, to be burned. As a special concession to humanity, however, he was strangled before his body was committed to the flames on August 3, 1546.

We now come to one who was perhaps the most versatile man ever associated with the craft of printing. Born about 1480, Geofroy Tory studied both at Bourges and in Italy and later became a professor of philosophy and an editor of the classics. His spare time he spent engraving ornamental letters, designs, and borders, at which he was so successful that about 1515 he gave up his professor's chair and devoted himself exclusively to graphic arts. Tory combined the erudition of a scholar with the genius of a true artist.

In 1523 he began a work which was an expression of two of his many interests. One of the manifestations of the spirit of nationalism which was growing strong in the sixteenth century was a new concern for the vernacular tongue. Tory opposed those who were introducing Latin words into French. He was also desirous of reducing French spelling into what he considered a logical system. Among his permanent reforms were the introduction of the accent, apostrophe, and cedilla into French orthography. Again, Tory desired to improve type design. He believed that the shapes of all roman capital letters were derived from the different parts of the human body and that the ideal letter must coincide with these proportions. In 1529 Tory published his great work, the *Champfleury*. In the first of the three books into which the work is divided he extols the French language and suggests improvements in its spelling, and in the second and third books he propounds, with the

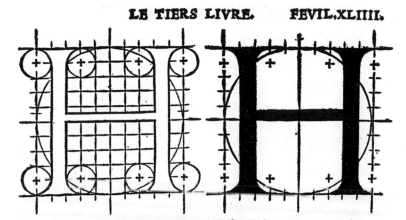

LA figure cy pres deſignee & faicte de le I.auec huit cētres, eſt de dix corps
en Quarre. Ceſt a dire, auſſi large que haulte. Les Grammairiens, & meſ=
mement ſelon Priſcian en ſon Premier liure ou il traicte De literarum poteſta=
te, diſent quelle neſt pas lettre, mais la note & enſeigne pour monſtrer quant
quelque vocale, ou lune de ſes quatre conſones, C.P.R.T.doibt eſtre pronū=
cee graſſe & a plaine voix venant du profond de leſtomac. Iceluy Priſcian dit.

» H.autem aſpirationis eſt nota, & nihil aliud habet literæ, niſi figuram, & quod
» in vſu ſcribit inter alias lřas. Ceſt a dire, H.eſt la note de laſpiratiō, & na aultre
choſe deficace de lettre, ſi non la figure, & auſſi que par vſage elle eſt eſcripte.

H.a ſi peu de vertus auec les vocales, q̃ ſi on len oſte, le ſens ne ſera point
diminue. mais ouy bien dauec leſſuſdictes quatre conſones. C.P.R.T.
Exemple des vocales. Erennius. Oratius. Exemple deſdictes cōſones. Cremes
pour Chremes. Et a ceſte cauſe comme dit Priſcian au ſuſdict lieu allegue, les
Grecs ont faict ces ſuſdictes conſones aſpirees. Car pour Th, ilz ont faict Θ.
pour Ph.Φ.pour Ch.X. Le Rho na point eſte mue de ſa figure, mais il prēt ſus
luy vne demye croix en lettres maiuſcules, ou vng point corbe en lettre courāt
qui denote la dicte aſpiration. cōme on peult cleremēt veoir es impreſſions du
feu bon imprimeur Alde, que Dieu abſoille.

» A Vlus Gellius au. III. Chapiſtre du Segōd liure de ſes nuyts Attiqués dit,
» que H.a eſte miſe des Anciens & inſeree es dictions pour leur bailler vng
» ſon plus ferme & vigoreux quant il dit. H.litera, ſiue illam ſpiritū magis quam
» literam dici oportet, inſerebant eam veteres noſtri pleriſq; vocibus verborū fir
» mandis roborādiſq; vt ſonus earum eſſet viridior vegetiorq;. Atq; id videntur
» ſeciſſe ſtudio & exemplo linguæ Atticæ. Satis notum eſt Attiquos ιχθυν ηϱον.
» Multa itidē alia citra morē gentiū Græciæ cæterarū inſpiratis primis literæ di=
» xiſſe ſic, lachrymas, ſic ſpechulū, ſic ahenū, ſic vehemēs, ſic ichoare, ſic helllua=
» ri, ſic hallucinari, ſic honera, ſic honuſtū dixerūt. In his verbis oïbus literæ ſeu
» ſpūs iſti⁹ nulla ratio viſa eſt, niſi vt firmitas & vigor vocis quaſi quibuſdā ner=
» uis additis iutēderet. Ceſt a dire. La lře H.ou ſil conuiēt myeulx la dire leſperit
· vocal, eſtoit ſouuāt iſeree des Anciēs Latins en beaucop de dictiōs pour les fir
· mer & roborer, afin q̃ leur ſon fuſt pl⁹ vertueux & vigoureux. Iceulx Anciēs le
faiſoiēt a limitatiō des Atheniēs, au lāgage deſqlz ιχθυν ηϱον. & beaucop de ſē
blables dictions eſtoiēt aſpirees hors la coſtume des aultres Nations de Grece.
Aiſi futēt aſpirez Lachrymæ, ſpechulū, ahenū, vehemēs, ichoare, hallucinari
honera, & honuſt⁹. En ces vocables ſuſeſcripts laſpiratiō na eſte veue raiſonna

I.ij.

aid of magnificent woodcuts, his theories of letter design. A page from this celebrated volume is reproduced on page 337.

Tory was appointed in 1530 or 1531 printer to the king, and he continued in the exercise of his craft until his death in 1533. He is famous as a scholar, reformer of spelling, type designer, and printer, but as a wood engraver he is preëminent. The delicacy and exquisite taste of his woodcut borders and the beauty of his mark, the *Pot cassé* (the broken vase), which commemorates the death of his brilliant ten-year-old daughter, are unsurpassed. His best woodcuts are found in the books of hours which he, Colines, and others printed. These will be discussed later in the chapter.

GEOFROY TORY'S PRINTER'S MARK.

Unlike Geofroy Tory, his versatile teacher, Claude Garamond was the master of but one of the arts of the book, but in that art, type designing, he has few rivals. In the design of his beautiful, clear, and open roman character, he drew upon the celebrated letter of Jenson and the less famed but meritorious roman of Aldus. But Garamond's roman was more conscious and elegant—less grave and simple. Garamond apparently cut a few italics, but he concentrated on the roman alphabet, leaving the supply of italic matrices, for the most part, to Robert Granjon, of Lyons, a friendly contemporary in the field of punch-cutting and matrix-making.

We find for example that Plantin, the Antwerp printer who also did his own type-casting, bought matrices for roman types from Garamond and for italic faces from Granjon. In the well-known 1592 specimen sheet of the Frankfurt typefounder Conrad Berner, the romans are ascribed to Garamond, the italics—or "cursives"—to Granjon. These two great punch-cutters thus appear to have made a friendly division of the market, each plowing the field of his own particular genius.

Had he not earned immortal renown as the designer of one of the greatest roman typefaces in printing history, Claude Garamond would still have earned a premier position in the typographic hall of fame by his masterful cutting of the punches of the Royal Greek types, produced under the patronage of Francis I.

The story of these Greek types is one of much interest. We learn from a manuscript in the Bibliothèque du Louvre that the king, on October 1, 1541, directed payment, through the hands of Robert Estienne, of 225 *livres tournois* to Claude Garamond, "cutter and founder of letters" toward the cost of Greek punches which he had undertaken to cut and "place in the hands of the said Estienne to use in printing books in Greek."

The first size of the Greek types to be completed was of comparatively large size, on a body about sixteen points high. It has generally been stated that the first use of this font was in printing the *Ecclesiastical History* of Eusebius, which was completed at the end of June, 1544. However, William Parr Greswell in 1833, in his comprehensive study of early Greek printing at Paris, made mention of an *Alphabetum Graecum* dated 1543 as being the work "in which the royal Greek characters were first exhibited." Although Greswell described this *Alphabetum* in considerable detail, as he could hardly have done without a copy before his eyes, he did not say where he had seen it. Auguste Bernard, therefore, writing on the

CHARACTERVM SEV
TYPORVM PROBATISSIMORVM,
INCONDITE QVIDEM, SED SECVN-
DVM SVAS TAMEN DIFFERENTIAS PRO-
POSITVM, TAM IPSIS LIBRORVM AVTORIBVS,,
QVAM TYPOGRAPHIS APPRIME VTILE
ET ACCOMMODATVM.

Efaiæ Caput
lo. LIII.

Canon de Ga
ramond.

¶ Quis credidit Auditui noſtro: & brachium Iehouæ cui Re-
uelatum eſt, Et aſcendit ſicut virgultum CORAM eo, & velut
radix de terra deſerti: Non erat forma ei, neque decor. ❦ Æ. Œ.

Petit Canon de Garamond.

Aſpeximus autem eum, & non erat aſpectus, & Non deſiderauimus eum videre. Deſpe
ctus fuit & Reiectus inter viros vir dolorum, & expertus Infirmitatem, & veluti abſconſio
faciei Ab eo, deſpectus inquam, & non putauimus eum. Verè languores noſtros ipſe tulit,
& dolores noſtros portauit, nos Autem reputauimus Eum plagis affectum, Percuſſum à
Deo & HVMILIATVM. ❦ W. H. S. G. ❦

Roman Paragon de Garmond.

Ipſe autem vulneratus eſt propter preuaricationes noſtras
Attritus eſt [&] propter iniquitates noſtraz caſtigatio pacis noſtræ ſuper eum
Et liuor eius ſanitas fuit nobis. Omnes nos ſicut oues erraui-
mus, vnuſquiſque ad viam ſuam. Declinauit, & Iehouah con
iecit in illum iniquitates omnium noſtrum. Oppreſſus fuit,
& ipſe afflictus, & non Aperuit os ſuum. Sicut agnus ad MA-
CTATIONEM ductus eſt, et velut ouis coram tondente ſe obm.

Gene. Paragon de Robert Grauon.

Nec aperuit os ſuum. A carcere & iudicio ſublatus eſt: & Gene
rationem eius Quis enarrabit, Quia abciſſus eſt è terra viuentium, propter pra
uaricationem populi Mei plaga fuit ei. Et dedit cum impijs ſepul
turam eius, & cum diuite in Morte ſua: Quamuis iniquitatem
non fecerit, Nec dolus fuerit in ore eius. Iehouah Autem voluit
conterere eum & egroture fecit eum: Quum poſuerit ſeipſum ſa
crificium pro delicto Anima eius.

Romain Gros Texte de Garmond.

Videbit prolongabit dies, & voluntas Iehouæ in Manu eius
proſperabitur. Propter laborem animæ ſuæ videbit fructum quo ſa
turabitur, ſcientia ſui iuſtificabit iuſtus ſeruus meus multos, & iniqui
tates ipſorum ipſe portabit. Ideo partem dabo ei cum multis & cum
fortibus diuidet ſpolia, Et quod effudit in MORTEM ANIMAM ſuam,

Curl Gros Texte de Garmond.

Et cum prœuaricatoribus Annumeratus eſt, ipſe quoque pecatum Multorum

Romain S. Auguſtin de Garmond.

Ad dexteram enim & ſiniſtram dilataberis, ſemen quoq; tuum Gentes hæredi
tate accipit ciuitates [ ]
deſolatas bitabit. Ne timeas, quia non afficieris pudore, nec erubeſces, Quia
non afficieris ignominia: pudoris enim adoleſcentiæ tuæ obliuiſceris. NAMMA
RITVS tuus, Iehouah exercituum nomen eius: Et redemptor tuus,
Sanctus Iſraelis, Deus vniuerſæ terræ vocatur

Gene S. Auguſtin de Gmalon.

Quam rependat afuera, dixit Deus tuus. Momento paruo dereliqui te, at in Miſeratio-
nibus magnu congregabo te In momento iræ abſcondi faciem Meam ad momentum à te,
In miſericordia ſempiterna Miſertus ſum tui, dixit Redemptor tuus Iehouah.

Roman Cicero de Garmond.

Nam vt aquæ Noha hoc michi, cui iuraui quod non tranſirent aquæ Noha vltra ſuper ter
ram, ſic iuraui quod non iraſcar contra te, neq;
nec in erepabo te Montes enim mouebunt ſeſe, & colles metabunt miſericordia autem mea
à te non recedet, & fœdus pacis meæ non nutabit dixit miſerator tuus IEHOVAH Pauper
cula in turbine verſans Non accepit conſolationem, en ego iacere faciam in Carbuncula la
pides tuos, & fundabo te in ſapphiris,

Gene. meue de Gmalon.

Et ponam ex Margarito fenſtram tuas & portas tuas ex lapidibus carbunculi, Atque omnem ter
minum tuum lapidibus deſiderabilibus Vni
nerſi quoque filij tui erunt docti à Iehouah, & Multiplicans pacem filiorum tuorum, In iuſtitia
fundaberis, longe aberis ab oppreſſione, quia Non timebu eam, & a contritione quia non appropin
quabit tibi En congrega congregabit ſe populus contra te abſque Me quiſquis congregue
rit ſe tecum contra te cadet

¶ Et hoc meliuru nota Litera Curreni, artifice Roberto Grantono Gallo prodita, vulgo Scolaſticalis dicta, Ea in lineas æſtimet componitur operaruum, magis patiens exiſtit.

Romain Guarmond de Guarlon.

Ecce ego creaui fabrum ferrarium ſufflantem in igne pr
& ego inquam ſtrieaui vaſtatorem ad abendum. Omne inſtru
mentum quod formabitur contra te, in proſperabitur, & omnem linguam quæ ſurget contra te in iudicium
condemnabis, hæc eſt hæreditas ſeruorum Iehouah, & iuſtitia eorum à me eſt, dixit Iehouah

Gene Garamond de Guarlon.

Rom. Galliard de Guarlon.

Ecce reſtem populo dedi eum, ducem, & preceptorem po
pulis. Ecce gen, quam non nouiſti, tu vocabis, & gen
noſti vocabis, ad te & genres quæ non nouerunt te, current propter Iehouah Deum tuum, & Sanctum Iſraelis, qui glorabit

Rom. Non parel.

Curl Petit Text de G.

Curl Non parel.

Estiennes and their Greek types in a monograph published in 1856, ventured to doubt that this *Alphabetum* of 1543 actually existed.

Alphabetum
Græcum.

CVM PRIVILEGIO REGIS.

PARISIIS
Ex officina Roberti Stephani typo-
graphi Regii.
M. D. XLIII.

TITLE PAGE OF ESTIENNE'S ALPHABETUM GRAECUM, PARIS, 1543.

There seemed to be good reason for Bernard's doubts, for no copy of it is to be found today in the Bibliothèque Nationale at Paris or in the British Museum at London, and no copy is located in any of

Upper section:

πω	παν	μετ μερ
ρα	παρ	μείνος. μετά
ρι	παρα	μη
ρο	παρο	μην
σα	παυ	μι
σαι	πε	μιν
σαρ	περ	μο μω μω
σας	περι	μυ
σαυ	πευ	μυι
σβ	πη	μων
σε	πι	οιον
σει	πο	ον
ση	πρ	ου
σθ	πρα	ουδε
σθα	πρβ	ουκ
σθε	πρω	ουρα ουκα
σθμ	πυ	τους τουτουτος
σθην	πυν	πα
σθι	πων	παν
σθο		

Lower section:

χι	θα	δυ δυν
χο χο	θη θμ	δω δων
χρ	θην	δυς.
χρα	θι	δω.
χρο	θν	ει ει ει.ει
χυ	θο	εναι.
χυι	θρ	εκ.
χω	θρο	εκ.
χων	θρα	ελ.
λλ	θυ	ελλ.
μμ	θω	εν.
μα	κα	εξ εξ επειδη
μαι	και καιι και	επι.
μαυ	καθω	επι.
μαρ	καν και καν	ετι.
μας	κας	ευ.
μαστον	κατα	η.
μαυ	κε	ην.
με	κεφαλαιον	θα.
μεθ	κη	θαρ.
μελ	κι	θαυ.
μελι	κλ	θε.

the leading libraries of the United States and Germany so far as can be ascertained from the union catalogues of these two countries. And Audin could not find a copy to describe in his recent bibliography of French typefounders' specimen books.

So the alleged *Alphabetum* of 1543 is an elusive book, to say the least. I may be pardoned, therefore, a small modicum of pride in having on the shelves of my personal library a copy of this first book printed from the Royal Greek types of Claude Garamond. And to guard against future question on this point, the title page and two pages showing the extravagant calligraphic ligatures are here reproduced. This copy, perfect in every respect except that its margins have been much trimmed down, comprises nineteen unnumbered pages. Later editions, which appeared in 1548 and 1568, showing other sizes of the Greek type and containing more material, are also in my collection, and I know of editions of 1550 and 1554, as well as of the 1548 edition in the British Museum and other libraries.

These Greek types of Garamond's, which were modeled after the handwriting of Angelos Vergetios, aimed to reproduce as faithfully as possible the best Greek calligraphy of the period, just as the earlier Aldine Greek had been designed with the same object in view. But it has since been discovered that there was Greek writing before the fifteenth century and that it was executed in a far nobler style. It has also been realized, as Robert Proctor so aptly stated it, that handwriting can be translated directly into the form of metal types "no more than a painting can be translated directly into a tapestry, except by losing in the process the best and most characteristic features of both."

While Parisian printing during the early years of the sixteenth century tended to discard the gothic letter and to adopt a more Italianate style of printing, in the books of hours a more conservative tone for a long time prevailed. The very success which met the

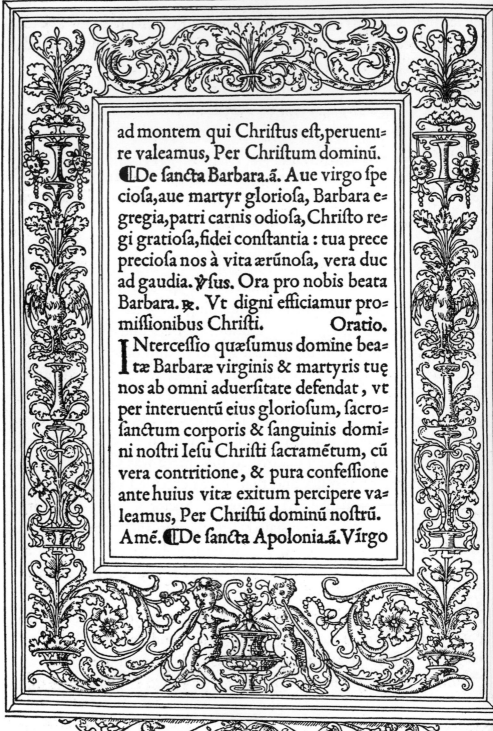

ad montem qui Christus est, perueni=
re valeamus, Per Christum dominū.
⸿De sancta Barbara.ā. Aue virgo spe
ciosa, aue martyr gloriosa, Barbara e=
gregia, patri carnis odiosa, Christo re=
gi gratiosa, fidei constantia : tua prece
preciosa nos à vita ærūnosa, vera duc
ad gaudia. ℣sus. Ora pro nobis beata
Barbara. ℞. Vt digni efficiamur pro=
missionibus Christi.   Oratio.
INtercessio quæsumus domine bea=
tæ Barbaræ virginis & martyris tuę
nos ab omni aduersitate defendat, vt
per interuentū eius gloriosum, sacro=
sanctum corporis & sanguinis domi=
ni nostri Iesu Christi sacramētum, cū
vera contritione, & pura confessione
ante huius vitæ exitum percipere va=
leamus, Per Christū dominū nostrū.
Amē. ⸿De sancta Apolonia.ā. Vírgo

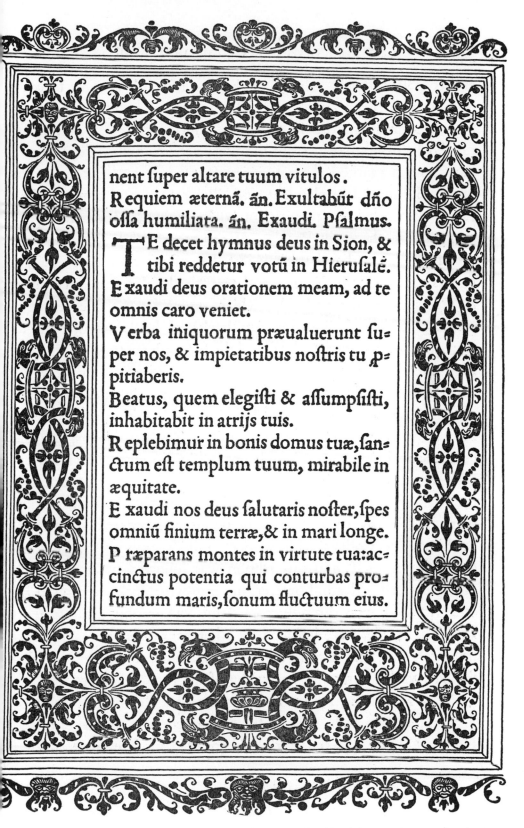

nent super altare tuum vitulos .

Requiem æternã. ãn. Exultabũt dño ossa humiliata. ãn. Exaudi. Psalmus.

TE decet hymnus deus in Sion, & tibi reddetur votũ in Hierusalẽ. Exaudi deus orationem meam, ad te omnis caro veniet.

Verba iniquorum præualuerunt super nos, & impietatibus nostris tu ꝑ= pitiaberis.

Beatus, quem elegisti & assumpsisti, inhabitabit in atrijs tuis.

Replebimur in bonis domus tuæ, san= ctum est templum tuum, mirabile in æquitate.

Exaudi nos deus salutaris noster, spes omniũ finium terræ, & in mari longe.

Præparans montes in virtute tua: ac= cinctus potentia qui conturbas pro= fundum maris, sonum fluctuum eius.

efforts of the French printers of the late fifteenth century to copy and even to surpass the beautiful illuminated manuscript prayer book rendered progress in the form difficult. The first period of fine books of hours was from the years 1490 to 1505. These *Horae* have certain marked characteristics. Printed in gothic type, often upon vellum, and resplendent with illustrations and borders, they closely resembled the manuscript books of hours. In their typography, then, the early Parisian *Horae* are of all books the most typical of the medieval spirit in art. In strange contrast to the religious nature of the pictures and text, the borders contain figures as grotesque as the gargoyles which stared from the eaves of a medieval cathedral. The Parisian books of hours, then, such as were produced in the last decade of the fifteenth century by Philippe Pigouchet, had all the coarseness and incongruity and all the vigor and freshness which characterized medieval art and life.

But after 1505 the beauty of the *Horae* steadily declined. The Parisian wood engravers began to imitate German models, and the borders and illustrations, though not lacking in vigor, became over-elaborate, unimaginative, and stupidly realistic. The task of restoring the book of hours to its former position of artistic merit was undertaken by Geofroy Tory. In 1524, he published a prayer book printed by Simon de Colines with borders, initials and illustrations engraved by himself, and this edition was followed by four or five others. After his death, however, his engraved blocks were used by other printers who carefully copied his typographic arrangement. His designs, too, were imitated by other engravers who were illustrating *Horae,* and as a result Tory's influence completely revolutionized the printing and decoration of the books of hours.

Tory substituted for medieval ornament a Renaissance form of decoration. As may be seen by the reproduction of the pages of the *Horae ad usum romanum,* printed in 1543 by Simon de Colines

(reproduced on pages 344 and 345), the borders by Geofroy Tory which appear in them are refined, balanced, restrained, and somewhat frigid. After attempting the use of black-letter type, Tory concluded that only roman could match the delicate borders, and his decision was approved by those who followed in his footsteps. The books of hours of Tory and his school are infinitely superior to the elaborate *Horae* of the 1520's, and if they lack the vigor of the early prayer book, they compensate for that deficiency by their elegance and dignity.

The printers of Paris who, with the support of Francis I, made the first sixty years of the sixteenth century the Golden Age of typography were scholars as well as artists. In them may be found an expression of the Renaissance ideal. They wrote books as well as printed them. They edited the classics which they issued from their presses. The art of the book, also, in the Golden Age was typically renaissance. In sharp contrast to the French book of the fifteenth century with its vigor, variety, and naïveté, the book of the Golden Age displayed a chaste simplicity, a classical restraint, and a delicate refinement which is typically renaissance in spirit.

The designers and printers of these books were not copying the styles of others, but were breaking new ground, and establishing styles of rare beauty and charm which have inspired the best book designers of the last three hundred years. If one traces back to its source the inspiration of many of the finest books produced in recent years, he will find their designers under deep obligation to the French practitioners of the arts of the book during this properly styled Golden Age.

Italian Book Illuſtration

ISTINGUISHED woodcut illustration is found in many Italian books of the fifteenth and early sixteenth centuries. The work of the Italian illustrators had a character and individuality of its own, making it of special interest to the student of bookmaking history.

The first woodcut illustrations to appear in a book printed on Italian soil were those in the *Meditationes* by Cardinal Torquemada, issued from the press of Ulrich Han at Rome in 1467. The simple line drawings were based on the frescoes in a church at Rome; the cutting of the blocks was relatively crude. The book proved a good seller, running through several editions. There were illustrations in other books printed at Rome during the remaining years of the century, but none of sufficient merit to demand our attention.

The first illustrated book printed at Naples appeared in 1478 from the press of Sixtus Riessinger, but we must skip to 1485 to find a noteworthy example of pictorial bookmaking. In this year Aesop's *Vita et fabulae* was printed at Naples by three *Germani fidelissimi* at the press of Francesco del Tuppo. The designs were enclosed in decorative borders cut on the block, which we will find to be the distinctive feature of the Florentine book illustrations. The drawing of the illustrations was rather amateurish, but the borders helped immensely toward making the blocks appear effectively in the book.

In *De re militari,* by Valturius, printed at Verona in 1472, we find illustrations which are of more interest to the student of mili-

tary history than to the bibliophile. The illustrations in an edition of Aesop printed in the same city by G. and A. Alvise in 1479 are of far greater interest. These latter blocks are enclosed within a border of type-cast ornaments.

While Venice was typographically the queen city of Italy, with many well-designed books issuing from its presses, it was not until the last ten or twelve years of the century that illustrated books of any importance made their appearance there. While a number of woodcuts are found in books of earlier dating, it was from 1488 onward that the work of local illustrators assumed importance.

We then find illustrations of two distinct schools, differentiated by Hind as *popular* and *classic,* and pointing to the existence of two master designers at work in Venice. The two types of design can be compared in two editions of the Bible, translated from Latin into Italian by Niccolò Malermi, one known as the Malermi Bible of 1490, illustrated in the popular style, and the other the Malermi Bible of 1493, with woodcuts in the classic style of drawing. In both editions were numerous small illustrations as well as some full pages of noble appearance, on which an illustration, an ornate border design, and a decorative initial were combined with type matter.

The Bible of 1490 with the popular style illustrations was printed by Giovanni Ragazzo for Lucantonio Giunta, an active and successful Venetian publisher, and actually proved popular, since it was at least twice reprinted. The Bible of 1493, illustrated in the classic style, was printed by Guliclmus Anima Mia and was not subsequently reprinted. The small cuts, which were scattered throughout the text of both editions, served, as Arthur Hind has pointed out, as "sign-posts to help the reader find his place without page headings or index."

Creditably illustrated editions of Boccaccio, Livy, Dante, Saint Jerome, Saint Thomas Aquinas, Saint Augustine, Voragine, and

AN ILLUSTRATION FROM ST. AUGUSTINE'S
DE CIVITATE DEI, VENICE, 1489.

other authors, too numerous to mention here in detail, issued from the Venetian presses during the last decade of the century. But two works cannot be passed by without special notice.

The first of these is Petrarch's *Trionfi,* which appeared in three Venetian editions from the offices of three different printers, between 1488 and 1493. Each included six full-page illustrations within decorative borders.

The masterpiece of Venetian book illustration, however, was the celebrated edition of the *Hypnerotomachia Poliphili* by Francesco Colonna, which was printed by Aldus Manutius in 1499. The text, a portion of which was later translated into English under the title of *The Strife of Love in a Dream,* recounted the love of Poliphilus for Polia. The book was of little significance as literature, but immensely important for the quality of its typography and illustration, and particularly for the perfect harmony between these two elements. Unfortunately, the artist responsible for the woodcuts, which are in the classic Venetian style, cannot be identified. A page of this remarkable book is reproduced on page 207.

The *Hypnerotomachia* was the only illustrated book of importance printed by Aldus, who, as we have seen, was interested primarily in the printing of editions of the Greek and Latin classics. Leonardus Crassus of Verona, who financed the making of this book, must have been responsible for Aldus having undertaken the printing and publishing of this "bright particular star" among the illustrated books of all time.

It should be added that some books of hours with woodcut illustrations and decorative borders were issued during the last decade of the century by a number of Venetian printers.

Excellent illustrated books were printed at Brescia, Vicenza, Verona, Saluzzo, Mantua, Bologna, and especially at Ferrara and Milan, as well as other cities of Italy, during the fifteenth century,

but book illustration at Florence was so notable in quality and character that it overshadows the work done elsewhere and demands, therefore, special consideration.

The earliest known illustrations in Florentine books were copperplate line engravings, but, as we have seen in Chapter XVII, the unsuitability of the process for use in type-set books produced by relief printing soon led to its abandonment. Following the failure of line engraving to meet the requirements, no illustrated books appeared from Florentine presses for eight or nine years, the few fully illustrated works being produced within the closing years of the century. Other books contained only one or two woodcuts. The typography and printing did not compare in quality with the best of the work at Venice. The texts were usually popular in character; romances, plays, poetry and the like—picture books made for the common people, which were read and re-read to the point of discard, with the consequence that many of them have become exceedingly rare.

That many of the Florentine books were printed anonymously has placed certain obstacles in the path of their study, but examination of the types used has resulted in attributing to Bartolommeo di Libri, whose name appears in only eight known volumes, over a hundred editions typographically unsigned.

It seems evident that the woodcutting shops or studios were independent of the printers, since some blocks appear in the books of more than one printing office. Whether the designers were identified with the cutters or not cannot be certainly determined.

The Florentine book illustrations have in common, almost without exception, one characteristic feature: a decorative border on four sides, cut on the block. This frame lends them charm as well as individuality.

In drawing, these illustrations are graphic and spirited, showing

ILLUSTRATION FROM PETRARCH'S SONETTI, VENICE, 1488.

TWO ILLUSTRATIONS FROM PULCI'S MORGANTE MAGGIORE, FLORENCE, 1501.

TWO ILLUSTRATIONS FROM THE CONTRASTO, FLORENCE, FIFTEENTH CENTURY.

them to be the work of artists who were true illustrators, to a degree not previously observed. Authorities see in them the style of great artists of the period, such as Botticelli and Ghirlandaio, but the best opinion assigns their authorship to lesser artists working under the tutelage and influence of these masters. There is some evidence to support the attribution of design of many of the fifteenth-century woodcuts to Bartolommeo di Giovanni, who is known to have collaborated with Ghirlandaio on several of the latter's paintings. But we can as yet make no certain statements regarding the obviously talented authorship of these illustrations.

Dr. Paul Kristeller, author of a two-volume work on Florentine woodcut illustrations, thus evaluates their artistic merit: "As the Athenian Lecythoi stand foremost amongst the Greek vases, so amongst Italian book-illustrations stand out the Florentine engravings used in books of the Quattrocento. Those relics of ancient Greek painting owe their surpassing importance to the fact that they are all which remain to us to represent it, but the beauty of the Florentine woodcuts is not, I think, less attractive because we may still enjoy the large frescoes and other paintings of contemporary Florentine artists. Never again, I am sure, has art, with all its refinements of technique, reached in book illustrations the same pitch of artistic perfection which, with all their unpretentious simplicity, the best woodcuts in the Florentine books of the Quattrocento, the true golden age of Italian art, never fail to exhibit."

A special group of Florentine publications were the *rappresentazioni,* or sacred plays, which were acted on certain saints' days. The individual plays could be printed in booklets of eight to twelve pages, but public demand required that they be illustrated. Those issued during the last decade of the fifteenth century, all lacking date and signatures of printer or publisher, have a charm and simplicity which have led to their high esteem by present-day biblio-

TWO ILLUSTRATIONS FROM THE QUADRIREGIO, FLORENCE, 1508.

philes. Many are exceedingly rare. As a matter of fact, out of eighty-five known *rappresentazioni,* the originals of only about fifty have been preserved to us.

Since we cannot discuss all the Florentine books or pamphlets issued before the close of the fifteenth century and during the first two decades thereafter, we will deal with a few of the outstanding issues from the viewpoint of illustration. The most ambitious undertaking was the edition of *Epistole e Evangile* published in 1495 by Piero Pacini and printed by Morgani and Petri, which was illustrated with upwards of a hundred and fifty woodcuts, many of which are of great interest. Another volume of importance was the same publisher's *Morgante maggiore,* by Luigi Pulci, printed by Societas Colubris, and illustrated by just short of a hundred and fifty woodcuts in the finest light-line manner, depicting scenes from the poem. Two of these scenes are reproduced on page 354.

A book announced by its title as dealing with the game of chess, the *Libro di giuoco di scacchi,* by Jacobus de Cessolis, pictured in its woodcuts the various activities of man. The frontispiece to the book, though somewhat inexact in perspective, has a vigor and charm not often found in woodcuts of the period. This book was printed by Miscomini in 1494, modern style.

Two scenes depicting the life of the day, here reproduced on page 355, figured among the interesting woodcuts illustrating the *Contrasto di carnevale e quaresima,* unsigned typographically, and the earliest edition not dated, though evidently printed in the fifteenth century. The only copy of this known to Dr. Kristeller is now in the British Museum.

Action pictures of the finest kind illustrated the *Quadriregio* by Frezzi, published in 1508 by Pacini. There is evidence that more than one printer worked on this book, part of which at least was produced in the office of Filippo Giunta. In my own opinion, this

is one of the great illustrated books of early printing history, and I hope I may some day have opportunity of issuing a complete facsimile of one of the three known copies, two of which are in the British Museum, the other being in the Biblioteca Corsiniana at Rome. He who will attentively examine the two woodcuts reproduced on page 357 will realize that their designer took one step nearer to the convincing representation, in a printed book, of human activity.

The blocks in the Florentine books were used again and again in editions of the more popular titles but, about the mid-point of the sixteenth century, the standard of printing and illustrating started on a decline. The anonymous artists and woodcutters of Florence had, however, written on a bright page in the chronicle of bookmaking a record of achievement which will never be erased.

XXIV

The Indomitable Plantin

THE name of Christopher Plantin is perhaps known to more people not identified with the bookmaking craft than that of any other early printer, with the possible exception of Gutenberg. Apart from the record of his distinguished career, this is due to the existence in Antwerp of a physical monument of great popular interest: the Plantin-Moretus Museum, in which has been preserved and is now exhibited the equipment of a sixteenth-century printing office. To this museum printers from all over the world make pilgrimage, for nowhere else is to be seen so comprehensive an exhibit of early printing methods. The museum is also visited annually by thousands of sightseers who find the ancient workrooms of compelling human interest.

A printer of great achievement and great misfortunes was Christopher Plantin, the Frenchman who won a place in the typographic hall of fame by his work in the Flemish city of Antwerp. Born about 1514, he learned the art of printing and bookbinding at Caen. Because of limitations on religious freedom in France, Plantin left Paris in 1548 and settled in Antwerp.

There were many printers then at work in Antwerp, and the prospects in this field did not look bright. So Plantin opened a shop where he sold prints and books, while his wife sold haberdashery "on the side." To employ his spare time he did bookbinding and decorated jewel boxes. He established an excellent reputation for work of this character but, just as fortune prepared to smile upon him, he had a tragic mishap. Mistaking him on a dark night for

someone else, a ruffian stabbed him in the arm and so disabled him that he could not again handle gilding tools.

Plantin thus had to make a new start in a somewhat different field and determined to try his luck at publishing. Starting in 1555, in a very small way, he issued more and more books each year, many of them being publications of considerable merit. Among them were a Latin Bible, texts in Greek and Latin, and a quadrilingual dictionary. He had meanwhile begun to print books as well as to publish them.

Again Plantin was prospering, but the old specter of religious intolerance which he had fled France to escape again raised its head. In 1562 the authorities ordered search for the printer of an unorthodox prayer book, and it was found that the book had been produced in Plantin's office, although without his knowledge. Being forewarned, our unlucky printer decamped abruptly, going to Paris, in which city he remained for twenty months. When he finally returned he found his business ruined; even his household furnishings had been sold at auction. In the words of the Salvation Army, Plantin was down but not out! Again he put his hand to the plough.

Four men backed Plantin in the re-establishment of his printing office. This time he managed to ingratiate himself with both church and state and was able to work without interruption. Perhaps he had found that heresy did not pay. The enterprise now prospered to a remarkable degree, and Plantin was able to commission types from the most renowned punch-cutters in Europe. In three short years he gathered a fine typographical equipment, as is evidenced by the specimen book which he issued in 1567.

Honors were now heaped on Plantin in quick succession. In 1570 he became, by appointment, printer to King Philip II of Spain and through Philip's influence obtained from the Holy See at Rome a monopoly of printing the liturgical books used in all the countries

under the rule of the Spanish monarch. He was invited to Paris by the king of France and was offered special inducements by the duke of Savoy to establish a printing office at Turin. But he "stuck to his last" and not only he, but all the members of his family, labored to build up the business. It is related that his youngest daughters were taught to read copy to the proof correctors at as early an age as twelve—often on books in foreign languages.

Plantin's ambition was to make his the greatest printing office in the world, and he certainly realized his ambition. By 1570 the institution was one of the show places of Europe. Twenty-two presses were working continually and—as one writer recorded with considerable awe—2,200 crowns daily were paid as wages to the workmen. The plant outgrew the four houses it occupied, and Plantin was soon under necessity of purchasing the property which has been preserved to the present day as the Plantin-Moretus Museum, to which reference has already been made.

The crowning glory of Plantin's printing career was the production of his Polyglot Bible. This was a project that he had long hoped to execute. The text was to run parallel in four different languages: Latin, Greek, Hebrew, and Chaldaic. To make possible the production of the six projected volumes, Plantin sought a subvention from the king of Spain which, after much deliberation, was granted, the king promising an advance of 6,000 ducats with the understanding that he was to receive equivalent value in copies of the completed book.

Like so many other projects, when the printer has his heart in the work, this one grew more ambitious as it went along. The six volumes became eight, and the cost ran much higher than had been anticipated. The edition, produced in the years from 1568 to 1573, consisted of 1,200 copies, divided up in much the manner of a French limited edition of the present day.

CAP. I.

Æc nomina filiorum Iſrael, qui ¹
ingreſſi ſunt in Ægyptum cum
Iacob patre eorum, vnuſquiſq;
cum domibus ſuis introierunt.

² Ruben, Symeon, Leui, Iudas, ²
³ Iſachar, Zabulon, & Beniamin, ³
min, ⁴ Dan, & Nephthali, Gad & Aſer. Ioſeph ⁴
autem erat in Ægypto. ⁵ Erant autem omnes animæ
quæ egreſſæ ſunt ex Iacob, quinque & ſeptuaginta.
⁶ Mortuus eſt autem Ioſeph, & omnes fratres e- ⁶
ius, & omnis generatio illa. ⁷ At filij Iſrael creuerũt
& multiplicati ſunt, & abundantes fuerunt, et inualuerunt valdè nimis. multiplicauit autem terra
illos. ⁸ Surrexit autem rex alter ſuper Aegyptũ, qui
non cognoſcebat Ioſeph. ⁹ Dixit autem genti ſuæ: Ecce
gens filiorum Iſrael magna valdè multitudo, et præ-
ualet ſuper nos. ¹⁰ Venite ergo ſapientes opprimamus ¹⁰
eos, ne forte multiplicetur: & quando acciderit nobis bellum, addentur & iſti ad aduerſarios: & de-
bellantes nos, egredientur de terra. ¹¹ Et præfecit eis ¹¹
præfectos operum, vt affligerent eos in operibus. &
ædificauerunt ciuitates munitas Pharaoni, & Phi-
thon, & Rameſſes, & On, quæ eſt Heliopolis.

¹² Quanto autem eos humiliabant, tanto plures ¹²
fiebant: & inualuerunt valdè. & abominatio-
nem habuerunt Aegyptij à filiis Iſrael. ¹³ Et op- ¹³
preſſerunt Aegyptij filios Iſrael vi: ¹⁴ Et afflixe- ¹⁴
runt eorum vitam in operibus duris in luto & la-
teritio, & omnibus operibus quæ in agris, ſecun-
dùm omnia opera quibus in ſeruitutem redegerunt
eos cum vi. ¹⁵ Et ait rex Aegyptiorum obſtetricibus ¹⁵
Hebræorum, vni earũ erat nomen Sephora, & nomen ſecundæ Phua: ¹⁶ Et ait illis: Quando obſte- ¹⁶
tricabitis Hebræas, et fuerint ad pariendum, ſi quidem maſculus fuerit, interficite illum: ſi autem fœ-
mina, reſeruate illam. ¹⁷ Timuerunt autem obſtetrices
Deum, & non fecerunt ſicut præcepit illis rex Aegypti: & viuificabant maſculos. ¹⁸ Vocauit autem ¹⁸
rex Aegypti obſtetrices, & ait illis: Quare feciſtis
rem hanc, & viuificaſtis maſculos? ¹⁹ Dixerunt ¹⁹
autem obſtetrices Pharaoni: Non ſicut mulieres
Aegyptiæ, Hebrææ: pariunt enim priuſquam ingre-
diantur ad eas obſtetrices, & pepererunt.

α'.

Αῦτα τὰ ὀνόματα τῶν υἱῶν ἰσραηλ, τῶν εἰ-
σπεπορευμζμ̓ων εἰς αἴγυπλον ἅμα ιακὼβ τῷ
πατεὶ αὐτῶν, ἕκαςος πανοικὶ αὐτῶν εἰσῆλ-
θοσαν· ῥουβίω̃, συμεὼν, λευὶ, ἰούλας,
ἰσάχαρ, ζαβουλὼν, καὶ βενιαμὶν,
δὰν, καὶ νεφθαλὶ, γὰδ, καὶ ἀσὴρ. ἰωσὴφ ἦ ἦν ἐν αἰγύπλῳ.
⁵ ἦ̃σαν ἢ πᾶσαι ψυχαὶ αἱ ἐξελθοῦσαι ἐξ ιακὼβ, πέντε
ἑβδομήκοντα. ⁶ ἐτελεύτησε ἢ ἰωσὴφ ⁊ πάντες οἱ ἀδελφοὶ
αὐτ̃ο, ⁊ πᾶσα ἡ γενεὰ ἐκείνη. ⁷ οἱ ἢ υἱοὶ ισραὴλ ηὐξήθησαν,
⁊ ἐπληθύνθησαν, ⁊ χυδαῖοι ἐγζμὀντο, καὶ κατίχυον σφόδ\
σφόδρα. ἐπλήθυνε ἢ ἡ γῆ αὐτούς. ⁸ ἀνέςη ἢ βασιλεὺς ἕτερος
ἐπ' αἴγυπλον, ὃς οὐκ ἤδει τὸν ἰωσήφ. ⁹ εἶπε ἢ τῷ ἔθνει αὐτ̃ο, ἰ-
δοὺ τὸ ἔθνο̃ τῶν υἱῶν ισραηλ μέγα πολὺ πληθο̃, καὶ ἰχύει
¹⁰ ὑπὲρ ἡμᾶς. δεῦτε οὖν κατασοφισώμεθα αὐτούς, μήπο-
τε πληθυνθῆ, ⁊ ἡνίκα ἂν συμβῆ ἡμῖν πόλεμο̃, πρ̃ος ἐθιο̃ν-
ται καὶ αὐτοὶ πρ̃ος τοὺς ὑπεναντίοις· καὶ ἐκπολεμήσαντες ἡ-
¹¹ μᾶς, ἐξελεύσονται ἐκ τῆς γῆς. ⁊ ἐπέςησεν αὐτοῖς ἐπι-
ςάτας τῶν ἔργων, ἵνα κακώσωσιν αὐτοὺς ἐν τοῖς ἔργοις. ⁊ ᾠκο-
δόμησαν πόλεις ὀχυρὰς τῷ φαραὼ, τήν τε φιθὼμ ⁊ ραμεσ-
¹² σῆ, ⁊ ὼν, ἥ ἐςιν ἡλιούπολις. ¹² καθ' ὅτι ἢ αὐτοὺς ἐταπεί-
νουν, τοσούτῳ πλείους ἐγίνοντο. ⁊ ἴχυον σφόδρα. ⁊ ἐβδελύ-
¹³ σσοντο οἱ αἰγύπλιοι ἀπὸ τῶν υἱῶν ισραηλ. ¹³ ⁊ κατεδυ̃νά-
¹⁴ ςευον οἱ αἰγύπλιοι τοὺς υἱοὺς ισραηλ βία· ¹⁴ ⁊ κατωδύνων
αὐτῶν τὴν ζωὴν ἐν τοῖς ἔργοις τοῖς σκληροῖς, ἐν τῷ πηλῷ ⁊ τῇ
πλινθεία, ⁊ πᾶσι τοῖς ἔργοις τοῖς ἐν τοῖς πεδίοις, κ̃ τὰ πάντα τὰ ἔρ-
¹⁵ γα, ὧν κατεδουλοῦντο αὐτοὺς μετ̃ βίας. ¹⁵ καὶ εἶπεν ὁ βασιλεὺς τῶν αἰγυπλίων ταῖς μαίαις τῶν ἑβραίων, τῇ μιᾷ αὐτῶ̃
ἦ ὄνομα σεφώρα, καὶ τὸ ὄνομα τῆς δευτέρας, φουά·
¹⁶ ⁊ εἶπεν αὐταῖς, ὅταν μαιοῦσθε τὰς ἑβραίας, ⁊ ὦσι πρ̃ος
τὸ τίκτειν, ἐὰν μεν ἄρσεν ᾖ, ἀποκλείνατε αὐτ̃ο· ἐὰν δὲ θῆλυ,
¹⁷ περιποιήσασθε αὐτὸ. ¹⁷ ἐφοβήθησαν ἢ αἱ μαῖαι τὸν θεὸν,
⁊ οὐκ ἐποίησαν καθ' ὅτι συνέταξεν αὐταῖς ὁ βασιλεὺς αἰγύπλου. καὶ ἐζωογόνουν τὰ ἄρσενα. ¹⁸ ἐκάλεσε ἢ ὁ βασιλεὺς αἰγύπλου τὰς μαίας, καὶ εἶπεν αὐταῖς, διότι ἐποιήσατε
¹⁹ τὸ πρᾶγμα τοῦτο, ⁊ ἐζωογονεῖτε τὰ ἄρσενα· ¹⁹ εἶπαν δὲ
αἱ μαῖαι τῷ φαραὼ, οὐχ ὡς αἱ γυναῖκες αἰγύπλιαι, αἱ ἑβραῖαι,
τίκτουσι γ̃ πρὶν ἢ εἰσελθεῖν πρ̃ος αὐτὰς τὰς μαίας, καὶ ἔτι-
κτον.

CHALDAICAE PARAPHRASIS TRANSLATIO.

CAP. I.

ET hæc ſunt nomina filiorum Iſrael, qui ingreſſi ſunt in Ægyptum cum Iacob, ſinguli cum viris domus ſuæ introierunt:
² Ruben, Symeon, Leui, & Iudas, ³ Iſachar, Zabulon, & Beniamin, ⁴ Dan, & Neptali, Gad & Aſer. ⁵ Mortuuſque
⁵ Erantque omnes animæ egredientium de femore Iacob, ſeptuaginta animæ, cum Ioſeph qui erat in Ægypto. ⁷ Filij autem Iſrael creuerunt, & nati ſunt in multitudinem, & roborati
ſunt vehementer nimis; & impleta eſt terra ex eis. ⁸ Et ſurrexit rex nouus in Ægypto, qui non confirmabat decreta Ioſeph.
⁹ Et ait ad populum ſuum: Ecce populus filiorum Iſrael multus & fortior nobis: ¹⁰ Venite, ſapienter agentes contra eos, ne fortè mul-
tiplicentur, & quando acciderit nobis bellum, addantur quoque ipſi inimici contra nos bellum, & aſcendent de terra. ¹¹ Et conſtituerunt ſuper eos principes malefacientes, vt affligerent eos in operibus ſuis, ædificaueruntque vrbes theſaurorum Pharaoni, Phi-
ton & Rameſes. ¹² Et quanto affligebant eos, tanto multiplicabantur, & tanto roborabantur. & tribulatio erat Ægyptiis propter filios
Iſrael. ¹³ Et ſeruire fecerunt Ægyptij filios Iſrael durè: ¹⁴ Et ad amaritudinem perduxerunt vitam eorum in ſeruitute dura, ¹⁵ Dixitque rex Ae-
in luto, & in lateribus, & in omni ſeruitute in agro, in omnibus operibus ſuis, quibus eos grauiter ſeruire fecerunt. ¹⁵ Dixitque rex Æ-
gypti obſtetricibus Iudæorum, nomen vnius Sephora, & nomen alterius Phua. ¹⁶ Et ait: Quando obſtetricabitis Iudæas, videbitis in partu
& filius fuerit, interficietis eum; & ſi filia fuerit, reſeruabitis eam. ¹⁷ Timueruntque obſtetrices à facie Dei, & non fecerunt ſicut locutus fuerat eis
rex Ægypti, ſed conſeruabant filios. ¹⁸ Vocauitque rex Ægypti obſtetrices, & ait: Cur feciſtis hanc rem, & reſeruatis filios? ¹⁹ Et dixerunt obſtetrices ad Pharaonem: Quia non ſunt ſicut mulieres Ægyptiæ, mulieres Iudææ; quia ipſæ ſapientes ſunt, & antequam veniat ad eas obſtetrix, pariunt.

Q 2

10 on grand imperial paper of Italy.............price not stated
30 on grand imperial, at the price of.................200 florins
200 on the fine royal paper of Lyons.................100 florins
960 on the fine royal paper of Troyes................. 70 florins

In addition, twelve copies on vellum were printed for the printer's royal patron.

Plantin's only troubles were not those involved in printing the book. The king would not permit its publication until the pope expressed his approval, and this sanction was denied. Arias Montanus, who had edited the book, traveled to Rome to petition for a revision of this fiat, but only when a new pope was elevated to office was the necessary approval obtained.

Even then the book was under the shadow of suspicion, one authority having denounced it as heretical and Judaistic. The Inquisition undertook to examine its text, but took many years to do so, and only in 1580 ruled that the book might properly be circulated. The strain of these delays on Plantin's finances can quite easily be imagined. The great Polyglot, therefore, on which a considerable share of his reputation was based, was not a very great satisfaction to him at the time of its production.

The king of Spain, who was Plantin's royal patron, was ready with promises in the grand manner but very remiss in meeting his obligations. He was lax in paying his grants to Plantin and just about the time that worthy printer was most sorely pressed, he would command him to print more service books for the church. But the king's financial derelictions had a direct effect even more disastrous. He committed the supreme error of neglecting to pay his soldiers, and as a result, the Spanish military threatened to plunder the city to obtain their compensation. In 1576, after Plantin was established in his new and handsome office, mutiny broke forth. In the sack of the city which ensued, eight thousand citizens were

BIBLIA SACRA

HEBRAICE,
CHALDAICE,
GRÆCE, &
Latine

PIETATIS CONCORDIÆ. Isaiæ.11

PHILIPPI II. REG. CATHOL. PIETATE,
ET STUDIO AD SACROSANCTÆ
ECCLESIÆ USUM

CHRISTOPH. PLANTINUS EXCUD. ANTVERPIÆ.

TITLE PAGE OF VOLUME I OF PLANTIN'S POLYGLOT BIBLE.

killed. The soldiers set fire to a thousand houses, and six million florins worth of property was consumed. Everything that could be moved was stolen, and hideous cruelties were perpetrated. When the smoke of the battle cleared away, Antwerp, one of the queen cities of Europe, was in ruins, never again to recover its former prosperity. The effect on Plantin's business was disastrous. According to his own account, "nine times did I have to pay ransom to save my property from destruction; it would have been cheaper to have abandoned it."

In the face of this last and greatest blow, Plantin still refused to admit he was beaten. He again vigorously attacked his work, but from that time to the end of his life he was severely cramped financially. To meet his most pressing obligations, he often had to sell books at sacrifice prices. Often he had to sell some of his equipment. In 1581 he sold his library in Paris for less than half its value. His predicament was that, although he had large resources in stock of books on hand, in printing plant equipment, and in accounts receivable, he had little ready cash with which to carry on his business. He was not, however, the first business man who has found himself in this position.

The political horizon once more becoming threatening, Plantin turned over his office to his sons-in-law and went to Leiden in 1582. Here the authorities of the university received him with open arms and appointed him as their printer; which function he discharged for a period of almost three years. Political conditions in Antwerp having then become more favorable, he returned to that city. The zenith of his career, however, had passed, and though he again went to work, the results obtained were not what they had been in the past. On July 1, 1589, Plantin passed to his heavenly reward which, let us sincerely hope, was more in consonance with his merits than that which had fallen to his lot this side of Saint Peter's Gate.

SIX DECORATIVE INITIALS USED BY PLANTIN.

We know more about Plantin than about most early printers, because not only his office and a great deal of its equipment but also his papers and records have been rather completely preserved. His correspondence, for example, has been published in a series of volumes, and his manuscript records and accounts, which were kept with commendable neatness and thoroughness, are preserved today in the collection of the Plantin Museum. In 1850 the building was falling into decay, but some public-spirited citizens of Antwerp induced the public authorities to purchase the property, which purchase was accomplished in 1875. The Museum, for by this name it is known, has been restored just as accurately as possible to the state in which it was in Plantin's day.

From Plantin's records we gain a pretty clear idea of the industrial conditions of his time. In his office work began at five o'clock in the morning, but the quitting time was not stated. Every workman coming into the organization had to pay as initiation eight sous which were devoted to buying drinks for the other employees of the office. He was also required to contribute two sous to the poor box. At the end of the month he had to put thirty sous in the poor box and pay ten sous to his comrades.

From the typographical point of view, Plantin was not a great printer. He contributed little to type design or to book design, but he was, in every sense of the word, a great publisher. And as a printer he was a thorough and conscientious craftsman.

As we have seen in this short sketch of his activities, on occasion after occasion, he started climbing the hill toward success, and every time some new disaster, for which he was in no way responsible, overwhelmed him and cast him back. Each time, however, he returned gamely to the struggle and, in the course of his continual battle with circumstances, he produced books which have made his name immortal in the annals of bookmaking.

XXV

The Vogue of Engraving

L IMITS of space prevent detailed discussion here of the role of intaglio engraving in the illustration of books during the sixteenth and seventeenth centuries. In that period fully engraved decorated title pages came into vogue, and late in the sixteenth century we find engraved illustrated title pages which show, in compartments, varied views referred to in the text of the book. A title of this character, done by one of the De Brys, is found in J. J. Boissard's *Theatrum vitae humanae,* printed at Metz in 1596.

Otherwise, engraving served well to illustrate books in which minute detail was necessary, as in atlases, herbals, anatomical works, and in series of portraits. And as fashionable books designed as objects of luxury for the wealthy amateur came more into vogue, the barrier of greater expense incident to the production of intaglio illustrations became of less effect.

The great period of copperplate engraving as related to printed books came in the eighteenth century, with the bulk of the best work being done in France. Able draughtsmen such as Hubert F. Gravelot, Charles Eisen, or Moreau *le jeune* conceived the compositions which they turned over to others to engrave on the copper plates. These men and others illustrated many handsome books, some of which were of literary mediocrity. They were at their best in depicting contemporary society.

Eisen is best known for the plates he designed for Dorat's *Les Baisers,* Paris, 1770, one of the most graceful books of the period. Gravelot is remembered for the plates he designed for Marmontel's

Contes moraux, Paris, 1765. Moreau *le jeune* was a keen observer of the details of life and manners. There is historical importance to the plates he engraved for De Laborde's *Chansons* of 1773, recording for us faithfully the atmosphere of the Dauphine and her court, as Hind has pointed out. He also illustrated most brilliantly J. J. Rousseau's *Œuvres completes,* 1774-1783, bearing a London imprint but probably actually printed at Brussels.

In addition to the illustrations they produced, the eighteenth-century French engravers made a notable contribution to the decoration of books, designing many head and tail pieces, frames for initial letters, and the like, of inescapable charm. Never before nor since has a style of bookmaking been more characteristic of a period. Cupids and urns, ribbons and wreaths, flowers and ringlets, these and other related elements were interwoven and made to grace the pages of books now highly esteemed by certain collectors. The leader in this decorative school was Pierre Choffard, whose work may be seen to good advantage in the 1762 edition of La Fontaine's *Contes* and the edition of Ovid's *Metamorphoses* printed between 1767 and 1771.

The name of Charles Nicolas Cochin the younger is known to many present-day printers through the typeface named after him, which is patterned after the copperplate lettering used to caption the engravings of his period. Cochin, unlike many of his contemporaries, was as much an engraver as a designer, being deeply interested in the technique of the art. His plates are fully representative of the best style of the period.

In a few books the vogue of engraving was carried to its ultimate conclusion by the graving on copper of text as well as illustrations. Pine's *Horace,* which appeared at London in 1733, was printed throughout from engraved plates, representing the last word in elegance as it was then conceived. This example was later emulated

112 *LES BAISERS.*

Avec toi croîtra mon amour :
Puissent tes feuilles quelque jour
Se voir tresser pour sa couronne !
Oui ; qu'elle t'envie à son tour,
Que ta verdure s'épaississe ;
Et que sa tige s'arrondisse,
Pour l'ombrager à son retour !

XVIII BAISER.

XVIII. BAISER.

L'IMMORTALITÉ.

De quels charmes tu m'environnes !
Que je sens près de toi d'amoureuses fureurs !
Comme ils sont parfumés les baisers que tu donnes !
En les cueillant, je crois cueillir des fleurs,
Telles que les vergers d'Hymette
En fournissent dès le matin
A ces filles de l'air qui sur le violette
Et l'oeillet et le lis vont chercher leur butin.

H

The Eye sees more than the Heart knows.

Printed by Will:^m Blake : 1793.

THE TITLE PAGE OF BLAKE'S VISIONS OF
THE DAUGHTERS OF ALBION, 1793.

in Paris in the production in 1772 by the same process of *Le Temple de Cnide,* illustrated after designs by Eisen.

This romantic and ornate school of engraving suffered an almost total eclipse with the French Revolution. The next flash of genius is found in England, incarnated in the person of William Blake. Among contemporary work of the most mediocre character, the imaginative engravings of this truly great artist are arresting indeed. Most amateurs of illustration become slightly incoherent when asked to evaluate artistically the better of Blake's compositions. And it is, in fact, difficult to overrate them.

The illustrations of Young's *Night Thoughts* of 1797, of *America, a Prophecy* of 1793, and of the *Book of Job* of 1825 are among the best of his work. He designed some fine illustrations for the writings of John Milton and at the time of his death he was at work on a series of illustrations for Dante's *Divina commedia.* His title page for the *Visions of the Daughters of Albion* of 1793 is reproduced in the plate facing this page.

William Blake was trained as an engraver and spent part of his life as a print seller, but during most of his career he was drawing and engraving. For many of his works he engraved text as well as illustrations, some of the publications being printed in colors, others hand-tinted. Blake was a mystic and visionary, and some of the subjects he put down on metal are weird and imaginative. But of such stuff are great artists made. As Collins Baker has eloquently written: "If, when we reflect on the titanic quality of his imagination and the godlike range of his endeavor, we relate these to his place in time and the limitations of his artistic training and experience, we must be amazed that he succeeds so often as he does in expressing the grandeur and supernatural content of his conceptions." At the end of his career, Blake was bedridden and suffered greatly. His end was in keeping with his work. We are told that

"having drawn for an hour, he began to sing Hallelujahs and songs of joy and triumph, loudly and with true ecstatic energy." Thus died the great English engraver on August 12, 1827.

Another of the greatest English artists was contemporary with Blake. I refer to Joseph Mallard William Turner, who lived 1775-1851. Turner's reputation rests first on his magnificent watercolors, spirited, imaginative, and wholly original in style. But he designed many plates which were engraved, or partly etched and partly engraved, by others, whose work he carefully checked and caused to be revised. Many of the subjects were issued as series of prints, but Turner also did some significant book illustrations, among them those for Rogers' *Italy* of 1830, and for Walter Scott's *Prose Works* printed in 1834-1836.

From this point onward, the work of the best artists designing for or making intaglio plates shifted from engraving to etching, which is less well adapted to the illustration of books.

XXVI

Baskerville and His Disciples

DO you remember the japanned trays, hairpin holders and knickknacks that were popular in the days of your youth? The profits on the manufacture of such japanned ware paid for the issue of some of the finest books ever produced. It came about this way. John Baskerville's first position was that of servant in a clergyman's household, in Birmingham, England. His employer found that he had more than ordinary skill in penmanship and enlisted his services in the instruction of poor boys in the parish in the art of writing. He soon secured an appointment as writing master in a local school. He also applied his skill in letter formation to cutting inscriptions on gravestones.

To make more money, Baskerville took up the production of japanned ware of high quality and with a superior type of decoration. At this business he made a great success and within a few years amassed a considerable fortune. He took a place in the outskirts of the city, which he called Easy Hill, and there built a handsome dwelling. Alexander Carlyle in his *Autobiography* describes it thus: "Baskerville's house was a quarter mile from the town, and in its way handsome and elegant. What struck us most was his first kitchen, which was most completely furnished with everything that could be wanted. Kept as clean and bright as if it had come straight from the shop, for it was used, and the fineness of the kitchen was a great point in the family, for here they received their company, and there we were entertained with coffee and chocolate."

When Baskerville was fifty years old he took up printing, the

avocation that was to make his name famous. He entered upon this work not as a business, but rather as a hobby. At this time printing as an art was still in eclipse in England. To be sure, Caslon, a generation earlier, had provided some good types for the use of printers, but they were seldom put to good use. Baskerville determined to print a few books just as well as they could be printed, so he started in at the beginning of the printing process—with the making of types. From 1750 to 1752 he devoted himself to this task, taking the greatest care to have every letter perfect. At the same time his printing equipment was being set up. His press was of the same kind as those commonly in use at the time, but it was made with greater precision. The paper available in the market did not suit his fastidious requirements, so he apparently had made to his own specifications the first wove paper—that is, paper which does not show the laid lines of the screens of the molds. This type of paper has since come into almost general use for book printing, so that laid paper is now the exception, rather than the rule.

The printer's ink then made did not come up to his standards, so he entered upon the manufacture of this accessory, boiling his own oil and burning his own lampblack. As fast as the sheets of dampened paper were printed, they were placed between hot plates of copper. The sheets were thus dried, the ink set, and the printed pages given a burnished appearance not found in any other printing of the period. In short, Baskerville's process of printing was original in many features, and each step was carried out with infinite care.

Seven years elapsed between the inception of the printing enterprise and the issue of the first book from the Baskerville press, the intervening period being occupied with the perfection of the materials and equipment. Again and again the publication date of the *Virgil*—the initial issue of the press—was postponed, in order that it might be just as perfect, in Baskerville's judgment, as human

PUBLII VIRGILII

MARONIS

BUCOLICA,

GEORGICA,

ET

AENEIS.

BIRMINGHAMIAE:

Typis JOHANNIS BASKERVILLE.

MDCCLVII.

THE TITLE PAGE OF BASKERVILLE'S VIRGIL.

effort could make it. When the book finally appeared its reception by the world of booklovers in Europe justified its printer's expectations. It was highly praised on all sides and, overnight, Baskerville became famous as a printer.

Baskerville's aim is well set forth in the preface to his second book, Milton's *Paradise Lost*—the only preface he ever wrote. In this he tells us:

Amongst the several mechanic Arts that have engaged my attention, there is no one which I have pursued with so much steadiness and pleasure, as that of *Letter-Founding*. Having been an early admirer of the beauty of Letters, I became insensibly desirous of contributing to the perfection of them. I formed to myself ideas of greater accuracy than had yet appeared, and have endeavoured to produce a *Set* of *Types* according to what I conceived to be their true proportion.

Mr. Caslon is an Artist, to whom the Republic of Learning has great obligations; his ingenuity has left a fairer copy for my emulation, than any other master. In his great variety of *Characters* I intend not to follow him; the *Roman* and *Italic* are all I have hitherto attempted; if in these he has left room for improvement, it is probably more owing to that variety which divided his attention, than to any other cause. I honor his merit, and only wish to derive some small share of Reputation, from an Art which proves accidentally to have been the object of our mutual pursuit.

After having spent many years, and not a little of my fortune in my endeavours to advance this art; I must own it gives me great satisfaction, to find that my edition of *Virgil* has been so favorably received. The improvement in the manufacture of the *Paper,* the *Colour,* and *Firmness* of the *Ink* were not overlooked; nor did the accuracy of the workmanship in general, pass unregarded. If the judicious found some imperfections in the *first attempt,* I hope the present work will shew that a proper use has been made of their Criticisms: I am conscious of this at least, that I received them as I ever shall, with that degree of deference which every private man owes to the Opinion of the public.

It is not my desire to print many books; but such only, as are *books* of *Consequence,* of *intrinsic merit,* or *established Reputation,* and which the

public may be pleased to see in an elegant dress, and to purchase at such a price, as will repay the extraordinary care and expence that must necessarily be bestowed upon them. ...

Though the issues of his press were well received, the financial returns were not such as "to repay the extraordinary care and expence," and the printing venture operated always at a loss. Baskerville had not expected the enterprise to show a profit. He had, for example, written Robert Dodsley, his publishing representative in London, regarding the projected printing of a "pocket Classick" as follows: "nor should I be very sollicitous whether it paid me or not." But he had not expected the operating deficit to be as great as it turned out to be. At one time he became disheartened and gave up printing for several years. But he was spurred again into activity by the attempt of a local competitor to print a Bible.

The Birmingham amateur printed many editions of classics, but his *chef d'œuvre* was the folio Bible which he printed at Cambridge under the auspices of the University. The printing of this book, completed in 1763, gratified a long-cherished ambition. The Bible was a noble volume, but out of an edition of 1,250 copies published at four guineas, he was able to sell less than half, and in 1768 he "remaindered" over five hundred at a sacrifice price to a London bookseller. That ardent bibliophile, Thomas Frognall Dibdin, characterized it, in an over-enthusiastic mood, as "one of the most beautiful printed books in the world."

Baskerville also issued a Book of Common Prayer which he intended to be "as perfect as I can make it." He wisely planned the typography "for people who begin to want spectacles, but are ashamed to use them in Church." He also designed and cut a font of Greek type for Oxford University, but this latter performance added nothing to his reputation.

In all, he printed about sixty-seven books—not a large total out-

put for a printer. But Baskerville was always interested in quality rather than quantity. Judged by current standards, his books were expensive and could be afforded only by collectors of means. Most of his books were delivered unbound, the purchasers having them bound up to suit their individual tastes.

All his books are characterized by great simplicity of typography. Of ornament he used almost none. He depended on well cast type carefully set and spaced and rightly positioned on the page. The simplicity and perfection of the Baskerville volumes made them stand out spectacularly among the ill-printed products of the contemporary English press.

Baskerville type was more than well executed mechanically. It represented a real departure in type design. His is generally considered as the first real "modern" typeface in contradistinction to the "old-style" types which had hitherto been in vogue. An *old-style* type is one in which the various elements of individual letters are of fairly uniform weight; in other words, the design is of approximately the same color throughout. A *modern* type varies in the weight of its elements, some strokes being relatively thick and others relatively thin. One other feature of old-style type is that the *serifs,* or terminals of the main strokes, are club-shaped and rounded at their extremities, while the extremities of the serifs in the modern type are pointed.

The sharp-pointed serifs, which printed well on Baskerville's smooth-finish paper, gave the printing an effect of brilliance never before seen. This effect was claimed by many contemporary critics to be dazzling and hard on the eyes, a criticism seized upon and propagated by the printers, with whom Baskerville was unpopular. For Baskerville was not highly regarded by other printers, probably because of the superior attitude he assumed, and his work was subjected to many unfounded criticisms.

CHRISTMAS-DAY.

The Epistle. Heb. i. 1.

GOD, who at sundry times, and in divers manners spake in time past unto the fathers by the prophets, hath in these last days spoken unto us by his Son, whom he hath appointed heir of all things, by whom also he made the worlds; Who being the brightness of his glory, and the express image of his person, and upholding all things by the word of his power, when he had by himself purged our sins, sat down on the right hand of the Majesty on high: being made so much better than the angels, as he hath by inheritance obtained a more excellent name than they. For unto which of the angels said he at any time, Thou art my Son, this day have I begotten thee? And again, I will be to him a Father, and he shall be to me a Son? And again, when he bringeth in the first-begotten into the world, he saith, And let all the angels of God worship him. And of the Angels he saith, who maketh his angels spirits, and his ministers a flame of fire. But unto the Son he saith, Thy throne, O God, is for ever and ever: a scepter of righteousness is the scepter of thy kingdom: Thou hast loved righteousness, and hated iniquity; therefore God, even thy God, hath anointed thee with the oil of gladness above thy fellows. And, Thou, Lord, in the beginning hast laid the foundation of the earth; and the heavens
are

Benjamin Franklin, who was a subscriber to Baskerville's editions and a regular correspondent of the Birmingham printer, wrote him regarding an amusing instance of this prejudice:

Let me give you a pleasant instance of the prejudice some have entertained against your work. Soon after I returned, discoursing with a gentleman concerning the artists of Birmingham, he said you would be the means of blinding all the readers of the nation, for the strokes of your letters being too thin and narrow, hurt the eye, and he could never read a line of them without pain. "I thought," said I, "you were going to complain of the gloss on the paper some object to." "No, no," said he, "I have heard that mentioned, but it is not that; it is in the form and cut of the letters themselves, they have not that height and thickness of the stroke which makes the common printing so much more comfortable to the eye." You see the gentleman was a connoisseur. In vain I endeavoured to support your character against the charge; he knew what he felt, and could see the reason of it, and several other gentlemen among his friends had made the same observation, etc. Yesterday he called to visit me, when, mischievously bent to try his judgment, I stepped into my closet, tore off the top of Mr. Caslon's Specimen, and produced it to him as yours, brought with me from Birmingham saying, I had been examining it, since he spoke to me, and could not for my life perceive the disproportion he mentioned, desiring him to point it out to me. He readily undertook it, and went over the several fonts, showing me everywhere what he thought instances of that disproportion; and declared that he could not then read the specimen without feeling very strongly the pain he had mentioned to me. I spared him that time the confusion of being told, that these were the types he had been reading all his life, with so much ease to his eyes; the types his adored Newton is printed with (for he himself is an author), and yet never discovered the painful disproportion in them, till he thought they were yours.

John Baskerville was personally a most interesting character. In dress, he was fastidious to a degree, verging on foppishness. He drove an elegant coach, with a pair of cream-colored horses, which was one of the marvels of Birmingham. He was vain and eccentric.

A Mrs. Eaves went to live at Easy Hill about 1750, probably in the role of housekeeper. She had been left destitute by her husband, who had been forced to flee the kingdom, with two daughters and a son on her hands. Soon afterwards she and Baskerville were living together and, though her husband was still living, she passed everywhere as Mrs. Baskerville. One is happy to report that his social position in Birmingham does not appear to have been prejudiced by this relation. Baskerville was very fond of her and, upon the death of Eaves, married her in 1764. To her he bequeathed most of his property. She bore him one son, who died in infancy to the great grief of the father.

Baskerville was a sincere unbeliever and he stated his convictions regarding theology in his will:

My further will & pleasure is and I Hearby Declare that the Device of Goods & Chattles as Above is upon this Express Condition that my Wife in Concert with my Exors do Cause my Body to be Buried in a Conical Building in my own premises, Heartofore used as a mill which I have lately Raised Higher and painted and in a vault which I have prepared for It. This Doubtless to many may appear a Whim perhaps It is so—But is a whim for many years Resolve'd upon as I have a Hearty Contempt of all Superstition the Farce of a Consecrated Ground the Irish Barbarism of Sure and Certain Hopes &c. I also consider Revelation as It is call'd Exclusive of the Scraps of Morality casually Intermixt with It to be the most Impudent Abuse of Common Sense which ever was Invented to Befool Mankind. I Expect some srewd Remark will be made on this my Declaration by the Ignorant & Bigotted who cannot Distinguish between Religion & Superstition and are Taught to Believe that morality (by which I understand all the Duties a man ows to God and his fellow Creatures) is not Sufficient to entitle him to Divine favour with professing to believe as they Call It Ceartain Absurd Doctrines & mysteries of which they have no more Conception than a Horse. This Morality Alone I profess to have been my Religion and the [Rule] of my Actions. to which I appeal how far my profession and practice have Been Consistant.

And finally he gave to his executors each "6 Guineas to Buy a Ring which I hope they will Consider as a Keepsake." To some questions of friends, regarding the manner in which he wished to be buried, he said they could "bury him sitting, standing or lying, but he did not think they could bury him flying." Baskerville died in 1795 and was interred in the vault as he had specified.

The name of John Baskerville will be immortal in the annals of printing—and rightly so, for he was one of the all-too-few idealists in the field of typography. Personally, I confess to a great admiration for him and for his work, and "in witness whereof," have named my younger son after him. The basis of Baskerville's fame is well outlined by Josiah Benton, at the conclusion of his excellent biographical essay:

What is it that makes the life and work of this middle-aged, vain, and silly Birmingham Englishman interesting to us? Why do we collect his imprints, and why do we talk about him? I think it is because he had the true artistic vision and courage. He conceived the idea of a perfect book. He conceived the book as an artist conceives a statue before he strikes a blow with his chisel into the marble. It was wonderful that he should have done so. He had grown up in a manufacturing and mercantile business, making japan work for sale, and profiting by its sale. Most men never get out of the work and the ideas of the work which they do until they are fifty years of age. He did. Why was it? I think as I have said, it was because he had an artistic perception and conceived the thing which he was to do, and adhered to his conception. Everything shows that he wrought in the true artistic spirit: having conceived the thing to be done he proceeded to do it. All his work was executed upon a hand-press His printing-office was what we should call a private printing-office in his house. He cut the type; he made the ink and improved the press; he devised the paper; and from start to finish the work was his. Everybody who will do better work than anybody else must adhere to it, or he will not produce perfect work. It is this that makes Baskerville interesting to us, and make the productions of his little private press treasures in the world of art.

Even more important than Baskerville's own work was the influence of that work on the development of typography in Europe. This became apparent first in the work of the Didots—the famous family of French printers. The Didot types reflected the *modern* character of the Baskerville types, their *papier vélin* imitated the paper he introduced, and their "classic" style of composition likewise showed evidence of his example. In part directly, and partly through the Didots, features of typographic style in which Baskerville was the pioneer exerted a great influence on Giambattista Bodoni, the eminent Italian printer who rose to fame during the last quarter of the eighteenth century.

The most celebrated of European printers thus became, in a sense, disciples of the English writing master who entered upon printing as an avocation.

The name of Didot is a familiar one in French typographic history for several reasons. The Didot family contributed a long line of illustrious printers and typefounders; from one the Didot point system (which is today the system of typographic mensuration in use throughout Europe) took its name; for another was named a type design which has exerted a consequential influence on the appearance of French printing up until the present time. The name, however, strange to relate, is not well known and would mean nothing to the present-day printer of average intelligence. Even the French have not properly appreciated the services of the Didots to their national typography. There is no book dealing adequately with their work, and authoritative information regarding this family of typographers is far to seek.

The founder of the line is usually considered to be François Didot born in 1689. One of his sons, François Ambroise Didot, was a typefounder of ability who brought out the first Didot types in the early 1770's or possibly before—types to which those later pro-

duced in Italy by Giambattista Bodoni bore an unmistakable family resemblance.

The question of precedence in the creation of this design has not been given the study it deserves, for the point is one of considerable importance if we are to give credit where credit is due. From the information I have been able to gather, it would seem that Bodoni, who was copying the designs and the composition style of Fournier, found that the Fournier typography was being superseded by the types and style of the Didots, and thereupon copied their types and adopted their style. We cannot, however, disparage the ability of the Italian, for he was an apt pupil and developed the inspiration perhaps thus gained in a splendid manner indeed.

François Ambroise, by the way, was the member of the family who instructed Franklin's grandson, Benjamin Franklin Bache, in the mysteries of typefounding. Young Bache referred to him in his diary as "the best printer of this age and even the best that has ever been seen," but added on the same page the very human entry "The meals are frugal." The subject of this comment had two sons Pierre *l'ainé* (born 1761) and Firmin (born 1764), the former succeeding to the printing office, the latter to the paternal typefoundry Pierre issued some fine monumental editions in a very severe style one of them, the Racine, receiving an official award as the finest book ever printed! It is a very impressive volume, but I have always had a failing for the Didot Bible, a copy of which on vellum is one of the most remarkable achievements in perfection of printing technique it has ever been my pleasure to see. The title page of this edition is here reproduced in slight reduction.

Firmin applied himself to typefounding and was responsible for the point system already mentioned. He did what no type founder ever did before or since: cut one design in a series of type a half a point apart in size. Most founders are content with a two

BIBLIORUM

SACRORUM

VULGATAE VERSIONIS

EDITIO.

TOMUS PRIMUS.

JUSSU CHRISTIANISSIMI REGIS

AD INSTITUTIONEM

SERENISSIMI DELPHINI.

PARISIIS,

EXCUDEBAT FR. AMB. DIDOT NATU MAJ.

M. DCC. LXXXV.

THE TITLE PAGE OF THE DIDOT BIBLE.

point step in progression of type sizes, but Didot divided this by four. There was, for example, a ten point, a ten and a half point, an eleven point, and so on.

There were many other members of the family all of whom did distinguished work in one or more fields. As Mr. Updike has aptly remarked, their family reunions must have resembled a meeting of the Royal Society!

Before discussing further the printing of the Didots we will turn for a moment to Giambattista Bodoni and his work, which ran parallel in so many ways with theirs.

Giambattista (John Baptist) Bodoni, born at Saluzzo in Italy in 1740, was the son of a printer and mastered in early life the principles of the paternal trade. While still a boy he cut some wood blocks of much merit, and the young printer was soon planning to go to Rome for further training in this art. He was especially interested in a visit to the great press of the Propaganda at Rome, which printed religious texts in a multitude of languages in order to further the evangelistic work of the Church. The director of this press was so impressed by the enthusiasm of Bodoni that he offered him a job as compositor—an offer immediately accepted.

Bodoni specialized in the typography of the Oriental languages and was soon able to put in order many of the ancient punches and matrices, some of which had been cut by Guillaume le Bé and Claude Garamond. These had fallen into utter confusion, but Bodoni managed to clean and sort them, and make them again ready for use. His interest in Oriental typography, acquired during this period, never deserted him, as is attested by the second volume of his *Manuale tipografico,* which is entirely given over to types for non-roman alphabets. This work with punches and matrices also led him to undertake punch-cutting on his own account.

At the age of twenty-eight, Bodoni was appointed director of

MANUALE

TIPOGRAFICO

DEL CAVALIERE

GIAMBATTISTA BODONI

VOLUME PRIMO.

PARMA

PRESSO LA VEDOVA

MDCCCXVIII.

the ducal press at Parma, established by Ferdinand I, duke of Parma. He bought the first supply of types and ornaments from Simon Pierre Fournier, the Paris typefounder, better known as Fournier *le jeune*. At this period Bodoni was strongly under the influence of Fournier, copying almost slavishly some of his models.

The period was one of classical influences, and the tendency was to simplify and regularize all forms of artistic expression. The florid style of the French eighteenth century was giving place to a colder and more formalistic manner. Garlands of flowers were being supplanted, so to speak, by icicles. These tendencies had their effect on Bodoni, who interpreted them typographically not only in the design of his types but also in their use. In the production of types of pointed serifs with a wide difference in color between the thick and thin strokes, Bodoni out-Baskervilled Baskerville—if we may be permitted the use of this cumbrous expression.

The Didots and Bodoni were active competitors, working in much the same style and on much the same type of material. Both concentrated their attention on monumental volumes of regal magnificence, though the Didots issued also charming little volumes for the general reader. Both used the "classical" types printed on plate-finish wove paper. The presswork of both was well-nigh flawless. The Didots claimed a higher degree of accuracy in their editions of the classics, and this claim could undoubtedly be sustained. Bodoni, on the other hand, can be credited with a greater inventiveness in type arrangement and make-up.

Both cut good types. As the new style swept over Europe, however, the design was generally credited to Didot. We find the German founders, for example, speaking often of *Didotsche Lettern*.

The tradition of modern types and plate-finish paper initiated by the writing master of Birmingham was thus carried forward in good hands in both France and Italy. My discussing together the

work of Bodoni and the Didots is by way of slight tribute to the memory of a great family of French printers who have gone down in typographic history, comparatively speaking, "unwept, un-honored, and unsung." Bodoni has received his meed of merited praise, in which I most cordially join, but he had contemporaries in France of stature fully equal to his own.

XXVII

The Press in the New World

ONE of the most astonishing facts in the history of printing is that, in less than a century after the invention, the new craft was being practiced on a continent the very existence of which had been unknown fifty years earlier. In 1539, at a time when printing had not yet found its way into a number of European cities of considerable importance, a printer and his assistants made the long and perilous voyage across the Atlantic to the viceroyalty of New Spain and there began to print in the city of Mexico.

This really remarkable enterprise had the hearty encouragement of Zumárraga, the Spanish archbishop in Mexico, and of the viceroy, Mendoza. The motive in establishing the press in Mexico was predominantly religious—a motive which in many other instances has sent a printer forth to follow close on the steps of the explorer. The archbishop wished to have books in the native languages for the use of priests and missionaries, and the function of the first printer in the New World was to print devotional books for the instruction of the natives in the Christian religion.

Confining ourselves first to facts established beyond dispute, we know that Juan Cromberger, the leading printer at Seville, in Spain, decided to start a printing office in Mexico to be operated as a branch of his main office. Archbishop Zumárraga had entrusted to him the printing of a catechism in the language of the Nahuatl, and a beginning of this work had been made at Seville. But the printer came to the conclusion that the work could be better done by a printer in immediate contact with the people who spoke that

language. Cromberger therefore entered into a contract, on June 12, 1539, with Juan Pablos (or Giovanni Paoli), an Italian printer then resident of Seville, to go to Mexico and there establish a shop. Fortunately, the original notarial record of this contract has recently been discovered, and the terms and conditions thereby imposed upon Pablos, which could hardly have been more rigorous, are thus fully known to us.

Pablos was to act as compositor and manager of the office in Mexico, but Cromberger reserved the right to place a representative beside him to check up on all his transactions. Neither Pablos nor his wife (who was to do the housekeeping for the printer and his assistant) was to receive any salary, nor were they to spend a cent of the income of the office in excess of bare living expenses. The printer was to print three thousand sheets daily and was to be held responsible for all errors in the original composition or in the correction of proofs. He was to seek out and procure the personnel requisite to the organization of the office, but at first must content himself with a pressman and a Negro as helpers. He was prohibited from entering into partnership for any business whatever, and any emoluments which he might receive personally were to go into the common fund. He was required to act as agent for the sale of books and merchandise sent to Mexico by his principal, but was entitled to no commission on such sales.

On the other hand, Pablos supplied no capital whatever. The traveling expenses of himself, his wife, and his pressman were defrayed by Cromberger, who also assumed the cost of shipping the printing press, materials, and equipment. The partnership was to last for ten years, counting from the day of the execution of the contract, and at the expiration of that term there was to be a settlement of accounts. After transportation costs, salaries, house rent, the personal expenses of Pablos and his wife, and depreciation of the

equipment were deducted from the income of the office, Pablos was to receive one-fifth of the net profits. The final settlement of the partnership accounts was to be made in Spain, to which country Pablos was to return for the purpose.

According to other clauses in the contract, it was stipulated that worn-out type was to be melted rather than sold, so that competition by other printers might not be encouraged. Before undertaking the printing of books from manuscripts brought to his press, Pablos was to obtain the permission of the bishop of Mexico and all the usual licenses. On all books printed in the Mexican printing office were to appear imprints specifying that they were printed "In the House of Juan Cromberger."

On the same day that Cromberger made his contract with Pablos he also made one with Gil Barbero, a pressman, employing him to exercise that function in the new office overseas.

We know little of Juan Pablos. He was a native of Brescia, in Lombardy, Italy. At the time of his departure for New Spain he was married to Jeronima Gutierrez, probably an Andalusian. We have no knowledge as to whether he had worked at the printing trade in his native country nor as to how long he had been in Spain. At the time the contract was made, it is most likely that he was employed in Cromberger's printing shop in Seville, so that the master was taking no chances on the ability and reliability of his typographic emissary.

The contract between Cromberger and Pablos was not long in effect, for it appears that the master printer died in Seville about September, 1540. After some interruption of operation, the Mexican printing office was taken over by Pablos and continued under his name. On February 17, 1542, the printer was admitted to citizenship in Mexico City, and on May 8 of the following year the district of San Pablo granted him a lot on which to build his house.

Before going on to an account of the earliest books which are known to have been printed in Mexico, it should be stated that the place of Juan Pablos as the first printer in the New World is subject to some dispute. The late José Toribio Medina, the foremost authority on Spanish-American printing, believed that there was a printer already at work in Mexico City from 1535 to 1538, before the arrival of Pablos, and that his name was Esteban Martin. Medina adduces considerable evidence in support of this contention. Martin is supposed to have printed the *Escala spiritual* of San Juan Climaco, but no copy of this or of any other book printed by him is now extant.

Evidence of vital importance to Martin's claim to priority is provided by a passage in a letter from Archbishop Zumárraga to the emperor-king of Spain, under date of May 6, 1538: "Little progress can be made in the matter of printing on account of the scarcity of paper, a difficulty in the way of many works which are ready here [to be printed] and of others which will have to be reprinted, because there is a scarcity of those most needed, and few are coming from overseas." To be sure, this does not mention Martin by name, but it clearly implies that a printer was there in Mexico in 1538, prepared to work if provided with the necessary supplies.

We have further to consider a statement made in 1599 by Davila Padilla, the earliest historian to mention the beginning of printing in Mexico, telling us that the first book written in the New World, and the first for which the printing press was used there, was by San Juan Climaco, translated from Latin into Spanish by Fray Juan de Estrada. He says further, however, that this was the first book printed by Juan Pablos but does not mention the date of its printing. Fray Alonso Fernandez, writing in 1611, apparently from independent sources, records the same book as the first printed in Mexico; he does not name the printer, but fixes the date of printing as 1535.

On this evidence, Medina holds that Padilla was right about the

book but in error as to the identity of the printer, naming Pablos because his was the only name appearing on other known early Mexican books, there being no imprint on the book in question. Medina accepts as correct the date 1535, as mentioned by Fernandez. Furthermore, there is no reason to doubt the date 1537 given by Beristain de Sousa as the date of printing the *Catecismo mexicano*.

Who was the printer at work in the city of Mexico before 1539? In the records of the *cabildo* of the city is found the following entry: "On Friday the fifth of September, 1539. On this day, being in meeting assembled . . . the aforesaid gentlemen received as resident Esteban Martin, a printer, and that he give security and, until he gives it, shall not enjoy. . . ."

As Juan Pablos is known to have left Spain in June, 1539; as he had as assistants only Gil Barbero, his pressman, and a Negro helper; and as a reasonable time almost invariably elapsed between the arrival of a stranger and his admission to citizenship, Medina concludes that Esteban Martin was responsible for the earlier printing activities recorded by various chroniclers and must therefore be regarded as the first typographer on the American continent. That Martin was a printer by trade and that he was in the city of Mexico before Juan Pablos arrived there may perhaps be conceded, but whether he actually did any printing in Mexico is still open to question. The claim that he printed certain books before 1539 has not been universally recognized by Spanish-American bibliographers, but the fact that it was advanced by so thorough a scholar as Señor Medina entitles it to very serious consideration.

To return to Juan Pablos, the first work for his press was undoubtedly the production of *cartillas,* or primers, for the instruction of the young, but none of these has survived. The earliest printed book of which we have a perfectly clear record was the *Breve y mas compendiosa doctrina christiana,* Mexico, 1539. A description of

this book was published in 1877 in the *Cartas de Indias,* but unfortunately this precious ancestor of books in the New World cannot now be located.

The next book of which we have definite evidence was the *Manual de adultos,* issued December 13, 1540. Of this there has survived only a fragment consisting of the last two leaves of the book discovered in a volume of miscellaneous papers in the Biblioteca Provincial at Toledo, Spain. The printer's note tells us that the book was printed "in the great city of Mexico by order of the very reverend bishops of New Spain, and at their expense, in the house of Juan Cromberger." In other words, the book was published by the Church. Two of the three pages are given over to errata, correcting mistakes of the "Typographers." The facts that the last correction relates to the 36th sheet, page 1, line 4, shows that the book was one of consequential proportions.

In 1541 there appeared a book on Guatemala by the notary Rodriguez, and from that date onward volumes appeared from the Mexican press with varying regularity, or perhaps we should better say with varying luck as to the preservation of copies, for many volumes may have been printed about which we know nothing.

During this period the types used were exclusively gothic in character, four sizes being in regular use. The printing office was evidently supplied with just two type ornaments, one being a Maltese cross and the other a unit of a vine pattern. Both were used regularly in the adornment of title pages. Pablos also had a miscellaneous lot of woodcut borders which he cut up and used indiscriminately in the weirdest of combinations. There was also a woodcut design representing a cardinal's hat with tassels hanging at the sides (see the illustration on page 397), which was apparently a favorite with the printer, as it was used on the title pages of at least five books, and perhaps more.

In 1554 there came a change in the character of the books printed by Pablos, which has not received adequate notice from bibliographers. During this year there appeared three books in folio format, the *Diálogos* by Cervantes de Salazar, the *Recognitio summularum*, and the *Dialectica resolutio*. In them we find the first use in Mexico of roman and italic types. We also find a new style in the composition of title pages, we encounter two or three new type ornaments, and we see in use some effective woodcuts, one of which (a title-page border) had been used a few years previously in London. Why the radical change in typographic style?

An answer to this question was offered by the writer in 1927. Antonio Espinosa, a skilled punch-cutter, had arrived in Mexico City, bringing with him a typefounder. Both contracted to enter the employ of Juan Pablos, thus making it possible for that printer to augment his type equipment as required, without recourse to distant European sources of supply. Judged by his own later work as a printer, Espinosa was a typographer of taste, who did much to improve the quality of the work done by the Pablos press.

The manner of Espinosa's affiliation with Pablos was in this wise. The Mexican printer in 1550 sent a commercial envoy to Spain with power of attorney to transact for him various items of business. One of the commissions with which this agent was entrusted was the employment of a typefounder. According to a document but recently discovered in the notarial archives of Seville, the envoy contracted with Espinosa and an assistant to make the journey to Mexico and work for Pablos, "cutting and casting type" for a period of three years. It was thus that the typography of the first Mexican press was rejuvenated.

During the succeeding years some fine books came from the Pablos press. In 1559 Pablos met with his first competition in a shop established by his former associate, Espinosa, who had returned to

TITLE PAGE OF THE DOCTRINA PRINTED
BY JUAN PABLOS, MEXICO CITY, 1543.

Spain and there obtained, on the plea that the prices charged for books printed by Pablos made it impossible for persons of moderate means to buy them, the privilege of operating a second printing office in the city of Mexico. Espinosa was undoubtedly a finer craftsman than his former master, and some fine volumes appeared from his press, the last of which was dated 1575.

In 1560 Juan Pablos, the pioneer typographer, brought out his last and most notable work, the *Manuale sacramentorum*. But he was then nearing the end of his career. His health must have been failing, for in that year he drew his will and before August 21, 1561, he had printed his last sheet. On that date we find his widow administering his estate.

The name of Pablos is little known in the English-speaking countries of the New World. Yet he is entitled to rank among the great pioneers in the development of civilization in the Americas.

The printing establishment of Juan Pablos passed in 1563 into the hands of Pedro Ocharte, who had married a daughter of Pablos. Ocharte, the third printer of definite record in Mexico, was a Frenchman who had been in the city of Mexico since 1558, doubtless as an employee in the Pablos printing office. His career as a master printer was beset with difficulties, as he came under the suspicion of the Inquisition in 1572 and thus was kept from any regular attention to the printing business for seven years. A specimen of his craftsmanship is shown in the title page here reproduced.

As to the other cities of Mexico, printing was introduced at Oaxaca in 1720 by a woman, Doña Francisca Flores, but it was soon discontinued there for reasons unknown and was not resumed in that city until 1812. Mariano Valdés Tellez Giron began to print at Guadalajara towards the end of 1792. At Vera Cruz, Manuel Lopez Bueno established a press in 1794, while the first printing at Mérida was done in 1813 by Francisco Bates. It may well be noted

PHILIPPVS HISPANIA
RVM ET INDIARVM
REX.

¶Prouisiões cedulas
Instruciones de su Magestad: orde
naças ò diffutos y audiêcia, pa la bue
na expediciõ delos negocios, y admi
nistraciõ ð justicia: y gouernaciõ ðsta
nueua España: y pa el buê tratamiê
to y pseruaciõ ðlos yndios, dende el
año 1525. hasta este presente ð. 63.

EN MEXICO EN CASA
De Pedro Ocharte. M.D.LXIII.

A TITLE PAGE OF PEDRO OCHARTE, MEXICO, 1563.

here that the first printing in California and in New Mexico was done under Mexican auspices and by Mexican craftsmen.

As we cannot trace here the further history of printing in Spanish America, suffice it to say that the next country in the western hemisphere to which type and printer's ink were to penetrate was Peru. There, in 1584, the first printing was done at Lima, "the city of kings," by Antonio Ricardo. This typographer, a native of Turin, Italy, had been printing in Mexico, but had found the competition there quite keen. Hearing of the fabulous riches of Peru, he emigrated to the land of the Incas. The only known copy of the earliest known product of the Peruvian press, an edict of Pope Gregory XIII, is now preserved as one of the treasures of the John Carter Brown Library at Providence, Rhode Island.

There is still a regrettable tendency, in popular thought, to belittle the part played by Spain in the settlement and civilization of the New World. It is salutary, therefore, for us to bear in mind that the Spanish had been using the press in Mexico and in South America for a full century before printing was introduced into English-speaking North America.

XXVIII

Printing on Massachusetts Bay

RINTING types and printing presses move with the pioneers in opening up new frontiers. When we investigate the coming of typography to English-speaking North America, and particularly to the territory which is now the United States, we find that there was no exception to the general rule. In 1620 the Pilgrims landed on Plymouth Rock. In 1638 the first printing press arrived in Massachusetts. In its coming there was much of romance. In its operation there was much of import to the development, intellectual and spiritual, of the infant colony.

Reverend Jose Glover of Sutton, England, was a clergyman of some wealth who had been suspended from his pastorate for non-conformity with the principles of the church. He decided to go to New England and probably sailed in his own ship, the *Planter,* early in 1634. He apparently liked the new country overseas and decided to make it his permanent home. He thereupon secured two pieces of property and ordered the erection of a house on one of them, in order to have ready accommodations for the members of his family when he brought them from England. The land records of Boston show that Glover was an inhabitant of that town, and a householder, in 1635.

At this time the American colonists were beginning to take an interest in education. Schools were started and the establishment of a college was discussed. Mr. Glover became interested in this project and returned to England to raise funds for the enterprise. For several reasons it seems probable that he had ambitions to be president

of the institution. While in England he permanently resigned the pastorate at Sutton from which he had been suspended.

It was evidently planned that a printing plant should be an important adjunct to the educational and religious work of the college. Mr. Glover bought a press with his own funds and a supply of type with money contributed by friends of the college. He also purchased supplies of paper, ink, and other accessories to take along when he and his family sailed for the New World in July or August, 1638.

Prior to his departure he contracted with Stephen Day (whose name is sometimes spelled Daye), his two sons, and another workman to go with him overseas. Stephen Day was a locksmith and a resident of Cambridge, England. It does not appear that he was a printer, but it seems that his two sons (who had not yet reached their majority) were probably apprentices in a Cambridge printing office. There is later evidence that Mr. Glover was counting principally on Matthew Day to do the composition.

Unfortunately, Jose Glover, who may properly be regarded as the father of printing in the United States, never reached the shores of America on this second trip, for during the voyage he fell ill and died—probably of smallpox.

In Winthrop's *Journal* is this entry:

> 1639, Mo. 1. A printing house was begun at Cambridge by one Daye, at the charge of Mr. Glover, who died on seas hitherward.

We thus learn that in March, 1639, the printing plant was in operation. Meanwhile the college (which it was decided to name Harvard College) had been organized. In 1640, Henry Dunster became its president.

Mrs. Glover and the workmen whom her husband had engaged arrived in Boston about the middle of September, 1638. In Cam-

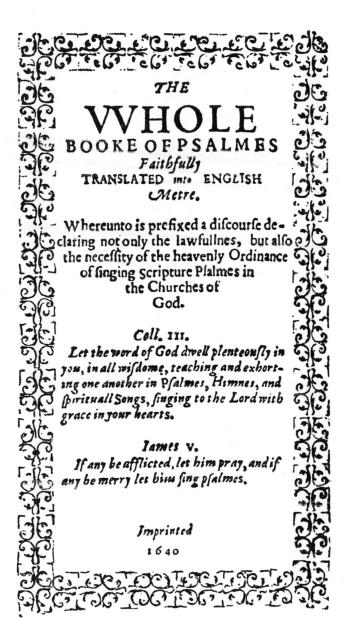

THE

VVHOLE

BOOKE OF PSALMES
Faithfully
TRANSLATED *into* ENGLISH
Metre.

Whereunto is prefixed a difcourfe de-
claring not only the lawfullnes, but alfo
the neceffity of the heavenly Ordinance
of finging Scripture Pfalmes in
the Churches of
God.

Coll. III.

*Let the word of God dwell plenteoufly in
you, in all wifdome, teaching and exhort-
ing one another in Pfalmes, Himnes, and
fpirituall Songs, finging to the Lord with
grace in your hearts.*

Iames v.

*If any be afflicted, let him pray, and if
any be merry let him fing pfalmes.*

Imprinted
1640

TITLE PAGE OF THE BAY PSALM BOOK, 1640.

bridge she promptly arranged first for the renting and then for the purchase of property to serve for a printing office and as a residence for the printers. Stephen Day, as has already been noted, was probably not a printer, but his son Matthew, in 1638 nineteen years of age, evidently had printing experience. His father, being a skilled locksmith, was qualified to erect the press and aid in the mechanical end of the work. He also undertook business direction of the office.

The first piece of work produced at the press was the *Freeman's Oath* printed on a half-sheet of small paper. Another item issued in 1639 was *An Almanac for 1639, calculated for New England, by Mr. William Pierce, Mariner*. No copies of either of these publications have been preserved.

In 1640 appeared the first publication of which copies are known to us: *The Whole Booke of Psalmes faithfully Translated into English Metre.* . . . "Imprinted 1640." This was a volume of 147 unnumbered leaves, the title page of which is shown on the preceding page. This is generally referred to as the Bay Psalm Book. There are ten copies of this American incunable known to be in existence, six of which are imperfect. It was far from an elegant piece of printing, but it served its purpose well.

This first existing book printed in what is now the United States must always have a well-nigh sacred interest to any cultivated American. A perfect copy, should it come up for public sale, would bring a fabulous figure—and properly so. For this book stands to American printing in the same relation as does the Gutenberg Bible to the printing of Europe.

About four other publications are supposed to have appeared before the printing of the next extant item, a *List of Theses* at the Harvard College Commencement in 1643, which showed considerable improvement in typography and presswork.

In 1647 appeared the first and only book bearing the imprint of

Matthew Day. Stephen Day had retired from active connection with the press and was devoting his time to other pursuits. His son took

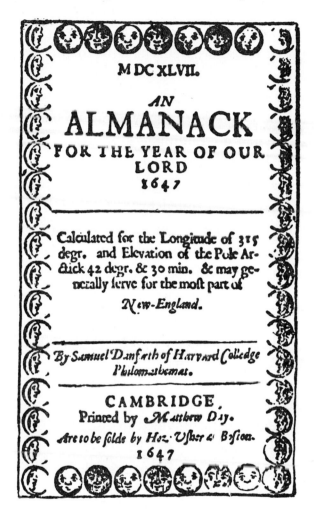

THE ONLY KNOWN TITLE PAGE WITH THE IM-
PRINT OF MATTHEW DAY, CAMBRIDGE, 1647.

it over and conducted it until his death on May 10, 1649, printing a number of other books, in the imprints of which, however, his name does not appear.

The widow of Jose Glover had married Henry Dunster, who thus, as president of the college (which owned some of the type) and as representative of the Glover estate, had a double interest in the direction of the press. On her death, however, the estate had to be settled, and the house originally bought for the Day family and the press was sold. The press was thereupon removed to the newly built "President's House," and Matthew Day bought a residence.

After Matthew Day's death, Samuel Green was chosen to take over the office. He had no training as a printer, but stepped into the breach and several years later was doing creditable work. The first known work bearing his name in the imprint is *A Platform of Church Discipline* . . . "Printed by S. G. at Cambridge in New England and are to be sold at Cambridge and Boston Anno Dom: 1649." He continued to print actively until he retired in 1692, the year in which his name last appears in an imprint.

The next factor of importance in the development of printing in the United States was the work of Rev. John Eliot, the missionary to the Indians. He spent a number of years learning their language and finally formulated it so that it could be reduced to print. He next became convinced of the necessity of some evangelistic and educational literature in the Indian tongue. Acting on suggestions from the new colony, Parliament provided in 1649 for the creation of "A Corporation for the Promoting and Propagating the Gospel of Jesus Christ in New England." This organization helped Mr. Eliot's work in many ways, including the contribution of money and materials to make possible the printing of texts in the Indian language.

Samuel Green was called on to print these books, the *Catechism* appearing before September, 1654, the *Book of Genesis* in 1655, the *Psalms in Metre* in 1658, and *Pierson's Catechism,* 1658-1659. Eliot had been working for some time on his translation of the whole Bible into the Indian tongue, and he found the typographic facili-

ties in Cambridge insufficient to its printing. On December 28, 1658, in a letter to the Corporation in London, he wrote:

I proposed this expedient for the more easie prosecution of this work, viz. that your selves might be moved to hire some honest young man, who hath skill to compose, (and the more skill in other parts of the work, the better) send him over as your servant, pay him there to his content, or ingage payment, let him serve you here in New-England at the presse in Harvard Colledge, and work under the Colledge printer, in impressing the Bible in the Indian language, and with him send a convenient stock of Paper to begin withal.

Meanwhile Hezekiah Usher had been in London and had purchased a press, type and other materials for the printing office. These were placed in the Indian College, to which the printing office had been moved when its chief concern had come to be the production of books for the Indians, and consigned to the care of Samuel Green.

On April 21, 1660, the Corporation in London records its action on Mr. Eliot's suggestion. It had contracted with Marmaduke Johnson, a skilled master printer of London, to go to New England for a period of three years. He was to receive £40 per annum in addition to board, lodging, and washing. In announcing Johnson's departure the Corporation requests "for his encouragement" that his name be mentioned in the imprint.

Marmaduke Johnson arrived in Boston in June, 1660, and immediately began working with Green on the Bible, which by the way, was the first edition of the Scriptures in any language to be printed in North America. Both the English and the Indian title pages of the volume, which was completed in 1663, are reproduced herewith.

This Indian Bible involved many typographical difficulties, and its execution was a great credit to the Cambridge printers. The New Testament was finished first and was issued with a separate title page dated 1661. It was then combined and issued with the Old

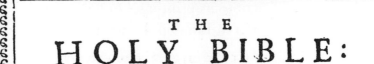

THE
HOLY BIBLE:
CONTAINING THE
OLD TESTAMENT
AND THE *NEW*.

Tranſlated into the

INDIAN LANGUAGE,
AND

Ordered to be Printed by the *Commiſſioners of the United Colonies*
in *NEW-ENGLAND*,

At the Charge, and with the Conſent of the

CORPORATION IN *ENGLAND*
For the Propagation of the Goſpel amongſt the Indians
in New-England.

CAMBRIDGE:

Printed by *Samuel Green* and *Marmaduke Johnſon.*

MDCLXIII.

ENGLISH TITLE PAGE OF ELIOT'S INDIAN BIBLE, 1663.

MAMUSSE
WUNNEETUPANATAMWE
UP-BIBLUM GOD
NANEESWE
NUKKONE TESTAMENT
KAH WONK
WUSKU TESTAMENT.

Ne quoſhkinnumuk naſhpe Wuttinneumoh *CHRIST*
noh aſᴏᴏweſit

JOHN ELIOT·

CAMBRIDGE:

Printcuᴏᴏp naſhpe *Samuel Green* kah *Marmaduke Johnſon.*

1 6 6 3.

Testament when that part of the work was finished. The volume was without doubt the most important production of the early press in the United States.

A copy of this Bible, which would today command a king's ransom, was purchased for Isaiah Thomas in 1791 for the extravagant sum of seven dollars, this copy being now in the collection of the American Antiquarian Society. Eben T. Andrews, who was his partner in a printing office which they operated jointly in Boston, wrote to Thomas under date of September 6 of that year as follows:

Mr. Harris was here today, and mentioned that he had procured an Indian Bible, which he had heard you express a wish to possess, and that you might have it if you please, as he supposes he can procure another for himself out of the College Library. He gave 7 dollars for the copy which he has, which he says is very good, excepting the binding, which is flattened. I enclose you some of his proposals.

Since the publication of any existing treatise on the early Massachusetts press, there have been made three very important finds. One was the discovery of a copy of the Indian version of Richard Baxter's *Call to the Unconverted,* which was known to have been printed, but no copy was thought to be extant. It turned up in the sale of non-scientific works from the library of the Royal Society which were sold at auction in London on May 4, 1925, and was purchased for the Henry E. Huntington Library at a price of approximately $38,000. Like the Bible, it was printed by Samuel Green and Marmaduke Johnson.

In 1661, Marmaduke Johnson fell in love with Green's daughter, but the latter objected to his attentions on the ground that he had a wife still living in England. Johnson failing to desist, Green took the matter to the courts, and Johnson was ordered to leave the country. Because of the value of his work on the Bible, however, the order was not enforced, but his further relations with his associate

must have been rather strained. In 1664, at the end of his period of employment, he returned to England.

The Corporation, however, transferred its printing equipment in Cambridge to the care of Mr. Eliot, who was very friendly to Johnson, and sent the latter back to New England with a new supply of type. Johnson also brought with him a press of his own and planned to set it up in Boston, where there would be more patronage than in Cambridge. This prospect was not at all pleasing to the authorities of the college press, to Green, and to his friends. So purely to hamper Johnson, the legislature, or General Court, issued an order on May 27, 1665, providing that no printing press should be erected in any town in the colony except Cambridge, and that any text to be printed must first be approved by a board of licensers. The result was that Johnson was forced to locate in Cambridge, which is across the river from Boston. The first book issued from the new office with the imprint of Marmaduke Johnson alone was the *Communion of Churches* by John Eliot, Cambridge, 1665.

In 1674 Johnson succeeded in having lifted the ban on printing in any other town but Cambridge, so he immediately made plans to remove to Boston, where he considered he could do more business. On July 18 of that year he bought a house on what is now known as Hanover Street, but the realization of his ambition was destined to be short-lived, for he passed to his heavenly reward on Christmas Day, 1674.

Though there is no publication of Johnson's with a Boston imprint, it was the belief of Mr. Littlefield that the later signatures of Torrey's *An Exhortation Unto Reformation* were printed after the removal of his office, thus constituting the first printing done in the city of Boston. After Johnson's death his equipment was bought and his office continued by John Foster.

To complete the present record of early printing in Cambridge,

it remains only to note that Samuel Green, who continued printing there, in 1691 took into partnership his son Bartholomew. Their joint imprint appeared in 1692 on *Ornaments for the Daughters of Zion,* which was the last book with which Samuel Green was associated. In that year he is supposed to have retired. No more printing was done in Cambridge for over a hundred years, with the exception of a brief period during the Revolutionary War when Boston was occupied by British troops.

Samuel Green's service in charge of the college press for over forty years entitles him to a position of distinction among American colonial printers, but perhaps his main claim to fame is that he was the ancestor of a long line of printers who carried the typographic art into many communities of the New World, members of the family being identified as pioneers in American printing for a period of almost two hundred years.

Typographer, Philosopher, Statesman

A CITIZEN of Boston returned from England about 1717 with an equipment of type and press and set up as a printer in his native city. At this time, his younger brother was casting about for a suitable trade to choose as his life work. A hard bargain was driven, and a nine-year apprenticeship contract was drawn, the father paying the fifty-dollar fee required.

In those days an apprentice was paid nothing except during the last year of his term of indenture, but he was lodged, fed, and clothed by his master. In this case, however, the master, being unmarried, did not keep house, so both he and his apprentice boarded with another family. The younger brother was a great reader and, although he was able to borrow many of the books he desired, there were others he wanted to buy. So he proposed that his brother pay him in cash one half the sum then being paid for his board, allowing him to provide his own meals. Out of this meager allowance he was able to save nearly a half, and with this income he began to acquire a small private library.

In the course of his business the older brother was commissioned to print for William Brooker, the postmaster at Boston, a weekly newspaper known as the *Boston Gazette*. But a new postmaster coming soon into office placed the job with a rival office, and our printer started a competitive sheet known as the *New England Courant,* the first newspaper in the United States not connected with a postoffice.

The first issue of the *Courant* appeared August 17, 1721. The

enterprise was undertaken contrary to advice of father and friends. These critics agreed that there were already three papers being published in the American colonies, and two of them in Boston. Another, therefore, could hardly be expected to succeed. But advice was of no avail. The young publisher proposed to issue a newspaper different in character from the existing publications. The editorial policy was hostile to the clergy, attacked some prevailing opinions on religion, and opposed various fads.

Expression of these opinions brought criticism from many quarters, but the young publisher soon ventured criticism in the more dangerous field of politics. Pirates were active in New England waters, and there was an idea current that the governmental authorities had not been very vigilant or effective in their suppression. In one issue appeared this sarcastic news note, purporting to come from Newport, R. I.:

"We are advis'd from Boston that the government of Massachusetts are fitting out a ship to go after the pirate to be commanded by Captain Peter Papillon and it is thought he will sail sometime this month, wind and weather permitting."

The Governor and Council took this as an affront and promptly committed the publisher of the *Courant* to jail. A week's incarceration put the offender in a repentant frame of mind; he duly apologized, entreated forgiveness, and sought his release.

Following release, however, the repentant spirit did not last long. Before long, a single issue of the *Courant* contained three articles, all objectionable to the authorities. After due consideration, the publisher was forbidden to print the *New England Courant* or any other similar publication, unless the copy was first approved by the secretary of the province.

The younger brother had meanwhile been learning the printing trade and making progress in other directions. He began to write

short pieces and slip them at night under the printing office door. Many were printed, and there was considerable speculation among the editorial circle as to their authorship. We can imagine the thrill of the young apprentice as he heard the names of various well known members of the community suggested as possible authors. Finally, the young apprentice revealed to his brother and friends the identity of the mysterious contributor, thereupon rising considerably in their estimation.

The printing office now faced a crisis, as the publisher had been forbidden to print further issues of the paper without official censorship. This condition being unacceptable, the publisher conceived the subterfuge of issuing the paper under the name of his apprentice. The name of this apprentice was Benjamin Franklin.

So we find the eightieth number of the *New England Courant* for the week of February 4 to February 11, 1723, published with this imprint: "Boston: Printed and sold by Benjamin Franklin in Queen Street, where Advertisements are taken in." To make this possible it had been necessary to cancel publicly the bonds of apprenticeship between James Franklin and his brother, but the former, seeking to preserve the advantage of a good agreement, executed secretly a new indenture, repeating the provisions of the original.

James Franklin was evidently an exacting master, ill-natured and sullen, and his apprentice brother had always had a difficult time getting along with him. Finally, hard words were superseded by blows, and young Benjamin announced a termination of agreement, knowing that James was not in position to enforce the secret contract. Being powerless to object to Benjamin's leaving his employ, James persuaded the other printers in Boston to refuse him employment. This boycott was serious, as there were only four printing offices in the colonies outside of Boston in which he could obtain employment in the trade to which he had devoted four years

of application. To reach either New London, New York, or Philadelphia, the points at which possible employment might be found, required either a long and dangerous journey on foot or a passage by boat. The latter required passage money, and Benjamin had no funds available for this purpose.

He could not appeal to his father, who had sided with the older brother in the dispute. In fact, he could not even disclose to his father his plan for leaving town for fear that he would be restrained. He was nevertheless determined to go through with the project. So he sold some of his books and secured passage on a sloop bound for New York City. He promptly presented himself at the only printing office in that town, conducted by William Bradford "at the Sign of the Bible" on Hanover Square.

The New York printer could offer him no employment, but suggested that he go on to Philadelphia, where Bradford's son Andrew was engaged in the business and was, by reason of the death of one of his workmen, in need of help. So thither Benjamin immediately repaired, reaching the city with which he was later so intimately associated on a Sunday morning in October, 1723.

Purchasing three-penny worth of bread in a bakery, he received much more than the same money would have purchased in Boston, Taking away with him three large rolls, he disposed one under each arm and was munching the third as he walked up Market Street. He wore his working garb, his "best clothes" having been shipped in his "chest" by another route. His pockets were stuffed with shirts and stockings and, all in all, he must have presented an uncouth figure indeed. So amusing did he appear that Miss Deborah Read, standing on the stoop of her house, snickered audibly as he passed. For this indignity Franklin later retaliated by marrying the young lady.

Monday morning, he applied for employment at the shop of

Andrew Bradford and was surprised to find there Andrew's father, who had made a faster trip to Philadelphia than Franklin. Bradford had no work immediately available, so the young man next applied for work to Samuel Keimer, the other printer who was then established in that city.

Keimer soon after gave Franklin employment in his ill-equipped office. The new workman saved a good share of his wages and made many friends. Keimer was unmarried and could thus offer him no place to live, so Franklin had continued to board with Andrew Bradford, to whose house he had first moved. The idea of his assistant lodging with his competitor did not appeal to Keimer, so he arranged to have him board with a Mr. Read, father of the young lady hereinbefore mentioned.

One new acquaintance was Sir William Keith, the governor of the Province of Pennsylvania. One day the governor and a friend called on young Franklin at his place of business and almost flabbergasted his employer. He invited Benjamin to dinner and talked with him regarding his plans. Keith deplored the poor workmanship of the Philadelphia printers and encouraged Franklin to set up in business for himself, promising him the public printing. He urged him to return to Boston and secure his father's financial backing, and gave him a letter to Josiah Franklin recommending his encouragement of the enterprise.

Franklin occasioned considerable surprise, particularly among the workmen in his brother's shop, by returning to Boston with money in his pockets and giving other evidences of prosperity. But his father was an ultra-conservative and viewed the proposition with disfavor. He thought little of Governor Keith's judgment in advocating the setting up in business of an eighteen-year-old lad. So he replied courteously to the governor, and Benjamin returned to Philadelphia with the parental blessing and a promise of assistance

later on if he should continue to make satisfactory progress in the business, and save up some money of his own.

On his return, Keith expressed regret at the elder Franklin's conservatism and proposed backing the boy himself. He instructed Benjamin to prepare a schedule of necessary equipment and an estimate of its cost, and promised to send to London for the material. Later he suggested that Franklin himself go to London to select the equipment, so a passage was duly engaged. Keith was to provide him with letters of introduction to persons of consequence in London and letters of credit wherewith to make his purchases. When Franklin called on the governor soon before sailing to obtain these letters, they were not ready, but according to the gubernatorial secretary they would be at Newcastle before the ship left that point. Keith was there, but was too busy to be seen, but the secretary assured him they would be sent on board before departure. The governor's mail was brought on board in a pouch which the captain of the vessel refused to open until later. When the sack was opened there were no letters for the young printer.

Franklin was thus disappointed by the governor but, had he discussed the project earlier with his friends, he would have learned this was just the outcome he might have expected in any dealings with Keith. So the dreams of setting up as a master printer faded into thin air. But the young printer faced the future undismayed.

Almost immediately upon his arrival in London, Franklin obtained employment with Samuel Palmer, a well-known printer of that city, who was also the author of a history of printing, only the first part of which was ever completed. In Palmer's office he was assigned to set type on the third edition of Wollaston's *Religion of Nature*. Disagreeing personally with certain theses in this work, Franklin wrote in refutation "a little metaphysical piece" called *A Dissertation on Liberty and Necessity, Pleasure and Pain*. This

brought him favorably to the attention of his employer, but Franklin is said to have endeavored to suppress the edition, regretting its publication on account of the atheistic views expressed. Be that as it may, four copies have survived. Once again, we find the young printer facile with the pen.

After a period of satisfactory service with Palmer, Franklin accepted a job from John Watts at a higher wage. Soon came an opportunity to return to America. Denham, a Quaker merchant whom he had met on the voyage to England and with whom he had kept in touch, was going to Philadelphia with an extensive stock of merchandise, to open a store in that city. He offered Benjamin a position as clerk and bookkeeper at lower wages than he was then drawing as a compositor. However, Franklin accepted, and sailed with Denham on July 23, 1726.

For six months all went well with Franklin in the Denham store. Then both master and clerk fell ill and the former did not recover. The store was taken over by executors, and Franklin had to look for another job. He tried first to obtain a mercantile position, but finding no opening, became foreman of the shop of Samuel Keimer, his former employer, who now had a force of several men. For the purpose of training these men and bringing the shop up to the best London standards of efficiency, Keimer paid Franklin what was then a comparatively high wage. The job had another element of attractiveness, however, in that the shop was closed Saturdays and Sundays, thus giving Franklin opportunity for reading and study.

After the men in the shop began to show the results of training, Keimer started to fret and fume over Franklin's wages, finally demanding a readjustment downward. They finally, however, broke over a trivial incident which is thus described by Franklin:

At length a trifle snapp'd our connections; for, a great noise happening near the Court-House, I put my head out of the window to see

what was the matter. Keimer being in the street look'd up and saw me, call'd out to me in a loud voice and angry tone to mind my business, adding some reproachful Words, that nettl'd me the more for their publicity, all the Neighbors who were looking out on the same occasion, being Witnesses how I was treat'd. He came up immediately into the Printing-House, continu'd the Quarrel, high Words pass'd on both sides, he gave me the quarter's Warning we had stipulat'd expressing a wish that he had not been obliged to so long a Warning. I told him his wish was unnecessary, for I would leave him that instant; and so, taking my Hat, walk'd out of doors, desiring Meredith, whom I saw below, to take care of some things I left, and bring them to my lodgings.

It was Franklin's idea to return to Boston, but he was stayed in this move by a visit from Hugh Meredith, the fellow printer just mentioned. Meredith proposed they go into business together, suggesting that his father might provide the necessary capital in consideration of Franklin's superior knowledge of the trade, the two partners to have an equal share in the profits. The father consenting, the equipment of a printing office was ordered from London.

There was, of course, a long wait to be contemplated before the equipment could arrive. Andrew Bradford could or would give Franklin no work, but Keimer, having a large job in prospect, soon re-employed him and sent him to Burlington, N. J., to print paper money for the province of New Jersey.

When the type and press arrived from London, the new firm of Franklin and Meredith began business. Almost immediately they received an order to print forty sheets of a large book on the history of the Quakers, which Samuel Keimer, their former employer, had started but had failed to finish on time. Franklin undertook this at too low a price, as he soon found out, so he resolved to finish a sheet each day, even though this often took him till late at night. On this book he did the composition and Meredith the presswork.

The new firm made a good impression with the accuracy of their

typesetting and the quality of their work, this being all the more noteworthy in comparison with the rather slipshod product of their two Philadelphia competitors. On one occasion, Bradford, who was the public printer, printed an address from the House to the Governor in a particularly careless manner. Franklin and Meredith promptly reprinted it accurately and well and sent a copy to each member of the House. Franklin writes: "They were sensible of the difference; it strengthened the hands of our friends in the House, and they voted us their printers for the year ensuing."

When the firm faced a financial crisis, Meredith withdrew and Franklin raised from his friends the funds necessary to meet outstanding obligations. From then on the title under which the enterprise operated was "B. Franklin, Printer."

His business prospered. Keimer went into bankruptcy in 1729 and the apprentice who succeeded him soon retired from the field. This left Andrew Bradford as Franklin's sole competitor in Philadelphia, and as Bradford was likewise postmaster, the duties of that office diverted much of his attention from the concerns of printing and publishing.

Franklin now began to think of getting married. One projected match falling through, he renewed his acquaintance with Miss Deborah Read and on September 1, 1730, she became his wife. Concerning his conjugal relations Franklin wrote: "She proved a good and faithful helpmate, assisted me much by attending the Shop; we strove together, and have ever mutually endeavored to make each other happy."

One of Franklin's important ventures in publishing was the issue of the *Pennsylvania Gazette*. When he embarked on the printing business the only newspaper being published in Philadelphia was the *American Weekly Mercury,* founded in 1719 by Andrew Bradford and published regularly thereafter. Though not well

edited, this paper had been profitable, and Franklin was sure there was room for a well edited competitive sheet. He confided his ideas to an English journeyman printer, George Webb, who promptly carried the news to Keimer. The latter appropriated the plan and lost no time in getting out the first issue of *The Universal Instructor in all Arts and Sciences; and Pennsylvania Gazette.* This paper limped along to its thirty-ninth number, when it went under, and its good will was purchased for a song by Franklin and Meredith, who abbreviated its title to *The Pennsylvania Gazette.* The paper contained much clever material and proved popular.

All through the columns of the *Gazette* ran a vein of good humor which was sadly lacking in most American literature of the period. The editor was always ready with a quip. One correspondent asked: "I am courting a girl I have but little Acquaintance with. How shall I come to a Knowledge of her Faults and whether she has the Virtues I imagine she has?" Franklin replied to the lovelorn inquirer: "Commend her among her female Acquaintances."

The second important publishing venture was the one with which Franklin's name is principally associated: *Poor Richard's Almanac.* Few know just how this name was derived.

At that period the annual publication of an almanac was a matter of great commercial importance to the American colonial printers. An almanac constituted the one item of printing that could be sold in quantity, for every household needed one, the booklet usually hanging by a string from a door jamb, available for ready reference. Almanacs also served as diaries or journals, and many important records have come down to us on the leaves or interleaves. The almanac was therefore a staple, and although a number were already published regularly in Philadelphia, Franklin was sure he could make profitable the issue of still another.

The chief expense of publication was for copy, as the "philo-

ANNO REGNI

GEORGII II.

R E G I S

Magnæ Britanniæ, Franciæ, & Hiberniæ,

VICESIMO PRIMO.

At a General Assembly of the Colony of
New-Jersey, continued by Adjournments to
the 17th Day of *November*, *Anno Dom.*
1747, and then begun and holden at *Burlington*, being the fifth Sitting of the second
Session of this present Assembly.

PHILADELPHIA:

Printed by B. FRANKLIN, Printer to the King's
most excellent Majesty for the Province of *New-Jersey*.

M,DCC,XLVIII.

maths" who compiled them charged a stiff fee. Franklin decided to avoid this cost by writing the copy himself and as he did not wish to appear as both author and publisher, decided to issue it under a *nom de plume* borrowed from an English almanac by Richard Saunders. The fictitious author of the same name of the American almanac was therefore known as "Poor Richard."

Through the pages of the successive issues appeared the homely wisdom which has crystallized into Poor Richard's philosophy. The success of the publication was very great. The almanac for the first year was twice reprinted to meet the demand. Of the almanac Franklin says: "I reaped considerable profit from it, vending annually near ten thousand."

Franklin summed up the maxims of Poor Richard in the preface to the 1758 almanac. This summary is sometimes known as "Father Abraham's speech to the American People" and sometimes as "The Way to Wealth." It has been reprinted again and again and translated into dozens of languages. Some sentences in it are better known than any other passages in American literature. We have only to recall:

> *Early to bed, Early to rise, makes a Man healthy, wealthy, and wise.*
> *God helps Them that help Themselves.*
> *Keep thy shop, and thy shop will keep thee.*
> *Diligence is the Mother of Good Luck.*

Do you recall the name of that valiant ship of John Paul Jones, the *Bon Homme Richard*? How came it by that name? During the American Revolution, the French government had promised John Paul Jones a new ship. He waited at Brest month after month for it to arrive, but it did not come. He wrote to everyone concerned, from the king of France down, pleading for fulfillment of the promise. Still the ship did not come. One day he read in Poor Richard this

maxim: "If you would have your Business done, go; if not, send."
He acted on the precept. He went. He got the ship. He named it
for his preceptor.

Franklin went to France in 1776 as one of the three commis-
sioners to represent the colonies. He took up his residence in the
village of Passy, now swallowed up in the growth of the French
capital. In his house there he established a little private press on
which he printed a number of items in blithesome mood, mostly for
the entertainment of his friends. Bagatelles, he called them. Until
recently most of these were believed to be lost, but an almost complete set was assembled by a distinguished American collector of
Frankliniana, who recently presented his collection to the library of
Yale University.

Benjamin Franklin's history as a patriot, statesman and diplomat,
as a scientist, and as the most distinguished American citizen of his
time, is too well known to require review here. The more we become familiar with his many-sided activities, the more we must
come to admire him. There is one point, however, that those of us
who are concerned with the making of books will never forget.
Though he was a signer of the Declaration of Independence, though
he had rendered to his country service of incalculable importance as
the ambassador of the colonies at the court of France, though he
had attained eminence in many branches of science—when he came
to write his last will and testament, he began it this way:

"I, Benjamin Franklin, Printer . . ."

XXX

Printer and Historian

THERE is one other personality which stands out among the printers of the American colonies. The name of Isaiah Thomas is not so well known as it deserves to be, perhaps because no undue political prominence or picturesque incident has led to its inclusion in the popular accounts of American history. Yet Thomas, a competent and conscientious printer of Boston and Worcester, rendered service of real importance in the building of these United States.

We are first introduced to Isaiah, born January 19, 1749, when he was apprenticed to Zechariah Fowle, a Boston printer, at the age of six. According to Isaiah's own story, he had no more than six weeks' schooling, "and poor at that." While other lads of his own age were getting their education in schools, the printing-office dictionary and the Bible were his only instructors, other than the trade which he was learning. But typography, as Dr. Charles L. Nichols, the competent biographer of Isaiah Thomas, pointed out, exercises in itself an educative force of no mean importance.

From Isaiah's record we find that Fowle was an "indifferent hand at presswork and much worse at the case." Thomas, however, took a vital and active interest in his work and made some good friends who gave helpful advice and practical assistance. When Isaiah was eight years old, he did the case work for ten thousand copies of the *New England Primer,* his first book; at the age of thirteen he printed and made woodcuts for the *New Book of Knowledge.* He says of these cuts that, as poorly executed as they

were, there were no better ones being made at that time in Boston, although there had been before and were shortly afterwards.

On September 19, 1765, at the age of sixteen, Thomas left Boston with the intention of going to England, but got no farther than Halifax, where he arrived four days later. He was disappointed in his hope to obtain passage to England and started to work with Anthony Henry, the indolent and unskillful printer of the *Halifax Gazette*. The management of this paper was left in Thomas's hands, but he remained with it a little less than six months.

In the spring of 1767 Thomas returned to Boston, but soon became restless again and obtained an apparently friendly release from Fowle. Isaiah's father had died in North Carolina, and he decided to go there. Unsuccessful in his efforts to establish himself at Wilmington in that province, he moved on to Charleston, where he became a journeyman in the shop of Robert Wells, publisher of the *South Carolina and American General Gazette*. He remained here for two years, during which time, on Christmas Day, 1769, he married Mary Dill, whom he divorced for infidelity on May 27, 1777.

In 1770 Isaiah again returned to Boston and entered into a partnership with his former master, the firm undertaking the publication of the *Massachusetts Spy* during a period rife with political dissension. There were five other papers being published in Boston, but that fact only made their venture more daring.

After three months of this partnership, the effort to continue the triweekly issues of the *Spy* proved too heavy a financial burden, and in October, 1770, Thomas bought out his partner and continued the publication as his own individual enterprise. The original aim of the *Massachusetts Spy* was to present impartially both sides of the argument between the royalists and the colonial patriots, but Thomas soon realized the impossibility of neutrality and cast his lot whole-heartedly with the patriots.

In the spring of 1771 Thomas began to print theses, in Latin, for students working for bachelor of arts degrees from Harvard. These papers had been printed for many years exclusively by the Drapers, the publishers of the *Massachusetts Gazette and Boston Weekly News Letter*. The audacity of Thomas in bidding for and winning this contract aroused great resentment, nor would he have escaped reminders of any misprints, had there been any, in the censorious articles that appeared in the *Massachusetts Gazette* after the young craftsman had won for himself the printing, not only of the bachelor of arts theses, but also those for the master of arts degree. Although Thomas had skilled and learned assistants, he held himself responsible for seeing that no textual or typographical errors occurred. Even political accusations and charges of wirepulling were brought against Thomas in the battle that was waged over the printing of these theses.

The Drapers, in retaliation for this invasion of their monopoly, and Governor Hutchinson, in anger at Isaiah's expressions of patriot sympathies, brought about the refusal by the customs-house officials of the "Shipping List" for publication in the *Spy*. The Drapers also accused Isaiah of changing the date of publication of his paper to Thursday just to conflict with that of their *News Letter*. Thomas retaliated with the statement that Richard Draper himself had formerly suggested Thursday as being the preferable day of issue.

In the *Spy* appeared articles specifically attacking Governor Hutchinson. As a result of these articles Thomas was summoned before the Governor's Council and the Supreme Judicial Court at Boston, but suit for the libel was dropped. After failure to obtain indictment in Suffolk County, there was talk of bringing suit in the Essex County court, but action was never pressed.

On the night of April 16, 1775, in order to save his life and machinery, Isaiah moved his press and some of his types to Wor-

A

NARRATIVE,

OF THE

EXCURSION and RAVAGES

OF THE

KING'S TROOPS

Under the Command of General GAGE,

On the nineteenth of APRIL, 1775.

TOGETHER WITH THE

DEPOSITIONS

Taken by ORDER of CONGRESS,

To fupport the Truth of it.

Publifhed by AUTHORITY.

This was the first printing done in Worcester Mass.

MASSACHUSETTS-BAY :

WORCESTER, Printed by ISAIAH THOMAS, by order

of the PROVINCIAL CONGRESS. *1775.*

AN EARLY TITLE PAGE FROM THE PRESS
OF ISAIAH THOMAS AT WORCESTER, 1775.

cester. In Worcester there was great resentment against any act of Parliament which curtailed liberty or freedom of the press. Isaiah set up his press in the cellar of Captain Timothy Bigelow's home. The first issue of the *Massachusetts Spy* in Worcester was that of May 3, 1775, within two weeks of its removal from Boston. For a year Thomas fought to maintain his paper and to finance his printing shop. Those were not prosperous days, for Benjamin Russell, one of Isaiah's apprentices, tells of sleeping on rags in the garret and eating with his master in the office bread and milk bought by the pennyworth. In the fall of 1775, Thomas succeeded in obtaining the establishment of a postoffice at Worcester, and the appointment of himself as postmaster.

A detailed story of Isaiah's misfortunes is told in vivid form in a letter, written October 2, 1775, addressed by him to Daniel Hopkins of the Massachusetts House of Assembly, then sitting (precariously) at Watertown. This letter, now preserved among the Thomas papers in the collection of the American Antiquarian Society at Worcester, was written after Thomas realized that he could not depend upon financial support from the government which the patriot forces had set up in Massachusetts.

On March 1, 1776, Thomas was forced to give up the publication of the *Spy* for the time being, and began to publish a handbill monthly which he sent to his old subscribers. On June 21, 1776, the names of William Stearns and Daniel Bigelow appeared as the printers of the *Massachusetts Spy,* Thomas having been compelled to lease its publication for two years, during which time it operated at a loss and deteriorated greatly from its former high standard. For two years, Thomas lived in such obscurity that nothing is known of his activities or place of residence. With the issue of June 25, 1778, Thomas's name again appeared on the Worcester newspaper, which was then renamed *Thomas's Massachusetts Spy.* On

May 26, 1779, Thomas married Mary Fowle, of whom little is known except that she was a "half-cousin" of Isaiah's. The two were unusually congenial.

By January, 1781, business began to prosper for Thomas. He was still using his old press, which had been stealthily removed from Boston on the night of April 16, 1775. This press is now preserved with the Thomas material in the American Antiquarian Society. He procured new types from England. Not only did Thomas build up his own office in Worcester to a commanding position, but he financed former apprentices to set up in business in other cities, forming partnerships with them. The firm of Thomas & Andrews in Boston built up an extensive and profitable business—a partnership with Ebenezer T. Andrews. Then there was Thomas & Carlisle at Walpole, New Hampshire, Thomas & Waldo at Brookfield, Massachusetts, Thomas & Tappan at Portsmouth, New Hampshire, Thomas & Merrifield at Windsor, Vermont, and Thomas & Tinges (later Thomas & Whipple) at Newburyport, Massachusetts. In 1784 was established in Baltimore the firm of Thomas, Andrews & Butler, and in 1796 in Albany the firm of Thomas, Andrews & Penniman. It is apparent from this that he directed what was almost—for those days—a printing "trust."

Thomas continued to print almanacs and juveniles, a style of publication which he had been issuing before he left Boston. The books for children were patterned after those published in London by John Newbery. In 1782 a bindery was added to his printing office. In 1785 Thomas began to print *Perry's Spelling Book,* a lucrative venture with a schoolbook which continued in popularity for forty years. In 1789, through permission of the author, his Boston office was printing still larger editions of Noah Webster's *Spelling Book.* He also issued many works of political character, Fourth of July orations, and Masonic orations, Thomas being an enthusiastic

adherent of Masonry and grand master for several terms of office. In 1793 Thomas erected a paper mill in Quinsigamond.

Religious works formed another important class, and the Bible was the best seller in this category. This was issued in all formats from folio to duodecimo. The text being so long, it was impossible for the average printer to set all the text in type at one time, much less to tie up such an amount of type to keep the job standing. The usual method was to set up several forms and print off the quantity of sheets required for the edition in hand, then distribute the type, print some more forms, and repeat until the book was completed. This involved the expense of composition for each edition printed, as well as the likelihood of errors creeping in each time. Thomas conceived the idea of buying enough type to set the whole Bible at one time and keep it standing, thus making the printing of a new edition a simple matter. An arrangement was made with the Fry Foundry in London to supply the type, and the pages were set in London and shipped to Worcester. The book was known as the "Standing Bible" and was the first edition of the Scriptures published on this plan in America.

Thomas also received from England a set of types to publish his "Musick Books," among which the most important is his *Laus Deo,* the first edition of which appeared in 1786.

In 1808 Thomas began that work which had been his ambition all through life—the writing and publishing of a *History of Printing in America.* This book was not to exhaust the history of printing, but "to collect and preserve materials for such a History." Thomas was the logical and best-equipped writer of such a history, having lived through the period of which he wrote and having had contacts, either personal or through correspondence, with the men of whom he wrote. But for his interest in the subject, record of the work of many pioneer American printers would have been lost.

While there have been published in recent years several monographs on the work of individual American printers, the Thomas book had remained up until 1936 the only general work on early printers and printing in the United States.

The first attempt at such a record could not, in the nature of things, be perfect, and no one realized this better than the author. No sooner was the book out than he began making notes and gathering material based on the correspondence he received, in preparation for a revised edition. At the beginning of his notes Thomas wrote: "If I should not live to fulfil my intention, and the books should be printed again, I hope that some friend will do it." This wish was carried out when the American Antiquarian Society, over a half century later, issued a revised edition of his *History of Printing in America.*

The problem of disposal of the large library which Thomas had collected during his life and more particularly during the writing of the *History* was solved by the decision to found a new historical society. In November, 1812, the American Society of Antiquaries met, and Thomas was elected president, which office he retained until his death in 1831. To this group, the present American Antiquarian Society, he gave his library, his collection of early American newspapers, and his papers and records. At his death he bequeathed to the society what was, in those days, a consequential fortune. Since its foundation the American Antiquarian Society has developed a library which constitutes now one of the most important sources for the study of American history anywhere to be found. Unlike many historical societies, it is operated on enlightened principles, the aim being to render to students all assistance within its power and to make its collection not a morgue for mummies but a laboratory for creative work. Perhaps, though, this is only a reflection of the spirit of its founder.

Starting with a good collection of early American newspapers, there have been constant additions of newspapers, which constitute one of the fundamental sources of historical fact. The present director, Dr. Clarence S. Brigham, has made and is now revising a census of American newspapers published before 1821 in all the libraries of the country, an invaluable contribution to American bibliography.

Regarding the aims of Isaiah Thomas in founding the American Antiquarian Society, his grandson, Judge Benjamin Franklin Thomas, wrote:

In his business as a printer and bookseller, in gathering the materials for his history of printing, having a deep personal interest in the annals of a country whose course he had watched, not idly, from colonial dependence to national greatness, a lover and reader of books, touched early by the gentlest of infirmities, bibliomania, he had collected a library especially rich as to the fountains and springs (*fontes et origines*) of American history. His researches had taught him the value of such a collection; his observation and experience had shown him how quickly the sources of our history were drying up, how rapidly the monuments of the past were crumbling and wasting away. He saw and understood, no man better, from what infinitely varied and minute sources the history of a nation's life was to be drawn; that the only safe rule was to gather up all the fragments so that nothing be lost. It was in the light of this experience, and with a view to garner up and preserve the materials of our history, that he conceived the plan of the American Antiquarian Society, of making his own library the basis of its collections, and of giving to the cause of good letters a liberal share of the fortune he had acquired in their service.

Ardent patriot, able typographer, successful printer, erudite historian, founder of a great learned society, respected citizen—such was the career of the lad apprenticed to typesetting at the age of six.

XXXI

The Spread of Printing in America

T HE spread of printing throughout the enormous areas of the two Americas presents a picture altogether different from that of the propagation of the art in Europe. In the Old World, printing developed and spread in communities which had each its background of centuries of culture. Across the Atlantic, on the other hand, printing became one of the implements of implanting and fostering the cultural heritage of European civilization in environments that were utterly new and strange. In the Americas the press accompanied the cross and the sword, the ax and the plow, in the world's most magnificent pioneering adventure.

Something has already been said about the first coming of the press to America and its establishment in Mexico and later in Peru before the close of the sixteenth century. And we have also noted the first appearance of printing in English-speaking America a full century after Juan Pablos began work as a printer in New Spain. Of the further spread of printing in North America no more than a brief survey can be offered here.

Nearly fifty years after the first establishment of the press in Massachusetts, William Bradford, a printer from London, came to Philadelphia and there began to print in 1685 under the auspices of the Society of Friends, or Quakers, headed by William Penn. In the same year another English printer, William Nuthead, set up his press at Saint Mary's City, in Maryland, after a futile attempt three years earlier to work at his craft in Virginia. At the time, the governmental authorities in Virginia resolutely forbade printing of

any kind in that dominion. In Pennsylvania there was no ban against printing, but its use was so hedged about with official regulations and limitations that William Bradford was often in trouble with the authorities. The first product of his press was a humble almanac for the year 1686, but in it occurred the term "Lord Penn," which the provincial council found so offensive that it reprimanded the printer and gave him strict instructions as to what he might or might not print.

After recurring conflicts with the authorities Bradford in 1692 printed a pamphlet for George Keith, a Quaker who at the time had come under the disapproval of the Society of Friends. The printer was arrested and imprisoned, together with several others involved in producing and distributing the offending pamphlet. Bradford appealed to Governor Benjamin Fletcher, who held the dual position of governor of New York and also of Pennsylvania. Fletcher disposed of the case quite simply by appointing Bradford the royal printer at New York. William Bradford, therefore, hurriedly departing from Philadelphia, became the first printer in the province of New York in 1693.

Philadelphia's outstanding claim to fame in the history of printing in colonial America is that that city was the home for nearly seventy years of the immortal Benjamin Franklin, whose career has been sketched—quite inadequately in so brief a space—in an earlier chapter. Philadelphia was also the focal point of the American Revolution, and the printers of that city, on both sides of the controversy, made important contributions to the history of the momentous struggle between the colonists and the mother country. Among Philadelphia's typographic distinctions is also the fact that in that city was printed the first American edition of the Bible in English, produced in 1782 from the press of Robert Aitken. It might further be noted that the large German immigration to Penn-

THE

HOLY BIBLE,

Containing the Old and New

TESTAMENTS:

Newly tranflated out of the

ORIGINAL TONGUES;

And with the former

TRANSLATIONS

Diligently compared and revifed.

PHILADELPHIA:

Printed and Sold by R. AITKEN, at Pope's
Head, Three Doors above the Coffee
House, in Market Street.
M.DCC.LXXXII.

TITLE PAGE OF THE FIRST AMERICAN
EDITION OF THE BIBLE IN ENGLISH.

sylvania resulted in the development, near Philadelphia, of an important German-language press in that colony, beginning in 1738.

In Maryland the printing career of William Nuthead was brief and unimportant except for the fact that he was the first to set up a press in that colony. He died in 1695 and was succeeded by his widow, Dinah—the first instance in America of a woman being in complete charge of a printing office. She was almost completely illiterate, however, and had little success with the printing business, which she relinquished in 1696. The first really successful printer to work in Maryland was William Parks, from Ludlow, in England, who printed at Annapolis for ten or eleven years beginning in 1726. In 1730 he set up a branch office at Williamsburg, Virginia, thus becoming the first printer actually to operate a printing plant in the Old Dominion. In 1737 he gave up his Annapolis office entirely and printed in Virginia until his death in 1750.

Parks was succeeded at Annapolis by Jonas Green, a grandson of that Samuel Green of Cambridge, Massachusetts, whose descendants appear in American printing history throughout two centuries. Green began to print in Maryland in 1739 and died there in 1767. His widow, three of his sons, and a grandson continued until 1839 the business which he had founded.

Another outstanding figure in the history of the American press was William Goddard, who set up a press in Baltimore in 1773 after a number of years of experience as a printer in Providence, Rhode Island, and in Philadelphia. Goddard was an ardent patriot and sensed the inevitably approaching conflict between the American colonies and Great Britain. In 1774 he put his Baltimore printing enterprise into the competent hands of his sister, Mary Katherine Goddard, and devoted all his time and energy to the creation of an American postal system which should take the place of the inefficient British colonial postal service. Though his "American

Post Office on constitutional principles" was adopted by the Continental Congress in 1775 as the official postal system of the new government, Goddard's two years of intensive work and the "Goddard post offices" in operation from Maine to Georgia brought almost no further official recognition to the creator of what has since become the United States postal service.

In New York, William Bradford from 1693 until his retirement from active work in 1744 made for himself an enviable reputation as a printer and as a citizen. In 1725 he began the printing and publication of the *New-York Gazette*. Andrew Bradford, one of his two sons, went to Philadelphia and established a successful printing business which was continued by his nephew and foster son, William Bradford. William's son and grandson maintained the tradition of the Bradfords as printers in Philadelphia until 1813.

The outstanding event in the history of the press in colonial New York was the famous trial of John Peter Zenger which established the principle of the freedom of the press in British North America. Zenger, an apprentice and later a partner of the pioneer William Bradford, was the printer and nominally the publisher in 1733 of the *New-York Weekly Journal,* which published some covert attacks on the administration of the province and particularly on William Cosby, the highly unpopular governor. For one of these publications the governor commanded that Zenger be imprisoned, although the grand jury had refused to return an indictment against the printer for libel. At the trial of the prisoner, in August, 1735, the defense was conducted by Andrew Hamilton, a venerable attorney of high reputation from Philadelphia. In spite of a packed court, the defendant was acquitted with a verdict which established for the first time the legal principle that in cases of libel the jury should be the judges of both the law and the facts. This marked an important step forward in the fight for the complete freedom of the

press, which almost since the first introduction of printing had been sternly limited in England and elsewhere.

In Connecticut the printing press first made its appearance in 1709, when Thomas Short arrived in New London from Boston and began to print the official documents of the Connecticut colonial government. For thirty years the laws, proclamations, and other official matters had been printed for Connecticut by Samuel Green in Cambridge or by Samuel's son Bartholomew in Boston. Short was a connection by marriage with the Green family and probably a member of Bartholomew's household. But the first Connecticut printer died in 1712, and the colony again applied to the Greens for help. This time Timothy Green, the younger brother of Bartholomew, answered the call in 1714. He and at least ten of his direct descendants printed in Connecticut for over a century.

William Bradford, who introduced printing in Pennsylvania and later in New York, was also the first to operate a press in New Jersey, where he printed a quantity of the colony's paper money and also an issue of the New Jersey laws at Perth Amboy in 1723. For some time before and after this date, Bradford printed for New Jersey in his New York shop. About 1728 Samuel Keimer, of Philadelphia, with a young man named Benjamin Franklin in his employ, set up a press in Burlington to print New Jersey's currency and also the current laws of the colony. But the first permanent press in New Jersey was not put in operation until about 1754, when James Parker began to print at Woodbridge, his birthplace, after having worked for ten years or so in the city of New York.

After New Jersey, the next of the American colonies to welcome the press was Rhode Island, where the first printer was James Franklin, older brother and one-time master in the printing trade of Benjamin Franklin. James was possibly influenced by the unfriendly attitude of the Boston authorities in his removal from that

city to Newport, where he set up shop in 1727. He died there in 1735, leaving his business to his widow, Ann Smith Franklin, who carried it on successfully for nearly thirty years. In her conduct of the printing office Ann Franklin was assisted by her son and two daughters, all of whom had been trained as printers. The son, James Franklin, Jr., after an apprenticeship in Philadelphia under his distinguished uncle Benjamin, returned to Newport when he came of age and became his mother's partner.

Historically important among the early printers of Rhode Island was William Goddard. After an apprenticeship under James Parker in New Haven and New York, Goddard set up the first press in the town of Providence in 1762. In this enterprise he was assisted as a business partner by his mother, Sarah Updike Goddard. His career took him

MDCCXXIX.

THE

Rhode-Island

ALMANACK,

For the Year, 1729.
Being the First after *Leap-Year.*
Carefully fitted, and exactly calculated to the Meridian of *NEW PORT* on *Rhode Island*; Whose Latitude North is 41 gr. 30 m. Longitude from *London*, 72 grs.
But may without sensible Error serve all Parts of *NEW-ENGLAND.*

By Poor *ROBIN.*

NEWPORT:
Printed and Sold by *J. Franklin*, at his Printing-House on *Tillinghast's* Wharf. Sold also by *T. Fleet*, in Pudding-Lane, *Boston.* 1729.

TITLE PAGE OF AN ALMANAC PRINTED BY JAMES FRANKLIN, 1729.

later to Philadelphia and finally to Baltimore. His part in the creation of the American postal system has already been mentioned, but it should also be noted that as a craftsman he was distinguished by the quality of his work, his typographic taste and skill being markedly superior to the then prevailing standards of American printing.

The resolute opposition of Virginia's government to the establishment of printing in that colony was not overcome until 1730, when William Parks began to print at Williamsburg. Parks was a good printer, with an intelligent interest not only in typography but also in literature. It is interesting to note that one of the very first things he printed at Williamsburg was a sixteen-page pamphlet containing *Typographia. An Ode, on Printing,* written by a local scholar and "occasion'd by the setting up a Printing Press in Williamsburg"—the earliest American appreciation of the press.

As early as 1722 the province of South Carolina began to make efforts to procure a printer to print its laws, but without success until 1731, when a bonus of £1,000—albeit in colonial currency—induced not one printer but three to move to Charleston and compete for the promised position of official printer. The three were George Webb, Thomas Whitmarsh, and Eleazer Phillips, Jr. Until recent years it was impossible to say which of the three was actually the first to print in South Carolina. But in 1932 the writer was fortunate enough to locate in the Public Record Office, London, the evidence which seems to settle the question. It is a printed document dated November 4, 1731, and bearing the imprint "Charles Town, Printed by George Webb." At the same time and place was also located another document with the imprint of Whitmarsh, but dated November 27, 1731.

Webb and Phillips, however, left but little trace in the records of South Carolina printing. Phillips is thought to have died in an epidemic which ravaged Charleston in 1732, and Webb may have died at the same time. Whitmarsh was left in command of the field. He had gone to Charleston as a partner of Benjamin Franklin, for whom he had worked in Philadelphia. When he died in 1733, he was succeeded as Franklin's Charleston partner by Lewis Timothy. Timothy with his widow Elizabeth, his son Peter, his daughter-in-

THE

RIGHTS

OF

COLONIES

EXAMINED.

PUBLISHED BY AUTHORITY.

PROVIDENCE:
PRINTED BY *WILLIAM GODDARD*.
M.DCC.LXV.

law Ann, and his grandson Benjamin Franklin Timothy formed an influential dynasty of printers which continued until 1802.

South Carolina was predominantly an agricultural province with few centers which could be called in any sense urban. In that region, therefore, the press developed but slowly, and hardly at all outside of Charleston before the end of the century. For the same reasons printing was late in finding a foothold in the neighboring province of North Carolina. Not until 1749 did James Davis move to New Bern, probably from Virginia, and set up his press in response to the government's urgent need of someone to print its laws. He continued to work there until his death in 1785. Printing in this slowly developing province was uneventful and was confined for many years to a few small towns on or near the seacoast.

Outside of the present borders of the United States, British North America had no press until 1752. In that year John Bushell, from Boston, moved his printing shop to Halifax, Nova Scotia, a town which had just been founded. The prime mover of the Halifax printing venture was Bartholomew Green, grandson of the Cambridge printer, who had the daring to try his fortunes in the Nova Scotian wilderness at the age of fifty. But he died in 1751, a few weeks after his arrival in Halifax, and his mantle of pioneering fell on the shoulders of Bushell, a Boston associate, whose principal claim to fame is that he thus became the first printer in Canada.

New Hampshire had no press until 1756, when Daniel Fowle, disgusted with the repressions of the authorities in Boston, departed from that city and set up shop in Portsmouth. In little Delaware, which was economically hardly more than a dependency of Pennsylvania, James Adams, at Wilmington in 1761, was the first to establish a press. And in far-off Georgia, the last of the colonies to be established, no printing was done until 1763—more than a hundred years after the introduction of printing in Massachusetts.

James Johnston, a recent immigrant from Scotland, was induced to procure the necessary equipment with which, in 1763, he set up a press at Savannah, primarily to serve the provincial government.

In 1764 William Brown and Thomas Gilmore, both from Philadelphia, ventured to seek their fortunes far to the north and became the first fully authenticated printers in Quebec. There is some reason to suspect, however, that Bishop Pontbriand, the last ecclesiastical head of the Quebec diocese under the French regime, may have had a small private press there as early as 1759. It was under distinctly French auspices that printing began in Louisiana in 1764 with Denis Braud as the pioneer craftsman. One of the very first things which Braud printed was a proclamation of the French king giving notice that Louisiana had been ceded to Spain.

The struggle of the American Revolution interrupted the spread of printing to new regions, but in 1780, as the war was drawing to its close, Judah Padock Spooner, a connection by marriage with the famous Green family, took the press to the new state of Vermont, where he set up shop at Westminster. The Revolution was over before Benjamin Titcomb, at Falmouth (now Portland) in 1785, became the first printer in Maine, which was then a "district" under the jurisdiction of Massachusetts.

Characteristic of the development of printing in the British American colonies is the fact that the pioneer printers, with very few exceptions, sought to support themselves by the printing of newspapers. In practically every case, too, the compelling motive for the introduction of printing into the different provinces was the urgent necessity of having the laws available in printed form. There was naturally much competition for the appointment as "royal printer," or "king's printer," or "printer to the crown," as such appointment gave the printer a certain official status as well as assuring him a fairly definite income. At centers such as Boston, New

York, and Philadelphia, the printing industry at the onset of the Revolution had developed into considerable importance, and the local presses were supplying a consequential part of their communities' cultural needs for reading matter.

The printers for the most part were their own publishers, although the trade of the publisher, whose books were printed for him, was beginning to appear. The printing office in many a town was also the local bookstore, and printers in many places regularly advertised the books which they had imported, from England or from the larger American centers, as well as the books and pamphlets which they themselves had printed.

Under British rule the colonial governments held the press under rather strict control and were quick to "crack down" on any printer who transgressed the limits of the freedom allowed him. The records contain innumerable instances of printers who were reprimanded, fined, or even imprisoned for daring to print something of which the authorities did not approve or for which the requisite permission had not been obtained. The colonial newspapers, therefore, were rather colorless affairs, their columns containing mostly "intelligence" from abroad, with almost no local news and (before the dissension with the mother country became acute) with barely a trace of real editorial opinion—particularly of opinion critical of the government.

But after independence had been achieved, restrictions upon the press were almost entirely removed. Furthermore, the establishment of the new government of the United States opened up for settlement a vast area of land in the "western country," and a new era of American pioneering began. A mass migration was soon under way, and the press was swept with it into almost uncharted regions beyond the Alleghanies.

Hugh Henry Breckenridge stood in the little settlement at the

confluence of the Monongahela and Alleghany rivers and pro-
phetically said of the site, "Nevertheless, it appeared to me as what
would one day be a town of note." He procured two young craftsmen from Philadelphia, John Scull and Joseph Boyd, and backed
them in establishing the *Pittsburgh Gazette*. Its first issue appeared
on July 29, 1786—a memorable date because it marked the first issue
of a press which definitely looked westward for its destiny.

The following year John Bradford, from Virginia, a surveyor
by profession, began the *Kentucky Gazette* at Lexington. Bradford's
brother, Fielding Bradford, learned what he could of the printing
craft in a few months' apprenticeship with John Scull in Pittsburgh,
procured a simple printing equipment, and brought it down the
Ohio. With such technical aid and advice as they could get from
Thomas Parvin, an aged and broken-down craftsman from Philadelphia, the Bradfords launched the press in Kentucky, where for
a generation it was to be the principal source of cultural material for
the whole western country. In 1791 George Roulstone, a printer
from Salem, Massachusetts, who had been working at Fayetteville,
North Carolina, with Robert Ferguson as partner, crossed the mountains with his equipment and set up a press at Rogersville, the first
in Tennessee. In 1793 William Maxwell, printer and former Revolutionary soldier, after working at his trade for a short time at Lexington, moved across the Ohio and established the first press in
Ohio at Cincinnati, publishing on November 9 of that year the initial issue of the *Centinel of the North-Western Territory*.

Growth of the western country was rapid as population poured
into it at an amazing rate. By 1804 there was sufficient settlement
in the wilds of Indiana to require the service of the press, and Elihu
Stout, formerly an employee under John Bradford in Kentucky,
introduced printing into that territory at Vincennes, then the seat
of territorial government. In 1808 the press crossed the Mississippi

River for the first time when Joseph Charless, an Irish printer who had worked in Philadelphia and later in Kentucky at Lexington and Louisville, established the *Missouri Gazette* at the old French settlement of Saint Louis. Printing took root in Michigan in 1809, under the direction of Rev. Gabriel Richard, a courageous and enterprising Catholic missionary priest, who brought James Miller from Utica, New York state, to print textbooks and religious works for him at Detroit. There had been some earlier printing at Detroit, however, the evidence showing that a printer named John McCall had worked there from 1796 to 1805.

Meanwhile, far to the south, the press had been introduced into Florida in 1783 by John Wells and William Charles Wells, loyalist refugees from revolutionary Charleston, who continued at Saint Augustine a newspaper which had earlier been published in the South Carolina town. It cannot be said, however, that the press became an established factor in Florida until 1821, two years after the United States had purchased that territory from Spain. In Mississippi, Andrew Marschalk, a printer who was also an army officer, introduced printing by the operation of a small printing shop at Walnut Hills, near Natchez, about 1798. Marschalk continued his career as a printer in Mississippi for about forty years. In Alabama, in 1807, an unidentified craftsman did the first printing, with types that were "old and much worn," at Wakefield, a site which has since vanished. The earliest Alabama printer whose name is known was P. J. Forster, whose imprint appeared at St. Stephens early in 1811. Later in the same year, Samuel Miller and John B. Hood began a newspaper at Fort Stoddert, a temporary military establishment a few miles above Mobile.

Illinois Territory, set off from Indiana in 1809, had its first capital at Kaskaskia, a settlement on the Mississippi River which has long since disappeared. As no press had as yet been set up in

the new territory, the first book of Illinois laws was printed in 1813 by Matthew Duncan at Russellville, Kentucky, the town from which had come Ninian Edwards, territorial governor of Illinois. But in the spring of 1814 the need for a printer in the territory had become so acute that Duncan was induced to remove his shop from Russellville to Kaskaskia and thus became the first printer in Illinois.

By 1830, five new states had been created out of the western wilderness and added to the Union. The population of these states was then served by some two hundred newspapers, while it also provided many other activities for the press in the varied demands of its political, economic, social, and religious life. Up to about this time, most of the migration into the western country had followed the Ohio River or had crossed the mountain passes from Virginia and North Carolina into Tennessee. But there then set in a second wave of migration, mostly from New England and New York, which followed the Mohawk Valley and passed over to the Great Lakes. This northern stream populated Michigan, the northern parts of Ohio, Indiana, and Illinois, and also reached into Wisconsin.

A birdseye view of the spread of the press throughout the region west of the Mississippi is presented in the following dates of the advent of printing in a number of the present states of the Union: Texas, 1817; Iowa, 1836; Minnesota, 1849; Nevada, 1858; Colorado, 1859. The Mormons operated a press at Salt Lake City, Utah, beginning in 1849. In California and in New Mexico, printing began in 1834, in both cases under Mexican auspices. Some crude, amateurish printing has been recorded in California two years or so before the regular establishment of the press there. Oregon had its first press in 1846, Washington in 1852, Arizona in 1859. The zeal of Christian missionaries to the Indians had taken printers, in advance of commercial need for the press, into the present areas of Kansas in 1834, Oklahoma in 1835, and Idaho in 1839. Last of the

states to receive the benefits of the press were Montana and Wyoming, in both of which printing began in 1863, and North Dakota, in which the first authenticated printing was done in 1864.

Wherever the settlers went, there too went the pioneer printers, with the materials for publishing their little newspapers in raw, frontier settlements, far from sources of supplies and beset with all the difficulties and dangers of life at the edge of the wilderness. Truly, these adventurous craftsmen played a notable part in the winning of the West and the making of America!

XXXII

The Revival of Craftsmanship

BRITISH printing standards were at their worst, and ugliness ran riot in the field of typography, when an artistic genius of amazing versatility turned his interests to bookmaking. The results were spectacular. William Morris, in 1888, was a poet and writer of eminence. He had revived fine standards of artistry in the weaving of tapestries, the making of furniture, the printing of cotton and linen, and other crafts. He was a prominent advocate of socialism. He was over fifty—the age at which most men begin to think of retiring—when the designing and printing of books came to be one of the major interests in his life. It came about in the following manner.

When materials were being gathered for the first Arts and Crafts Exhibition, Morris found that there were none of the books which he had written or with which he had been otherwise concerned which were worthy, on the basis of their artistic merit, of inclusion among the exhibits. Among the arts and crafts in intimate contact with daily life, printing was conspicuous as one to which he had made no contribution, and he now became aware of the importance of the omission.

His good friend, Emery Walker, delivered at that exhibition an illustrated lecture on printing. In preparing the slides for this address, he discussed his material with Morris, and the two made a joint examination of incunabula as well as of manuscripts which might have served the first printers as models. This circumstance served to awaken his latent interest in bookmaking, and Morris then

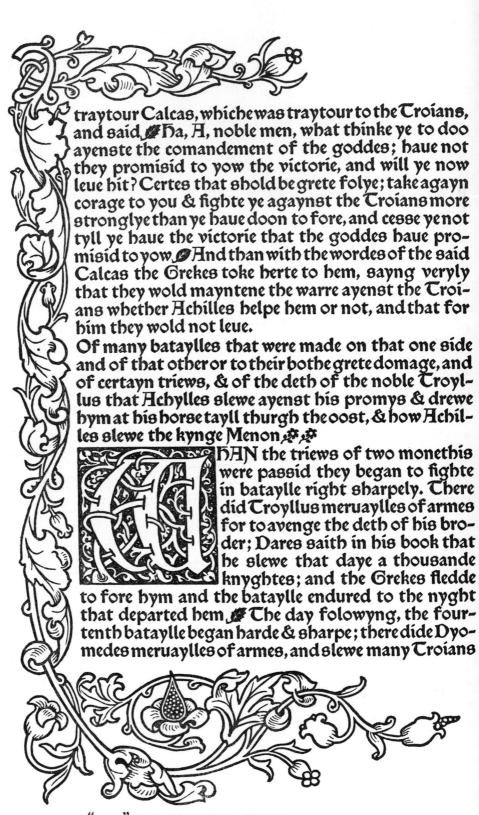

traytour Calcas, whiche was traytour to the Troians, and said, Ha, A, noble men, what thinke ye to doo ayenste the comandement of the goddes; haue not they promisid to yow the victorie, and will ye now leue hit? Certes that shold be grete folye; take agayn corage to you & fighte ye agaynst the Troians more stronglye than ye haue doon to fore, and cesse ye not tyll ye haue the victorie that the goddes haue promisid to yow. And than with the wordes of the said Calcas the Grekes toke herte to hem, sayng veryly that they wold mayntene the warre ayenst the Troians whether Achilles helpe hem or not, and that for him they wold not leue.

Of many batoylles that were made on that one side and of that other or to their bothe grete domage, and of certayn triews, & of the deth of the noble Troyllus that Achylles slewe ayenst his promys & drewe hym at his horse tayll thurgh the oost, & how Achilles slewe the kynge Menon.

HAN the triews of two monethis were passid they began to fighte in bataylle right sharpely. There did Troyllus meruaylles of armes for to avenge the deth of his broder; Dares saith in his book that he slewe that daye a thousande knyghtes; and the Grekes fledde to fore hym and the bataylle endured to the nyght that departed hem. The day folowyng, the fourtenth bataylle began harde & sharpe; there dide Dyomedes meruaylles of armes, and slewe many Troians

A PAGE SHOWING THE "TROY" TYPE OF WILLIAM MORRIS.

resolved to design and cut a font of type and re-establish long lost standards of craftsmanship in printing.

He thought of this entirely as an enterprise to be undertaken at his own cost and for his own gratification, having no thought of selling any volume or volumes to be produced. Though enthusiastic, his work was deliberate, for he spared no pains to attain perfection. The chronology of his early efforts was:

November, 1888. Emery Walker's lecture.
December, 1889. Type designing begun.
December, 1890. Last punches of the Golden type cut.
January, 1891. Proof of specimen page of *Glittering Plain*.

The general model for the Golden type was the roman of Jenson and his contemporaries. The best obtainable examples of such letters were enlarged photographically and, with these before him, Morris drew the designs for the new type in large scale. These were next reduced photographically to the size in which the type was to be cut and were studied, in consultation with Emery Walker, in this scale. Each letter was revised and restudied with unstinted pains until, when the designs met with the approval of the collaborators, they were turned over to Edward Prince for rendering in the form of steel punches. After cutting by this expert and sympathetic engraver, the punches were "smoked" and proofs drawn. These were likewise studied, again considered, and the punches altered when alteration was considered necessary by the ultra-exigent critics. The punches were now driven, types cast, and the specimen page above referred to was set up.

The results so far were encouraging to the apprentice printer now past the half century mark. The original idea was that Morris should have a small composing room and that the presswork be done outside. As his study of the elements of bookmaking prog-

Hesperides   Let bounteous Fates your spindles full
Fill, and wind up with whitest wool.
Let them not cut the thread
Of life until ye bid.
May death yet come at last,
And not with desp'rate haste;
But when ye both can say,
Come, let us now away.
Be ye to the barn then borne,
Two, like two ripe shocks of corn.

TO ELECTRA.

'LL come to thee in all those shapes
As Jove did when he made his rapes:
Only I'll not appear to thee
As he once did to Semele.
Thunder and lightning I'll lay by
To talk with thee familiarly.
Which done, then quickly we'll undress
To one and th' other's nakedness.
And, ravisht, plunge into the bed,
Bodies and souls commingled,
And kissing, so as none may hear,
We'll weary all the fables there.

50

ressed, however, it became evident that all the processes must be done under one roof and under one direction. A cottage was taken at Hammersmith, near his residence, and the equipment of a small press installed. So the Kelmscott Press, since become so celebrated in the annals of fine bookmaking, came into being. Its name was derived from Kelmscott Manor, near Lechlade on the upper Thames, concerning which Morris wrote: "It has come to be the type of the pleasant places of earth, and of the homes of harmless, simple people not overburdened with the intricacies of life; and, as others love the race of man through their lovers or their children, so I love the Earth through that small space of it."

The first book was to have been Caxton's translation of the *Golden Legend,* but this proved too lengthy for fairly prompt production, Morris being impatient to produce his first book. So a shorter composition of his own, the *Story of the Glittering Plain,* was selected and put into work at once. In the engraving of a border designed for this book by Morris, the services of William Harcourt Hooper, a retired wood engraver, were enlisted. The relation thus established continued throughout the life span of the press, it being Hooper who rendered on wood the great illustrative work of Sir Edward Burne-Jones and the inimitable book decorations from the hand of the master of the press.

The plan was to print twenty copies of the *Glittering Plain* for presentation to Morris's friends, the "adventure" being a purely private and personal one. But an unexpected announcement in the *Athenaeum* regarding the work of the press gave rise to many urgent requests that copies be made available for purchase. After many misgivings, Morris decided to print what seemed to him the large number of two hundred copies of the *Glittering Plain,* twenty for presentation as originally contemplated, and one hundred and eighty for sale through his regular publishers, Reeves and Turner.

The edition was promptly oversubscribed, before any price had been announced. The price when it was fixed represented only actual cost, as indeed, throughout the history of the press, the books were sold only at rates calculated to save Morris from being out of pocket on the enterprise.

Other books followed, and soon Morris projected an edition of Caxton's *Recuyell of the Historyes of Troye,* designing for this the Troy type, a letter of strongly Gothic character. A move was made to larger quarters, and a second press was installed. On New Year's Day, 1895, still another move was made to afford larger space, and at this time a third press was added to the equipment. And the steady flow of fine books, mostly printed in editions of about three hundred copies, continued to be taken up by enthusiastic subscribers.

The third type, which was projected for the Chaucer, the majestic volume destined to be the crowning glory of the press, and known as the Chaucer type, was simply a recutting in smaller size of the Troy type. This type was first used in the *Recuyell* above referred to, which was published late in 1892.

The *Works of Geoffrey Chaucer,* which had been projected in 1891, was finally issued in large folio format in 1896. It included no less than eighty-seven illustrations by Sir Edward Burne-Jones and many elaborate borders, initial letters, and initial words, as well as a decorative title page designed by Morris and engraved on wood. There were 425 copies on paper issued at £20 and 13 on vellum issued at 120 guineas.

The earliest Kelmscott books were bound in "half holland," that is, board sides with a canvas back, but the standard form of binding soon established was limp vellum with silk ties.

A word must be said about materials and processes of production. William Morris felt that much of the degradation of standards in contemporary craftsmanship was due to mechanical methods

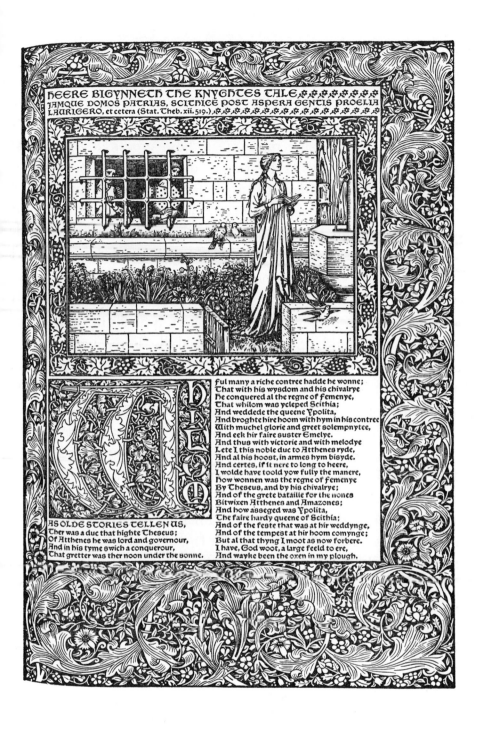

A PAGE (GREATLY REDUCED) FROM THE
WILLIAM MORRIS EDITION OF CHAUCER.

designed to promote speed. In seeking high standards, therefore, he found his inspiration in the work and methods of the early craftsmen who worked by hand. So his type punches were produced in exactly the same manner as those produced by Claude Garamond centuries earlier by purely manual processes. Casting, however, was done by machine, as he found he could thus obtain better results than by the ancient typefounder's method of "pour and jerk" with a hand mold.

With paper, however, he decided that hand fabrication could give him the only satisfactory product and, early in the career of the Kelmscott Press, he was fortunate in enlisting the enthusiastic cooperation of Joseph Batchelor of Little Chart, near Ashford in Kent, a papermaker of high ideals and great skill. Three papers, each named from a watermark designed by Morris, the Flower, the Perch, and the Apple, were especially made for the Kelmscott Press at the Batchelor mill.

But as to vellum for the special copies, a product satisfactory to Morris was practically non-existent. The entire output of one Italian maker had been bespoken by the Vatican. A commercial maker of binding vellum, drum heads, and so forth, was interested in the quest, however, and after many experiments produced an excellent vellum. It was made with special care from the skins of calves not yet six weeks old.

A source of good ink was another worry. The attitude of the English and American makers was, as Sparling tells us: "Take it or leave it; what's good enough for others is good enough for you!" Jaenecke, the celebrated inkmaker of Hanover, Germany, however, offered an ink said to be made of the old-fashioned pure materials, and this satisfied our fastidious printer.

The noteworthy characteristic of the Kelmscott publications was their rich decoration, as may be seen from the pages of the books

A BURNE-JONES ILLUSTRATION (REDUCED) FROM
MORRIS'S LOVE IS ENOUGH, PRINTED IN 1897.

reproduced in the present chapter. The illustrations, most of which were from drawings made originally in pencil by Burne-Jones, translated into line by R. Catterson-Smith, provided with borders by Morris, and the whole rendered on wood by Hooper, were also part of the decoration of the book, all the elements of which were planned in harmony.

The criticism leveled by competent critics against the Kelmscott books holds that the fundamental purpose of books is to be read and that the Morris books are neither legible in their type matter nor convenient for handling in their format. They contend that they are, first, exercises in decorative design and only secondarily, books intended for reading; that even if one endeavors to read them, the mind is distracted from the sense of the author by spots or masses of decoration so insistent in area and color as to completely overshadow the text.

Even the most enthusiastic admirers of William Morris must admit that there is much of truth in these criticisms. They must further admit that the Kelmscott books are not to be handed to the neophyte in book design as models for him to emulate.

Why is it, then, that the Kelmscott books mark the beginning of the modern revival of fine printing, for such is unquestionably the case? In the first place, whether easy to read or not, they are things of great beauty and the work of a decorative artist of unparalleled genius. As such they will always be prized by the collectors and amateurs of fine bookmaking to whom they were addressed. Never again will be offered them a like orgy of beauty in the embellishment of books.

But in the second place, the master of the Kelmscott Press is revered by succeeding generations because he led printers back to the fundamental principles of fine craftsmanship. He taught them that when good types were not available for their use, the remedy

was not dumbly to complain but to go forthwith and make them. He demonstrated that fine paper could still be made; that careful presswork was not a lost art. Above all, he taught them that infinite care and patience in the design of the book and infinite pains in its execution, are still not only possible, but profitable as well.

Other presses which owed their existence to Morris's example and the success of his pioneer enterprise printed books conceived in a mood of far greater simplicity and undoubtedly better exemplars of the principles of fine bookmaking. But they all built on principles which Morris evolved single-handed in the face of difficulties apparently insuperable. And all of them cordially acknowledge him as their mentor.

Thus, if I am asked to point to the greatest achievements of William Morris, I will find them in the printed books produced by the disciples whom he inspired.

XXXIII

The Private Presses

A PERSONAL enthusiasm for fine printing and bookmaking, rising above considerations of commercial return, or in some cases a yearning for literary self-expression in print, is responsible for the birth of any private press. The master of such a press regards printing as a hobby—as an avocation rather than a vocation—printing texts he personally admires, because he enjoys doing so. This does not mean, as the issues of the press become consequential, that copies cannot be offered for subscription, but it does mean that the principal return to the owner is in the satisfaction he takes in the quality of the books produced rather than in the income from their sale. The most that the conductors of the most distinguished presses have hoped for is that the returns should equal the out-of-pocket expenses.

Will Ransom, author of the most valuable treatise on private presses, aptly refers to their work as "the typographic expression of a personal ideal conceived in freedom and maintained in independence." Such an enthusiasm for printing is one that might be expected to come naturally to a man possessed of good taste, literary and artistic. For a book can be a thing of beauty and it can also be the vehicle of world-changing ideas.

Ever since the fifteenth century, when Johann Müller (Regiomontanus) printed at Nuremberg astronomical works which he and his friends had written, the private press has played a part in the production of books. In the early days of the craft, however, both the commercial printer and the state authorities frowned upon this

form of book production. This was especially true in England during the sixteenth and seventeenth centuries, when private presses had the dangerous habit of issuing books which the Star Chamber deemed "naughtie & seeditious." The Martin Marprelate tracts, a series of Puritan attacks upon the bishops, for instance, were the product of a printing office which, in an unsuccessful attempt to avoid detection, was moved from place to place in a wagon. Needless to say, the typography of private presses working under these conditions was extremely poor. But when men of means and ability such as John Baskerville, Horace Walpole, and William Morris took up printing as a hobby and established private presses, the quality of the books produced was quite different in character.

In any consideration of private presses, however, we must note the work of at least two in the pre-Kelmscott years. First was the press established in 1757 by Horace Walpole at his Strawberry Hill estate, near Twickenham on the banks of the Thames. The first editions of many of Walpole's own writings were printed at this press, which he called the Officina Arbutcana. Two odes by Thomas Gray, an intimate personal friend of Walpole's, constituted the text of the first volume printed at Strawberry Hill.

Walpole was well born and adequately provided with means to gratify his often bizarre interests. He was a prolific writer, but his historical works were regarded as better than his attempts at imaginative literature. His best writing, however, is represented by his correspondence with friends, much of which was published after his death. His press functioned until 1789, and a detailed account of its activities has been preserved to us in the manuscript journal kept by Walpole, and recently published. Walpole had a number of printers working for him at various times, but the name of Thomas Kirgate, who worked the press from 1765 onward, is best known in connection with the enterprise, his name appearing in some of the

imprints. All the work of the press was simple and restrained in typography. Walpole thus expressed his ambitions regarding the press: "I hope future edition-mongers will say of those of Strawberry Hill, they have all the beautiful negligence of a gentleman."

The Daniel Press, at Oxford, was the most truly private of all the English private presses. Printing was from boyhood the hobby of Charles Henry Olive Daniel, D.D. Born in 1836, he began his typographic activities at the age of nine. Till 1863, the press was just a plaything devoted to printing small items relating to his family, his father's parish, or his neighbors. During ten years which Daniel devoted to higher education, the activities of the press were suspended, but were resumed in 1874. Two years later, types cast in the rediscovered matrices of the Fell types were provided by the Oxford University Press for Dr. Daniel and used in printing subsequent issues of the Daniel Press, all in exceedingly limited editions. Any reader interested in the work of this unique press is referred to the excellent account of the Daniel Press edited by Falconer Madan.

Since the death of Morris his ideals have, to a large degree, been fostered and propagated by private presses. This is partly because such establishments, printing only a few copies addressed to a discriminating clientèle and regarding profits as a secondary consideration, can carry out experiments which commercial plants would not dare attempt. The private press, also, is able to perform the different processes of bookmaking by hand and in its endeavor to obtain the Morris results is able to use the Morris methods.

The first important disciple of the typographical messiah was Charles Ricketts, who in 1896 issued from the Vale Press an edition of Milton's *Early Poems*. The actual printing of the Vale Press was done at the Ballantyne establishment under the immediate supervision of Mr. Ricketts, who designed the type and cut most of the borders, ornaments, and initials, the decoration being influenced

largely by the work of William Morris. Three types were used: the Vale, Avon, and King's fonts. The most famous production of the press is the *Works of Shakespeare* (1900-1903) in thirty-nine volumes. After continuing for seven years, the operation of the press was terminated in 1904, with a *Bibliography of the Vale Press* by Ricketts. Then, in fear lest, drifting into the hands of unskilled printers, the type should "become stale by unthinking use," the punches and matrices were thrown into the Thames and the letters were melted down.

The Eragny Press at Hammersmith was started in 1894 by Lucien Pissarro, a French painter and engraver. He used at first the Vale type of his friend Ricketts, but in 1903 he began the use of the Brook type, designed by himself and based upon the Vale letter. The designing, wood engraving, and printing of the books of the Eragny Press are all the work of Pissarro and his wife, Esther. His productions are famous for their beautiful colored wood-block prints; in fact, as one critic has pointed out, "Mr. Pissarro's aim is rather to print illustrations with a suitable text than to print an illustrated book." The last volume produced by the Eragny Press appeared in 1914.

The first important private press, the establishment of which was inspired largely by Morris, was the Ashendene Press of C. H. St. John Hornby. In a summer house on his father's estate, Ashendene, in Hertfordshire, he set up some type cases and a hand press and began printing small books in his spare time "solely for the sake of the interest and amusement" he expected to derive from it. In 1895 appeared the first publication of the press, *The Journal of Joseph Hornby,* being the diary of the printer's grandfather on a trip to Brussels and Paris in 1815. Only thirty-three copies were printed "for private circulation only amongst the printer's friends," showing the press to have been truly an amateur venture. The un-

distinguished typography and poor presswork of the early books produced by Hornby in comparison with the distinguished composition and flawless printing of the later issues of his press may well serve to encourage others undertaking similar ventures.

The first books of the Ashendene Press were set in Caslon and in the Fell types obtained from the Oxford University Press. Hornby was ambitious, however, to have a private typeface of his own. The type used in printing the *Lactantius* at Subiaco, Italy, in 1465, which combined characteristics of both gothic and roman letter forms, was selected as a model. Redrawings of the alphabet were made with the help of Emery Walker and Sydney Cockerell, and the punches were cut by E. P. Prince. The type, christened Subiaco, was completed in 1901, and the first book set in it, *Lo Inferno di Dante,* appeared the following year. A page from the *Carmina Sapphica* of Horace (1903) set in the Subiaco type, is here reproduced.

Another typeface, patterned after that used by F. Holle of Ulm in 1482 in printing Ptolemy's *Geographia,* was produced twenty-five years later and christened Ptolemy. This proved a highly legible and satisfactory face.

In 1899 the Ashendene Press was moved to Shelley House, Chelsea, where a small house was built to accomodate it. With the production of more ambitious works, it became impossible for St. John Hornby to perform all the work with his own hands, and one assistant was employed in 1902. In that year began the practice of offering the books of the press for subscription by interested collectors. But the press remained an amateur enterprise, the proceeds from the sale of books serving only to defray expenses. In the introduction to the valedictory volume of the press, Hornby tells us that, over the years of its operation—1895-1935—the press "about paid its way without gain or loss."

The later books were printed on hand-made papers, with some

Dic & argutae properet Neaerae
Murreum nodo cohibere crinem;
Si per invisum mora ianitorem
    Fiet, abito.
Lenit albescens animos capillus
Litium et rixae cupidos protervae;
Non ego hoc ferrem calidus iuventa
    Consule Planco.

FAUNE, Nympharum fugientum amator,
  Per meos finis et aprica rura
Lenis incedas abeasq3 parvis
    Aequus alumnis,
Si tener pleno cadit haedus anno,
Larga nec desunt Veneris sodali
Vina craterae, vetus ara multo
    Fumat odore.
Ludit herboso pecus omne campo,
Cum tibi Nonae redeunt Decembres;

29

copies on vellum. Many were ably illustrated by Charles M. Gere, R. Catterson-Smith, and others, and cut on wood by W. H. Hooper (who had worked for Morris), C. Keates, and J. B. Swain. Some books were printed in red and blue, in addition to black. Graily Hewitt contributed hand-drawn initial letters to many of the Ashendene Press Books.

Among the more important productions of St. John Hornby's private press are the *Dante* of 1909, the *Malory* of 1913, the *Spenser* of 1923, and the *Don Quixote* of 1927, all folios noble in design and exceedingly fine in execution. Fortunately, the master of the Ashendene Press has given us in 1935 a final volume, which contains an account of the venture and a bibliography of the forty books produced in the forty years during which the press functioned. I have unbounded admiration for the purposes, ideals, taste, and production standards of this truly private press.

The Essex House Press was an expression of a desire to put "idealism in industry." Founded in 1898 by the Guild of Handicraft under the leadership of C. R. Ashbee, the establishment acquired two of the printing presses and the empty type cases of the Kelmscott Press. Plans were made to complete the *Froissart* which Morris had begun and to print some of the works which he had planned to undertake, but these designs were never carried out. The first productions of the Essex House Press in Caslon type are delightfully simple, but later works are printed in characters designed by Ashbee. These may be dismissed as interesting but unsuccessful experiments, and the later work of the establishment is greatly handicapped by their use. The woodcuts, however, are always excellent. The best known production of the Essex House Press is the *Prayer Book of King Edward VII* (1903).

The Doves Press was established at Hammersmith in 1901 by T. J. Cobden-Sanderson—then sixty-one years old—in cooperation

TITLE PAGE OF THE ASHENDENE DANTE, 1909.

❡ THE DOVES PRESS was founded in 1900 to attack the problem of Typography as presented by ordinary Books in the various forms of Prose, Verse, and Dialogue and, keeping always in view the principles laid down in the Book Beautiful, to attempt its solution by the simple arrangement of the whole Book, as a whole, with due regard to its parts and to the emphasis of its capital divisions rather than by the addition & splendour of applied ornament.

II

❡ The Books selected for this purpose have been chosen partly for the sake of the particular typographical problems presented by them, but partly also in view of the second object of the Press, viz., to print in a suitable form some of the great literary achievements of man's creative or constructive genius. To-day there is an immense reproduction in forms at once admirable & cheap of all books which in any language have stood the test of time. But such reproduction is not a substitute for the more monumental production of the same books, and such a production, expressive of man's admiration, is a legitimate ambition of the Printing Press & of some Press the imperative duty.

III

❡ THE ENGLISH BIBLE is a supreme achievement of English Literature, if not of English

8

A PAGE OF THE DOVES PRESS CATALOGUE RAISONNÉ.

with Emery Walker. These two men pooled their genius in the production of a remarkable roman letter based on that of Jenson. The books of the Doves Press are characterized by a majestic simplicity of design, meticulous typesetting, flawless presswork on the finest of papers, and workmanlike binding. Free from all ornament, save for an occasional colored initial, they form a contrast to the works of Morris and show the influence of the Kelmscott Press chiefly in their close spacing. The Doves Bible (1903-1905), the masterpiece of the press, is a monument of dignity and restraint. The five large quarto volumes of this work presented no small task to the single compositor who so skilfully put it into type.

In 1909, Emery Walker retired from the partnership and Cobden-Sanderson continued the press alone until 1916, when he printed the *Catalogue Raisonné of Books Printed and Published at the Doves Press,* in which he bade his press an eternal farewell. A page of this beautiful book is shown on the opposite page. After the last leaf had been printed he took in his arms the type, matrices and punches of the Doves Press and threw them into the Thames, with this invocation: "May the River in its tides and flow, pass over them to and from the great sea for ever . . . untouched of other use." In referring to the books issued by the Doves Press, Will Ransom writes: "When it is said that they approach dangerously near to absolute perfection in composition, presswork, and page placement, everything has been said."

The Golden Cockerel Press, founded in 1921 at Waltham St. Lawrence, in Berkshire, by Harold M. Taylor and taken over in 1923 and continued by Robert Gibbings, has, in co-operation with able wood engravers, produced many illustrated books of much merit. It is now operating under the direction of Christopher Sandford and F. J. Newbery. The shop is located in a pleasant garden, shaded by fruit trees.

The Cuala Press, in Dublin, is distinctive among the private presses in being a wholly feminine enterprise. It is different also in its purposes, the production of books being incidental to the encouragement of crafts among Irish women. Founded in 1902 by Miss Elizabeth Corbet Yeats and Miss Evelyn Gleeson in connection with their embroidery and rug-making enterprise, it was called at first the Dun Emer Press, after Miss Gleeson's home in Dundrum, near Dublin, where the press was originally set up. In 1908 the press was moved into another cottage and, as Miss Gleeson kept Dun Emer for her rug-making, was then renamed Cuala, after one of the five famous roads that led to Tara, on which stood the new home of the press. In 1929 the Cuala Press was moved into the city of Dublin.

Simplicity is the keynote of the work of this press. "We simply started the press to give work to Irish girls and to enable us to live in Ireland doing good work" is the simple explanation given by Miss Yeats for the existence of the press. An Albion press and Caslon type form its equipment. An all-rag paper machine-made in Ireland is used. Composition is excellent, but for some time the work showed that the women in the shop had difficulty with presswork. Decorative and illustrative material is sparingly used.

The Cuala Press has the further distinction of association with its director's two brothers, Jack P. Yeats, the artist, and William Butler Yeats, the poet, many of whose works appeared in their first editions from the press over which his sister presided.

In Wales, the Gregynog Press at Newtown is concerned for Welsh art and craftsmanship much as the Cuala Press is devoted to similar interests in Ireland. It has had generous financial backing from two women, the Misses G. E. and M. S. Davies, of Llandinam, and was directed until 1930 by Robert Ashwin Maynard. Within its own organization it has not only the requisite typographic per-

sonnel, but also competent editorial scholarship, art in woodcut illustration and decoration, and its own bindery. It was founded on an intention "to print a series of volumes, chiefly by authors related to Wales, in which at the very least the typography shall be clean and honest."

Much of the charm of the Gregynog books is found in the combination of their truly "clean and honest" typography with woodcut illustrations carefully made to harmonize with the type page. The woodcuts are the work of Mr. Maynard, Horace Walter Bray, Blair Hughes-Stanton, Gertrude Hermes, Agnes Miller Parker, and William MacCance.

St. Dominic's Press at Ditchling, in Sussex, England, is ably conducted by H. D. C. Pepler, who has been successful in making his press the means of earning for himself a modest livelihood through the interest of booklovers in his work. Mr. Pepler contents himself with sincere and careful craftsmanship, with paper and other materials of excellent quality, in books of simple formats, with no striving for spectacular effects.

The Pear Tree Press was begun in 1899 by James Guthrie, an artist, who was then living in Pear Tree Cottage at Ingram, Essex. After 1907 Mr. Guthrie operated his press at Bognor, in Sussex. Much of the beauty of the Pear Tree books is derived from the decorations and illustrations provided by the proprietor of this press.

It has sometimes happened that presses first established for the personal delectation of their owners have grown into commercial enterprises. Such was the case with the Hogarth Press, instituted in 1917 by Leonard and Virginia Woolf, who described themselves as "two amateur and incompetent printers." Although the Hogarth Press has since developed into a publishing firm, the Woolfs continue to divert themselves, from time to time, with efforts at typographic self-expression.

When the activities of the Hogarth press began, Cyril W. Beaumont, bookseller, of London, also began to print, but with motives quite different from those which actuated the owners of other private presses. As a bookseller, Beaumont had noticed that the finely printed books which passed through his hands were almost invariably reprints of editions of the classic authors. He felt it to be "a pity that modern writers should not be afforded an opportunity of having their works published in a choice form during their lifetime." His press, therefore, specialized in contemporary literature and especially in works which had not previously appeared in book form. The titles in his list contain the first editions of many distinguished contemporary authors, printed in a style which Will Ransom has well described as "a sort of sophisticated naïveté entirely delightful."

In America, Morris speedily gained many enthusiastic admirers who imitated his typographical style with great zeal but little taste. Few, indeed, are the type-specimen books issued in the United States during the late 90's which do not contain an ugly, blotchy, black type with some fantastic ornaments intended to accompany it. These found a ready market among printers who supplied themselves with some thick paper and a quantity of red ink and set out to do artistic printing, but succeeded only in perpetrating inconceivable typographical monstrosities.

The Elston Press at New Rochelle, New York, however, was more fortunate in its results. Its books were frank, but by no means servile imitations of those of the Kelmscott Press. In type, ornament, illustration, and design *The Vision of William Concerning Piers the Plowman,* printed in 1901, for example, closely follows the Kelmscott *Chaucer,* but by 1904 the edition of Longus' *Daphnis and Chloe* issued by this press, though it retains the main characteristics of a book printed by Morris in the Golden type, still, in

INVICTUS

I

INE EYES LOOK UP,
exalted, to the height
Whereto thy spirit, thou
my love, has led,
To find the endless rapture
of the dead
Beyond my realm of touch
and sound and sight.
Thy love glows radiant as a guiding light
Unto the shrine where godhead waits—and thou!
I have not failed, nor shall I fail thee now,
But I shall follow, as the day the night.

So, when my little sunless hour is past,
And death shall summon, I shall rise arrayed
In joy, as to the thrill of phantom drums.
In high fulfilment, soul to soul at last,
I unto thee, in smiles and unafraid,
Shall come, triumphant, as the victor comes!

[11]

A PAGE FROM BANNING'S SONGS OF THE
LOVE UNENDING, VILLAGE PRESS, 1912.

the use of a title page and in other features, shows some degree of typographic independence.

The Village Press was founded in July, 1903, and was first located in the barn of its proprietor at Park Ridge, Illinois. The working force of the establishment consisted of the owner, Frederic W. Goudy, his wife, Bertha, and a promising young apprentice by the name of Will Ransom.

Goudy had begun life as a bookkeeper, but gradually succumbed to his love for the graphic arts. After doing some commercial lettering and advertising work, he set up, in 1895, the Booklet Press in Chicago, where he printed the *Chap Book*. In 1903, when Goudy had returned to lettering and design, Will Ransom sought him out, filled with a desire to learn the art of designing types, and soon the two enthusiasts decided to found a private press. A new face, the now famous Village type No. 1, was designed by Goudy and cut by Robert Wiebking, and the work of the press was begun, with Mrs. Goudy doing most of the composition. In March, 1904, the press was moved to Hingham, Massachusetts, and two years later to the Parker Building in New York, where it was destroyed when that building burned in 1908. The Village Press, however, was soon re-established and is still in operation at Marlborough-on-Hudson, N. Y.

The Village Press is important because it provided the training ground of a great type designer. The intrinsic merit of its productions, though sometimes marred by traces of advertising technique, is high. Besides the excellence of their type, the books show much skill and originality in design.

Perhaps the most interesting private press in America was that operated by Dard Hunter in a room of his home at Chillicothe, Ohio. Dard Hunter was taught the art of printing by his father and later worked for seven years at the Roycroft shops. Then, dissatisfied with the condition of American typography, he went to

¶ I greet you on CHRISTMAS DAY!
And if you have a Moment,
hear my Story. Its Title is

THAT ENDETH NEVER

·∞ I ∞·

N the West of this
Country, beside the
Ocean that is called
Gentle, there dwelt
a Knight. He lived
upon a Hill, in a
Tower of Ivory as
all good Knights should. And with him on
the Hill lived his Lady. She was slender &
tall as is the very New Moon when it is come
to Earth above the Fig-tree Gardens. Also

◄►(I)►◄

A PAGE FROM "THAT ENDETH NEVER," LABORATORY
PRESS (PORTER GARNETT), PITTSBURGH.

T.J. COBDEN-SANDERSON

By William Rothenstein

FTER a visit to Cobden-Sanderson I usually had the sense of a cushion of air between my feet and the ground. Intercourse with a few rare spirits has brought a similarly inspiring experience; and though only fleeting forms are given to a speaker's play of wit and wisdom, they can convey something of the convincing and exalting power which belongs to material creations. ¶ Craftsmen are by nature idealists; but their vision is sometimes dimmed by a doctrinaire tendency & confused by a misapprehension of what constitutes tradition. The writer has learned much from the scrupulous order and scholarly methods of craftsmen, but he has been sometimes aware of a hesitation in saying 'Yes' to certain robuster impulses of life, a reluctance to respond to Mistress Truth's appeal for reasonably fashionable garments in which to clothe herself. ¶ Cobden-Sanderson knew that the greatest of all traditions is the impulse to do honest work, an impulse the artist must obey, no matter where it leads him. He knew that mere likeness to a tradition of good workmanship or subject matter does not imply true relationship. Further, he did not mistake Puritanism of outlook for austerity of style. I think the peculiar interest of Cobden-Sanderson's conversation came from this: that he held, certainly in his later years, the aim of the practice of an art to lie in the steady education of the individual human spirit.

Herein lay, for him, the importance of the pursuit of beauty. Each new triumph of his own lovely work was another milestone in his pilgrimage through life. Good craftsmanship is necessary because it brings to him who passionately desires it the ripe and sound fruits of wisdom and understanding, respect and tolerance. He believed the influence of works of art upon other people to be of less moment than the spiritual experience which gave them birth. So he devoted his ripe age to threshing the knowledge he had garnered throughout a long life of noble practice. Those who had not the privilege of listening to his talk may find its essence in his last work, *Cosmic Vision*. In this book one of his most delightful qualities is apparent—his generous response to all that seemed to him gallant, humane, and vital in life and in art. He understood clearly that each generation must express its vision in its own way, and that this way is likely to shock, for a time, previous judgments. His culture was too broad to permit of his misreading the past, or of his saying aught but God-speed to the present and future. His own pursuit of beauty had led him to certain conclusions, and he desired to adjust his faith and his conclusions to the values he believed to be permanent, before he looked from the windows for the last time on the river he loved. ¶ These conclusions, this faith, Cobden-Sanderson expressed up to the end with singular power. Fastidious in taste, a little precious in manner, with something of the dandy and much of the man of the world in his social bearing and outlook, he was possessed by a demonic spirit of faith in the power of human idealism. Yet, like most men who dwell apart from their fellows, he seemed to know more of the ways of the great world than those who live in it. He had a mordant wit, a keen judgment of men and manners. Those with whom he fell out he was inclined to judge unreasonably. But his firm belief in the opportunity which lies before every man to attain spiritual equilibrium as the end and object of his life, will be remembered by his friends as the dominant characteristic of one of the most significant and attractive figures of our time.

Reprinted from The Fleuron, *A Journal of Typography,* Nº 1, *(London, 1923), with the permission of the editor,* Mr Oliver Simon, *and of* Professor Rothenstein. (*The initial is an adaptation of a design by* Cobden-Sanderson.)

A STUDENT PROJECT EXECUTED AT THE LABORATORY PRESS, PITTSBURGH.

Europe, where he studied papermaking and type design in England, Germany, and Italy. Upon his return to America, he began with the equipment of a three-hundred-year-old Wiltshire paper mill, some ancient typefounder's tools, and an old hand press, to make all the implements needed in his private press. He succeeded in manufacturing excellent paper from fine Irish linen and in cutting a roman type somewhat resembling that of Jenson. Hunter has printed at his private press a number of books of his own authorship, all dealing with the manufacture of paper, the first being *Old Papermaking,* which appeared in 1923. For all these books he wrote his own copy, made the paper, designed, cast, and set the type, and printed, bound, and published his books. His works are said to be the first books printed in modern times which were produced entirely by the labor of one man.

A noteworthy American private press was the late lamented Laboratory Press established in 1923 by Porter Garnett, in connection with the course in fine printing which he directed at the Carnegie Institute of Technology, at Pittsburgh. I have high respect for the work of this press, which has fortunately been permanently recorded in a volume issued in 1926. The ideals of this press were well expressed in its motto *Nil vulgare, nil pertriti, nil inepti,* which can be translated as "nothing commonplace, nothing hackneyed, nothing inept."

The majority of the imprints of the Laboratory Press were student "projects" which showed the solution of varied problems of typographic design by individual students. The most important book bearing the imprint of this press was an allegory by Hildegarde Flanner entitled *That Endeth Never,* designed by Professor Garnett and printed with meticulous care in an edition of fifty-three copies.

Private presses, too numerous to mention in any but a specialized work on that subject, have been established during recent years in

the United States, "from coast to coast," as the radio announcers put it. Among those of special distinction are the press At the Sign of the Chorobates, conducted by Carl Purington Rollins at New Haven; the Spiral Press of Joseph Blumenthal in New York; the Overbrook Press maintained by Frank Altschul and operated by Margaret Evans at Stamford, Connecticut; and Hawthorn House, the imprint of Edmund B. Thompson of Windham, Connecticut. Peter Beilenson's Peter Pauper Press and the Black Cat Press of Chicago started as private presses, but have grown into printing and publishing enterprises, both retaining, however, much of the private press tradition.

Germany also has a number of interesting private presses. Best known of these is perhaps the Bremer Press, founded at Munich in 1911 by Ludwig Wolde and Willi Wiegand. Its two special types, an Italianate roman following the roman of Nicolas Jenson and a fine Greek, were designed by Dr. Wiegand and cut by Louis Hoell.

At the time the European war broke out in 1914, the Bremer Press had produced but one book, and its work was not resumed until 1919. Although, by their uniform character, Bremer books are apt to impress one as monotonous, they display good taste and sound craftsmanship. The superb editions of the *Iliad* and *Odyssey* of Homer will stand as enduring monuments to the merit of this press.

The Officina Serpentis, established in 1911 at Berlin by E. W. Tieffenbach, was inspired by the Kelmscott influence. It uses only the hand press for its impressions. A letter based upon that used by Peter Schoeffer in his Bible of 1462 is employed, together with ornaments and initials in keeping with the type but rather too archaic in character for present-day taste. The books of the Officina Serpentis also lack variety, but the technical work is always good, particularly in the clear beauty of their red and black printing inks.

The Ernst-Ludwig Press was founded at Darmstadt in 1907 as the private printing plant of the Grand Duke Ernst Ludwig of Hesse. Friedrich Wilhelm Kleukens, who established it, was succeeded in 1914 by his brother, Christian Heinrich Kleukens. It has specialized in simple and dignified books printed in an austere classical style.

Really the first of the German private presses, the Janus Press was founded in 1907 by Dr. Carl Ernst Poeschel and Walter Tiemann, who were evidently under the influence of the Doves Press in England. It issued a few books of high quality, with types and initials designed by both Poeschel and Tiemann. In 1918 its business management, but not its typographic direction, were taken over by the Insel-Verlag, a large publishing firm. The operations of the Janus Press ceased in 1923.

In the Netherlands, the Zilverdistel Press at The Hague has produced excellent books under the direction of J. F. van Royen, an enthusiastic bibliophile and a meticulous amateur printer. The first book produced by this press appeared in 1915. In it the Zilver type, designed by S. H. de Roos, was used for the first time. Two years later the English artist Lucien Pissarro, already mentioned as the moving spirit of the Eragny Press, designed the Distel type for this Dutch press. Based upon old Dutch handwritten letters, the Distel type has an effect not unlike that of the Ashendene face.

In 1923 Van Royen rechristened his enterprise the Kunera Press and issued three more well printed books. In composition as well as in its typefaces, the Zilverdistel Press clearly shows the influence of English typography.

S. H. de Roos, a designer for a prominent Dutch typefoundry, established at Hilversum about 1928 the Heuvel Press, second private press in the Netherlands, and created for its use the Meidoorn type.

The private press, as we have seen, has had its richest flowering

in England, in which country a number of men of means have devoted ability and resources to turning out truly magnificent books. In the United States, however, there have been few men or women of financial independence who have undertaken the printing of fine books for their own satisfaction, rather than for profit. And the majority who have cultivated this field have dropped it after a relatively brief effort. American genius, it would appear, takes more kindly to fine printing done under commercial stimulus, the best typography having been produced in offices where the receipts must meet the weekly payroll.

Holbrook Jackson, well fitted to arrive at an intelligent evaluation of endeavors in the bookmaking field, writes thus of the products of the private presses:

The show book in the early stages of the printing revival of our own time served the excellent purpose of making an indifferent age sit up and take notice of its typographical shortcomings. The best books of that impulsion towards good printing are protests of beauty against ugliness, rather than precepts and examples for ordinary practice. They bear much the same relation to books in general that monuments do to life in general. ... Nothing could be more appropriate than the Doves Bible. Its typographical austerity, its monumental simplicity, are the supreme compliment to our 'well of purest English undefiled;' but you would not read the Doves Bible even if you could afford to. Such books are monuments, homage to great authorship, and it is encouraging to feel that good printing has now come down to earth once more and is addressing itself with no little success to the problem of making books which shall satisfy at one and the same time the aesthetic sense and the need for utility.

Julius Rodenberg, the German authority on private presses, makes this criticism of their output:

If some feel that the books printed by the private presses are in themselves unimportant, it is doubtless due to the fact that the conductors of these presses have unquestionably backward-looking tastes and preferences

and seem to withdraw from the contemporary clashes and struggles. They are interested chiefly in making what are, to them, beautiful books. But they are books which do not in the remotest way touch the common life— they appeal to a very small number of exquisites. They have not solved the problem of bringing good typography into the matter which the common man reads....

Private presses, it is true, have produced during the last half century but an infinitesimally small proportion of the printed matter of Europe and America, and—considered by themselves—might be regarded as of minor importance. But the private press has been the pioneer and pathfinder of present-day typography, the "bell cow," so to speak, of contemporary bookmaking. The private-press books, produced by the loving care of printers devoted to their art, provide models which the commercial craftsman has learned to copy. From this emulation, workaday typography has reaped a rich harvest. The private press has therefore performed real service in bringing appreciably closer to realization the dream of William Morris: a world redeemed from ugliness.

XXXIV

Contemporary Fine Printing

WHILE the efforts of idealists with private incomes in the conduct of private presses are inspiring and interesting, the work which exerts the most profound influence on standards of printing is done by the men who produce books as a business, with the receipts meeting the expenses and providing a decent living as well.

In the words of Mr. A. J. A. Symons, William Morris and his Kelmscott Press had "set the trade printer a standard which he could never hope to reach, and . . . widened rather than diminished the gap between the ideal book, as they represented it, and the book of every day." And some of the other private presses, when the best is said of them, still must be charged with an attitude of exclusiveness which separated them from the currents of everyday life. They produced beautiful books, but only by accident, so to speak, did they produce useful books—books which were made to be read rather than merely admired.

And the private presses, beginning with Morris, in their disgust with the banality and ugliness of the trade typography of their day, sought escape in an attempt to return to the techniques of a monastic age. The beauty that they produced was for the favored few, and their methods could not be adapted to the production of beauty for the multitude.

Yet the printing of the private presses stimulated an appreciation of fine printing which opened a new market for books produced by the few printers with the taste and inclination to put out books

sound alike in design and execution. It is encouraging to observe that printers on both sides of the Atlantic who have consistently brought out finely printed books have prospered. And fine books, produced under commercial conditions, are coming from the presses of—not one or two—but of a considerable number of printers.

Before discussing contemporary work in the United States, I wish to pay tribute to two notable printers of the past generation: Theodore L. De Vinne and Walter Gilliss. The former made a distinguished success as a commercial printer, always standing for good business methods. In the printing of the *Century Magazine* De Vinne contributed largely to progress in the reproduction of illustrations. He was an indefatigable student of the history of printing and author of numerous books on the typography of the past and on composing-room practice of his own period. In addition, he printed many fine books for the Grolier Club, in which he was most active, and for wealthy book collectors.

The late Walter Gilliss, with whom I was privileged to collaborate in the printing of a number of notable volumes, was a typographer of distinguished ability. For most of his life he was a manufacturing printer, turning out work ranging from the earliest issues of *Vogue* to exquisite volumes for William Loring Andrews, J. Pierpont Morgan, the Metropolitan Museum of Art, and other clients. The outstanding typographic monument with which his name is associated is the *Iconography of Manhattan Island* by I. N. Phelps Stokes, one of the most important books, from a number of viewpoints, ever printed in this country. For many years Walter Gilliss was the beloved secretary of the Grolier Club. In later years he retired from the production end of the printing business, but continued to design and supervise the production of books for his customers. Gilliss was a traditionalist in every sense of the word, but his judgment in the use of type, the selection of sizes, and the

spacing of matter on a page was sure to an uncanny degree. He is permanently assured of a niche in America's typographical hall of fame, beside that of his illustrious contemporary, De Vinne.

The most important figure in modern fine printing in the United States is Bruce Rogers, whose books are collected enthusiastically by an ever-widening circle of amateurs, with a consequent appreciation in the market value of his best books. This market situation is not artificial, however, because his work is deserving of the esteem in which it is held, its most commendable feature being variety.

With many of the modern private presses, to have seen one of their books is almost equivalent to having seen them all. Instead of using one type only and sticking to one style, Rogers has used a myriad of types and has adapted his style to the subject in hand. He must be regarded as a traditionalist, for practically all his work follows the typography of one classic school or another, but in following the masters a native inventiveness bubbles to the surface, and we have traditional typography plus a verve which captivates us.

Rogers' abilities as an artist carry him through the whole range of the book arts. He draws his own decorations, designs his own types, makes the typographical arrangement, oversees the composition with a critical eye, and creates the style of binding. He is thus practically independent of assistance from others. In recent years he has devoted considerable attention, with gratifying results, to a rather fanciful and often playful use of type ornaments. We can conceive of no more masterful use of such ornament than in the title page of *The Pierrot of the Minute,* reproduced on page 487, which he did for the printers' series of the Grolier Club. In the book, the title page is printed in two colors: rose and black.

His most celebrated book, perhaps, is a mere pamphlet entitled *The Centaur* which, partly because of its perfection as a piece of typography and partly because of the extremely limited edition in

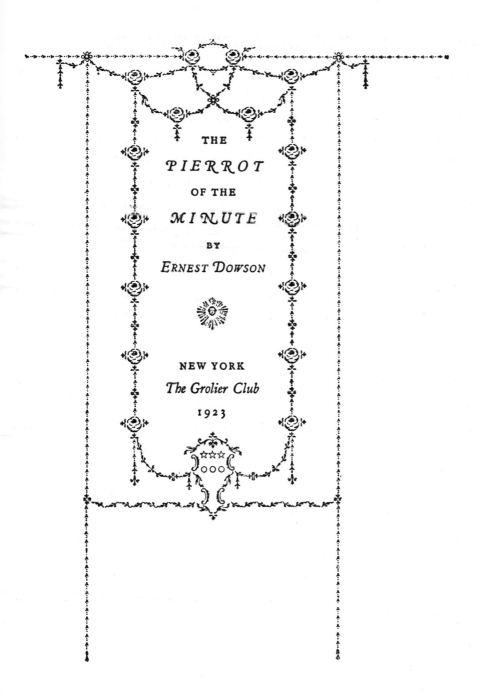

THE

PIERROT

OF THE

MINUTE

BY

ERNEST DOWSON

NEW YORK

The Grolier Club

1923

TITLE PAGE OF THE PIERROT OF THE MINUTE, DESIGNED
BY BRUCE ROGERS ORIGINAL PRINTED IN TWO COLORS.

which it was printed, has risen to dizzy heights in the auction room. A page from this booklet, in which the Centaur type, designed by Rogers in faithful imitation of the roman type of Jenson, was first used, is shown in slight reduction on the opposite page.

This is no place for a biography of Bruce Rogers, but we may recall that his first noteworthy work was done at the Riverside Press in Cambridge, Massachusetts, between the years 1903 and 1912, during which period he issued fifty books of a standard not heretofore known in this country. Since the termination of that connection he served for some time as printing adviser to the Cambridge (England) University Press. After his return to this country he became typographic adviser to the Harvard University Press and designer of books for my friend and neighbor, the late William Edwin Rudge, in whose printing office at Mount Vernon many of the Rogers-designed books were produced. The latest *chef d'œuvre* of Bruce Rogers is the great lectern Bible printed at the Oxford University Press. He designed and supervised the production of this truly noteworthy edition of the Scriptures, the title page of which is reproduced in considerable reduction on page 491.

The other master of typography in recent years in America was the late Daniel Berkeley Updike, of the Merrymount Press in Boston. Updike, unlike Rogers, was an employing printer who, in addition to winning fame as a designer of books, made a success in building up a printing office of the highest standard. He was not himself a designer of type, though his judgment undoubtedly influenced largely the drawing of the several special types designed for his use. In planning books he relied almost entirely on the use of type alone, but the results he accomplished in this medium are little short of remarkable. I can recall, in the history of typography, no one who used type more skilfully or with a surer hand.

Strange to say, the collectors of modern fine printing are not

THE CENTAUR. WRITTEN BY MAURICE DE GUÉRIN AND NOW TRANSLATED FROM THE FRENCH BY GEORGE B. IVES.

Was born in a cavern of these mountains. Like the river in yonder valley, whose first drops flow from some cliff that weeps in a deep grotto, the first moments of my life sped amidst the shadows of a secluded retreat, nor vexed its silence. As our mothers draw near their term, they retire to the caverns, and in the innermost recesses of the wildest of them all, where the darkness is most dense, they bring forth, uncomplaining, offspring as silent as themselves. Their strength-giving milk enables us to endure without weakness or dubious struggles the first difficulties of life; yet we leave our caverns later than you your cradles. The reason is that there is a tradition amongst us that the early days of life must be secluded and guarded, as days engrossed by the gods.

My growth ran almost its entire course in the darkness where I was born. The innermost depths of my home were so far within the bowels of the mountain, that I should not have known in which direction the opening lay, had it not been that the winds at times blew in and caused a sudden coolness and confusion. Sometimes, too, my mother returned, bringing with her the perfume of the valleys, or dripping wet from the streams to which she resorted. Now, these her home-comings, although they told me naught of the valleys or the streams, yet, being attended by emanations therefrom, disturbed my thoughts, and I wandered about, all agitated, amidst my darkness. 'What,' I would say to myself, 'are these places to which my mother goes and what power reigns there which summons her so frequently? To what influences is one there exposed,

awake to the merits of Updike's printing, and in failing to acquire examples of it while they are still to be obtained are, I feel sure, missing an opportunity. While his work is appreciated now, it is of a kind which will be still more admired by generations to come.

Updike was a student of type history as well as a typographer of renown, and he has made a contribution to the literature of typography which will not soon be superseded. His *Printing Types,* in two volumes, constitutes an invaluable textbook for all who use type, and in writing it he rendered a lasting service to the art of which he was a distinguished exponent. He was also the author of a volume of charming essays on printing and bookmaking entitled *In the Day's Work,* the reading of which I heartily commend to anyone seriously interested in the planning of printing.

On the Pacific Coast we find at work a distinguished pair of brothers, Edwin and Robert Grabhorn, still young enough and amply enthusiastic to have ahead of them many more years in which to produce fine books. In their shop on a narrow San Francisco street, the Grabhorns do their hand composition, presswork, and binding. With meticulous care, they have produced certain books by hand processes entirely, among which their *Mandeville* comes first to mind. Many of these volumes were hand-illuminated, also in the same office, by Valenti Angelo. In later years the Grabhorns have designed other books just as carefully, had them set by machine, printed them well, and distributed them at prices bringing them within the reach of average mortals not possessed of overfat purses. In their series of western Americana are many excellently printed books presenting material of real historical importance. The standard of taste evidenced in the books produced by the Grabhorns entitles them to rank among the finest printers in the United States.

My good friend, Dr. John Henry Nash of San Francisco, is a notable printer who has made a successful business of fine printing.

THE

HOLY BIBLE

Containing the Old and New
Testaments : Translated out
of the Original Tongues and
with the former Translations
diligently compared and revised by His Majesty's special
Command

Appointed to be read in Churches

OXFORD
Printed at the University Press
1935

TITLE PAGE (MUCH REDUCED) OF THE GREAT
LECTERN BIBLE DESIGNED BY BRUCE ROGERS.

All of his composition is set by hand, with the details of spacing checked most carefully. Many fine books have been produced in his office for the late William Andrews Clark, Jr., William Randolph Hearst, and other clients. Dr. Nash has taken meticulous care with the materials and execution of these volumes. The paper for many has been specially made for him in Europe, and the bindings of others were executed overseas, in order to obtain the best of quality in skins and workmanship.

His monumental edition of Dante is, I believe, regarded by Dr. Nash as the most important production of his office. Much of his work has been done in a rather decorative style, which is distinctly individual, but he has also printed volumes of chaste simplicity. An enthusiasm which I most heartily approve has led him to collect a splendid library of books on printing, which is handsomely housed and is open to the inspection and use of both friends and visitors. This library has certainly helped him in his effort to do fine work. Several years ago, Dr. Nash announced his retirement from the printing business, but evidently the lure of type and ink proved too strong, and he has since gratified his friends by announcing his return to the active typographic arena. He is now planning a great edition of the Bible in Latin, following the text of the Vulgate.

Among other printers of distinction on the Pacific coast are the Johnson Brothers in San Francisco, Bruce McCallister in Los Angeles, and the irrepressible and idealistic Frank McCaffrey in Seattle.

In New York one of the most interesting offices was that of the Pynson Printers, operated by Elmer Adler. Drawn into bookmaking from another line of work by an irresistible interest in typography, Adler made a notable contribution to the cause of fine printing. He would not compromise on quality, being interested only in turning out the best work it was possible for him to produce. Though by nature conservative, he has been willing to pioneer in the use of new

WHITSUNDAY. THE COLLECT.

GOD, who as at this time didst teach the hearts of thy faithful people, by sending to them the light of thy Holy Spirit: Grant us by the same Spirit to have a right judgment in all things, and evermore to rejoice in his holy comfort; through the merits of Christ Jesus our Saviour, who liveth and reigneth with thee, in the unity of the same Spirit, one God, world without end. Amen.

FOR THE EPISTLE. Acts ii. 1.

WHEN the day of Pentecost was fully come, they were all with one accord in one place. And suddenly there came a sound from heaven as of a rushing mighty wind, and it filled all the house where they were sitting. And there appeared unto them cloven tongues like as of fire, and it sat upon each of them. And they were all filled with the Holy Ghost, and began to speak with other tongues, as the Spirit gave them utterance. And there were dwelling at Jerusalem Jews, devout men, out of every nation under heaven. Now when this was noised abroad, the multitude came together, and were confounded, because that every man heard them speak in his own language. And they were all amazed and marvelled, saying one to another, Behold, are not all these which speak Galilæans? And how hear we every man in our own tongue wherein we were born? Parthians, and Medes, and Elamites, and the dwellers in Mesopotamia, and in Judæa, and Cappadocia, in Pontus, and Asia, Phrygia, and Pamphylia, in Egypt, and in the parts of Libya about Cyrene, and strangers of Rome, Jews and proselytes, Cretes and Arabians, we do hear them speak in our tongues the wonderful works of God.

THE HUNTER'S FAMILY

THERE is quite a large race or class of people in America, for whom we scarcely seem to have a parallel in England. Of pure white blood, they are unknown or unrecognisable in towns; inhabit the fringe of settlements and the deep, quiet places of the country; rebellious to all labour, and pettily thievish, like the English gipsies; rustically ignorant, but with a touch of woodlore and the dexterity of the savage. Whence they came is a moot point. At the time of the war, they poured north in crowds to escape conscription; lived during summer on fruits, wild animals, and petty theft; and at the approach of winter, when these supplies failed, built great fires in the forest, and there died stoically by starvation. They are widely scattered, however, and easily recognised. Loutish, but not ill-looking, they will sit all day, swinging their legs on a field fence, the mind seemingly as devoid of all reflection as a Suffolk peasant's, careless of politics, for the most part incapable of reading, but with a rebellious vanity and a strong sense of independence. Hunting is their most congenial business, or, if the occasion offers, a little amateur detection. In tracking a criminal, following a particular horse along a beaten highway, and drawing inductions from a hair or a footprint, one of those somnolent, grinning Hodges will suddenly display activity of body and finesse of mind. By their names ye may know them, the women figuring as Loveina, Larsenia, Serena, Leanna, Or-

52

A PAGE FROM THE SILVERADO SQUATTERS DESIGNED AND
PRINTED BY JOHN HENRY NASH, SAN FRANCISCO.

types and materials. He has been wise in enlisting the co-operation on various projects of such distinguished artists as Rockwell Kent, Thomas M. Cleland, and Lucian Bernhard. Walter Dorwin Teague drew his printer's mark.

The finest book, in my own opinion, that Elmer Adler has produced is Voltaire's *Candide,* illustrated by Rockwell Kent. In addition to printing many other well-designed books, Adler has acted as adviser to Alfred A. Knopf on the design of the *American Mercury* in its original form and of many trade books, the printing of which could not be undertaken in his own office. He was also a prime mover in the establishment and publication of *The Colophon,* a finely printed quarterly devoted to the interests of bibliophiles. Now associated with Princeton University, Adler appreciates the value of books about books and has assembled a fine typographical library.

A number of other printers in and around New York have done or are doing book printing of a high character. Among these are the Harbor Press, in which John Fass was active; the Walpole Printing Office operated by Edna and Peter Beilenson; the Powgen Press of Ted Gensamer; the Spiral Press of Joseph Blumenthal; Hawthorn House at Windham, Conn., presided over by Edmund B. Thompson; and Valenti Angelo's Golden Cross Press, under the imprint of which have appeared a number of exquisite but precious items. Helen Gentry, formerly of San Francisco, is now continuing her sound work in book design in New York City. In Portland, Maine, at the Southworth-Anthoensen Press, Fred Anthoensen has printed numerous books of real textual value, giving evidence of excellent taste and high standards of craftsmanship.

Among the designers planning the books of trade publishers, the names of Robert Josephy, Ernst Reichel, S. A. Jacobs, Evelyn Harter, and Arthur Rushmore come to mind. Richard Ellis has designed some outstanding books for the Haddon Craftsmen at Camden, N. J.

The Yale University Press is fortunate in having enlisted the services as typographer of Carl Purington Rollins, who is responsible for many distinguished books issued by that publishing organization. His work is guided but not subjugated by the dictates of tradition, and is leavened by a temptation to spontaneity that he is unable completely to resist. Rollins is a scholar as well as an artist in the typographic field, his knowledge of the historical background of bookmaking being attested by his critical yet lively columns which used to appear every other week under the heading of "The Compleat Collector" in the *Saturday Review of Literature*.

In Chicago, William A. Kittredge, with the unmatched resources of the Lakeside Press at his disposal, has been identified with the design and production of many finely printed volumes. Through special ability on the part of several members of its staff, the University of Chicago Press has turned out books of surprising virtuosity of design. Among the younger men of promise in the midwestern bookmaking field is Norman Forgue who, after finding his feet in the selection of texts, has printed over the imprint of the Black Cat Press a number of interestingly designed books. Another midwestern printer who will bear watching is Carroll D. Coleman, master of the Prairie Press of Muscatine, Iowa. Further west we find Walter Goodwin making some highly creditable books at the Rydal Press, Santa Fe, New Mexico.

A project in the United States which has had an important influence in raising popular standards of taste in bookmaking is the Limited Editions Club, conceived and developed by George Macy. The avowed purpose of this organization is "to furnish to lovers of beautiful books unexcelled editions of their favorite works; to place beautifully printed books in the hands of book lovers at commendably low prices; to foster in America a high regard for perfection in bookmaking; by publishing for its members twelve books each

year, illustrated by the greatest of artists and planned by the greatest of designers." Each year since 1929 the club has distributed to its restricted list of fifteen hundred subscribers its quota of twelve books, each volume designed and printed by a different printer of ability and reputation, either in the United States or overseas, and nearly all the volumes containing illustrations by distinguished artists.

Among the artists who have contributed their talents to the books issued by the Limited Editions Club are to be found Allen Lewis, Rudolph Ruzicka, René Clarke, C. B. Falls, W. A. Dwiggins, Edward A. Wilson, Zhenya Gay, Hugo Steiner-Prag, Frans Maseréel, Vojtech Preissig, Lynd Ward, Alexander King, Pablo Picasso, Rockwell Kent, Richard Floethe, Sylvain Sauvage, Thomas Maitland Cleland, George Grosz, Valenti Angelo, Miguel Covarrubias, Henri-Matisse, and other artists. Books have been designed and printed by D. B. Updike at the Merrymount Press, Boston; John Henry Nash, San Francisco; the Marchbanks Press, New York; Frederic W. Goudy's Village Press; Edwin and Robert Grabhorn, San Francisco; the Harbor Press, New York; the Oxford University Press, England; Poeschel and Trepte, Leipzig, Germany; Hans Mardersteig's Officina Bodoni, Verona, Italy; the Czechoslovakian Government Printing Office, Prague; J. Enschedé en Zonen, Haarlem, Netherlands; Elmer Adler's Pynson Printers, New York; the Golden Cockerel Press, Waltham St. Lawrence, England; the Lakeside Press, Chicago; Hawthorn House, Windham, Connecticut; the Curwen Press, London; the Southworth-Anthoensen Press, Portland, Maine; and many other printing offices throughout the world.

Each volume is independent in size, style, and treatment, and the total output presents a wide variety of typographic design of distinctly high quality. As a result of Macy's efforts, therefore, collections of finely printed books are to be found today in many private

libraries throughout the land, giving pleasure and satisfaction to their possessors.

The Limited Editions Club has recently taken over the Nonesuch Press of London, whose work is discussed below, and is issuing in the United States another series of books under the imprint of the Heritage Press.

Passing now to a consideration of fine printing in England done under commercial conditions, we encounter first the work of the Nonesuch Press. This unique organization was established at London in 1923 by Francis Meynell and his associates, who saw the problem of practical typographic progress from a point of view varying widely from that of the private-press enthusiasts. Mechanical devices, such as typesetting machines and high-speed presses, were, it is true, producing work of banality and ugliness. But machines were able to produce books more cheaply and in greater quantities than was possible by hand processes. If the machines produced ugliness, the remedy was not to discard the machines and revert to hand labor, but to improve the machines. "Our stock in trade," Meynell has written, "has been the theory that mechanical means could be made to serve fine ends; that the machine in printing was a controllable tool."

With this theory, Francis Meynell, Vera Mendel (later Vera Meynell), and David Garnett started the Nonesuch Press in 1923 in a cellar under Birrell and Garnett's bookshop. From the start there was nothing "arty" about the Nonesuch, and its staff did not share the belief that virtue lay in getting their own fingers inky or in tiring their own muscles by pulling the lever of an old-fashioned hand press. They sought, rather, to mobilize the resources available for book production in a modern city and to use them for their own purposes; to be "designers, specifiers, rather than manufacturers; architects of books rather than builders."

The output of the Nonesuch Press has displayed as much variety in format and typographic style as in subject-matter. Meynell did not want people to be able to say, "Oh, yes, that must be a Nonesuch book." He preferred to have them say, "That's not a bad-looking book." And time has shown that in both theory and practice the Nonesuch Press has succeeded. Its books are machine-made, but they are well made and attractively, even beautifully printed. And large numbers of people buy them, not as museum pieces or "collector's items" but as books to be used and enjoyed.

The proudest achievement of the Nonesuch Press has been the seven-volume edition of the works of Shakespeare, issued in 1929-1933, which an English bibliographer has called "the finest of all editions of our greatest poet." With this ranks the edition of Dante's *La Divina Commedia,* containing the Italian text with an English translation by H. F. Cary, published in 1928. The editorial scholarship in these and other works of the Nonesuch Press is on a par with the excellence of their typography.

Through the work of the Nonesuch Press the ideal of fine typography in the books for everyday use has influenced the commercial printer. "It has demonstrated," says Mr. Symons, "that the machine can be as much an agent of beauty as the hand, and its practice has been, both to printers and publishers, part of a new trade education."

XXXV

Modern Typography

THE art of book design during the past generation was almost wholly dependent upon tradition. Bookmakers were content to follow quite slavishly the models of one or another of the masters of bygone ages who had made their impress on the typography and format of the book. The typefaces in use were practically all revivals of those designed by master punch-cutters of the past, recut versions of these being used in a few well-established and standardized styles. Individual features of book-making, such as title pages, chapter heads, initials, and the like, all followed along strictly traditional channels. Title pages, for example, were cast in standard molds, balanced carefully on a central axis. Exhibitions of well-made books could not fail to impress the careful observer with the extent of our dependence upon the work of our typographic ancestors.

Ten or fifteen years ago we could well have questioned whether we had not reached the end of possible typographic creation, having settled back comfortably to imitate the work of others. We seemed the more satisfied the more closely the present-day replica resembled its classical model. It could hardly be denied that little new was visible on the bookmaking horizon.

Even the work of the best private presses, with real ideals and aspirations, which had achieved a certain individuality of style, did not maintain a reasonable degree of inventiveness. One book from a given press was disappointingly similar to another. To have seen three books from the Kelmscott Press is nearly equivalent to having

seen them all. To have examined two characteristic volumes produced by the Doves Press gives us a good idea of all the rest.

That typography was held so firmly in the vise of traditionalism was surprising, to say the least, when one observed the fundamental changes which had already taken place in a number of the fine and applied arts. Painting, sculpture, architecture, furniture design, had all given evidence of the stirring of a new spirit and a new freedom in design. Yet the users of type were not swayed to any appreciable degree from their traditional course.

The end of the first quarter of the twentieth century marked the beginning of the long overdue typographic revolution. The younger designers of printing in the central European countries, inspired by the new concept of design that was making itself felt in other applied arts, began experiments toward the development of a typographic style with its roots in the life of the present rather than in that of the past.

It will readily be understood that the great art of any period is that art which best expresses, typifies, and satisfies the needs of the life of its own time. When styles of art live over, as they do, into a period not their own, their vitality is sapped for lack of the milk from their mothers' breasts. When art is not in the generative stage, it becomes slowly but surely degenerative.

This is why creativeness in art is of such supreme importance. No artist ever attained lasting fame by working "in the style of" someone else. Giotto and Rembrandt and Cézanne alike were great painters because their work was the untainted expression of their respective ages, interpreted through the medium of their own individual genius. It is for this reason that the enlightened amateur heeds and appreciates the work of new artists of ability and inventiveness, painting in a style of their own rather than resting content to copy the work of their elders.

The twentieth-century concept of design is based on the principles of the engineer, who learned early in his work the apparently simple axiom that form should follow function. Asking first the purpose for which the object or structure was intended, and analyzing the possibilities and limitations of the materials to be used, the engineer proceeded in a businesslike and unromantic way to design his product so that it would serve most efficiently its intended use. When design had been so determined, the engineer stopped, superadding no furbelows to the simple elementary plan.

Examples of sound modern engineering design are to be seen in recently erected skyscrapers, in the cradle telephone, in present-day airplanes, and in thousands of objects of everyday use, where intelligent planning has replaced the old rule of "doing it that way because grandfather did it that way." Perhaps the most graphic symbol of modern design is the streamlined railroad train.

All these products of modern engineering design, when viewed through twentieth-century eyes, are seen to have a beauty of form so elementary and fundamental that scant training in art is essential to its appreciation. The most important feature of modern design is simplicity. Rococo ornament, furbelows, and "gingerbread" are taboo. We have learned a new respect for the beauty of pure form, without benefit of decoration.

When the engineering principles of design were applied to typography, they brought about important changes, particularly in advertising and commercial printing. An analysis of the purposes which printed advertising was to serve brought about a realization of the steadily decreasing time the average citizen has free for reading, in the face of numerous recently developed attractions competing for his attention. The typographers concluded, therefore, that the prospect must be able to "read as he runs" if the selling story was to bring results.

Uber die Ausdrucksmittel der neuen Typographie

Was hat das alles mit Typographie zu tun? So wird man unwill-
kürlich fragen, wenn man die Typographie als ein selbständiges
Gebiet des Formschaffens ansieht. Aber das ist sie nie gewesen
und kann sie auch niemals sein. Immer war sie gebunden an das
Formempfinden ihrer Zeit, und immer wird sie ein Widerschein
sein vom Wollen und Vollbringen auf dem Gebiete des for-
malen Ausdrucks, der Kunst.

Also auch in der Typographie wird man an den grundsätzlichen
Änderungen auf dem Gebiet des allgemeinen Formschaffens
nicht achtlos vorübergehen können. Das heißt nun keineswegs,
daß man etwa die neue Form der Stütze, unten schmal, oben
breit, einfach ins Typographische übertragen soll. Nein, auch hier
heißt es, aus dem Material heraus im Sinne der neuen Lebens-
auffassung und des Zeittempos, des gesamten Lebensrhythmus,
zu gestalten und zu formen.

Das Bewegungsmoment ist auch für uns ausschlaggebend. Der
Empfänger einer Drucksache, die im Stil der geruhsamen Zeit aus-
geführt ist, wird unangenehm berührt, wenn er sich plötzlich um-
stellen muß, sich aus dem Moment der Bewegung, in dem er sich
befindet, in das der Ruhe versetzen soll, um die empfangene
Drucksache ganz auf sich wirken lassen zu können.

Und so ist das charakteristischste Merkmal in der neuen Typographie die Betonung eines Bewegungsrhythmus — die asym-
metrische Anordnung der Zeilen und Satzgruppen — gegen-
über der Stellung auf Mitte, der Arbeit mit einem Ruhepunkt,
der symmetrischen Satzanordnung früherer Zeiten.

Es tut dabei nichts zur Sache, daß auch früher gelegentlich einmal
eine Verschränkung der Zeilen vorgenommen wurde. Denn es
ist doch ein Unterschied, ob man etwas bewußt, als Ergebnis

2*

A PAGE IN THE GERMAN "NEW" TYPOGRAPHY,
WITH UNUSUAL MARGINS.

This realization brought about a new respect for legibility, for type large enough to be read with comfort, for headings set in capitals and small letters (upper and lower case to printers) rather than in capitals only, which are far less easy to read. It was also found that dynamic or unbalanced arrangements were more likely to arrest the eyes of hurried readers than the static, balanced layouts favored by tradition. Display types were simplified in design and reduced to their most elementary form, and serifs, which accented and finished off the main strokes of letters, went into the discard. Simplicity in layout led to arrangements of illustrations and type areas in geometrical forms.

Especially in post-war Germany were strenuous efforts made to burst the bonds of typographic tradition. These efforts produced a "lunatic fringe" of typographic experimenters whose "creations" were, to say the least of them, startling. But there were sound technicians at work also, and much that they did and advocated has been stimulating and helpful.

The famous Bauhaus, at Dessau, was a center of revolutionary typographic ideas, as it was of radical departures from tradition in architecture. "Scientific" alphabets were developed in a laudable (though unsuccessful) effort to get to the essential elements of letter forms. Particularly in Germany the cult of the sans-serif typefaces flourished, and a number of type families in the "new" style appeared. Printers in the United States will remember the sudden vogue of Erbar, Futura, Kabel, and other like typefaces. The sans-serif cult in Germany was related to a renewal of the revolt against the traditional Fraktur, the crabbed black letter of German texts. A side issue to this revolt was a determined effort on the part of some leaders of the "new typography" to remedy the excessive use of capitals in German orthography by doing away entirely with capital letters. There were sporadic attempts in other countries to

abolish the capitals, but in the United States at least the attempts were half-hearted or were made in a humorous mood.

The Nazi government was unfriendly to innovations in typography, and the search by German typographers for outlets into new fields of expression in and with types ceased rather abruptly. But not until something had been contributed to the improvement of typography in general. At least, in the strenuous years of attempting to keep up with the swift and startling developments of the "new typography," printers learned that their ancient craft was still flexible enough to permit of experiment and innovation.

"Modern typography" effected notable changes in the style of printing in the service of sales. But the principles and practices found so useful in the design of commercial printing have effected changes of far less significance in the field of book design.

We will all readily approve the modern dictum that "form follows function." As the primary function of a book is to present a written text to a reader in such a form that he can read it, for hours if need be, with perfect ease, we strive to find the most legible possible typeface of adequate size, and set it in lines not too long for the eye to follow easily, with ample space between lines to lead the eye back unerringly to the start of the next line. Ease of reading requires that the type pages be evenly printed in black ink on a nearly white paper, free from glare, with opacity enough so that the type printed on the other side will not show through and confuse the vision. The book intended to be read for enjoyment will be of such a size and weight that it can be held comfortably in the hand, and will open easily and stay open.

Even typographers free from traditional prejudices, and definitely committed to new practices in the commercial printing field, agree that there are comparatively few changes which can be made advantageously in the general form of soundly designed books. The

JAN TSCHICHOLD

DIE NEUE TYPOGRAPHIE

EIN HANDBUCH. FÜR ZEITGEMÄSS SCHAFFENDE

BERLIN **1928**

VERLAG DES BILDUNGSVERBANDES DER DEUTSCHEN BUCHDRUCKER

A TITLE PAGE ILLUSTRATING THE GERMAN "NEW" TYPOGRAPHY OF 1928, WITH THE FACING PAGE IN SOLID BLACK.

general trend, however, has made for freedom from stereotyped pattern in certain elements of book design. For example, a new spontaneity is observable in the arrangement of title pages. Contemporary designers now feel free to place the main title on the page wherever they please, with no fixed relation to a central axis. A spot of illustration, tied up with the subject-matter of the book, is used in ways which are often surprising. Sometimes the type occupies an exceedingly small proportion of the page, and at other times it takes up the whole page. We have observed some striking modern title pages with all lines starting flush to the left and set in the block or sans-serif types. Such an arrangement for title pages as well as for newspaper heads eliminates the necessity of writing copy to fit or of contorting or modifying it to meet physical limitations.

In other words, the inventiveness of the designer can be given full play without risk of calling down upon him the wrath of critics whose sole complaint is that "Bodoni would not have done it that way." A large share of credit for this new freedom must be given to the pioneers of "modern typography."

Efforts to supplant the traditional typefaces by modern sans-serifs have proved unsuccessful, so far as book composition is concerned. Serifs seem to contribute to legibility by tying individual letters together into words. Furthermore, eyes trained in reading types with serifs do not find it so easy to read matter which is set in types lacking these familiar stroke terminals.

Modern book designers have also experimented with the proportion and area of margins. Some have placed left- and right-hand type pages in uniform, rather than reversed, position on the page with relation to margins. Others have made the inner margins wider than the outer ones, to no apparent advantage. Still others have set type in larger size and with more generous leading, to occupy almost the whole area of the page, thus achieving greater

legibility by utilizing space that is usually unprinted. This is the most constructive of the experiments.

Book jackets (or "dust wrappers," as our English friends call them) have, however, shown the influences of the new practices in commercial typography, and rightly so, for they act, as it were, as the sales agent of the publisher and bookseller. The jacket's function is to attract the attention of the passing reader and to proclaim the merits of the book that it enfolds. To achieve these ends, the jacket designer employs all the features of the modern poster and modern commercial printing: striking layout, emphatic display lines, and vivid color.

XXXVI

Modern Book Illustration

SINCE the time of the Kelmscott Press there has been much encouraging activity in the field of book illustration. After the processes of photo-engraving had apparently smothered the old-fashioned wood engraver, who was content to render technically the artistic creations of others, the air was cleared, so to speak, for a renaissance of creative engraving, with the artist cutting his own blocks. Other artists, equally competent, have chosen to work with pen or brush on paper, entrusting to mechanical means the reproduction of compositions so rendered.

Here, it seems to me, issue may well be taken with those who express abhorrence of the use of anything mechanical in connection with the arts. For to the extent, at least, that art serves the purposes of book illustration, the recent developments of photo-mechanical methods, particularly in color printing, have enormously increased the range of techniques available to the artist-illustrator. No matter what different mediums or manners of expression he may wish to select in order to produce results in harmony with the character of the book he is illustrating, the artist will find some photo-mechanical method of reproduction that will meet his requirements.

It is a matter of regret to the writer that it is not possible here to undertake a comprehensive review of book illustration during recent years, but limitations of space constitute an insuperable handicap to any effort to give some view of the beginnings of bookmaking and the development of the book arts across five centuries —and more. The subject of contemporary illustration needs a book

to itself. We are reduced, therefore, to mentioning only a few artists whose work promises to be reasonably permanent in interest.

In what may be called a period of transition, between 1850 and 1880, a number of distinguished English artists contributed to the illustration of books. To name any of them is to incur criticism as well for the names mentioned as for those omitted. But surely those of an older generation, at least, will pardon me for recalling to their memories the book illustrations by Ford Madox Brown, Edward Burne-Jones, Birket Foster, John Gilbert, Frederick Leighton, John Millais, George du Maurier, Dante Gabriel Rossetti (of the famed pre-Raphaelites), Frederick Sandys, and John Tenniel (creator of the immortal Alice of Looking-Glass Land and of Wonderland). And what oldster among us will not forever associate the people of Dickens' novels with the vivid characterizations of them in the drawings made by George Cruikshank and by Hablôt K. Browne, who signed his pen-name "Phiz"? Also remembered will be the spirited illustrations with which Howard Pyle delighted thousands of boy and girl readers of fifty years and more ago.

In the late years of the nineteenth century in England, some of the most talented drawing ever undertaken for the embellishment of books was done by Aubrey Beardsley, a mere lad in delicate health who died at the age of twenty-six. He left an influence on draftsmanship that will never be forgotten. It is specially noteworthy, from our point of view, that practically all his drawing was done specifically for books or other matter appearing in print. It may also be noted here that Beardsley made his drawings with a view to their reproduction by photo-mechanical means. A typical example of his work is reproduced on the opposite page.

In the same period numerous books were decorated by Charles Ricketts, of the Vale Press; but the more ambitious of this artist's ornament pressed hard on the sphere of illustration. With Ricketts

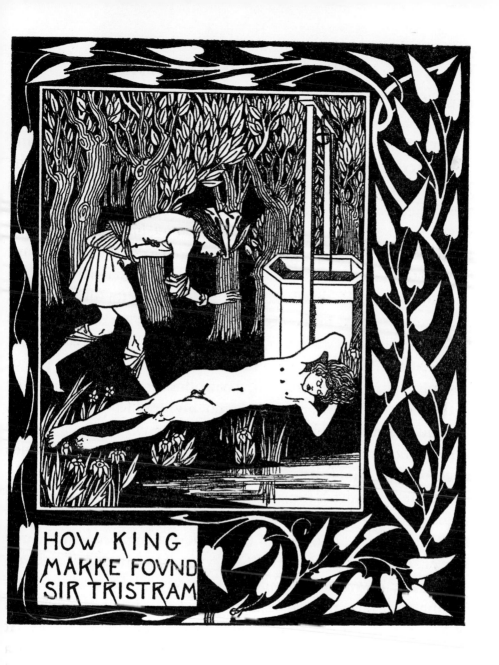

HOW KING
MARKE FOVND
SIR TRISTRAM

AN AUBREY BEARDSLEY ILLUSTRATION, FROM
THE MORTE D'ARTHUR, LONDON, 1893-1894.

must also be mentioned Lucien Pissarro, of the Eragny Press. Laurence Housman, best known to us now as an author, did excellent work early in his career as a book decorator and illustrator.

Walter Crane, son of an artist, fellow worker with William Morris, was a distinguished illustrator who emphasized in all his work the decorative function of book illustration. His drawings served not merely to interpret the text of the author, but also contributed to the printed pages an atmosphere of dignity, charm, and beauty. Crane's great talents as an illustrator covered the whole range of literature from Shakespeare to fairy tales for children. His outstanding interest in the decorative function of art also expressed itself in designs for wallpaper, printed textiles, stained glass, metal work, pottery, and house ornaments.

Outstanding, too, among the book illustrators of his time was Arthur Rackham, an artist of thoroughly original genius, whose work identifies itself by its subtly imaginative charm. Rackham, it would almost seem, must have had a personal acquaintance with the elves, gnomes, and witches whose activities he so intimately and delightfully portrayed. It may also be said of this artist that no little of his success was derived from his sympathetic understanding of the capacities and limitations of the photographic processes of reproduction, especially in his inimitable illustrations in color.

Coming down to the contemporary period, the work of nine English book illustrators appeals to me as being truly distinguished: Albert Rutherston, Eric Gill, Paul Nash, the American-born E. McKnight Kauffer, Robert Gibbings, Blair Hughes-Stanton, Edmund Dulac, David Jones, and Eric Ravilious. Exceedingly fine book illustration has come also from the hands of John Austen, Douglas Percy Bliss, Barnett Freedman, Vera Willoughby, John Nash, Zhenya Gay, Thomas Lowinsky, Keith Henderson, Ethelbert White, Robert Ashwin Maynard, Horace Walter Bray, Hal Collins,

M ANE AUTEM FACTO, CONSILIUM
inierunt omnes principes sacerdotum et se-
niores populi adversus Jesum, ut eum morti
tradcrent. Et vinctum adduxerunt eum, et
tradiderunt Pontio Pilato præsidi. Tunc videns Judas, qui
eum tradidit, quod damnatus esset, pœnitentia ductus,
retulit triginta argenteos principibus sacerdotum et senio-

BOOK PAGE WITH WOODCUT ILLUSTRATION EXECUTED
BY ERIC GILL FOR THE GOLDEN COCKEREL PRESS, 1926.

E. Fitch Daglish, John F. Greenwood, Ralph Keene, Wyndham Payne, F. L. Griggs, Marcia Lane Foster, and others. Good illustrations in the copperplate medium are credited to Hester Sainsbury and Edward Wadsworth.

In France, the interest in fine books is centered almost exclusively on beautifully illustrated books. Though there are no private presses in France, there are numerous associations of bibliophiles who have done much to encourage high standards of illustrated bookmaking. Léon Pichon, the publisher, has made a notable contribution to the art of the book in the volumes brought out over his imprint, illustrated with wood engravings by Carlègle and others. Figuring prominently in recent French publishing are the wood engravers Hermann-Paul, J. L. Perrichon, Jou, Fernand Siméon, Deslignières, Jean Lebédeff, Georges Bruyer, Maximilien Vox, Émile Bernard, Alfred Latour, P. E. Vibert, Paul Baudier, and a number of others.

Book illustrators in France have been ready to use other techniques of reproduction, such as etching, intaglio, line engraving, and dry point. In these fields we find work by Hermine David, J. E. Laboureur, Bernard Naudin, Pierre Brissaud, Charles Martin, André E. Marty, A. Alexeieff, André Dignimont, and Gaston Nick, among many. Lithography has been invoked for the illustration of numerous books by such artists as Charles Guérin, L. A. Moreau, René Ben Sussan, Marcel Vertès, and Lucien Boucher.

Distinguished book illustrations have been executed by F. L. Schmied, whose woodcuts in colors are splendid. P. E. Colin, Sylvain Sauvage, Pierre Falké, and Raphaël Drouard have worked in the same medium. Other books in which colors have been introduced into the illustrations by the stencil or *pochoir* process, so popular in France, are credited to the artists Georges Lepape (known to Americans by his covers for *Vogue*), Pascin, and Laprade.

A BOOK ILLUSTRATION BY FRANS MASERÉEL, DEPICTING
OPERATION OF A HAND PRESS IN THE OFFICINA BODONI.

In Germany there is an exceedingly active interest in book design and decoration, but relatively little in illustration, though we may not properly overlook the woodcuts of Ludwig von Hoffman, Rudolf Wirth, and Hans Alexander Miller, the woodcuts in color by Willi Harwerth, the lithographic illustrations by Georg A. Mathéy, and the work of Fritz Kredel and Richard Seewald. In other European countries there is some interest in illustrations but not much outstanding work. Among the exceptions must be named the Hollander Frans Maseréel, the Hungarian Ludovic Kozma, and the Swede Akke Kumlien.

In the United States first-quality work has been done by Rudolph Ruzicka, who illustrated numerous fine books in black and white and in colors for Updike and other printers. Allen Lewis followed, giving evidence of outstanding artistic ability. Many of his best subjects have been cut on wood for printing in colors.

Rockwell Kent, a distinguished artist in a variety of media, has made some book illustrations in woodcut, but has done many more in black and white drawings in the woodcut technique, to be reproduced as line engravings. The finest book that he has illustrated, in my opinion, is Voltaire's *Candide,* printed by Elmer Adler's Pynson Printers for Random House. Also distinguished are his vigorous illustrations for Melville's classic tale of the sea, *Moby Dick,* so ably printed by the Lakeside Press of Chicago. For Covici-Friede Kent illustrated *The Canterbury Tales.* And situations in many other fine volumes have been pictured by his gifted hand. Kent must be ranked today as America's Number One book illustrator.

Thomas Maitland Cleland, whose name has been identified with many fine books, has long ranked high among American illustrators and decorators. His illustrations, restrained in style and color, are largely of a decorative character.

Edward A. Wilson, one of the ablest American draftsmen, has

ETCHING BY PABLO PICASSO IN OVID'S MÉTAMOR-
PHOSES, LAUSANNE: SKIRA, 1931.

From Wheeler, *Modern Painters and Sculptors as Illustrators,* by
courtesy of the Museum of Modern Art.

devoted a share of his attention, in recent years, to book illustrations, and his contribution to this field has been notable indeed. His drawings are all free and spirited, and their charm is enhanced by rendering in the liveliest of colors. Pictures by Wilson give me, personally, more pleasure than those of any other contemporary illustrator.

W. A. Dwiggins, whose talents have made themselves felt in several features of bookmaking, is a decorator by inclination, who achieves some fine illustrations in his own individual style. Dwiggins is an artist of high ability, and every book on which he works gives clear evidence of this fact.

Valenti Angelo did excellent work for the Grabhorns in San Francisco in the illumination of books. He has since moved East, where he has designed and decorated numerous volumes, many of which could properly be characterized as precious. His illustrations are strongly decorative in character, and again and again he gives evidence that he thinks and works in the tradition of the early book illuminator. Angelo is, however, a competent artist in his own particular sphere of work.

George Grosz, now working in the United States, is a book illustrator of real virtuosity, his colorful paintings being generally reproduced by offset lithography. His work is decidedly more modern in slant than that of any of the artists heretofore mentioned. It is vigorous and impressive.

Miguel Covarrubias, the Mexican cartoonist, has won rank as one of the foremost book illustrators now working in America. His individuality is greatly to his credit, for he copies the work of no other artist. His colorful and imaginative illustrations can be counted on to enhance the interest of any book the text of which he undertakes to interpret pictorially.

Alexander King has been responsible for the vigorous and unconventional illustration of numerous books published in the United

LE FAVNE

*C*es nymphes, je les veux perpétuer.

                                        Si clair,
Leur incarnat léger, qu'il voltige dans l'air
Assoupi de sommeils touffus.

                              Aimai-je un rêve?

AN ETCHING BY HENRI-MATISSE IN MALLARMÉ'S
POÈMES, LAUSANNE: SKIRA, 1932.

From Wheeler. *Modern Painters and Sculptors as Illustrators,*
by courtesy of the Museum of Modern Art.

CALLIGRAMME

ombre   *Vous voilà de nouveau près de moi*
Souvenirs de mes compagnons morts à la guerre
L'olive du temps
Souvenirs qui n'en faites plus qu'un

LITHOGRAPH BY GIORGIO DE CHIRICO IN APOLLI-
NAIRE'S CALLIGRAMMES, PARIS: GALLIMARD, 1930.

From Wheeler, *Modern Painters and Sculptors as Illustrators*, by
courtesy of the Museum of Modern Art.

States within recent years. His interpretations usually border on the weird and exotic.

Lynd Ward is a gifted wood engraver, with a special flair for and interest in book illustration. His work is always creditable. One novelty for which Ward was responsible was a novel, the story of which is told entirely in woodcuts, without accompanying text.

The limitations of space forbid discussion of the work of many other American book illustrators of acknowledged ability. Among them (to name but a few) are Gordon Ross, René Clarke (best known as art director of a distinguished advertising agency), Carlotta Petrina, Mallette Dean, Maxwell Simpson, Fritz Eichenberg, Richard Floethe, Susanna Suba, Joseph Low, Thomas W. Nason, Charles Turzak, C. B. Falls, John Held, Jr., and Howard Simon.

A most interesting development in the field of book illustration in recent years has been the application to this purpose of the talents of outstanding painters and sculptors, including Pablo Picasso, Henri-Matisse, Marie Laurencin, and many others. In this movement a few publishers have specially commissioned leading artists of our own generation to interpret and supplement pictorially the texts of certain literary works that they were planning to print.

Foremost among these publishers has been Ambroise Vollard, of Paris, one of the greatest contemporary publishers of illustrated books. Beginning as an art dealer and becoming the friend and confidant of the artists whose works he handled, he turned first to the publication of prints. Then it became his ambition to devote his wealth and abounding energy to the production of the finest possible illustrated books. In 1900 he issued his first great book, Verlaine's *Parallèlement,* illustrated with nearly a hundred lithographs by Bonnard. Since then he has published twenty or more volumes, in each of which he has stubbornly insisted on flawless impressions of type and illustrations, regardless of cost.

It is true that Vollard's interest is primarily in the artist and that the text of the books which he publishes is largely subordinate to the illustrations. In his volumes is to be found the work of such artists as Pierre Bonnard, Georges Braque, Marc Chagall, Hilaire-Germain-Edgar Degas, André Derain, Raoul Dufy, Aristide Maillol, Pablo Picasso, Auguste Rodin, Georges Rouault, and André Dunoyer de Segonzac. Other publishers also have sought the aid of a number of the artists named and in addition have enlisted the talents of Giorgio de Chirico, Marie Laurencin, Jean Lurçat, Henri-Matisse, Henri de Toulouse-Lautrec, and others of equal rank. The catalogue of a recent exhibition, at the Museum of Modern Art in New York, of the work of modern painters and sculptors as illustrators lists over two hundred books illustrated by a hundred contemporary artists, published since Vollard's pioneering in 1900. A few typical illustrations by outstanding artists, which are here reproduced, show pages with drawings by Picasso from Ovid's *Metamorphoses,* published by Skira at Lausanne in 1931 (on page 517); by Matisse, from Mallarmé's *Poèmes,* published at Lausanne by Skira in 1932 (on page 519); and by Chirico, from Apollinaire's *Calligrammes,* published by Gallimard at Paris, 1930 (on page 520).

Thus contemporary artists are now being brought into the service of book production very much as Albrecht Dürer, Hans Holbein, and others, were employed to provide illustrations for fifteenth-century books. The results have varied widely in quality and appropriateness, as was to have been expected, but in a large number of cases the illustrations thus produced, in a variety of techniques, have set new standards in bookmaking with promising possibilities for future development.

The last cry in book illustration is found in work of the surrealist school, which aims to picture concepts beyond the realm of reality. The efforts are startling and interesting, but do not give

evidence of very sound or permanent worth. Books illustrated by surrealists, however, have achieved a published check list in which the following artists figure: Hans Arp, Salvador Dali, M. Janso, Max Ernst, and Pablo Picasso.

Within the past two decades there have been executed more book illustrations of originality and true artistic merit than can be credited to all the preceding century. A more active appreciation of pictures has established a reader demand which has inevitably stimulated the supply. Present indications are that, in the future, more and more books will be provided with adequate illustrations to complement the text.

XXXVII

Processes of Bookmaking

THE first operation in the process of printing is the making of type. And the first step in the making of type is the preparation of the matrix in which the letters are cast. From the earliest stages of the art, and up until a few decades ago, punches were cut by hand on the end of steel billets from which the temper had been removed to make them easy to work. A so-called counter-punch was first cut by hand in the shape of the inside contour of the letter, such as the inside oval of an *O*. This, after hardening, was driven into the end of the punch, thus depressing the portion corresponding to the inside of the letter, known to typefounders as the "counter." The outside contour of the letter was then made by cutting or filing the outer edges. When the correct shape of the letter was thus punched and engraved on the end of the piece of steel, the latter was hardened by tempering. This completed punch was then driven in copper or some other comparatively soft metal to form the matrix. When this matrix is placed at one end of a rectangular mold, so arranged that the width can be regulated, and molten metal is poured into the mold, it is apparent that the resulting cast will bear on one end, in relief, a letter similar in design to that cut on the end of the punch. This cast is a piece of type. Copy is set up for printing by arranging in the proper sequence types of the various letters of the alphabet.

In any book page it is apparent that all the types of all letters are uniform in height, while they vary widely in width; an *M,* for example, requiring a wider shank or body than an *i*. The common

way of adjusting this width was to "fit" the matrices, that is, to cut them to varying widths, in keeping with the widths of the characters punched in them. When the jaws of the hand mold closed on the matrix, the mold was thereby set to just the right width for casting the letter in question.

In the latter part of the nineteenth century, an American, Linn Boyd Benton, invented a punch-cutting machine which eliminated the laborious and costly process of engraving the steel punch by hand and thus made the process of punch production much easier. Punches so produced were driven in copper the same as before. It was soon found, however, that with this engraving machine a matrix could be cut in intaglio in the first instance, without going through the intermediate process of punch-cutting. It is thus that most typefoundry matrices are produced today.

Type-casting was for centuries done in a hand mold, the molten metal being dipped from a crucible and poured into the mouth of the mold. As it was poured, the founder gave the mold a quick jerk that forced the metal into the opening and against the face of the matrix. After ejection of the type from the mold the jet, similar to the jets inseparable from all casting operations, was broken off, and the type was then rubbed and finished by hand. In recent years there have been developed automatic casting machines which perform all the operations of casting and finishing, delivering perfect type at high speed.

Type so cast is laid in a compositor's case, the arrangement of divisions of which is determined not alphabetically but according to the frequency with which letters are used. The compartment for the letter e, for example, is large and conveniently located, while that for x is smaller and more remote. The first task of the apprentice compositor, therefore, is to learn the "lay" of the case.

With the copy before him and a case of type of the desired size

and style pulled out from the cabinet, the compositor begins to pick up one by one the letters called for by the copy, depositing them in his stick, a holder which can be set to the width or measure of the column or page which he is setting. Each line being set upside down, in order to appear correctly when printed, it is necessary that each character be inverted when placed in the stick. To aid the compositor in positioning it correctly, the bottom side of each piece of type is marked with a groove or "nick." On types of European manufacture the nick is on the top side of each character.

As the letters are set, the compositor drops in between words a "normal" space, usually a three-to-em space, called by printers for short a "three-em" space, the width of which is one-third the height of the types being used. When as much copy as will come within the line has thus been set, the compositor goes back over the line adding thin spaces between words to "justify" the line—that is, to make its length come out to the exact width of column being set. Less frequently, the spacing already inserted between words has to be reduced, in which case the original spaces have to be removed and other thinner ones substituted. After the spacing is approximately correct, the compositor feels the line to find whether it is sufficiently tight so that the individual types will be held securely in place when the whole page is locked up in the chase. If the line feels at all loose, the compositor goes over it again inserting exceedingly thin brass or paper "hair" spaces, in order to make the line, in printer's parlance, "tight to lift." It will thus be seen that the spacing of hand composition is done by the trial-and-error method, though a skilful compositor accomplishes it quite deftly and quickly.

Book or magazine composition is first set in "galleys," that is, in long columns, so called from the name for the trays on which the type is placed and stored. A first proof, drawn from the newly set type, together with the author's copy, is then sent to the proofreader.

A "copyholder" reads aloud the original copy, indicating all paragraph breaks, punctuation, italicization, and so forth, in a proofroom jargon almost unintelligible to a bystander, while the reader follows the copy in proof. This enables the proofreader not only to correct obvious errors of spelling and punctuation, but also to detect the omission of words or sentences, errors in dates, wrong forms of proper names, and so forth. The errors are marked on the margins of the proof according to a code of symbols, and the proof is then returned to the compositor so that he may make in the type the changes called for by the proofreader. A second proof is then drawn and sent to the proofreader, who compares it with the first corrected proof to check whether the changes called for have been accurately made. After this checking, the revised proof goes out to the author for reading.

After the author has corrected the galley proofs and all desired changes have been made, the type is ready for "make-up" into pages. At this point page headings and page numbers are added, and when proof next goes out the book is in practically final form for printing.

Setting extensive manuscripts by hand is, of course, a very slow and laborious process, and as the printing industry grew in extent and importance it was only natural that efforts should be made to devise a means of setting type mechanically at greater speed and less cost. This problem intrigued the minds of many, and the record of experiments in the field of typesetting machinery is a dizzy one. The failures were myriad. All efforts to take the foundry type used by the compositor and set it up mechanically came to naught. Finally, however, Ottmar Mergenthaler invented a machine which, by the action of a keyboard somewhat resembling that of a typewriter, assembled not type but matrices and, when a whole line was set and spaced, cast this line in one piece, or "slug," of type metal. This machine, which was first put into practical use in 1886, and appro-

priately christened a "linotype," gave a revolutionary impetus to the printing industry. It is often said to have made possible the modern newspaper. As with all new inventions of importance it was expected that thousands of compositors would be thrown out of work. But, again as usual, the industry grew so fast that more men were employed than before. The text of this book is linotype-set.

The next practical machine devised to set type mechanically was the monotype, the invention of Tolbert Lanston, which came on the market soon after the linotype. The monotype comprises two separate units. The keyboard, which resembles a large typewriter, is actuated by compressed air, punching in a strip of paper a succession of holes which record the succession of letters on the keys struck by the operator. The operation of the caster, the second unit of the equipment, is directed by compressed air blowing through the holes in this paper ribbon. The letters are cast one type at a time and, by mechanism of extraordinary ingenuity, are spaced out in lines of uniform width.

The third equipment of importance in expediting composition and reducing its cost is one of comparatively recent development: the Ludlow. With this system matrices are set and spaced by hand, in a special stick, and the line cast in slug form by an exceedingly simple method. The Ludlow was originally devised to set job and advertising display composition, one of its principal features being easy change from one typeface size and style to another, but it can also be used to advantage on hand-set book composition when meticulous spacing is required. The title page, initials, and chapter headings of the present volume are Ludlow-set.

With all three mechanical methods of composition, one great advantage to the printer is unlimited type supply, since he has matrices rather than type. Today machine composition has reached such high standards of quality that most fine books are now set

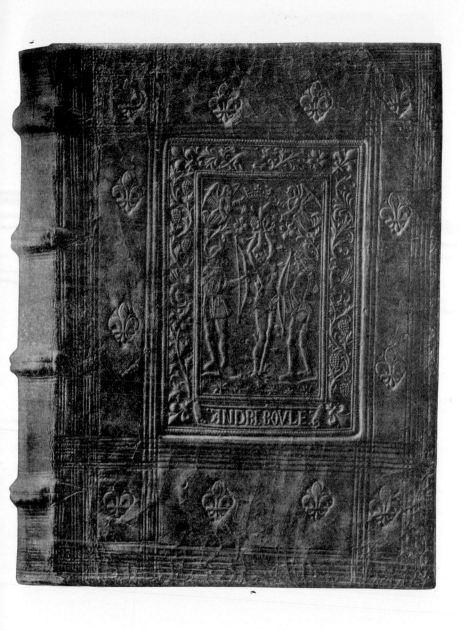

A BINDING BY ANDRE BOULE, PARIS, ABOUT 1510.

A CAMEO BINDING MADE AT ROME ABOUT 1520.

mechanically. The book set by hand in foundry type is now the rare exception rather than the rule.

When a book has been set—either by hand composition or by machine—and made up into pages, it is now ready to print either directly from type or slugs or from plates made from them. The next process is "lockup," which involves the placing of pages in the position in which they are to print, filling in the spaces between the pages with wood or metal "furniture," and locking them in place by the use of "quoins"—wedge-shaped units which are drawn together by the rotary motion of a key engaging in teeth on the facing sides of two quoins. Pulling the angular units together naturally increases the width of the pair and thus exerts pressure to close the form and hold the type in place.

The arrangement of the pages is dependent on two factors: the margins desired on the four sides of the page and the manner in which the sheet is to be folded. The first printers printed one page of a folio at a time, but they soon learned to print at the same time the two pages of a folio which came on the same side of a sheet. If four leaves of paper were each folded once and gathered together to make a quaternion, or what we should call a "signature" of sixteen pages, it is obvious that pages 1 and 16 would fall on the same side of one sheet and could thus be printed together. If the book were of quarto format and the gathering were to be made up of two sheets folded twice, making again sixteen pages, we find by actually folding two such sheets and numbering the pages, that pages 1, 4, 13, and 16 fall on the same side of one sheet and can thus be printed together. Even this simple combination is difficult to work out without actually folding the paper, and the problems of "imposition" (for such the arrangement of pages in forms is termed) of the modern printer are far more complicated. Modern novels are commonly printed with sixty-four pages in one form on

one side of a sheet and sixty-four pages on the other side. A book of 256 pages would therefore be printed in four forms on only two sheets of paper, which in the case of an ordinary novel are 41 by 61 inches in size.

In the imposition of a form the distance between pages determines the relative proportions of the margins, but the general arrangement of the pages is dependent on the working of the folding machine on which the printed sheets are later to be folded, and they must be properly laid for printing in order that the pages, after the sheet is folded, shall follow one another in the proper sequence.

Properly imposed and locked up, a form is now ready to print. The earliest form of hand press used in the early days of printing has already been described. The pressure of a screw was next replaced by pressure through a toggle joint with a spring to return the platen to its original position after the pull was made. The invention of the power press and its development historically makes a fascinating story, but one which we cannot here recount in detail.

Suffice it to say that today most book printing is done on cylinder presses which are known technically as two-revolution flat-bed presses. The type form is placed on a bed which travels from one end of the press to the other. The ink is carried from a fountain at one end of the press through a series of distributing rollers onto an ink plate which travels with the same motion as the type form. A film of the ink is taken from the ink plate by the form rollers as it passes under them and immediately thereafter these same rollers contact with the type form, leaving on the type face an even film of ink.

Above this reciprocating bed is a cylinder, the periphery of which revolves at exactly the same speed as the linear travel of the bed. As the bed moves toward the ink fountain end of the press, the axle of the cylinder is slightly raised and its surface does not contact with the type, making one revolution without printing.

Meantime a sheet of paper has been fed to guides at the top of the cylinder, and half a revolution before the bed reverses its travel, grippers on the cylinder seize the edge of the waiting sheet and start to carry it around on its surface. When the front end of the sheet reaches the bottom of the cylinder, which has now returned to a position of contact with the type surface, the bed has started to travel in the other direction, and the paper meets the inked type at the point of impression. As the cylinder completes this revolution the grippers release the sheet, which is carried along by tapes and dropped on a delivery board, equipped with joggers which leave the sheets of paper in an even pile.

With sheets printed on cylinder presses the next process is folding. This is done on folding machines, the most common type being known as "drop roll" folders. The sheet travels into the folder under the control of tapes and, on reaching a certain point, is struck by a blade at the point where the first fold should be made and carried by this blade in between two knurled rolls which engage the folded edge and carry it through with the fold creased and completed. It is then carried by another set of tapes to the point where it is struck by another blade and the process repeated. When more than four successive folds are required, the sheet is divided in the folder by a slitting roll and each portion folded independently. Another type of folding machine which is tapeless, a development of recent years, is useful for small work or folds of unusual character.

With the sheets in folded form the next step is binding. With pamphlets or magazines the signatures are commonly fastened together by wire staples inserted by a stitching machine—with signatures placed one inside the other and "saddle stitched" through the fold, or placed one on top of the other in sequence and "side wired" through all of them a short distance from the binding edge. The covers can then be pasted on or included in the stitching.

With the average book, however, the wiring method is not practical. Books of normal size are folded in sixteen- or thirty-two-page signatures and then gathered in sequence. The principle of hand-sewing books will be described later. There are today machines for sewing book signatures. Schoolbooks are sometimes sewed on tapes, but the signatures of the average trade book are usually held together only by the sewing thread. The end leaves, half of which paste down on the inside covers, are tipped with a narrow strip of paste to the first and last signatures of the book before they are sewed. After sewing, the books are trimmed to the desired size and then rounded and backed. This process gives the curvature to the fore edges of the book and makes a swell at the back which helps the book to fit snugly into its case. To the rounded back of the books is then pasted some crash and paper which extend beyond the back on each side and help to strengthen the binding.

Meanwhile the cases are being made. Binders' board, a composition made of fibrous substances, or a cheaper substitute known as "chip board," is cut to the right size for the sides. Binders' cloth, if it is to be a cloth-bound book, is cut to the appropriate size to cover the boards and paste down on the inside edges. This process is known as casemaking and it may be done by hand for small editions or on a casemaking machine for quantity work. For board-bound books, paper instead of cloth is used to cover the boards.

The cover design is preferably engraved on brass (as is the cover of this volume) and the brass die placed in a stamping press, the head of which is heated by electricity or gas flame to keep the brass hot. Gold leaf or some other kind of foil is either laid on the cover or pulled over it in a roll form; the case in its flat state, already sized, is fed into the press against guides, and the impression applied. Where the hot die strikes the leaf or foil the latter adheres to the cover and the excess material is rubbed off. Many inexpensive

books are now stamped with ink, the cases being printed on an ordinary platen press of strong construction, with a heavy ink.

With covers stamped the final process is casing-in. This is done by applying paste to the outside of the sewed book, which is then inserted into the case. The crash and paper protruding a half-inch or so beyond the back are thus pasted to both the boards and the end papers, and hidden by the latter, which neatly line the inner sides of the case. The cased-in books are then held under heavy pressure, overnight or longer, until the paste is thoroughly dried.

Books bound this way in quantity are technically not *bound,* but *cased.* In unusual instances, when signatures are sewed on tapes, the ends of the tapes are also pasted to the inside of the case, but the strength of the binding does not exceed the strength of the paste. Though exigent critics may for this reason cavil at modern edition bookbinding, the fact is that the average book, so bound, satisfactorily fulfils its purpose. It is only when books so bound are put to extraordinary use—as in the circulation department of a public library—that they fail to measure up to requirements. On the other hand, the mechanical methods make possible the production of books at low cost and so increase their range of circulation and usefulness. According to the law of compensation, for every drawback there is an advantage.

The Art of Bookbinding

S OME form of covering was of course essential for texts designed for reading as well as for preservation. The character of such a covering, which would permit convenient use and at the same time provide protection of contents, was naturally enough determined in large degree by the form of the book. Assyrian clay tablets of the eighth century B. C. were thus enclosed in clay "envelopes" stamped with a short title. The papyrus rolls of ancient Egypt were housed in wooden cases.

At Pompeii were found "diptychs," which consisted of two wooden leaves bound together at one side by leather thongs which served as hinges—in other words, in the form of a double photograph frame made for traveling. The facing sides were hollowed out and filled with wax, on which the text was scratched with a stylus. One such diptych, recording a financial transaction, is dated A. D. 55, and is the oldest existing Latin manuscript. During the next few centuries, some extremely handsome diptychs for presentation to personages of importance were made of ivory and elaborately carved.

The usual form of writing a papyrus, in columns with the writing itself parallel to the length of the roll, made it possible to fold it accordion fashion, with the folds coming in the spaces between the columns. Since the reverse side of the roll was blank, this method brought blank sides of the resulting pages facing each other, and written sides facing each other, presenting an ensemble much resembling a modern book. When we paste the blank sides together or pierce the book at one side and fasten it together with

A SPECIMEN OF THE WORK OF JEAN GROLIER'S
FIRST BINDER, PARIS, ABOUT 1540.

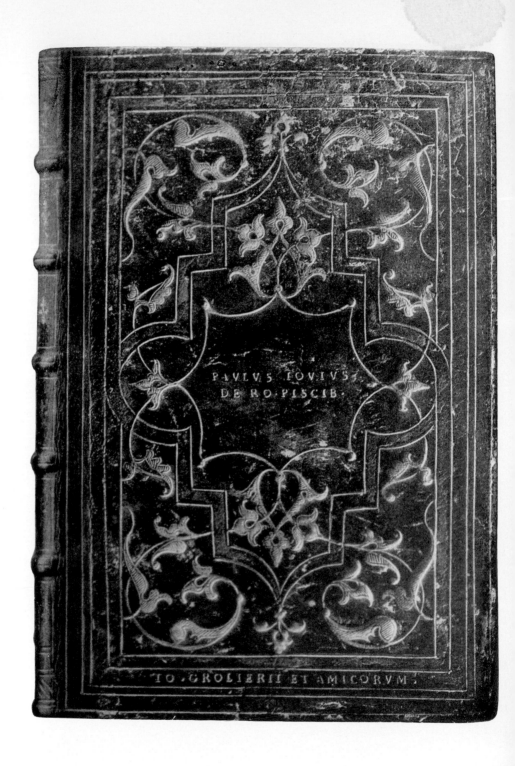

A BINDING EXECUTED FOR JEAN GROLIER.

ties, the resemblance becomes even more marked. Books are still bound in this way in China and Japan.

With the coming of paper and parchment, the book made up of folded sheets became more logical, and we find this type of book from the fifth century on. The sheets were folded once, and four or more of these folded sheets were arranged inside of one another so as to make what is known as a gathering or quire. A stitch through the fold would thus hold all the sheets. When the practice arose of sewing a number of these gatherings, with the threads passed around two or more thongs of leather at the back of the book, the essentials of modern binding came into being.

These thongs at the back needed protection, and the first move was to paste over them a covering of leather. But the vellum leaves would then tend to curl and, in use, the pages would become worn at the corners. The obvious remedy was to apply thin wooden boards front and back, and by lacing into them the protruding ends of the thongs on which the book was sewed, a hinged joint was conveniently obtained.

The rough leather then pasted onto the back came a few inches over on the boards in order to give a neat finish. The next step was to extend this leather to cover the whole area of the boards. On books of value, beautifully written and illuminated, it was only natural to decorate the leather-covered sides of the binding.

In the tenth century, Suidas gives us confirmation in picturesque form of the use of leather in the bindings of books. He tells us that the Golden Fleece, which was the object of search by Jason and the Argonauts, was really a book bound in sheepskin which taught the art of making gold. There is a still earlier reference (A. D. 450) to large square books of the Byzantine emperor's instructions, bound in red, blue, or yellow leather, bearing on their covers a gilt or painted portrait of the emperor.

The earliest form of embellishment of bindings invoked the art of the goldsmith and jeweler. Bindings covered with gold, silver, and precious stones were probably Byzantine in origin but were introduced farther westward earlier than the sixth century. Seneca and other Roman philosophers criticized the extravagant ornamentation of books. In this connection may be recalled the plaint of St. Jerome: "Your books are covered with precious stones, and Christ dies naked before the door of His temple."

The oldest binding now extant is on a copy of the Scriptures in Greek bound in two plates of gold bearing a cross set with precious stones and cameos, which was given by the queen of the Lombards to the basilica of St. John the Baptist at Monza at the end of the sixth century. A binding of the seventh century, of boards covered with velvet and embellished with silver, is preserved in the Laurentian Library at Florence. Carved ivory and enamels were also used in the fabrication of elaborate bindings.

It will be recalled that there was a brilliant school of manuscript writing and illumination in Ireland in the fifth, sixth, and seventh centuries (see page 80). Most of the bindings of this period were, however, quite plain, for the ecclesiastics using the books had to travel in sparsely settled territory, and it was needful for the books to be light in weight and to lack obvious attraction for bandits. For books which were presented to churches, however, richly decorated "book shrines" were provided.

Though most of the Irish bindings were plain, some elaborate work was done. Dagaeus, a monk of the sixth century, is reported to have been adept with both leather and metal. The Molaise Gospels of the eleventh century were bound in bronze plates with silver and gold ornaments riveted on.

In England the monastic organizations became interested in bookbinding, the finest work being done at Durham and Winches-

ter. As a matter of fact, in the thirteenth century the English binders gained supremacy over their Continental confrères.

The earliest decoration of leather bindings, without the aid of jeweler or goldsmith, was by means of points and lines impressed into the leather. The next development, which took place in the twelfth century, consisted in stamping leather bindings with heated metal dies, which left relief impressions on the book covers. This new technique appeared full-blown, rather suddenly, and after use for a period of about fifty years between 1140 and 1190 practically disappeared. On the Durham Bible no less than fifty-one different stamps were used, showing that binding was far from being an amateur operation. Evidence points to the probability that these stamped bindings were produced in one or two monastic binderies.

Most of these metal stamps or tools were cut in intaglio so that impressions from them gave a cameo effect. With a limited number of these tools it is apparent that a wide variety of combinations and arrangements could be achieved. Incidentally, such tools, though now in relief rather than intaglio, constitute the equipment of the fine binder of today. These punches had still another great advantage in that they could be stamped hot, making a deeper impression, changing slightly the color of the leather, and giving, all in all, a more effective result.

During the thirteenth and fourteenth centuries practically no stamped bindings seem to have been produced, but at the start of the fifteenth century there was a revival of such work, traceable to the revival of piety and activity on the part of the clergy and the monastic orders, already referred to in Chapter IX. Many of the houses of the two orders founded by Gerard Groot, the Brothers of the Common Life and the Windesheim Congregation, maintained binderies. We have highly satisfactory evidence to this effect in the identification of binders' marks of ten Windesheim priories.

Manuscripts were costly, and it had been thought appropriate to enshrine them in costly bindings. But with the invention of printing at the midpoint of the fifteenth century, a new situation confronted the binders. Books were produced in quantity. Some were of course handsome and important and demanded a fine dress, but many were cheap and of small importance comparatively and required only the most utilitarian form of binding. The ordinary run of books were thus bound quite simply in leather and, if decorated at all, stamped in blind.

The fifteenth-century bindings were of strong leather, usually calf or pigskin, over wooden boards. The decoration consisted first of ruled lines breaking up the area of the cover into compartments, which were then decorated by stamps repeatedly impressed into the leather. Characteristic styles of cover decoration grew up in the various regions in which such work flourished, as in the neighborhood of Erfurt, Augsburg, Nuremberg, Vienna, and Paris. Many stamped bindings, fortunately for the student of book history, are signed by the craftsmen who made them.

One of the most interesting of stamped bindings, reported upon by Goldschmidt, is found on a manuscript *Epistolae* of St. Augustine written and bound in 1410, in sheepskin dyed red, at the Benedictine monastery of St. Justine at Padua, Italy. It is the earliest known monastic binding with a note of its origin clearly stamped upon it. This was the first of the monasteries to take on a new lease of piety and activity, under the inspired leadership of Ludovico Barbo, who became its abbot one year before the production of this particular volume.

A further development of the stamp idea, made necessary by the increasing production of printed books during the last half of the fifteenth century, was the engraving in metal of panel dies with which the sides of books might be impressed with a design of con-

AN ENGLISH BINDING MADE FOR THE EARL OF
LEICESTER BETWEEN 1554 AND 1588.

AN EARLY 17TH CENTURY DUTCH BINDING
IN EMBROIDERED WHITE SATIN.

siderable size, in a single operation. The book covers were wet, and the dies were tied onto the front and back of the book, which was then subjected to pressure in a screw press. The images thus impressed into the leather became permanent when the covers dried.

These paneled bindings were produced almost exclusively in the Netherlands, France, and the Lower Rhine district of Germany. Those of Flemish origin are particularly delicate and charming, figures of saints being frequently chosen as subjects. Some of the French panels made use of acorns or other decorative elements.

The Italian equivalent for these panel stamps was the cameo, which was impressed on the binding with casts from antique coins or medals or cut specially for the purpose in hand. Heads of classical characters or other portraits were the usual subjects.

The highest manifestation of the medieval bookbinder's art, however, was in the *cuir-ciselé* bindings, each of which represented an independent artistic production. The design was first outlined with a pointed tool on the dampened book cover and then deepened. The subject was brought into relief by depressing the background, usually by stamping a succession of dots, very close together, into the leather with a pointed tool. Certain parts of the design were sometimes embossed from the back.

This method of decorating bookbindings, in spite of the beauty of the results, was in use only during the fifteenth century and only in certain localities, principally in southeastern Germany and in Spain. No English or Flemish and practically no Italian bindings of this character are known. The finest *cuir-ciselé* bindings known have recently been identified as the work of Mair Jaffe, a Jewish artist-binder of Nuremberg.

The next forward step in the decoration of bookbindings was an epochal one: the introduction of gold tooling. In this process, an adhesive size is first applied to the leather, and then sheets of gold

leaf beaten exceedingly thin are laid down upon it. The heated tools are next pressed down where it is desired to have the decoration appear, and wherever the heat and pressure are applied, the gold leaf adheres to the leather, the excess gold not so impressed being afterwards rubbed off. When properly applied by this method, the affinity of gold for the leather is remarkable. Once on, it will practically never come off.

Oriental binders working at Venice in the fifteenth century had produced bindings with gilt decoration, but these were made in an entirely different way. The designs were impressed in blind or cut out of the top layer of a two-ply board, and the recesses were then colored with a liquid gold paint. This method has, of course, no relationship to gold tooling with hot stamps.

Matthias Corvinus, from 1458 to 1490 king of Hungary, was a bibliophile of truly noble stature. He had in his service scribes to write manuscript books, distinguished miniature painters to illuminate them, and binders to put them into handsome covers. These artists, probably all Italians, produced for the royal collector some of the finest manuscript books, which he preferred to volumes produced by printing. Some of the bindings, of morocco leather or velvet, were decorated with gold tooling, in addition to inlays of varicolored leathers, cameos and precious stones.

The relations of Corvinus with Italy were close; in 1476 he married the daughter of the king of Naples. We find a clue to the early use of gold tooling in a document of 1480, from Naples, recording payment to Baldassare Scariglia for binding seven volumes in Cordovan leather "decorated with borders of foliage and flowers, tooled in gold (*impressi in oro*) and enameled in blue." This reference is quite specific and constitutes the earliest clear record of gold-tooled binding. Goldschmidt considers it "fairly established" that the binders who taught and practiced the art of gold tooling in the

palace of Corvinus at Buda came from Naples. A number of gold-tooled bindings executed at Naples prior to 1490 are also extant.

The origin of gold tooling at Venice, where much binding in the Oriental style was being done, presents some rather complicated questions. Some bindings executed between 1480 and 1488 for Peter Uglheimer, partner of Jenson and organizer of the important Venetian publishing firm of "Jo. de Colonia, Nic. Jenson et socii," have their main decoration done in the brush technique on a blind outline, but with borders around the edge stamped in gold leaf. Other Venetian bindings showing a similar dual technique are known. All are apparently from the same bindery, which used as its mark a small scallop shell.

The commonly accepted view that Aldus Manutius, the Venetian printer, first introduced the gold tooling of bindings appears, in the light of recent research, to be nothing more than legend. Whence the art came to Naples and Venice is not known, but the most likely hypothesis seems to be that it was an invention of the Moorish leather workers at Cordova.

Gold tooling next made its appearance in France, the earliest bindings in this technique appearing soon after the return of Charles VIII from the conquest of Naples. While the early work was not distinguished, the Parisian gold toolers, or *doreurs sur cuir,* were soon doing the finest work in Europe.

It is now clearly established that the finely gold-tooled bindings executed for Jean Grolier and contemporary bibliophiles were all done in Paris, about 1535 and later. Because of the fact that Grolier was treasurer of the French duchy of Milan for certain years between 1499 and 1521, and because he was a close friend of Aldus who dedicated some books to him, it had been concluded that Grolier's finely bound Aldines were executed in Venice at the Aldine bindery. Critical study has shown this widely accepted theory to be

without foundation. Watermarks in the end papers, dates in the books themselves, and other evidences of like character have contributed to the revised conclusion.

Recent research has also disclosed the identity of "Maioli," a bibliophile whose name is often associated with Grolier's, as Thomas Mahieu, secretary of Catherine de' Medici. Grolier had stamped on his books "Io. Grolierii et amicorum" (belonging to Jean Grolier and his friends), and Mahieu made use of a like statement of communal ownership.

The earlier bindings executed for Grolier were decorated with solid leaf tools and simple geometrical interlacings, while the later ones showed the use of shaded or azured leaves and interlaced strapwork, the latter often in color.

During this period a binder often sewed the book and encased it in a leather cover, which was then decorated by another artist who specialized in gold tooling. The finest Parisian *doreurs sur cuir* were far more than craftsmen. They worked with comparatively few and simple tools, but accomplished with them bindings of a high degree of personal artistry, comparable in virtuosity to the German *cuir-ciselé* bindings already mentioned.

From this point on, we can only touch briefly on the work of several of the most important binders, who have left a definite impress on binding style. Nicholas Eve was at work in France late in the sixteenth century. The bindings done under his supervision are characterized by the use of allover or diaper patterns of small units, such as fleurs-de-lis, tears, or two lambdas (representing the initials of Louise de Lorraine, wife of Henri III). His name is also associated with the so-called "fanfare" style, in which the space was broken up into geometric compartments which were filled in with shaded or azured tools of a floral character.

Clovis Eve followed in the post of "binder to the King" after

the decease of his brother Nicholas, but there is little specific evidence regarding bindings which he executed.

Our next figure of note is a mysterious personage—Le Gascon. There has been some question as to whether such a person ever existed, but Thoinan has proved, by documentary evidence, that such a binder and gilder was at work in Paris in the second quarter of the seventeenth century and that his work was well regarded. At any rate, a very definite style of binding is named for him—a style in which the lines of the decoration are broken up into a succession of fine dots. In fact, all the elements are rendered as fine dots rather than solids, by the use of what are known to binders as "pinhead" tools. This made for a style of great delicacy.

Antoine Michel Padeloup, referred to as Padeloup *le jeune,* was the most renowned member of a large family of binders. He worked in Paris during the early part of the eighteenth century, his style being characterized by lace-pattern borders of great luxuriance.

Nicholas Denis Derôme was the most brilliant of another large family of binders which contributed to the art no less than eighteen members by the name of Derôme. Many of Derôme's bindings resemble Padeloup's, and it is possible that he may have taken over the business and the tools of the latter. Derôme is best known, however, for his dentelle borders—borders with salients toward the center. In these he introduced a small bird with outstretched wings. He also drew on the grammar of ornament of other crafts for other dentelle designs.

The first name known in English fine binding is that of Thomas Berthelet, a Frenchman, bookseller and "printer to the King" from 1530 to 1555. He is known to have supplied bindings "bounde after the Venecian fascion" and in other styles, but it is not known that he was personally a craftsman or artist in the bookbinding field. Samuel Mearne, who became bookbinder to the king in 1660, has

been regarded as outstanding in the English record of fine book-making, but it has recently been proved that the finest gold-tooled "Mearne" bindings were executed by a Dutch artist named Sucker-man. These bindings are associated with the "cottage pattern," so called because of the pentlike arrangement of lines at top, bottom, and sides. Sprays and branches, combined with lacework, fill in the spaces, or small tools are used in fan ornament. Though the crafts-manship leaves something to be desired, many English bindings of this type have much charm.

It is of interest to observe that gold-tooled bindings were exe-cuted at Cracow, Poland, both before and after 1500.

Gold tooling, *mirabile dictu,* did not come into use in Germany until about 1540, and little distinguished binding was done in that country until recent years, when some of the book artists have pro-duced excellent bindings of modern, rather than traditional design.

Only recently have the facts regarding early American book-binding been firmly established. John Sanders, bookbinder, took the freeman's oath in Boston in 1636, three years before any printing is known to have been done in Massachusetts. It seems likely that he may have bound copies of the Bay Psalm Book printed in 1640 and other works issued by the early Cambridge press. All the earliest bindings we know are of plain leather, without ornamentation or gold tooling of any description.

John Ratcliff came to America about 1661-1663, for the purpose of binding the Eliot Indian Bible, and we find him complaining in 1664 about the small pay he received for this work. He appears to have returned to England about 1682. In addition to his work in binding the Bibles, he is known, by documentary record in the book itself, to have bound in 1677 Samuel Sewall's *Commonplace Book,* which was stamped with tools, but without gold leaf. With some of the same tools Ratcliff stamped in gold a crudely bound and deco-

A 17TH CENTURY AMERICAN BINDING BY JOHN RATCLIFF.

BINDING EXECUTED BY KATHERINE ADAMS FOR THE
ASHENDENE DANTE, 1909.

rated volume of *A Call from Heaven,* by Increase Mather, 1679. Another gold-tooled binding ascribed to Ratcliff covers a copy of the Psalms printed at Cambridge in 1651 but probably bound later.

Another early New England binder was Edmund Ranger, who was admitted a freeman of Boston in 1671. He continued his business as publisher, bookseller, and bookbinder until his death in 1705. He probably executed numerous plain bindings. At present writing the earliest gold-tooled bindings ascribed to him are on two different copies of *Practical Truths,* by Increase Mather, Boston, 1682, the bindings being thought to be approximately contemporary with the printing. It seems probable that Ranger acquired Ratcliff's tools when the latter sailed back to his native shores.

Collectors of modern first editions are not interested, however, in copies which have been rebound by the fine binder; they seek rather the book in the exact and unaltered form in which it originally appeared. For nineteenth-century titles this often requires the work to be in parts, with paper wrappers, or in original paper boards. The rarest items are today enclosed in handsome slipcases by the discriminating collector, rather than rebound.

At the end of the first quarter of the nineteenth century, however, a new form of clothing books at the time of their original appearance came into being—the now universal publishers' binding in cloth. Only recently has the origin and history of cloth binding, now so important a factor in the bookmaking industry, been adequately investigated. The question has lately been studied by Michael Sadleir and by John Carter, two competent English bibliographers. Credit for introducing the new style of cloth binding goes to William Pickering, who first made use of it on volumes of his Oxford Classics in or about the year 1825. The first material used was calico, which was later sized to stiffen and glaze it. However, it took a good many years for cloth binding to win popular favor, the idea

that all books were ultimately to be bound in leather holding on with remarkable tenacity.

Having briefly traced the historical development of the art of bookbinding, we may now consider some of the present-day aspects. The stronghold of "fine binding" today is in England. In that country are located several establishments with a complement of conscientiously trained craftsmen, and a labor cost infinitely less than for similar work done in the United States. There are, however, in New York and Chicago several shops operating with London-trained finishers whose work is of high standard but whose costs are necessarily high.

The fine binders of today work in the same manner as their predecessors for centuries back. The signatures are sewed on cords, and these cords are interlaced into the boards (now made of composition) which, in the next step, are covered with leather. A flexible back is greatly to be desired so that a book will open easily and lie flat and close easily and stay closed. It is a rule of informed binders to trim the books they handle just as little as possible, in books printed on deckle-edge paper confining this trim to the top only, which is then frequently gilded. Many binders in ages past have mangled books in a distressing way by cutting down their margins so radically that there were almost no margins left. When a book already severely cropped is to be rebound, the fine binder "rough gilds" the edges before he starts his work so that he may avoid the necessity of further cropping.

The sewing, gilding of edges, covering, and so forth, are known as "forwarding"; the decoration of the cover as "finishing." The design is first made up on paper with inked impressions of the tools, and when the arrangement has been worked out to satisfaction, it is transferred to the leather by light impressions through the paper pattern onto the leather, which has previously been dampened to soften

it. The portions of the cover thus lightly impressed are then sized and the gold leaf is laid. This is so thin that the impressions show through clearly. The finisher, thus having a guide for his work, makes a second and more vigorous impression with his hot tools, which causes the gold to adhere to the leather, and the book is now ready for delivery to an expectant collector.

Almost all binding in England and the United States is wholly traditional in character, and there is in evidence practically no inventiveness in design. Books are executed in the style of one or another of the masters whose work has been discussed, and their merit appears to hinge on how faithfully those styles are reproduced.

Toward the end of the nineteenth century, a great service to the cause of bookbinding was rendered by T. J. Cobden-Sanderson—a disciple of William Morris. This remarkable man, who gave up a career in the legal profession to become a bookbinder through choice, made fruitful contributions to the art, particularly in introducing new forms of design and in freeing the binders from a too servile allegiance to the classical styles. His motifs of decoration, while still within the bounds of conventionalism, were much more naturalistic than the tools which had been used by his predecessors. His pupil, Douglas Cockerell, writes: "Before his time there had been few attempts to combine tools to form organic patterns. Mr. Cobden-Sanderson's tools were very elementary in character, each flower, leaf or bird being the impression of a separate tool. These impressions were combined in such a way as to give a sense of growth, and yet in no way overlapped the traditional limitations and conventions of the craft. Mr. Cobden-Sanderson got his results by sheer genius in the right use of simple elements."

There is an entertaining story told of Cobden-Sanderson's rejoinder to a lady client who came to protest a charge of six pounds for binding a book on which, as she pointed out, there was little

gold tooling. "Madam," replied the master binder, "I charge as much for my restraint as for my elaboration."

The main present source of original ideas in bookbinding design —as in book-printing design—is on the Continent. European artists are binding books with entire freedom from the restrictions of tradition, and they are being followed by a few on this side of the ocean who are interested in the modern movement. Many of the results are weird, but many of the designs show much promise. From this free experimentation, there is bound to result much good. As in all fields, the best course will be found in a synthesis of the best elements in the old leavened by the best elements in the new.

XXXIX

The Printing of Illustrations

URING the eighteenth century wood engraving increased in volume, because of improvements in printing and paper-making which made possible the production of more and more books and magazines, and also because of a growing popular demand for pictures—the end of which demand is not yet in sight. But as the volume of engraving rose, the quality of the work fell. Wood engraving became a trade rather than an art. No longer did creative artists cut their own designs on wood. Instead, a group of artisans reproduced their drawings and paintings on wood blocks, with a widely varying degree of skill.

The decline of the art of wood engraving was sharply arrested, however, in the later years of the eighteenth century by an original genius in the person of Thomas Bewick. At the age of fourteen, Bewick was apprenticed to a copperplate engraver at Newcastle, England. Turning early in his career to the engraving of wood, he pioneered, if he did not indeed originate, two new practices in the making of blocks for illustrations.

First, he developed the picture in white lines on a black ground, rather than continuing the method of his predecessors, whose pictures were printed in black lines on a white background. The difference in technique, which is important to understand, is thus explained by Woodberry: "By the old method . . . the block was treated as a white surface, on which the designer drew with pen and ink and obtained grays and blacks by increasing the number of cross-strokes, as if he were drawing on paper; by the new method

the block was treated as a black surface, and the color was lessened by increasing the number of white lines."

At the same time Bewick abandoned the use of planks of soft woods such as pear or apple, substituting in their stead the hard wood of the box tree, with the blocks cut across the grain. Whereas the former were cut on the side grain with a knife, held like a pen, and drawn toward the engraver, the end-grain boxwood was best worked with a graver pushed away from the engraver. The new technique was expeditious as well as effective, providing black-and-white illustrations of a new brilliance and strength.

The first book of importance illustrated by Thomas Bewick was the *Select Fables,* which was published at Newcastle during 1784. William Bulmer, the printer, also of Newcastle, was a friend of Bewick's, the two collaborating on the illustration and production of many fine books. Bewick died in 1828, after making an enduring impression on the art of wood engraving. Among the engravers whose work was very largely influenced by Bewick was Alexander Anderson, the first American engraver whose work is regarded as of artistic significance.

Toward the close of the eighteenth century came a new process for the printing of pictures which was destined to exert a great influence on the illustration of books. I refer to the invention of lithography by Alois Senefelder. The story of the discovery is so romantic as to deserve recountal here.

At the age of eighteen, Senefelder wrote for the carnival at Munich a short dramatic sketch, which was well received and subsequently printed. The young author's future career was determined by the fact that he made a profit of fifty gulden on the publication of his first opus. The publication of later plays not proving so successful, Senefelder sought means for doing his own printing. Since he could not afford the purchase of a press and type, he

experimented with a method of writing reversed letters directly on a plate of copper, which was then etched. This process provided a plate which would print successfully, but the effort of grinding down and repolishing it for further use, together with the waste of the copper involved, made it impractical for regular use. Senefelder then tried zinc plates, but the action upon them of the acid which he used for etching proved unsatisfactory.

The young experimenter's attention was next drawn to the slab of Kellheimer stone which he used for grinding his inks. He tried polishing a block of this stone and then etching the surface. But such plates would not outlast the printing of fifty impressions. This, however, was no discovery, for etched stone plates had earlier been used by music printers.

The next stage in our story concerns what may well have been the most important laundry list in all history. In 1793, Senefelder's mother asked him to write down a record of the family wash. Having no paper immediately at hand, he wrote the list on a polished stone with which he was working, using an ink made of wax, soap, and lampblack. He intended to copy the list on paper, but curiosity led him to etch the stone just as it was. This produced a plate with the written characters in low relief, which looked exceedingly encouraging. But practical difficulties in printing, which developed in the attempt to print from the plate thus produced, led Senefelder to continue his experiments along other lines.

To obviate the difficulty of writing on the stone in reverse, the inventor tried writing on paper and transferring the writing from the sheet onto the stone. Senefelder himself, in telling us of several thousand experiments in making such transfers, including moistening the paper before laying it on the stone, wrote: "I noticed that if there happened to be a few drops of oil in the water into which I dipped paper inscribed with my greasy stone-ink, the oil would

distribute itself evenly over all parts of the writing, whereas the rest of the paper would take no oil."

Senefelder then conceived the idea of transferring to a stone surface so prepared that it would take ink only on the portions covered with a fatty pigment. Solenholfer limestone proved to have a great affinity for oil or fat. Three more days of experimentation, we are told, sufficed for "such handsome, clean, and strong impressions . . . that few better ones have been made since." The great invention of lithography had been made. Claims were filed in the British patent office in 1800 and in other countries soon after, and the patient experimenter was on his way to wealth and renown.

The use of lithography spread rapidly, its chief importance lying in the facility it afforded for the printing of pictures, either in black and white, or in colors.

As the art of photography developed, it was applied to lithography, providing an exact and economical mechanical means of transferring a drawing to the stone and giving a further impetus to the art of picture printing invented by Senefelder. Some creative artists, however, who were familiar with the technique, preferred to make their drawings directly on the stone.

Offset lithography, a recent development of the process, made it possible to discard the cumbrous stones. In this process the image is etched on zinc or aluminum plates with a grained surface, which are then printed on presses with three cylinders. The first cylinder carries the plate, which prints onto a rubber blanket on the second cylinder. The image on the rubber is then printed or "offset" onto the sheet of paper around the third, or impression, cylinder. This development has made lithographic printing faster and less costly and has taken certain classes of work away from the printers using the standard relief or letterpress process. Practically all posters are printed by offset lithography, which has also proved adaptable to

fine book illustrations in color. One of the principal advantages of offset is that it does not require paper with a highly coated surface to achieve a satisfactory printed result.

There was still a demand, however, for relief plates of illustrations mechanically produced, which could be printed in the same forms and on the same presses as pages of type. Wood engraving continued to provide for this ever-increasing demand until 1880 and for a few years thereafter. Soon after this date, however, wood engraving as a handicraft was practically wiped out by the new industry of photo-engraving. The last standouts were engravers of considerable virtuosity, such as Timothy Cole, who interpreted paintings in minute and exquisite detail, achieving reproductions of unquestionable charm.

The foundations of photo-engraving, the process which has made possible the wealth of pictures which prove so popular in the books, magazines, and newspapers of the present day, were laid in the experiments of Joseph Nicéphore Niepce, the colleague of Louis Jacques Daguerre in the development of photography. In 1824 Niepce produced successfully a portrait of Cardinal d'Amboise on a plate etched in intaglio. Mungo Ponton made a discovery of great importance in 1839, when he found that bichromate of potash in combination with albumen or some other colloid became hard and insoluble in water through exposure to light. Fox Talbot pointed the way to a photographic negative, from which prints could be made in positive. When light is thrown through a negative onto a film of bichromate and albumen, the latter will be hardened and rendered insoluble at different points in proportion to the amount of light which reaches them. The blacks in the original, showing white and transparent in the negative, will thus be hardened on the bichromate film. The areas which are white on the original will be black in the negative, which will shield the film from light at these

points and thus leave them soluble, to be washed out with water. When the film is superimposed on a plate of copper or zinc and the hardened portions dusted with asphalt, which is melted by heat, these portions are protected from the action of acid, which etches away the portions of the plate not covered by portions of the film hardened by light. This etching process leaves the protected areas in relief, which can be inked like type and printed on a press, thus reproducing the blacks and whites of the original copy.

While such a process would reproduce the blacks and whites of a pen-and-ink drawing, it would not reproduce the varied gray tones of a photograph or wash drawing. This was accomplished by the invention of "halftone" engraving, in which the image projected on the bichromate film was broken up by a screen. Without entering into the technicalities of the process, we may say that the resulting plate shows a succession of dots of various sizes, which make a picture. In the dark areas the dots are large, so that their outside edges come close together. In the light areas the dots are small, leaving considerable white space between them.

Whether the screen through which the original is photographed is coarse or fine depends upon the paper on which the plate is to be printed. For newsprint and rough papers the screen is coarse. The character of the resulting plate can be seen in any photograph printed in a newspaper. Where a smooth-finish or coated paper is used, the screen becomes finer, as in the halftones used throughout this volume to reproduce bindings, manuscript pages, and so forth.

The invention of the halftone process was one of great importance in the development of printing and bookmaking. Fox Talbot conceived, in 1852, the idea of a screen, using at first an open-weave fabric to break up the picture. In 1879 Joseph Swan, in England, patented a screen ruled in one direction which was moved during the exposure to obtain a cross-ruled effect. In 1882 Georg

Meisenbach, a German, patented a similar method, having produced his first successful halftone in the previous year.

Meanwhile, in the United States, Frederick E. Ives, generally regarded as the inventor of a practical halftone process, who died in May, 1937, was doing his pioneer work, and my good friend the late Stephen H. Horgan reproduced direct from a photograph the now celebrated "Shantytown," the first halftone to be printed in a newspaper. This appeared in the issue of the New York *Daily Graphic* for March 4, 1880.

The perfection of the halftone process waited, however, on the development of a cross-ruled screen. Max Levy, of Philadelphia, made a ruling machine accurate enough for the ruling of satisfactory screens. In 1886, Ives used two such screens at different angles, sealed face to face, thus producing the cross-ruled screen which is in general use today. It is pleasant to report that almost all halftone screens are still made by Levy.

Color printing was still to be provided for, working on the theory that all colors could be produced by the proper combination of the three primaries: yellow, red, and blue. Frederick Ives experimented with the photography of three negatives through the appropriate color filters, making halftones from each negative. He succeeded in producing in 1881 the first three-color engravings for letterpress printing.

In the photogravure process, copper plates were etched in intaglio. Such plates were inked all over, the top surface was wiped clean, and dampened paper was pressed against them under heavy pressure, which drew the ink out of the depressions onto the sheet. In 1879 Karl Klic substituted for the bichromate film a gelatine film pigmented with carbon, paving the way for rotary photogravure or rotogravure, a process popularized in the pictorial sections of our larger newspapers. In this process a screen is also used.

The resulting holes in the plate are all of the same diameter, but vary in depth and thus in the quantity of ink which they will hold. A group of deep holes discharge much ink on the paper, thus printing a dark area, while shallow holes deposit little color on the sheet, producing a highlight in the picture.

There is another process known as collotype or gelatine printing, in which inked impressions are made directly from a bichromated gelatine film, without the necessity of breaking up the image by a screen. The plates can be used for only a limited number of impressions, which must be printed slowly. It is used mostly for fine illustrations printed in limited editions.

There are three general methods of printing illustrations. The first is *planographic,* comprising lithography, offset lithography, and collotype, all being printed from approximately plane or level plates, various portions of which accept or reject ink in differing degree. The second method is *relief,* which comprises line engravings, halftones, and wood engravings, the non-printing portions of which are etched or cut away, the remaining upper surface of the plate being inked by the roller and being impressed on the paper. The third type of plates are *intaglio,* the pictures on which are cut or etched into the plate below the surface. After inking, the top surface is wiped clean, and the ink in the depressions is sucked out onto the sheet of paper. Copperplate engravings, etchings, photogravure, and rotogravure are comprehended within this classification.

XL

The Title Page

A STRIKING peculiarity of books printed in the earliest years of printing is that they almost invariably lack that familiar feature of modern books—the title page. To use McKerrow's definition, a title page is "a separate page setting forth in a conspicuous manner the title of the book which follows it and not containing any part of the text of the book itself." To waste a precious leaf of parchment or paper merely to set forth the title of the book was an extravagance not permitted to the penman who wrote books in manuscript. In fact, it probably never occurred to scribes that such a thing was necessary. Could not the user of the book identify the book at a glance by looking at the three or four lines at the beginning of the text?

For the scribes as a matter of course put the essential information —the title and authorship of the text which followed—at the top of the page on which the text began. This paragraph was frequently written in red, to distinguish it from the text, and usually began with the word *Incipit*, "Here begins"—or its equivalent in the vernacular tongues. Further identification of the book was often provided by a *titulus* ("label") pasted on the back of the binding, if not stamped into the leather of the binding itself.

The earliest printers followed the usage of the scribes. We therefore find that most of the early printed books start with an *Incipit*, or *Cy commence*, or *Hier begynneth*. As the text of the earliest books was printed in black, their printers generally left to the handwork of professional rubricators the insertion, usually in red,

of the headings of chapters or sections, the insertion of paragraph marks, and the rather inept practice of making a pen stroke in red through all capital letters, making them much less readable than if they had been left alone. To the rubricator also was frequently left the writing of the *Incipit,* for which the printer left a sufficient blank space at the top of the page, though later this was printed in type along with the text making up the remainder of the page. Pages beginning in the manner described may be seen in the illustrations on pages 155, 271, and 285.

These introductory headings usually gave the title of the book and the name of the author, but never, so far as I recall, the name of the printer, the place of printing, or the date of issue. They thus performed but one of the functions of the title page with which we are familiar. As did manuscript books before them, the earliest printed books reserved any complete statement as to authorship, production, and place and date of issue for a position at the very end of the volume. Here the information, so far as the printer cared to impart it, was set in a paragraph which has come to be known as the colophon—the term being a Greek word meaning "finishing stroke." The first appearance of a printed colophon was in the celebrated Mainz Psalter of 1457, which we have already had occasion to describe, and which is reproduced on page 290.

The colophons of many early incunabula make interesting reading. In addition to such information as the title of the book, the name of the author, the printer's name, and the place and date of printing, they not infrequently contain notes invaluable to modern scholars as to the editor who corrected and prepared the text, the patron who made possible the publication of the book, and so on. We have already seen how adulatory verses added to certain early colophons have been used as clues to the identification of the inventor of printing. The colophon, in fact, often included much that

in our present-day books is expanded into the author's or editor's preface or introduction.

In their introductory and terminal paragraphs taken together, early printed books provided the information that we find on our title pages, but in an ineffectual and clumsy manner at best. Yet the title page, like many another improvement, was a slow and gradual development. As Mr. Alfred W. Pollard puts it, in his admirable monograph on the history of the title page, "It is hard to understand how the first printers, who had introduced so mighty a revolution in the art of multiplying books, hesitated for so long over so simple and so sorely needed a reform as the introduction of the title page."

Where and when did the title page first make its appearance in any form comparable to our present-day title pages? Strangely enough, it first appeared in manuscript books, although in very few of them. Pollard, in his article on title pages in some Italian manuscripts, brings to attention what may have been the earliest page of this character. It was a "general title page" to the four gospels in the manuscript Bible known as the Codex Aureus, produced about 800 A. D. in the school of calligraphy founded at Aix by Charlemagne. But this innovation upon the standard practice of manuscript production seems to have found no imitators. The innovation did not appear again until the fifteenth century, when title pages were introduced in a few handsomely written Italian manuscripts.

In these exceptional Italian manuscripts the title was engrossed on the first leaf in a well-proportioned central space which was then surrounded with elaborate ornament in the illuminator's most effective style. In some cases this *tour de force* of the penman was put on the reverse of the first leaf, as if to protect it from the wear to which the outside of the leaf would be subjected. In fact, the function of these manuscript title pages seems to have been primarily the

embellishment of the books in which they appeared. But in the sense of McKerrow's definition quoted at the beginning of this chapter, they were none the less true title pages.

No case can be cited of the imitation of this style of page by any fifteenth-century printer, though Pollard notes one printed book of 1501 in the title page of which some such influence was evident— *La vita de la beata Catherina da Siena,* printed in Venice by Albertinus Vercellensis. But as to printed books in general, the title page seems rather to have come into being through an evolution of the colophon. This statement by the printer at the end of his work came in many cases to have the typographic form, as well as the literary content, of our title pages. The final steps in this evolution were the segregation of the "finishing stroke" from the text by putting it on a separate page, and the placing of this page in the front instead of at the back of the book. Haebler makes note of some forty incunabula which have true title pages at the end, the earliest being a Dutch imprint of 1483.

The earliest use of a separate page at the beginning of a book to set forth the title and authorship is found in the *Bul zu dutsch* ("Papal Letter in German") of Pope Pius II, which was printed in Mainz in 1463. From the reproduction on the opposite page it will be seen that the material was set forth typographically like a solid paragraph of text, without any display. Also there is no indication on this page of the place of printing, name of printer, and date. The next such page in point of date is in the *Sermo ad populum,* a "sermon suitable to be preached on the Feast of the Assumption of the Most Blessed ever Virgin Mary," printed at Cologne by Arnold ther Hoernen in 1470. In this form of title page, which is known as the "label" title, the title of the book in the briefest possible compass was printed at the top of the first leaf.

An early example of such a title page in English occurs in a

Diß ist die bul zu dutsch die vn=
ser allerheiligster vatter der babst
Pius heruß gesant hait widder
die snoden vngleubigen turcken.

book printed in London by William Machlinia at an undetermined date, but certainly before 1490. It reads:

A passing gode lityll boke necessarye &
  behouefull agenst the Pestilens.

Interpreting this title phonetically, as is necessary in reading the English of this period, we find the volume to contain a treatise on the plague.

Caxton, though a near neighbor of Machlinia, did not follow this example, but printed his statements of authorship, title, date, and so forth at the beginning or at the end of the prologue, or of the table of contents, text, or epilogue—anywhere, in fact, except in the obvious place, the first page of the book, which he left blank. Wynkyn de Worde, however, further developed the use of the title page in English printing.

The earliest title page with any display arrangement is a beautiful one indeed. The book is the *Calendarium* of Regiomontanus which was printed by Erhard Ratdolt and his associates at Venice in 1476. As we pointed out in Chapter XVIII, Ratdolt was a pioneer in the decoration of books, and in this volume he does not disappoint his admirers. The title page was printed in two colors. Its details were set forth in verse, as was so frequently done in early colophons, and there follow the date of issue and the names and native cities of the three men who collaborated in the production of the book. The verse, to be sure, is rather like a publisher's "blurb," eulogizing the book; but such adulatory comments on the excellence of books became familiar features of the title pages of later years. This Ratdolt title page is reproduced on the opposite page.

In the case of early printed books of importance it was customary to have the first page of the text embellished with a border in florid and colorful style, supplied by a professional illuminator. See, for

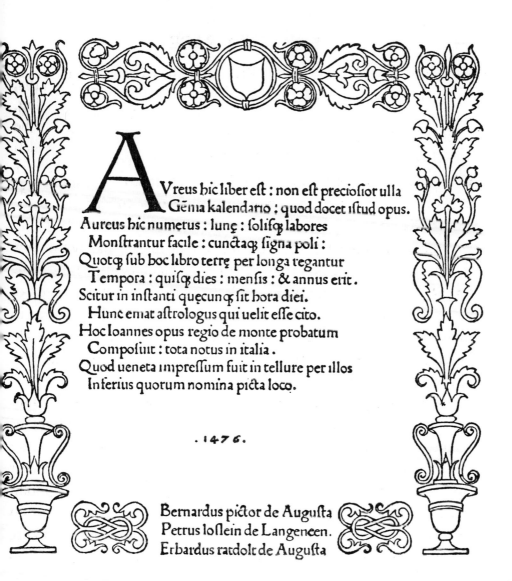

AVreus hic liber eſt : non eſt precioſior ulla
Gēma kalendario : quod docet iſtud opus.
Aureus hic numetus : lunę : ſoliſꝗ labores
Monſtrantur facile : cunctaꝗ ſigna poli :
Quotꝗ ſub boc libro terrę per longa tegantur
Tempora : quiſꝗ dies : menſis : & annus erit .
Scitur in inſtanti quęcunꝗ ſit hora diei .
Hunc emat aſtrologus qui uelit eſſe cito .
Hoc Ioannes opus regio de monte probatum
Compoſuit : tota notus in italia .
Quod ueneta impreſſum fuit in tellure per illos
Inferius quorum nomina picta loco.

. 1476 .

Bernardus pictor de Auguſta
Petrus loſlein de Langeneen.
Erbardus ratdolt de Auguſta

THE FIRST COMPLETE TITLE PAGE, IN THE CALENDARIUM PRINTED
IN 1476 BY ERHARD RATDOLT AND ASSOCIATES, VENICE.

example, the first page of the Fust and Schoeffer Bible of 1462, illustrated on page 155. In the development of the art of printing, however, less and less of this kind of ornamentation was left to be supplied by hand. We may therefore expect to find books in which such decoration or illustration is printed from woodcuts. Chapter XVIII deals in more detail with this subject. It was inevitable that such woodcut decorations should find their way to the title page. In fact, for several generations of printers, highly embellished title pages became an almost invariable feature of their books.

An early form of this treatment of the title page was an illustration intended to convey the subject matter of the book, headed with a short title such as was used on the "label" title pages. An example of such a page, reproduced on the opposite page, which should have a special interest for Americans, is from an early version of the famous letter in which Christopher Columbus reported his discoveries. The illustration depicts the arrival of the daring navigator in the New World. The reader will note with interest the great distance between Spain and the coast of America.

The decorated title page had a unique development in France. This took the form of an exaggerated and highly embellished initial letter, usually the *L* of the French definite article, at the beginning of a title set in type of modest size. The development of these initials as ornaments in many cases seriously impaired or altogether destroyed their legibility as letters. The drawings with which they were embellished were often pure products of the artist's fantasy, but sometimes were designedly suggestive of the subject-matter of the books in which they appeared. A few Spanish title pages of a similar character show that this French influence penetrated beyond the Pyrenees. The illustration on page 567 shows one of these highly ornamented initials.

At a somewhat later date we encounter title pages on which

¶ La lettera dellisole che ha trouato nuouamente il Re dispagna.

TITLE PAGE OF AN ITALIAN VERSION OF THE
COLUMBUS LETTER, PRINTED AT FLORENCE, 1495.

the printers have put their devices or distinctive printers' marks. In some instances, also, the title pages bore independent woodcut illustrations. The former style, as followed by Badius of Paris in a book dated 1522, is represented by the title page illustrated in Chapter XV on page 236, showing the printer's device of his printing press.

Aldus used pages with the title simply set, but embellished with his celebrated device of the anchor and dolphin. Sometimes he elaborated on the title by including in it a summary of the contents of the volume. The printers at Lyons and elsewhere who pirated Aldus's texts followed him also in the typographic arrangement of their title pages.

In the Parisian books of hours, those highly characteristic products of the French press which are discussed in more detail in Chapter XXII, the title pages developed a style of their own. Decoration is the outstanding feature of these books, and their title pages are almost completely covered with elaborate decoration, with the title itself relegated to a relatively unimportant position on the page. An example of this style is presented in the illustration on page 569, from an issue of the *Horae Beatae Mariae Virginis* printed by Simon Vostre. It will be noted that the decorative feature of this page is an elaboration of Vostre's printer's mark.

It is not uncommon to find fifteenth-century books provided with title pages which were added at a later date. In such cases it would appear that unsold copies of the books were "remaindered" to later printers, who printed title pages for the volumes which did not originally have them.

Early title pages not infrequently contained a notice of the place where the books could be bought. The practice of naming on title pages the bookseller or agent for the sale of the books persisted until well into the nineteenth century and is not altogether unknown even today. It originated, it would seem, among early printers who kept

INITIAL "L" FROM TITLE PAGE OF LA MER DES
HISTOIRES BY ANTOINE VÉRARD, PRINTED BY P.
LE ROUGE, PARIS, 1488.

their title pages standing and used them for printing posters or handbills advertising their books.

In the second quarter of the sixteenth century we find a general use of complete title pages as we know them now. They were especially well set at that time by Robert Estienne, the distinguished Parisian printer.

Once it had been universally adopted as an essential feature of a printed book, the title page was never displaced, and never will be. But the manner of setting it has varied greatly with different periods and with different printers. Many such variations will be noted among the illustrations throughout this volume, showing the work of eminent printers. The most common fault in composition which the evolution of the title page has had to remedy has been the attempt to list the whole contents of the book, or to set forth a biography of the author, or otherwise to crowd it to a point not only of unsightliness but even of illegibility. Thirty or more lines of type, interspersed with various rules and printers' ornaments, is somewhat too much for the title page of a duodecimo, or even of an octavo. But such crowded title pages were common enough until relatively recent times. At all times, however, the best printers have always set the simplest title pages.

What may be called the architecture of the title page has also passed through many variations. Type has been set in square or oblong blocks, or with lines of graduated lengths to form rhomboids, funnels, hourglasses, circles, or ellipses. Lines have been bent into curves and waves, and the whole has been complicated with almost every type ornament which the printer could find in his cases and crowd into the page. But the day has gone forever (we hope) when the printer took pride in making type play impossible tricks, and the title page has taken on beauty and dignity.

The best practice calls for the use of the fewest possible different

SIMON · VOSTRE ·

Hore beate marie virginis secundu vsu R o-
manum absq; requisitione aliqua cu pluribus orationibus in gallico et latine.

TITLE PAGE OF A BOOK OF HOURS PRINTED BY
SIMON VOSTRE.

sizes and faces of type compatible with the proper display emphasis of the main title. The predominant weight of the page is at the top. The principal words in the title are not divided, and the typography is planned to meet this requirement. The prevailing usage is to set title pages in capitals, as it is easier, on the whole, to work out an acceptable page with letters which are all of the same height than with capitals and lower case. But, as we point out elsewhere, the lower-case letters are decidedly more legible and should be used in cases where they appear to advantage.

Simplicity, the right proportional relations between the several blocks of type, and the correct positioning of these blocks on the page are the main desiderata in the composition of title pages. In books in which it is appropriate, some border or decoration in a mood of restraint is a welcome addition.

Good book printers give thoughtful consideration to the title page—and rightly. For, as the late George Sargent so aptly termed it, the title page is "the door to the book" and it should invite to entrance the visitor who approaches its threshold.

XLI

Concerning Type Design

S INCE the aim of the first printers was to reproduce manuscripts in quantity, it is not unnatural that the design of the first types was based upon the prevailing book hand of the scribes working in the region in which the printers set up their presses. As a matter of fact, the early printers made matrices for many more characters than the letters in the two alphabets of capitals and lower case, for they provided variants for many letters in order to make it possible for the compositor more nearly to approximate the appearance of text as it would have been written by a scribe.

As already noted, the types of Gutenberg and his associates and immediate successors were of the German pointed gothic style, which may be seen in illustrations facing pages 144 and 160 and in the large-type lines of the Indulgence on page 148 of the present volume. The next development was a rounded gothic which was considerably more legible and functioned successfully in sizes smaller than were practical with the pointed gothic types. Rounded gothics are shown in the small-type lines on pages 148 and 155 and facing page 161.

In Italy the Humanists favored what has since come to be known as the roman form of letter, and their influence spread beyond the Alps. Believe it or not, the first appearance of the roman alphabet in printing types is noted at Strasbourg, then a German city, where a long-unidentified printer began about 1464 to use an alphabet with a bizarre form of R, wherefore he became known to historians of bookmaking as the "R Printer." In later years, however, his name

was found to be Adolf Rusch. The next appearance of roman type was in the books printed at Rome by Sweynheym and Pannartz in 1467, but the face was inferior in quality to the cross between gothic and roman (reproduced on page 185) that they had used earlier at Subiaco. Also at Rome, in 1468, Ulrich Han made use of still another roman typeface which, in quality, left much to be desired. All these types, however, showed in their design a residuum of gothic influence.

The first typeface which was purely roman in origin and appearance was that used by John of Spire at Venice in 1469. This face has so many elements of design in common with the type produced by Nicolas Jenson during the following year that we cannot well escape the suspicion that the master of roman typeface design was the punch-cutter.

In 1470, however, appeared at Venice the first great roman typeface, the punches for which were cut by Nicolas Jenson. This face was used in printing *De praeparatione evangelica* by Eusebius. While its design was inspired by the humanistic hand written by the Italian scribes, the Jenson face gives some evidence of a realization on the part of its creator that he was working in a new medium, making metal types for printing on paper. The variant forms of each letter were resolved into a single standardized character, for use whenever called for by the copy. That Jenson was a man of great native genius requires no argument to prove. Through the combination of his artistic ability with his technical experience as a die-cutter, he crystallized the roman alphabet into forms so satisfactory that they have never since been materially improved upon. He thus left to that important portion of the civilized world depending upon the roman alphabet a legacy of immeasurable value.

In 1495 Aldus began the use of a roman letter of marked simplicity and strength, cut for him by Francisco Griffo, already

referred to and reproduced on page 209. The italic type, first cut for and used by Aldus, is discussed and reproduced on pages 210-212.

The next high spot in the development of type design is seen in the work of Claude Garamond, a French punch-cutter of superlative genius working in Paris during the first half of the sixteenth century. His roman types show a conscious striving for beauty in design, supcradded to legibility and utility. It was his great merit that he achieved this beauty without resort to mannerisms. Garamond's types were, to all intents and purposes, lost to the printing world during the eighteenth and nineteenth centuries, being revived in the second decade of the present century. In their recent reincarnation, they have again proved their merits so conclusively that we can safely regard them as a permanent asset on our typographic ledger.

It is a little surprising that the designs of most of the present-day typefaces named after Garamond have been based, not on the types of Claude Garamond, but on an early seventeenth-century recutting by Jean Jannon of Sedan, France. In 1642 the Protestant city of Sedan came under the power of Cardinal Richelieu, and Jannon's punches and matrices were transferred to the Imprimerie Nationale at Paris. After lying in disuse for many years, they were brought out again early in the present century, and Arthur Christian, then director of the French national printing office, definitely, though erroneously, ascribed them to Garamond. True authorship of these punches was made clear by Mrs. Beatrice Warde, writing under the pen name of Paul Beaujon, who discovered in the Mazarin Library in Paris, and reproduced, an apparently unique copy of Jannon's own type specimen book.

Our best authority for the typefaces actually engraved by Claude Garamond is a type specimen sheet (reproduced on page 340) issued at Frankfurt am Main in 1592 by the typefounder Conrad Berner, who had acquired the punches sold at auction in Paris in

1561, after the death of the great French punch-cutter. The Garamond produced by the Ludlow Typograph Company is the only typeface currently used in the United States or in England which is based directly on this authentic showing of Garamond designs.

Most of the good italics produced in France during the sixteenth century and purchased by Dutch and German typefounders and printers are ascribed to Robert Granjon of Lyons, a punch-cutter of great artistic and technical skill. Granjon is also known for his first interpretation, in types, at Lyons about 1557, of a cursive gothic handwriting which was then popular. These new and ingenious but illegible types cut by Granjon became known as *lettres de civilité,* from the titles of two volumes in which they were used.

Geofroy Tory, whose work has already been mentioned, influenced type design as well as other features of book art. Like the English prototypographer Caxton, he rendered a great service in reforming and stabilizing French orthography. It is interesting to recall that he introduced accents and was the author of a celebrated book on letter design entitled *Champfleury,* which appeared at Paris in 1529 and is now rare. An excellent translation has recently been published by the Grolier Club of New York. Tory exerted an important influence on the adoption of the roman alphabet as the standard letter for French printing.

In the seventeenth century in France, Pierre Moreau brought out interesting but undistinguished types of calligraphic character designed to reproduce handwriting. The cutting of a new series of type for the exclusive use of the Imprimerie Nationale was authorized in 1692 by Louis XIV. The Académie des Sciences instituted research to determine what the form of the letters should be. Philippe Grandjean de Fouchy cut the typeface thus projected, a specimen of the resulting *romain du roi* being shown in a specimen booklet printed in 1702.

The most colorful French punch-cutter and founder of the eighteenth century was Fournier *le jeune,* who made his name immortal through the authorship of a valuable treatise on typefounding, the *Manuel typographique.* The most significant typefounder of that century, however, was François Ambroise Didot, a member of a family which left an indelible impress on subsequent French printing. An able typefounder, he began about 1775 the production of typefaces prefiguring the style of design later crystallized by his son Firmin Didot. These Didot types and Fournier's ornaments exerted a profound influence on the typefounding and printing of the Italian Giambattista Bodoni.

The Didot types were perfected by François Ambroise's youngest son Firmin, who was responsible for cutting the faces used in the monumental editions of Racine and Horace which appeared in the opening years of the nineteenth century. These cold and geometrical types, with their sharp contrasts and fine straight-line serifs, enjoyed a great vogue for printing in the "classical" style. They became highly popular not only in France, but also with the printers and typefounders of Germany.

Typefounding was an active industry in the Netherlands during the seventeenth and eighteenth centuries. The work of the Dutch founders, however, has little special interest to us, except in the influence it had on English typefounding in general and on William Caslon in particular. The Dutch punch-cutter of real genius was Christophel van Dyck; the one of greatest industry with the minimum of artistry was J. M. Fleischman. Other punch-cutters of note were Dirk Voskens and Jacques François Rosart. The Enschedé foundry, established at Haarlem in 1703, and still in active operation today, fell heir to the equipments of most of the Dutch foundries and today possesses the most remarkable collection anywhere to be found of ancient punches and matrices. Charles Enschedé has writ-

ten a monumental work on typefounding in the Low Countries, making excellent use of the noteworthy materials available to him in the archives of the Enschedé foundry and printing office.

One of the important products of Dutch typefounding is the Fell type, punches and matrices of which were imported into England about 1693 by Bishop Fell, for use of the Oxford University Press.

In the modern period, several fine book faces have come out of Holland, notably the Lutetia designed by J. Van Krimpen and the Medieval authored by S. H. de Roos.

To return to England, an important opportunity here awaited any competent typefounder at the beginning of the eighteenth century. The efforts in this field of Nicholas Nicholls, Joseph Moxon, and others had been nothing short of pitiful. The James foundry had obtained matrices for most of its types from Holland but, even then, its casting was poor. It was, as one writer remarked, an era of "brown sheets and sorry letter." Judged by the books issued by the publishers of the day, the type supply could not have been worse.

In 1716, William Caslon, who had been previously apprenticed to a London engraver of gunlocks and barrels, set up a shop of his own in which he did similar work; also silver chasing and the cutting of binders' gilding tools and letter stamps. Under the patronage of William Bowyer, Caslon undertook typefounding, the first font which we know he cut being an Arabic. Other faces were added, and in 1734, when his first specimen sheet was issued, we find him with the equipment of a complete foundry. His types met with immediate success.

To the question, "What is the best type for all purposes which has been designed from the beginning of printing until the present day?" there can be no uncertain answer. The type is that designed and cut by William Caslon. It can be used for years for all purposes without palling on the taste. One American printer, who was among

WILLIAM CASLON.

AN ENGRAVED PORTRAIT OF WILLIAM CASLON.

the first to establish a reputation for fine and forceful composition in the field of commercial printing, had for many years nothing in his cases but Caslon. And his work never lacked sparkle and spontaneity. The type is today, in spite of all the good faces now available, still the dependable standby of advertising typographers. Caslon is, too, as good a book type as has ever been produced. It is legible in the highest degree, yet is not monotonous in color.

What is the reason for this undisputed supremacy? I think the secret lies in the stress placed comparatively, in the mind of the designer, on legibility and beauty. When we seek legibility only, we obtain a readable type which is stupid and monotonous; when we seek alone beauty of form, we obtain a type of great charm in individual letter forms but tiring in mass, because the element of design is too consciously apparent. In Caslon we have the product of a master designer who made drawing the servant of readability rather than its master.

Caslon's type could not be regarded as an entirely original creation on the part of its designer. It represented a synthesis of the best elements in the letter designs of the Dutch founders. But in adopting the best features of the Dutch types Caslon went further, putting into his design a spirit and virility that makes his types far greater than the models on which they were based. The reason for the difference is simple: William Caslon was a master of surpassing genius rather than a mere craftsman. That genius has left an influence on typography which seems destined never to be effaced.

The bright particular star in Italian typefounding history was Giambattista Bodoni, whose work has already been discussed (see pages 386-389). He drew his inspiration in typeface design from the Didots and in typographic ornament from Fournier *le jeune*. His types, characterized by a mechanical draftsmanship, with radical contrast in weight between main strokes and hairlines, and fine

straight-line serifs, are brilliant but dazzling in effect. They may be seen in the title page reproduced on page 387.

In Germany, almost up until the end of the nineteenth century, there was practically no type designing of permanent significance or interest to Anglo-Saxons, or, for that matter, to those Teutons who believe that the alphabet represented in Fraktur or Schwabacher is doomed to yield to the roman alphabet, because of the superior legibility of the latter. Several efforts were made toward reforming the design of Fraktur, notably that of Johann Friedrich Unger toward the end of the eighteenth century. But the traditional German typeface persisted in popular use.

In the last fifty years the popularity of the roman alphabet has increased notably in Germany. There seemed to be no difference in impartial opinion as to its greater readability. The scientific journals and books led in its adoption. The distinguished German type designers of recent years, such as Walter Tiemann, F. H. Ehmcke, Emil Rudolf Weiss, Rudolf Koch, and others, devoted their best efforts to the creation of many original and distinguished roman alphabets. Jacob Erbar, Paul Renner, Rudolf Koch, and others made an epochal contribution to publicity printing by the design of the geometric sans-serif typefaces demanded by the school of modern typography, already discussed. The next development was the flat-serif typefaces, which proved more legible than the sans-serifs. Among the names figuring in recent annals of German type design are those of Imre Reiner and Heinrich Jost.

The trend in Germany toward the adoption of roman types for book and magazine printing has, however, received two formidable setbacks. The first occurred at the time of the World War, when the Kaiser called upon printers and publishers to return to the truly German types of their forefathers. More recently the Hitler régime has exerted potent influence in favor of a return to the use of the

nationalistic Fraktur typefaces. We may be confident, however, that the moot question of *Fraktur oder Antiqua* will be settled eventually on sound principles of optics.

In England, apart from a number of admirable typefaces developed for the use of the private presses, the important developments of recent years have been in the field of book types. Among the productions of the Lanston Monotype Corporation, we think first of the important revivals—Poliphilus, Blado italic, Bembo, Fournier, Baskerville, Bell, Bulmer, and others. Among the original typefaces produced by this competent organization are two by that outstanding British artist, Eric Gill—Perpetua, a bookface, and Gill Sans, the modern type most popular in England for advertising composition. Another face recut for the recent lectern Bible designed by the American Bruce Rogers is a recutting of that designer's Centaur. Pastonchi, designed by Professor Eduardo Cotti, is another recent production of merit.

The British company manufacturing the linotype has had the benefit of typographic advice by that genial and gifted London printer "at the sign of the Dolphin," the late George W. Jones. Under his direction was produced Granjon, the most successful of faces for text composition available to the printer of today. It is the face in which the present volume is set, so the reader will already have had opportunity to judge for himself how easy it is to read and how well it wears. Personally, I know of no typeface which rates higher on these counts. I once told Mr. Jones that Granjon appeared to me to be fifty per cent Garamond and fifty per cent Caslon. He replied: "Your diagnosis is just about correct." Certainly he drew on sound precedents! A later typeface produced by the same organization is Estienne. Few typefaces of outstanding merit have been produced by British typefoundries in recent years.

In the United States there has been more activity in the pro-

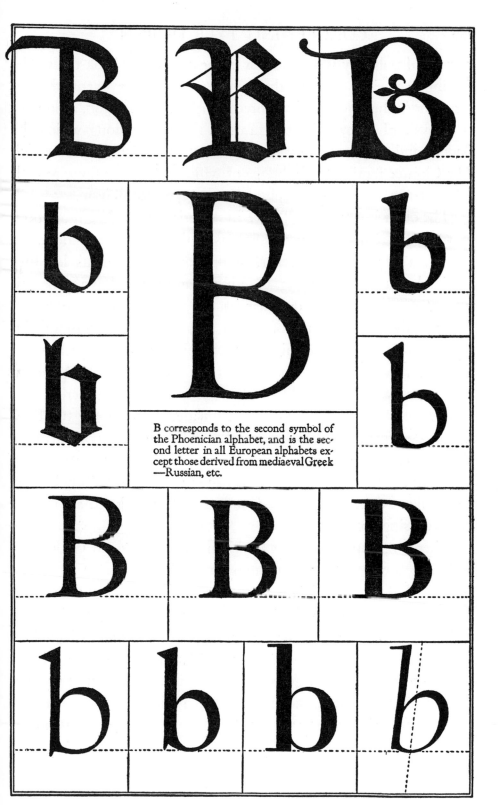

B corresponds to the second symbol of the Phoenician alphabet, and is the second letter in all European alphabets except those derived from mediaeval Greek —Russian, etc.

INTERPRETATIONS OF THE LETTER B BY FREDERIC W. GOUDY.

duction of publicity types and less in the creation of book faces. The leading American typefoundry began, early in the twentieth century, under the able technical direction of Morris Benton, a number of revivals of noteworthy typefaces of the past, among which the Bodoni and Garamond families stand out as particularly successful. The Cloister family, the lightface of which is a prime favorite with John Henry Nash, was inspired by the types of Jenson.

The other important influence in American type design has been exerted by a remarkable native genius in the person of Frederic W. Goudy, a Chicago bookkeeper, whose tastes and talents led him inevitably into typefounding. Goudy has a gift for drawing beautiful letters second to no designer of this or any other generation. He recently designed his hundredth type face. Of outstanding interest and charm is one of his earliest, the Village type, which is still held as a private face. His most important face, beyond all question, is Kennerley, a completely original design with a superb italic. Goudy Oldstyle is probably the most widely used of the typefaces he has designed, being a highly acceptable face, the popularity of which has been increased by the addition of bold and other versions, produced by the typefoundry, in the design of which Goudy had no part. One of these adaptations, Goudy Bold, has enjoyed a wide use in advertising composition.

There are numerous other beautiful typefaces which Goudy has designed, among the more important being Italian Old Style, Goudy Modern, Hadriano, Forum capitals, and Deepdene. But, perhaps because of Goudy's irresistible urge to draw beautiful letters, the emphasis on beauty has prejudiced their complete legibility. Many Goudy types have been and will be used in privately printed books set in relatively large point sizes, and his types work successfully in magazine heads, advertising display lines, and so forth. But there are few six-hundred page novels set in Goudy's types and no

dictionaries or encyclopedias. All this simply indicates that Goudy's genius is great but not universal.

A demonstration of Frederic Goudy's versatility may be seen in the page from his book, *The Alphabet,* reproduced on page 581, showing a variety of treatments of the letter *B*. This illustration also provides an object lesson in the possible range of type design.

Other recent American contributions to type design are largely in the field of publicity types. The late Oswald Cooper met one important need. R. Hunter Middleton has designed for the Ludlow a number of highly successful modern and traditional typefaces. The most important typefaces lately produced for book composition have been Electra and Caledonia, both designed for the linotype by W. A. Dwiggins, and Fairfield, designed by the distinguished wood engraver, Rudolph Ruzicka.

Almost all the American composing-machine companies have produced satisfactory versions of the various standard book faces, such as Jenson, Caslon, Garamond, Bodoni, Baskerville, and so forth. It is on these, and on the recent British-produced faces, that American book printers currently depend.

When we consider recent type design in its relation to the composition of books, the conclusion is inescapable that practically all the important achievements are to be found in the revivals of outstanding typefaces produced by the punch-cutters of the past.

XLII

The Printer's Ideals

IN the chapters preceding, we have endeavored to trace, albeit briefly, the efforts of man, from the beginning down to the present time, to make permanent record of his achievements and aspirations, of his loves and hates, and of the widely varying opinions which have been the fruit of his thinking. Most of the record which has come within our own knowledge has been in the form of books. The supreme importance of the book to the development—in the past, present, or future—of either the individual or the race has been pointed out and needs here no further emphasis.

The approach to the problems of bookmaking has been historical, and we believe rightly so, for the bookmaking practice of any period has been based in large degree on the experience of the past, with a more or less generous admixture of originality—contributed by printers of various countries at different times. It seems likely that we shall continue to draw heavily on the experience of past generations in the planning and production of books. It behooves us only to keep alert and to be hospitable at all times to ideas for improving styles and methods of bookmaking.

In the course of our discussion we have considered in some detail many of the elements entering into the making of a book. It is important that we should have an intelligent understanding of these elements. But it is more essential that we should understand and acknowledge the supreme importance of coherence of all the elements. For only when all the elements interfit perfectly do we achieve a sound structure of the whole.

The modern school of design has taught us one approach to the planning of any product on which we may confidently depend. This requires first that we analyze the function, and next that we permit the functional requirements thus developed to control, without question, the design of the product. There can be no argument as to the soundness of such a procedure.

The first object of our thought, then, will be the average reader. Our duty to consult his needs, tastes, and comfort works to our own advantage also, for it is the ever widening circle of average readers who buy books and pay indirectly the living of authors, illustrators, papermakers, printers, and binders.

If we set up the average reader as the patron we shall strive to please, we automatically exclude from our practical conception of the ideal book the various precious or monumental volumes which many eminent printers have delighted to produce. We must regard these museum pieces as hothouse products, off the main stream of a busy world's bookmaking. In setting these volumes aside, however, in a niche of their own as exhibits of bookmaking history, we must do honor to the inspiration and enthusiasm of their makers, many of whose improvements in typefaces and printing styles have been appropriated to advantage by printers of books intended to serve exceedingly practical uses. We cannot forget that the idealistic printers of many impractical books have done much to inspire higher standards of workaday production.

When we come to observe and record the need, convenience, and comfort of the average reader, there can be little conflict between the findings of different investigators. My own report would be that the average reader demands a book easy and comfortable to read, easy and comfortable to handle, and easy and comfortable to purchase. Whatever of beauty, grace, and verve we can superadd to these primary functional demands will contribute to the interest

and attractiveness of the volume. These are simple requirements to state, but they are likely to prove more difficult of fulfillment than of formulation.

The demand for ease and comfort of reading calls first for a well-designed typeface, free of affectation or labored drawing, which we can read for hours on end without undue fatigue. The best typefaces are those having a design of which we are not sensible. As Beatrice Warde has so aptly put it, type for extended text composition should be "invisible." These requirements narrow down our choice to the simplest typefaces, most of which have successfully stood the test of time.

The type design selected should be used in a size large enough to be read with ease under average lighting, or worse, by readers of average acuity of eyesight, or worse. If we make our selection according to the functioning of a specially effective pair of young eyes, under a reading lamp behind the desk, casting ample light over the left shoulder, we prejudice the interests of many readers with older eyes who may try to read our book on a street car or railroad train. It will always be safe to err on the side of greater reader comfort.

The design of the book will limit the width of the type page to a sensible measure, so that the eye may take in the span without undue difficulty, and we will make sure that there is enough white space or "leading" between lines to direct the eye back from the end of one line to the beginning of the next without possibility of confusion. We will keep the spacing between words and between sentences reasonably snug, but will avoid the ridiculous and nonfunctional extremes to which some alleged fine printers have gone in the effort to achieve close spacing. When it is difficult for a reader to tell where one word ends and another begins, or where one sentence leaves off and the next one starts, we have passed

beyond the sphere of good printing into the lunatic fringe of indefensible affectation.

Realizing that the "lower case" or small letters are more readable than lines set entirely in capitals, we will avoid the latter so far as we can in chapter heads, subheads, and the like.

The usual break between paragraphs, with one line ending short and the following line slightly indented, provides to the eye of the reader a "pause that refreshes." An editor who permits copy to run on and on in long unbroken paragraphs is taking a great risk of losing the interest of the reader.

Books for study or reference should be as liberally provided with signposts in the way of subheads, and so forth, as the well-marked highway. It is easy for an editor to put in these aids to the reader, who will not fail to appreciate them. An adequate, well set-up index is another *sine qua non* of sound bookmaking whenever the subject-matter indicates the need.

While not a feature of design, sound proofreading is certainly a feature of workmanlike production. The book without a typographic error is difficult if not impossible of accomplishment, but every self-respecting printer will strive to make books as free as possible from obvious and annoying misprints. I confess to writing this statement with no inconsiderable trepidation, trusting hopefully that no typographical error will creep into this very page!

After our type pages are set, we will make sure that margins of a book in the traditional style are properly proportioned. The accepted relationship is for the margin toward the binding edge or gutter to be the narrowest, with the margins to the top, outer edge, and bottom of the page increasing progressively. Should we be planning a book along modern non-traditional lines, there is wider latitude in the arrangement of margins, but designers of modest ability will do well to stick to the time-tried style.

After we have achieved a legible setting of type pages, it is essential, if we are to safeguard the legibility at which we aim, that the pages be printed sharply and clearly in good black ink, with a uniform color and strength of impression maintained throughout the book. More well-designed and well-set volumes have been disqualified from consideration in bookmaking contests for poor presswork than for any other cause.

Book presswork may seem simple, but it is not; and the pressman who can print type forms with just the right amount of ink and the proper degree of impression, and maintain these factors constant, is the exception rather than the rule. The fraternity of American pressmen have come to look on halftone forms or process color printing with respect, as being truly worthy of their skill, dismissing a chase of book pages with the contemptuous remark that it is "only a type form."

If our finished book is to be a workmanlike product the pages must be accurately "lined up" before printing, so that the pages will face each other accurately when the sheets are folded. It is essential, too, that the pages printed on the second side of the sheet shall "back up" accurately the pages first printed. The precision of back-up, page for page and line for line, achieved in some continental pressrooms would prove a revelation to many American pressmen, should they take the trouble to examine some carefully produced European books. It is only fair to say, however, that the better American book-printing plants have effected a notable improvement in the quality of presswork during the last decade.

Recognition of words in reading reaches the maximum of efficiency when type is printed in an intense but dull black on white paper. Whenever the contrast is reduced, either by graying the ink or tinting the paper, or both, we must face the realization that legibility is to some extent jeopardized. This loss can be compensated

for by an increase in the size and weight of the type, but the safest formula for book printing calls for black ink on white paper.

We next come to our average reader's demand for a book easy and comfortable to handle. This brings up considerations of size, weight, paper stock, and binding, regarding all of which decisions must be made.

The dimensions of a book will turn largely on the character of the manuscript. If the book is one to be read for pleasure, the volume should be kept within such range of size as can be held comfortably in the hand. As Aldus once learned to make, for the convenience of the reader, small books instead of ponderous folios, so can many of our better printers advantageously reduce the magnificent but unwieldy dimensions of some of the volumes they produce. If, on the other hand, we have to deal with a scientific monograph requiring large-scale illustrations, which will in practical use be consulted on a desk or reading table, the size of the volume may quite properly be radically increased. Here again function can and should control the form to be adopted.

The weight of the book to be held in the hand and read for pleasure is a feature of importance, the possibilities of which we have failed to appreciate. It will require no labored argument to prove that such a book should be as light as possible. British publishers achieve light weight in popular books through the use of light papers made from the esparto grass, which appears to be grown exclusively in Spain and northern Africa. In the United States "high-bulking" papers are used almost universally by publishers, not because anyone likes them, but because the public seems to have fallen into the habit of judging the market value of a book by its physical bulk. Since publishers must live, improvement in this particular can be expected only from the public's expressed willingness to pay as much for a small convenient-to-handle book with a given

literary content as for a clumsy "stuffed-shirt" presentation of the same text in artificially bulked-up form. The least indication of a change of heart in this connection on the part of book-buyers would encourage publishers to abandon a practice which is distressing to everyone concerned with the production of books.

Not alone does bulking paper produce froth without substance, but its spongy and porous formation puts sharp and clear presswork almost beyond the bounds of possibility. The best printing can be done on paper of solid, even texture, with a surface relatively smooth, but not so smooth as to make it shiny.

What quality of paper should be used? Here is a knotty problem indeed, for we must reconcile the ideal with the practical. All-rag paper is acknowledged to be the best, especially so far as permanence is concerned, but it often costs ten times as much per pound as another paper, made from cheaper materials, which is entirely acceptable from the viewpoint of appearance.

We hear a good deal today about the quick disintegration of modern papers; such discussion relates mostly to newsprint, which is made of ground wood and is not designed to last. The cheapest book papers will discolor in five or ten years, but a fair grade of paper, sold at a price within the budget of the average book publisher, will last long enough, in good condition, for most practical purposes. For the printing of a text which is likely to be consulted for the next two hundred years, a permanent all-rag paper should be used. But most novels will go out of circulation before the paper on which they are printed begins to discolor, and many books of other character become obsolete almost before the ink with which they are printed has a good chance to dry. A handbook of aviation mechanics need not last very long, because ten successively revised and rewritten editions will have appeared before the paper of the first printing turns yellow. I think reasonable people will agree that

it is sensible to have books of ephemeral usefulness produced at a cost which justifies prices the reader can afford to pay.

Perhaps we can here take a leaf from the experience of several important daily newspapers which print a small number of each issue on all-rag paper for preservation by libraries. This is a wise move, for the newspaper provides an historical record of primary importance which should be permanently preserved.

The greatest complaints about book papers come also from libraries, where books are used not by one reader but by hundreds. Under this strain it is natural that books manufactured primarily for the individual reader should go to pieces. The newspapers have suggested a solution: that a special library edition of important and even of unimportant books should be printed on rag paper and specially bound. The libraries could well afford to pay the extra cost of materials, for it would amount to less than the present cost of replacement copies. This special library edition, which might be run first, could also be bought by collectors of first editions.

It appears today that the problem of permanent preservation of material which is essentially ephemeral is likely to be solved by photographing it on microfilm. This film requires for storage but an infinitesimal fraction of the space required for shelving newspaper files and sets of books. Technical developments in this field are being made rapidly, and the "filmbook" appears to have important possibilities.

One of the essentials to comfortable reading of any printed book is that it shall open easily and stay open. Fortunately, the prevailing practice of sewing even the least expensive books meets this requirement, when there are not too many pages in a signature and when the paper used is not too stiff. It is important, however, that the "grain" of the paper, which runs the length of the papermaking machine, should run parallel with the binding edge of the book.

Most books which will not lie flat when opened are printed on paper with the grain in the wrong direction.

To be of true importance in the work of the world, books must be read, and as a condition precedent thereto they must be sold. This injects into the planning problem certain economic considerations. For if good bookmaking is to become and continue possible, books must be produced at a cost within reason and sold at a price within reason, and yet yield to the publisher a profit which will justify his investment in brains and money—with the emphasis, if you please, on the first-named ingredient. Fortunately, fine bookmaking from the point of view of artistry does not necessarily mean expensive bookmaking, but it does demand something approaching genius in planning, and infinite pains in supervising production.

The average printer has little conception of the care required to produce a fine book. In this connection I always think of the motto chosen by Walter Gilliss as a rule of work as well as to embody his printer's mark: "Trifles make perfection, but perfection is no trifle." For a memorial volume in honor of Gilliss, which I endeavored to print in a format which he would have approved, Dr. John H. Finley deftly wove this motto into these lines of affectionate tribute:

> For his enduring epitaph we take
> His Printer's Motto, set in jeweled ring:
> *Though little things perfection make*
> *Perfection is no little thing.*

But while we strive for perfection, we can do so along sensible and efficient lines. The theorists do a great deal of talking about the degradation incident to machine production. It is beyond denial that the change from a hand to a mechanical method of production generally results at first in lower standards of execution. But as the machine process becomes perfected, the printers interested in a high standard of work can regain that standard in machine operation.

In presswork, for example, I can see no characteristic in hand-press printing which cannot be obtained with careful and competent operation of a modern power press. The first type composition by mechanical process was of poor quality indeed, but there can now be produced by machine excellent typesetting, in faces of good design, well spaced and well cast. And the difference in cost between setting body matter by hand and machine is, of course, spectacular.

In one day's reading I recently ran across statements of two opinions on this question which were so diametrically opposed as to be startling. I cannot resist the temptation to quote them both here. The first was written by Hans Mardersteig in his excellent book on the aims and work of the Officina Bodoni, now at Verona, Italy, which has produced many fine books:

Just as in all other arts and crafts which were the bearers of an old tradition, so did the invention of machinery imply the destruction of the art of printing. The printing of books became a set, commercial affair, in fact a mechanical achievement. Men like William Morris, Charles Ricketts, T. J. Cobden-Sanderson, Emery Walker and others, artists or men imbued with noble culture and a far-reaching education were the saviors of this chaotic period in which the mechanic determined the artistic level of typography. These men returned to the hand-press and by hand labor, comparable only to that of the earliest printers, they regained a lost territory for art. Once more books were produced which from their conception down to the last detail of their material completion were the outcome of one idea and animated by one and the same spirit. The work of those Englishmen sounded an alarm to the whole world, did indeed meet with response in a few countries, and it is essential that their labor shall be fructified and kept alive. The book in its highest achievement must always be a work of art, and the instrument with which such an aim may undoubtedly best be achieved is the hand-press.

The other was written by a brilliant English author, Aldous Huxley, a man concerned with the writing rather than the manu-

facture of books, but apparently seeing clearly the principles that must control the effective distribution of modern literature. Huxley wrote in *Printing of To-Day* this pungent comment:

The problem which confronts the contemporary printer may be briefly stated as follows: to produce beautiful and modern print-patterns by means of labor-saving machinery. There have been numerous attempts in recent years to improve the quality of printing. But of these attempts too many have been made in the wrong spirit. Instead of trying to exploit modern machinery, many artistic printers have rejected it altogether and reverted to the primitive methods of an earlier age. Instead of trying to create new forms of type and decoration, they have imitated the styles of the past. This prejudice in favor of hand-work and ancient decorative forms was the result of an inevitable reaction against the soulless ugliness of nineteenth-century industrialism. Machines were producing beastliness. It was only natural that sensitive men should have wished to abandon the use of machines and to return to the artistic conventions in vogue before the development of machinery. It has become obvious that the machine is here to stay. Whole armies of William Morrises and Tolstoys could not now expel it. Even in primitive India it has proved itself too strong for those who would, with Gandhi, resist its encroachments. The sensible thing to do is not to revolt against the inevitable, but to use and modify it, to make it serve your purposes. Machines exist; let us then exploit them to create beauty—a modern beauty, while we are about it. For we live in the twentieth century; let us frankly admit it and not pretend that we live in the fifteenth. The work of the backward-looking hand-printers may be excellent in its way; but its way is not the contemporary way. Their books are often beautiful, but with a borrowed beauty expressive of nothing in the world in which we happen to live. They are also, as it happens, so expensive, that only the very rich can afford to buy them. The printer who makes a fetish of hand-work and medieval craftsmanship, who refuses to tolerate the machine or to make any effort to improve the quality of its output, thereby condemns the ordinary reader to a perpetuity of ugly printing. As an ordinary reader, who cannot afford to buy hand-made books, I object to the archaizing printer. It is only from the man with the machine that I can hope for any amelioration of my lot as a reader.

It seems to me that the book artist of the present and future should take advantage of the economies of mechanical processes, while insisting upon a high standard of product. When men of real ability turn their attention to obtaining the best work by the most effective means, real progress will surely result. The cause of fine bookmaking will not be served by a stupid and unthinking loyalty to antiquated production methods.

In our formula for a book to meet the needs and wishes of the average reader, beauty, grace, and verve were specified as plus values greatly to be desired after the purely functional demands have been met. Certainly a degree of charm will make soundly planned books more attractive and pleasant to read and handle. Functional considerations will prevent us from making bad books, but to make great books we must pass the boundary of negative rules and give rein to creative abilities.

Some extremists may urge that, since the purpose of books is to be read, any features which do not promote legibility are excrescences and tend to diminish rather than increase the merit of the book. That a book unfitted to its purpose is wrong, and that an illegible book is pernicious, all will be ready to admit. It is further true that a logically planned book, like a logically planned building, has in it many elements of beauty. But these principles alone will not suffice to produce the best books of which we are capable. Were they carried to their logical conclusion, we would never have an initial letter, a headband, a border, a decoration on a title page, a touch of color, or any of the gracious features which can contribute so largely to make a book charming.

In many books, beauty is an end in itself to be sought beyond strict fitness to purpose. This statement implies that there are some books in which beauty is a desideratum and others in which charm is not a factor of material importance. When we attempt a classi-

fication, the distinction appears to lie between a work of utility only and a work of literary art. Even the most enthusiastic typographer could hardly summon much enthusiasm for the embellishment of a dictionary or a trade directory or a cable code book, though he might be sincerely interested in their sound typographical design. For works of this character, legibility and convenience of consultation may well be the features exclusively sought.

But when we turn to works of creative literary art—novels, poetry, essays, and the like—a different situation prevails. It is not essential to the physical actualities of life that such books should be read. They are read for pleasure: for gratification of our artistic perceptions. They are, in other words, food for the spirit. Can we not then enjoy them esthetically at the same time, not only for the text we read, but also for the beauty of their appearance, which we likewise perceive through our eyes? I think so. I believe it is a crying shame that so much beautiful literature of the present day comes to us in such unesthetic form as it does.

The object of any work of art is to evoke an emotion. Does a poem of real significance run a better chance of gaining its object when it comes to us in the crowded columns of a newspaper, or when the page is not only clear typographically, but beautiful as well? We react to art not through one sense at a time. It is on rare occasions that we can see a work of art in any medium, independent of its environment. We absorb unconsciously other impressions than those gained from the object nominally holding our attention.

This certainly is true of books, or so many people would not appreciate finely made books. And it is worthy of note that the modern books most in favor with present-day booklovers are not those of the severely plain school, but those to which the creative fancy of the designer has made a contribution. As a picture frame executed by a master of the framing art can help present a great

oil painting more favorably than when the canvas is stretched bare over its frame, so can the artist in bookmaking present to the reader a literary composition in a setting favorable to its esthetic appreciation and enjoyment.

Then there is the element of variety. I do not believe in standardization in book plan or design. There is in progress a crusade to effect standardization in the sizes of printed matter. Such a course deadens interest and increases monotony. In other applied arts we have decided that standardization is depressing. In architecture, we do not design all houses of the same shape and size. In town planning and landscape work we endeavor to attain variety rather than uniformity. I believe the same principles apply to book design.

The unofficial standardization of novel format, I must confess, annoys me. I should find refreshing a novel a little taller or a little wider or a little thinner than usual. I believe publishers would find it worth while occasionally to break away from the standard and do a bit of pioneering. Individuality is surely a desideratum. Just so long as a book does not become freakish, the more it has in the way of personality the better.

We can conceive of a committee of experts in typography and book design meeting in council and determining upon the most logical form for the novel. They might fix, by common consent, on a good type-page size, the paper size, the face and size of type in which the text should be set. They could select the type for chapter headings, running heads, and the like. Basing their decisions wholly on functional considerations, they would eschew decoration. Let us then presume that publishers adopted this as a standard novel format. I can conceive reading the first novel in this form and appreciating its legibility and the logic of its plan. When I had read the fourth novel so standardized in format I should be losing some appreciation of its merits, and after the twentieth I am sure I would

wish the twenty-first were printed in red ink! No, there are other desiderata than legibility in reading purposed for esthetic enjoyment.

The appreciation of charmingly designed books being so general among readers, it seems probable that more effort could profitably be devoted to make more attractive books of wide trade circulation. It would be so simple to lend a little more grace to the average novel, and the effort would be all in the composition. Paper can remain cheap, cloth inexpensive, yet with a little more thought given to tasteful design, a book can be made charming instead of bleak. I believe, therefore, in good book decoration, sparingly but feelingly used. I believe in putting more into books than the bare demands of fitness to purpose. Sound in kind and right in measure, decoration will add to the beauty of widely read books. It will make them more worthy the attention of those accustomed to high standards of artistry in other objects of daily use. It will make them more pleasing to read. It will sell more books.

A title page offers special opportunity for a graceful touch in the way of picture or ornament. The copy on the modern title page is usually brief, and after this is set in type ample space remains for other use. Too much decoration is, of course, worse than none at all; but a little, tastefully applied, is generally a help, except in cases where the subject and character of the book demand severity and simplicity of treatment.

The binding of modern books offers a wide range of opportunity to the book designer. Here again I would consider variety and individuality to be cardinal virtues. In the past, books have looked too much alike and, in general, have been too drab. Binding cloths are available in a wide range of subdued or lively colors, finished or unfinished, in considerable variety of texture. Decorative binding cloths are beginning to appear in Europe and it is only a matter of time when they will come into use here. Meanwhile, a few enter-

prising publishers have begun the interesting experiment of printing, by the offset process, illustration or decoration directly on the binding cloth. A number of publishers have used decorative papers to cover the boards of the binding. Many of these papers are charming. The only drawback is that paper over board sides makes a much less durable binding; though, with a cloth backbone, the result is fairly satisfactory. In the book proper the binding is often the gayest feature so far as color and design are concerned.

In present-day commercial book design there is one feature in the conception of which fancy can run riot: the jacket. The attractiveness of the jacket is known to have an important influence on the sale of the book, for the volume is clothed in its jacket when it stands on the table or shelf of the bookseller. Naturally, a jacket which arrests attention runs a far better chance of being, in the first instance, inspected and, in the second instance, sold, than a jacket which plays the part of the shrinking violet among its neighbors.

It is encouraging to report that more and more trade books, sound in legibility and in standards of manufacture, and possessed in addition of the precious assets of individuality and charm, are coming from the presses each year. Bookmaking standards have improved more in the last fifteen years than in any preceding half century. Many talented designers are devoting their attention exclusively to the planning of books, better typefaces are becoming available for machine composition, more pressrooms are setting up workmanlike standards of printing.

It finally remains to point out that we are in the midst of a veritable renaissance in book illustration. The newspaper rotogravure sections started public appreciation of and interest in pictures, the daily newspapers played up news photographs, and the new and successful picture magazines have capped the pictorial climax. Meanwhile the art of the photographer has kept pace with the demand.

The public interest in pictures has likewise made itself felt in the book-publishing field, and the services of many able artists have been drafted to enliven books with interesting and vital illustrations, as has already been pointed out. It seems likely that more and more books of general interest will be illustrated.

First-rate contemporary writing is, I believe, the meat into which the best book printers of the present day should sink their teeth. It seems to me a depressing anomaly that, with isolated exceptions, our best printing talent is devoted to the reprinting of standard texts already available in dozens of more or less satisfactory editions. This accounts for many finely printed books being placed promptly and permanently on the shelves, after one examination, by the purchasers of their typography and illustrations. The weakness of the private presses and of printers working in the private-press tradition is that instead of putting into type new and significant manuscripts, they spend their energy in bringing out the ninety-seventh printing of *A Sentimental Journey* or the forty-ninth of *The Scarlet Letter*. At the same time, the best of our contemporary literature is being printed in exceedingly shoddy form. It is encouraging, however, to note that when original writing of merit is made into a finely printed book, its market value often reflects the potency of this praiseworthy alliance.

A large audience is an inspiration to any public speaker. In just the same way, thousands of prospective readers should prove an inspiration to a book designer to give these readers the best that it is possible for him to achieve in functional effectiveness and beauty of form, within practical limitations of cost.

In the manuscript of an outstanding novel, or able biography, or some distinguished work of non-fiction, I see a challenge to our highest abilities in book design and production to make contemporary books of the greatest human significance the best exemplars

of the bookmaking art. We must not and shall not fail to rise to this great opportunity.

Books were not made more beautiful by the invention of printing, the five-hundredth anniversary of which is upon us; but by the use of the new process beautiful books were produced in quantity and, through wider consequent circulation, became—instead of decorations on the shelves of the wealthy and powerful—vital forces in molding the thought of the people. From this precedent is logically derived the objective we have stated: the fine making of common books. Is not this an ambition to challenge the imagination of the bookmaker of idealism?

Bibliographies

S INCE this volume undertakes to present a consecutive account of the historical development and present status of printing and book-making, rather than a series of technical monographs on various aspects of the subject, a series of notes compiled during the examination of the many authorities consulted is omitted for practical reasons. But fairly complete bibliographical references to source material on the subjects dealt with in the chapters of this book are appended, for the benefit of those who may wish to devote further study to any particular features of bookmaking history or practice.

On one point, however, I wish to report here some supplementary information. On page 116 of the text, in Chapter VIII, there is a brief reference to an important piece of evidence which I had only recently seen. After this chapter had been made up in page form, during a visit to the Henry E. Huntington Library in San Marino, California, my attention was directed by Mr. Roland O. Baughman to an exceedingly interesting manuscript volume illustrated with woodcuts which were not tipped in but were integral parts of the volume. This *Beichtbüchlein* (HM 195) is a manuscript on vellum of 159 leaves, with 18 woodcut illustrations, the printing of which "was obviously done in collaboration with the scribe." It was written and printed at Nonnberg in Salzburg, Austria, *circa* 1435, and is known from the place of its production as the Nonnberg Passion. Its date is determined from two inscriptions in the text—one, 1433, on fol. 53; the other, 1435, on fol. 70. Authorities who have seen the woodcuts agree that 1435 is a sound dating for the blocks.

This volume cannot be regarded as a chiroxylographic block book, but it certainly represents a stage in the transition from the manuscript book, through the chiroxylographic block book like the *Exercitium super Pater Noster* (described on page 116), to the block book proper in which both the text and the illustrations were printed from woodblocks. It is thus of great importance to the history of bookmaking and will well repay further study.

For full information regarding the Nonnberg Passion I am indebted to Mr. Reginald B. Haselden, the distinguished curator of manuscripts of the Henry E. Huntington Library.

Chapter I: PRIMITIVE HUMAN RECORDS

BARTON, GEORGE A. [A note on the "monuments Blau"], *Journal of the American Oriental Society,* Vol. 22, 1901, pp. 118-126.

———. "Interpretation of the archaic tablet of the E. A. Hoffman collection," *Journal of the American Oriental Society,* Vol. 23, 1902, pp. 21-28.

BREASTED, JAMES HENRY. "The physical processes of writing in the early Orient and their relation to the origin of the alphabet," *American Journal of Semitic Languages and Literatures,* Vol. 32, 1916, pp. 230-249.

CLAY, ALBERT TOBIAS. Documents from the temple archives of Nippur. The Babylonian Expedition of the University of Pennsylvania, Series A: Cuneiform Texts, Vol. 14, 1906, pp. 17-20.

EVANS, ARTHUR JOHN. "The European diffusion of primitive pictography and its bearing on the origin of script," in *Anthropology and the Classics* (R. R. Marett, editor), Oxford, 1908, pp. 9-43.

———. *Scripta Minoa.* Oxford, 1909.

FAULMANN, KARL. *Illustrierte Geschichte der Schrift.* Leipzig, 1880.

GARDINER, ALAN HENDERSON. "The nature and development of the Egyptian hieroglyphic writing," *Journal of Egyptian Archaeology,* Vol. 2, 1915, pp. 61-75.

HEMPL, GEORGE. "The genesis of European alphabetic writing," in his *Mediterranean Studies* (edited by Frederick Anderson), Stanford University Publications, Language and Literature, Vol. 5, No. 1, 1930.

HUMPHREYS, HENRY NOEL. *The Origin and Progress of the Art of Writing.* London, 1853.

JENSEN, HANS. *Geschichte der Schrift.* Hannover, 1925.

LAYARD, AUSTEN HENRY. *Monuments of Nineveh,* Vol. V, London, 1853.

MASON, WILLIAM A. *A History of the Art of Writing.* New York, 1920.

MÖLLER, GEORG C. *Hieratische Palaeographie.* Vol. 1. Leipzig, 1927, pp. 4-7.

PETRIE, WILLIAM MATHEW FLINDERS. "The royal tombs of the First Dynasty," Part 1. *Memoirs of the Egypt Exploration Fund,* No. 18, 1900, pp. 31-32.

VAN HOESEN, HENRY BARTLETT. "History of Writing," in Van Hoesen and Walter, *Bibliography, Practical, Enumerative, Historical.* New York, 1928, pp. 259-315.

WARD, WILLIAM HAYES. [A note on the "thin greenish stone belonging to Dr. A. Blau, said to have been obtained near Warka"], *Proceedings of the American Oriental Society,* October, 1885, p. lix.

WEICHBERGER, KONRAD. "Die minoischen Schriftzeichen," *Buch und Schrift,* Vol. 4, 1930, pp. 29-46.

WILLIAMS, HENRY SMITH. *Manuscripts, Inscriptions and Muniments, Oriental, Classical, Medieval and Modern, Comprehending the History of the Art of Writing.* London and New York, 1902. (Consists of four portfolios containing 228 facsimile reproductions.)

Chapter II: THE ORIGIN OF THE ALPHABET

BLEGEN, CARL W. "Inscriptions on geometric pottery from Hymettus," *American Journal of Archaeology,* Vol. 38, 1934, pp. 10-28.

BÖMER, ALOYS. "Die Schrift und ihre Entwicklung," *Handbuch der Bibliothekswissenschaft* (edited by Fritz Milkau), Vol. 1, Leipzig, 1931, pp. 27-149.

BUTIN, ROMAIN F. "The Serâbît inscriptions," *Harvard Theological Review,* Vol. 21, 1928, pp. 9-67.

——. "The protosinaitic inscriptions," *Harvard Theological Review,* Vol. 25, 1932, pp. 130-203.

CAPART, JEAN. "Quelques découvertes récentes rélative à l'histoire de l'alphabet," Académie Royale de Belgique, *Bulletin,* Classe des Lettres, 1920, pp. 408-421.

CARPENTER, RHYS. "The antiquity of the Greek alphabet," *American Journal of Archaeology,* Vol. 37, 1933, pp. 8-29.

——. "The Greek alphabet again," *idem,* Vol. 42, 1938, pp. 58-69.

CLODD, EDWARD. *The Story of the Alphabet.* New York, 1905.

DUNAND, MAURICE. "Nouvelle inscription découverte à Byblos," *Syria,* Vol. 11, 1930, pp. 1-10.

DUSSAUD, RENÉ. "Les inscriptions phéniciennes du tombeau d'Ahiram, roi de Byblos," *Syria,* Vol. 5, 1924, pp. 135-157.

EVANS, ARTHUR JOHN. "The palace of Knossos in its Egyptian relations," *Archaeological Report of the Egypt Exploration Fund,* 1899-1900, pp. 64-65.

FRIES, D. S. A. [Article in] *Zeitschrift des Palästina Vereins,* Vol. 22, 1900, pp. 118-126.

GARDINER, ALAN HENDERSON. "The Egyptian origin of the Semitic alphabet," *Journal of Egyptian Archaeology,* Vol. 3, 1916, pp. 1-16.

——. "The Sinai script and the origin of the alphabet," *Palestine Exploration Fund Quarterly Statement,* January, 1929, pp. 48-55.

GRIMME, HUBERT. "Die Südsemitische Schrift, ihr Wesen und ihre Entwicklung," *Buch und Schrift,* Vol. 4, 1930, pp. 19-27.

HARLAND, J. PENROSE. "Scripta Helladica," *American Journal of Archaeology,* Vol. 38, 1934, pp. 85-92.

HOMMEL, FRITZ. *Geschichte Babyloniens und Assyriens*. Berlin, 1885-1888.

KIRCHHOF, ADOLF. *Studien zur Geschichte des griechischen Alphabets*. 4th edition. Gütersloh, 1887.

MENTZ, ARTHUR. *Geschichte der griechisch-römischen Schrift bis zur Erfindung des Buchdrucks mit beweglichen Lettern*. Leipzig, 1920.

MERRIAM, AUGUSTUS C. "The law code of the Kretan Gortyna," *American Journal of Archaeology*, Vol. 1, 1885.

PETERS, JOHN P. "Notes on recent theories of the origin of the alphabet," *Journal of the American Oriental Society*, Vol. 22, 1901, pp. 177-198.

PETRIE, WILLIAM MATHEWS FLINDERS. "Résumé of recent investigations into the sources of the alphabet," *Journal of the Anthropological Institute*, Vol. 29, 1899, pp. 205-206.

———. "The formation of the alphabet," British School of Archaeology in Egypt, *Studies*, Vol. 3, 1912.

ROUGÉ, EMMANUEL, VICOMTE DE. *Mémoire sur l'origine egyptienne de l'alphabet phénicien*. Paris, 1874.

SCHMIDT, KURTZ. "Warum ABC? Der Ursprung unsrer Alphabetfolge, ein uraltes Misverständnis," *Buch und Schrift*, Vol. 5, 1931, pp. 47-50.

SETHE, KURT HEINRICH. *Der Ursprung des Alphabets; die neu entdeckte Sinai-schrift. Zwei Abhandlungen zur Entstehung unserer Schrift*. Neudruck aus den Nachrichten der Gesellschaft der Wissenschaften zu Göttingen, 1916-1917. Berlin, 1926.

SPRENGLING, MARTIN. "The alphabet, its rise and development from the Sinai inscriptions." Oriental Institute of the University of Chicago, *Communications*, No. 12, 1931.

STILLWELL, AGNES NEWHALL. "Eighth century B.C. inscriptions from Corinth," *American Journal of Archaeology*, Vol. 37, 1933, pp. 605-610.

STUBE, RUDOLF. *Ursprung des Alphabets und seine Entwicklung*. Berlin [1921].

TAYLOR, ISAAC. *The History of the Alphabet, an Account of the Origin and Development of Letters*. New edition. 2 volumes. New York, 1899.

TORREY, CHARLES C. "The Ahiram inscription of Byblos," *Journal of the American Oriental Society*, Vol. 45, 1925, pp. 269-279.

ULLMAN, BERTHOLD LOUIS. "The origin and development of the alphabet," *American Journal of Archaeology*, Vol. 31, 1927, pp. 311-328.

———. *Ancient Writing and Its Influence*. New York, 1932.

———. "How old is the Greek alphabet?" *American Journal of Archaeology,* Vol. 28, 1934, pp. 359-381.

ZIMMERN. "Zur Frage nach dem Ursprung des Alphabets," *Zeitschrift der deutschen morgenländischen Gesellschaft*, Vol. 50, 1896.

Chapter III: THE ALPHABET IN WESTERN EUROPE

ABBOTT, F. F. "The evolution of the modern forms of the letters of the alphabet," in *Society and Politics in Ancient Rome*. New York, 1909, pp. 234-259.

DEGERING, HERMANN. *Die Schrift*. Berlin, 1929. (A collection of 240 plates illustrating the Roman alphabet from the 6th century B.C. to the 18th century A.D.)

GRENIER, A. "L'alphabet de Marsiliana et les origines de l'écriture à Rome," École Française de Rome, *Mélanges d'archéologie et d'histoire*, Vol. 41, 1924, pp. 3-41.

HILL, GEORGE FRANCIS. *The Development of Arabic Numerals in Europe Exhibited in Sixty-four Tables*. Oxford, 1915.

LOWE, ELIAS AVERY. "Handwriting," in George Crump and E. F. Jacobs, *The Legacy of the Middle Ages*. Oxford, 1925, pp. 197-226.

STEFFENS, FRANZ. *Lateinische Paläographie*. Second edition. Trier, 1909. (Sheets of plates with transliterations and explanatory text.)

SULLIVAN, EDWARD. *The Book of Kells, described by Sir Edward Sullivan, bart., and illustrated with twenty-four plates in colours*. Third edition. London, 1927.

THOMPSON, EDWARD MAUNDE. *Introduction to Greek and Latin Palaeography*. Oxford, 1912.

ULLMAN, BERTHOLD LOUIS. "The Etruscan origin of the Roman alphabet and the names of the letters," *Classical Philology*, Vol. 22, 1927, pp. 372-377.

Chapter IV: PAPER AND ITS ORIGINS

BLUM, ANDRÉ. *On the Origin of Paper*. Translated from the French by Harry Miller Lydenberg. New York, 1934.

BOCKWITZ, HANS H. "Zur Kulturgeschichte des Papiers," Sonderdruck aus *Die Chronik der Feldmühle*, Festschrift der Feldmühle A. G., Stettin, 1935.

CARTER, THOMAS FRANCIS. *The Invention of Printing in China and Its Spread Westward*. New York, 1925. Chapter I, "The invention of paper."

CLAPPERTON, ROBERT HAMILTON. *Paper, an Historical Account of Its Making by Hand from the Earliest Times Down to the Present Day*. Oxford, 1934.

HUNTER, DARD. "Fifteenth century papermaking," *Ars Typographica*, Vol. 3, No. 1, July, 1926, pp. 37-51.

———. *Papermaking through Eighteen Centuries*. New York, 1930.

———. "The use and significance of the ancient watermarks," *Paper and Printing Digest*, February, 1937. (An extract from the author's *Papermaking*.)

LAUFER, BERTHOLD. *Paper and Printing in Ancient China*. Chicago, 1931.

SCHULTE, ALFRED. "Papiermühlen- und Wasserzeichenforschung," *Gutenberg Jahrbuch,* 1934, pp. 9-27.

[STEIN, HENRI]. "Fondation de papeteries près de Troyes au XV siècle," *Bibliographe moderne,* Vol. 5, 1901, pp. 412-419.

———. "La papeterie de Saint-Cloud (près de Paris) au XIV siècle," *Bibliographe moderne,* Vol. 8, 1904, pp. 108-112.

WEISS. "Papiergeschichte und Wasserzeichenkunde," *Archiv für Buchgewerbe,* Vol. 63, 1926, pp. 292-308.

Chapter V: HANDWRITTEN BOOKS

DESTREZ, JEAN. *La pecia dans les manuscrits universitaires du XIIIe et du XIVe siècle.* Paris, 1935.

MADAN, FALCONER. *Books in Manuscript, a Short Introduction to Their Study and Use.* Second edition, revised. London, 1920.

POLLARD, ALFRED WILLIAM. "The title pages in some Italian manuscripts," *The Printing Art,* Vol. 12, No. 2, October, 1908, pp. 81-87.

THOMPSON, EDWARD MAUNDE. "The grotesque and the humorous in illuminations of the Middle Ages," *Bibliographica,* Vol. 2, 1896, pp. 309-332.

———. "English illuminated manuscripts," *Bibliographica,* Vol. 1, 1895, pp. 129-154, 385-403, and Vol. 2, 1896, pp. 1-22.

———. "Calligraphy in the Middle Ages," *Bibliographica,* Vol. 3, 1897, pp. 257-290.

TISCHENDORF, CONSTANTIN VON. *Die Sinaibibel, ihre Entdeckung, Herausgabe und Erwerbung.* Leipzig, 1871.

———. *Codex sinaiticus, the ancient biblical manuscript now in the British Museum; Tischendorf's story and argument related by himself.* Eighth edition. London, 1934.

Chapter VI: PRINTING IN THE FAR EAST

CARTER, THOMAS FRANCIS. *The Invention of Printing in China and Its Spread Westward.* New York, 1925.

DALAND, JUDSON. "The evolution of modern printing and the discovery of movable metal types by the Chinese and Koreans in the fourteenth century," *Journal of the Franklin Institute,* Vol. 212, No. 2, August, 1931, pp. 209-234.

FORTHUNY, PASCAL. "La richesse graphique des ideogrammes chinois," *Arts et metiers graphiques,* No. 10, March, 1929, pp. 609-613.

LAUFER, BERTHOLD. Descriptive account of the collection of Chinese, Tibetan, Mon-

gol, and Japanese books in the Newberry Library. Publications of the Newberry Library, No. 4. Chicago [1914].

LAUFER, BERTHOLD. *Paper and Printing in Ancient China.* Chicago, 1931.

PEAKE, CYRUS H. "The origin and development of printing in China in the light
of recent research," *Gutenberg Jahrbuch,* 1935, pp. 9-17.

This chapter is based to a large extent on Professor Carter's fundamental
work. Carter made extensive use of Chinese sources in the preparation of this
book, which treats every aspect of the subject in the most thorough manner. The
book contains an extensive bibliography in which will be found the references
necessary for an extended study of the subject. Some errors and omissions in
Carter's work have been noted by Cyrus H. Peake in his article in the *Gutenberg
Jahrbuch.* A briefer treatment of the subject will be found in Laufer's *Paper and
Printing in Ancient China.*

Chapter VII: EARLY EUROPEAN WOODCUTS

BREITKOPF, JOHANN. *Versuch, den Ursprung der Spielkarten, die Einführung des
Leinenpapieres, und den Anfang der Holzschneidekunst in Europa zu erfor-
schen.* Leipzig, 1784, 1801.

CLEMEN, OTTO CONSTANTIN. *Alte Einblattdrucke.* Berlin, 1911.

DODGSON, CAMPBELL. *Catalogue of early German and Flemish woodcuts preserved
in the Department of Prints and Drawings in the British Museum.* London,
1903-1911.

———. *Woodcuts of the fifteenth century in the John Rylands Library, Manchester, reproduced in facsimile with an introduction and notes.* Manchester,
1915.

FRITZ, GEORG. "Die Entwicklung der Buchillustration," *Gutenberg Festschrift,*
Mainz, 1925, pp. 167-174.

GUPPY, HENRY. "Stepping-stones to the art of typography," *Bulletin of the John
Rylands Library,* Vol. 12, No. 1, January, 1928.

———. *The Beginnings of Printed Book Illustration.* Manchester, 1933. (A descriptive catalogue of an exhibition of printed book illustrations of the fifteenth century in the John Rylands Library.)

HARGRAVE, CATHERINE PERRY. *A History of Playing Cards and a Bibliography of
Cards and Gaming.* Boston and New York, 1930. ("Compiled and illustrated
from the old cards and books in the collection of the United States Playing
Card Company in Cincinnati.")

HELLER, JOSEPH. *Geschichte der Holzschneidekunst . . . , enthaltend den Ursprung der Spielkarten. . . .* Bamberg, 1823.

HIND, ARTHUR MAYGER. *A History of Engraving and Etching, from the Fifteenth Century to the Year 1914.* Being the third and fully revised edition of his *A Short History of Engraving and Etching.* Boston and New York, 1923.

——. *An Introduction to a History of Woodcut, with a Detailed Survey of Work Done in the Fifteenth Century.* 2 vols. London, 1935.

SCHREIBER, WILHELM LUDWIG. *Manuel de l'amateur de la gravure sur bois et sur métal au XV siècle.* 8 vols. Berlin and Leipzig, 1891-1911.

——. *Handbuch des Holz- und Metallschnittes des XV Jahrhunderts.* . . . 8 vols. Leipzig, 1926-1930. (A second edition, but in German, of the first three volumes and a translation of the other volumes of his *Manuel.*)

The best general account of early European woodcuts will be found in the recent two-volume *Introduction to a History of Woodcut* by Arthur M. Hind, of the British Museum; a comprehensive and scholarly work, profusely illustrated. The standard catalogue of fifteenth-century prints is Schreiber's *Handbuch,* in which are recorded not only all the known early prints, but also all illustrations in fifteenth-century printed books. The writings of Dodgson and Guppy on the collections in the John Rylands Library are important here because that library (of which Dr. Guppy is librarian) contains a number of the rarest of the early woodcut prints.

Chapter VIII: THE BLOCK BOOKS

The *Ars moriendi* . . . a reproduction of the copy in the British Museum. Edited by W. Harry Rylands . . . with an introduction by George Bullen. London, 1881. (Volume 14 of the Holbein Society's facsimile reprints.)

CUST, LIONEL. *The master E. S. and the Ars moriendi.* Oxford, 1898.

HAEBLER, KONRAD. "Xylographische Donate," *Gutenberg Jahrbuch,* 1928, pp. 15-31.

HOCHEGGER, R. "Über die Entstehung und Bedeutung der Blockbücher," *Beihefte zum Centralblatt für Bibliothekswesen,* 2, Heft 7. Leipzig, 1891.

KRISTELLER, PAUL. *Decalogus; Septimia poenales; Symbolum apostolicum: Drei Blockbücher der Heidelberger Universitäts-bibliothek.* Graphische Gesellschaft, Bd. 4, Berlin, 1907.

——. *Die Apokalypse, älteste Blockbuchausgabe in Lichtdrucknachbildung.* Berlin, 1916.

LEHRS, MAX. "Der Kunstler der *Ars moriendi* und die wahre erste Ausgabe derselben," *Repertorium,* Vol. 11, 1888, p. 51.

SCHREIBER, WILHELM LUDWIG. "Darf der Holzschnitt als Vorläufer der Buchdruckerkunst betrachtet werden?" *Centralblatt für Bibliothekswesen,* Vol. 12, 1895, p. 201 ff.

SCHREIBER, WILHELM LUDWIG. "Vorstufen der Typographie," *Mainzer Festschrift zum fünfhundertjährigen Geburtstage von Johann Gutenberg,* Mainz, 1900, pp. 25-58.

SOTHEBY, SAMUEL LEIGH. *Principia typographica.* 3 vols. London, 1858.

For a more extended account of the block books the reader is referred first to the chapter on block books in Hind's *History of Woodcut,* Vol. 1, pp. 207-264. The works by Dodgson, Guppy, and Schreiber, as well as Hind, cited in the bibliography for the preceding chapter, also contain pertinent material.

Chapter IX: THE STAGE SETTING FOR TYPOGRAPHY

BOUCHOT, HENRI. *Un ancêtre de la gravure sur bois.* Paris, 1902.

DEPIERRE, JOS. *L'impression sur tissus, spécialement l'impression à la main, à travers les âges et dans les divers pays.* Mulhouse, 1910.

FALK, FRANZ. "Der Stempeldruck vor Gutenberg und die Stempeldrucke in Deutschland," *Mainzer Festschrift zum fünfhundertjährigen Geburtstage von Johann Gutenberg,* Mainz, 1900, pp. 59-64.

FLEURY, ED. *Les manuscrits à miniatures de la bibliothèque de Laon,* Part 2, 1863, p. 4 ff.

FORRER, ROBERT. *Die Zeugdrucke der byzantinischen, romanischen, gothischen, und späteren Kunstepochen.* Strasbourg, 1894.

———. *Les impressions de tissus dans leurs relations historiques et artistiques avec les corporations.* Strasbourg, 1898.

———. *Die Kunst des Zeugdrucks vom Mittelalter bis zur Empirezeit.* Strasbourg, 1898.

HUSUNG, MAX JOSEPH. "Neues Material zur Frage des Stempeldrucks vor Gutenberg," *Gutenberg Festschrift,* Mainz, 1925, pp. 66-72.

SCHREIBER, WILHELM LUDWIG. "Vorstufen der Typographie," *Mainzer Festschrift,* Mainz, 1900, pp. 25-58.

THEELE, JOSEPH. "Einzeltypenstempel auf Kölner Einbänden, ein weiterer Beitrag zu dem Stempeldruck vor Gutenberg," *Gutenberg Jahrbuch,* 1926, pp. 9-13.

Chapter X: JOHANN GUTENBERG'S INVENTION

BÖMER, ALOYS. "Die Schlussschrift des Mainzer Catholicon Drucks von 1460," Kuhnert Festschrift, *Von Büchern und Bibliotheken,* Berlin, 1928, pp. 51-55.

BUTLER, PIERCE. *The Invention of Printing in Europe.* Chicago, 1940.

DEVINNE, THEODORE LOW. *The Invention of Printing.* A collection of facts and opinions descriptive of early prints and playing cards, the block-books of the

fifteenth century, the legend of Lourens Janszoon Coster, of Haarlem, and the work of John Gutenberg and his associates. New York, 1877. (Illustrated with facsimiles of early types and woodcuts.)

DZIATZKO, KARL. "Die gedruckten Ablassbriefe von 1454 und 1455," in his *Beiträge zur Gutenbergfrage,* Berlin, 1889, pp. 56-86. Sammlung bibliothekswissenschaftlicher Arbeiten herausgegeben von Karl Dziatzko, Heft 2.

———. "Das Helmasperger'sche Notariatsinstrument vom 6 November, 1455," *idem,* pp. 1-40. (With a facsimile of this important document.)

———. "Die Ordonnanz Karls VII von Frankreich vom 4. Oktober 1458," *idem,* pp. 41-55.

———. *Gutenbergs früheste Druckerpraxis auf Grund einer . . . Vergleichung der 42 zeiligen und 36 zeiligen Bibel dargestellt.* Sammlung bibliothekswissenschaftlicher Arbeiten, Heft 4. Berlin, 1890.

———. "Was wissen wir von dem Leben und der Person Joh. Gutenbergs?" *Sammlung bibliothekswissenschaftlicher Arbeiten,* Heft 8, Leipzig, 1895, pp. 34-51.

———. "Satz und Druck der 42-zeiligen Bibel," *Beiträge zur Kenntnis des Schrift-, Buch- und Bibliothekswesen,* Vol. 7, 1902, pp. 90-108. *Sammlung bibliothekswissenschaftlicher Arbeiten,* Heft 15.

ENSCHEDÉ, CHARLES. *Technisch onderzoek naar de uitvinding van de boekdrukkunst.* Haarlem, 1901.

FUHRMANN, OTTO W. *Gutenberg and the Strasbourg Documents of 1439; an Interpretation.* To which has been appended the text of the documents in the original Alsatian; the French of Laborde, and modern German and English translations. New York, 1940.

———. "The modern conception of Gutenberg," *Papers of the Bibliographical Society of America,* Vol. 35, 1941, p. 1-16.

GOTTSCHALK, PAUL. *Die Buchkunst Gutenbergs und Schöffers, mit einem einleitenden Versuch über die Entstehung der Buchkunst von ihren frühesten Anfangen bis auf die heutige Zeit.* Berlin, 1918.

HAEBLER, KONRAD. "Warum tragen Gutenbergs Drucke keine Unterschrift?" *Zentralblatt für Bibliothekswesen,* Vol. 19, 1902, pp. 103-108.

———. *Die Erfindung der Druckkunst und ihre erste Ausbreitung in den Ländern Europas.* Kleiner Druck der Gutenberg Gesellschaft, No. 14. Mainz, 1930.

HARTWIG, OTTO, editor. *Festschrift zum fünfhundertjährigen Geburtstage von Johann Gutenberg,* herausgegeben von Otto Hartwig; mit einem Atlas von 35 Tafeln. Leipzig, 1900. (Also issued at Mainz, 1900, and as Beiheft zum *Centralblatt für Bibliothekswesen,* Band 8, Heft 23.)

HEIDENHEIMER, HEINRICH. "Das Begleitgedicht zum Justiniani Institutiones Druck von 1468," *Gutenberg Festschrift,* Mainz, 1925, pp. 108-117.

HEIDENHEIMER, HEINRICH. *Vom Ruhme Johannes Gutenbergs, eine literärge-schichtliche Studie.* Mainz, 1930.

HESSEL, ALFRED. "Von der Schrift zum Druck," *Zeitschrift des deutschen Vereins für Buchwesen und Schrifttum,* Vol. 6, 1923, pp. 89-105.

HUPP, OTTO. *Ein Missale speciale Vorläufer des Psalteriums von 1457.* Munich, 1898.

———. *Gutenbergs erste Drucke.* Munich, 1902.

———. *Zum Streit um das Missale speciale Constantiense, ein dritter Beitrag zur Geschichte der ältesten Druckwerke.* Strasbourg, 1917.

———. "Gutenberg und die Nacherfinder," *Gutenberg Jahrbuch,* 1929, pp. 31-100.

———. "Ein Zahlenbeweis für Gutenberg," *Gutenberg Jahrbuch,* 1931, pp. 9-27.

———. "Das Bild Gutenbergs," *Gutenberg Jahrbuch,* 1935, pp. 18-64.

JOACHIM, JOHANNES. [Article on "Eyn manung der cristenheit widder die durken"], *Beiträge zur Kenntnis des Schrift-, Buch- und Bibliothekswesens,* Vol. 6, 1901, pp. 87-102. *Sammlung Bibliothekswissenschaftlicher Arbeiten* herausgegeben von Karl Dziatzko, Heft 14.

JOSEPHSON, AKSEL G. S. "The literature of the invention of printing," *Papers of the Bibliographical Society of America,* Vol. 11, 1917, pp. 1-14.

KAPP, FRIEDRICH. *Geschichte des deutschen Buchhandels bis in das siebzehnte Jahrhundert.* Leipzig, 1886.

KEOGH, ANDREW. "The Gutenberg Bible as a typographical monument," *Yale University Library Bulletin,* Vol. 1, 1926, pp. 1-6.

LABORDE, LÉON DE. *Débuts de l'imprimerie à Strasbourg, ou récherches sur les travaux mystérieux de Gutenberg dans cette ville, et sur le procès qui lui fut intenté en 1439 à cette occasion.* Paris, 1840.

———. *Débuts de l'imprimerie à Mayence et à Bamberg, ou description des lettres d'indulgence du pape Nicolas V, pro regno Cypri imprimées en 1454.* Paris, 1840.

LA CAILLE, JEAN DE. *Histoire de l'imprimerie et de la librairie, où l'on voit son origine et son progrés, juqu'en 1689.* Paris, 1689.

LANGE, ADOLPH. *Peter Schöffer von Gernsheim, der Buchdrucker und Buchhändler.* Leipzig, 1864.

LINDE, ANTONIUS VAN DER. *Gutenberg, Geschichte und Erdichtung, aus der Quellen nachgewiesen.* Stuttgart, 1878.

———. *Geschichte der Erfindung der Buchdruckkunst.* 3 vols. Berlin, 1886.

McMURTRIE, DOUGLAS C. *The Fichet letter, the earliest document ascribing to Gutenberg the invention of printing.* With a reproduction of the letter in collotype and a translation of the text by W. A. Montgomery, Ph.D. New York: Press of Ars Typographica. 1927.

McMurtrie, Douglas C. *The Gutenberg Documents;* with translations of the texts into English, based with authority on the compilation by Dr. Karl Schorbach. New York, 1941.

———. *The Invention of Printing: a Bibliography.* Chicago, 1942. (More than 3,000 titles on the invention of printing, with an author index.)

Martineau, Russell. "The Mainz Psalter of 1457," *Bibliographica,* Vol. 1, 1895, pp. 308-323.

Meyer, Wilhelm. "Bücheranzeigen des 15. Jahrhunderts," *Centralblatt für Bibliothekswesen,* Vol. 2, No. 11, November, 1885, pp. 437-463.

Mori, Gustav. *Was hat Gutenberg erfunden? Ein Rückblick auf die Frühtechnik des Schriftgusses.* Beilage zum XIXten Jahresbericht der Gutenberg Gesellschaft, 1919-1920. Mainz, 1921.

———. "The essence of Gutenberg's invention," *Ars Typographica,* Vol. 2, No. 2, October, 1925, pp. 101-144.

———. *Der Türkenkalender für das Jahr 1455, eine druckhistorische Studie.* Kleiner Druck der Gutenberg Gesellschaft, No. 9b. Mainz, 1928.

Mortet, Charles. *Les origines et les débuts de l'imprimerie d'après les récherches les plus récentes.* Paris, 1922.

Ottley, William Young. *An Inquiry Concerning the Invention of Printing . . .* With an introduction by J. Ph. Berjeau. London, 1863.

Pollard, Alfred William. "Gutenberg, Fust, Schoeffer, and the invention of printing," *The Library,* n.s. Vol. 8, 1907, pp. 69-99.

Ricci, Seymour de. *Catalogue raisonné des premières impressions de Mayence 1445-1467).* Veröffentlichungen der Gutenberg Gesellschaft, 8-9, Mainz, 1911.

Roth, F. Wilhelm Emil. "Die Mainzer Buchdruckerfamilie Schoeffer." *Beihefte zum Centralblatt für Bibliothekswesen,* Band 3, Heft 9, Leipzig, 1892.

———. *Die Druckerei zu Eltville im Rheingau und ihre Erzeugnisse, . . .* Augsburg, 1886.

Ruppel, Aloys. *Mainz als Gutenbergstadt.* Kleiner Druck der Gutenberg Gesellschaft, No. 8. Mainz, 1928.

———. "Über den Wohnort Gutenbergs in seinen letzten Lebensjahren," *Gutenberg Jahrbuch,* 1928, pp. 58-68.

———. *Das Grab Gutenbergs.* Kleiner Druck der Gutenberg Gesellschaft, No. 13. Mainz, 1930.

———. *Johannes Gutenberg, sein Leben und sein Werk.* Berlin, 1939.

———. *Peter Schoeffer aus Gernsheim.* Kleiner Druck der Gutenberg Gesellschaft, No. 26, Mainz, 1937.

———. "Der Totenschild am Grabe Gutenbergs," *Gutenberg Jahrbuch,* 1937, pp. 35-42.

SCHENK ZU SCHWEINSBERG, GUSTAV. "Genealogie des Mainzer Geschlechtes Gäns-
fleisch," *Mainzer Festschrift,* Mainz, 1900, pp. 65-131.

SCHOLDERER, VICTOR. "The invention of printing," *Transactions of the Bibliographical Society (The Library),* n.s., Vol. 21, 1940, p. 1-25.

SCHORBACH, KARL. "Die urkundlichen Nachrichten über Johann Gutenberg, mit
Nachbildungen und Erläuterungen," *Mainzer Festschrift,* Mainz, 1900, pp.
135-256. (Previously published in *Beiheft zum Centralblatt für Bibliothekswesen,* Vol. 8, no. 23, Leipzig, 1900, p. 163-319.)

——. "Neue Strassburger Gutenbergfunde," *Gutenberg Festschrift,* Mainz,
1925, pp. 130-143. (With additions in *Gutenberg Jahrbuch,* 1926, pp. 14-31.)

SCHRÖDER, EDWARD. *Das Mainzer Fragment vom Weltgericht, der älteste Druck
mit der Donat-Kalender-Type Gutenbergs.* Veröffentlichungen der Gutenberg Gesellschaft, 3, Mainz, 1904, pp. 2-10.

——. *Das Mainzer Fragment vom Weltgericht, ein Ausschnitt aus dem
deutschen Sibyllenbuche.* Veröffentlichungen der Gutenberg Gesellschaft, 5-7,
Mainz, 1908, pp. 1-9. (On the language and literary origin of the poem.)

SCHWENKE, PAUL. *Untersuchungen zur Geschichte des ersten Buchdrucks.* Festschrift zur Gutenberg Feier 1900. Berlin, 1900.

——. "Gutenberg und die Type des Türkenkalenders," *Zentralblatt für Bibliothekswesen,* Vol. 18, 1901, pp. 289-296.

——. *Die Donat- und Kalender-Type; Nachtrag und Uebersicht.* Veröffentlichungen der Gutenberg Gesellschaft, 2, Mainz, 1903.

——. *Die Türkenbulle Pabst Calixtus III; ein deutscher Druck von 1465 in
der ersten Gutenbergtype.* In Nachbildung herausgegeben und untersucht von
Paul Schwenke, mit einer geschichtlich-sprachlichen Abhandlung von
Hermann Degering. Berlin, 1911.

——. *Johann Gutenbergs zweiundvierzigzeilige Bibel.* Ergänzungsband zur
Faksimile-Ausgabe. Herausgegeben von Paul Schwenke. Leipzig, 1913-1914.
(With an appendix on the Helmasperger document.)

STAMMLER, RUDOLF. "Die Rechtshandel des Johann Gutenbergs," *Festschrift . . .
für Wilhelm von Brünneck,* Halle, 1912, pp. 1-25.

TRONNIER, ADOLPH. *Die Missaldrucke Peter Schöffers und seines Sohnes Johann.*
Veröffentlichungen der Gutenberg Gesellschaft, 5-7, Mainz, 1908, pp. 28-220.

VELKE, WILHELM. *Zu den Bücheranzeigen Peter Schöffers.* Veröffentlichungen
der Gutenberg Gesellschaft, 5-7, Mainz, 1908, pp. 221-235.

WALLAU, HEINRICH. *Das Mainzer Fragment vom Weltgericht, . . . Technische
Untersuchungen des Weltgericht-Druckes und seiner Typen.* Veröffentlichungen der Gutenberg Gesellschaft, 3, Mainz, 1904, pp. 21-36.

WALLAU, HEINRICH. "Die zweifarbigen Initialen der Psalterdrucke," *Mainzer Festschrift,* Mainz, 1900, pp. 261-304.

WEALE, WILLIAM HENRY JAMES. *Historical Music Loan Exhibition . . . a Descriptive Catalogue . . .* London, 1886. (Contains a study of the Fust and Schoeffer Psalter of 1457.)

WETTER, JOHANN. *Kritische Geschichte der Erfindung der Buchdruckerkunst durch Johann Gutenberg zu Mainz, begleitet mit . . . einer neuen Untersuchung der Ansprüche der Stadt Haarlem. . . .* Mainz, 1836.

WINSHIP, GEORGE PARKER. *Gutenberg to Plantin: Outline of the Early History of Printing.* Cambridge, Mass., 1926.

WYSS, ARTHUR. "Die Türkenkalender für 1455, ein Werk Gutenbergs," *Mainzer Festschrift,* Mainz, 1900, pp. 305-321.

ZEDLER, GOTTFRIED. *Gutenbergforschungen.* Leipzig, 1901.

———. *Die älteste Gutenbergtype.* Veröffentlichungen der Gutenberg Gesellschaft, 1. Mainz, 1902.

———. *Das Mainzer Fragment vom Weltgericht, . . . Typographische und zeitliche Stellung.* Veröffentlichungen der Gutenberg Gesellschaft, 3. Mainz, 1904, pp. 10-21.

———. *Das Mainzer Catholicon.* Veröffentlichungen der Gutenberg Gesellschaft, 4. Mainz, 1905.

———. "Das Helmaspergersche Notariatsinstrument und die 42zeilige Bibel," *Zentralblatt für Bibliothekswesen,* Vol. 24, 1907, pp. 193-207.

———. *Die 42zeilige Bibeltype im Schöfferischen Missale Moguntinum von 1493.* Veröffentlichungen der Gutenberg Gesellschaft, 5-7. Mainz, 1908, pp. 10-27.

———. *Die Bamberger Pfisterdrucke und die 36zeilige Bibel.* Veröffentlichungen der Gutenberg Gesellschaft, 10-11. Mainz, 1911.

———. *Die Mainzer Ablassbriefe der Jahre 1454 und 1455.* Veröffentlichungen der Gutenberg Gesellschaft, 12-13. Mainz, 1913.

———. "Die Erfindung Gutenbergs und der chinesische und frühholländische Bücherdruck," *Gutenberg Jahrbuch,* 1928, pp. 50-57.

———. *Die sogenannte Gutenbergbibel, sowie die mit der 42zeiligen Bibeltype ausgeführten kleineren Drucke.* Veröffentlichungen der Gutenberg Gesellschaft, 20. Mainz, 1929.

———. *Gutenbergs älteste Type und die mit ihr hergestellten Drucke.* Veröffentlichungen der Gutenberg Gesellschaft, 23. Mainz, 1934.

The literature concerning Gutenberg and the invention of printing is of vast extent, and most of it is in German. The recognized center of scholarly investigations in this field is the Gutenberg Gesellschaft in Mainz, and the publications

of that society (the *Gutenberg Jahrbuch,* the *Veröffentlichungen,* and others) contain the most authoritative statements on the many controversial questions involved in the study of Gutenberg and his invention. The scope of the literature on the subject is shown in *The Invention of Printing: a Bibliography,* edited by McMurtrie.

In English, the subject is best presented in the volumes by DeVinne and by Winship. Ottley's *Inquiry Concerning the Invention of Printing,* valuable in its day, is now mostly out of date. Several valuable articles, and abstracts or reviews of others, appeared in the issues of *Ars Typographica.*

In other languages, the subject has been surveyed in the contributions by Haebler (*Die Erfindung der Druckkunst*), Ruppel, Hessel, Gottschalk, Hupp (*Das Bild Gutenbergs*), Laborde, van der Linde, Mortet, and Wetter.

On Gutenberg himself, the contributions by Schorbach are fundamental, as they present in full the text of the twenty-eight documents thus far discovered in which Gutenberg is mentioned. Fuhrmann's work on the Strasbourg documents of 1439 and McMurtrie's *The Gutenberg Documents* are important in this connection. The studies by Dr. Aloys Ruppel are full of interest, as are the studies of the life and personality of the inventor by Dziatzko, Haebler, Heidenheimer, and Hupp, recorded in the foregoing bibliography.

Chapter XI: THE CASE OF RIVAL CLAIMANTS

BRADSHAW, HENRY. *List of the Founts of Type and Woodcut Devices Used by Printers in Holland in the Fifteenth Century.* London, 1871. Also in *Collected Papers of Henry Bradshaw,* Cambridge, 1889, pp. 258-280.

CLAUDIN, ANATOLE. "Les origines de l'imprimerie en France; premiers essais à Avignon en 1444," *Bulletin du bibliophile,* Paris, 1898.

DUHAMEL, L. *Les origines de l'imprimerie à Avignon; notes sur les documents découverts par M l'Abbé Requin.* Avignon, 1890.

ENSCHEDÉ, CHARLES. *Technisch onderzoek naar de uitvinding van de boekdrukkunst.* Haarlem, 1901.

———. Laurens Janzs. Coster, de uitvinder van de boekdrukkunst. Haarlem, 1904.

HAEBLER, KONRAD. "Zum Studium der altniederländischen Donate," *Zentralblatt für Bibliothekswesen,* Vol. 35, 1918, pp. 242-254.

HESSELS, JAN HENDRIK [JOHN HENRY]. *Gutenberg: Was He the Inventor of Printing?* London, 1882.

———. *Haarlem the birthplace of printing, not Mentz.* London, 1887. (An edition in Dutch was issued at Haarlem in 1888.)

———. "Typography," in Encyclopædia Britannica, 11th ed., 1911, Vol. 27.

HESSELS, JAN HENDRIK [JOHN HENRY]. *The Gutenberg Fiction; Showing That He Was Not the Inventor of Printing.* London, 1912.

KRUITWAGEN, BONAVENTURA. "Die Ansprüche Hollands auf die Erfindung der Buchdruckerkunst," *Gutenberg Festschrift,* Mainz, 1925, pp. 353-370.

LINDE, ANTONIUS VAN DER. *The Haarlem Legend of the Invention of Printing by L. J. Coster Critically Examined.* From the Dutch by J. H. Hessels, with an introduction and a classified list of the Costerian incunabula. London, 1871.

McMURTRIE, DOUGLAS CRAWFORD. *The Dutch Claims to the Invention of Printing.* Second and revised edition. Chicago, 1928.

MÜLLER, G. H. "Die Quellen der Costerlegende," *Zentralblatt für Bibliothekswesen,* Vol. 28, 1911, pp. 145-167, 193-207.

OTTLEY, WILLIAM YOUNG. *Inquiry into the Origin and Early History of Engraving.* 2 vols. London, 1816.

PANSIER, PIERRE. *Histoire du livre et de l'imprimerie à Avignon du XIVe au XVIe siècle.* 3 vols. Avignon, 1922.

POLLARD, ALFRED WILLIAM. *Fine Books.* London, 1912.

REQUIN, Abbé PIERRE HENRI. *L'imprimerie à Avignon en 1444.* Paris, 1890.

———. *Origines de l'imprimerie en France* (Avignon, 1444). Paris, 1891.

———. "Documents inédits sur les origines de la typographie," *Bulletin historique et philologique,* 1890.

SCHRIJVER, PIETER. (PETRUS SCRIVERIUS). *Laure-crans voor Laurens Coster van Haerlem, eerste Vinder van de Boeckdruckery.* Haarlem, 1628.

SEYL, A. "Qui inventa l'imprimerie en Europe?" *La Chronique graphique,* Vol. 10, 1934, pp. 2541-2545. ("Belgium can and should claim this honor for Jean Brito, the first printer of Bruges.")

———. "Jean Brito et l'invention de l'imprimerie," *La Chronique graphique,* Vol. 10, 1934, pp. 2577-2583.

———. "Une gloire nationale reconquise; Bruges, berceau de l'imprimerie," *La Chronique graphique,* Vol. 10, 1934, p. 2617-2623.

SOMEREN, JAN FREDERIK VAN. *De Gutenberg-Legende.* Utrecht, 1913.

VINCENT, A. "Jean Brito, l'imprimeur brugeois, inventa-t'il la typographie?" *Bulletin mensuel du Musée du Livre,* Vol. 17, Nov., 1934.

ZEDLER, GOTTFRIED. *Von Coster zu Gutenberg; der holländische Frühdruck und die Erfindung des Buchdrucks.* Leipzig, 1921.

———. *Die neuere Gutenbergforschung und die Lösung der Costerfrage.* Frankfurt, 1923.

———. "Der holländische Frühdruck und die ersten Versuche Gutenbergs in Strassburg," *Gutenberg Jahrbuch,* 1930, pp. 53-66.

Chapter XII: THE DISSEMINATION OF PRINTING

BINZ, GUSTAV. "Die Anfänge des Buchdrucks in Basel," *Gutenberg Festschrift,* Mainz, 1925, pp. 385-397.

BOGENG, GUSTAV ADOLF ERICH. *Geschichte der Buchdruckerkunst.* Hellerau bei Dresden, 1930.

BÖMER, ALOYS. "Die älteste Druckwerk Italiens," *Zentralblatt für Bibliotheks-wesen,* Vol. 45, 1928.

CANIBELL Y MASBERNAT, EUDALDO. "Precedentes e introducción de la imprenta en España," *Gutenberg Festschrift,* Mainz, 1925, pp. 241 247.

CLAUDIN, ANATOLE. *The First Paris Press, an Account of the Books Printed for G. Fichet and J. Heynlin in the Sorbonne, 1470-1472.* Illustrated monographs of the Bibliographical Society, No. 6, London, 1898.

———. *Histoire de l'imprimerie en France au XVe et au XVIe siècle.* 4 vols. Paris, 1900-1914.

DZIATZKO, KARL. "Der Drucker mit dem bizarren R," *Sammlung bibiotheks-wissenschaftlicher Arbeiten,* Heft 17, Halle, 1902, pp. 13-24.

FALK, FRANZ. "Die Schuler Gutenbergs, Fusts und Schöffers," *Centralblatt für Bibliothekswesen,* Vol. 4, 1887, pp. 216-218.

FINKENSTÄDT, FRITZ. "Ein Druck Berthold Ruppels mit Rubrizierungsdatum 1464," *Beiträge zur Forschung aus dem Antiquariat Jacques Rosenthal,* neue Folge, 4, Munich, 1932, pp. 7-33.

HAEBLER, KONRAD. *The early printers of Spain and Portugal.* Illustrated monographs of the Bibliographical Society, No. 4, London, 1897.

———. "Deutsche Buchdrucker in Spanien und Portugal," *Mainzer Festschrift,* Mainz, 1900, pp. 393-405.

———. *Geschichte des spanischen Frühdruckes in Stammbäumen.* Leipzig, 1923.

———. *Die deutschen Buchdrucker des XV. Jahrhunderts im Auslande.* Munich, 1924.

———. "Die italienischen Fragmente vom Leiden Christi, das älteste Druckwerk Italiens," *Beiträge zur Forschung aus dem Antiquariat Jacques Rosenthal,* neue Folge, 1, Munich, 1927.

HARRISSE, HENRI. *Les premiers incunables bâlois et leurs dérivés.* Paris, 1902.

JOHNSON, ALFRED FORBES. *The First Century of Printing at Basle.* New York, 1926.

LABANDE, LÉON-HONORÉ. "L'imprimerie en France au XVe siècle," *Mainzer Festschrift,* Mainz, 1900, pp. 347-391. (Principally on the first printers at Paris and at Lyons.)

MCMURTRIE, DOUGLAS C. "The introduction of printing into Italy," *Inland*

Printer, Vol. 83, No. 1, April, 1929, pp. 90-92. (On the Italian translation of the *Leiden Christi*.)

MARZI, DEMETRIO. "I tipografi tedeschi in Italia durante il secolo XV," *Mainzer Festschrift*, Mainz, 1900, pp. 407-453. (An important summary of facts, documents, etc.)

NIJHOFF, WOUTER. *L'art typographique dans les Pays-Bas, pendant les années 1500 à 1540*. The Hague, 1902-1926. (More than 2,000 facsimile reproductions.)

PEDDIE, ROBERT ALEXANDER, editor. *Printing, A Short History of the Art*. London, 1927. (Contains chapters by several authorities on the spread of printing throughout Europe and in other parts of the world.)

RENOUARD, PHILIPPE. *Imprimeurs parisiens, libraires, fondeurs de caractères, et correcteurs d'imprimerie, depuis l'introduction de l'imprimerie à Paris (1470) jusqu'à la fin du XVIe siècle*. Paris, 1898. (Also similar title in *Revue des bibliothèques*, Vols. 32-34 and 36, 1922-1926.)

——. *Documents sur les imprimeurs, libraires, cartiers, graveurs, fondeurs de lettres, relieurs ... ayant exercé à Paris de 1450 à 1600*. Paris, 1901.

SCHOLDERER, VICTOR. *Vom italienischen Frühdruck*. Kleiner Druck der Gutenberg Gesellschaft, No. 19, Mainz, 1932.

SCHORBACH, KARL. *Der strassburger Frühdrucker Johann Mentelin, 1458-1478*. Veröffentlichungen der Gutenberg Gesellschaft, 22. Mainz, 1932. (With a descriptive bibliography of Mentelin imprints.)

STEHLIN, K. "Regesten zur Geschichte des Buchdrucks bis zum Jahre 1500," published as Vols. 11 and 12 of the *Archiv für die Geschichte des deutschen Buchhandels*, Leipzig, 1888-1889. (Presents original fifteenth century documents from Basel archives which concern printers or printing.)

UHLENDORF, B. A. "The invention of printing and its spread until 1470, with special reference to social and economic factors," *Library Quarterly*, Vol. 2, No. 3, July, 1932, pp. 179-231.

VELKE, WILHELM. "Zur frühesten Verbreitung der Druckkunst," *Mainzer Festschrift*, Mainz, 1900, pp. 323-346.

VOULLIÉME, ERNST HERMANN. *Die deutschen Drucker des fünfzehnten Jahrhunderts*. 2e Aufl. Berlin, 1922.

Chapter XIII: THE MASTER PRINTERS OF VENICE

BROWN, HORATIO R. F. *The Venetian Press; an Historical Study*. London, 1891.

BULLEN, HENRY LEWIS. *Nicolas Jenson, Printer, of Venice: his famous type designs and some comments upon the printing types of earlier printers*. San Francisco: John Henry Nash. 1926.

CASTELLANI, CARLO. *La stampa in Venezia dalla sua origine alla morte di Aldo Manuzio seniore.* Venice, 1889.

DE VINNE, THEODORE LOW. *Aldus Pius Manutius.* San Francisco: The Grabhorn Press. 1924.

DIBDIN, THOMAS FROGNALL. *Early Printers in the City of Venice.* Mt. Vernon, N. Y., 1924. (From the author's *Bibliographical Decameron,* the Fourth Day.)

DIEHL, ROBERT. *Erhard Ratdolt, ein Meisterdrucker des XV. und XVI. Jahrhunderts.* Vienna, 1933.

GOLDSMID, EDMUND MARSDEN. *A Bibliographical Sketch of the Aldine Press at Venice, forming a catalogue of all works issued . . . from 1494 to 1597 . . .* Edinburgh, 1887. (An abridged translation of Renouard's *Annales de l'imprimerie des Aldes,* with revisions and corrections.)

JENSON, NICOLAS. *The last will and testament of the late Nicolas Jenson, who departed this life at the city of Venice in the month of September, A.D., 1480.* Chicago, 1928. (Translated from the Latin original by Dr. Pierce Butler, and privately printed by the Ludlow Typograph Company, in its re-cutting of Jenson's roman type.)

JOHNSON, ALFRED FORBES, and STANLEY MORISON. "The Chancery types of Italy and France," *The Fleuron,* No. 3, 1924, pp. 23-51.

MARX, ALEXANDER. "Aldus and the first use of Hebrew type in Venice," *Papers of the Bibliographical Society of America,* Vol. 13, 1919, pp. 64-67.

MORISON, STANLEY. *Four centuries of Fine Printing.* London, 1924. (On the developments of the roman typefaces at Venice, in the Introduction.)

RENOUARD, ANTOINE AUGUSTIN. *Annales de l'imprimerie des Alde; ou, Histoire des trois Manuce et leurs éditions.* 3e édition. 2 vols. in one. Paris, 1834. (See the title above, under Goldsmid.)

SCHOLDERER, VICTOR. "Printing at Venice to the end of 1481," *The Library,* 4th series, Vol. 5, No. 2, September, 1924, pp. 129-152.

———. "Introduction" in *Catalogue of Books Printed in the Fifteenth Century, now in the British Museum,* Vol. 5, London, 1924.

Chapter XIV: THE FIRST PRINTING IN ENGLISH

ALLNUTT, W. H. "English provincial presses," *Bibliographica,* Vol. 2, 1896, pp. 23-46, 150-180, 276-308.

[BLADES, ROWLAND HILL.] *Who Was Caxton? William Caxton, merchant, ambassador, historian, author, translator and printer.* London, 1877. (Mainly founded on William Blades' biography of Caxton, but presents a different view of Caxton's early connection with printing at Cologne and Bruges.)

BLADES, WILLIAM. *The Life and Typography of William Caxton, England's First Printer; with Evidences of His Typographical Connection with Colard Mansion, the Printer at Bruges.* 2 vols. London, 1861-1863.

——. *A Catalogue of Books Printed by (or Ascribed to the Press of) William Caxton.* London, 1865.

——. *The Biography and Typography of William Caxton, England's First Printer.* London, 1882. (An epitomized revision of his earlier *Life and Typography of William Caxton.*)

BYLES, A. T. P. "William Caxton as a man of letters," *The Library,* 4th series, Vol. 15, 1934-1935, pp. 1-25.

CROTCH, W. J. BLYTH. "Caxton on the continent," *The Library,* 4th series, Vol. 7, 1927, pp. 387-401. (New documentary material bearing on Caxton's activities on the continent.)

DUFF, EDWARD GORDON. *Early English Printing; a series of facsimiles of all the types used in England during the XVth century.* London, 1896.

——. *William Caxton.* Chicago: The Caxton Club, 1905.

——. *Fifteenth Century English Books; a Bibliography.* Illustrated monographs of the Bibliographical Society, No. 18, Oxford, 1917.

OAKESHOTT, WALTER F. "Caxton and Malory's Morte d'Arthur," *Gutenberg Jahrbuch,* 1935, pp. 112-116. (On Caxton's editorial activities.)

PLOMER, HENRY ROBERT. *Wynkyn de Worde and His Contemporaries, from the Death of Caxton to 1535.* London, 1925. (Includes chapters on Richard Pynson, John Lettou, William de Machlinia, Julyan Notary, and others.)

POLLARD, ALFRED WILLIAM. "Printing in England, 1476-1580," in his *Fine Books,* London, 1912.

RICCI, SEYMOUR DE. *A Census of Caxtons.* Illustrated monographs of the Bibliographical Society, No. 15. Oxford, 1909.

SMITH, GEORGE. *William de Machlinia; the primer on vellum printed by him in London about 1484, . . . with facsimiles of the woodcuts.* London, 1929. (Contains an account of Machlinia and his work.)

WINSHIP, GEORGE PARKER. *William Caxton;* a paper read at a meeting of the Club of Odd Volumes in Boston, . . . in January 1908. Printed by T. J. Cobden-Sanderson at the Doves Press, 1909.

Chapter XV: THE PRODUCTION OF THE INCUNABULA

DIETERICHS, KARL. *Die Buchdruckpresse von Johannes Gutenberg bis Friedrich König.* Beilage zum 28. Jahresbericht der Gutenberg Gesellschaft. Mainz, 1930. (A brief illustrated history of the printing press.)

HAEBLER, KONRAD. "Schriftguss und Schrifthandel in der Frühdruckzeit," *Zentral-blatt für Bibliothekswesen,* Vol. 41, 1924, pp. 81-104. (Also reprinted by the H. Berthold Schriftgiesserei, Leipzig, 1925.)

————. "Typefounding and commerce in type during the early years of printing," *Ars Typographica,* Vol. 3, 1926, pp. 3-35. (A translation of the preceding, by Otto W. Fuhrmann.)

KLEUKENS, CHRISTIAN HEINRICH. *Die Handpresse.* Kleiner Druck der Gutenberg Gesellschaft, No. 4. Darmstadt, 1927.

McMURTRIE, DOUGLAS C. *The Corrector of the Press in the Early Days of Printing.* Greenwich, Conn., 1922.

————. *Proofreading in the Fifteenth Century.* Greenwich, Conn., 1921.

MADAN, FALCONER. "Early representations of the printing-press, with special reference to that by Stradanus," *Bibliographica,* Vol. 1, 1895, pp. 223-248, and "Addenda," pp. 499-502.

MOXON, JOSEPH. *Moxon's Mechanick Exercises, or, the Doctrine of Handy-Works Applied to the Art of Printing. . . .* With preface and notes by Theo. L. De Vinne. 2 vols. New York, 1896. (A literal reprint of the first edition published in 1683.)

SCHOTTENLOHER, KARL. "Handschriftforschung und Buchdruck im XV. und XVI. Jahrhundert," *Gutenberg Jahrbuch,* 1931, pp. 73-106. (On the editorial correction and preparation of the MS texts reproduced by the early printers.)

THEVET, ANDRÉ. *Jean Guttemberg, Inventor of Printing;* a translation by Douglas C. McMurtrie of the essay in André Thevet's *Vie des hommes illustrés,* Paris, 1589. New York, 1926. (Contains the first explicit printed account of the technique of punch-cutting, typecasting, composition, and printing.)

Chapter XVI: WOODCUT BOOK ILLUSTRATION

FRITZ, GEORG. "Die Entwicklung der Buchillustration," *Gutenberg Festschrift,* Mainz, 1925, pp. 167-174.

HIND, ARTHUR MAYGER. *A History of Engraving and Etching, from the 15th Century to the Year 1914.* Boston and New York, 1923.

————. *An Introduction to a History of Woodcut, with a Detailed Survey of Work Done in the Fifteenth Century.* 2 vols. London, 1935.

KRISTELLER, PAUL. *Die strassburger Bücher-illustration im XV und im Anfange des XVI Jahrhunderts.* Leipzig, 1888. Also *Beiträge zur Kunstgeschichte,* neue Folge, Vol. 7.

————. *Kupferstich und Holzschnitt in vier Jahrhunderten.* 2e Auflage. Berlin, 1911.

LYELL, JAMES PATRICK RONALDSON. Early book illustration in Spain. With an introduction by Dr. Konrad Haebler. London, 1926. (Finely illustrated.)

MUTHER, RICHARD. *Die deutsche Buchillustration der Gothik und Frührenaissance, 1460-1530.* Munich and Leipzig, 1884.

OTTLEY, WILLIAM YOUNG. *An Inquiry into the Origin and Early History of Engraving, upon Copper and in Wood.* London, 1816.

POLLARD, ALFRED WILLIAM. *Fine Books.* London, 1912.

———. *Early Illustrated Books; a history of the decoration and illustration of books in the 15th and 16th centuries.* Second edition. London, 1917.

RATH, ERICH VON. "Buchdruck und Buchillustration bis zum Jahre 1600," *Handbuch der Bibliothekswissenschaft,* Vol. 1, Leipzig, 1931, pp. 332-460.

SCHRAMM, ALBERT. *Der Bilderschmuck der Fruhdruck.* 19 vols. Leipzig, 1924-1936. (Reproducing all the illustrations in the incunabula.)

SCHREIBER, WILHELM LUDWIG. "Das erste Zusammenwirken von Bild- und Typendruck," *Gutenberg Festschrift,* Mainz, 1925, pp. 164-166. (On Boner's *Edelstein* and Voragine's *Heiligenleben.*)

SCHRETLEN, MARTIN JOSEPH. *Dutch and Flemish Woodcuts of the 15th Century.* London, 1925.

Chapter XVII: ENGRAVED BOOK ILLUSTRATION

HOFER, PHILIP. "Early book illustration in the intaglio medium," *Print Collector's Quarterly,* Vol. 21, 1934, pp. 203-227, 295-316.

KRISTELLER, PAUL. *Kupferstich und Holzschnitt in vier Jahrhunderten.* 2te Auflage. Berlin, 1911.

OTTLEY, WILLIAM YOUNG. *An Inquiry into the Origin and Early History of Engraving, upon Copper and in Wood.* London, 1816.

RATH, ERICH VON. "Kupferstichillustration im Wiegendruckzeitalter," *Archiv für Buchgewerbe,* Vol. 64, 1927, pp. 1-27.

Chapter XVIII: EARLY BOOK DECORATION

KRISTELLER, PAUL. *Florentinische Zierstücke in Kupferstich aus dem XV Jahrhundert.* Berlin, 1909.

MCMURTRIE, DOUGLAS C. *Book Decoration.* Pelham, N. Y., 1928.

———. *The Earliest Use of Type Ornament.* Chicago, 1933. (This statement appeared originally in the *American Printer* for December, 1924.

MEYNELL, FRANCIS, and STANLEY MORISON. "Printers' flowers and arabesques," *The Fleuron,* No. 1, 1923, pp. 1-43.

Nijhoff, Wouter. *L'art typographique dans les Pays-Bas, pendant les années 1500 à 1540*. The Hague, 1902-1926. (With many facsimiles, including book ornaments.)

Pollard, Alfred William. *Early illustrated books; a history of the decoration and illustration of books in the 15th and 16th centuries*. Second edition. London, 1917.

——. "Some pictorial and heraldic initials," *Bibliographica*, Vol. 3, 1897, pp. 232-252.

Redgrave, Gilbert Richard. *Erhard Ratdolt and His Work at Venice*. Illustrated monographs of the Bibliographical Society, No. 1, London, 1894. (A supplement of additions and corrections was issued in 1895, and the work was reprinted in 1899.)

Schottenloher, Karl. "Der Farbenschmuck der Wiegendrucke," *Buch und Schrift*, Vol. 4, 1930, pp. 81-96.

Smith, Percy J. "Initial letters in the printed book," *The Fleuron*, No. 1, 1923, pp. 61-91.

Chapter XIX: SOME SPECIAL PROBLEMS

British Museum; Department of Printed Books. *A guide to the exhibition in the King's Library illustrating the history of printing, music-printing and bookbinding*. London, 1926. Early printing of music, pp. 105-114.

De Morgan, Augustus. *On the Study and Difficulties of Mathematics*. Second edition. Chicago, 1902.

Frank, Rafael. *Über hebräische Typen und Schriftarten*. Mit einem Nachwort von Dr. Jacques Adler. Herausgegeben von der Schriftgiesserei H. Berthold. Berlin, 1926.

Friemann, Aron, editor. *Thesaurus typographiae hebraicae saeculi XV*. Berlin, 1924.+ (Contains facsimiles of typographically significant pages from all Hebrew incunabula.)

Guégan, B. "Histoire de l'impression de la musique," *Arts et métiers graphiques*, No. 37, 1933, pp. 26-34; No. 39, 1934, pp. 16-26; No. 41, 1934, pp. 39-46; No. 43, 1934, pp. 15-20.

Kinkeldey, Otto. "Music and music printing in incunabula," *Papers of the Bibliographical Society of America*, Vol. 26, 1932, pp. 89-118. (With a bibliography of the subject.)

Lyell, James P. R. *Cardinal Ximenes, Statesman, Ecclesiastic, Soldier and Man of Letters, with an Account of the Complutensian Polyglot Bible*. London, 1917.

PROCTOR, ROBERT G. C. *The Printing of Greek in the Fifteenth Century.* Illustrated monographs of the Bibliographical Society, No. 8, London, 1900.

SCHMID, A. *Ottaviano dei Petrucci da Fossombrone, der erste Erfinder des Musiknotendruckes mit beweglichen Metalltypen, und seine Nachfolger im sechzehnten Jahrhunderte.* Vienna, 1845.

SCHOLDERER, VICTOR. *Greek Printing Types, 1465-1927: facsimiles from an exhibition illustrating the development of Greek printing shown in the British Museum, 1927.* London, 1927.

SQUIRE, WILLIAM BARCLAY. "Notes on early music printing," *Bibliographica,* Vol. 3, 1897, pp. 99-122.

STEELE, ROBERT. *The Earliest English Music Printing, a description and bibliography of English printed music to the close of the sixteenth century.* Illustrated monographs of the Bibliographical Society, No. 11, London, 1903.

THOMAS-STANFORD, CHARLES. *Early Editions of Euclid's Elements.* Illustrated monographs of the Bibliographical Society, No. 20, London, 1926.

VERNARECCI, A. *Ottaviano de' Petrucci da Fossombrone, inventore dei tipi mobili metallici fusi della musica nel secolo XV.* Ed. 2. Bologna, 1882.

Chapter XX: PRINTERS' MARKS

BERJEAU, JEAN PHILIBERT. *Early Dutch, German and English Printers' Marks.* London, 1866-1867.

DAVIES, HUGH WILLIAM. *Devices of the Early Printers, 1457-1560, their history and development, with a chapter on portrait figures of printers.* London, 1935. (Another authoritative book on the subject.)

DELALAIN, PAUL ADOLPHE. *Inventaire des marques d'imprimeurs et de libraires de la collection du Cercle de la Librairie,* 2e édition. Paris, 1892.

HAVRE, GUSTAVE VAN. *Marques typographiques des imprimeurs et libraires anversois.* Antwerp, 1883-1884.

————. *Les marques typographiques de l'imprimerie plantinienne.* Antwerp, 1911.

HEITZ, PAUL, editor. *Die Büchermarken, oder Buchdrucker- und Verlegerzeichen.* 7 vols. Strasbourg, 1892-1908.

HUSUNG, MAX JOSEPH. *Die Drucker- und Verlegerzeichen Italiens im fünfzehnten Jahrhundert.* Munich, 1929.

JUCHHOFF, RUDOLF. *Die Drucker- und Verlegerzeichen des XV Jahrhunderts in den Niederlanden, England, Spanien, Böhmen, Mähren und Polen.* Munich, 1927.

KRISTELLER, PAUL. *Die italienischen Buchdrucker- und Verlegerzeichen bis 1525.* Strasbourg, 1893.

LAURENT-VIBERT, ROBERT, and MARIUS AUDIN. *Les marques de libraires et d'im-primeurs en France aux dix-septième et dix-huitième siècles.* Paris, 1925.

MCMURTRIE, DOUGLAS C. *Printers' Marks and Their Significance.* Chicago, 1930.

MADDEN, JOHN PATRICK AUGUSTE. *Lettres d'un bibliographe.* 6 vols. in 4. Versailles, 1868-1886.

MEINER, ANNEMARIE. *Die deutsche Signet, ein Beitrag zur Kulturgeschichte.* Leipzig, 1922.

MEYER, WILHELM JOSEF. *Die französischen Drucker- und Verlegerzeichen des fünfzehnten Jahrhunderts.* Munich, 1826.

NIJHOFF, WOUTER. *L'art typographique dans les Pay-Bas, pendant les années 1500 à 1540.* Reproduction en facsimile des caractères typographiques, marques d'imprimeurs, gravures sur bois et autres ornements employés pendant cette period. The Hague, 1902-1926.

POLAIN, LOUIS. *Marques des imprimeurs et libraires en France au XVe siècle.* Paris, 1926.

RENOUARD, PHILIPPE. *Les marques typographiques parisiennes des XVe et XVIe siècles.* Paris, 1926-1928.

ROBERTS, WILLIAM. *Printers' Marks, a Chapter in the History of Typography.* London and New York, 1893.

ROTH-SCHOLZ, FRIEDRICH. *Thesaurus symbolorum ac emblematum, i. e., insignia bibliopolorum et typographorum.* Nuremberg, 1730.

SCHECHTER, FRANK ISAAC. "Early printers' and publishers' devices," *Papers of the Bibliographical Society of America,* Vol. 19, 1925, pp. 1-28. (Reprinted from the author's *Historical Foundations of the Law Relating to Trade Marks,* Columbia Legal Studies, Vol. 1.)

SCHRETLEN, MARTIN JOSEPH. "Printers' devices in Dutch incunabula," *Ars Typographica,* Vol. 3, 1926, pp. 53-64.

SILVESTRE, LOUIS CATHERINE. *Marques typographiques en France . . . 1470 jusqu'à la fin du XVIe siècle.* Paris, 1853-1867.

WEIL, ERNST. *Die deutschen Druckerzeichen des XV Jahrhunderts.* Munich, 1924.

Chapter XXI: THE STUDY OF INCUNABULA

BALLARD, JAMES F., compiler. *A catalogue of medical incunabula contained in the William Norton Bullard Loan Collection.* Boston, 1929.

CONSENTIUS, ERNST. *Die Typen der Inkunabelzeit.* Berlin, 1929. (A critical discussion of Haebler's *Typenrepertorium.*)

COPINGER, WALTER A. Supplement to Hain's *Repertorium bibliographicum.* 3 vols. London, 1895-1902.

CROUS, ERNST. "Die Abkürzungszeichen in den Wiegendrucken," *Gutenberg Festschrift,* Mainz, 1925, pp. 288-294.

ELTON, C. and M. "Little books," *Bibliographica,* Vol. 3, 1897, pp. 197-211 and 485-486. (The addendum contains a note on the miniature Sarum missal printed by Julian Notary, Westminster, 1499.)

FISCHER, GOTTHELF. Beschreibung einiger typographischen Seltenheiten.

FREIMANN, ARON, editor. *Thesaurus typographiae hebraicae saeculi XV.* Berlin, 1924.+ (Contains facsimiles of typographically significant pages from all Hebrew incunabula.)

Gesamtkatalog der Wiegendrucke. Leipzig, 1925.+

HAEBLER, KONRAD. *Handbuch der Inkunabelkunde.* Leipzig, 1925.

——. *Italian incunabula;* 110 original leaves, translated from the German by André Barbey. Munich, 1927.

——. *The Study of Incunabula,* translated from the German by Lucy Eugenia Osborne, with a foreword by Alfred W. Pollard. New York, 1933. (Translated from the German edition of 1925, but with "certain revisions of the text made by the author in 1932.")

——. *Typenrepertorium der Wiegendrucke.* 6 vols. Halle and Leipzig, 1905-1924.

——. *Der deutsche Wiegendruck in Original-Typenbeispielen; 115 Inkunabelproben.* Munich, 1927.

HAIN, LUDWIG F. T. *Repertorium bibliographicum, in quo libri omnes ab arte typographica inventa usque ad annum MD typis expressi.* Stuttgart, 1826-1838.

IVINS, WILLIAM M., JR. "Artistic aspects of fifteenth-century printing," *Papers of the Bibliographical Society of America,* Vol. 26, 1932, pp. 1-51.

KLEBS, ARNOLD C. "Incunabula of science and medicine," *Papers of the Bibliographical Society of America,* Vol. 26, 1932, pp. 52-88.

McMURTRIE, DOUGLAS C. *Miniature Incunabula; some preliminary notes on small books printed during the fifteenth century.* Chicago, 1929.

MAITTAIRE, MICHAEL. *Annales typographici.* 5 vols. The Hague, Amsterdam, and London, 1719-1741.

OSLER, WILLIAM. *Incunabula medica; a study of the earliest printed medical books.* Illustrated monographs of the Bibliographical Society, No. 19, Oxford, 1923. (With list of medical books printed before 1481.)

PEDDIE, ROBERT A. *Conspectus incunabulorum,* London, 1910.+

——. *Fifteenth Century Books; a Guide to Their Identification.* London, 1913.

POLLARD, ALFRED WILLIAM. "Introduction," in *Catalogue of books printed in the fifteenth century, now in the British Museum,* Vol. 3, London, 1905, pp. ix-xxvi.

POLLARD, ALFRED WILLIAM. "Incunabula," in Encyclopædia Britannica, 11th ed., Vol. 14, pp. 369-370.

PROCTOR, ROBERT G. C. *An index to the early printed books in the British Museum, from the invention of printing to the year MD, with notes on those in the Bodleian Library.* London, 1898.

SMITH, DAVID EUGENE. *Rara arithmetica; a catalogue of the arithmetics written before the year MDCI, with a description of those in the library of George Arthur Plimpton.* Boston and London, 1908.

STEELE, ROBERT. "What fifteenth century books are about," *The Library,* n.s., Vol. 4, 1903, pp. 235-254 (scientific books); Vol. 5, 1904, pp. 337-358 (divinity); Vol. 6, 1905, pp. 137-155 (law); Vol. 8, 1907, pp. 225-238 (literature).

STILLWELL, MARGARET BINGHAM. *Incunabula and Americana, 1450-1800; a Key to Bibliographic Study.* New York, 1931. (A comprehensive guide to the literature of the subject.)

TIERSOT, J. "Les incunables de la musique," *Bulletin du bibliophile et du bibliothecaire,* n.s., Vol. 13, 1934, pp. 110-116.

Chapter XXII: TYPOGRAPHY'S GOLDEN AGE

AUDIN, MARIUS. *Les livrets typographiques des fonderies françaises créées avant 1800, étude historique et bibliographique.* Paris, 1933.

BERNARD, AUGUSTE JOSEPH. *Les Estienne et les types grecs de François Ier.* Paris, 1856.

——. *Notice sur Geofroy Tory, rénovateur de l'imprimerie et de la gravure en France au commencement du 16e siècle.* Brussels, 1853.

——. *Geofroy Tory, Painter and Engraver: first royal printer: reformer of orthography and typography under François I; an account of his life and works.* Translated by George B. Ives. Boston and New York, 1909.

DIDOT, AMBROISE FIRMIN. *Poésies . . . suivies d'observations littéraires et typographiques sur Robert et Henri Estienne.* Paris, 1834.

——. "Les Estienne: Henri I; François I et II; Robert I, II, et III; Henri II; Paul et Antoine." Extrait de la Nouvelle Biographie Générale. Paris, 1858.

GRESWELL, WILLIAM PARR. *A view of the Early Parisian Greek Press; including the lives of the Stephani; notices of other contemporary Greek printers of Paris; and various particulars of the literary and ecclesiastical history of their times.* 2 vols. Oxford, 1833. (The "Stephani" were the Estiennes.)

JOHNSON, ALFRED FORBES. *French sixteenth century printing.* With fifty illustrations. London and New York, 1928.

McMURTRIE, DOUGLAS C. *The Type Punches Cut by Garamond and Le Bé, a Discussion Regarding Their Preservation or Loss.* New York, 1926.

McMurtrie, Douglas C. *Garamond; a note on the transmission of the design of the roman typeface cut by Claude Garamond in the sixteenth century, with a discussion regarding the ultimate disposition of the punches cut by the celebrated French typefounder.* Chicago: Ludlow Typograph Company, 1930.

Omont, Henri Auguste. *Alphabets grecs & hébreux publiées à Paris au XVIe siècle.* Paris, 1885.

Pollard, Alfred William. "The books of hours of Geofroy Tory," *Bibliographica,* Vol. 1, 1895, pp. 114-122.

———. "The illustrations in French books of hours, 1486-1500," *Bibliographica,* Vol. 3, 1897, pp. 430-473.

Proctor, Robert G. C. "The French royal Greek types and the Eton Chrysostom," *The Library,* n.s., Vol. 7, 1904, pp. 89-119.

Renouard, Antoine Augustin. *Annales de l'imprimerie des Estienne; ou, Histoire de la famille des Estienne et de ses éditions . . .* 2e édition. Paris, 1843.

Renouard, Philippe. *Bibliographie des éditions de Simon de Colines, 1520-1546 . . .* Avec une notice biographique et 37 reproductions en fac-simile. Paris, 1894.

———. *Bibliographie des impressions et des œuvres de Josse Badius Ascensius, imprimeur et humaniste, 1462-1535 . . .* Avec une notice biographique et 44 reproductions en fac-simile. Paris, 1908.

Sabbe, Maurits. *Die Civilité-Schriften des Robert Granjon in Lyon und die flämischen Drucker des 16 Jahrhunderts.* Vienna, 1929.

Scholderer, Victor. *Greek Printing Types, 1465-1927: facsimiles from an exhibition illustrating the development of Greek printing shown in the British Museum, 1927.* London, 1927. (The French royal Greek types, pp. 10-12.)

Chapter XXIII—ITALIAN BOOK ILLUSTRATION

Ivins, William Mills, Jr., compiler. *A Catalogue of Italian Renaissance Woodcuts.* New York: Metropolitan Museum of Art, 1917.

Kristeller, Paul. "Florentine book-illustrations of the 15th and early 16th centuries," *Bibliographica,* Vol. 2, London, 1896, pp. 81-111, 227-256.

———. *Early Florentine Woodcuts. With an annotated list of Florentine illustrated books.* 2 vols. London, 1897.

———. *Eine Folge venezianischer Holzschnitte aus dem XV Jahrhundert im Besitze der Stadt Nürnberg.* Berlin, 1909.

———. *Die lombardische Graphik der Renaissance, . . . nebst einem Verzeichnis von Büchern und Holzschnitten.* Berlin, 1913.

LIPPMANN, FRIEDRICH. *The art of Wood-Engraving in Italy in the Fifteenth Century*. English edition. London, 1888.

POLLARD, ALFRED WILLIAM. *Italian Book Illustrations, Chiefly of the Fifteenth Century*. London, 1894.

POPPELREUTER, JOS. *Des anonyme Meister des Poliphilo, eine Studie zur italienischen Buchillustration und zur Antike in der Kunst des Quattrocento*. Strasbourg, 1904.

VARNHAGEN, HERMANN. *Ueber eine Sammlung alter italienischer Drucke der Erlanger Universitatsbibliothek*. Erlangen, 1892.

Victoria and Albert Museum. *A Picture Book of 15th Century Italian Book Illustrations*. London, 1927.

WEITENKAMPF, FRANK. "The Malermi Bible and the Spencer Collection," *Bulletin of the New York Public Library*, Vol. 33, 1929, pp. 779-788.

Chapter XXIV: THE INDOMITABLE PLANTIN

HAVRE, GUSTAVE VAN. *Les marques typographiques de l'imprimerie plantinienne*. Antwerp, 1911.

McMURTRIE, DOUGLAS C. *Plantin's Index Characterum of 1567*. Facsimile reprint with an introduction. New York: Pynson Printers, 1924.

ROOSES, MAX. *Christophe Plantin, imprimeur anversois*. Antwerp, 1882-1883.

———. *Le Musée Plantin Moretus*. Antwerp, 1914. (Printed with type, copperplates, and woodcuts from the Plantin workshop preserved in the museum.)

———. *Plantijn en de Plantijnsche drukkerij*. Brussels, 1877.

SABBE, MAURICE. "Dans les ateliers de Plantin: règlement du travail, discipline, et prévoyance social," *Gutenberg Jahrbuch*, 1937, pp. 174-192.

TARR, JOHN C. *A Visit to the Workshop of Christophe Plantin in the City of Antwerp*. Salt Lake City: Porte Publishing Co., 1936.

Chapter XXV: THE VOGUE OF ENGRAVING

BOUCHOT, HENRI. *Livres à vignettes, 15e-19e siècles*, Paris, 1891.

DUPLESSIS, GEORGES. *Histoire de la gravure en France*. Paris, 1861.

GONCOURT, EDMOND and JULES DE. *Les vignettistes*. Paris, 1868.

Chapter XXVI: BASKERVILLE AND HIS DISCIPLES

BASKERVILLE CLUB [CAMBRIDGE UNIVERSITY], *No. 1 Handlist*. Cambridge, 1904.

BENNETT, WILLIAM. *John Baskerville, the Birmingham Printer, His Press, Relations, and Friends*. Birmingham, 1937.

BENTON, JOSIAH HENRY. *John Baskerville; Type-Founder and Printer, 1706-1775.* Boston, 1914.

BERTIERI, RAFFAELLO. *L'arte di Giambattista Bodoni; . . . con una notizia biografia a cura di Giuseppe Fumagalli.* Milan, 1913.

BROOKS, H. C., compiler. *Compendiosa bibliografia di edizioni Bodoniane.* Florence, 1927.

FOURNIER, SIMON PIERRE (*le jeune*). *Manuel typographique.* 2 vols. Paris, 1764-1766.

————. *Fournier on Typefounding.* The text of the *Manuel typographique* (1764-1766) translated into English and edited with notes by Harry Carter. London, 1930.

STRAUS, RALPH, and R. K. KENT. *John Baskerville; a Memoir.* Cambridge, 1907.

Chapter XXVII: THE PRESS IN THE NEW WORLD

GARCÍA ICAZBALCETA, JOAQUÍN. *Bibliographía mexicana del siglo XVI.* Catalogo razonado de libros impresos en México de 1539 á 1600 . . . Precedido de una noticia acerca de la introducción de la imprenta en México. Mexico, 1886.

JOHN CARTER BROWN LIBRARY. *Books Printed in South America Elsewhere Than at Lima before 1801.* Boston, 1908.

McMURTRIE, DOUGLAS C. *The First Printing in South America.* Facsimile of the unique copy of the *Pragmatica sobre los diez dias de año,* Lima, 1584, preserved in the John Carter Brown Library, with a note on Antonio Ricardo, the printer. Providence, 1926.

————. "The first typefounding in Mexico," *The Library,* 4th series, Vol. 8, 1928, pp. 119-122.

MEDINA, JOSÉ TORIBIO. *La imprenta en México (1539-1821).* 8 vols. Santiago de Chile, 1908--1912. (Vol. I has account of the introduction of the press in Mexico.)

————. *La imprenta en Oaxaca (1720-1820); notas bibliográficas.* Santiago de Chile, 1904.

————. *Notas bibliográficas referentes á las primeras producciones de la imprenta en algunas ciudades de América Española (1754-1823).* Santiago de Chile, 1904.

SMITH, DAVID EUGENE. *The* Sumario compendioso *of Brother Juan Diez, the earliest mathematical work of the New World.* Boston, 1921.

VALTON, EMILIO. *Impresos mexicanos del siglo XVI (incunables americanos); estudio bibliografico con una introducción sobre los origines de la imprenta en América.* Mexico, 1935.

WAGNER, HENRY R. "Sixteenth-century Mexican imprints," in *Bibliographical essays, a Tribute to Wilberforce Eames*, Cambridge [Mass.], 1924, pp. 249-268.

WINSHIP, GEORGE PARKER. "Spanish America," in R. A. Peddie (editor), *Printing, a Short History of the Art*, London, 1927, pp. 306-318.

WROTH, LAWRENCE C. "The origins of typefounding in North and South America," *Ars Typographica*, Vol. 2, No. 4, April, 1926, pp. 273-307.

Chapter XXVIII: PRINTING ON MASSACHUSETTS BAY

The Bay Psalm Book; being a facsimile reprint of the first edition, printed by Stephen Daye at Cambridge in New England in 1640, with an introduction by Wilberforce Eames. New York, 1903.

EAMES, WILBERFORCE. *Bibliographic Notes on Eliot's Indian Bible and on His Other Translations and Works in the Indian Language of Massachusetts,* Washington, 1890. Also in James C. Pilling's *Bibliography of the Algonquian Languages,* Washington, 1891, pp. 127-184.

GREEN, SAMUEL ABBOTT. *John Foster, the Earliest American Engraver and the First Boston Printer.* Boston, 1909.

KIMBER, SIDNEY A. *The Story of an Old Press; an account of the hand press known as the Stephen Daye Press, upon which was begun in 1638 the first printing in British North America.* Cambridge [Mass.], 1937.

LITTLEFIELD, GEORGE EMERY. *The Early Massachusetts Press, 1638-1711.* 2 vols. Boston, 1907.

McMURTRIE, DOUGLAS C. "The Green family of printers," *Americana*, Vol. 26, 1932, pp. 364-375.

———. "Die ersten Drucke im Englisch-sprachigen Nord-Amerika," *Gutenberg Jahrbuch,* 1926, pp. 136-143.

RODEN, ROBERT F. *The Cambridge Press, 1638-1692; a history of the first printing press established in English America, together with a bibliographical list of the issues of the press.* New York, 1905.

THOMAS, ISAIAH. *The History of Printing in America, with a Biography of Printers and an Account of Newspapers.* Second edition, 2 vols. Albany, 1874. (Vol. 1, pp. 38-84 contains a full account of the first Cambridge printing.)

WINSHIP, GEORGE PARKER. *The First American Bible;* a leaf from a copy of the Bible translated into the Indian language by John Eliot and printed at Cambridge in New England in the year 1663, with an account of the translator and his labors and of the two printers who produced the book. Boston, 1929.

Chapter XXIX: TYPOGRAPHER, PHILOSOPHER, STATESMAN

CAMPBELL, WILLIAM J., compiler. *The Collection of Franklin Imprints in the Museum of the Curtis Publishing Company,* with a short-title check list of all the books, pamphlets, broadsides, &c., known to have been printed by Benjamin Franklin. Philadelphia, 1918. (This collection is now in the library of the University of Pennsylvania.)

EDDY, GEORGE SIMPSON. *Account Books Kept by Benjamin Franklin (1728-1747).* 2 Vols. New York, 1928 and 1929.

——. *A Work-Book of the Printing House of Benjamin Franklin and David Hall, 1759-1766.* New York, 1930. Reprinted from the *Bulletin of the New York Public Library,* August, 1930.

FAŸ, BERNARD. *Franklin, the Apostle of Modern Times.* Boston, 1929.

McMURTRIE, DOUGLAS C. *Benjamin Franklin, Type Founder.* New York, 1925.

OSWALD, JOHN CLYDE. *Benjamin Franklin, Printer.* Garden City, N. Y., 1917.

Chapter XXX: PRINTER AND HISTORIAN

McMURTRIE, DOUGLAS C. *The Isaiah Thomas "Standing Bible."* Chicago, 1928.

MARBLE, ANNIE RUSSELL. *From 'Prentice to Patron. The life story of Isaiah Thomas.* New York, 1935.

NICHOLS, CHARLES LEMUEL. *Isaiah Thomas, Printer, Writer and Collector. . . .* With a bibliography of the books printed by Isaiah Thomas. Boston: The Merrymount Press. 1912.

——. *A list of books, pamphlets, newspapers and broadsides, printed in the town of Worcester, from 1775 to 1848.* Worcester, 1899. (Contains titles printed by Isaiah Thomas and by his son, Isaiah Thomas, Jr.)

——. *Some Notes on Isaiah Thomas and His Worcester Imprints.* Worcester, 1900. (From the *Proceedings of the American Antiquarian Society,* April 25, 1900.)

——. editor. *Extracts from the Diaries and Accounts of Isaiah Thomas, from 1782 to 1804, and His Diary for 1808.* Worcester, 1916.

THOMAS, BENJAMIN FRANKLIN. "Memoir of Isaiah Thomas, by his grandson." In Isaiah Thomas, *The History of Printing in America,* second edition, Albany, 1874, pp. xvii-lxxxvii.

Chapter XXXI: THE SPREAD OF PRINTING IN AMERICA

Note. The literature on the introduction of the press in the different states and provinces of the United States and Canada is so extensive that it would

exceed permissible limits to list even the more significant contributions. The bibliography for this chapter therefore undertakes to list only general works on the diffusion of printing throughout North America.

BRIGHAM, CLARENCE S. "Bibliography of American newspapers, 1690-1820." (Published serially in *Proceedings of the American Antiquarian Society*, n.s., Vol. 23, 1913, to Vol. 37, 1927.)

DUFF, LOUIS BLAKE. "The journey of the printing press across Canada," *Gutenberg Jahrbuch*, 1937, pp. 228-238.

EVANS, CHARLES. *American Bibliography*. 12 vols. Chicago, 1903-1934. (More than 35,000 titles of American imprints, 1639-1799. Left unfinished at the death of the compiler, but will probably be completed through 1800 by the American Antiquarian Society.)

FAUTEUX, AEGIDIUS. *The Introduction of Printing into Canada; a Brief History*. Montreal, 1930.

FAŸ, BERNARD. *Notes on the American Press at the End of the Eighteenth Century*. New York, 1927.

GRESS, EDMUND GEIGER. *Fashions in American Typography, 1780 to 1930*. New York, 1931. ("With brief illustrated stories of the life and environment of the American people in seven periods . . . profusely illustrated with examples of typography drawn from American life for the last 150 years.")

McMURTRIE, DOUGLAS C. "The westward migration of the printing press in the United States, 1786-1836," *Gutenberg Jahrbuch*, 1930, pp. 269-288. (With a map showing the distribution of the press in the Middle West to 1836.)

——. *Beginnings of Printing in the Middle West*. Chicago, 1930.

——. "The printing press moves westward," *Minnesota History*, Vol. 15, 1934, pp. 1-25.

——. *A History of Printing in the United States*. Vol. 2: Middle and South Atlantic states. New York, 1936. Vols. 1, 3 and 4 are still to be published.

MOTT, FRANK LUTHER. *A History of American Magazines, 1741-1850*. New York, 1930.

RICHARDSON, LYON N. *A History of Early American Magazines, 1741-1789*. New York, 1931.

RUTHERFORD, LIVINGSTON. *John Peter Zenger, His Press, His Trial, and a Bibliography of Zenger Imprints*. New York, 1904.

SEIDENSTICKER, OSWALD. *The First Century of German Printing in America, 1728-1830*. Philadelphia, 1893.

THOMAS, ISAIAH. *The History of Printing in America, with a Biography of printers and an account of newspapers*. Second edition. 2 vols. Albany, 1874. (Covers, in the main, the spread of printing to the year 1810 only.)

Winship, George Parker. "The literature of the history of printing in the United States: a survey . . ." *The Library,* 4th series, Vol. 3, No. 4, March, 1923, pp. 288-303.

Wroth, Lawrence C. *The Colonial Printer.* New York, 1931. (On the operation, equipment, supplies, and product of American colonial printing offices.)

———. "North America (English-speaking)," in R. A. Peddie (editor), *Printing, a Short History of the Art,* London, 1927, pp. 319-373.

Chapter XXXII: THE REVIVAL OF CRAFTSMANSHIP

Colebrook, Frank. *William Morris, Master Printer.* London, 1897.

Cowan, Robert Ernest, and Cora Edgerton Sanders, compilers. *The Library of William Andrews Clark, Jr.: The Kelmscott and Doves Presses.* San Francisco: John Henry Nash. 1921. (With Foreword and Introduction by Alfred W. Pollard, and "Note by William Morris on his aims in founding the Kelmscott Press.")

Jacobi, Charles Thomas. "The work of the private presses: I. The Kelmscott Press, 1891-1898," *Penrose's Annual,* Vol. 24, 1922, pp. 17-22.

Marrot, H. V. *William Bulmer and Thomas Bensley, a Study in Transition.* London, 1930.

Morris, William. *A Note by William Morris on His Aims in Founding the Kelmscott Press, together with a short description of the press by S. C. Cockerell.* Hammersmith: The Kelmscott Press. 1898. (This was the last book printed at the Kelmscott Press.)

Ricketts, Charles, and Lucien Pissarro. *De la typographie et de l'harmonie de la page imprimée; William Morris et son influence sur les arts et métiers.* London, 1898.

Scott, Temple, compiler. *A Bibliography of the Works of William Morris.* London, 1897. (In addition to a complete bibliography of the Kelmscott Press, contains a valuable bibliography of works about Morris.)

Sparling, Henry Halliday. *The Kelmscott Press and William Morris, Master-Craftsman.* London, 1924.

Steele, Robert, editor. *The Revival of Printing; a bibliographical catalogue of works issued by the chief modern English presses, with an introduction by Robert Steele.* London, 1912.

Chapter XXXIII: THE PRIVATE PRESSES

Ashbee, Charles Robert. *The Private Press: a Study in Idealism.* Chipping Campden, England, 1909. (Contains a bibliography of the Essex House Press.)

Ashbee, Charles Robert. "The Essex House Press," *The Book-Collector's Quarterly*, Vol. 11, 1933, pp. 69-86.

Claudin, Anatole. "Private presses in France during the fifteenth century," *Bibliographica*, Vol. 3, 1897, pp. 344-370.

Cobden-Sanderson and the Doves Press. The history of the press and the story of its types told by Alfred W. Pollard. The character of the man set forth by . . . Edward Johnston, with The Ideal Book or the Book Beautiful, by Thomas James Cobden-Sanderson, and a list of the Doves Press printings. San Francisco: John Henry Nash. 1929.

Cobden-Sanderson, Thomas J. *Catalogue raisonné of books printed at the Doves Press, 1900-1916*. Hammersmith: The Doves Press. 1916. (The third and last catalogue of the Doves Press books.)

——. The Doves Press: *salve aeternum aeternumque vale*. Hammersmith: The Doves Press. 1916. (A three-page résumé of the work of the Doves Press and an announcement of its closing.)

Cowan, Robert Ernest, and Cora Edgerton Sanders, compilers. *The Library of William Andrews Clark, Jr.: The Kelmscott and Doves Presses*. San Francisco: John Henry Nash. 1921. With Foreword and Introduction by Alfred W. Pollard.

Haas, Irvin. *A Bibliography of Material Relating to Private Presses*, with an introduction by Will Ransom. Chicago: The Black Cat Press. 1937.

Hornby, C. H. St. John. *The Ashendene Press, a Descriptive Bibliography*, with a foreword by C. H. St. John Hornby. London: The Ashendene Press. 1935. (The last volume issued by this famous private press.)

Jacobi, Charles Thomas. "The work of the private presses," *Penrose's Annual*, Vols. 24-33, London, 1922-1931. (Ten brief surveys of the work of private presses, as follows: Kelmscott, Vol. 24, 1922; Doves, Vol. 25, 1923; Ashendene, Vol. 26, 1924; Daniel, Vol. 27, 1925; Eragny, Vol. 28, 1926; Essex House, Vol. 29, 1927; Golden Cockerel, Vol. 30, 1928; Nonesuch, Vol. 31, 1929; Oxford University, Vol. 32, 1930; Cambridge University, Vol. 33, 1931.)

Madan, Falconer. *The Daniel Press; memorials of C. H. O. Daniel, with a bibliography of the press*. Oxford, 1921. ("Printed on the Daniel Press in the Bodleian Library." A record by a distinguished bibliographer of the work of the most truly "private" of all the private presses.)

Martin, John. *A bibliographical catalogue of books privately printed; including those of the Bannatyne, Maitland and Roxburghe clubs, and of the private presses at Darlington, Auchinleck, Lee Priory, Newcastle, Middle Hill, and Strawberry Hill*. London, 1834.

Moore, Thomas Sturge. *A Brief Account of the Eragny Press, and a Note on*

the Relation of the Printed Book as a Work of Art to Life. . . . Hammersmith: Eragny Press. 1903. (Contains "A bibliographical list of the Eragny books printed in the Vale type by Esther and Lucien Pissarro on their press . . . in the order in which they were printed.")

MORISON, STANLEY, and HOLBROOK JACKSON. *A Brief Survey of Printing History and Practice.* New York, 1923.

NEWDIGATE, BERNARD H. "Mr. C. H. St. John Hornby's Ashendene Press," *The Fleuron,* No. 2, 1924, pp. 77-85. (With a list of the Ashendene books, 1895-1923.)

POLLARD, ALFRED WILLIAM. "Private presses and their influence on the art of printing," *Ars Typographica,* Vol. 1, No. 4, 1934, pp. 36-42.

RANSOM, WILL. *Private presses and Their Books.* New York, 1929.

RICKETTS, CHARLES P. *A Bibliography of the Books Issued by Hacon and Ricketts.* Vale Press, 1904.

RODENBERG, JULIUS. *Deutsche Pressen, eine Bibliographie, mit vielen Schriftproben.* Zurich, 1925. (A supplement was published in 1931.)

STEELE, ROBERT, editor. *The Revival of Printing; a bibliographical catalogue of works issued by the chief modern English presses,* with an introduction by Robert Steele. London, 1912.

TOMKINSON, G. S., compiler. *A select bibliography of the principal modern presses, public and private, in Great Britain and Ireland,* with an introduction by B. H. Newdigate. London, 1928.

WALPOLE, HORACE. *Journal of the Printing-Office at Straberry Hill,* now first printed from the MS of Horace Walpole, with notes by Paget Toynbee. London, 1923.

WHEATLEY, H. B. "The Strawberry Hill Press," *Bibliographica,* Vol. 3, 1897, pp. 83-98. (With a short list of books and pamphlets printed at the Strawberry Hill Press.)

Chapter XXXIV: CONTEMPORARY FINE PRINTING

BARTLETT, EDWARD EVERETT. *The Typographic Treasures of Europe, and a Study of Contemporaneous Book Production in Great Britain, France, Italy, Germany, Holland and Belgium.* With an addendum by J. W. Muller giving the principal dates and personalities in printing history. New York and London, 1925.

DWIGGINS, WILLIAM ADDISON. "D. B. Updike and the Merrymount Press," *The Fleuron,* No. 4, 1924, pp. 1-8. ("Commercial printing under a more enlightened dispensation.")

GARNETT, PORTER. *A Documentary Account of the Beginnings of the Laboratory Press*. Pittsburgh, 1927.

GOUDY, FREDERIC W. *The Story of the Village Type*. With an introduction by Melbert B. Cary, Jr. New York, 1933.

HAAS, IRVIN. *Bibliography of Modern American Presses, with an Introduction by Will Ransom*. Chicago: The Black Cat Press. 1935.

HARASZTI, ZOLTÁN. "Mr. Updike and the Merrymount Press," *More Books*, Bulletin of the Boston Public Library, Vol. 10, 1935, pp. 157-173. (A comprehensive review of the *Notes on the Merrymount Press*, with comments on the work of the Press.)

HOLME, CHARLES, editor. *Modern Book Production: an International Survey*. London, 1928. (Contains articles by B. H. Newdigate, Clement Janin, Julius Zeitler, Jarmil Krecor, S. H. de Roos, Augusto Calabi, Rudolph Junk, P. Ettinger, Julius De Vegh, Alfred Altherr, Arthur Schneider, Anders Billow, and Will Ransom, on contemporary book production in various countries.)

JOHNSTON, PAUL. *Biblio-typographica, a study of contemporary fine printing style*. New York, 1930.

LEHMANN-HAUPT, HELLMUT. *Das amerikanische Buchwesen; Buchdruck und Buchhandel, Bibliophilie und Bibliothekswesen in den Vereinigten Staaten von dem Anfängen bis zur Gegenwart*. Leipzig, 1937. (Contains sections on the history of the American book trade by Lawrence C. Wroth, and on American collectors and libraries by Miss Ruth S. Grannis.)

MARDERSTEIG, HANS. *The Officina Bodoni; the operation of a hand-press during the first six years of its work*. Paris and New York, 1929. (With woodcut illustrations by Frans Maseréel.)

MEYNELL, FRANCIS. "A bibliography of the first ten years of the Nonesuch Press," *The Book-Collector's Quarterly*, Vol. 13, 1934, pp. 45-69, and Vol. 14, 1934, pp. 54-59.

MORISON, STANLEY. *Four Centuries of Fine Printing*. London, 1924. ("Upwards of six hundred examples of the work of presses established during the years 1500 to 1914, with an introductory text and index by Stanley Morison." See the comprehensive review of this work by D. B. Updike in *The Fleuron*, No. 3, 1924, pp. 107-116.)

MORISON, STANLEY, and HOLBROOK JACKSON. *A Brief Survey of Printing History and Practice*. New York, 1923.

——. *Modern Fine Printing. An exhibit of printing issued in England, the United States of America, France, Germany, Italy, Switzerland, Czecho-Slovakia, Holland and Sweden during the twentieth century and with few exceptions since the outbreak of the War*. London, 1925.

NOVAK, ARTHUR. "Die buchkünstlerischen Bestrebungen in der Tschechoslovakei," *Buch und Schrift*, Nos. 7-8, 1933, 1934, pp. 51-71.

O'DAY, NELL. *A Catalogue of Books Printed by John Henry Nash,* compiled and annotated, including a biographical note. San Francisco: John Henry Nash. 1937.

POLLARD, ALFRED WILLIAM. *Modern Fine Printing in England and Mr. Bruce Rogers, with a list of books and other pieces of printing designed by Mr. Rogers.* Newark, N. J., 1916.

ROGERS, BRUCE. *An Account of the Making of the Oxford Lectern Bible.* Phila-adelphia, 1936.

ROLLINS, CARL PURINGTON. "A survey of the making of books in recent years: The United States of America," *The Dolphin*, No. 1, 1933, pp. 288-301.

———. "A survey of contemporary bookmaking: The United States of America," *The Dolphin*, No. 2, 1935, pp. 259-268.

ROOS, S. H. DE "Ueber die neuzeitliche Buchkunst und Schriftgestaltung in der Niederlanden," *Buch und Schrift*, Nos. 7-8, 1933-1934, pp. 3-17.

SIMON, OLIVER, and others. *Printing of To-day.* An illustrated survey of post-war typography in Europe and the United States, with a general introduction by Aldous Huxley. London and New York, 1928. (Contains accounts of printing in England, by Oliver Simon; Printing in the United States, by Paul Beaujon [Mrs. Beatrice L. Warde]; and Continental printing, by Julius Rodenberg.)

STEINER-PRAG, HUGO. "European books and designers," *The Dolphin*, No. 1, 1933, pp. 209-249.

———. "A survey of the making of books in recent years," *The Dolphin*, No. 1, 1933, pp. 253-363.

———. "A survey of contemporary bookmaking," *The Dolphin*, No. 2, 1935, pp. 257-329.

SYMONS, A. J. A. "Die Englischen Pressen der Gegenwart," *Buch und Schrift*, Nos. 7-8, 1933-1934, pp. 19-24.

———, with Francis Meynell and Desmond Flower. *The Nonesuch Century;* an appraisal, a personal note, and a bibliography of the first hundred books issued by the press, 1923-1934. London: The Nonesuch Press, 1936. (Appraisal, by A. J. A. Symons; the personal element, by Francis Meynell; the bibliography, by Desmond Flower.)

VOX, MAXIMILIEN. "Das schöne Buch in Frankreich; eine übersicht über zehn Jahre," *Buch und Schrift*, Nos. 7-8, 1933-1934, pp. 25-31.

WARDE, FREDERIC. *Bruce Rogers, Designer of Books;* with a list of the books printed under Mr. Rogers's supervision. Cambridge: Harvard University Press. 1925. (Reprinted with a few alterations from *The Fleuron*, No. 4.)

WINSHIP, GEORGE PARKER. *The Merrymount Press of Boston, an account of the work of Daniel Berkeley Updike.* Vienna, 1929.

Chapter XXXV: MODERN TYPOGRAPHY

ALBINUS, PHILIPP. *Grundsätzliches zur neuen Typographie.* Berlin, 1929.

McMURTRIE, DOUGLAS C. *Modern Typography and Layout.* Chicago and London, 1929.

MOHOLY-NAGY, LADISLAUS. "Zeitgemässe Typographie—Ziele, Praxis, Kritik." *Gutenberg Festschrift,* Mainz, 1925, pp. 307-317.

TSCHICHOLD, JAN. *Die neue Typographie.* Ein Handbuch fur zeitgemäss Schaffende. Berlin, 1928.

———. *Typographische Gestaltung.* Basel, 1935.

Chapter XXXVI: MODERN BOOK ILLUSTRATION

ANTHONY, A. V. S., and others. *Wood-Engraving;* three essays, by A. V. S. Anthony, Timothy Cole, and Elbridge Kingsley, with a list of American books illustrated with woodcuts. New York, 1916.

BAKER, C. H. COLLINS. "William Blake, 1757-1827," in *An Exhibition of William Blake's Watercolor Drawings of Milton's "Paradise Lost."* San Marino, California: Henry E. Huntington Library and Art Gallery [1936], pp. 3-7.

BEWICK, THOMAS. *Memoir of Thomas Bewick Written by Himself, 1822-1828,* with an introduction by Selwyn Image. New York, 1925. (Edited by Jane Bewick and first published in 1862.)

BLISS, DOUGLAS PERCY. *A History of Wood-Engraving.* London, Toronto and New York, 1928.

———. "Modern English book illustration," *Penrose's Annual,* Vol. 31, 1929, pp. 107-115.

———. "The last ten years of wood engraving," *Print Collector's Quarterly,* Vol. 21, London, 1934, pp. 250-271.

CUNDALL, JOSEPH. *A Brief History of Wood-Engraving from Its Invention.* London, 1895.

DARTON, F. J. HARVEY. *Modern Book-Illustration in Great Britain and America.* London and New York: The Studio, 1931.

FLETCHER, JOHN GOULD. "Blair Hughes-Stanton," *Print Collector's Quarterly,* Vol. 21, London, 1934, pp. 353-372.

FURST, HERBERT E. A. *The Modern Woodcut, a Study of the Evolution of the Craft.* London [1924].

HUGO, THOMAS. *The Bewick Collector.* A descriptive catalogue of the works of Thomas and John Bewick. London, 1866. With two supplements. London, 1868.

KONODY, P. G. *The Art of Walter Crane.* London, 1902.

NAMÉNYI, ERNST. "Ungarische Buchkunst," *Buch und Schrift,* Vols. 7-8, 1933-1934, pp. 73-81; plates 75-91.

PICHON, LÉON. *The New Book Illustration in France.* Translated by Herbert B. Grimsditch. London, 1924.

ROBINSON, ROBERT. *Thomas Bewick; His Life and Times,* Newcastle, 1887.

RODENBERG, JULIUS. "Geschichte der Illustration von 1800 bis heute," *Handbuch der Bibliothekswissenschaft, herausgegeben von Fritz Milkau,* Vol. 1. Leipzig, 1931, pp. 625-665.

SALAMAN, MALCOLM CHARLES. *Modern Book Illustrators and Their Work.* Edited by C. Geoffrey Holme and Ernest G. Hatton. Text by M. C. Salaman. London, Paris, New York: The Studio, 1914.

SKETCHLEY, R. E. D. *English Book-Illustration of To-day—appreciations of the work of living English illustrators with lists of their books.* With an introduction by Alfred W. Pollard. London, 1903.

STEPHENS, FREDERIC GEORGE. *Notes by F. G. Stephens on a collection of drawings and woodcuts by Thomas Bewick, exhibited at the Fine Arts Society's rooms, 1881; also a complete list of all works illustrated by Thomas and John Bewick* [compiled by David Croal Thomson]. London, 1881.

TUGENHOLD, I. "Die Kunst des Buchgewerbes in der Sowjetunion," *Buch und Schrift,* Vols. 7-8, 1933-1934, pp. 83-89, plates 92-107.

VOX, MAXIMILIEN, and A. H. MARTINE. "Fernand Siméon," *Buch und Schrift,* Vols. 7-8, 1933-1934, pp. 33-36, plates 30-37.

WALKER, R. A. "The engravings of Eric Gill," *Print Collector's Quarterly,* Vol. 15, London, 1928, pp. 144-166.

WEITENKAMPF, FRANK. *American graphic art.* New edition. New York, 1924.

——. *Wood-Engraving To-day.* New York, 1916. (A reprint from the *Bulletin of the New York Public Library.*)

WHEELER, MONROE, editor. *Modern Painters and Sculptors as Illustrators.* New York: The Museum of Modern Art, 1936.

WHITE, GLEASON. *English Illustration, "the Sixties."* London, 1906. (Reprint of the original edition, 1897.)

WIJNGAERT, FRANK VAN DEN. "Die belgische Holzschnittkunst von heute," *Buch und Schrift,* Vols. 7-8, 1933-1934, pp. 37-50, plates 40-50.

WOODBERRY, GEORGE EDWARD. *A History of Wood-Engraving.* New York, 1883.

Chapter XXXVIII: THE ART OF BOOKBINDING

ADAMS, CHARLES M. "Illustrated publishers' bindings." *Bulletin of the New York Public Library,* Vol. 41, 1937, pp. 607-611.

BENDIKSON, LODEWYK. "The House of Magnus, Famous Bookbinders of the Seventeenth Century," *Pacific Bindery Talk,* Vol. 8, No. 6, Los Angeles, February, 1936, pp. 94-100.

CARTER, JOHN. *Binding variants in English publishing, 1820-1900.* London, 1932.

——. *Publisher's Cloth; an outline history of publishers' binding in England, 1820-1900.* New York, 1935.

COCKERELL, DOUGLAS. *Bookbinding and the Care of Books;* a textbook for bookbinders and librarians. 4th edition. London and New York, 1920.

COOK, DAVIDSON. Illustrations on bindings. *Times Literary Supplement,* London, April 17, 1937, p. 296.

DAVENPORT, CYRIL JAMES HUMPHRIES. "The decoration of book-edges," *Bibliographica,* Vol. 2, London, 1896, pp. 385-406.

——. *Thomas Berthelet, Royal Printer and Bookbinder to Henry VIII, King of England, with Special Reference to His Bookbindings.* Chicago: The Caxton Club, 1901.

——. *The Book, Its History and Development.* New York, 1908.

GIBSON, STRICKLAND. *Early Oxford Bindings. Bibliographical Society Illustrated Monographs,* No. 10. Oxford, 1903.

GOLDSCHMIDT, ERNST PHILIP. *Gothic and Renaissance Bookbinding,* exemplified and illustrated from the author's collection. London, Boston, and New York, 1928.

GOTTLIEB, THEODOR. *K. K. Hofbibliothek Bucheinbünde.* Auswahl von technisch und geschichtlich bemerkenswerten Stücken. Vienna, 1911.

GRUEL, LÉON. *Manuel historique et bibliographique de l'amateur de reliures.* 2 vols. Paris, 1887, 1905.

HEVESY, ANDRÉ DE. *La bibliothèque du Roi Matthias Corvin.* Paris, 1923.

HOBSON, GEOFFREY DUDLEY. *Maioli, Carnevari and others.* London, 1926. (The author shows that "Carnevari" bindings were executed for the Italian collector Pierluigi Franesi [1503-1547].)

HOLMES, THOMAS JAMES. "The bookbindings of John Ratcliff and Edmund Ranger, seventeenth century Boston bookbinders," *Proceedings of the American Antiquarian Society,* Vol. 38, 1928, pp. 31-50.

——. "Additional notes on Ratcliff and Ranger bindings," *Proceedings of the American Antiquarian Society,* Vol. 39, 1929, pp. 291-302.

HORNE, HERBERT PERCY. *The Binding of Books;* an essay in the history of gold-tooled bindings. London, 1894.

HUSUNG, MAXIMILIAN JOSEPH. *Bucheinbände aus der Preussischen Staatsbibliothek zu Berlin in historischer Folge erläutert.* Leipzig, 1925.

———. "Geschichte des Bucheinbandes," *Handbuch der Bibliothekswissenschaft herausgegeben von Fritz Milkau,* Vol. 1. Leipzig, 1931, pp. 666-716.

LAND, WILLIAM G. "Further notes on Ratcliff and Ranger bindings," *Proceedings of the American Antiquarian Society,* Vol. 39, 1929, pp. 302-306.

LOUBIER, HANS. *Der Bucheinband von seinen Anfängen bis zum Ende des 18. Jahrhunderts.* 2te Aufl. Leipzig, 1926.

MITTIUS, O. Fränkische Lederschnittbände des XV. Jahrhunderts; ein burgeschichtlicher Versuch. *Sammlung bibliothekswissenschaftlicher Arbeiten,* Heft 28 (2te ser. Heft 11). Leipzig, 1909.

RHEIN, ADOLF. "Einband-Pressendruck vor Gutenberg," *Archiv für Buchgewerbe und Gebrauchsgraphik,* Vol. 73, 1936, pp. 283-286.

ROQUET, ANTOINE ERNEST. Les relieurs français (1500-1800). Biographie critique et anecdotique, précédée de l'histoire de la communauté des relieurs et doreurs de la ville de Paris et d'une étude sur les styles de reliure, par Ernest Thoinan [pseud.] Paris, 1893.

SADLEIR, MICHAEL. *Evolution of Publishers' Binding Styles, 1770-1900.* London, 1930.

SCHMIDT, ADOLPH. *Bucheinbände aus dem XIV. bis XIX. Jahrhundert in der Landesbibliothek zu Darmstadt.* Leipzig, 1921.

THOINAN, ERNEST (pseud.) See Roquet, A. E.

VICTORIA AND ALBERT MUSEUM [London]. *A Picture Book of Bookbinding.* Part I: Before 1550; Part II: 1550-1800. London, 1933. (With forty illustrations.)

Chapter XXXIX: THE PRINTING OF ILLUSTRATIONS

ALBERT, KARL. "The beginning of rotogravure in America," *Penrose's Annual,* Vol. 30, 1928, pp. 127-128.

———. "The history of rotogravure in America," *Penrose's Annual,* Vol. 33, 1931, pp. 162-163. (With illustrations of the first machines used.)

BROWNE, WARREN CRITTENDEN. *Offset Lithography; a treatise on printing in the lithographic manner from metal plates on rubber blanket offset presses.* New York, 1917.

HAGEDOORN, LEO H. M. "The first century of photo-engraving," *Penrose's Annual,* Vol. 19, 1917, pp. 189-197.

HORGAN, STEPHEN HENRY. "The beginnings of halftone," *Penrose's Annual,* Vol. 30, 1928, pp. 93-94.

Ives, Frederic Eugene. *The Autobiography of an Amateur Inventor*. Philadelphia, 1928. (By the man who is generally regarded as the inventor of the halftone process.)

Nordquist, Nils. "Fifty or sixty years of letterpress halftone," *Penrose's Annual*, Vol. 35, 1933, pp. 62-65. (Recognizes Carl Carleman, of Sweden, as "one of the inventors" of halftones.)

Schreiber, Wilhelm Ludwig. "Die Anfänge des Buntfarbendrucks," *Gutenberg Jahrbuch*, 1928, pp. 87-88.

Senefelder, Alois. *The Invention of Lithography*, translated from the original German by J. W. Muller. New York, 1911.

——. *A Complete Course of Lithography*: . . . to which is prefixed a history of lithography from its origin to the present time . . . Translated from the original German by A. S. London, 1819.

Chapter XL: THE TITLE PAGE

Bammes, Reinhold. *Der Titelsatz, seine Entwicklung und seine Grundsätze*. Leipzig, 1911.

De Vinne, Theodore Low. *A Treatise on Title-Pages*, with numerous illustrations in facsimile and some observations on the early and recent printing of books. New York, 1902. (In his series of volumes entitled "The Practice of Typography.")

Johnson, Alfred Forbes. *One Hundred Title-Pages, 1500-1800*, selected and arranged with an introduction and notes. London, 1928.

Kiessling, Gerhard. "Die Anfänge des Titelblattes in der Blütezeit des deutschen Holzschnitts (1470-1530)," *Buch und Schrift*, Vol. 3, 1929, pp. 9-45.

Pollard, Alfred William. *Last Words on the History of the Title-Page, with notes on some colophons and 27 facsimiles of title-pages*. London, 1891.

——. "The title-pages in some Italian manuscripts," *The Printing Art*, Vol. 12, No. 2, October, 1908, pp. 81-87.

Sondheim, Moriz. Das Titelblatt. Kleiner Druck der Gutenberg-Gesellschaft, No. 5, 1927.

Chapter XLI: CONCERNING TYPE DESIGN

Berry, William Turner, and Alfred Forbes Johnson, compilers. *A catalogue of specimens of printing types made by English and Scottish printers and founders, 1665-1830*. London, 1935. (With an introduction by Stanley Morison.)

Bruce, David, Jr. *The History of Typefounding in the United States, . . .* with an introduction by Douglas C. McMurtrie. New York, 1925.

The Earliest American Type Specimens from American Foundries. New Haven, 1936. (With an introduction by Carl Purington Rollins on the history of typefounding in British North America and the United States up to 1812. Illustrated with facsimile reproductions in collotype.)

ENSCHEDÉ, CHARLES. *Fonderies de caractères et leur matériel dans les Pays-Bas du 15e au 19e siècle.* Haarlem, 1908. (It is understood that Stanley Morison is preparing for publication an English translation of this valuable work.)

GOUDY, FREDERIC WILLIAM. *The Alphabet;* fifteen interpretative designs drawn and arranged with explanatory text and illustrations. Second edition. New York, 1922.

——. "On designing a type face," *The Dolphin,* No. 1, 1933, pp. 3-23.

——. *The Story of the Village Type.* With an introduction by Melbert B. Cary, Jr. New York, 1933. (Contains a chronological list of Goudy's types.)

JOHNSON, ALFRED FORBES. *Type Designs, Their History and Development.* London, 1934.

LEGROS, L. A., and J. C. GRANT. *Typographical Printing-Surfaces; the Technology and Mechanism of Their Production.* London and New York, 1916.

McMURTRIE, DOUGLAS C. *American Type Design in the Twentieth Century, with Specimens of the Outstanding Types Produced during This Period.* With an introduction by Frederic W. Goudy. Chicago, 1924.

——. *Type Design; an Essay on American Type Design with Specimens of the Outstanding Types.* With an introduction by Frederic W. Goudy. Pelham, N. Y., 1927. (A revision of the preceding.)

McRAE, JOHN FINDLAY, compiler. *Two Centuries of Typefounding;* annals of the letter foundry established by William Caslon in Chiswell Street, London, in the year 1720. London, 1920.

MORES, EDWARD ROWE. *A Dissertation upon English Typographical Founders and Founderies,* with appendix by John Nichols, edited by D. B. Updike. New York, 1924. (Originally printed in a private edition in 1778, with the later addition, in 1779, of an appendix by John Nichols.)

MORISON, STANLEY. "Towards an ideal type," *The Fleuron,* No. 2, 1924, pp. 57-75.

——. *Type Designs of the Past and Present.* London, 1926.

REED, TALBOT BAINES. *A History of the Old English Letter Foundries,* with notes, historical and bibliographical, on the rise and progress of English typography. London, 1887.

UPDIKE, DANIEL BERKELEY. *Printing Types, Their History, Forms, and Use; a Study in Survivals.* With illustrations. 2 vols. Cambridge [Mass.], 1922. (Revised edition, Cambridge, 1937.)

The Index

Abrahamson, Ben, acknowledgment to, vii

Ackermann von Böhmen, first illustrated printed book, 239-241

Adams, James, first printer in Delaware, 444

Adler, Elmer (Pynson Printers), 493, 495, 497

Advertising, printed, 502

Ahiram, tomb of, 30-31

Aitken, Robert, printer at Philadelphia, 436

Alabama, first printing in, 448

Aldus Manutius, 197; as editor and publisher, 205-206; Greek types of, 208, 280; roman typeface designed for, 208-209, 572-573; italic type cut for, 210-213, 573; works of, pirated, 213; academy founded by, 213; business difficulties of, 213-214; trade-mark of, 215, 300; not the originator of gold tooling, 541

Alexeieff, A., illustrator, 514

Allen, Albert H., acknowledgment to, viii

Almanacs, American colonial, 422

Alphabet, 20-39; phonetic, 21; origin of, 21; consonantal, 29, 36; function of, 30; in western Europe, 40-59
See also Arabic, Aramaean, Etruscan, Greek, Hebrew, Latin, Phoenician, Samaritan, Slavic, Yiddish; capital letters, majuscule, minuscule, small letters, uncial.

Alphabetum Graecum of 1543, 339, 341-343

Altschul, Frank (Overbrook Press), 480

Alvise, G. and A., first to use type ornaments, 272, 273; illustrated *Aesop* printed by, 349

Amerbach, Johann, printer of early illustrated books at Basel, 246; miniature book printed by, 308, 309

America, first papermaking in, 63; first printing in, 390-400

American Antiquarian Society, founded by Isaiah Thomas, 433-434

American Institute of Graphic Arts, xii, xiii

Amman, Jost, illustration of early type-casting by, 232; representation of early printing press by, 237-238

Anderson, Alexander, early American engraver, 550

Andrews, Eben T., on Indian Bible bought for Isaiah Thomas, 410; partner of Thomas, 431

Angelo, Valenti, modern hand illumination by, 490; Golden Cross press of, 495; illustrator, 497, 518

Anglo-Saxon half-uncials, 54

Anima Mea, Gulielmus, printer at Venice, 349

Anthoensen, Fred (Southworth-Anthoensen Press), 495

Apocalypse, block book, 114, 116; printed with Dürer woodcuts, 252

Arabic alphabet, 21

Arabic numerals, 59-60

Arabs, diffusion of papermaking by, 63-65

Aramaean alphabet, 39

Arizona, date of first printing in, 449